Advancements, Applications, and Foundations of C++

Shams Al Ajrawi
Wiley Edge, USA & Alliant International University, USA

Charity Jennings
Wiley Edge, USA & University of Phoenix, USA

Paul Menefee
Wiley Edge, USA

Wathiq Mansoor
University of Dubai, UAE

Mansoor Ahmed Alaali
Ahlia University, Bahrain

IGI Global
PUBLISHER of TIMELY KNOWLEDGE

A volume in the Advances in Systems Analysis, Software Engineering, and High Performance Computing (ASASEHPC) Book Series

Published in the United States of America by
IGI Global
Engineering Science Reference (an imprint of IGI Global)
701 E. Chocolate Avenue
Hershey PA, USA 17033
Tel: 717-533-8845
Fax: 717-533-8661
E-mail: cust@igi-global.com
Web site: http://www.igi-global.com

Library of Congress Cataloging-in-Publication Data

CIP DATA PROCESSING

Advancements, Applications, and Foundations of C++
Shams Al Ajrawi, Charity Jennings, Paul Menefee, Wathiq Mansoor, Mansoor Ahmed Alaali
2024 Engineering Science Reference

ISBN: 9798369320075(hc) | ISBN: 9798369349984(sc) | eISBN: 9798369320082

This book is published in the IGI Global book series Advances in Systems Analysis, Software Engineering, and High Performance Computing (ASASEHPC) (ISSN: 2327-3453; eISSN: 2327-3461)

British Cataloguing in Publication Data
A Cataloguing in Publication record for this book is available from the British Library.

For electronic access to this publication, please contact: eresources@igi-global.com.

Advances in Systems Analysis, Software Engineering, and High Performance Computing (ASASEHPC) Book Series

Vijayan Sugumaran
Oakland University, Rochester, USA

ISSN:2327-3453
EISSN:2327-3461

Mission

The theory and practice of computing applications and distributed systems has emerged as one of the key areas of research driving innovations in business, engineering, and science. The fields of software engineering, systems analysis, and high performance computing offer a wide range of applications and solutions in solving computational problems for any modern organization.

The **Advances in Systems Analysis, Software Engineering, and High Performance Computing (ASASEHPC) Book Series** brings together research in the areas of distributed computing, systems and software engineering, high performance computing, and service science. This collection of publications is useful for academics, researchers, and practitioners seeking the latest practices and knowledge in this field.

Coverage

- Performance Modelling
- Distributed Cloud Computing
- Computer Networking
- Software Engineering
- Computer Graphics
- Engineering Environments
- Metadata and Semantic Web
- Parallel Architectures
- Network Management
- Storage Systems

IGI Global is currently accepting manuscripts for publication within this series. To submit a proposal for a volume in this series, please contact our Acquisition Editors at acquisitions@igi-global.com or visit: https://www.igi-global.com/publish/.

The Advances in Systems Analysis, Software Engineering, and High Performance Computing (ASASEHPC) Book Series (ISSN 2327-3453) is published by IGI Global, 701 E. Chocolate Avenue, Hershey, PA 17033-1240, USA, www.igi-global.com. This series is composed of titles available for purchase individually; each title is edited to be contextually exclusive from any other title within the series. For pricing and ordering information please visit https://www.igi-global.com/book-series/advances-systems-analysis-software-engineering/73689. Postmaster: Send all address changes to above address.

Titles in this Series

For a list of additional titles in this series, please visit: https://www.igi-global.com/book-series/advances-systems-analysis-software-engineering/73689

Big Data Quantification for Complex Decision-Making
Chao Zhang (Shanxi University, China) and Wentao Li (Southwest University, China)
Engineering Science Reference • copyright 2024 • 312pp • H/C (ISBN: 9798369315828) • US $315.00 (our price)

Digital Technologies in Modeling and Management Insights in Education and Industry
G. S. Prakasha (Christ University, India) Maria Lapina (North-Caucasus Federal University, Russia) Deepanraj Balakrishnan (Prince Mohammad Bin Fahd University, Saudi Arabia) and Mohammad Sajid (Aligarh Muslim University, India)
Information Science Reference • copyright 2024 • 409pp • H/C (ISBN: 9781668495766) • US $250.00 (our price)

Serverless Computing Concepts, Technology and Architecture
Rajanikanth Aluvalu (Chaitanya Bharathi Institute of Technology, India) and Uma Maheswari V. (Chaitanya Bharathi Institute of Technology, India)
Engineering Science Reference • copyright 2024 • 310pp • H/C (ISBN: 9798369316825) • US $300.00 (our price)

Developments Towards Next Generation Intelligent Systems for Sustainable Development
Shanu Sharma (ABES Engineering College, Ghaziabad, India) Ayushi Prakash (Ajay Kumar Garg Engineering College, Ghaziabad, India) and Vijayan Sugumaran (Oakland University, Rochester, USA)
Engineering Science Reference • copyright 2024 • 327pp • H/C (ISBN: 9798369356432) • US $385.00 (our price)

Technological Advancements in Data Processing for Next Generation Intelligent Systems
Shanu Sharma (ABES Engineering College, Ghaziabad, India) Ayushi Prakash (Ajay Kumar Garg Engineering College, Ghaziabad, India) and Vijayan Sugumaran (Oakland University, Rochester, USA)
Engineering Science Reference • copyright 2024 • 357pp • H/C (ISBN: 9798369309681) • US $300.00 (our price)

Advanced Applications in Osmotic Computing
G. Revathy (SASTRA University, India)
Engineering Science Reference • copyright 2024 • 370pp • H/C (ISBN: 9798369316948) • US $300.00 (our price)

Omnichannel Approach to Co-Creating Customer Experiences Through Metaverse Platforms
Babita Singla (Chitkara Business School, Chitkara University, Punjab, India) Kumar Shalender (Chitkara Business School, Chitkara University, India) and Nripendra Singh (Pennsylvania Western University, USA)

IGI Global
PUBLISHER of TIMELY KNOWLEDGE

701 East Chocolate Avenue, Hershey, PA 17033, USA
Tel: 717-533-8845 x100 • Fax: 717-533-8661
E-Mail: cust@igi-global.com • www.igi-global.com

Table of Contents

Detailed Table of Contents

This first chapter acts as an entry point into the world of C++ programming equipping readers with the knowledge and skills to start their coding journey successfully. The authors begin by discussing the importance of C++ in the programming landscape and explore the intricacies of its compilation process shedding light on types of errors that programmers may encounter. The chapter introduces integrated development environments (IDEs). It provides step-by-step guidance on how to write your first C++ program called "Hello World." Detailed explanations, including code examples, token explanations and line-by-line breakdowns ensure an understanding of the basics. Readers will also delve into essential language features like values, statements, operators, and data types encompassing both value and reference types. The chapter explores declaration, initialization, and assignment using examples while offering insights into leveraging the "auto" keyword. Furthermore, it covers input methods coding conventions or standards to follow when writing code professionally and debugging techniques.

Chapter 2 delves deep into the world of algorithms and control structures, setting the foundation for effective programming in C++. Beginning with an overview of algorithms and their representation in pseudocode, it progresses to explore various control structures essential to the development of robust software. Core selection statements in C++, including the 'if', 'if...else', and nested 'if...else' are elucidated, with special attention given to common issues like the dangling-else problem. Logical operators—AND, OR, and NOT—are demystified, highlighting key differences between equality and assignment operations. Practical examples elucidate key concepts, followed by an in-depth look at repetition statements such as 'while', 'for', and 'do...while'. This chapter also introduces nested loops and their interactions with 'break' and 'continue' statements. Finally, the art of generating random numbers in C++ is unraveled, offering insights into seeding and calculating numbers within a desired range. The chapter concludes with hands-on exercises to fortify learning.

Chapter 3 dives deep into the core data structures of C++: arrays and vectors. Beginning with the fundamentals, it introduces the basic syntax and declaration of arrays and vectors, illustrated through concise examples. It elaborates on accessing array elements and efficiently iterating over them using loops. The chapter emphasizes array initialization techniques—ranging from direct initialization lists to loops. A focus on the range-based 'for' loop brings modern C++ practices to the fore. The intricate dynamics of parallel arrays, comparing arrays, and leveraging arrays in functions are explored. Diverse array structures, including static and multidimensional arrays, are expounded upon, offering insights into 2D arrays and jagged arrays. The chapter proceeds to discuss search and sort techniques, comparing their efficiencies. The versatility of the C++ Standard Library's vector template is introduced, diving into vector declaration, initialization, and algorithms. The latter section offers a deep dive into vector performance and its underlying intricacies.

Chapter 4 delves into the heart of modular programming in C++: functions. Starting with an introduction, it establishes the significance of functions in the realm of programming. The chapter systematically dissects the nuances of function prototypes and underscores the importance of function signatures and argument coercion. By elaborating on the intricacies of argument promotion, the reader gains a profound understanding of the subtleties in function calls. A categorization of functions based on return type and argument passing offers clarity and depth to the topic. The chapter elucidates the pivotal concept of scope, supported by a practical "Yes or No" program example. A deep dive into references and the distinct differences between pass-by-value and pass-by-reference paves the way for more advanced topics. Highlights include the exploration of default arguments, the power of function overloading, and the magic of recursion juxtaposed against iteration. The discussion on storage classes, with an emphasis on static storage, reinforces understanding.

Chapter 5 delves deep into one of the foundational and powerful concepts in C++: pointers. The chapter embarks with an enlightening introduction, elucidating the importance and utility of pointers in programming. Readers are guided through pointer variable declaration, initialization, and are introduced to pivotal pointer operations. The nuances of pointer arithmetic and expressions unfold, paving the way for a detailed discussion on pass-by-reference mechanisms with pointers. A significant focus is given to the interplay of 'const' with pointers, elaborating on varying degrees of pointer and data constancy. The chapter then demystifies the intricate relationship between pointers and arrays, leading into the intriguing world of arrays of pointers and function pointers. The 'sizeOf' operator's interaction with pointers is explored. Practical applications emerge through bubble sort and selection sort examples utilizing pass-by-reference. Closing the chapter is an engaging segment on pointer-based string processing.

Chapter 6 provides a comprehensive exploration of file processing in C++. It commences with an enlightening introduction, setting the tone for the intricate world of file operations. A deep dive into data hierarchy establishes a foundational understanding of organized data storage. Practical segments on appending data to files, whether it be characters or whole lines, are provided with illustrative examples. The chapter introduces the utility of the getline function for formatted input and delves into manipulating both input and output streams. As the chapter progresses, readers are shown the methods to create files and write data into them, followed by techniques to efficiently read from files. The concept of a file position pointer is introduced, allowing for intricate file manipulations. Essential to any file operation, the chapter concludes by highlighting the importance of recognizing exceptions and strategies for robust error handling. With hands-on exercises, readers are ensured a holistic understanding of file processing in C++.

Chapter 7 offers a meticulous exploration of the cornerstone of C++: classes and objects, ushering readers into the object-oriented paradigm. It commences with foundational topics on classes, their data members, and member functions. A thorough introduction to object-oriented analysis and design (OOAD) and the historical development of the unified modeling language (UML) creates a framework for understanding modern software design. As readers progress, the chapter unfolds the nuances of defining classes, with a UML representation of a sample class 'GradeCourse'. Emphasis is placed on software engineering principles, encompassing set and get functions, constructors, and destructors. The crucial concept of encapsulation is elucidated with detailed discussions on header files, source files, and client files. This chapter delves deep into advanced topics such as constructors (default and overloaded), destructors, static members, operator overloading, and the significance of the 'this' pointer.

Chapter 8 embarks on a detailed journey into the heart of object-oriented programming (OOP) by focusing on inheritance and polymorphism. It begins with an introductory discourse, highlighting the advantages of the OOP paradigm, and establishing a foundation with concepts like class hierarchy. The relationship between base and derived classes is elucidated, with focus given to access control specifiers, discussing their advantages and drawbacks. This sets the stage for understanding inheritance in depth, emphasizing the significance of constructors and destructors within derived classes. Public, protected, and private inheritance are examined meticulously. Polymorphism, one of the pillars of OOP, is expounded upon, with distinctions drawn between static and dynamic binding. Further, the chapter demystifies complex relationships among objects in inheritance, assignments between base and derived classes, and touches upon critical topics like overloading, virtual functions, pure virtual functions, abstract classes, and virtual destructors.

This chapter delves into the sophisticated facets of modern C++ programming, aiming to equip developers with the knowledge and skills necessary to leverage advanced features and best practices in their software development endeavors. It begins with an introduction to the significance of modern C++ practices and an overview of the advanced features that have been introduced in recent versions of the C++ standard. In summary, this chapter serves as a comprehensive guide to advanced C++ programming techniques, from theoretical concepts to practical applications, offering valuable insights into modern C++ practices and how they can be applied to develop high-quality, efficient, and scalable applications.

Preface

Within the pages of *Advancements, Applications, and Foundations of C++*, a symphony of knowledge orchestrated by Shams Al Ajrawi, Charity Jennings, Paul Menefee, Wathiq Mansoor, and Mansoor Alaali awaits your eager exploration. As editors, it is our honor to present this meticulously crafted reference book, a beacon of enlightenment in the ever-evolving landscape of programming education.

This book is not merely a collection of words on paper; it is a manifesto of empowerment, a gateway to mastery. With fervor and dedication, we have curated its contents to serve as a transformative force in your journey toward C++ proficiency.

Embark with us on an odyssey through the fundamental principles and advanced techniques that define the C++ programming paradigm. Each chapter is meticulously crafted to unravel the mysteries of the language, from its foundational elements to its most intricate nuances.

As you navigate through the chapters, you will discover a treasure trove of knowledge awaiting your grasp. From the rudiments of control structures to the elegance of object-oriented programming, every concept is presented with clarity and depth, empowering you to wield C++ with confidence and finesse.

But our mission extends beyond mere instruction; we aspire to ignite a passion for programming within you. Through immersive exercises, real-world examples, and supplementary materials, we aim to cultivate a dynamic learning experience that transcends the boundaries of the classroom.

Join us in revolutionizing the way C++ is taught and learned. Whether you are an aspiring programmer, a seasoned professional seeking to sharpen your skills, or an educator shaping the minds of tomorrow, *Advancements, Applications, and Foundations of C++* is your indispensable companion on the path to greatness.

As you embark on this transformative journey, remember that knowledge is power, and mastery is within your reach. Let this book be your guide, your ally, and your inspiration as you conquer the complexities of C++ programming.

While our primary audience comprises undergraduate students, we believe that this book will also resonate with professionals seeking to enhance their programming prowess, educators tasked with imparting programming knowledge, and self-learners eager to delve into the depths of C++.

W extend our gratitude to our readers for embarking on this journey with us. May *Advancements, Applications, and Foundations of C++* serve as a guiding light in your quest for programming proficiency.

ORGANIZATION OF THE BOOK

The book comprises nine meticulously structured chapters, each meticulously designed to guide readers through key aspects of C++ programming. Beginning with an elucidation of the fundamentals in Chapter 1, we progress through control structures, data structures, functions, and pointers, gradually unfolding the intricacies of memory management and algorithmic thinking.

As we delve deeper into the realms of C++, Chapters 6 and 7 usher readers into the realm of object-oriented programming, shedding light on classes, objects, inheritance, and polymorphism. Building upon this conceptual framework, Chapter 8 delves into the nuances of inheritance hierarchies and abstract classes, enriching readers' understanding of object-oriented design principles.

Finally, in Chapter 9, we embark on a voyage into the realm of advanced C++ programming techniques, equipping readers with the tools and insights necessary to navigate the complexities of modern software development.

Beyond its pedagogical content, this book aspires to leave a lasting impact on the academic community. By bridging the gap between theoretical knowledge and practical application, we aim to empower learners to wield C++ as a potent tool in their educational and professional endeavors.

To facilitate learning, each chapter is accompanied by practice exercises, real-world examples, and supplementary online materials. These resources aim to reinforce comprehension and provide avenues for further exploration.

IN CONCLUSION

In closing, dear readers, let us extend our heartfelt gratitude for accompanying us on this exhilarating expedition through the vast expanse of C++ programming. As the final pages of *Advancements, Applications, and Foundations of C++* draw near, we are filled with a profound sense of pride and accomplishment.

Together, we have embarked on a transformative journey, delving deep into the heart of one of the most powerful programming languages known to humanity. From the rudiments of syntax to the intricacies of object-oriented design, we have traversed a landscape teeming with knowledge and discovery.

But our voyage does not end here. Armed with the insights gleaned from these pages, you are poised to embark on your own adventures in the world of C++ programming. Let this book be your compass, guiding you through the complexities of code and the marvels of software design.

As you venture forth, remember the lessons learned within these pages: the importance of diligence, the power of perseverance, and the boundless potential that lies within each line of code. Whether you are a novice programmer taking your first steps or a seasoned veteran seeking new horizons, may the wisdom contained herein serve as your steadfast companion on your quest for mastery.

In the ever-evolving landscape of technology, the journey of learning is perpetual. As you continue to hone your skills and expand your knowledge, remember that the spirit of exploration and discovery is the fuel that propels us forward.

With that, we bid you farewell, dear readers. May your code be elegant, your algorithms efficient, and your passion for programming ever-ignited. Until we meet again on the shores of knowledge, may your journey be filled with wonder, curiosity, and boundless possibility.

Shams Al Ajrawi
Wiley Edge, USA & Alliant International University, USA

Charity Jennings
Wiley Edge, USA & University of Phoenix, USA

Paul Menefee
Wiley Edge, USA

Wathiq Mansoor
University of Dubai, UAE

Mansoor Ahmed Alaali
Ahlia University, Bahrain

Chapter 1 Introduction

ABSTRACT

This first chapter acts as an entry point into the world of C++ programming equipping readers with the knowledge and skills to start their coding journey successfully. The authors begin by discussing the importance of C++ in the programming landscape and explore the intricacies of its compilation process shedding light on types of errors that programmers may encounter. The chapter introduces integrated development environments (IDEs). It provides step-by-step guidance on how to write your first C++ program called "Hello World." Detailed explanations, including code examples, token explanations and line-by-line breakdowns ensure an understanding of the basics. Readers will also delve into essential language features like values, statements, operators, and data types encompassing both value and reference types. The chapter explores declaration, initialization, and assignment using examples while offering insights into leveraging the "auto" keyword. Furthermore, it covers input methods coding conventions or standards to follow when writing code professionally and debugging techniques.

1.1 INTRODUCTION

Welcome to the world of C++, a programming language that has stood the test of time and continues to be a cornerstone in the development of modern software. Since its inception in the early 1980s by Bjarne Stroustrup, C++ has evolved from its roots in the C language to become one of the most versatile and powerful programming languages in use today. Its ability to seamlessly blend high-level abstractions with low-level system access makes it uniquely capable of creating efficient, scalable, and high-performance applications.

C++ is more than just a programming language; it's a foundation that underpins much of the world's technology. From operating systems and system drivers to game development and high-frequency trading platforms, C++ plays a pivotal role in the infrastructure that powers our digital lives. Its significance lies not only in its performance and efficiency but also in its rich feature set that supports object-oriented, generic, and functional programming paradigms.

Learning C++ is an investment in your future as a developer. Mastering this language opens doors to a wide range of programming disciplines, including systems programming, application development, game development, and even embedded systems. The journey through C++ is one of discovery and

DOI: 10.4018/979-8-3693-2007-5.ch001

empowerment, as you'll learn to write code that's as close to the machine as possible while still maintaining portability and high-level abstractions.

This book, "Mastering C++," is designed to guide you through the intricacies of C++ from the fundamentals to advanced concepts. Whether you're new to programming or looking to deepen your understanding of C++, this book offers a structured path to enhancing your skills. Through clear explanations, practical examples, and in-depth discussions, you'll explore the breadth and depth of C++ and its applications.

As we embark on this journey together, remember that mastering C++ is not just about learning syntax or memorizing functions. It's about developing a mindset that values efficiency, performance, and the ability to think at multiple levels of abstraction. This book is your companion in building a solid foundation in C++, enabling you to tackle complex problems with confidence and creativity.

Let's begin this exciting journey into the world of C++, where every chapter brings you closer to mastering a language that shapes the backbone of modern computing.

Prerequisites and Target Audience

To effectively engage with "Mastering C++," readers should have a basic understanding of programming concepts such as variables, control structures (if statements, loops), functions, and an idea of how computer programs work. Familiarity with another programming language could be beneficial but is not mandatory. For those new to programming or needing a refresher, it's recommended to start with introductory materials on programming fundamentals and logic.

The target audience includes beginners who have grasped basic programming concepts, as well as intermediate programmers looking to deepen their knowledge in C++. For complete beginners, exploring resources on general programming principles and practicing with a simpler language like Python might make the transition to C++ smoother.

To ensure readers are well-prepared for "Mastering C++," it's important to outline more detailed prerequisites:

1. **Basic Programming Concepts**: A solid grasp of fundamental programming concepts such as variables, data types, control structures (if-else statements, loops), and basic input/output operations is essential. This foundational knowledge can be acquired through introductory programming courses or self-study materials focused on any high-level language.
2. **Problem-Solving Skills**: The ability to think logically and solve problems systematically is crucial. Readers should be comfortable with breaking down complex problems into manageable parts and developing step-by-step solutions.
3. **Understanding of Basic Computer Science Principles**: Familiarity with basic computer science concepts such as algorithms, data structures (arrays, lists), and the concept of memory management will greatly enhance the learning experience. These principles underpin many advanced topics in C++.
4. **Exposure to Object-Oriented Programming (OOP)**: While not strictly necessary, some exposure to object-oriented programming concepts such as classes, objects, inheritance, and polymorphism can be advantageous, as C++ is heavily object-oriented.

5. **Development Environment Setup**: Readers should be ready to set up a development environment for C++. This includes installing a C++ compiler and becoming familiar with a text editor or Integrated Development Environment (IDE).

For those needing to brush up on any of these areas, it's recommended to explore introductory resources in programming, computer science fundamentals, and object-oriented concepts.

This book is best suited for individuals with some programming experience, whether in C++ or another language, looking to deepen their understanding of C++ and its applications. Absolute beginners might find it challenging but not insurmountable, provided they are willing to put in extra effort to build the necessary foundational knowledge concurrently.

The Advantages

Conciseness

We can express repeated command sequences more accurately by using programming languages. Shorthand in C++ is particularly useful.

Maintainability

It is much simpler to change a few lines of text than it is to rearrange hundreds of processor instructions. Maintainability is improved even further in C++ due to its object-oriented nature.

Portability

Various processors offer various instructions. A benefit of C++ is that it can be used to write programs for almost any processor. Text programs can be converted into instructions for a variety of processors.

Many applications use C++, especially those that need speed and/or access to low-level features. Bjarne Structure developed it in 1979 as a set of additions to the C programming language. Although graphical programs can be created using C++, they are much more difficult to create and have much less portability than text-based (console) programs. This book will only cover console programs. SomeName and SomeName are not the same thing because of the case-sensitivity of C++. Because C++ is a high-level language, you don't have to be concerned about the specifics of processor instructions when writing programs in it. Access to some lower-level functionality that other languages do not offer is provided by C++ (e.g., memory addresses).

1.1.1 Compilation Process

The following is how a program moves from text files (or source files) to processor instructions:

Because each source file only shows a small part of the program, when it is turned into an object file, the object file has some marks that show which missing pieces it needs. Object files are intermediate files that represent an incomplete copy of the program. The connecter fills in the gaps between those object files and the precompiled libraries on which they depend, producing the finished program that the operating system can then execute (OS). Compiler and linker software is just another type of program. In the decoding stage of compilation, the compiler reads the file. In C++, each of these steps is completed in advance before a program is run. They are carried out during the lengthy execution process in a few different languages. Because of this, C++ code runs much faster than code written in many other contemporary languages. In C++, the compilation process includes an additional step where the source code is modified by a preprocessor before being sent to the compiler. Thus, the altered diagram is as follows:

Figure 1. Program moves from text files to processor instructions

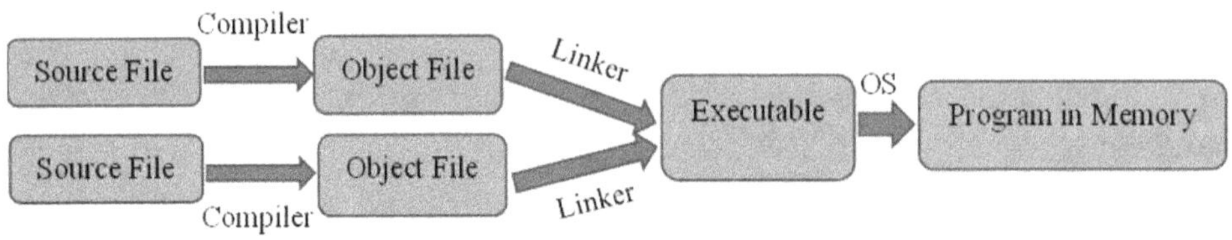

Figure 2. Altered diagram

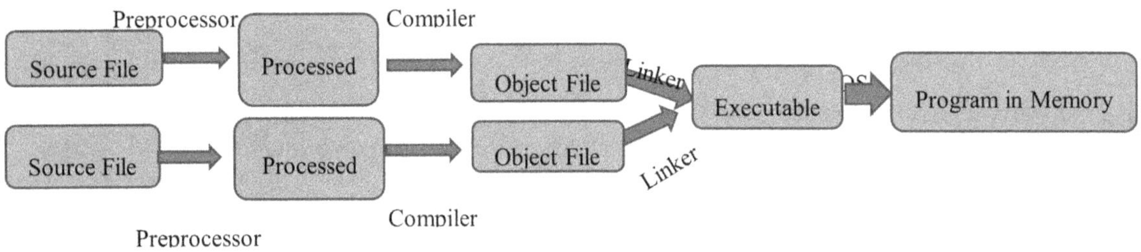

Programmers must fix the errors listed below in the Executable file generated from the C++ source.

1.1.2 Error Types

Compilation errors:

These occur during the compilation of code. As a result, no object file is generated. These could be syntax errors, indicating that the compiler does not comprehend something. They are frequently the result of something as simple as a typo. Compilers can also generate warnings. Although you are not required to heed the warnings, you should treat them as errors and fix and recompile them.

Link errors:

Occur during the linking process and may indicate that something the program refers to outside of the program cannot be found. These errors are typically fixed by modifying the offending reference and restarting the compile or link process.

Run-time errors:

Occur when the executable is executed. If the program commits an illegal act, it may crash unexpectedly. However, a more subtle type of run-time error, a logical error, can cause the program to behave in unexpected ways.

1.2 Integrated Development Environment IDE

Based on the developer's needs and preferences, C++ may be utilized with several different IDEs. A few examples of well-liked C++ integrated development environments are:

- Microsoft's Visual Studio is an integrated development environment (IDE) that has many useful features, such as syntax highlighting, code completion, and code debugging.
- Code::Blocks is an open-source IDE (integrated development environment) that is free to use and supports many compilers (such as GCC, Clang, and Visual C++).
- Eclipse is a free and open-source integrated development environment (IDE) that may be used for C++, among other languages. In addition to standard capabilities like code completion and debugging, it also provides several advanced options.
- You can use NetBeans, an open-source integrated development environment that works with several languages, to write code in C++.Code highlighting, code completion, and debugging are just some of the capabilities it provides.
- Apple made Xcode, which is an integrated development environment (IDE) that works with a wide range of languages, including C++. It has a lot of useful extras, like syntax highlighting and bug fixing.

1.3 First C++ Program "Hello World"

We'll start by introducing the fundamental C++ features with a "Hello, world!" program, as is the custom for all programmers.

1.3.1 Code

```
1 // A Hello World program
2 # include <iostream >
3 int main () {
4 std:: cout << "Hello, world !\n" ;
5 return 0;
}
```

C++ Notes:

- As shown in line 4, every C++ program requires a main function.
- Braces must be properly balanced.
- Semicolons are used to end statements.
- C++ is a case-sensitive programming language.
- C++ source code is saved in a file with the extension.cpp.
- The compiler ignores comments.

Line 2: The directive # include

- Preprocessor instruction
- No; after #include

Line 3: main int ()

Every C++ program requires an entry point; the main function is the C++ application's entry point.

The main function, like any other function, has a header and a body.

The return type, function name, and parameter list are enclosed in parentheses in the header. The return type may be void or int. There is no need to use the return statement in line 4 if it is void. However, if it is int, we must return it as an integer to the operating system, and we return zero to indicate that there is no error.

Line 4: std:: cout << "Hello, world !\n" ;

Cout is an object that displays messages.

To use it, please follow the steps below:

Include iostream> is required.

The cout Object

<< Insertion Stream Operator

1.3.2 Tokens

Tokens are the smallest meaningful symbols in the language and are the smallest chunk of a program that has meaning to the compiler. Our code displays all six types of tokens, but the usual use of operators is absent:

Table 1. Token type – purpose and examples

Token Type	Purpose	Examples
Keywords	For the Compiler, words with special meaning.	In int, double, char, for, while, auto, void, … etc.
Identifiers	User-defined names are, not built into the language.	cin, std, x, myArray, … etc.
Literals	Values specified directly in the code.	" Welcome to C++", "Hello", 20, 0.5 'A', … etc.
Operators	Logical or Mathematical operations.	+, -, &&, %, >>, <<, … etc.
Punctuation	Defining the program structure.	{ }, (),,, ;, …. etc.
Whitespace	Blank spaces ignoring by the compiler.	Tap, "\n", newline, spaces, me comments,…. etc.

1.3.3 Lines-by-Line Explanation

The // character tells the compiler to ignore the comments that follow it up until the end of the line. Between /* and /*/, a comment can also be written (for instance, x = 1 + /*sneaky comment here*/ 1);). A comment on this form may take up multiple lines. Not immediately obvious aspects of the code are explained in the comments. Make use of them by writing up your code in detail.

Preprocessor commands that start with # are lines that typically alter what code is being compiled. In this case, the iostream file, which describes the input and output procedures, is the other file whose #include instruction instructs the preprocessor to load its contents.

The code that should run when the program is implemented is defined by the int main()... statement. The curly braces signify the collection of several commands into a block. More info on this is in the next lectures. cout <<: This is the syntax for printing some text to the screen.

cout: This syntax is used to print text to the screen.

Namespaces: A namespace is a context in C++ where identifiers can be defined. It resembles a directory of names. The scope resolution operator is used to instruct the compiler to look for an identifier defined in a namespace when we want to access it (::).

We're instructing the compiler to search the std namespace, which is home to many common C++ identifiers, for cout. After line 2, insert the following line:

using namespace std;

The std namespace is utilized; This line instructs the compiler to look for any undefined identifiers in the std namespace. We can omit if we carry out this.

Line 4. Strings: A string is a group of characters, such as the phrase "Hello, world." A string that is explicitly specified in a program is known as a string literal.

The character "\n" stands for a newline in the escape sequence. It serves as an example of an escape sequence, a symbol that can be found in text literals and used to indicate special characters. The following is a list of the C++ escape sequences that can be used in strings:

Escape Sequence	Description
\a	System alert (beep bell)
\b	Backspace
\f	Page break(formatted)
\n	A line break (new line)
\r	Return the cursor to the start of the line
\t	Vertical tap
\\	Backslash
\'	Single quote
\"	Double quote
\ integer x	The character represented by X

Line 5. Returning 0 instructs the program to notify the operating system that it has completed its task successfully. For the time being, simply add it as the last line in the main block. We'll discuss this syntax in terms of functions.

Every statement, with the exception of preprocessor commands and blocks using, ends with a semicolon. New C++ programmers frequently make the error of forgetting these semicolons.

Using cout

Each time you invoke the cout object, you generate a lot of program overhead. So, doing a bunch of them all one after the other, takes a lot of processing time (relatively speaking):

```
cout << "Your 1st answer is: " << total1 << endl;
cout << "Your 2nd answer is: " << total2 << endl;
cout << "Your 3rd answer is: " << total3 << endl;
cout << "Your 4th answer is: " << total4 << endl;
```

You can do the same exact thing with less than half the amount of processing by re-writing those statements like:

```
cout << "Your 1st answer is: " << total1 << endl
<< "Your 2nd answer is: " << total2 << endl
<< "Your 3rd answer is: " << total3 << endl
<< "Your 4th answer is: " << total4 << endl;
```

1.3.4 Long lines

When your C++ source code is printed, long lines cause "wrap around," ruining the formatting of your source code. In the source code editor, long lines are also more difficult to manage, which forces the programmer to use the horizontal scroll bar needlessly. The most common reason for wrap around is writing a cout statement that is improperly formatted.

Here is a typical format error with the string written as one long line:

```
int main()
{
cout << "Peter Piper picked a peck of pickled peppers.\nHow many pickled pep-
pers did Peter Piper pick?\n";
return 0;
}
```

However, the same statement can be written like this, avoiding wrap - around:

```
int main()
{
cout << "Peter Piper picked a peck of pickled "
"peppers.\nHow many pickled peppers did "
"Peter Piper pick?\n";
cout << "Peter Piper picked a peck of pickled "
<< "peppers.\nHow many pickled peppers did "
<< "Peter Piper pick?\n";
return 0;
}
```

The output stream receives a single lengthy string in the first example. Three shorter strings are sent to the stream in the second example. Either option is effective.

What Does Cout Actually Do?

The cout object is typically used when creating a straightforward program in Win32 Console C++. I created the following program and used the debugger to trace it:

```
#include <iostream>
void main()
{
std::cout << ""Hello, world!"";
}
```

Even though this program is as basic as they come, when I traced the code, I found that one call to the cout object revealed the following. The cout object's source code, written in C++ and Assembly, can be found below.

This code is executed with each cout call. Naturally, this is only a portion of it. The #include files are also a part of cout, so if you wanted to see everything that it does, you would also need to look at all the code in those files.

When you next come across a program in your textbook that operates in a manner similar to this:

The code below is run separately every time the cout object appears in the program. cout "The Grande Hotel has " floors " floorsn"; cout "with " rooms " rooms and " suites; cout " suites.n"; keep in mind that this is how it will appear in the program. The three lines above would never be written by a programmer who works on embedded systems, operating systems, games, or device drivers. The majority of compilers' compiler optimizers compensate for some of the inefficiency of multiple consecutive calls, but C++ programmers should begin their training with efficiency in mind.

Here is some of the cout code you run each time you send a stream to the output device:

```
*fputc.c - write a character to an output stream
* Copyright (c) Microsoft Corporation. All rights reserved.
*Purpose:
* defines fputc() - writes a character to a stream
* defines fputwc() - writes a wide character to a stream
#include <cruntime.h>
#include <stdio.h>
#include <dbgint.h>
#include <file2.h>
#include <internal.h>
#include <mtdll.h>
*int fputc(ch, stream) - write a character to a stream
*Purpose:
* Writes a character to a stream. Function version of putc().
*Entry:
* int ch - character to write
* FILE *stream - stream to write to
*Exit:
```

```
* returns the character if successful
* returns EOF if fails
*Exceptions:
******************************************************************************
*/
```

The code specifies the fputc() and fputwc() methods, which are used to write a character or wide character to a given output stream. These functions are specified in the stdio.h header file of the standard library.

The goal of the comments at the start of the code is to convey information about the source file, copyright, and function definitions.

To execute input/output operations in C++, you would normally use the iostream library instead of the stdio.h library. In the iostream library, std::putchar() and std::putwchar() correspond to fputc() and fputwc(), respectively.

These functions serve a similar purpose as the ones you developed in C, but their syntax and use are distinct. Typically, the insertion operator () is used to send data to an output stream, whereas the extraction operator (>>) is used to read data from an input stream in C++.

1.4 Basic Language Features

Our program hasn't accomplished much thus far. Let's change it in different ways to show off some more intriguing constructs.

1.4.1 Values and Statements

A statement is a piece of code that accomplishes a task and is the fundamental building block of a program.

A statement with a value, such as a number, a string, the sum of two numbers, etc., is called an expression. Expressions include "Hello, world! n," "4 + 2," and "x - 1.

"Statements aren't always expressions. For instance, discussing the value of a #include statement is absurd.

1.4.2 Operators

With operators, we can perform arithmetic calculations. Expressions can be changed by operators to create new expressions. For instance, replacing "Hello, world!" with (4 + 2) / 3 would result in the program printing the number 2. The expressions 4 and 2 are affected by the + operator in this situation (its operands).

Operator varieties

Mathematical

The standard mathematical meanings for +, -, *, /, and parentheses apply, including the use of - to signify negation. The remainder of two numbers is taken by the modulus operator, which is %: 6% of five equals one.

Logical

used for "and," "or," and other similar terms. In the following lecture, more will be said about those.

Bitwise

used to change how numbers are represented in binary. We won't pay attention to these.

Assignment Operators

For shortening assignment expressions, C++ offers a number of assignment operators. The expression c = c + 3; can be condensed using the addition assignment operator += as c+= 3; as an example. The += operator calculates the sum of the value of the expression to its right and the value of the variable to its left, then stores the result in the variable to its left. This format can be used to write any sentence with the formula Variable = variable operator expression, where the same variable appears on both sides of the assignment operator and operator is one of the binary operators +, -, *, /, or% (or others we'll cover later in the text). As an illustration, the assignment c += 3 increases the value of the variable c by 3.

Assume: int c = 3, d = 5, e = 4, f = 6, g = 12;

Table 2. Assignment operator

Assignment Operator	Sample Expression	Explanation	Assigns
+=	c += 7	c = c + 7	10 to c
-=	d -= 4	d = d - 4	1 to d
*=	e *= 5	e = e * 5	20 to e
/=	f /= 3	f = f / 3	2 to f
%=	g %= 9	g = g % 9	3 to g

1.4.3 Increment and Decrement Operators

In addition to the arithmetic assignment operators, C++ offers two unary operators for modifying the value of a numeric variable by adding or removing 1. These are the unary increment and decrement operators, denoted by ++ and --, respectively. A program can use the increment operator, ++, in place of the expressions c = c + 1 or c += 1, to increase the value of a variable called c by 1. The terms "prefix increment" and "prefix decrement operator" refer to an increment or decrement operator that is prefixed to (placed before) a variable. The terms "postfix increment" and "postfix decrement operator" refer to an increment or decrement operator that is postfixed to (placed after) a variable.

Using the prefix increment (or decrement) operator, you can add (or take away) 1 from a variable to pre-increment (or pre-decrement) it. When a variable is pre-incremented (or pre-decremented), it is increased (decremented) by 1 before its new value is used in the expression in which it appears. Post-incrementing (or post-decrementing) a variable is the process of adding (or subtracting) 1 from it using the postfix increment (or decrement) operator. The variable's current value is used in the expression

Table 3. Operator and explanation

Operator	Called	Sample Expression	Explanation
++	Pre- increment	++a	Increment a by 1, then use the new value of an in the expression in which a resides.
++	Post- increment	a++	Use the current value of a in the expression in which a resides, then increment a by 1.
--	Pre- decrement	--b	Decrement b by 1, then use the new value of b in the expression in which b resides.
--	Post- decrement	b--	Use the current value of b in the expression in which b resides, then decrement b by 1.

in which it appears before being increased or decreased by 1 as a result of post-incrementing (or post-decrementing). As the program explains, post-increment and post-decrement deal with two values, the current value and the next value in memory, as opposed to pre-increment and pre-decrement, which only deal with one value. A has two values for post-decrement and post-increment (current and future in memory), but only one for pre-increment and pre-decrement.

```
/* Pre-increment/Post-increment
Pre-decrement/Post-decrement*/
#include <iostream>
using namespace std;
void main()
{
int A=20;
cout << "++A = " <<++A << '\n'; // A= 21
cout << "A++ = " << A++ << '\n'; // A= 21 22
cout << "--A = " << --A << '\n'; // A= 21
cout << "A-- = " << A-- << '\n'; // A= 21 20
system("pause");
}
```

The code illustrates the pre- and post-increment and decrement operators on an integer variable A.

The ++A operator performs an increment of 1 on the value of A and returns that value. The first cout line uses the pre-increment operator to increase the value of A by 1, and then outputs A as 21.

In contrast to pre-increment operators, the post-increment operator (A++) adds 1 to A but returns A's previous value. The post-increment operator is used to increase the value of A by 1, but the previous value of A (21), is written before the increment takes effect in the second cout statement.

The —->A operator performs a 1-by-1 decrement on A and returns the resulting value. By applying the pre-decrement operator, the value of A is decreased by 1, and the resulting value (20) is written in the third cout statement.

The post-decrement operator (A—) takes away 1 from A but puts it back to what it was before. The value of A is decreased by 1 in the fourth cout line, but the previous value of A (21), which is written before the decrement, is shown. The post-decrement operator is used for this decrease.

After pausing console output with system("pause"), the application ends normally.

In programming, these operators are often used to work with numbers and change the values of variables.

1.4.4 Operator Precedence

Table 4. Operator precedence

C						Associativity	Type
()						**Left to Right**	**Parentheses**
++	--	Static _cast<type>()				Left to right	Unary(postfix)
++	--	+	-			Right to left	Unary(prefix)
*	/	%				Left to right	Multiplicative
+	-					Left to right	Additive
<<	>>					Left to right	Insertion/ Extraction
<	<=	>	>=			Left to right	Relational
= ==	! =					Left to right	Equality
?:						Right to left	Conditional
=	+ =	-=	* * =	/=	%=	Right to left	Assignment

1.5 Data Types

Data types in C++ are used to specify the type of data that a variable or expression can hold. C++ has several built-in data types that can be categorized into four main categories:

1. Basic Data Types: C++ provides several basic data types that are used to represent simple values. These data types include:
   - **bool**: A Boolean data type that can hold true or false values.
   - **char**: A character data type that can hold a single character.
   - **int**: An integer data type that can hold whole numbers.
   - **float**: A floating-point data type that can hold decimal numbers with single precision.
   - **double**: A floating-point data type that can hold decimal numbers with double precision.
2. Derived Data Types: Derived data types in C++ are created by combining basic data types. These data types include:
   - **array**: A collection of values of the same data type.
   - **pointer**: A data type that holds the memory address of a variable.
   - **reference**: A data type that is an alias for an existing variable.
   - **function**: A data type that represents a function
3. User-defined Data Types: User-defined data types are created by the programmer to meet specific requirements. These data types include:
   - **struct**: A data type that groups related data elements together.

- class: A data type that encapsulates data and functions into a single entity.
- union: A data type that allows multiple data types to share the same memory location.

4. Enumeration Data Types: Enumeration data types are used to create a list of named constants. These data types include:
   - **enum**: A data type that defines a set of named constants.

Data types are important in C++ because they help the compiler allocate the appropriate amount of memory for a variable or expression, and they also determine the range of values that a variable or expression can hold. Understanding data types is essential for writing efficient and bug-free C++ programs.

When assigning or initializing data, it's important to understand conversions (from one data type to another) so that you can either control them or avoid them. Here are two illustrations of bad initializations:

float gallons equal 5.3 double miles, and an integer (123) is implicitly converted to a double in the first illustration. A double (5.3) is implicitly changed to a float in the second example (with possible loss of data, and a warning from the compiler).

The proper method for performing these initializations is:

123.0 double miles; 5.3 float gallons;

Using the phrase "integer frustration" as an example:

/*Using integers with division.

This program takes several attenpts to achieve the "desired

```
result" (1) when dividing 2 by 3 (2/3) using integers.
With floats or doubles, 2/3 = .6666667 or .666666666666667
With integers, 2/3 = 0 (actually 0 remainder 2, but C++
throws away the remainder)
*/
#include <iostream>
using namespace std;
int main()
{
int iDividend = 2, iDivisor = 3, iAnsw = 0;
// 2/3 is zero
iAnsw = iDividend / iDivisor;
cout << iAnsw << endl;
// attempting to "round up" to reach 1.
iAnsw = iDividend / iDivisor + 0.5;
cout << iAnsw << endl;
// Fails because division occurs first (result = 0)
// adding .5 to 0 is still less than 1
// explicitly casting to double gives an answer of .666667
iAnsw = static_cast<double>(iDividend) / iDivisor;
cout << iAnsw << endl;
// but, assigning .6666667 to an integer results in 0
// casting to double for the division, and rounding by
// adding .5 to the double result
```

```
iAnsw = static_cast<double>(iDividend) / iDivisor + 0.5;
cout << iAnsw << endl;
// finally, displays 1
return 0;
}
//Output:
/*
0
0
0
1
*/
```

Every expression has a type – a formal description of what kind of data its value is. For instance, 0 is an integer, 3.142 is a floating-point (decimal) number, and "Hello, world! \n" is a string value (a sequence of characters). Data of different types take different amounts of memory to store. Here are the built-in datatypes we will use most often.

Table 5. Data type

Data Type	Bytes	Also called	Example	Numeric Range
INTEGER				
Char	1	signed char	'A', 97	–128 to 127
unsigned char	1		'Z', 200	0 to 255
Short	2	Short int, signed short int	20000, -1	-32,768 to 32,767
unsigned short	2	unsigned short int	1, -60000	0 to 65,535
Int	4	(defalut)	-1, 200000000	–2,147,483,648 to 2,147,483,647
Unsigned int	4	unsigned	400000000	0 to 4,294,967,295
long[1]	4	long int, signed longint	-200000000	–2,147,483,648 to 2,147,483,647
unsigned long[2]	4	unsigned long int	400000000	0 to 4,294,967,295
long long	8			–9,223,372,036,854,775,808 to 9,223,372,036,854,775,807
unsigned long long	8			0 to 18,446,744,073,709,551,615
REALS:				
Float	4		10.0F	3.4E +/- 38 (7 digits)
double	8		10.0	1.7E +/- 308 (15 digits)

Notes on this table:

Because a signed integer can never be read as a negative number, an unsigned integer can represent a wider range of positive integers. If not provided, the majority of compilers assume it is signed. Most compilers assume signs when specified.

In non-descending order of size, short, int, and long are the three types of integers (int is usually a synonym for one of the other two). You shouldn't have to worry about which type to use unless you need to work with a lot of numbers or are worried about how much memory is being used. The three floating point types, float, double, and long double, which are specified in non-descending precision order, are the same (there is usually some imprecision in representing real numbers on a computer).

The sizes and ranges for each type are not fully standardized; those shown above are the ones used on most 32-bit computers. Only suitable types may be used in an operation. It is possible to add 34 and 3, but you cannot subtract a floating-point number from an integer addition.

When an operator is used with two integer operands, the result is truncated to an integer, so 1 / 4 evaluates to 0. An operator typically also returns a value of the same type as its operands. You would need to enter a value like 1 / 4.0 to obtain 0.25.

1.5.1 Value Types

- Value Types directly contain the data.
- Value Types are fixed-length data structures that are kept on stack memory; when a variable's value is assigned to another variable, it actually copies that value.

1.5.2 Reference Types

- Reference Types stores a reference to the value i.e. it stores address.
- Reference types are kept on the heap in memory and are available in a variety of sizes.

Note:

Only the reference, not the actual value stored in the memory address, is duplicated when one reference variable is assigned to another.

A heap is a portion of memory that has been set aside for a program to use for long-term storage of data structures, the existence of which or their size cannot be known until the program has begun to execute.

1.6 Variables

Identifiers with values are called variables. They are created by writing the type, name, and optionally the initial value for the variable in the same statement. Values are stored in variables.

1.6.1 Syntax:

Datatype varname=value; Datatype any datatype

Varname is identifier provided i.e. name of variable. Value is value of the variable.

1.6.2 Declaring a Variable

```
int MyInt; // Declaring an uninitialized variable called 'MyInt', of type 'int'
Initialize
```

```
int MyInt; // Declaring an uninitialized variable MyInt = 35; // Initializing
the variable
```

1.6.3 Declare and Initialize Variables

```
int a, b; // Declaring multiple variable of the same type
int a = 2, b = 3; // Declaring and initializing multiple variables of the same
type
```

In order to use a value later on, we might want to give it a name. We use variables to accomplish this. A variable is a specific place in memory with a name. Let's take the case where we intended to use 4 + 2 several times. It might be designated as x and used as follows:

```
1 # include <iostream >
2 using namespace std ;
3
4 int main () {
5 int x;
6 x = 4 + 2;
7 cout << x / 3 << ' ' << x * 2;
8
9 return 0;
10 }
```

(Note how we can print a sequence of values by "chaining" the << symbol.)

A variable's name serves as its identifying token. Identifiers may not begin with a number, but they may contain letters, digits, and underscores. The variable x is declared in line 5. In order for the compiler to know how much memory to set aside for type x and what sorts of operations can be performed on it, we must specify what type x will be. The initialization of x is done at line 6, where we give it a starting value. The assignment operator, denoted by the new operator =, is now used. Using this operator, we can later on in the code modify the value of x. Lines 5 and 6 might be swapped out for a single statement that does both initialization and declaration:

int x = 4 + 2; // This form of declaration/initialization is cleaner, so it is to be preferred.

Understanding type modifiers

Modifiers can be used to change a type. A modifier called short can limit the total number of values that a variable can contain. Can a variable retain a greater range of values if the modifier long is used? Long may require more storage space for a variable than short, and vice versa. Long can also alter double, while short and long can modify int. Modifiers like signed and unsigned only apply to integer type data. Unsigned variables can only store positive values, but signed variables can store both positive and negative values. The overall number of values that a variable can retain is unaffected by whether it is signed or unsigned; only the range of values is altered.

The default for the integer type is signed. Okay, feeling confused by your variety of type choices? Anyway, don't be. Commonly used kinds are shown in Table 1.1, along with a few modifiers. A possible range of values for each is also shown in the table.

1.6.4 Examples

1.6.4.1 Variables and Literals

C++ also has literals, which are fixed values used in expressions. There are several types of literals in C++:

Integer literals: Integer literals can be represented in decimal, hexadecimal (prefixed with 0x or 0X), and octal (prefixed with 0) formats. For example:

```
int decimalLiteral = 42;
int hexLiteral = 0x2A;
int octalLiteral = 052;
```

Floating-point literals: Floating-point literals can be represented in decimal or exponential notation (using e or E). For example:

```
float floatLiteral = 3.14;
double doubleLiteral = 6.02e23;
```

Boolean literals: Boolean literals can have two values, true or false. For example:

```
bool trueLiteral = true;
bool falseLiteral = false;
```

Character literals: Character literals are enclosed in single quotes (‘) and can represent a single character or an escape sequence. For example:

```
char charLiteral = 'A';
char escapeLiteral = '\n';
```

String literals: String literals are enclosed in double quotes (“) and represent a sequence of characters. For example:

```
const char* stringLiteral = "Hello, world!";
```

Variables and literals are fundamental concepts in C++ and are used extensively in programming. It is important to choose appropriate variable names and use literals properly in order to write clear and maintainable code.

1.6.4.2 Identifiers

Identifier - programmer-defined name for some part of a program

In C++, an identifier is a name used to identify a variable, function, class, or any other user-defined object. Identifiers are case-sensitive and can consist of letters, digits, and underscores (_), but cannot begin with a digit. There are some naming conventions for identifiers in C++, such as starting with a lowercase letter for variable names and starting with an uppercase letter for class names.

Here are some examples of valid C++ identifiers:

```
int myVariable;
double pi;
const int MAX_VALUE = 100;
void printHello();
class MyClass;
struct MyStruct;
```

In the examples above, myVariable, pi, MAX_VALUE, printHello, MyClass, and MyStruct are all valid identifiers. myVariable and pi are variable names, MAX_VALUE is a constant name, printHello is a function name, and MyClass and MyStruct are class and struct names.

Here are some examples of invalid C++ identifiers:

int 123myVariable; // identifier cannot begin with a digit

double my-variable; // identifier cannot contain a hyphen

const int max value = 100; // identifier cannot contain a space

void int(); // identifier cannot be a reserved keyword

In the examples above, 123myVariable is invalid because it begins with a digit, my-variable is invalid because it contains a hyphen, max value is invalid because it contains a space, and int is invalid because it is a reserved keyword in C++.

First character: A-Z a-z _

After first character: A-Z a-z _ 0-9

Table 6. Identifier

Identifier	Valid?	Reason if Invalid
totalSales	Yes	
total_Sales	Yes	
total.Sales	No	Cannot contain
4thQtrSales	No	Cannot begin with digit
totalSale@	No	Cannot contain @

1.6.4.3 Integer Data Types

In C++, integer data types are used to store whole numbers without any fractional part. There are several integer data types available in C++, with varying ranges and sizes. Here are the commonly used integer data types in C++:

Table 7. INT data

INT Data types	Bytes	Range
short int	2	-32,768 to 32,767
unsigned short int	2	0 to 65,535
int	4	-2,147,483,648 to 2,147,483,647
unsigned int	4	0 to 4,294,967,295
long int	4	-2,147,483,648 to 2,147,483,647
long long int	8	-9,223,372,036,854,775,808 to 9,223,372,036,854,775,807
unsigned long int	4	0 to 4,294,967,295
unsigned long long int	8	0 to 18,446,774,073,709,551,615 x 10 ^ 19

When declaring integer variables, it is important to choose the appropriate data type depending on the range and precision of the values to be stored. For example, if you know that the value will always be positive, you can use an unsigned integer data type to increase the range of values that can be stored.

1.6.4.3 Char Data Type

The char data type is used to represent single characters. It is a built-in data type and can be used to store any ASCII character. The char data type occupies 1 byte of memory and can hold values ranging from -128 to 127 or 0 to 255, depending on whether it is signed or unsigned.

To declare a char variable, you can use the following syntax:

```
char myChar = 'a';
```

Here, myChar is the name of the variable and 'a' is the value assigned to it. The value must be enclosed in single quotes to indicate that it is a character literal.

You can also assign the ASCII value of a character to a char variable. For example:

```
char myChar = 65; // Assigns the ASCII value of 'A' to myChar
```

To output the value of a char variable, you can use the cout object from the iostream library:

```
cout << myChar << endl; // Outputs the value of myChar
```

The output will be the character 'a', as assigned to the variable in the example above.

In C++, you can also use escape sequences to represent non-printable characters or characters that cannot be easily typed on a keyboard. For example:

```
char newLine = '\n'; // Represents the newline character
char backslash = '\\'; // Represents the backslash character
```

Here, \n represents the newline character and \\ represents the backslash character. The backslash is used to indicate that the next character should be interpreted as a special character.

Overall, the char data type is useful for storing individual characters and can be used in a variety of applications, such as text processing and encryption.

```
#include <iostream>
using namespace std;
int main() {
char firstInitial = 'A'; char middleInitial = 'J'; char lastInitial = 'S';
cout << "Your initials are: " << firstInitial;
cout << " " << middleInitial << " " << lastInitial << endl;
system("pause");
return 0;
}
```

In the above example we declared three **char** variables: **firstInitial**, **middleInitial**, and **lastInitial**. These variables are assigned the characters 'A', 'J', and 'S', respectively.

The program then uses the **cout** object from the **iostream** library to output a message to the console. The message includes the values of the **char** variables separated by spaces, using the **<<** operator to concatenate the values.

Finally, the **system("pause")** function is used to pause the console output so that the user can view the results before the program exits. The **return 0** statement at the end of the **main** function indicates that the program executed successfully.

When this program is executed, the output will be:

```
lessCopy code
Your initials are: A J S
```

This program demonstrates the use of **char** variables to store and output individual characters. It also shows how the **cout** object can be used to output multiple values on a single line.

1.6.4.4 The C++ String

In C++, a string is a sequence of characters stored in a contiguous block of memory. The string class is part of the C++ standard library and provides a convenient way to work with strings.

To use strings in a C++ program, you need to include the string header file:

```
#include <string>
```

Once you have included the header file, you can declare a string variable like this:

```
std::string myString;
```

You can also initialize the string with a value like this:

```
std::string myString = "Hello, world!";
```

To access the characters in a string, you can use the square bracket [] operator, just like you would with an array:

```
char firstChar = myString[0];
```

You can also use the at() member function to access characters, which performs bounds checking to ensure that you don't access characters beyond the end of the string:

```
char secondChar = myString.at(1);
```

The string class provides many useful member functions for working with strings, including:

```
length() or size(): Returns the length of the string
substr(): Returns a substring of the string
find(): Searches for a substring within the string
replace(): Replaces a portion of the string with a new substring
append(): Appends a string or character to the end of the string
insert(): Inserts a string or character at a specified position in the string
erase(): Removes a portion of the string
```

For example, to get the length of a string and output it to the console:

```
std::string myString = "Hello, world!";
std::cout << "Length of string: " << myString.length() << std::endl;
```

This would output:

Length of string: 13

Overall, the string class in C++ provides a flexible and convenient way to work with strings, making it easy to manipulate and modify string data in a program.

String – is an array of characters **OR** Series of characters stored in adjacent memory locations

Ex. "Hello"

```
H
E
```

```
L
L
O
\0
\0 null terminator
```

This example demonstrates the usage of the string class.

The program starts by including the necessary header files - iostream for input/output operations and string for string manipulation using the string class.

In the main() function, a variable movieTitle of type string is declared. It is then assigned the value "The Notebook" using the assignment operator =.

Finally, the program outputs the string "My favorite movie is " concatenated with the value of movieTitle using the insertion operator <<. The output is displayed on the console using cout.

Overall, this program shows how to declare and initialize a string variable, and how to output its value.

1.6.4.5 Floating-Point Data Type

In C++, floating-point data types are used to represent real numbers with fractional parts. The two primary floating-point data types in C++ are float and double.

The float data type can represent real numbers with up to 7 decimal digits of precision, while the double data type can represent real numbers with up to 15 decimal digits of precision.

Here's an example program that demonstrates the usage of floating-point data types in C++:

```
#include <iostream>
using namespace std;
int main() {
float f = 3.14159f;
double d = 3.141592653589793;
cout << "Float value: " << f << endl;
cout << "Double value: " << d << endl;
return 0;
}
```

In this program, a float variable f is declared and initialized with the value 3.14159f, where the f at the end indicates that the value should be treated as a float.

A double variable d is also declared and initialized with the value 3.141592653589793.

Finally, the program outputs the values of f and d using cout.

Output:

Float value: 3.14159

Double value: 3.14159

Note that although the value of d has more decimal places than f, they are both displayed with the same precision of 6 decimal digits by default

The floating-point data types are:

Float

Double
long double
Float has 7 digits of accuracy.
Double has 15 digits of accuracy.

Float	4 bytes
Double	8 bytes

Floating-point literals are stored as doubles by default.
3.5
3.5f (to use as float).

1.6.4.6 The Bool Data Type: True or False

The bool data type is used to represent boolean values, which can either be true or false. bool is a built-in data type, and it is used to store variables that can have only two possible values: true or false.

Here is an example program that demonstrates the usage of bool data type:

```
#include <iostream>
using namespace std;
int main() {
bool isTrue = true;
bool isFalse = false;
cout << "isTrue = " << isTrue << endl;
cout << "isFalse = " << isFalse << endl;
return 0;
}
```

In this program, isTrue and isFalse are two bool variables that are initialized with true and false, respectively. The cout statement is used to output the values of these two variables.

```
Output:
isTrue = 1
isFalse = 0
```

In C++, true is represented by the value 1 and false is represented by the value 0. When a bool value is output using cout, true is displayed as 1, and false is displayed as 0.

```
//Another example demonstrate Bool data type
#include <iostream>
using namespace std;
int main() {
```

```
bool firstValue = true;
bool secondValue = false;
cout << "firstValue is " << firstValue << endl;
bool firstValue = true;
bool secondValue = false;
cout << "firstValue is " << firstValue << endl; cout << "secondValue is " <<
secondValue << endl; secondValue = true;
cout << "firstValue is " << firstValue << endl; cout << "secondValue is " <<
secondValue << endl;
return 0;
}
```

The program declares two bool variables named firstValue and secondValue and assigns them the values true and false, respectively.

Then, it prints the values of these variables using the cout statement. Since true is equivalent to the value 1 and false is equivalent to 0, the output will be:

```
firstValue is 1
secondValue is 0
```

Next, the value of the secondValue variable is changed to true and the values of both variables are printed again using cout. The output will be:

```
firstValue is 1
secondValue is 1
```

This program illustrates the use of boolean variables and how they are treated as 1 or 0 when printed to the console.

1.6.5 Variable Assignments and Initialization

A variable is a named memory location that stores a value of a particular data type. Assigning a value to a variable involves storing a value in its memory location. Initialization is the process of assigning an initial value to a variable when it is created.

Variable Assignments:

Variable assignments are done using the assignment operator "=", which assigns a value to a variable. For example, the following code assigns a value of 10 to the variable num:

```
int num;
num = 10;
```

Variable Initialization:

Variable initialization is the process of assigning an initial value to a variable when it is created. Initialization is done using the assignment operator "=", and it can be done in the declaration statement of the variable. For example, the following code initializes the variable num with a value of 10:

```
int num = 10;
```

If the variable is not initialized when it is declared, it will contain a garbage value that is the value of the memory location where the variable is stored.

```
int num; //num is not initialized
```

It is always recommended to initialize variables when they are declared to avoid unexpected behavior in the program.

```
int a; // <====declaration
a = 10; //<=====assigned (initialized)
a = 20; //<=====assigned (but not initialized)
int b = 10; //<=======declaration and assignment (initialized)
```

Declare	Reserve a space in memory for a variable
Assign	Change the contents of the variable
Initialize	Assigning a variable a value for the first time

1.6.6 Auto Keyword

The auto keyword is used to automatically deduce the data type of a variable from its initializer. When a variable is declared using the auto keyword, its type is inferred from the expression used to initialize it.

Here's an example:

```
auto x = 10; // x is an integer
auto y = 3.14; // y is a double
auto z = "hello"; // z is a string
```

In the above example, the type of the variables x, y, and z is inferred from their respective initializers. The auto keyword is especially useful when the type of the variable is complicated or difficult to write out explicitly.

Note that the auto keyword can only be used for variables declared with an initializer. It cannot be used for function arguments, return types, or class member variables.

```
auto interestRate = 12.0; auto stockCode = 'D';
```

1.7 Input

Now that we know how to give names to values, we can have the user of the program input values. This is demonstrated in line 6 below:

```
1 # include <iostream >
2 using namespace std ;
3
4 int main () {
5 int x;
6 cin >> x;
7
8 cout << x / 3 << ' ' << x * 2;
9
10 return 0;
```

Just as cout << is the syntax for outputting values, cin >> (line 6) is the syntax for inputting values.

Memory trick: Think of the angle brackets for cout and cin as arrows pointing in the direction of data flow if you have difficulties remembering which way they go. In the same way as cout represents the terminal and your data flow to it, cin symbolizes the terminal with data flowing from it to your variables. cin.getline (for char[]) and getline combined (for string) Run this program by copying it into a source file. It's ineffective, isn't it? The names are left blank as the application never stops asking the user to enter them. This happens as a result of how cin.getline/getline and cin function differently. When reading a non-character value, cin leaves a n character in the input buffer.

When cin.getline notices that \n, it assumes that the string being entered has come to an end (before the user enters anything). The cin.getline/getline is ignored by the program, which proceeds as if it never existed.

```
int number; //any number entered just to leave a \n in the buffer
string sName; //a string class string which includes spaces
char cName[80]; //a character array type string that includes spaces
cout << "Enter a number: ";
cin >> number; //leave a \n in buffer
//[Solution: add this line]cin.ignore(); //clear the buffer
cout << "Enter a name: ";
getline(cin, sName); //input a name into the string object
cout << "Enter a number: ";
cin >> number; //leave a \n in buffer
//[Solution: add this line]cin.ignore(); //clear the buffer
cout << "Enter another name: ";
cin.getline(cName, 79, '\n'); //input a name into the character array
cout << "You entered:\n"
<< sName << "\nand\n"
<< cName << endl;
```

The solution to this problem is to clear the input buffer after the **cin**, but before the **cin.getline** or **getline**. You can clear the buffer with this statement:

```
cin.ignore();
/*
Without the cin.ignore():
Enter a number: 1
Enter a name: Enter a number: 2
Enter another name: You entered:
and
With the cin.ignore():
Enter a number: 1
Enter a name: Mrs. Sarah Cynthia Sylvia Stout
Enter a number: 2
Enter another name: Master Reginald Peaquot Thorton III, Esq.
You entered:
Mrs. Sarah Cynthia Sylvia Stout
and
Master Reginald Peaquot Thorton III, Esq.
*/
//Another example:
#include <iostream>
#include <string>
using namespace std;
int main()
{
string make;
int cylinders;
double mpg;
const int MODEL_SIZE = 80;
char model[MODEL_SIZE];
int topspeed;
//priming read
cout << "\n\nEnter name ('Q' or Enter to quit): ";
getline(cin, make); //input a name into a string
if (make != "Q" && make != "")
{
cout << "Enter number cylinders: ";
cin >> cylinders;
cout << "Enter mpg: ";
cin >> mpg;
cin.ignore(); //clear the buffer
cout << "Enter model: ";
cin.getline(model, MODEL_SIZE-1, '\n'); //input a name into a character array
```

```
cout << "Enter top speed: ";
cin >> topspeed;
cin.ignore(); //clear the buffer between number and string
}
//main loop
while (make != "Q" && make != "")
{
cout << "Make: " << make << " Model: " << model << " cylinders: "
<< cylinders << " mpg: " << mpg << " Top speed: " << topspeed << endl;
//see if user wants another
cout << "\n\nEnter name ('Q' or Enter to quit): ";
getline(cin, make); //input a name into a string
if (make != "Q" && make != "")
{
cout << "Enter number cylinders: ";
cin >> cylinders;
cout << "Enter mpg: ";
cin >> mpg;
cin.ignore(); //clear the buffer between number and string
cout << "Enter model: ";
cin.getline(model, MODEL_SIZE-1, '\n'); //input a name into a character array
cout << "Enter top speed: ";
cin >> topspeed;
cin.ignore(); //clear the buffer between number and string
}
}
return 0;
}
```

Defining New Names for Types

For a type that already exists, a new name can be defined. In fact, I proceed in the following manner: unsigned short int ushort typedef; The type unsigned short int is also referred to as ushort in this code. Use typedef, the current type, the new name, and then the current type to define new names for existing types. Types with lengthy names are frequently given shorter ones using typedef. Your new type name can be used the same way as the original type. I create the additional ushort variable, which is really simply an unsigned short int, and set its initial value before displaying it.

Understanding Which Types to Use

When it comes to the basic types, you have several options. How then do you decide which type to employ? Well, using int is usually ideal if you need an integer type. This is due to the fact that integers are typically constructed so that they take up the least amount of memory possible. Use unsigned int to represent integer values that are larger than the maximum int or that will never be negative. Use a kind that requires less storage if your memory is limited. However, memory shouldn't be a major problem on the majority of machines. (Programming for game consoles or portable electronics is a different matter.) Last but not least, if you require a floating point number, it is usually better to use a float, which is again likely to be built so that it takes up the least amount of memory possible for the computer to manage.

Using Constants

For the purpose of expressing the point value of an alien, I define the constant ALIEN POINTS. I simply alter the declaration with the prefix const, as in Const int ALIEN POINTS = 150. ALIEN POINTS can now be used like any other integer literal. Take note of the constant's name, which is written in all caps. Although only a convention, this one is widely used. Programmers can detect that an identifier is a constant value by the capitalization.

Using Enumerations

Unsigned int constants, often known as enumerators, make up an enumeration. In most cases, the enumerators are linked and follow a specific order. An illustration of an enumeration is given here: This specifies the enumeration "difficulty," which has the values "NOVICE, EASY, NORMAL, HARD, UNBEATABLE." Enumerators have an initial value of zero and an increasing value of one by default. Therefore, NOVICE is 0, EASY is 1, NORMAL is 2, HARD is 3, and UNBEATABLE is 4. Use the term enum, an identifier, a list of enumerators enclosed in curly braces, and the phrase "define" to define your own enumeration.

This new enumeration type is then used to construct a variable. difficulty The value of the variable myDifficulty is set to EASY (which is equal to 1). Being of the type difficulty, myDifficulty can only store one of the values listed in the enumeration. NOVICE, EASY, NORMAL, HARD, UNBEATABLE, 0, 1, 2, 3, or 4 are the only options for myDifficulty.Using Constants as a Resource 31.

I define another enumeration after that.

```
FIGHTER COST = 25, BOMBER COST = 30, and CRUISER COST = 50;
```

This line of code establishes the definition of the enumeration shipCost, which in a strategy game denotes the price in resource points for three different types of ships, In it, I give some of the enumerators particular integer values. The figures show how many resource points each ship is worth. If you want, you can give the enumerators values. Enumerators without values are given the value of the preceding enumerator plus one. BOMBER COST is initially set to 26 because I didn't give it a value.

I then define a variable that belongs to this new enumeration type. Afterwards, I give an example of how to use enumerators in arithmetic calculations by setting shipCost myShipCost = BOMBER COST; myShipCost - (CRUISER COST). Returning 0 instructs the program to notify the operating system that it has completed its task successfully. For the time being, simply add it as the last line in the main block. We'll discuss this syntax in terms of functions.

Dealing with Integer Wrap Around

What occurs when you raise an integer variable above its upper bound? It appears that you don't produce an error. The value "wraps around" to the minimum value for the type instead. I'll then show you this phenomenon.

I start by giving the score the highest possible value.

I increase the variable after setting score to 4294967295.

Then I increment the variable.

```
++score;
```

Score becomes 0 as a result of the value wrapping around, similar to what happens when a car odometer exceeds its maximum value (see Figure). An integer variable is "wrapped around" to its maximum value when it is decremented past its minimum value.

1.8 Coding Standards

Coding standards in C++ are a list of rules and best practices that should be used when writing code. These rules make sure that the code is easy for other developers to read, fix, and understand. Some common coding standards followed in C++ are:

- Naming conventions: consistent naming conventions should be followed for all variables, functions, and classes. Names should be descriptive and meaningful to convey their purpose.
- Indentation and formatting: Code should be properly indented and formatted to enhance readability. The placement of curly braces and blank lines between code blocks should be consistent.
- Comments: Comments should be added wherever they are needed to explain what code blocks are for and how they work. Comments should be concise and to the point.
- Handling errors: The right ways to handle errors should be used to keep programs from crashing and doing things that aren't clear. Exceptions should be used for error handling where applicable.
- Code reuse: Code should be modular and reusable to reduce duplication and improve maintainability. Functions and classes should be designed to be independent and reusable.
- Performance: Performance considerations should be taken into account while designing and writing code. Efficient algorithms and data structures should be used wherever possible.

If you follow these coding standards, you can write C++ code that is consistent, easy to maintain, and works well.

Nearly every programming shop has some kind of standard for programmers to follow. They do this to "standardize" their code, making it easier and faster for others to read, modify, and debug their code. This course also has a simple set of standards for all the work you submit. The following standards were compiled from Cubic Corp., Inspirel.com, Boost.org, and Dartmouth.

1.8.1 Things to Do

Avoid leading and trailing blank lines in your source file. Avoid trailing whitespace on a line. Don't exceed the maximum line length of 70 characters. Use no more than two consecutive blank lines anywhere in your source code. Avoid "pasting" anything other than common ASCII characters into your code.

Start your source file with a comment block that has your name, the name of the assignment, and a description of the assignment.

Use "student style" compound statements (bracketed blocks of code) by always placing your brackets alone on a line and aligning your brackets with each other and with the first character of the control statement they follow (if, else, while, for, switch, etc.). Use a compound statement for each control statement, even those with a single line of code.

Separate major sections of your code (preprocessor directives, comment blocks, input, loops, and output) with blank lines. Do not separate lines of code within major sections.

Block comment each function (other than main) with a brief description of what the function does, a description of each parameter, and the return value.

Use ALL_CAPS for *#define* and *const* identifiers. Do not use all capital letters for any variables not qualified as constants.

Put a space before and after each operator (x >= y, not x>= y).

Single-line comment only those statements that might be confusing to another programmer.

Write "safe" code. Use const whenever a value doesn't change. Don't pass reference parameters or pointers to a function unless the function **needs** to change a value declared elsewhere. Be aware of buffer overflows whenever user input is involved.

Always validate user input using the methods shown elsewhere (after learning the *while* statement).

Always include identifiers in function prototypes.

Fix all compiler **warnings** before finalizing the code.

Design and develop your program using the shortest, most efficient code possible. Exception: Where readability or maintainability would suffer, choose a longer, clearer approach.

Always adhere to the best programming practices as shown in your text but be aware that it does deviate from the guidelines provided above (which you must follow).

Add some sample output as a comment after your source code; you can do this with a comment block.

1.8.2 Things to Avoid

Goto, break, and continue statements, the exit () function and all "system" functions. Exceptions: break may be used inside a switch statement.

Magic numbers. Use named const declarations or #define statements instead.

Global variables. Global **const** declarations may be made if they are required in 2 or more functions.

Multiple 'cout' objects placed one after the other in code. When possible, break a single long 'cout' statement onto multiple lines, but don't invoke the cout object itself more than once without intervening statements.

Placing code on the same line as control statements. Always indent dependent code on the line(s) following your control statements.

Determining the Size of a Data Type

```
//sample program that determines the sizes of data types
#include <iostream>
using namespace std;
int main() {
```

```
double amount;
cout << "An int is stored in " << sizeof(int) << " bytes.\n";
cout << "Variable amount is stored in " << sizeof(amount) << " bytes.\n";
system("pause");
return 0;
}
```

The above C++ program uses the sizeof operator to determine the sizes of different data types in memory. The program declares a double precision floating-point variable amount, and then uses the sizeof operator to determine the size of the int and double data types.

The sizeof operator returns the size of its operand in bytes, so sizeof(int) will give the size of an integer in bytes, and sizeof(amount) will give the size of the amount variable in bytes.

The program then outputs the size of an int and the size of the amount variable using cout. The system("pause") statement is used to pause the console window so that the user can see the output before the window closes.

Output:

An int is stored in 4 bytes.

Variable amount is stored in 8 bytes.

1.9 Debugging

Debugging in C++ is the process of finding errors or bugs in a program and fixing them. Debugging is an important part of the development process, as even small errors can cause unexpected results or program crashes.

There are several techniques and tools available for debugging in C++, including:

- Using a debugger: A debugger is a tool that allows you to step through your code and examine the state of variables and memory at various points in the program. Popular debuggers for C++ include GDB and LLDB.
- Printing debug statements means adding statements to the code that show the values of variables or the program's execution path. This can help you identify where a program is going wrong.
- Using assertions: Assertions are statements that check a condition and stop the program if the condition is false. Assertions are useful for checking assumptions about the state of the program and can help you catch errors early in development.
- Code review: Code review involves having other developers review your code and provide feedback. This can help you identify errors or areas for improvement in your code.

Before putting your code into production, you should test it thoroughly, as even small mistakes can have big effects. Good debugging practices, such as using a debugger, writing clear and understandable code, and testing your code thoroughly, can help you catch errors early and ensure that your code is robust and reliable When writing C++ programs, you'll encounter two types of errors: compilation errors and runtime errors. Compiler errors are issues that are typically brought on by misuse of types or violations of syntax rules. These are frequently brought on by mistakes like typos. Runtime errors are issues that you only discover when you run the program; even though you specified a legitimate program, it doesn't perform the task you intended. Since the compiler won't alert you to them, these are typically more difficult to find.

Advanced Practice Exercises with Answers

1. Example 1: Hello, World! Program

Question: How do you write a simple C++ program to display "Hello, World!" on the console?

Objective: To understand the structure of a C++ program and practice compiling and running a basic application.

```
#include <iostream>

int main() {
    std::cout << "Hello, World!" << std::endl;
    return 0;
}
```

Explanation:

This C++ program is the classic "Hello, World!" example, commonly used as the first program when learning a new programming language. It consists of a single function, **main()**, which is the entry point for C++ programs. Inside the **main()** function, it uses **std::cout**, a standard output stream, to print the message "Hello, World!" to the console. The **<< std::endl;** part is used to insert a newline character after the message and flush the output buffer, ensuring that the message is immediately displayed. The program then returns 0, signaling successful execution to the operating system.

2. EXAMPLE 2: GREETING USER

Question: How can you modify the "Hello, World!" program to ask for the user's name and greet them personally?

Objective: To learn how to use **cin** for input and concatenate strings for personalized output.

```
#include <iostream>
#include <string>

int main() {
    std::string name;
    std::cout << "Enter your name: ";
    std::cin >> name;
    std::cout << "Hello, " << name << "!" << std::endl;
    return 0;
}
```

Explanation:

This simple C++ program prompts the user to enter their name and then greets them by name. It starts by declaring a string variable **name** to store the user's input. It then displays a message, "Enter your name: ", and waits for the user to input their name. The input is captured using **std::cin >> name;**, and the program proceeds to greet the user with "Hello, [name]!", where **[name]** is replaced by the user's input. Finally, the program ends its execution and returns 0, indicating successful completion.

3. EXAMPLE 3: VARIABLE MANIPULATION

Question: How do you declare, initialize, and modify an integer variable in C++?

Objective: To understand the process of working with variables including declaration, initialization, and assignment.

```
#include <iostream>

int main() {
    int number = 5; // Declaration and initialization
    number = 10; // Assignment
    std::cout << "The number is " << number << std::endl;
    return 0;
}
```

Explanation:

This C++ program demonstrates variable declaration, initialization, and assignment. Initially, the variable **number** is declared as an **int** and initialized with the value **5**. Then, **number** is reassigned the value **10**. Finally, the program outputs the current value of **number**, which is **10**, to the console.

4. EXAMPLE 4: USING AUTO KEYWORD

Question: How can you use the **auto** keyword for type inference in variable declaration?

Objective: To demonstrate the use of **auto** in simplifying variable declarations by allowing the compiler to infer the type.

```
#include <iostream>

int main() {
    auto number = 15; // 'auto' infers 'int' from the initialization
    std::cout << "The number is " << number << std::endl;
    return 0;
}
```

Explanation:

This C++ program demonstrates the use of the **auto** keyword to automatically deduce the type of the variable **number** from its initializer. Here, **number** is initialized to **15**, so **auto** deduces its type as **int**. The program then prints the value of **number** to the console.

5. EXAMPLE 5: BASIC ARITHMETIC OPERATIONS

Question: How do you perform basic arithmetic operations and display the results in C++?

Objective: To practice using arithmetic operators in C++ and understand operator precedence.

```
#include <iostream>

int main() {
    int a = 10, b = 3;
    std::cout << "a + b = " << (a + b) << std::endl;
    std::cout << "a - b = " << (a - b) << std::endl;
    std::cout << "a * b = " << (a * b) << std::endl;
    std::cout << "a / b = " << (a / b) << " (integer division)" << std::endl;
    std::cout << "a % b = " << (a % b) << " (remainder)" << std::endl;
    return 0;
}
```

Explanation:

This C++ program demonstrates the use of basic arithmetic operators. Here's what it does:

1. **Initialization**: Two integer variables, **a** and **b**, are declared and initialized with values **10** and **3**, respectively.
2. **Addition (+)**: The program calculates the sum of **a** and **b** using the **+** operator and prints the result (**13**).
3. **Subtraction (-)**: It calculates the difference between **a** and **b** using the **-** operator and prints the result (**7**).
4. **Multiplication (*)**: It multiplies **a** by **b** using the * operator and prints the product (**30**).
5. **Integer Division (/)**: It divides **a** by **b** using the **/** operator and prints the quotient (**3**). Since both operands are integers, the result is also an integer, meaning any fractional part is discarded.
6. **Modulus (%)**: It calculates the remainder of the division of **a** by **b** using the % operator and prints the result (**1**). The modulus operator is useful for finding remainders in integer division.
7. **Program Completion**: The program successfully ends with **return 0;**.

This simple program effectively illustrates how arithmetic operations are performed in C++, highlighting the integer division behavior where the decimal part is truncated, and how the modulus operator can be used to find division remainders.

6. EXAMPLE 6: INCREMENT AND DECREMENT OPERATORS

Question: How do you use the increment and decrement operators in C++?

Objective: To understand and demonstrate the use of prefix and postfix increment/decrement operators.

```
include <iostream>

int main() {
    int counter = 10;
    std::cout << "Counter: " << counter << std::endl;
    std::cout << "Counter++: " << counter++ << std::endl; // Postfix increment
    std::cout << "++Counter: " << ++counter << std::endl; // Prefix increment
    std::cout << "Counter--: " << counter-- << std::endl; // Postfix decrement
    std::cout << "--Counter: " << --counter << std::endl; // Prefix decrement
    return 0;
}
```

Explanation:

This C++ program demonstrates the use of both postfix and prefix increment and decrement operators. Here's a detailed breakdown:

1. **Include the I/O Stream Library**: **#include <iostream>** allows the program to use input and output streams. It enables displaying outputs to the console using **std::cout**.
2. **Main Function**: The program's entry point is defined by **int main()**. It returns an **int**, signifying the program's execution status.
3. **Initialize Counter**: A variable named **counter** is initialized with the value **10**.
4. **Postfix Increment**: **std::cout << "Counter++: " << counter++ << std::endl;** displays the current value of **counter** (10), and then increments it. The postfix increment operator (**counter++**) increases the value of **counter** by 1 after its current value is used.
5. **Prefix Increment**: **std::cout << "++Counter: " << ++counter << std::endl;** increments **counter** first (from 11 to 12, since it was incremented in the previous step), and then displays its value. The prefix increment operator (**++counter**) increases the value of **counter** by 1 before it is used in the expression.
6. **Postfix Decrement**: **std::cout << "Counter--: " << counter-- << std::endl;** shows the current value of **counter** (12), and then decrements it. The postfix decrement operator (**counter--**) decreases the value of **counter** by 1 after its current value is displayed.
7. **Prefix Decrement**: **std::cout << "--Counter: " << --counter << std::endl;** decreases **counter** first (from 11 to 10, since it was decremented in the previous step), and then displays its value. The prefix decrement operator (**--counter**) decreases the value of **counter** by 1 before it is used in the expression.
8. **Program Completion**: The program ends with **return 0;**, signaling successful completion.

This program illustrates how the postfix (**var++**, **var--**) and prefix (**++var**, **--var**) increment and decrement operators work in C++. The postfix version modifies the variable's value after the current expression is evaluated, while the prefix version does it before evaluating the expression.

7. EXAMPLE 7: INPUT AND OUTPUT

Question: How do you read an integer from the user and display it?

Objective: To practice using **std::cin** and **std::cout** for basic input and output operations.

```
#include <iostream>

int main() {
    int number;
    std::cout << "Enter an integer: ";
    std::cin >> number;
    std::cout << "You entered: " << number << std::endl;
    return 0;
}
```

Explanation:

This C++ program reads an integer from the user and then displays the entered value. Here’s a detailed explanation:

1. **Include the Input/Output Stream Library**: The program begins with **#include <iostream>**, which includes the C++ Standard Library’s Input/Output stream. This allows the program to use **std::cin** for input and **std::cout** for output.
2. **Main Function Definition**: **int main()** marks the entry point of the program. It’s where the execution starts. The function returns an **int**, which is a status code to the operating system. A return value of **0** typically signifies successful execution.
3. **Declare an Integer Variable**: Inside **main()**, an integer variable named **number** is declared with **int number;**. This variable is used to store the integer value input by the user.
4. **Prompt the User for Input**: The program then outputs a prompt to the console, asking the user to enter an integer. This is done with **std::cout << “Enter an integer: “;**, which displays the message without moving to a new line.
5. **Read User Input**: **std::cin >> number;** reads the next integer value entered by the user and stores it in the **number** variable. If the user enters a non-integer value, **std::cin** will enter a failed state, and no assignment will be made to **number**.
6. **Display the Entered Value**: The program outputs the text “You entered: ” followed by the value stored in **number**. This is accomplished with **std::cout << “You entered: ” << number << std::endl;**. The **std::endl** inserts a newline character after the output and flushes the output buffer, ensuring that the output is immediately displayed.
7. **Return from Main**: The program ends with **return 0;**, signaling successful completion of the program to the operating system.

This program demonstrates basic C++ input and output operations using **std::cin** and **std::cout**, variable declaration, and the reading and printing of an integer value.

8. EXAMPLE 8: CODING STANDARDS

Question: How can you follow basic coding standards for readability?

Objective: To understand and apply basic coding conventions like naming variables properly and using comments.

```
#include <iostream>

int main() {
    // Variable to hold the sum of two numbers
    int sum = 0;
    int num1 = 5, num2 = 15; // First and second number

    // Calculating the sum
    sum = num1 + num2;

    // Displaying the result
    std::cout << "The sum of " << num1 << " and " << num2 << " is " << sum <<
std::endl;

    return 0;
}
```

Explanation:

This C++ program calculates the sum of two numbers and displays the result. Here's a step-by-step explanation:

1. **Include the Input/Output Stream Library**: **#include <iostream>** includes the standard Input/Output stream library, which is necessary for using **std::cout** to output to the console.
2. **Define the main Function**: **int main()** is the starting point of any C++ program. This function must return an integer, with **0** typically indicating successful completion.
3. **Declare and Initialize Variables**:
   - **int sum = 0;** initializes an integer variable named **sum** to **0**. This variable will hold the result of the addition.
   - **int num1 = 5, num2 = 15;** declares two integer variables, **num1** and **num2**, and initializes them to **5** and **15**, respectively. These variables represent the two numbers to be added.
4. **Calculate the Sum**: **sum = num1 + num2;** performs the addition of **num1** and **num2**, storing the result in **sum**.
5. **Display the Result**:
   - **std::cout << "The sum of " << num1 << " and " << num2 << " is " << sum << std::endl;** uses **std::cout** to output a formatted string to the console. It concatenates fixed strings with the values of **num1**, **num2**, and **sum**, resulting in a statement like "The sum of 5 and 15 is 20".

- ◦ **std::endl** is used to insert a newline character and flush the output stream, ensuring the output is immediately visible.

6. **Return from main**: **return 0;** exits the **main** function, returning **0** to indicate that the program completed successfully.

This program demonstrates basic variable declaration and initialization, arithmetic operations (addition), and output formatting in C++.

9. EXAMPLE 9: DISPLAYING USER INPUT

Objective: To demonstrate basic input and output operations in C++ by accepting a string from the user and displaying it.

```
#include <iostream>
#include <string>

int main() {
    std::string userInput;
    std::cout << “Please enter your name: “;
    std::getline(std::cin, userInput);  // Reads a full line including spaces
    std::cout << “Hello, ” << userInput << “! Welcome to the C++ world.” <<
std::endl;
    return 0;
}
```

Explanation:

This C++ code snippet is a straightforward program designed to prompt the user for their name and then greet them. Here's a breakdown of how it works:

1. **#include <iostream>**: This line includes the standard Input/Output stream library, enabling the program to perform input and output operations, like reading from the keyboard and writing to the console.
2. **#include <string>**: This directive includes the string library, which provides the **std::string** class. **std::string** is a versatile data type for handling text strings in C++.
3. **int main() { ... }**: Defines the entry point of the program. The **main** function is where the execution starts, and it returns an integer value. In this case, **0** is returned at the end, indicating successful execution.
4. Inside the **main** function:
   - ◦ **std::string userInput;**: Declares a variable named **userInput** of type **std::string**. This variable will store the name entered by the user.
   - ◦ **std::cout << “Please enter your name: “;**: Uses **std::cout** to print a prompt asking the user to enter their name. **std::cout** is used for console output, and the **<<** operator is used to send the string to the output stream.

- **std::getline(std::cin, userInput);**: This function call reads a line of text from the standard input (**std::cin**) and stores it in the **userInput** variable. Unlike **std::cin >> userInput;**, which stops reading at the first whitespace character, **std::getline** reads the entire line, including spaces, until it encounters a newline character.
- **std::cout << "Hello, " << userInput << "! Welcome to the C++ world." << std::endl;**: Constructs a greeting message using the user's input and outputs it to the console. The message is concatenated with the user's name in the middle. **std::endl** is used to insert a newline character at the end of the output and flush the output stream.

5. **return 0;**: Signals the end of the **main** function and returns **0** to the operating system, indicating that the program executed successfully.

This program illustrates basic string handling, how to read a full line of input from the user, and how to concatenate and output strings.

10. EXAMPLE 10: SIMPLE ARITHMETIC CALCULATOR

Objective: To show how to perform a basic arithmetic operation (addition) on two numbers provided by the user.

```
#include <iostream>

int main() {
    double num1, num2;
    std::cout << "Enter the first number: ";
    std::cin >> num1;
    std::cout << "Enter the second number: ";
    std::cin >> num2;
    // Since we're avoiding conditional and loop structures, we'll directly
perform an operation
    double sum = num1 + num2;
    std::cout << "The sum of " << num1 << " and " << num2 << " is " << sum <<
"." << std::endl;
    return 0;
}
```

Explanation:

This C++ code is a simple program that calculates the sum of two numbers entered by the user. Here's a detailed explanation of each part:

1. **#include <iostream>**: This line includes the Input/Output stream library in C++. It allows the program to use **std::cin** for input from the user and **std::cout** for output to the console.
2. **int main() { ... }**: This is the main function where the execution of the program begins. In C++, every program must have a main function. The type **int** indicates that the function returns an inte-

ger, which is a status code to the operating system. Returning 0 typically means that the program executed successfully.

3. Inside the main function:
   - **double num1, num2;**: Two variables **num1** and **num2** of type **double** are declared. **double** is a data type used for storing floating-point numbers, which can contain decimal points and larger ranges of values.
   - **std::cout << "Enter the first number: ";**: This line uses **std::cout** to print a message asking the user to enter the first number. << is the insertion operator, used to send data to the output stream.
   - **std::cin >> num1;**: This line uses **std::cin** to read the value entered by the user and stores it in the variable **num1.** >> is the extraction operator, used to get data from the input stream.
   - A similar pair of **std::cout** and **std::cin** statements are used to ask for and read the second number into **num2**.
   - **double sum = num1 + num2;**: A new variable **sum** of type **double** is declared and initialized with the result of adding **num1** and **num2**. This line performs the actual addition operation.
   - **std::cout << "The sum of " << num1 << " and " << num2 << " is " << sum << "." << std::endl;**: This line outputs the result of the addition back to the user. It shows the values of **num1**, **num2**, and their sum. **std::endl** is used to insert a newline character and flush the output stream, ensuring that all output is written to the console immediately.
4. **return 0;**: The main function returns 0, signaling successful execution of the program to the operating system.

This program demonstrates basic input and output operations in C++, variable declaration and initialization, arithmetic operation, and the use of the standard library for IO operations.

SUMMARY

Chapter 1 of this C++ programming guide serves as an essential starting point for beginners, providing all the foundational knowledge needed to embark on the journey of becoming proficient in C++. It begins with a compelling introduction to the significance of C++ in today's programming world, emphasizing its widespread use and the advantages it offers.

The chapter methodically breaks down the C++ compilation process, illuminating the types of errors programmers might encounter, such as syntax, runtime, and logical errors. This insight helps budding programmers understand common pitfalls and how to navigate them effectively.

A substantial section is devoted to Integrated Development Environments (IDEs), where readers are guided through selecting and setting up an IDE for C++ programming. This includes practical steps for writing, compiling, and running the quintessential "Hello World" program in C++, accompanied by a detailed explanation of the code structure, tokens, and a line-by-line breakdown to ensure a deep understanding of what's happening behind the scenes.

Focusing on the core language features, the chapter delves into values, statements, operators, and data types, including both value and reference types. Through illustrative examples, it explains variable declaration, initialization, and assignment, shedding light on the utility of the "auto" keyword for type inference, which simplifies code.

Input methods are covered, providing readers with knowledge on how to receive input from users, enhancing the interactivity of C++ programs. The chapter also introduces coding standards and best practices to follow, ensuring that readers not only write code that works but also adheres to professional quality and readability standards.

The chapter wraps up with debugging techniques, offering strategies to identify and fix errors, an indispensable skill for any programmer. By the end of this chapter, readers are equipped with a solid foundation in C++ and are prepared to tackle more advanced topics in subsequent chapters. This groundwork ensures that readers understand the basic constructs of C++ programming, setting the stage for a successful coding journey.

Multiple Choice

1. What is the primary use of Integrated Development Environments (IDEs) in C++ programming?
   - A) To create complex data structures
   - B) To write, compile, and run C++ programs
   - C) To increase the execution speed of programs
   - D) To debug third-party code libraries
2. Which of the following errors is typically caught during the compilation process?
   - A) Syntax errors
   - B) Runtime errors
   - C) Logical errors
   - D) All of the above
3. What is the output of a "Hello World" program in C++?
   - A) Hello World
   - B) hello world
   - C) Hello, World!
   - D) "Hello World"
4. Which keyword in C++ is used for automatic type inference?
   - A) auto
   - B) var
   - C) let
   - D) const
5. How can C++ programmers receive input from users?
   - A) Using the **input** function
   - B) Using the **scanf** function
   - C) Using the **cin** object
   - D) Using the **get** method
6. Which operator is used for incrementing a variable's value by one?
   - A) ++
   - B) --
   - C) +=
   - D) =+

7. What does IDE stand for in the context of C++ programming?
   - A) Integrated Debugging Environment
   - B) Integrated Development Environment
   - C) Internal Development Environment
   - D) Integrated Deployment Environment
8. Which statement correctly declares and initializes an integer variable in C++?
   - A) int x = 10;
   - B) x = 10;
   - C) int x: 10;
   - D) integer x = 10;
9. What is the purpose of using coding standards and best practices in C++?
   - A) To make code run faster
   - B) To enhance the security of the code
   - C) To ensure code quality and readability
   - D) To reduce the size of the compiled program
10. Which of the following is a common technique for debugging C++ programs?
    - A) Using the **debug** keyword
    - B) Writing tests for each function
    - C) Running the program on different operating systems
    - D) Adding print statements to track variable values

Exercises

1- Declare and Initialize Variables Declare and initialize the following variables:
   - an integer variable named age with a value of 30
   - a double variable named salary with a value of 50000.50
   - a string variable named name with a value of "John Doe"
   - a boolean variable named isMarried with a value of true
   - a char variable named gender with a value of 'M'

2- Write a program that asks the user to enter their name, age, and salary, and then prints out this information.

3- Write a program that calculates the area of a circle given its radius. The formula for the area of a circle is A = pi*r^2. Assume that the value of pi is 3.14159.

4- Write a program that asks the user to enter their age and prints out whether they are eligible to vote or not. Assume that the legal voting age is 18.

5- Declare an integer variable num and initialize it to 5. Use post-increment to increment the value of num by 1 and print the result.

6- Declare a float variable price and initialize it to 10.5. Use pre-decrement to decrement the value of price by 1 and print the result.

7- Declare a double variable balance and initialize it to 100. Use post-decrement to decrement the value of balance by 1 and print the result.

8- Declare a char variable letter and initialize it to 'a'. Use pre-increment to increment the value of letter by 1 and print the result.

9- Declare a boolean variable isTrue and initialize it to true. Use post-increment to increment the value of isTrue by 1 and print the result.
10- What is the significance of C++ in today's programming world, and what advantages does it offer?
11- Describe the C++ compilation process. What types of errors might programmers encounter during this process?
12- How can Integrated Development Environments (IDEs) enhance the C++ programming experience, and what steps are involved in setting one up?
13- Explain the purpose of the "Hello World" program in C++ and what beginners can learn from writing and running this program.
14- What are the core language features of C++, and how do values, statements, operators, and data types play a role in programming?
15- How do you declare, initialize, and assign variables in C++, and what role does the "auto" keyword play in type inference?
16- What methods can be used to receive input from users in C++ programs, and why is user input important?
17- Discuss the importance of adhering to coding standards and best practices in C++. Provide examples of do's and don'ts.
18- How can debugging techniques be applied in C++ to identify and fix programming errors?
19- What foundational knowledge do readers acquire by the end of Chapter 1, and how does it prepare them for more advanced C++ topics?
20- Why is understanding the basic constructs of C++ programming crucial for beginners embarking on their coding journey?

ENDNOTES

[1] Same as **int** data type. With the 64 bit compiler, it is a separate data type.
[2] Same as **unsigned int** data type. With the 64 bit compiler, it is a separate data type.
[3] Same as **double** data type. With the 64 bit compiler, it is a separate data type.

Chapter 2
Control Structures Algorithms

ABSTRACT

Chapter 2 delves deep into the world of algorithms and control structures, setting the foundation for effective programming in C++. Beginning with an overview of algorithms and their representation in pseudocode, it progresses to explore various control structures essential to the development of robust software. Core selection statements in C++, including the 'if', 'if...else', and nested 'if...else' are elucidated, with special attention given to common issues like the dangling-else problem. Logical operators—AND, OR, and NOT—are demystified, highlighting key differences between equality and assignment operations. Practical examples elucidate key concepts, followed by an in-depth look at repetition statements such as 'while', 'for', and 'do...while'. This chapter also introduces nested loops and their interactions with 'break' and 'continue' statements. Finally, the art of generating random numbers in C++ is unraveled, offering insights into seeding and calculating numbers within a desired range. The chapter concludes with hands-on exercises to fortify learning.

2.1 INTRODUCTION

Control structures are the fundamental building blocks of algorithms. They allow the programmer to specify the flow of control in a program, including decisions, loops, and branching. Common control structures include:

- If and if-else statements, which allow the program to make decisions based on certain conditions.
- for loops, which allow the program to repeat a block of code a certain number of times.
- while loops, which allow the program to repeat a block of code as long as a certain condition is true.
- do-while loops, which are similar to while loops but the code block inside it will be executed at least once.
- switch-case statement, which allows the program to make decisions based on a specific value or variable.

DOI: 10.4018/979-8-3693-2007-5.ch002

These structures allow the programmer to create more complex and powerful algorithms by combining simple operations in different ways.

2.2 ALGORITHM

Any solvable computing issue can be resolved by carrying out a string of operations in a particular order. a method for resolving a dilemma in terms of

1. the actions to execute.
2. the order in which these actions are performed.

referred to as an algorithm. The example that follows shows how crucial it is to accurately specify the order in which the actions execute.

2.3 PSEUDOCODE

("fake" code) is a made-up, informal language that allows programmers to create algorithms without worrying about the exact specifics of the C++ language syntax. This pseudocode is especially useful for making algorithms that will be turned into sections of a structured C++ program. Although pseudocode isn't a real programming language, it is convenient and user-friendly and is similar to everyday English.

Computers do not execute pseudocode. Instead, it aids in "thinking out" a program before attempting to create it in a programming language like C++.

Programmers can easily type pseudocode using any editor program because the way we show pseudocode is based only on characters. On demand, the computer can print a new copy of a pseudocode program. It is simple to translate a carefully crafted pseudocode program into a corresponding C++ program. This frequently just entails swapping out pseudocode statements for their C++ equivalents.

When a programmer changes a program from pseudocode to C++ and runs it on a computer, only statements that can be run and cause certain things to happen are usually described by pseudocode. Declarative statements (that don't include constructor calls or initializers) cannot be executed. Variable declarations are typically absent from our pseudocode. Some programmers, however, prefer to list variables and explain their functions at the start of pseudocode programs.

Now, we will look at an example of pseudocode that a programmer could use to help them write the addition program.

1. Prompt the person to go into the primary integer.
2. Input the first integer.
3. Prompt the consumer to go into the second integer.
4. Enter the second integer.
5. Add the first and second numbers and store the result.
6. Exhibit result.

Activity Diagram for the above pseudocode:

Figure 1. Activity diagram

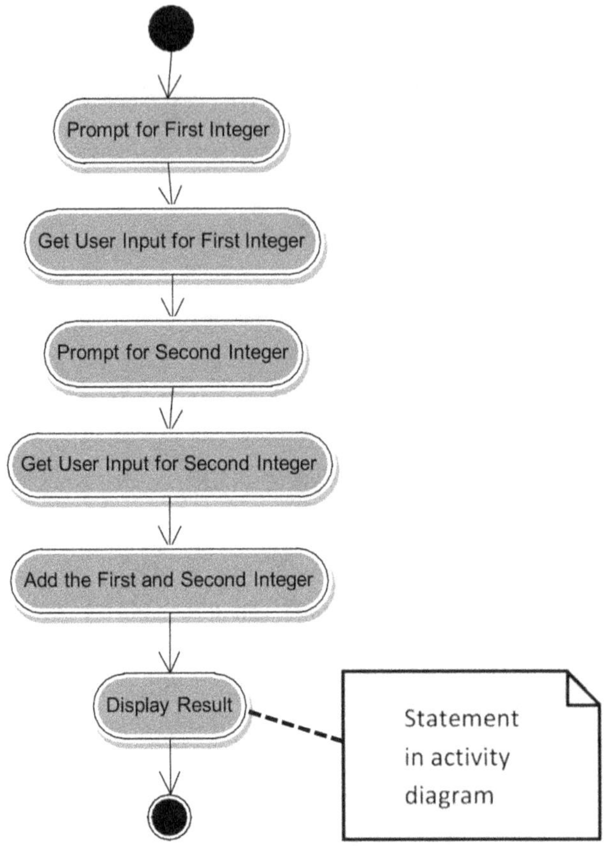

C++ includes the sequence structure by default. Unless otherwise instructed, the computer executes C++ statements sequentially, in the order in which they are written.

The activity diagram in the Unified Modelling Language (UML) above shows a typical sequence structure where calculations are carried out sequentially. In a sequence structure, C++ enables us to have as many actions as we like.

A component of the UML are activity diagrams. An activity diagram represents the workflow, which is also known as the activity, of a particular piece of software. These processes could incorporate a section of an algorithm, like the sequence structure. The special-purpose symbols used in activity diagrams include action state symbols (an elongated circle), diamonds (typically used for decisions/conditions), and small circles (known as start and end states); these symbols are connected by transition arrows, which show how the activity progresses.

Although many programmers prefer pseudocode, activity diagrams can be used to develop and represent algorithms. Activity diagrams make it easy to understand how control structures work.

Take a look at the activity diagram above. It includes a number of action states that stand in for actions to take. Each action state has an action expression that specifies the specific action to be taken, such as "prompt for an integer" or "display result." Calculations and input/output operations are examples of additional actions. Transition arrows are what the arrows in the activity diagram are called. These arrows stand for transitions, which show the sequence in which the program that implements the activities performs the actions represented by the action states.

The activity's initial state (also known as the start state), which occurs before the program executes the modelled activities, is represented by the solid circle at the top of the activity diagram. The final state (or end state), the point in the workflow where the program has completed its activities, is represented by the solid circle surrounded by a hollow circle at the bottom of the activity diagram.

Rectangles with the upper-right corners bent over are also shown in the diagram. The UML refers to these as notes. Notes are illustrative remarks that explain the significance of the diagram's symbols. Not only activity diagrams but any UML diagram can use notes. Each note is linked to the element it describes by a dotted line. The C++ code used to implement an activity is typically not displayed in activity diagrams. Here, we demonstrate how the diagram relates to C++ code using notes. Visit www.uml.org for more information on the UML.

The single-selection if statement is demonstrated in the diagram below. It contains the diamond symbol, which denotes a decision that needs to be made, which is possibly the most significant symbol in an activity diagram. When a decision symbol is present, the workflow will proceed in accordance with the associated guard conditions, which may be true or false. There is a guard condition on each transition arrow that emerges from a decision symbol (specified in square brackets above or next to the transition arrow). The workflow enters the action state to which that transition arrow points if a specific guard condition is true. If the grade in the aforementioned diagram is greater than or equal to 60, the program prints "Passed" to the screen before moving on to the activity's final state. The program switches directly to the final state without displaying a message if the grade is less than 60.

2.4 CONTROL STRUCTURES

In a program, statements typically run in the order they were written, one after the other. Sequential execution is the term used for this. Programmers can specify that the next statement to execute may not be the next in the sequence using a variety of C++ statements. Control is transferred in this situation.

Only three control structures—the sequence structure, the selection structure, and the repetition structure—could be used to describe all programs. The discipline of computer science is where the term "control structures" originated.

Sequence Structure in C++

C++ includes the sequence structure by default. Unless otherwise instructed, the computer executes statements sequentially, in the order in which they are written.

Statement 1 asks the user to enter an integer, Statement 2 gets the user's input, and so on until the end of the statements. In a sequence structure, C++ enables us to have as many actions as we like.

Figure 2.

```
if ( grade >= 60 )
cout << "Passed";
else
cout << "Failed";
```

```
if ( grade>=60 )
  cout << "passed";
```

```
switch ( grade)
{
    case 90:
        cout<<"A"; break;
    case 80:
    cout<<""; break;
    case 70:
    cout<<"C"; break;
    .
    .
    .
    Default:
    Cout<"Error";
    }
```

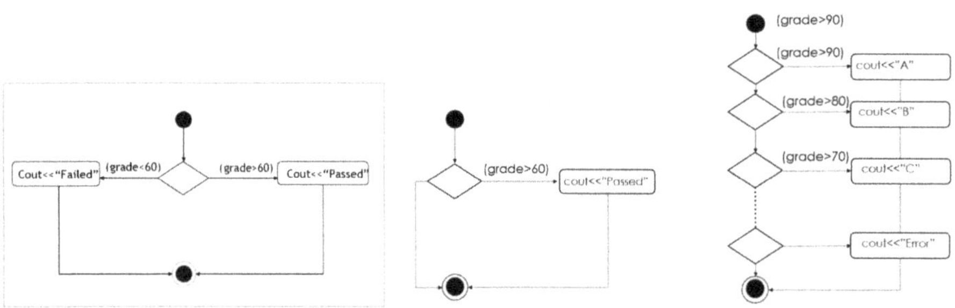

2.5 SELECTION STATEMENTS IN C++

C++ provides three different types of selection statement.

If a condition (predicate) is true, the if selection statement either executes (selects) the action or skips it if the condition is false. If a condition is true, the if...else selection statement takes a certain action; if it is false, a different action is taken. The switch selection statement does one of many things, depending on the result of an integer expression.

Because it chooses to take or reject a single action, the if selection statement is a single-selection statement (or, as we will soon see, a single group of actions). Because it chooses between two separate actions, the if...else statement is called a double select (or group of actions) will soon see, a single group of actions). Because it chooses between two separate actions, the if...else statement is called a "double select" (or "group of actions"). Because it chooses from a variety of actions, the switch selection statement is also known as a multiple-selection statement (or group of actions).

2.5.1 if Selection Statement

Programs use selection statements to decide between various options. Let's say, for instance, that a test's passing score is 70. The statement in pseudocode evaluates the truth or falsity of the statement "Student's grade is greater than or equal to 70." The next orderly pseudocode statement is "performed" and "Passed" is printed if the condition is true (remember that pseudocode is not a real programming language). The print statement is disregarded and the subsequent pseudocode statement in the order is executed if the condition is false. This selection statement's second line has an indentation, as you can see. Although this type of indentation is optional, it is advised because it draws attention to the inherent structure of structured programs. The C++ compiler ignores white-space characters (such as blanks, tabs, and newlines) used for indentation and vertical spacing when converting your pseudocode into C++ code.

Figure 3. Selection statements

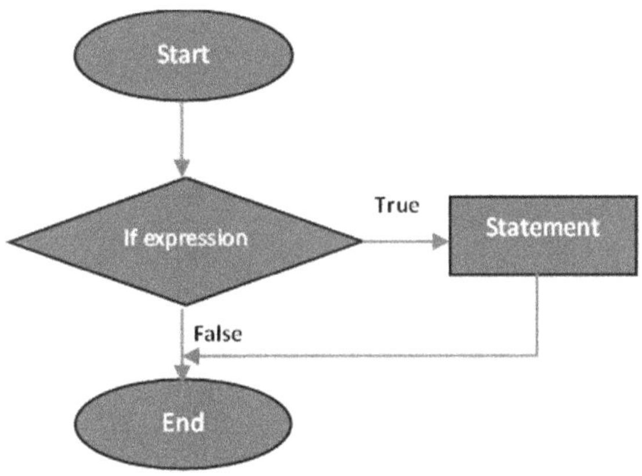

Program readability is greatly enhanced by consistently using reasonable indentation conventions throughout your programs.

The pseudocode before In C++, an if statement can be written as

```
if (grade >= 70)
cout << "Passed";
```

Take note of how closely the pseudocode and C++ code match. One of the qualities that makes pseudocode such a helpful tool for program development is this.

Any expression may be used as the basis for a decision in C++. If an expression evaluates to zero, it is considered false; if it evaluates to nonzero, it is considered true. For variables that can only hold the values true and false, C++ offers the data type bool. Each of these is a C++ keyword.

2.5.2 if...else Double-Selection Statement

When the condition is True, the if single-selection statement executes the indicated action; otherwise, it skips it. Programmers can specify one action to be taken when a condition is true and another action to be taken when a condition is false using the if...else double-selection statement.

Figure 4. Double-selection statement

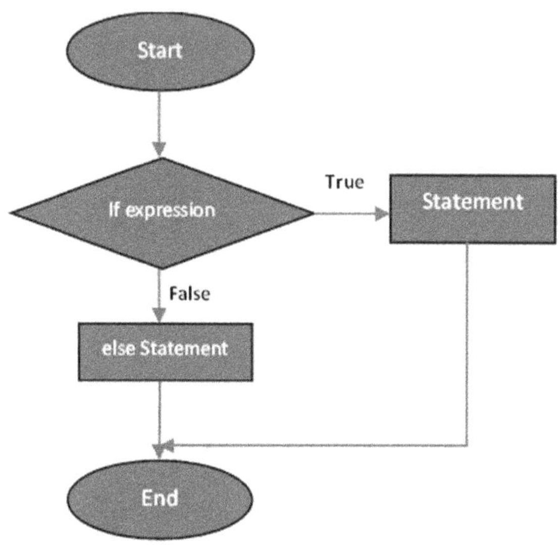

For instance, the cryptic phrase

If student's grade is greater than or equal to 70 Print "Passed"

```
Else
Print "Failed"
```

Prints "Passed" if the student's grade is greater than or equal to 70, but prints "Failed" if the student's grade is less than 70. In both the cases, after printing occurs, the next pseudocode statement in sequence is "performed."

The preceding pseudocode If...Else statement can be written in C++ as

```
if (grade >= 70)
cout << "Student Passed";
else
cout << " Student Failed";
```

Keep in mind that the else's body is also indented. You should use the indentation style you decide on consistently throughout all of your programs. Programs that do not adhere to consistent spacing conventions are challenging to read.

2.5.3 Conditional Operator (?:)

In the C++ programming language, the conditional operator (?:) functions similarly to the if...else statement. The conditional operator is the only ternary operator in C++ that allows three operands. The components of a conditional expression are the operands, the conditional operator, and the operands. The first operand represents a condition, the second operand represents the value for the full conditional expression if the condition is true, and the third operand represents the value for the entire conditional expression if the condition is false. Example: the output declaration.

```
cout << (grade >= 70 ? "Student Passed" against "Student Failed"
```

Is the conditional statement graded greater than or equal to 70? The phrase "Student Passed" evaluates to the string "Passed" if the condition grade >= 70 is true; otherwise, it evaluates to the string "Failed." As a consequence, the conditional operator statement acts similarly to the preceding if...else statement. As we will see, the preceding phrase requires parenthesis because the conditional operator has a low precedence.

The above conditional phrase is as follows: "If rank is 70 or more, then cout is activated.

Figure 5.

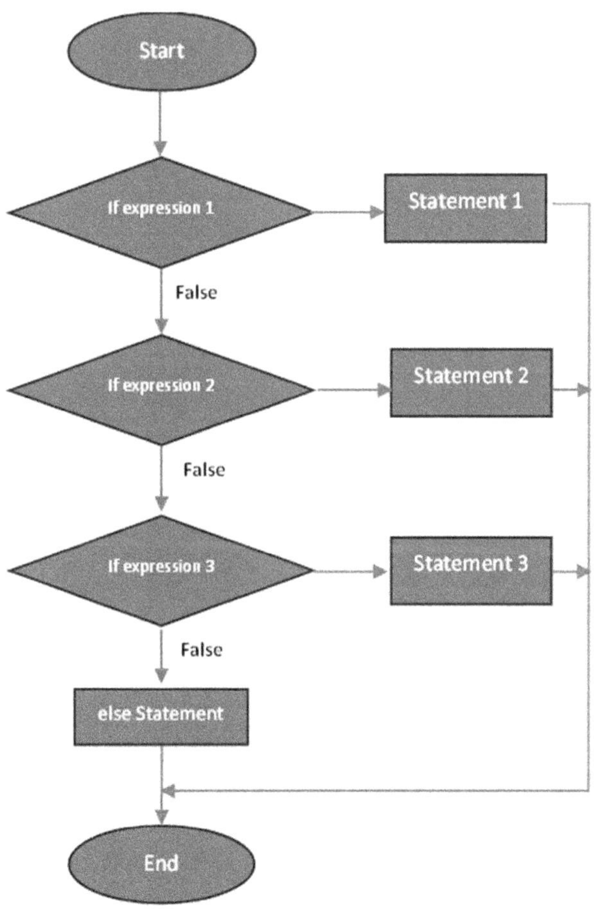

" Student Passed;" if not, cout failed." This is also equivalent to the previous if-then-else expression. Conditional expressions may be used in places where if...else statements are inapplicable.

2.5.4 Nested if...else Statements

Nested if...then...else statements test for more than one condition by putting one if...then...else statement inside of another. For instance, the if...else statement in the following pseudocode returns A for test scores over 90, B for scores between 80 and 89, C for scores between 70 and 79, D for scores between 60 and 69, and F for all other grades:

If the student's grade is at least 90, they obtain an A.

```
Type "A"
Else
```

If the student's grade is 80 or above, they pass the course.

```
Print "B"
Else
```

If the student's grade is 70 or higher or is equal to or greater than 70

```
Type "C"
Else
```

If the student's grade is 60 or higher or is equal to or greater than 60

```
Print "D"
Else
Print "F"
```

This pseudocode is equivalent to C++ code.

```
if (studentGrade >= 90) // Any grade of 90 or above is considered a "A"
cout << "A";
else
If(studentGrade >= 80) // 80 - 89, the student receives a "B"
cout << "B";
else
if (studentGrade >= 70) // 70 - 79 receives a grade of "C"
cout << "C";
else
if (studentGrade >= 60) //60 - 69 earn a "D"
cout << "D";
```

```
other // less than 60 gets an "F"
cout << "F";
```

If studentGrade is at least 90, the first four conditions will be met, but only the last statement after the first test will be executed. The computer skips the else section of the "outermost" if...else expression when this cout is run. Typically, the statement before an if...then clause is structured as follows:

```
cout "A" if (studentGrade >= 90) // grades of 90 and above get a "A"
otherwise if (studentGrade >= 80) // 80-89 receives "B" cout << "B";
otherwise if (studentGrade >= 70) // 70-79 gets "C" cout << "C";
otherwise if (studentGrade >= 60) // 60-69 gets "D" cout << "D";
cout "F"; else // less than sixty instances of "F"
```

The only difference between the two versions is the use of spaces and tabs, which the compiler doesn't care about.Since it prevents the right side of the code from being pushed in too far, the second version is preferable. This kind of indentation leaves little space on a line, which forces lines to be broken and makes it harder to understand programs.

Due to the potential for an early exit when one of the conditions is met, nested if...else statements may execute significantly quicker than a series of single-selection if statements. At the start of nested if...else statements, you should verify the most likely correct assumptions. By considering instances that occur often first, the nested if...else expression will run more quickly and complete earlier.

2.5.5 Dangling-else Problem

Unless told otherwise by the placement of braces (and), the C++ compiler always connects an else to the if that came right before it.This behavior may result in the "dangling-else problem," as it is known. For instance,

```
if (x > 5)
if (y > 5)
cout << "x and y are > 5";
else
cout << "x is <= 5";
```

Looks like the nested if statement checks to see if y is greater than 5 if x is greater than 5. If so, the output reads "x and y are > 5". Otherwise, it appears that the else portion of the if...else statement outputs "x is <= 5" if x is not greater than 5.

Beware! This nested if-then-else statement doesn't actually work as intended. Actually, the compiler interprets the statement as

```
if (x > 5) if (y > 5)
cout << "x and y are > 5";
else
cout << "x is <= 5";
```

where the first if's body is a nested if...else. The outer if clause determines whether x exceeds 5. Execution then checks to see if y is also greater than 5 in that case. In that case, the appropriate string "x and y are > 5" will be shown. Even though we are aware that x is greater than 5, the string "x is = 5" is displayed if the second condition is false.

To make the nested if-then-else statement work as intended, it needs to be written like this:

```
if (x > 5)
if (y > 5)
cout << "x and y are > 5";
else
cout << "x is <= 5";
if (x > 5)
{
if (y > 5)
cout << "x and y are > 5";
}
else
cout << "x is <= 5";
```

The braces ({}) indicate to the compiler that the second if statement is in the body of the first if and that the else is associated with the first if.

2.6 LOGICAL OPERATORS

We have only looked at basic criteria so far, like counter = 10, total > 1000, and number! = sentinel-Value. The equality operators == and! = and the relational operators >, >=, and = were used to come up with these conditions. Each option was an examination of a particular situation. In order to evaluate several circumstances while making a choice, we ran these checks in independent statements or inside nested if or if...else expressions.

Logic operators in C++ may be used to generate more complicated conditions by combining simpler ones. The logical operators are && (logical AND), || (logical OR), and! (logical NOT, also called logical negation).

2.6.1 Logical AND (&&) Operator

Before deciding what to do, let's say we want to make sure that two conditions are met in each case.The && (logical AND) operator can be used in the following way:

This if statement contains two basic conditions: (gender == 1 and age >= 65) seniorFemales++. Here, a person's gender is established using the formula gender == 1. A person is regarded as a senior citizen if their age exceeds 65. Since == has a greater precedence than &&, the condition to the left of && evaluates first. As >= has a greater precedence than &&, the simple condition to the right of && is evaluated next, if required. As we shall soon explore, the right side of a logical AND statement is only evaluated if the left side is true. Then, the if clause takes the combined condition into consideration.

```
gender == 1 && age >= 65
```

This condition is true if and only if both of the basic criteria are met. Lastly, if the combined condition is true, the statement in the body of the if statement raises the number of seniorFemales. If either of the two basic conditions is untrue, the program avoids incrementing and instead proceeds to the sentence that follows the if (or both are). To improve readability, repetitive parentheses may be appended to the above combined condition:

```
(gender == 1) && (age >= 65)
```

2.6.2 Logical OR (||) Operator

Now, let's examine the || (logical OR) operator. Before picking a certain line of action, we want to ensure that one or both of two requirements are met at some point in the program. Here, the || operator is used, as seen in the following program segment:

```
if ((semesterAverage >= 90) || (finalExam >= 90)) then cout "Student received
an A" endl;
```

There are also two simple requirements in the preceding condition. The uncomplicated semester If the student has done well during the semester, they should get an A (average >= 90) in the course. The basic premise Exam >= 90 determines if a student's performance on the final test merits a "A" in the course. Then, the if clause takes the combined condition into consideration.

```
(semesterAverage >= 90) || (finalExam >= 90)
```

and declares the student successful if one or both of the straightforward conditions are true. Notice that until all of the simple criteria are incorrect, the message "Student's grade is an A" will be shown.

2.6.3 Logical Negation (!) Operator

The! (logical NOT, also called "logical negation") operator is a tool in C++ that lets programmers "reverse" what a condition means.The unary logical negation operator only accepts a single condition as an operand, unlike the binary operators && and || which combine two conditions.

We use the unary logical negation operator before a condition to decide what to do if the initial condition (without the logical negation operator) is false. For example, in the following code segment:

```
if (!(grade == sentinelValue))
cout << "The next grade is " << grade << endl;
```

Since the logical negation operator comes before the equality operator, the statement grade == sentinelValue needs to be surrounded by parentheses.

Most of the time, a programmer can avoid using logical negation by using the right relational or equality operator to state the condition.The if statement that comes before this, for instance, can also be written as follows:

```
if (grade != sentinelValue)
cout << "The next grade is " << grade << endl;
```

This adaptability frequently enables a programmer to express a condition in a way that feels more "natural" or practical.

2.6.4 Confusing Equality (==) and Assignment (=) Operators

No matter how skilled they are, there is one mistake that C++ programmers tend to make so frequently that we feel it needs its own section. Accidentally switching the operators = and == (equality) results in that error (assignment). The fact that these swaps typically do not result in syntax errors is what makes them so harmful. Instead, the programs run successfully even though the statements with these errors frequently produce incorrect results due to runtime logic errors. [Note: When = is used in a context where == is typically expected, some compilers issue a warning.]

Two features of C++ are responsible for these issues. One is that any expression that generates a value may be used in any control statement's decision section. The expression is treated as false if the value is zero and as true if the value is greater than zero. The second is that assignments result in a value, specifically the value that is assigned to the variable on the assignment operator's left side. Let's say, for instance, that we want to write.

```
if (payCode == 4)
cout << "You get a bonus!" << endl;
but we accidentally write
if (payCode = 4)
cout << "You get a bonus!" << endl;
```

The individual whose payCode equals 4 is duly given a bonus by the first if statement. The assignment expression in the if condition is evaluated and applied to the constant 4 in the second if statement—the one with the error. The condition in this if statement is always true and the individual always receives a bonus regardless of what the actual paycode is because any nonzero value is interpreted as true!

Even worse, the paycode was only supposed to be examined, but it was actually modified!

Due to their ability to be used on the left side of an assignment operator, variable names are referred to as "left values" or "lvalues." Because they can only be used on the right side of an assignment operator, constants are referred to as "right values" (or "rvalues"). Keep in mind that rvalues cannot be used as lvalues and vice versa.

NOTE: Adding a semicolon after the condition in a single-selection if statement or a double-selection if...else statement with a body statement in the if part causes a logic error.

2.7 EXAMPLES

```
// Menu Chooser
//
Demonstrat
es the
switch
statement
#include <iostream>
using namespace std;

void main()
{
  cout << "Difficulty Levels\n\n"
       << "1 - Easy\n"
       << "2 - Normal\n"
       << "3 - Hard\n"
       << "4 - Exit\n\n";
  int choice;
  cout << "Choice: ";
  cin >> choice;
  switch (choice)
  {
  case 1:
    cout << "You picked Easy.\n";
       break;
  case 2:
    cout << "You picked Normal.\n";
       break;
  case 3:
    cout << "You picked Hard.\n";
    break;
  case 4:
    cout << "Exit.\n";
    break;
```

```
#include <iostream>
using namespace std;

void main()
{
    cout << "Difficulty Levels\n\n"
         << "1 - Easy\n"
         << "2 - Normal\n"
         << "3 - Hard\n"
         << "4 - Exit\n\n";
    int choice;
    cout << "Choice: ";
    cin >> choice;
   if (choice ==1)
        cout << "You picked Easy.\n";
   else if (choice == 2)
        cout << "You picked Normal.\n";
   else   if (choice == 3)
        cout << "You picked Hard.\n";
   else   if (choice == 4)
        cout << "Exit.\n";
   else
        cout << "You made an illegal
choice.\n";


    system("pause");
}
```

2.8 REPETITION STATEMENTS IN C++

As long as a certain condition, called the loop-continuation condition, is true, a program can use one of three types of repetition statements, also called looping statements or loops, to run statements over and over again.While, do...while, and for statements are repetition statements. If the loop-continuation condition is initially true, the action (or group of actions) in the while and for statements will execute zero or more times. Otherwise, the action (or group of actions) will not execute. The action (or set of actions) in the do...while statement is carried out at least once. If, else, switch, while, do, and for are all C++ keywords. The C++ programming language reserves these words to implement a number of features, including control statements. It is forbidden to use keywords as identifiers, like variable names.

NOTE: A syntax error occurs when a keyword is used as an identifier.

NOTE: A syntax error occurs when a keyword is spelled with any uppercase letters. The keywords in C++ are all lowercase only.

Table 1.

While() // Pre-Test Loop	**For() // Pre-Test Loop**	**Do ... While() // Post-Test Loop**

while (condition)
{
statement;
increment;
}
	initialization;
	for (initialization; condition; increment)
	{
	statement;
	}
		do {
		statement;
		}
		increment;
		}while (condition);

#include <iostream>
using namespace std;
void main()
(
int num = 1;
while (num <= 10)
{
cout << "Employee #" << num << endl;
num++; // Cv as control variable to stop the loop
}
}
	#include <iostream>
	using namespace std;
	void main()
	{
	for (int num = 1; (num <= 10); num++)
	{
	cout << "Employee #" << num << endl;
	}
	system("pause");
	}
		#include <iostream>
		using namespace std;
		void main()
		{
		int num = 1;
		do
		{
		cout << "Employee #" << num << endl;
		num++; // Cv as control variable to stop the loop
		} while (num <= 10);
		}

2.8.1 While Repetition Statement

Programmers can tell a computer to repeat an action as long as a certain condition is true by using repetition statements, also known as looping statements or loops. The pseudocode statement While there are more items on my shopping list The repetition that happens while shopping. There are two possible outcomes for the statement "There are more items on my shopping list." If so, the action of "buying the next item and crossing it off my list" is carried out. As long as the circumstance is true, this action will be repeated. The body of the while, which can be a single statement or a block of statements, is the statement that is contained in the while repetition statement. The condition will eventually turn false (when the last item on the shopping list has been purchased and crossed off the list). The repetition ends at this point, and the first pseudocode statement that follows the repetition statement is then executed.

General format:

Declare and initialize the control variable.

```
While(condition)
{
Statement;
```

```
Update the control variable;
}
```

Example:

```
int i = 0;
while (i < 5)
{
Cout << "i = " << i << endl;
i++;
}
```

As an example of the while repetition statement in C++, take a piece of code that finds the first power of 3 greater than 100.Assume that the initial value of the integer variable product is 3. The product will contain the following result once the while repetition statement has completed running:

```
int product = 3;
while (product <= 100)
product = 3 * product;
```

The value of product is 3 when the while statement starts to run. Product is multiplied by 3 after each iteration of the while clause, resulting in successive values of 9, 27, 81, and 243 for product. The while statement condition that product = 100 is false when product is 243. This ends the cycle of repetition, making the product's final value 243. The next statement after the while statement is now run as part of the program.

NOTE: A logic error called an infinite loop happens when a while statement's condition is not followed by an action that eventually makes it false. In this case, the repetition statement never ends. If there are no statements that talk to the user in the body of the loop, the program may seem to "hang" or "freeze."

Counter-Controlled Repetition: Formulating Algorithms:

Introducing the Play Again Program

```
// Play Again
// Demonstrates while loops
#include <iostream>
using namespace std;
void main()
{
char again = 'y';
while (again == 'y')
{
cout << "\n**Played an exciting game**";
cout << "\nDo you want to play again? (y/n): "; cin >> again;
}
cout << "\nOkay, bye.";
```

```
system("pause");
}
```

This C++ program is demonstrating the use of while loops to create a "Play Again" program. The program first initializes a variable "again" to the value of 'y'. It then enters a while loop, which will continue to execute as long as the value of "again" is 'y'.

Within the while loop, the program prints out a message indicating that the game has been played. It then prompts the user with a message asking if they want to play again and reads in their response using the "cin" command. The value of the "again" variable is set to the user's response, which will determine if the loop should continue or not.

When the user enters a response other than 'y', the while loop will exit, and the program will print a message indicating that the program is ending. The "system("pause")" command is used to pause the program before it exits, allowing the user to see the final message before the program terminates.

Pseudocode Algorithm With Counter-Controlled Repetition

Let's make a list of the steps to be taken and the order in which they should be done using pseudocode. We enter the grades one at a time, using counter-controlled repetition. This method limits the number of times a collection of statements will run by using a variable called a counter (also known as the number of iterations of the loop).

Because the number of repetitions is known before the loop starts running, counter-controlled repetition is frequently referred to as definite repetition. In this illustration, repetition stops when the counter reaches 10. The algorithm is implemented in a C++ member function and is presented as a fully developed pseudocode algorithm in this section.

```
// Counters
#include <iostream>
using namespace std;
void main()
{
int num = 1;
while (num <= 10)
{
cout << "Employee #" << num << endl;
num++; // Cv as control variable to stop the loop
}
system("pause");
}
```

This C++ program demonstrates the use of a while loop to print out a series of messages.

The program first includes the iostream header file to allow for input and output operations, and uses the "std" namespace to simplify the code.

The program then initializes an integer variable "num" to the value of 1. It enters a while loop, which will continue to execute as long as the value of "num" is less than or equal to 10.

In the while loop, the program prints a message with the employee number, using the value of "num" to show which employee is being talked about. It then increments the value of "num" by 1, using it as a control variable to stop the loop when it reaches the value of 11.

When the loop has finished executing, the program uses the "system("pause")" command to pause the program before it exits, allowing the user to see the final message before the program terminates.

Essentials of Counter-Controlled Repetition

Counter-controlled repetition requires

1. the name of a control variable (or loop counter)
2. the initial value of the control variable
3. the loop-continuation condition that checks the final value of the control variable (i.e., whether looping should continue).
4. the amount by which the control variable is changed each time through the loop. This can be either an increase or a decrease.

Using the while loop for input validation for a Repetition Statement

It is possible to implement any counter-controlled loop using the while statement. The for-repetition statement, which specifies the counter-controlled repetition details in a single line of code, is another feature offered by C++.

The control variable counter is declared and set to 1 when the for statement starts to run. The loop-continuation condition counter is then checked to see if it equals 10. Since the condition is met and the counter's initial value is 1, the body statement (line 12) prints the value of the counter, which is 1. The control variable counter is then increased by the expression counter++, and the loop is restarted with the loop-continuation test. The final value is no longer exceeded because the control variable has been set to 2, and the program executes the body statement once more.

2.8.2 For Statement Header Components

The general form of the for statement is

Figure 6. Statement header components

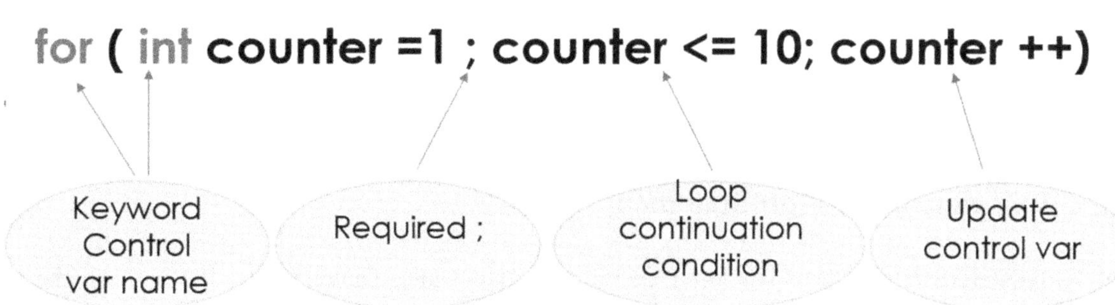

```
// for Counters
#include <iostream>
using namespace std;
void main()
{
for (int num = 1; (num <= 10); num++)
{
cout << "Employee #" << num << endl;
}
system("pause");
}
```

where the loopContinuationCondition determines whether the loop should continue running (this condition typically contains the final value of the control variable for which the condition is true), increment increases the control variable, and the initialization expression initializes the loop's control variable. Comma-separated lists of expressions can be used for the initialization and increment expressions. These expressions' use of commas, known as comma operators, ensures that expression lists evaluate from left to right. Of all the C++ operators, the comma operator has the lowest precedence. The value and type of the rightmost expression in a list of expressions separated by commas represent the value and type of the entire list. For statements, the comma operator is used the most. Its main use is to give programmers the ability to use multiple increment expressions and/or multiple initialization expressions. For instance, multiple control variables may need to be initialized and increased in a single for statement.

The statement header's three expressions are optional, but the two semicolon separators are required. In the absence of the loopContinuationCondition, C++ assumes the condition to be true and starts an infinite loop. If the control variable is initialized earlier in the program, it is possible to omit the initialization expression. If the increment is determined by statements in the for's body or if no increment is required, the increment expression may be omitted.

Most of the time, the for statement can be replaced by the following while statement:

```
initialization;
while (loopContinuationCondition)
{
statement increment;
}
```

The control variable can only be used in the for statement's body because it won't be known outside of it if the initialization expression in the header declares it (that is, if the control variable's type is specified before the variable name). The variable's scope refers to this constrained use of the control variable name. Where a variable can be used within a program is determined by its scope.

2.8.3 do...while Repetition Statement

The while statement and the do...while repetition statement are related. Before the body of the loop executes in the while statement, the loop-continuation condition test takes place at the start of the loop.

The loop body always runs at least once because the do...while statement checks the loop-continuation condition after the loop body has finished running. The statement that comes after the while clause is executed when a do...while ends. Though most programmers include the braces to prevent confusion between the while and do...while statements, braces are not required if there is only one statement in the body of the code. For instance, while (condition.while repetition statement are related. Before the body of the loop executes in the while statement, the loop-continuation condition test takes place at the start of the loop. The loop body always runs at least once because the do...while statement checks the loop-continuation condition after the loop body has finished running. The statement that comes after the while clause is executed when a do...while ends. Though most programmers include the braces to prevent confusion between the while and do...while statements, braces are not required if there is only one statement in the body of the code. For instance, "while" (condition) is normally regarded as the header of a while statement. A do...while with no braces around the single statement body appears as a do statement while (condition), which may be confusing. The reader might mistakenly think that the last line, "while (condition), is a while statement with an empty body. To avoid confusion, the phrase "do while with one statement is frequently written as follows:

```
do
{
statement
} while (condition);
```

Example of Counters

```
#include <iostream>
using namespace std;
void main()
{
int num = 1;
do
{
cout << "Employee #" << num << endl;
num++; // Cv as control variable to stop the loop
} while (num <= 10);
system("pause");
}
```

This C++ program explains how to print a sequence of messages using a do-while loop.

The program begins by including the iostream header file to enable input and output operations, followed by the "std" namespace to simplify the coding.

The program then assigns the value 1 to the integer variable "num." It enters a do-while loop, which is identical to a while loop but guarantees that the loop runs at least once before evaluating its state.

The software publishes a message displaying the employee number inside the do-while loop, utilizing the value of "num" to identify which employee is being referred to. It then increases "num" by 1, utilizing it as a control variable to exit the loop when its value reaches 11.

Figure 7.

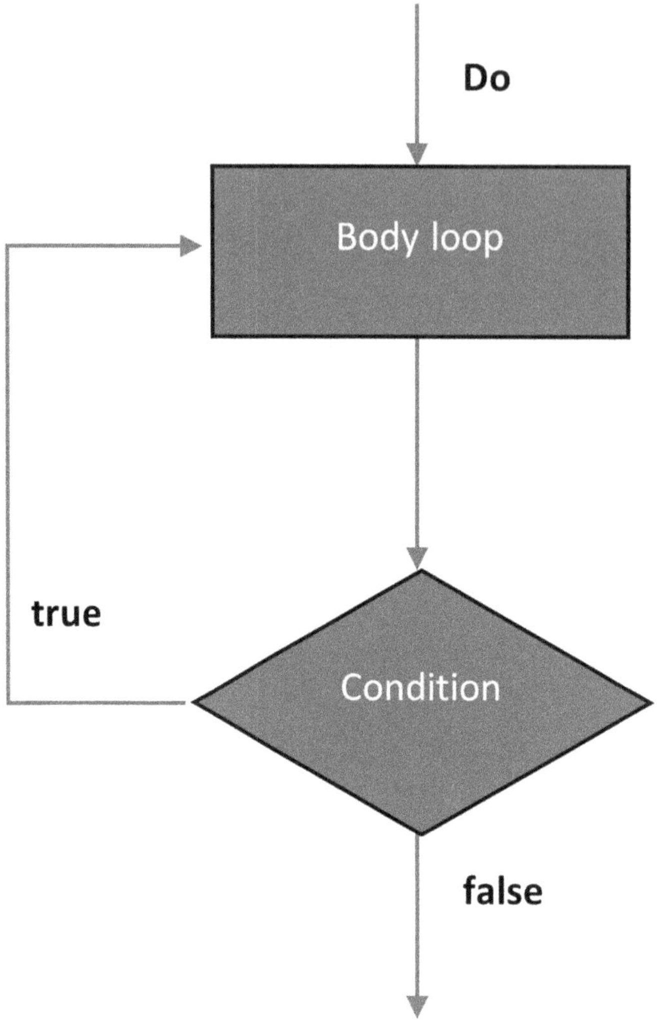

After performing the loop, the program checks the loop condition in the while statement. If the condition is met (i.e., "num" is still less than or equal to 10), the program returns to the beginning of the do-while loop and executes it again. This will continue till the condition of the loop is false (i.e., when "num" is greater than 10).

The program utilizes the "system("pause")" command to halt the application before to exiting, enabling the user to see the last message before the program closes.

2.8.4 Examples

1. Using the while Loop for input Validation

```
// Program asks you to enter a 1 through 50
#include <iostream>
using namespace std;
void main()
{
int number = 1;
cout << " Please enter a number between 1 and 50: ";
cin >> number;
while (number > 50 || number < 0)
{
cout << "The number was not within range. " << endl;
cout << " Please enter another number:";
cin >> number;
}
system("pause");
}
```

This C++ software invites the user to enter a number between 1 and 50, reads the user's input using the "cin" command, and employs a while loop to ensure that the value is inside the given range.

The application utilizes the "std" namespace to simplify the code and includes the iostream header file to enable input and output operations.

The program initializes the integer variable "number" with the value 1, but quickly replaces this value with the user's input using the "cin" command.

The while loop determines if the value of "number" exceeds 50 or falls below 0. If the number is beyond the range, the program displays an error message, asks the user to enter another number using the "cout" and "cin" commands, and then reads in the new number.

As long as "number" is beyond the defined range, the loop will continue to run. After the value of "number" falls inside the specified range, the loop terminates and program execution resumes.

The software then utilizes the "system("pause")" command to halt the application before exiting, enabling the user to see the last message before the program closes.

2. do-while loop input validation.

```
#include <iostream>
using namespace std;
void main()
{
int value;
bool flag = false;
cout << " This program will prompt user to enter"
<< "a numerical value within the range of 1 to 50. \n";
cout << " Please enter a value: ";
cin >> value;
do
```

```
{
if (cin.fail()) //will sets an error flag if the input does not fit the vari-
able
{
cin.clear(); // corrects the stream.
cin.ignore(50, '\n'); //skips the left over data stream
cout << " Please enter an Integer value only: ";
cin >> value;
}
else if (value < 1 || value > 50)
{
cout << " Invalid entry, not within the ranger from 1-50. \n"
<< " Please enter another value: ";
cin >> value;
}
else {
flag = true;
cout << " Good Job!\n";
}
} while (!flag);
system("pause");
}
```

This C++ software invites the user to enter a number between 1 and 50, reads the input using the "cin" command, then validates the input using a do-while loop.

The application utilizes the "std" namespace to simplify the code and includes the iostream header file to enable input and output operations.

The program assigns an undefined value to the integer variable "value" and false to the boolean variable "flag."

The program then requests the user to input a numeric number between 1 and 50 using the "cout" and "cin" commands, and produces a message informing the user that he or she would be prompted to enter a value between 1 and 50.

The do-while loop runs the code enclosed by curly brackets and uses the "cin.fail()" function to determine if the input is an integer value. If the input is not an integer, the software sets an error flag with the "cin.clear()" function, clears the stream with the "cin.ignore()" function, produces a message to the user requesting that they only enter integer values, and asks the user to enter another value with the "cin" command.

If the input is an integer, the program use a "if-else" statement to determine whether the value is within the defined range. If the value is beyond the range of 1 to 50, the program displays an error notice and encourages the user to submit a new number using the "cout" and "cin" commands if the input is invalid.

If the value is between 1 and 50, the software changes the value of the boolean variable "flag" to true, indicating that the input is legitimate, and displays a message to the user stating that they have submitted a valid input.

The loop executes until the value of "flag" is true, at which time it exits and the program proceeds.

Lastly, the program utilizes the “system(“pause”)” command to pause before exiting, enabling the user to see the final message before the program closes.

2.8.5 Nested Loops

In C++, a nested loop is a loop that is inside another loop. This allows you to execute a block of code multiple times for each iteration of the outer loop. Here is an example of a nested loop that prints a multiplication table:

```
for (int i = 1; i <= 10; i++) {
for (int j = 1; j <= 10; j++) {
cout << i << " x " << j << " = " << i * j << endl;
}
}
```

In this example, the outer loop iterates from 1 to 10, and the inner loop iterates from 1 to 10. For each iteration of the outer loop, the inner loop is executed 10 times, resulting in a multiplication table that shows the products of the numbers from 1 to 10.

Another example of a nested loop is printing a triangle pattern using

```
for (int i = 0; i < 5; i++) {
for (int j = 0; j <= i; j++) {
cout << "*";
}
cout << endl;
}
```

In this example, the outer loop iterates from 0 to 4, and the inner loop iterates from 0 to i, so in the first iteration the inner loop only runs once, the second time twice, and so on. This will print a triangle pattern of stars.

These are just a couple examples of how nested loops can be used in C++. The possibilities are endless, and nested loops can be used to solve many different types of problems. However, it’s important to use nested loops with caution, as they can lead to complexity and make the code harder to understand and maintain if not used appropriately.

2.8.6 Nested Loops With Break and Continue Statements

The break statement can be used to exit a loop early before the loop’s normal termination condition is met. When a break statement is found inside a nested loop, the innermost loop ends. Here is an example of using the break statement inside a nested loop:

```
for (int i = 1; i <= 10; i++) {
for (int j = 1; j <= 10; j++) {
if (i * j == 50) {
```

```
cout << "Found 50 at i = " << i << ", j = " << j << endl;
break;
}
}
}
```

In this example, the outer loop iterates from 1 to 10, and the inner loop iterates from 1 to 10. For each iteration of the outer loop, the inner loop is executed 10 times. When the product of the two numbers, i and j, is equal to 50, the inner loop will be exited and the program will continue with the next iteration of the outer loop.

Another example is finding the prime number in a range of numbers.

```
for (int i = 1; i <= 100; i++) {
for (int j = 2; j <= i / 2; j++) {
if (i % j == 0) {
break;
}
if (j == i / 2) {
cout << i << " is a prime number" << endl;
}
}
}
```

In this example, the outer loop iterates from 1 to 100, and the inner loop iterates from 2 to half of the number. If the number is divisible by any number other than 1 and itself, it means it's not prime, so the inner loop is broken; otherwise, it continues, and if the inner loop completes successfully, it means it's a prime number.

It's important to note that the break statement only exits the innermost loop it is inside of, so if you have multiple nested loops and you want to exit more than one level of loops, you can use a labeled break statement and use the label to specify which loop you want to exit.

The continue statement can be used to skip the current iteration of a loop and move on to the next iteration. When a continue statement is found inside a nested loop, the innermost loop skips the current iteration and moves on to the next one. Here is an example of using the continue statement inside a nested loop:

```
for (int i = 1; i <= 10; i++) {
for (int j = 1; j <= 10; j++) {
if (i * j % 2 == 1) {
continue;
}
cout << i * j << " ";
}
cout << endl;
}
```

In this example, the outer loop iterates from 1 to 10, and the inner loop iterates from 1 to 10. For each iteration of the outer loop, the inner loop is executed 10 times. When the product of the two numbers, i and j, is odd, the inner loop will skip the current iteration and continue with the next one, and if the product is even, it will be printed. This will print only even numbers in a multiplication table format.

Another example is finding the sum of even numbers.

```
int sum = 0;
for (int i = 1; i <= 10; i++) {
for (int j = 1; j <= 10; j++) {
if ((i * j) % 2 != 0) {
continue;
}
sum += i * j;
}
}
cout << "The sum of even numbers is: " << sum << endl;
```

In this example, the outer loop iterates from 1 to 10, and the inner loop iterates from 1 to 10. For each iteration of the outer loop, the inner loop is executed 10 times. When the product of the two numbers, i and j, is not even, the inner loop will skip the current iteration and continue with the next one, and if the product is even, it will be added to the sum variable. This will give the sum of all the even numbers.

Like the break statement, the continue statement only affects the innermost loop it is inside of. If you want to skip an iteration of an outer loop, you will need to use a labeled continue statement to specify which loop you want to skip the iteration on.

2.9 REPETITION STRUCTURE NOTES

A control structure known as a "loop" makes a statement or group of statements repeat.

Three loops are covered:

1. Using a while loop (pre-test loop). Conditional loop, pretest loop (useful with an unknown number of iterations when you don't want the loop to iterate when a condition is false from the start).

   For instance, input validation

2. Using a do-while loop (post-test loop), a while loop-like conditional loop that is in the posttest (ideal when you want the loop to iterate at least once)

   Instance: menus

3. The for loop (pre-test loop). built-in expressions for initialization, testing, and updating; a pretest loop

Example: Entering multiple values and transferring data
Common Errors to Avoid

1. Semicolon after the loop header (null statement)
2. Lack of brackets results in an infinite loop.

Counters are constants that are changed every time a loop iterates, either by going up or down.This allows you to control the number of times a loop iterates and how strings are concatenated to avoid repeated string editing.

The do-while loop is a posttest loop; expressions are not tested until after the first iteration. Using a for loop There are two types of loops:

1. Conditional loops only run if an expression is true.
2. Count-controlled loop, where the user controls the loop's iteration cycle.
3. The user can decide how many times a for loop runs by comparing the counter variable to a variable that has already been set.
4. There is no cap on the number of initialization and update expressions.
5. Ignoring the expressions in the for loop

Nested Loops:

1. Each time an outer loop iterates, the inner loop completes all of its iterations.
2. Inner loops finish iterations more quickly than outer loops.
3. To determine how many times a nested loop has been iterated, multiply that number by the sum of all the loop iterations.

Breaking and Continuing a Loop

1. The break statement causes an early loop termination.
2. helpful for ending or exiting loops
3. "Continue" tells a loop to stop the current iteration and begin a new one.
4. The program jumps to the expression at the top of the while loop. The program jumps to the bottom of a do-while loop.
5. Before the test expression is checked, the update expression is run in a for loop.
6. Useful for programs that track the costs of items brought and give an item away after n purposes, for

2.10 GENERATING RANDOM NUMBERS

A sense of unpredictability can make a game more exciting. Players thrive on a certain level of surprise, whether it's a sudden shift in the strategy of a computer opponent in an RTS or the appearance of an alien creature through an arbitrary door in an FPS. To achieve this kind of surprise, one method is to generate random numbers.

Introducing the Die Roller Program

The Die Roller program simulates the roll of a six-sided die. The computer uses a randomly generated number to calculate the roll. The results of the program are displayed in the figure below.

```
//Die Roller
// Demonstrates generating random numbers.
#include <iostream>
#include <cstdlib>
#include <ctime>
using namespace std;
void main()
{
srand(static_cast<unsigned int>(time(0))); // seed random number generator
int randomNumber = rand(); // generate random number
int die = (randomNumber % 6) + 1; // get a number between 1 and 6
cout << "You rolled a " << die << endl;
system("pause");
}
```

Calling the rand() function

I add a new file as one of the first things I do in the program: #include <cstdlib>. Among other things, the cstdlib file contains functions for generating random numbers. I am free to call the functions in the file, including the function rand(), because I have included it, and this is what I do in main(): Create a random number using int randomNumber = rand();// Code segments known as functions are capable of performing tasks and producing results. A function is called or invoked by using its name followed by two parentheses. You can give a function's return value, if one exists, to a variable. This is what I do in this instance with the assignment statement. I give randomNumber the random number that rand() returned.

Aside from values, functions can also take values to work with. After the function name, you supply these values by putting them between parentheses and separating them with commas. These values are known as arguments, and you pass them to the function when you supply them. Since rand() doesn't accept arguments, I didn't pass it any values.

2.10.1 Seeding the Random Number Generator

Based on a formula, computers produce pseudorandom numbers—not truly random numbers. Consider using the computer to read from a large book of predetermined numbers as one way to approach this. The computer can appear to generate a series of random numbers by reading from this book. The issue is that the computer always begins reading the book at the beginning. As a result, whenever a program is run, the computer will always generate the same set of "random" numbers. This is not something we would want in a game. For instance, we wouldn't want the same set of dice rolls in a round of craps every time.

This problem can be fixed by telling the computer to start reading the book from a random spot every time a game program starts.The seeding of the random number generator is the name of this procedure. The starting position in this series of pseudorandom numbers is determined by the game programmers by providing the random number generator with a number known as a seed.

The random number generator is seeded with the code below: time(0)); srand(static castunsigned int>); generator of random numbers, seed Wow, that line seems pretty cryptic, but it does something very straightforward. The current date and time are used to seed the random number generator, which is ideal because they will change for each run of the program.

In the actual code, you can seed the random number generator by passing an unsigned int to the srand() function. The return value of time(0), a number based on the current system date and time, is what is given to the function in this case. The static castunsigned int> function is used to turn this value into an unsigned int.Now, you don't have to understand all the subtleties of this line; the bare minimum you need to know is that your program should execute this line once before calling rand() if you want it to generate a series of random numbers that are unique every time the program is run.

2.10.2 Calculating a Number Within a Range

After generating a random number, randomNumber holds a value between 0 and 32767 (based on my implementation of C++). But I need a number between 1 and 6, so next I use the modulus operator to produce a number in that range. int die = (randomNumber % 6) + 1; // get a number between 1 and 6. Any positive number divided by 6 will give a remainder between 0 and 5. In the preceding code, I take this remainder and add 1, giving me the possible range of 1 through 6—exactly what I wanted. You can use this technique to convert a random number to a number within the range you're looking for.

Advanced Practice Exercises With Answers

1. **Example 1: Complex Condition Handling in User Authentication**
    - **Objective**: To implement a user authentication system using complex conditional statements to verify username and password combinations. This system should lock the user out after a certain number of unsuccessful attempts, showcasing the use of if-else and nested if statements.

```
#include <iostream>
#include <string>
int main() {
    std::string correctUsername = "admin";
    std::string correctPassword = "password123";
    std::string username, password;
    int attemptCount = 0;
    bool accessGranted = false;
    while (attemptCount < 3 && !accessGranted) {
        std::cout << "Enter username: ";
        std::cin >> username;
        std::cout << "Enter password: ";
        std::cin >> password;
        if (username == correctUsername && password == correctPassword) {
            accessGranted = true;
            std::cout << "Access granted.\n";
```

```
        }
        else {
            attemptCount++;
            std::cout << "Incorrect username or password. ";
            if (attemptCount < 3) {
                std::cout << "Please try again.\n";
            }
            else {
                std::cout << "Account locked due to too many failed 
attempts.\n";
            }
        }
    }

    return 0;
}
```

Explanation:

This C++ program is designed to simulate a basic user authentication system. Here's how it works:

1. **Initialization**: It starts by defining the correct username and password that are required to gain access. These are stored in **correctUsername** and **correctPassword** variables. It also initializes variables to store user input (**username** and **password**), an **attemptCount** to keep track of the number of login attempts, and a boolean **accessGranted** to indicate whether access has been successfully granted.
2. **Authentication Process**:
    - A **while** loop is used to repeat the authentication process until the user either successfully logs in (**accessGranted** becomes **true**) or exceeds the maximum number of login attempts (defined here as 3 attempts).
    - Inside the loop, the program prompts the user to enter a username and password.
    - It then compares the entered credentials with the predefined correct ones. If they match, **accessGranted** is set to **true**, and a message indicating successful access is displayed.
    - If the credentials do not match, the **attemptCount** is incremented, and the user is informed that the username or password was incorrect. The loop then iterates again, asking for the credentials, unless the maximum number of attempts is reached.
3. **Lockout Mechanism**:
    - If the user fails to provide correct credentials after the specified number of attempts, the loop exits, and a message is displayed informing the user that the account has been locked due to too many failed attempts.

This program demonstrates basic control flow in C++, utilizing conditional statements (**if** and **else**) and a loop (**while**) to manage user inputs and control access based on the correctness of the credentials provided.

2. **Example 2: Multi-level Menu Using Switch-Case**
    - **Objective**: To create a multi-level menu system for an application's settings. This program should use nested switch-case statements to allow users to navigate through menus and modify settings, demonstrating the application of switch-case in creating user interfaces.

```
#include <iostream>
void showMainMenu() {
    std::cout << "Main Menu:\n";
    std::cout << "1. Settings\n";
    std::cout << "2. About\n";
    std::cout << "3. Exit\n";
    std::cout << "Enter your choice: ";
}

void showSettingsMenu() {
    std::cout << "Settings Menu:\n";
    std::cout << "1. Display\n";
    std::cout << "2. Sound\n";
    std::cout << "3. Back\n";
    std::cout << "Enter your choice: ";
}
int main() {
    int choice;
    showMainMenu();
    std::cin >> choice;
    switch (choice) {
    case 1:
        showSettingsMenu();
        std::cin >> choice;
        switch (choice) {
        case 1:
            std::cout << "Display settings.\n";
            break;
        case 2:
            std::cout << "Sound settings.\n";
            break;
        case 3:
            showMainMenu();
            break;
        default:
            std::cout << "Invalid choice.\n";
        }
        break;
    case 2:
```

```
        std::cout << "About the application.\n";
        break;
    case 3:
        std::cout << "Exiting application.\n";
        break;
    default:
        std::cout << "Invalid choice.\n";
    }

    return 0;
}
```

Explanation:

This C++ program demonstrates the implementation of a simple multi-level menu system using selection structures (switch-case statements). It begins by defining two functions, **showMainMenu()** and **showSettingsMenu()**, which display the main menu and the settings menu, respectively. Each menu provides users with a list of options they can select by entering a corresponding number.

In the **main()** function, the program starts by showing the main menu and prompting the user for a choice. Based on the user's input, the program enters one of the switch-case blocks:

1. If the user selects "Settings" (option 1 from the main menu), the program displays the settings menu. It then prompts the user again for a choice, this time to select either "Display" settings, "Sound" settings, or to go "Back" to the main menu. Depending on the choice, the program either displays a message related to the selected settings option or goes back to the main menu.
2. If the user selects "About" (option 2 from the main menu), the program prints information about the application.
3. If the user chooses to "Exit" (option 3 from the main menu), the program prints a message indicating that the application is exiting.
4. If the user enters an invalid choice at any point, the program notifies the user of the invalid selection.

This program effectively demonstrates the use of nested switch-case statements to create a navigable multi-level menu system in a console application, allowing for structured and user-friendly interaction.

3. **Example 3: Automated Grading System with Loops**
    - **Objective**: To build an automated grading system that employs loops to iterate through a series of student responses, match them with a predefined answer key, and tally up scores and grades. This exercise showcases the utility of loops in handling sequential data and making calculations based on conditional checks.

```
#include <iostream>
#include <string>
int main() {
    // Preset answers for demonstration (e.g., A, B, C, D, A)
    char answer;
```

```
    int score = 0;
    std::cout << "Enter student answers for 5 questions (A/B/C/D):\n";
    std::cout << "Question 1 answer: ";
    std::cin >> answer;
    if (answer == 'A') score++;
    std::cout << "Question 2 answer: ";
    std::cin >> answer;
    if (answer == 'B') score++;
    std::cout << "Question 3 answer: ";
    std::cin >> answer;
    if (answer == 'C') score++;
    std::cout << "Question 4 answer: ";
    std::cin >> answer;
    if (answer == 'D') score++;
    std::cout << "Question 5 answer: ";
    std::cin >> answer;
    if (answer == 'A') score++;
    std::cout << "Total correct answers: " << score << "\n";
    std::cout << "Grade: ";
    switch (score) {
    case 5: std::cout << "A"; break;
    case 4:
    case 3: std::cout << "B"; break;
    case 2:
    case 1: std::cout << "C"; break;
    default: std::cout << "F"; break;
}
    std::cout << std::endl;

    return 0;
}
```

Explanation:

This C++ program simulates an automated grading system that processes student answers for five questions. Here's a breakdown of how it operates:

1. **Variable Declaration:**
    - **answer** stores the student's answer for each question.
    - **score** keeps track of the total correct answers.
2. **Collecting Answers:**
    - The program prompts the user to input answers for five questions, expecting characters 'A', 'B', 'C', or 'D' as valid inputs.

3. **Scoring:**
   - For each question, the program compares the input with the correct answer (presumed here as 'A' for Q1, 'B' for Q2, 'C' for Q3, 'D' for Q4, 'A' for Q5). If the answer matches, it increments the **score** by one.
4. **Calculating Grade:**
   - After all answers are inputted and scored, the program calculates the grade based on the total score:
   - **5** correct answers result in an 'A' grade.
   - **3-4** correct answers result in a 'B' grade.
   - **1-2** correct answers result in a 'C' grade.
   - **0** correct answers result in an 'F' grade.
5. **Output:**
   - It outputs the total correct answers and the calculated grade.

This program is a simple illustration of using conditionals (**if** statements) and a **switch** statement to process a sequence of inputs and make decisions based on those inputs, simulating an automated grading system.

4. **Example 4: Pattern Generation with Nested Loops**
   - **Objective**: To implement a program capable of generating complex patterns (e.g., fractals or chess boards) on the console. This program should utilize nested loops to control the pattern generation, showing the power of looping structures in creating intricate designs.

```
#include <iostream>
int main() {
    int n = 5; // Example size
    // Generate a square pattern
    for (int i = 0; i < n; ++i) {
        for (int j = 0; j < n; ++j) {
            std::cout << "* ";
        }
        std::cout << std::endl;
    }
    return 0;
}
```

Explanation:
This C++ program generates a square pattern of asterisks on the console. Here's how it works:

1. **Initialization:**
   - The integer variable **n** is initialized to **5**, which represents the size of the square (both its width and height).
2. **Generating the Pattern:**
   - The program uses two nested **for** loops to generate the square pattern.

- The outer loop runs **n** times, once for each row of the square.
- The inner loop also runs **n** times for each iteration of the outer loop, once for each column in a row.

3. **Printing Asterisks:**
   - Inside the inner loop, **std::cout << "* ";** prints an asterisk followed by a space, representing a single cell of the square pattern.
4. **New Line after Each Row:**
   - After completing each iteration of the inner loop (i.e., after printing **n** asterisks for a row), the outer loop's body executes **std::cout << std::endl;**. This command moves the cursor to the next line, ensuring that each row of asterisks is printed on a new line.
5. **Output:**
   - The program outputs a 5x5 square made of asterisks, with each row containing 5 asterisks separated by spaces.

In summary, this program demonstrates the use of nested loops to create a simple geometric pattern on the console, illustrating basic loop control structures in C++.

5. **Example 5: Simulation of a Banking System**
   - **Objective**: To write a banking system simulation where the control flow dictates operations such as account creation, deposits, withdrawals, and account closure. This system should implement error handling for invalid operations, highlighting the use of control structures in managing program flow and user input validation.

```
#include <iostream>
#include <string>
int main() {
    double balance = 0.0;
    std::string command;
    double amount;
    std::cout << "Simple Banking System\n";
    while (true) {
        std::cout << "\nEnter command (deposit, withdraw, check, exit): ";
        std::cin >> command;
        if (command == "exit") {
            break;
        }
        else if (command == "deposit") {
            std::cout << "Enter amount to deposit: ";
            std::cin >> amount;
            if (amount < 0) {
                std::cout << "Invalid amount. Please enter a positive 
number.\n";
            }
            else {
```

```
                balance += amount;
                std::cout << "Amount deposited successfully.\n";
            }
        }
        else if (command == "withdraw") {
            std::cout << "Enter amount to withdraw: ";
            std::cin >> amount;
            if (amount < 0) {
                std::cout << "Invalid amount. Please enter a positive 
number.\n";
            }
            else if (amount > balance) {
                std::cout << "Insufficient funds.\n";
            }
            else {
                balance -= amount;
                std::cout << "Amount withdrawn successfully.\n";
            }
        }
        else if (command == "check") {
            std::cout << "Current balance: $" << balance << std::endl;
        }
        else {
            std::cout << "Invalid command. Please try again.\n";
        }
    }
    std::cout << "Thank you for using our banking system.\n";
    return 0;
}
```

Explanation:

The provided C++ program simulates a simple banking system that allows a user to deposit money, withdraw money, check the current balance, or exit the program. The program continues running until the user decides to exit by entering the command "exit".

Here's a breakdown of its functionality:

1. **Initialize the Banking System**: The program starts by initializing a **balance** variable to store the current balance of the bank account, which is initially set to 0.0.
2. **User Interaction Loop**: It enters an infinite loop, displaying a message to the user to enter a command. The available commands are "deposit", "withdraw", "check", and "exit".
3. **Process Commands**:
    - **Deposit**: If the user enters "deposit", the program prompts them to enter an amount to deposit. It checks if the amount is a positive number. If it is, the amount is added to the **balance**. If not, it displays an error message.

- **Withdraw**: If the user enters "withdraw", the program asks for the amount to withdraw. It checks if the amount is positive and if the balance is sufficient for the withdrawal. If both conditions are met, the amount is subtracted from the **balance**. Otherwise, appropriate error messages are displayed.
- **Check**: If the command is "check", the current **balance** is displayed.
- **Exit**: If the command is "exit", the loop breaks, effectively ending the program.
- For any other input, the program displays an "Invalid command" message and prompts again.

4. **Program Termination**: Once the loop exits, a thank you message is displayed, signaling the end of the program.

This program effectively demonstrates the use of a loop to keep the program running until a specific user command, conditional statements to handle different user commands, and basic input/output for interaction with the user.

6. **Example 6: Dynamic Group Filtering with Looping and Conditional Structures**
   - **Objective**: To develop a program that filters group of integers based on specific conditions (e.g., prime numbers, even numbers) using loops and conditional statements.

```
#include <iostream>
int main() {
    // Hardcoded integers for demonstration
    int num1 = 12, num2 = 15, num3 = 8, num4 = 23;
    std::cout << "Identifying even numbers:\n";
    // Manually check each number and identify if it's even
    if (num1 % 2 == 0) {
        std::cout << num1 << " is even.\n";
    }
    if (num2 % 2 == 0) {
        std::cout << num2 << " is even.\n";
    }
    if (num3 % 2 == 0) {
        std::cout << num3 << " is even.\n";
    }
    if (num4 % 2 == 0) {
        std::cout << num4 << " is even.\n";
    }
    return 0;
}
```

Explanation:

- This program defines four integers (**num1** through **num4**) directly in the **main** function, simulating a fixed set of data to be processed.

- For each integer, an **if** statement checks whether the number is even by using the modulus operator (%). If the number is divisible by 2 (i.e., **number % 2 == 0**), it is considered even, and a message indicating that the number is even is printed to the console.
- This approach manually iterates through each hardcoded integer, applying the even-number filter directly via conditional checks without the use of external functions, arrays, vectors, or maps, adhering to the constraints provided.

7. **Example 7: Simple C++ Program that Simulates a Basic ATM Machine**
   - **Objective**: To create a simple C++ program that simulates a basic ATM machine, demonstrating the use of loops for repeating operations and selection structures (if-else statements) for making decisions. The ATM allows the user to check their balance, deposit money, and withdraw money. The program runs in a loop, so the user can perform multiple operations until they choose to exit.

```
#include <iostream>
int main() {
    int choice;
    double balance = 1000.00; // Starting balance
    do {
        std::cout << "\n*** Basic ATM ***\n";
        std::cout << "1. Check Balance\n";
        std::cout << "2. Deposit Money\n";
        std::cout << "3. Withdraw Money\n";
        std::cout << "4. Exit\n";
        std::cout << "Enter your choice: ";
        std::cin >> choice;
        if (choice == 1) {
            // Check Balance
            std::cout << "Your current balance is: $" << balance << std::endl;
        }
        else if (choice == 2) {
            // Deposit Money
            double depositAmount;
            std::cout << "Enter amount to deposit: $";
            std::cin >> depositAmount;
            if (depositAmount <= 0) {
                std::cout << "Please enter a positive amount.\n";
            }
            else {
                balance += depositAmount;
                std::cout << "$" << depositAmount << " deposited
successfully.\n";
            }
        }
```

```
        else if (choice == 3) {
            // Withdraw Money
            double withdrawAmount;
            std::cout << "Enter amount to withdraw: $";
            std::cin >> withdrawAmount;
            if (withdrawAmount <= 0) {
                std::cout << "Please enter a positive amount.\n";
            }
            else if (withdrawAmount > balance) {
                std::cout << "Insufficient funds.\n";
            }
            else {
                balance -= withdrawAmount;
                std::cout << "$" << withdrawAmount << " withdrawn
successfully.\n";
            }
        }
        else if (choice == 4) {
            std::cout << "Exiting ATM. Have a nice day!\n";
        }
        else {
            std::cout << "Invalid choice. Please try again.\n";
        }
    } while (choice != 4);

    return 0;
}
```

Explanation:

This C++ program simulates a basic ATM (Automated Teller Machine), showcasing fundamental programming constructs such as loops and conditional statements. It starts with a preset balance and presents a menu to the user with four options: checking balance, depositing money, withdrawing money, and exiting the program.

- The program uses a **do-while** loop to repeatedly show the menu and process user input until the user chooses to exit (option 4).
- Within the loop, **if-else** statements determine which action to take based on the user's menu selection:
- **Option 1** prints the current account balance.
- **Option 2** prompts the user for a deposit amount, checks if it's a positive number, then adds it to the account balance if it is.
- **Option 3** asks the user for a withdrawal amount, verifies that it's positive and that there are sufficient funds, then deducts it from the balance if both conditions are met.
- **Option 4** exits the loop, ending the program with a farewell message.

- If the user enters an invalid choice, the program advises them to try again, thus ensuring the user is guided back to valid options.

By repeating the menu after each operation until the user decides to exit, the program demonstrates effective use of loops for creating interactive, user-driven programs. Conditional logic via **if-else** statements enables decision-making processes based on user input, ensuring the program behaves correctly according to different scenarios, such as handling insufficient funds or invalid deposit and withdrawal amounts.

8. Example 8: Temperature Conversion Tool
   - **Objective**: To create a simple C++ program that converts temperatures between Fahrenheit and Celsius. The program uses loops to allow continuous conversion until the user decides to exit. Selection structures (if-else statements) determine the direction of conversion based on user input.

```
#include <iostream>
using namespace std;
int main() {
    int choice;
    double temperature;
    do {
        cout << "\n*** Temperature Conversion Tool ***\n";
        cout << "1. Fahrenheit to Celsius\n";
        cout << "2. Celsius to Fahrenheit\n";
        cout << "3. Exit\n";
        cout << "Enter your choice: ";
        cin >> choice;
        if (choice == 1) {
            cout << "Enter temperature in Fahrenheit: ";
            cin >> temperature;
            double celsius = (temperature - 32) * 5.0 / 9.0;
            cout << "Temperature in Celsius: " << celsius << "°C\n";
        }
        else if (choice == 2) {
            cout << "Enter temperature in Celsius: ";
            cin >> temperature;
            double fahrenheit = (temperature * 9.0 / 5.0) + 32;
            cout << "Temperature in Fahrenheit: " << fahrenheit << "°F\n";
        }
        else if (choice == 3) {
            cout << "Exiting Temperature Conversion Tool.\n";
        }
        else {
            cout << "Invalid choice. Please try again.\n";
```

```
        }
    } while (choice != 3);

    return 0;
}
```

Explanation:

Key Components

- **Loop Structure (do-while)**: Allows the program to present the menu repeatedly and perform temperature conversions until the user chooses to exit by entering '3'.
- **Selection Structure (if-else)**: Determines the action based on the user's menu selection. It handles three scenarios: converting Fahrenheit to Celsius, converting Celsius to Fahrenheit, and exiting the program. An additional condition handles invalid choices.
- **Temperature Conversion Formulas**: For converting Fahrenheit to Celsius, the formula is **(Fahrenheit - 32) * 5/9**. For converting Celsius to Fahrenheit, the formula is **(Celsius * 9/5) + 32**.

This program exemplifies how loops and selection structures can be effectively used in C++ to create a simple, interactive application that responds to user input and performs specific actions based on that input.

9. **Example 9: Debugging Practice: Identifying and Fixing Logical Errors**
    - **Objective**: To enhance debugging skills by identifying and fixing logical errors intentionally placed within complex C++ code. This exercise focuses on understanding control flow and the common pitfalls in logical operations.

```
#include <iostream>
int main() {
    // Intentional logical errors for debugging practice
    // Error 1: Incorrect comparison leading to unexpected behavior
    int a = 5, b = 10;
    if (a = b) { // Assignment instead of comparison
        std::cout << "a is equal to b\n";
    }
    else {
        std::cout << "a is not equal to b\n";
    }
    // Error 2: Infinite loop due to incorrect loop condition
    for (int i = 0; i < 5; i--) { // Decrement instead of increment
        std::cout << "i = " << i << std::endl;
    }
    // Error 3: Incorrect logical operator leading to wrong branch execution
    int age = 20;
    if (age > 18 && age < 30 || age > 60) { // Confusing logical operation
```

```
precedence
        std::cout << "Young adult or senior\n";
    }
    else {
        std::cout << "Child or middle-aged\n";
    }
    // Error 4: Dangling else problem
    int score = 85;
    if (score > 90)
        std::cout << "Grade A\n";
    else if (score > 75)
        std::cout << "Grade B\n";
    else if (score > 60)
        std::cout << "Grade C\n";
    else
        std::cout << "Grade F\n";
    std::cout << "Better luck next time!\n"; // Intended to be part of the
else block
    return 0;
}
```

Explanation:

For this example, we'll present a program with several intentional logical errors related to control flow and logical operations. The task is to identify and correct these errors.

Fixes

1. Change **if (a = b)** to **if (a == b)** to correct the comparison.
2. Change the loop condition to **i++** to prevent the infinite loop.
3. Clarify logical operations by using parentheses: **if ((age > 18 && age < 30) || age > 60)**.
4. Enclose the intended else block in braces **{}** to avoid the dangling else problem.

```
// Corrected version
#include <iostream>
int main() {
    // Fixed Error 1
    int a = 5, b = 10;
    if (a == b) {
        std::cout << "a is equal to b\n";
    }
    else {
        std::cout << "a is not equal to b\n";
    }
    // Fixed Error 2
```

```
    for (int i = 0; i < 5; i++) {
        std::cout << "i = " << i << std::endl;
    }
    // Fixed Error 3
    int age = 20;
    if ((age > 18 && age < 30) || age > 60) {
        std::cout << "Young adult or senior\n";
    }
    else {
        std::cout << "Child or middle-aged\n";
    }
    // Fixed Error 4
    int score = 85;
    if (score > 90)
        std::cout << "Grade A\n";
    else if (score > 75)
        std::cout << "Grade B\n";
    else if (score > 60)
        std::cout << "Grade C\n";
    else {
        std::cout << "Grade F\n";
        std::cout << "Better luck next time!\n";
    }
    return 0;
}
```

This program now accurately reflects the intended logic and serves as a practice tool for identifying and fixing common logical errors in C++.

Example 10: Simple Quiz Game

- **Objective**: Design a basic quiz game in C++ that tests the user's knowledge with a single-choice question. The program will utilize loops to ask the question repeatedly until the user selects the correct answer. Selection structures (if-else statements) will be used to provide feedback based on the user's choice and to determine whether the loop continues or ends.

```
#include <iostream>
using namespace std;
int main() {
    int answer;
    cout << "Welcome to the Simple Quiz Game\n";
    cout << "Question: What is the capital of France?\n";
    cout << "1. Berlin\n";
    cout << "2. Madrid\n";
```

```
    cout << "3. Paris\n";
    cout << "4. London\n";
    do {
        cout << "Enter your answer (1-4): ";
        cin >> answer;
        if (answer == 3) {
            cout << "Correct! Paris is the capital of France.\n";
            break; // Exit the loop when the user chooses the correct answer.
        }
        else {
            cout << "Incorrect. Please try again.\n";
        }
    } while (true); // Loop indefinitely until the correct answer is given.
    return 0;
}
```

Explanation:

This is a simple C++ example program that utilizes loops and selection structures to create a basic quiz game. The program asks the user a question and continues to prompt for an answer until the correct option is chosen.

Key Components

- **Infinite Loop (do-while loop with true condition)**: The program uses an infinite loop to continuously prompt the user for an answer until the correct one is given.
- **Selection Structure (if-else)**: The program checks the user's input against the correct answer. If the user selects option '3', the program acknowledges the correct answer and breaks the loop. Otherwise, it informs the user that their choice is incorrect and prompts for another attempt.
- **User Interaction**: Through standard input (**cin**) and output (**cout**), the program interacts with the user, providing a question, accepting an answer, and giving feedback based on the user's input.

This example demonstrates how loops and selection structures can be combined in C++ to create interactive, user-friendly applications that respond to user input and control the flow of the program based on conditions.

SUMMARY

Chapter 2 of this C++ guide takes readers through the essential concepts of algorithms and control structures, which are fundamental for crafting efficient and effective programs. It starts by demystifying what algorithms are and how they can be succinctly represented using pseudocode, providing a bridge between theoretical solutions and their practical implementation in C++.

As the chapter unfolds, it delves into control structures, beginning with selection statements such as 'if', 'if...else', and the complexities of nested 'if...else' statements. It addresses the dangling-else problem, ensuring readers understand how C++ interprets ambiguous else statements. The chapter also clarifies the usage of logical operators (AND, OR, NOT), and educates on the crucial differences between equality and assignment operations, a common source of bugs in programming.

The narrative then transitions into repetition statements, with a comprehensive exploration of 'while', 'for', and 'do...while' loops. These structures are the backbone of executing code blocks multiple times based on certain conditions. The section on nested loops further expands on this concept, explaining how loops can be combined and how 'break' and 'continue' statements alter the flow of control within these loops.

A particularly intriguing section of the chapter is dedicated to generating random numbers in C++. This includes a discussion on seeding the random number generator to produce truly random sequences and techniques for calculating numbers within a specified range, which are invaluable for simulations, games, and testing scenarios that require random data.

To cement the concepts introduced, the chapter includes practical examples illustrating each control structure in action. These examples not only help to clarify theoretical concepts but also offer hands-on experience with writing C++ code that implements various control structures effectively.

The chapter wraps up with a set of exercises designed to challenge the reader's understanding and proficiency with algorithms and control structures in C++. Through these exercises, readers can practice writing their own C++ programs that leverage the power of control structures to solve complex problems, thereby reinforcing their learning and preparing them for more advanced topics in programming with C++.

Multiple Choice

Q1- Find the error in each code segment below and explain how to fix it.

```
a. x = 1;
while (x <= 10); x++;
}
b. for (y = .1; y != 1.0; y += .1)
cout << y << endl;
c. switch (n)
{
case 1:
cout << "The number is 1" << endl; case 2:
cout << "The number is 2" << endl; break;
default:
cout << "The number is not 1 or 2" << endl; break;
}
d. The following code should print the values 1 to 10.
n = 1;
while (n < 10)
cout << n++ << endl;
```

Q2- What represents a black circle surrounded by a white circle in an algorithm's activity diagram?

a. Initial state.
b. Final state.
c. Action state.
d. Transition.

Q3- Which of the following statements is a double select?

a. if.
b. if…else.
c. do…while.
d. switch.

Q4- Which of the following is a repeating structure?

a. if.
b. if…else.
c. do…while.
d. switch.

Q5 - What does the following code mean if the grade is 60?

```
if (grade >= 60)
cout << "Passed";
```

a. nothing.
b. 60
c. Passed
d. cout << "Passed";

Q6-. The conditional operator (?:):

a. The only ternary operator in C++.
b. Unary operator.
c. Colleagues from left to right.
d. Accepts two operands.

Q7- What is wrong with the following while loop?

```
while (sum <= 1000) sum = sum - 30;
```

a. The parentheses should be braces.
b. Braces are required around sum = sum – 30;.
c. There should be a semicolon after while (sum <= 1000).
d. sum = sum – 30 should be sum = sum + 30 or else the loop may never end.

Q8- How many times will the following loop print hello?

```
i = 1;
while (i <= 10)
cout << "hello";
```

a. 0
b. 9
c. 10
d. An infinite number of times.

Q9- Having a loop within a loop is known as:

a. Recursion.
b. Doubling up.
c. Nesting.
d. Stacking.

Q10- Assuming that x and y are equal to 3 and 2, respectively, after the statement x -= y executes, the values of x and y will be:

a. x: 5; y: 3
b. x: 3; y: -1
c. x: 3; y: 5
d. x: 1; y: 2

Exercises:

1- What is the purpose of control flow statements in C++ programming?
2- How is a choice made in a C++ application using an if statement?
3- What is the difference between C++'s if-else and switch-case statements?
4- How can you continually run a piece of code using a while loop in C++?
5- How can a for loop be used to traverse over an array or a range of values in C++?
6- How can you manage the flow of execution inside a C++ loop using the break and continue statements?
7- What is the difference between a C++ for loop's post-increment and pre-increment operators?
8- When is the do-while loop beneficial in C++, and how is it used?
9- How do you decide what to do and give values in C++ by using the ternary operator (?:)?
10- Write a C++ statement or series of C++ statements to achieve the following:

1. Use the for statement to sum the odd integers from 1 to 99. b. Suppose you have declared integer variables sum and count.
2. Print an integer between 1 and 20 using a while loop and a counter variable x. Suppose a variable x is declared but not initialized. Print only 5 integers per line. [caution: Use the calculation x % 5. A value of 0 here outputs a newline character. Otherwise, print a tab character].

11- Design a console-based dynamic menu system using **if**, **else if**, and **else** statements that reacts to user input to perform different operations like add, delete, display, and exit.
12-Write a program to print a complex pattern (e.g., a pyramid or a diamond) using nested loops, demonstrating the use of **for** or **while** loops within another loop.
13-Develop an advanced calculator that takes a mathematical expression as input and correctly applies control structures to respect operator precedence without using existing parser libraries.
14-Implement a custom random number generator that seeds itself based on the current time and provides options to generate random integers, floats, and within user-defined ranges.
15-Create a program that validates the strength of a password based on criteria such as length, inclusion of numbers, symbols, uppercase, and lowercase letters using control structures.
16-Simulate a traffic light system where the program cycles through green, yellow, and red lights, using **switch** cases or **if-else** statements, including conditions for pedestrians.
17-Design an automated quiz system that asks the user multiple-choice questions and tracks scores, implementing control flow to respond to correct and incorrect answers.
18-Write a program that recursively traverses directories and prints the hierarchy of files and folders, demonstrating the use of recursion for nested directories.
19-Develop a file processing application that reads, modifies, and writes to files, implementing control structures for error handling and validation of file operations.
20-Implement a command-line argument parser that processes flags and parameters passed to a C++ program, using control structures to handle various options and display help text.

Chapter 3
Arrays and Vectors

ABSTRACT

Chapter 3 dives deep into the core data structures of C++: arrays and vectors. Beginning with the fundamentals, it introduces the basic syntax and declaration of arrays and vectors, illustrated through concise examples. It elaborates on accessing array elements and efficiently iterating over them using loops. The chapter emphasizes array initialization techniques—ranging from direct initialization lists to loops. A focus on the range-based 'for' loop brings modern C++ practices to the fore. The intricate dynamics of parallel arrays, comparing arrays, and leveraging arrays in functions are explored. Diverse array structures, including static and multidimensional arrays, are expounded upon, offering insights into 2D arrays and jagged arrays. The chapter proceeds to discuss search and sort techniques, comparing their efficiencies. The versatility of the C++ Standard Library's vector template is introduced, diving into vector declaration, initialization, and algorithms. The latter section offers a deep dive into vector performance and its underlying intricacies.

3. INTRODUCTION

An array is a data structure composed of similar data items. When an array is declared, its size is specified and cannot be changed at runtime. The elements of an array are all of the same kind and are stored in a continuous pool of memory regions. To refer to a particular position or element in the array, we must supply both the array's name and the element's position number. Elements of an array may be accessed using their index, which starts at 0 for the first item.

Vectors are comparable to arrays, although there are significant distinctions. Vectors are dynamic, meaning that their dimensions might vary during execution. In addition, vectors have operations for adding, deleting, and accessing items. Typically, vectors are used when the amount of the data to be stored is unknown in advance or if the size of the data may vary during runtime.

C++ uses both arrays and vectors to store collections of data, but the decision between the two depends on the unique use case and application needs.

DOI: 10.4018/979-8-3693-2007-5.ch003

Array Example: int c[5];

```
c[0]=10;
c[1]=10;
c[2]=10;
c[3]=10;
c[4]=10;
```

This array has five items. A program may refer to any of these items by surrounding the array's name and the element's position number inside square brackets ([]). Formally, the slot number is called as the index or index (this number specifies the number of elements from the beginning of the array). The initial element of any array has an index of 0 (zero) and is sometimes referred to as the zero element. So, the elements of the array 'c' are c[0],c[1], c[2], etc. The greatest index of array c is 4, which is 1 less than the array's capacity of 5 items. Using the same naming guidelines as other variable names, array names must be identifiers.

Index must be an integer or integer [deleted] using any integral type. If a program uses an expression as an index, the expression is evaluated to determine the index. c[a + b] += 2; adds 2 to the array member c[3] if we believe that variable an equals 1 and variable b equals 2. Notice that the indexed array name is a value that may be used on the left side of an assignment, similar to a variable name that is not an array.

Vector Example

```
#include <iostream>
#include <vector>
using namespace std;
int main() {
vector<int> myVector; // create an empty vector of integers
// add elements to the vector
myVector.push_back(10);
myVector.push_back(20);
myVector.push_back(30);
// print out the contents of the vector
cout << "The elements of the vector are: ";
for (int i = 0; i < myVector.size(); i++) {
cout << myVector[i] << " ";
}
return 0;
}
```

In this example, the program contains the <iostream> and <vector> header files. The <iostream> header offers input and output capabilities, whereas the vector> header defines the vector class.

The program then writes a main() method that uses the vector class to make a vector of integers called myVector that is empty. The pushback() technique is then used to add three numbers (10, 20, and 30) to the vector.

The program then uses a for loop to run through the vector and the cout instruction to output the vector's contents. The loop iterates for the vector's size (myVector.size()) and utilizes the square bracket notation (myVector[i]) to access each vector member.

The software then returns 0 to signify successful completion.

3.1 Declaring Arrays

Declaring an array in C++ involves defining the data type of the array's elements, the array's name, and the number of items it may carry.

Arrays take up space in memory. The programmer specifies the element type and required number of elements of an array as follows:

```
<datatype> <array_name>[<array_size>];
```

The compiler reserves the amount of RAM required. array_size must be a positive integer larger than zero. Use the declaration, for instance, to instruct the compiler to reserve 12 members for the integer array c.

```
int c[ 12 ];
```

c is an array of 12 integers, uninitialized array elements are ones that don't have a value until they are given one.

Memory can be reserved for multiple arrays with a single statement. The following statement dedicates 100 elements to the integer array b and 27 elements to the integer array x.

```
int b[ 100 ], // b is an array of 100 integers
int x[27 ]; // x is an array of 27 integers
```

Arrays can be declared to hold values of any non-reference data type. For example, an array of type char can be used to store a string of characters. So far, we have used string objects to store strings.

3.2 Accessing Array Elements Values

Array elements may be accessed in C++ using the square bracket syntax [].

Assuming that the array variable myArray has a size of n, the syntax to get its elements is:

myArray[index]; // Accessing the value corresponding to the index "index"

To retrieve the first member of an array called myArray, for instance, you would use:

myArray[0]; //Accessing the index 0 value

You may also use a variable for the index instead of a constant value.

myArray[index]; // Accessing the value at the index "index"

Remember that array indexing in C++ is 0-based; therefore, the index of the first element is 0, the index of the second element is 1, and so on.

Accessing items outside of the array's limits is not a good idea because it could lead to strange behavior and memory problems.

To access element in the array, we need to call array name with subscript (index) surrounded by the square brackets:

```
cout << values[2]; // prints 5
cin >> numbers[6];
//stores user input to numbers[6]
```

3.3 Using a Loop to Step Through an Array

To walk through an array in C++, you may cycle over each member of the array using a for loop. The basic idea is to set a loop variable to 0 (which represents the first element in the array) and then increase it by 1 after each iteration until it reaches the size of the array minus 1 (which represents the last element in the array).

Here are the steps for using a loop in C++ to move through an array:

- Declare an array and populate it with values.
- Use a loop to traverse over each array member.
- Access each array member throughout the loop using the square bracket syntax [].
- Execute some action on each member of the array (e.g., print it out, modify it, etc.).

For each iteration of the loop,

- increment the loop variable by 1.

By following these steps, you can do something with each element of any C++ array. Depending on the unique use case, the actual code for the loop may change, but the fundamental principles stay the same.

```
for (int count = 0; count < SIZE; count++)
{
numbers[count] = 99;
}
```

This C++ code fragment inserts each entry of an array called numbers with the value 99. This is how it operates:

int count = 0 initializes count, a loop counter variable, to zero.

count SIZE is a loop condition that determines if the value of count is smaller than the array's size.

numbers[count] = 99 gives the array element whose value is the current value of count the value 99.

The ++ operator adds one during each loop iteration to the loop counter.

So, the loop is run SIZE times, and at each iteration, the value 99 is given to the current member of the numbers array. At the conclusion of the loop, all array items will have the value 99. For the code to function correctly, SIZE should be substituted with the actual size of the array of integers.

3.4 Default Initialization

When a C++ array is defined with no initialization, all of its elements are set to their default values.The precise behavior of default initialization depends on the element type of the array.

The default initialization for built-in types (such as int, double, etc.) sets the components to zero. The default initialization for class types depends on whether the class contains a default constructor. If the class contains a default constructor, then the array components are initialized using the default constructor. If the class does not have a default constructor, then the array cannot be default-populated, and each element must be initialized explicitly. The default initialization of pointers sets the components to a null pointer value.

Value initialization, which gives each array member a certain value, is different from default initialization.If you want to be sure that your array starts out with the right values, you should use value initialization or an explicit initialization list when you declare the array.

In C++, default initialization of arrays is the process of giving each array component a default value based on its data type.

Global Array	Declared Outside Any Function	All Elements Would Initialized to 0
Local array	Declared inside any function	All elements uninitialized by default

C++ Bounds Checking

No bounds checking in C++, for example:

```
const int SIZE = 100;
int numbers[SIZE];
for (int count = 1; count <= SIZE; count++)
numbers[count] = 0;
```

This code has an off-by-one error

```
0 0 0 0 0 0
0 1 2 3 … 98 99
```

This case causing error (overflow error). Attempting to reach unavailable item. While using count less than the array size working perfectly.

Using a loop, this code initializes to zero an array called “numbers of size SIZE.” This is how it operates:

1- ‘const int SIZE = 100;’ declares and sets the value of a constant integer called SIZE to 100.
2- ‘int numbers[SIZE];’ defines an integer array with SIZE entries called numbers.
3- ‘for (int count = 1; count < SIZE; count++) iterates through the loop as long as count is less than or equal to SIZE.

4- 'numbers[count] = 0;' assign the value 0 to the member of the array numbers whose index is the same as the current count.
5- The ++ operator adds one during each loop iteration to the loop counter.

Notice that the loop sets up the array starting at index 1 and going all the way to index SIZE.This code will actually leave the first member of the array uninitialized and set the remaining SIZE-1 items to zero since C++ arrays are 0-indexed.

To initialize the whole array to zero, the loop should instead begin at 0 and go up to SIZE - 1.

```
const int SIZE = 100;
int numbers[SIZE];
for (int count = 0; count < SIZE; count++)
numbers[count] = 0;
```

This will guarantee that every element of the array of numbers is set to zero.

```
0 0 0 0 0 0
0 1 2 3 … 98 99
```

3.5 Array Initialization

3.5.1 Initialization List

Arrays may be initialized in C++ when defined with an initialization list. The initialization list is a comma-separated list of values surrounded by braces.

Here is an example of array initialization:

```
int myArray[5] = {1, 2, 3, 4, 5};
```

This makes a five-element array of integers called myArray and gives each of its entries the values 1, 2, 3, 4, and 5.

If the number of values in the initialization list is less than the size of the array, the remaining items in the array are set to zero for built-in types and to the default for class types.

```
int myArray[5] = { 1, 2, 3 };
```

In this example, the first three array items are initialized to 1, 2, and 3, while the remaining two are initialized to zero.

If the number of values in the initialization list is greater than the size of the array, this is called a compile-time error.

```
int myArray[3] = { 1, 2, 3, 4, 5 }; //error: excessive number of initializers
```

Arrays may also be initialized with default values. If no values are specified in the initialization list, the array components are initialized with default values.

```
int myArray[5] = {}; // All items are initialized to zero by default.
```

In this example, each array entry is initialized at zero.

The initialization of arrays It is handy to use an initialization list to initialize arrays with precise values at the time of declaration.

Initialization List: we can use data type, array name and array size inside the square brackets or initialization list (the compiler is going to set the size based on how many items we have in the list:

```
int tests[] = { 79, 82, 91, 77, 84 };
int tests[5] = { 79, 82, 91, 77, 84 }; // OK
int tests[3] = { 79, 82, 91, 77, 84 }; // BAD
int tests[5] = { 79, 82, 91 }; // Positions 3 & 4
// will be set to
79
82
91
0
0
```

3.5.2 Direct Access

You may initialize array items using either direct access or individual access in C++.

Direct access means that you may directly initialize array items by providing their indices and setting their values. Here's one instance:

```
myArray[0] = 1;
myArray[1] = 2;
myArray[2] = 3;
myArray[3] = 4;
myArray[4] = 5
```

In this example, a five-element integer array called myArray is defined. The array elements are then initialized via direct access by assigning values to each element individually. Direct access is often used when you know exactly what value to give each member of an array.

3.5.3 Loops

Array elements may be initialized by using a loop to go over each element and give it a value. Here's one instance:

```
int myArray[5];
for (int i = 0; i < 5; i++) {
myArray[i] = i + 1;
}
```

In this example, a five-element integer array called myArray is defined. The array items are then populated using individual access by iterating over each element using a for loop and assigning it a value. Individual access is often used to give array items values that are computed or made at runtime.

3.6 The Range-Based for Loop

The range-based for loop in C++11 makes going through the items in a container, like an array or vector, easier and more comfortable.

Following is the syntax for the range-based for loop:

```
for (element: container) {
// code block
}
```

So, element is a variable that stands for each element in the container, and container is the container that holds the iterable components.

Using a range-based for loop, the following code goes through all the items in an array:

```
int myArray[] = { 1, 2, 3, 4, 5 };
for (int element: myArray) {
std::cout << element << " ";
}
```

Declare and initialize an integer array called myArray with 5 items. A range-based for loop is then used to traverse through the array's members. The loop variable element represents each array element in succession, and the loop body sends each element's value to the console.

The range-based for loop simplifies the syntax of iterating through a container's elements, making the code more understandable and less prone to mistakes. It is especially handy when you do not need to know the index of each element and just need to conduct an action on each element of the container.

General Format:

```
for (data-Type rangeVariable: array)
statement;
```

Example:

```
#include <iostream>
using namespace std;
int main() {
```

```
int number[] = { 10, 20, 30, 40, 50 };
for (int val: number)
cout << val << endl;
return 0;
}
```

The code begins by including the iostream library, which offers input and output capabilities. The using namespace std; directive instructs the compiler to use the std namespace, which contains the standard C++ library.

Next, the numbers array is declared and initialized with five values.

The range-based for loop is then used to traverse through the numbers array's elements. The loop variable val represents each member of the array, and the loop body uses the cout object and the operator to display the value of val to the console.

The return 0; statement tells the operating system that the program has finished running, and the program then closes.

This program shows how the range-based for loop can be used to make the syntax for going through the items in an array and doing something with each one, like publishing its value, easier to read.

You cannot use a range-based for loop to modify elements in an array unless you declare the range variable as a reference.

```
#include <iostream>
using namespace std;
int main() {
const int SIZE = 5;
int numbers[SIZE];
for (int& val: numbers) {
cout << "Enter an integer value: ";
cin >> val;
}
cout << "Here are the values you entered:\n";
for (int val: numbers)
cout << val << endl;
return 0;
}
```

The code begins by utilizing the std namespace and including the iostream library.

The SIZE variable is then set to 5, which means that the array of numbers will have five items.

Declare an integer array called numbers with SIZE elements.

The range-based for loop is then used to read integer user input and store it in the numbers array. The loop variable val stands for each member of the array in turn, while the loop body uses the cout object to ask the user for an integer value and the cin object to read the value from the console.

When all the values from the console have been read and put into the numbers array, another range-based for loop sends the contents of the array to the console.The loop variable val represents each member of the array, and the loop body uses the cout object to print the value of val to the console.

The program concludes by returning 0 to the operating system.

This program shows how the range-based for loop can be used to make the syntax for iterating through array items and doing something with each one, like reading the user's input or making the array's contents public, simpler.

To declare a scope variable as a reference, simply write an & before its name in the loop header. Range based for loop can be used in any situation when you need to iterate over array elements without using element index. If you need the element's index for some purpose, use a regular for loop.

3.7 Parallel Arrays

In C++, parallel arrays are two or more arrays that are used to show related data at the same time.In a parallel array, each member represents a single record or data point, and the data for each record is spread out among the many arrays.

Consider a piece of software that must maintain information on a group of students, such as their names, ages, and grades. This might be expressed using three distinct arrays, one for each data item:

```
string names[] = { "Alice", "Bob", "Charlie", "Dave" };
int ages[] = { 18, 19, 20, 18 };
double grades[] = { 3.8, 3.2, 3.9, 3.5 };
```

Each index in the names array is the same as an index in the ages and grades arrays, which hold information about a particular student.By indexing into the associated arrays, this method lets the application quickly get to and change the data for each student.

Parallel arrays may be helpful for arranging similar data in a manner that is simple to maintain and modify, but they can be more challenging to deal with than alternative data structures like structs or classes, which enable related data to be kept in a single object. Furthermore, modifications to one array must be carefully coordinated with modifications to the other arrays to preserve data consistency.

Example 1:

```
#include<iostream>
#include<string>
#include<iomanip>
using namespace std;
int main() {
const int SIZE = 24;
string names[] = { "Lina", "Gina", "Ryan", "Aparna", "Yang","Prateek", "Zach",
"Joshi", "Eric", "Roger",
"Ben", "Rohan", "Johanan", "Todd", "Eric", "Jocksan",
"Michael", "David", "Roman", "Jaymar", "Vidya",
"Olivia", "Rachel", "Daniel" };
int nSiblings[] = { 2, 1, 1, 1, 0, 1, 3, 5, 2, 3, 1, 1, 2, 1, 2, 0,
2, 1, 4, 3, 2, 1, 1, 1 };
int sum = 0;
for (int i = 0; i < SIZE; i++) {
```

```
cout << names[i] << "\t" << nSiblings[i] << endl;
sum += nSiblings[i];
}
cout << fixed << showpoint << setprecision(2);
cout << "Total: " << sum << endl;
//greatest
int max = nSiblings[0];
for (int i = 0; i < SIZE; i++) {
if (nSiblings[i] > max)
max = nSiblings[i];
}
cout << "Maximum: " << max << endl;
//least
int min = nSiblings[0];
for (int i = 0; i < SIZE; i++) {
min = (nSiblings[i] < min) ? nSiblings[i]: min;
}
cout << "Minimum: " << min << endl;
//average
cout << "Average: " << static_cast<double>(sum) / SIZE << endl;
system("pause");
return 0;
}
```

This C++ code sets up two parallel arrays, named "names" and "nSiblings," before processing them to get statistics about the data.The names array keeps the names of 24 people, whereas the nSiblings array records the number of siblings each person has.

The code used a for loop to traverse over each array member and print the sibling name and count for each person. It also computes the sum of all the nSiblings array items.

After processing the data, the code figures out the most and least siblings, as well as the average number of siblings, and reports them.The cout commands prepare the output using the fixed, showpoint, and setprecision manipulators.

The system("pause") command is used to halt the program before it ends, allowing the user to see the output.

3.8 Comparing Arrays

To compare two parallel arrays in C++, you have to compare the parts of the arrays that are the same.If we have two parallel arrays arr1 and arr2, for instance, we may compare their items at position I by writing arr1[i] == arr2[i]. This comparison returns true if the items at index I are identical and false otherwise.

We may use a loop to compare all the entries in the two arrays that correspond. If any pair of items does not match, we may deduce that the two arrays do not match. If every pair of items is the same, we may infer that the two arrays are identical.

It is essential to notice that when comparing parallel arrays, both arrays must have the same length. If the lengths of the arrays vary, we cannot compare them element by element and must use an alternative comparison method.

```
#include <iostream>
using namespace std;
const int SIZE = 5;
int main() {
int first_Array[SIZE] = { 5, 10, 15, 20, 25 };
int second_Array[SIZE] = { 5, 10, 15, 20, 25 };
bool arraysEqual = true; // flag variable
int count = 0;
while (arraysEqual && count < SIZE) {
if (first_Array[count] != second_Array[count])
arraysEqual = false;
count++;
}
return 0;
system("pause");
}
```

The code verifies the equality of two arrays of integers, first_Array and second_Array. The software employs the following elements:

- The preprocessor directive #include <iostream> tells the compiler to include the iostream input/output library.
- This line tells the compiler to use functions and objects from the C++ standard library that are in the std namespace without prefixing them with std::.
- const This line establishes a constant integer size with the value 5 that will be used to indicate the size of the arrays.
- This is the program's main purpose, and it is done when the program is run.
- This line defines and initializes an array of integers named first_Array with SIZE items having the values 5, 10, 15, 20, and 25.
- This line sets up a second array of integers called second_Array with the same size and values as the first array, first_Array.
- bool arraysEqual = true;: This line sets up the arraysEqual variable and gives it the value true as its first value.
- int count = 0; This line defines a variable of type integer whose initial value is 0.
- This line initiates a while loop that will continue so long as arraysEqual is true and count is smaller than SIZE.
- This line checks to see if the item at index count in first_Array is the same as the item at index count in second_Array.
- If they are not equal, false is returned for arraysEqual.
- count++;: This line adds 1 to the count variable.

- This line notifies the operating system that the program has concluded properly and returns the value 0.
- system ("pause");: This line invokes the system function to stop the program before quitting, enabling the user to see the output before the program is terminated. It is important to note, however, that this line is unreachable since it follows the return statement, therefore, it will never be performed.

3.9 Arrays as Function Arguments

In C++, arrays can be passed to functions as parameters, which lets the function change or work with the array's elements.When an array is provided to a function, the first element is really pointed to. So, the method gets an array pointer and can use pointer arithmetic to access and change array items.

To send an array as an argument to a function, you may define the function to accept an array parameter.

```
void functionName(type arrayName[], int arraySize)
{
// function code
}
```

Here, functionName is the name of the function, type is the data type of the array members, arrayName[] (which may be any valid identifier) is the name of the array parameter, and arraySize is the size of the array.

Consider the following function, which calculates the sum of the integer array's elements:

```
int arraySum(int arr[], int size)
{
int sum = 0;
for (int i = 0; i < size; i++)
{
sum += arr[i];
}
return sum;
}
```

This method takes as parameters the array of integers arr and the size of that array, size.The function then uses a for loop to add up all of the items in the array and gives the result back as an integer.

To use an integer array with this method, give the array's name and size as parameters.

```
int myArray[] = { 1, 2, 3, 4, 5 };
int arraySize = 5;
int sum = arraySum(myArray, arraySize);
```

Here, myArray is a five-element integer array, and arraySize is a variable that stores its size. MyArray and arraySize are passed to the arraySum function as arguments, and the result is stored in the integer variable sum.

When passing an array as a function parameter, the array's size must be given explicitly, either as a constant or as a variable holding the array size. This is due to the fact that the array's size is not contained inside the array itself but rather is set by its declaration.

It is common to pass array size so function knows how many elements to process for example:

```
showScores(tests, ARRAY_SIZE);
void showScores(int[], int); // prototype
void showScores(int tests[], int size) // function header
```

Example:

```
#include <iostream>
using namespace std;
void showValues(int[], int); // prototype
int main() {
const int ARRAY_SIZE = 8;
int numbers[ARRAY_SIZE] = { 5, 10, 15, 20, 25, 30, 35, 40 };
showValues(numbers, ARRAY_SIZE);
system("pause");
return 0;
}
void showValues(int nums[], int size) {
for (int index = 0; index < size; index++)
cout << nums[index] << endl;
}
```

The given code contains the C++ standard library iostream, which provides fundamental input/output functions and defines the std namespace for application usage. The program also contains the function prototype for the showValues function, which accepts two parameters: an integer array int[] and an integer int.

A constant integer ARRAY SIZE is defined and assigned the value 8 in the main function. Next, an ARRAY SIZE-by-ARRAY SIZE array of integers is formed and populated with eight integer values. showValues is invoked with the parameters numbers and ARRAY SIZE.

The function showValues, which was prototyped before main, is subsequently declared in the code. The function accepts two parameters: an array of integers, nums[, and a size parameter, int. The function iterates through each member of the array using a for loop, writing each element to the console using the cout instruction.

In the end, the program makes an array of integers and a function that sends the array's contents to the screen. The array and its size are sent to the method as parameters. The program's output consists of the printed values of the integer array.

3.10 Static Arrays

In C++, a static array is a group of items with the same data type and a size that has already been set.A constant number that must be known at the time of compilation determines the size of a static array.

After the name of a static array, square brackets [] are used to define it and say how big it is.For instance, the code below sets up a static array of 5 integers:

```
int myArray[5];
```

This defines a five-element array of integers called myArray with the indexes myArray[0] through myArray[4].

The elements of a static array are kept in a single memory block. Memory allocation for the array is fixed and cannot be altered at runtime.

With the index notation, the elements of a static array may be accessed. For instance, the expression myArray[0] = 10 assigns the value 10 to the first member of the array.

With curly brackets, values can be added to static arrays at the time they are declared.In the code below, for example, a static array of integers with a size of 3 is defined and set up.

```
int myArray[] = {1, 2, 3};
```

Static arrays may be supplied as parameters to functions, but their size must be specified at build time. When given as function parameters, a pointer to the first array element is supplied, enabling the function to access and alter array items.

Static arrays are easy to use and make good use of memory and speed. Nevertheless, they have the drawback of having a fixed size that cannot be altered during runtime, and they may waste RAM if the array size is larger than required.

```
//Static arrays are initialized to zero.
#include <iostream>
using namespace std;
void staticArray(void); // function prototype
void automaticArray(void); // function prototype
const int arraySize = 3;
void main()
{
cout << "First call to each function:\n";
staticArray();
automaticArrayInit();
cout << "\n\nSecond call to each function:\n";
staticArray();
automaticArrayInit();
cout << endl;
system("pause");
} // end main
```

```
// function to demonstrate a static local array
void staticArray(void)
{
// initializes elements to 0 first time function is called
static int array1[arraySize]; // static local array
cout << "\nValues on entering staticArray:\n";
// output contents of array1
for (int i = 0; i < arraySize; ++i)
cout << "array1[" << i << "] = " << array1[i] << " ";
cout << "\nValues on exiting staticArray:\n";
// modify and output contents of array1
for (int j = 0; j < arraySize; ++j)
cout << "array1[" << j << "] = " << (array1[j] += 5) << " ";
} // end function staticArray
// function to demonstrate an automatic local array
void automaticArray(void)
{
// initializes elements each time function is called
int array2[arraySize] = { 1, 2, 3 }; // automatic local array
cout << "\n\nValues on entering automaticArray:\n";
// output contents of array2
for (int i = 0; i < arraySize; ++i)
cout << "array2[" << i << "] = " << array2[i] << " ";
cout << "\nValues on exiting automaticArray:\n";
// modify and output contents of array2
for (int j = 0; j < arraySize; ++j)
cout << "array2[" << j << "] = " << (array2[j] += 5) << " ";
} // end function automaticArray
```

The difference between a local static array and a local automated array is shown in this C++ code.

Each of the two methods, staticArray() and automaticArray(), sets up and updates an array of size arraySize, which is a global constant with the value 3.

The staticArray() method declares a local array of size arraySize that is static. When this method is invoked for the first time, the array items are automatically initialized to zero. The code then returns the array values before and after adding 5 to each member of the array.

The automaticArray() method defines a local array of size arraySize that is initialized automatically. When this function is used, the array elements are initialized to the values 1, 2, and 3, respectively. The code then returns the array values before and after adding 5 to each member of the array.

The two functions are called twice in the main() method: once to display the original values of the arrays and once to demonstrate the updated values.

The output of the application displays the array values before and after alteration. The static local array preserves its values across function calls, but the automatic local array is reinitialized on every function call.

3.11 Multidimensional Arrays

A multidimensional array in C++ is an array with several dimensions. Each member of the outer array includes another array as its value.

Here is the C++ syntax for defining a multidimensional array:

```
type array name [size 1] [size 2]... [size N];
```

Here, type is the data type of the array elements, array name is the array's name, and size1, size2,..., sizeN are the sizes of each array dimension. To define a 2-dimensional array of numbers with 3 rows and 4 columns, for example, we may write:

```
int my_array[3][4];
```

This produces a 12-element array with three rows and four columns. We may access the array's elements using the row and column indexes as follows:

```
my_array
[row index]
[column index]
```

To assign the value 42 to the element in the second row and third column of the array my_array, for instance, we may write:

```
my_array[1][2] = 42;
```

We may also explore the elements of a multidimensional array using stacked loops. To print all the items in my array, for instance, we may write:

```
for (int i = 0; i < 3; i++) {
for (int j = 0; j < 4; j++) {
cout << my_array[i][j] << " ";
}
cout << endl;
}
```

This will display the array with each row on a distinct line, in row-major order.

Remember that multidimensional arrays in C++ are stored in row-major order, meaning that the items of each row are kept in memory consecutively. This may have performance ramifications, particularly when accessing components column-wise.

3.11.1 Two-Dimensional Arrays

A Two-Dimensional Arrays are commonly used to represent arrays of values that include information arranged in rows and columns. To define a specific table element, two indices must be specified. By convention, the first specifies the item's row, and the second defines the item's column. Two-dimensional arrays, or 2D arrays, are arrays that need two indices to identify a specific element. Remember that multidimensional arrays may have dimensions beyond two (i.e., indices). A table having m rows and n columns is referred to as an m-by-n table.

Each member of array an has a name of the form a[i][j], where an is the name of the array and I and j are indices that identify each member of the array uniquely.Observe that each element name in row 0 has a leading index of 0 and that each element name in column 3 has a second index of 3.

Similar to a one-dimensional array, a multidimensional array may be initialized in its definition. For instance, a two-dimensional array b containing the values 1 and 2 in its row 0 elements and the values 3 and 4 in its row 1 elements may be defined and initialized as follows:

```
int b[ 2 ][ 2 ] = { { 1, 2 }, { 3, 4 } };
```

Values are grouped by line in curly brackets. Hence, 1 and 2 respectably initialize b[0][0] and b[0][1], but 3 and 4 respectably initialize b[1][0] and b[1][1]. If there are insufficient initializers for a row, the remaining items are initialized to 0.

. Hence the declaration

```
int b[ 2 ][ 2 ] = { { 1 }, { 3, 4 } };
initializes b[ 0 ][ 0 ] to 1, b[ 0 ][ 1 ] to 0, b[ 1 ][ 0 ] to 3 and b[ 1 ][ 1
] to 4
```

For example:

```
const int ROWS = 4, COLS = 3;
int exams[ROWS][COLS];
```

	0	1	2
0	exams[0][0]	exams[0][1]	exams[0][2]
1	exams[1][0]	exams[1][1]	exams[1][2]
2	exams[2][0]	exams[2][1]	exams[2][2]
3	exams[3][0]	exams[3][1]	exams[3][2]

```
exams[2][2] = 86;
const int ROWS = 4, COLS = 3;
Example:
int exams[ROWS][COLS] = { {84, 78}, {92, 97} };
```

```
84 78
92 97
```

Example 1:

```
#include <iostream>
#include <iomanip>
using namespace std;
const int COLS = 3;
void showArray(int[][COLS], int); // prototype
int main() {
int nStudents[][COLS] = { {9999, 22000, 11000},
{8000, 20000, 10500},
{7500, 18500, 9500} };
showArray(nStudents, 3); system("pause");
return 0;
}
void showArray(int array[][COLS], int rows) {
for (int x = 0; x < rows; x++) {
for (int y = 0; y < COLS; y++) {
cout << setw(4) << array[x][y] << " ";
}
cout << endl;
}
}
```

This C++ code has the input/output stream library (<iostream>) and the input/output manipulation library (<iomanip>), as well as the constant COLS with the value 3. It also defines the function showArray, which accepts a two-dimensional array of integers (int[][COLS]) and an integer (int) and returns void.

The two-dimensional integer array nStudents is declared and filled with three rows and three columns in the main() method.The method showArray is then called with the inputs nStudents and 3 to display the array's contents.

Two nested loops are used by the showArray function to explore and show the contents of a two-dimensional array.The outer loop goes through each row in the array, while the inner loop goes through each column (COLS) in the array.To align the columns of output, the setw() function from the iomanip library is used to set the width of the output field to 4 characters.

The application pauses the console using the system() method before departing.

Example 2:

```
#include <iostream>
using std::cout;
using std::endl;
void main()
{
```

```
const int ROWS = 4;
const int COLS = 5;
int multiArr[ROWS][COLS] = {
{1111, 78, 45, 65, 12},
{ 2222, 78, 65, 24, 98},
{3333, 87, 54, 89, 78},
{7, 4, 9, 0, 6} };
for (int i = 0; i < 20; ++i)
{
cout << multiArr[i] << "\t";
}
system("pause");
}
```

This C++ code defines and initializes a 2-dimensional integer array called multiArr with 4 rows and 5 columns. The cout command is then used to display the values of each of the 20 array items, separated by tabs (t), using a for loop.

This method main() in this code does not have a return type, which is invalid C++ syntax. int main is the right form for the main() function in C++ ().

Also, the loop in this code only goes through each item in the array in a linear way, which may not give the results that were wanted or expected.Most of the time, you use two indices to get to the items in a two-dimensional array: one for the row and one for the column.The loop in this code needs to be nested, with one loop for the rows and one for the columns, so that it can go through the array's items in the right way.

The system() method is then used to stop the console before leaving. This is not a good way to do C++ programming in the 21st century. Use a return statement to end the function or application or use the right method for input/output processing to talk to the user.

3.11.2 Jagged Array

A jagged array (also known as a ragged array) in C++ is an array in which each element might be another array of varying size. In a standard (or rectangular) two-dimensional array, there are the same number of elements in each row and column. This array, on the other hand, is not standard.

Using pointers, a jagged array may be defined in C++. The following code, for example, creates a jagged array of integer pointers:

```
int* jaggedArray[] = {
new int[3] {1, 2, 3},
new int[2] {4, 5},
new int[4] {6, 7, 8, 9}
};
```

jaggedArray is an array of integer pointers. Each member of jaggedArray is another array of variable-sized integers. The first element is an array of three integers, whereas the second and third elements are arrays of two and four integers, respectively.

To get to the items in a jagged array, you must first look at the outer array, which gives you a pointer to the inner array. With the pointer, you can then access the items in the inner array. For instance:

```
cout << jaggedArray[0][1] << endl; // prints 2.
cout << jaggedArray[1][0] << endl; // prints 4.
cout << jaggedArray[2][2] << endl; // prints 8.
```

jaggedArray[0][1] accesses the second member of the first inner array (2), jaggedArray[1][0] accesses the first element of the second inner array (4), and jaggedArray[2][2] accesses the third element of the third inner array (which has a value of 8).

When using jagged arrays in C++ (like new and delete), remember that memory allocation and deallocation must be done by hand using pointers and dynamic memory allocation routines. Memory leaks and unclear behavior may result from improper memory management.

Example:

```
#include <iostream>
using namespace std;
int main()
{
const int ROWS = 4;
int* jaggedArr[ROWS]; // declare a jagged array of pointers to integers
jaggedArr[0] = new int[3]{ 1, 2, 3 }; // initialize the first row with 3 ele-
ments
jaggedArr[1] = new int[2]{ 4, 5 }; // initialize the second row with 2 ele-
ments
jaggedArr[2] = new int[4]{ 6, 7, 8, 9 }; // initialize the third row with 4
elements
jaggedArr[3] = new int[1]{ 10 }; // initialize the fourth row with 1 element
// access and print the elements of the jagged array
for (int i = 0; i < ROWS; i++) {
for (int j = 0; j < (i + 1); j++) {
cout << jaggedArr[i][j] << " ";
}
cout << endl;
}
// free the memory allocated for the jagged array
for (int i = 0; i < ROWS; i++) {
delete[] jaggedArr[i];
}
return 0;
}
```

This program begins by declaring a jagged array. jaggedArr of integer pointer arrays with four rows Instead of creating a single contiguous block of memory for the whole array, the new keyword is used to allocate each row of the jagged array individually. Each row may have a varied number of entries, making it a "jagged" array.

Using the brace-initialization syntax for arrays, each row of the jagged array is then initialized with a unique number of entries. In this example, the first row has three items, the second row contains two items, the third row contains four items, and the fourth row contains one item.

We then use nested for loops to access and output the jagged array's elements. The outer loop iterates through the array's rows, while the inner loop iterates over each row's items. Notice that we chose (i+1) as the limit for the inner loop since the number of items in each row varies.

Lastly, we free the memory allocated for the jagged array by deleting each row of the array using the delete[] operator.

When the program is run, the following is the output:

```
1 2 3
4 5
6 7 8 9
10
```

indicating that the jagged array has been appropriately initialized and the items have been read and printed.

3.12 Constant Keyword

There may be situations in your program where a function is not allowed to modify array elements. C++ provides a const qualifier that can be used to prevent array values in the caller from being modified by code in the called function. When a function provides an array argument before the const qualifier, the array items become constants in the body of the function, and any attempt to alter an array element in the function body results in a compiler error. This enables the programmer to avoid the unintentional alteration of array items inside the function's body.

3.13 Searching Arrays With Linear Search

A programmer often works with enormous quantities of data contained in arrays. It may be essential to determine if an array includes a value that corresponds to a certain key. The search for a particular element inside an array is referred to as searching. In this part, basic linear search is discussed.

3.13.1 Linear Search

Linear search compares each array element to a search key. As the array is not in any specific order, it is possible that the value exists in both the first and final elements. Therefore, the program must, on average, compare the search key with fifty percent of the array's elements. To ascertain if a particular value does not exist in the array, the software must compare the search key to each member of the array.

The linear search approach performs well with tiny arrays or arrays that are not sorted (i.e., arrays with elements that are not in any particular order). Yet, linear search in large arrays is inefficient. If the array is sorted (e.g., the items are in ascending order), you may use the high-speed binary search approach described in the section Searching and Sorting.

Steps:

1. Start from the first element
2. Sequentially go through the table
3. Check each item until the search item is found

```
#include <iostream>
using namespace std;
// Function prototype
int linearSearch(const int[], int, int);
// Main function
void main()
{
const int arraySize = 100; // size of array
int a[arraySize]; // create array a
int searchKey; // value to locate in array a
// Fill the array with some data
for (int i = 0; i < arraySize; ++i)
{
a[i] = 2 * i;
cout << a[i] << endl;;
}
// Prompt the user to enter the search key
cout << "Enter integer search key: ";
cin >> searchKey;
// Call the linear search function
int element = linearSearch(a, searchKey, arraySize);
// Check if the value was found or not
if (element != -1)
cout << "Found value in element " << element << endl;
else
cout << "Value not found" << endl;
system("pause"); // pause the program
}
// Linear search function
int linearSearch(const int array[], int key, int sizeOfArray)
{
// Search for the key in the array
for (int j = 0; j < sizeOfArray; ++j)
```

```
if (array[j] == key) // if found,
return j; // return location of key
return -1; // key not found
}
```

This C++ application illustrates linear search. This is a concise description of the program:

- For input/output operations, the software includes the iostream> library.
- The linearSearch function takes three parameters: an array of constant integers, an integer key, and an integer sizeOfArray.
- At the beginning of the main function, arraySize is set to be a 100-valued constant integer that represents the size of the array.
- Using a for loop, an integer array of size arraySize is constructed and populated with values.
- The user is requested to input a searchKey integer.
- The array a, searchKey, and arraySize are sent to the linearSearch function as parameters.
- The element is discovered, and its index is shown if the linearSearch function returns a value other than -1. If not, the value not found will be shown.
- Before a program quits, the system("pause") statement is used to halt the program.

3.13.2 Binary Search

Binary Search is a technique for efficiently searching for an element in a sorted array. It works by periodically halving the search interval until the target element is located or the interval is empty.

The method compares the target element to the array's middle element. If the target matches the element in the center, the search is complete. If the target is less than the middle element, the algorithm searches the left half of the array again. Otherwise, the algorithm restarts its search on the array's right half.

By halving the search interval with every iteration, Binary Search achieves a time complexity of O(log n), where n is the array size. This is far more efficient than linear search, which has a temporal complexity of O. (n).

Unfortunately, Binary Search is only applicable to sorted arrays. If the array is not sorted, a time-consuming sorting procedure must be implemented first.

(Requires items to be in order)

1- Divide the board into 3 parts
  - middle element (1/2 path between array[first] and array[last]
  - element on one side of the middle element
  - elements on the other side of the middle element

2- If array[between] is equal to the search element, return between

3- Different if array[middle] > search element
  - Place the last in the middle - 1

4- Different if array[between] < search item
  - Set in the center before +1

5- Continue steps 1-4 until a value is found or there are no items left to check

Example:

```
#include<iostream>
#include<string>
using namespace std;
int binarySearch(int[], int, int);
void main()
{
int myArray[8] = { 2, 3, 5, 11, 17, 23, 29, 31 };
//find the 5 in myArray
int result = binarySearch(myArray, 100, 8);
if (result != -1) {
cout << "Your item was found at position " << result << endl;
}
else
cout << "Your item was not found." << endl;
system("pause");
}
int binarySearch(int array[], int value, int arraySize) {
int first = 0;
int last = arraySize - 1;
int position = -1; // we'll change this if we find the value
bool found = false;
//Search for the value
for (int i = 0; i < arraySize; i++) {
//if we still haven't found it
if (!found) {
//calculate the midpoint
int middle = (first + last) / 2;
//Case 1: if value is found at midpoint,
//set found to true,position to middle
if (array[middle] == value) {
found = true;
position = middle;
} //Case 2: else if value is in lower half,
        //set last = middle - 1
else if (value < array[middle]) {
last = middle - 1;
} //Case 3: else if value is in upper half,
//set first = middle + 1
else if (value > array[middle]) {
first = middle + 1;
}
}
```

```
}
return position;
}
```

This C++ application illustrates the usage of the Binary Search algorithm to locate an element inside a sorted array. The software then invokes the "binarySearch" method to search the array for the number 100.

The "binarySearch" function accepts three arguments: the array to search, the value to search for, and the array's size. It starts by setting the beginning and end positions of the array and the position variable to -1, which means that the value hasn't been found yet.

The program then starts a loop to look for the value. At each iteration of the loop, the formula (first + last) / 2 is used to determine the midpoint of the search interval. Then, it examines three cases:

If the value is located at the midpoint, the "found" variable is set to true, and the "position" variable is updated to the middle.

If the value is smaller than the value at the halfway point, the "last" variable is updated to the position shortly before the halfway point.

If the value is larger than the midway value, the "first" variable is updated to the place shortly after the midpoint.

The iteration continues until the value is located or until the search period expires.

The function returns the index of the value inside the array, or -1 if the item could not be located.

In the main function, the binary search result is examined. If the value is discovered, the software outputs the value's location in the array. If not, it produces a message stating that the value could not be found. Before ending, the software waits for the user to touch any key.

3.13.3 Linear Search vs. Binary Search

Linear search and binary search are two techniques for searching an array for an element.

The target element is compared to each element in the array in a planned way until a match is found or the end of the array is reached.The temporal complexity is O(n), where n is the array's size. Simple to build, linear search may be used for both sorted and unordered arrays. Yet, for big arrays, its temporal complexity is inefficient.

In contrast, binary search works by halving the time between each search until the target element is found or the time between searches runs out.The temporal complexity is O(log n), where n is the array's size. Binary search is limited to sorted arrays only. For large arrays, it is more efficient than linear search since each iteration halves the search interval, resulting in quicker search times.

Linear search is easier to construct and can be used for both sorted and unsorted arrays, but its time complexity is O. (n). Binary search is more effective on large, sorted arrays, with a time complexity of O(log n), although it can only be used for sorted arrays. The method used depends on the particular use case and the size of the array being searched.

3.14 Array Sort

Sorting the items in an array, usually in ascending or descending order, is a common way to use array sorting in computer programming.There are various ways to sort an array in C++, but the "sort" built-in function is one of the most used.

The "sort" function is part of the C++ Standard Template Library (STL). It can be found in the algorithm> header file.The first parameter is the beginning of the array to be sorted, and the second is the end of the array. The function arranges the array items between the array's beginning and finish.

Depending on the comparison function used, the "sort" function may be used to sort an array either ascending or descending. By default, the "sort" function sorts the array using the less-than operator in ascending order. You can sort an array in descending order by passing a comparison function that reverses the order of the items.

Here's how to use the "sort" function to put an array in ascending order:

Example

```
#include <iostream>
#include <algorithm>
using namespace std;
int main() {
int arr[] = { 3, 5, 1, 9, 2 };
int n = sizeof(arr) / sizeof(arr[0]);
sort(arr, arr + n);
for (int i = 0; i < n; i++) {
cout << arr[i] << " ";
}
return 0;
}
```

In this example, the "sort" function is used to ascendingly sort an array of numbers. The first argument to the function is the array, and the second argument is the end of the array. In this case, the end is calculated by adding the beginning of the array to the size of the array. The function sorts the array in situ, so the original array is sorted in ascending order after the function call.

The "sort" function in C++ is a valuable tool for sorting arrays. It is simple to use and can be modified to sort arrays in a number of ways, making it a useful programming tool for a range of jobs.

3.14.1 Bubble Sort

Bubble Sort is a simple way to put things in the right order by constantly swapping items next to each other that are in the wrong order.At each run of the method, smaller items "bubble" to the top of the array, giving the algorithm its name.

The basic idea behind Bubble Sort is to loop over the array and swap nearby items that are out of order until the array is in the right order.The algorithm is implemented as follows:

- Beginning at the array's beginning, compare the first two members. If the first element is bigger than the second, switch the two elements.
- Repeat step 1 for the next pair of items.
- Continue until the end of the array has been reached.
- At this moment, the array's last member is assured to occupy its final place.
- Repeat steps 1-4 for the remaining array items.

This is a C++ implementation of the bubble sort:

```
#include <iostream>
using namespace std;
void bubbleSort(int arr[], int n) {
for (int i = 0; i < n - 1; i++) {
for (int j = 0; j < n - i - 1; j++) {
if (arr[j] > arr[j + 1]) {
int temp = arr[j];
arr[j] = arr[j + 1];
arr[j + 1] = temp;
}
}
}
}
int main() {
int arr[] = { 5, 2, 8, 6, 1, 9 };
int n = sizeof(arr) / sizeof(arr[0]);
bubbleSort(arr, n);
cout << "Sorted array: ";
for (int i = 0; i < n; i++) {
cout << arr[i] << " ";
}
return 0;
}
```

In this example, the "bubbleSort" function receives as input an array of numbers and the array's size and sorts the array using Bubble Sort. The main function initializes an array of integers, invokes the "bubbleSort" function to sort the array, and then outputs the array once it has been sorted.

Bubble Sort's worst-case time complexity of O(n2) makes it less efficient than merge sort and quick sort. Yet, it is simple to comprehend and apply, making it a viable option for tiny arrays or a straightforward illustration of the notion of sorting algorithms.

Example:

```
#include <iostream>
#include <iomanip>
using namespace std;
void main()
{
const int arraySize = 10;
int a[arraySize] = { 2, 6, 4, 8, 10, 12, 89, 68, 45, 37 };
int hold;
cout << "Data items in original order\n";
for (int i = 0; i < arraySize; i++)
```

```
cout << setw(4) << a[i];
for (int pass = 0; pass < arraySize - 1; pass++)
{
for (int j = 0; j < arraySize - 1; j++)
{
if (a[j] > a[j + 1])
{
hold = a[j];
a[j] = a[j + 1];
a[j + 1] = hold;
} // end if
} // end for
} // end for
cout << "\nData items in ascending order\n";
for (int k = 0; k < arraySize; k++)
cout << setw(4) << a[k];
cout << endl;
system("pause");
} // end main
```

This C++ code explains the Bubble Sort algorithm's implementation.

The software makes an array of 10 integers and gives it some random values to start off with. The values are then printed in their original sequence.

The bubble sort method is constructed with two for loops nestled inside one another. The outer loop iterates through each iteration of the method, while the inner loop examines nearby array items and swaps them if their order is incorrect.

When the method is complete, another for loop is used to output the data in sorted order.

Overall, the software sorts the array in ascending order using the bubble sort method and shows the sorted array.

Example: Enhanced bubble sort

```
#include <iostream>
#include <iomanip>
using namespace std;
void main()
{
const int SIZE = 10; // size of array
int a[SIZE] = { 2, 6, 4, 8, 10, 12, 89, 68, 45, 37 };
int hold;
int numberOfComp = 0; // number of comparisons made
int comp; // used to control for loop and for subscripts
cout << "Data items in original order\n";
for (int i = 0; i < SIZE; ++i)
cout << setw(4) << a[i];
```

```
cout << "\n\n";
for (int pass = 1; pass < SIZE; pass++)
{
cout << "After pass " << pass - 1 << ": ";
for (comp = 0; comp < SIZE - pass; comp++)
{
numberOfComp++;
if (a[comp] > a[comp + 1])
{
hold = a[comp];
a[comp] = a[comp + 1];
a[comp + 1] = hold;
} // end if
cout << setw(3) << a[comp];
} // end inner for
cout << setw(3) << a[comp] << '\n'; // print last array value
} // end outer for
cout << "\nData items in ascending order\n";
for (int j = 0; j < SIZE; j++)
cout << setw(4) << a[j];
cout << "\nNumber of comparisons = " << numberOfComp << endl;
system("pause");
} // end main
```

The enhanced bubble sort algorithm is a type of bubble sort that stops if the array is already in the right order.In C++, the implementation requires a flag variable to keep track of whether any swaps were performed during a particular pass.

The improved bubble sort algorithm is conceptually similar to bubble sort. On the first pass, the first and second array items are compared and swapped if they are in the incorrect order. This procedure is then performed for each remaining array element. The procedure is continued until no further exchanges are made.

The primary distinction between enhanced bubble sort and standard bubble sort is that the enhanced version maintains a note of whether or not any swaps occurred during a given pass. If no swaps are performed, the array is already sorted, and the algorithm may end. This makes the improved bubble sort more efficient than the standard bubble sort for partially sorted arrays.

Using the C++ code given, the extended bubble sort method sorts an array of numbers in ascending order. Moreover, the number of comparisons performed throughout the sort is sent to the console.

3.14.2 Selection Sort

Selection Sort is a straightforward sorting algorithm that works by continually locating and inserting the least element from the unsorted portion of the array. The method maintains two subarrays: the sorted subarray, which is incrementally constructed from left to right, and the unsorted subarray, which includes any leftover unsorted items.

In C++, the algorithm operates as follows:

- From the first element through the n-1th element, traverse the array.
- Determine the smallest element in the array's unsorted portion.
- Switch the minimal element with the first member in the array's unsorted portion.
- Repeat steps 2 and 3 for the remainder of the unsorted array.

Here is an example of Selection Sort implementation in C++:

```
#include <iostream>
#include <iomanip>
using namespace std;
void selectionSort(int arr[], int n)
{
int i, j, minIndex, temp;
// One by one move boundary of unsorted subarray
for (i = 0; i < n - 1; i++)
{
// Find the minimum element in unsorted array
minIndex = i;
for (j = i + 1; j < n; j++)
{
if (arr[j] < arr[minIndex])
minIndex = j;
}
// Swap the found minimum element with the first element
temp = arr[minIndex];
arr[minIndex] = arr[i];
arr[i] = temp;
}
}
int main()
{
const int arraySize = 10;
int a[arraySize] = { 2, 6, 4, 8, 10, 12, 89, 68, 45, 37 };
cout << "Data items in original order\n";
for (int i = 0; i < arraySize; i++)
cout << setw(4) << a[i];
selectionSort(a, arraySize);
cout << "\nData items in ascending order\n";
for (int k = 0; k < arraySize; k++)
cout << setw(4) << a[k];
cout << endl;
system("pause");
```

```
return 0;
}
```

This selection sort implementation has a time complexity of O(n2), making it inefficient for big arrays. Still, it is effective for sorting tiny arrays and has the benefit of needing just a fixed amount of extra memory.

This C++ code illustrates how the Selection Sort algorithm may be implemented to sort an integer array in ascending order. The code provides a function selectionSort that accepts an array of integers arr and its length n as inputs. The function executes the following operations:

Iterate across the array, beginning at index 0 and ending at index n-2.

Get the index of the smallest element in the unsorted subarray at each iteration (from the current index to the end of the array).

Exchange the smallest member in the unsorted subarray with the initial element.

The main function creates a ten-element array of integers and shows them in their original order. The array is then sorted using the selectionSort function, and its members are shown in ascending order. The system ("pause") command is used to pause the console window, allowing the user to observe the output.

The steps are listed below:

1. Locate the smallest element
   a. Swap it with the element at position 0
2. Locate the next smallest array element
   a. Swap it with the element at position 1
3. Continue until all elements are sorted

3.14.3 Insertion sort

Insertion Sort is a straightforward sorting algorithm that sorts an array element by element. It iterates over an array, selecting and inserting the current element into the right place in the sorted subarray at each iteration.

Example:

```
// This program sorts an array's values into ascending order.
#include <iostream>
#include <iomanip>
using namespace std;
void main()
{
const int arraySize = 10; // size of array a
int data[arraySize] = { 34, 56, 4, 10, 77, 51, 93, 30, 5, 52 };
int insert; // temporary variable to hold element to insert
cout << "Unsorted array:\n";
for (int i = 0; i < arraySize; ++i)
cout << setw(4) << data[i];
for (int next = 1; next < arraySize; ++next)
```

```
{
insert = data[next];
int moveItem = next;
while ((moveItem > 0) &&
(data[moveItem - 1] > insert))
{
data[moveItem] = data[moveItem - 1];
moveItem--;
} // end while
data[moveItem] = insert;
} // end for
cout << "\nSorted array:\n";
for (int i = 0; i < arraySize; ++i)
cout << setw(4) << data[i];
cout << endl;
system("pause");
}
```

This C++ program uses the insertion sort method to put the array's items in ascending order.The software defines and initializes an array of data of size arraySize with values. The output is then an unsorted array.

The array is then sorted using the insertion sort method by going through the array from the second element (next = 1) to the last element (next = 1).The software gets the value of each element and then goes backwards from the current index until it finds the right place to put the extracted value. This makes sure that the values before the insertion point are in order.After locating the correct spot, the computer puts the extracted value into that location.

The program ends after printing the sorted array.

3.14.4 Merge Sort

Merge sort is a common algorithm for sorting things. It uses the "divide and conquer" method to sort a set of items.This method splits the input array in half, sorts each half separately, and then puts the two sorted arrays back together to make the final sorted array.

Here's how C++'s merge sort works:

- First, we split the array into two halves until each half has exactly one entry or is empty.
- Next, we combine the halves by comparing the initial elements of each half and picking the one with the least value.
- This procedure is repeated until all items have been combined into a single, sorted array.

We return the array's sort order.

Example:

```
#include <iostream>
using namespace std;
void merge(int arr[], int left, int mid, int right) {
int i, j, k;
int n1 = mid - left + 1;
int n2 = right - mid;
int leftArr[n1], rightArr[n2];
for (i = 0; i < n1; i++)
leftArr[i] = arr[left + i];
for (j = 0; j < n2; j++)
rightArr[j] = arr[mid + 1 + j];
i = 0;
j = 0;
k = left;
while (i < n1 && j < n2) {
if (leftArr[i] <= rightArr[j]) {
arr[k] = leftArr[i];
i++;
}
else {
arr[k] = rightArr[j];
j++;
}
k++;
}
while (i < n1) {
arr[k] = leftArr[i];
i++;
k++;
}
while (j < n2) {
arr[k] = rightArr[j];
j++;
k++;
}
}
void mergeSort(int arr[], int left, int right) {
if (left < right) {
int mid = left + (right - left) / 2;
mergeSort(arr, left, mid);
mergeSort(arr, mid + 1, right);
merge(arr, left, mid, right);
}
}
```

```
int main() {
int arr[] = { 12, 11, 13, 5, 6, 7 };
int arrSize = sizeof(arr) / sizeof(arr[0]);
cout << "Original array: ";
for (int i = 0; i < arrSize; i++)
cout << arr[i] << " ";
mergeSort(arr, 0, arrSize - 1);
cout << "\nSorted array: ";
for (int i = 0; i < arrSize; i++)
cout << arr[i] << " ";
return 0;
}
```

In this implementation, we start by defining a merge() method that takes three arguments: the input array, the starting index of the left subarray, and the ending index of the right subarray.The merge() method combines the two subarrays by comparing and sorting their respective components.

The mergeSort() function is then set up. It takes three arguments: the input array, the index of where the left subarray starts, and the index of where the right subarray ends. The mergeSort() method splits the array recursively into two halves until each subarray has a single element and then combines the subarrays to get the final sorted array. In the main method, we call the mergeSort() function with the beginning index set to 0 and the ending index set to the size of the array minus one.

3.14.5 Bubble Sort vs. Insertion Sort vs. Selection Sort vs. Merge Sort

In computer science, bubble sort, insertion sort, selection sort, and merge sort are common sorting algorithms. Below is a concise description of each algorithm:

Bubble Sort is a simple algorithm for sorting that keeps swapping pieces next to each other if their order is wrong. The method compares each element of the array to the one next to it and, if necessary, swaps their positions. With each iteration, the smallest element "bubbles" to the top of the array, thus the name bubble sort.

Insertion Sort is another basic sorting algorithm that sorts an array by inserting each element into its proper location one at a time. The algorithm compares each element to the items that came before it, pushing the bigger components forward to make way for the smaller ones.

It is a sorting algorithm that always picks the smallest unsorted element left and swaps it with the next one in the array.The method keeps track of two sub-arrays in an array: the sorted sub-array and the unsorted sub-array.The sorted sub-array starts out empty, and the algorithm keeps adding the smallest item from the unsorted sub-array to the sorted one.

Merge Sort is a divide-and-conquer sorting algorithm that splits an array into two halves, sorts each half recursively, and then combines the two halves to create a sorted array. The method continually splits the array in half until it cannot be further subdivided, sorts the smaller sub-arrays, and then combines them until the whole array is sorted.

While comparing these algorithms, trade-offs must be taken into account. Bubble sort and selection sort are simple to comprehend and apply but may be time-consuming for big datasets. For small datasets, insertion sort is quicker than bubble sort and selection sort, but slower for big datasets. Merge sort is widely regarded as the most effective technique; however, it consumes more memory than the other algorithms since it uses extra arrays to sort and combine the subarrays.

In conclusion, the selection of a sorting method depends on the specifics of the job, the amount of the dataset to be sorted, and the computational resources available.

3.15 Introduction to C++ Standard Library Class Template Vector

We now provide the C++ Standard Library class template vector, a more robust array type with several extra capabilities. C-style pointer-based arrays (i.e., the array type shown so far) have the potential to include significant errors. A program may easily "get lost" at either end of an array since C++ does not verify whether the indices are beyond the array's range. Comparing two arrays with the equality or relational operators is not useful.

The value of a pointer variable (also known as a pointer) is a memory address. The name of the array is just a reference to where in memory the array starts, and the two arrays will always be in different parts of memory.When giving an array to a general-purpose function that can take arrays of any size, the size of the array must also be given.A constant pointer cannot be used on the left side of the assignment operator, and an array cannot be assigned to a different array than the array name of the assignment operator.When working with arrays, these and other features may seem "natural," but C++ doesn't have them.Still, the C++ Standard Library has a set of class templates that programmers can use to make an alternative to arrays that is more reliable and less likely to make mistakes.The vector class paradigm is accessible to all C++ application developers. While vectors use model notation, you may be unfamiliar with the notations used in the vector example. For the time being, you should feel confident utilizing class template vectors by imitating the syntax shown in this section. As we examine the course examples, your comprehension will grow.

Vector containers are implemented as dynamic arrays. Similar to ordinary arrays, components of vector container arrays are kept in contiguous storage locations, so they may be accessed without the need for loopers. Iteratively, as well as with standard pointer-to-element shifts. But unlike regular arrays, vector storage is handled automatically, allowing it to be expanded and collapsed as needed.

Vectors are good for:

1. Access specific items using their position index (constant time).
2. Repeat the items in any sequence (linear time).
3. Add or delete components at the conclusion (constant amortization time).

In addition to providing almost the same speed as arrays for certain jobs, they are readily resizable. Nonetheless, when their capacity is handled automatically, they often require more memory than arrays (this is intended to provide more storage space for future growth).

Vectors, like other containers, have an internal size that indicates the number of items they hold. Nevertheless, vectors also possess capacity, which controls the amount of assigned storage space and might be equal to or more than the actual size. The allotted additional storage is not utilized, but is reserved for use by the vector in the growth scenario. This manner, the vector does not have to reallocate memory each time it expands, but only when the additional space is used up and a new element is added (this only happens at logarithmic frequency vs. its size).

3.15.1 Declaring and Initializing Vectors

In C++, a vector is a dynamic array that can grow or shrink as the program runs.To use a vector, it must first be declared and then initialized with data. This is how vectors may be declared and initialized in C++:

Declaring a vector:

```
#include <vector>
// Define a vector of integers that is empty
// Declare a string vector with an initial size of five
std::vector<std::string> my_strings(5);
```

In the code above, we added the <vector> header file so that we could use the vector container. Next, we define my vector and my strings as vectors. The starting size of the first vector is zero, whereas the initial size of the second vector is five.

Initializing a vector:

```
#include <vector>
// Assign some values to a vector of integers.
std::vector<int> my_vector = { 1, 2, 3, 4, 5 };
// Initialize a string vector with some values
std::vector<std::string> my_strings = { "apple", "banana", "orange" };
```

In the above code, the two vectors are initialized with certain values. The first vector consists of the numbers 1 through 5, while the second vector has three strings: "apple," "banana," and "orange."

Instead, the push back() function may be used to add items to a vector one by one:

```
#include <vector>
// Declare an empty vector of integers.
std::vector<int> my_vector;
// Add some elements to the vector.
my_vector.push_back(1);
my_vector.push_back(2);
my_vector.push_back(3);
```

In the above code, an empty vector of integers is declared, and subsequently, entries are added using the push back() function.

Standard Template Library vector<int> scores;

Dynamically resize - automatically add more space as needed You must #include <vector>

vector<int> scores;	vector to hold ints
vector<int> scores(30);	vector to hold 30 ints
vector<int> scores(30, 0);	Vector to initialize all 30 elements to 0

Table 1. Non-modifying operations

Operation	Effect
v1.size()	Returns the actual number of elements
v1.empty()	Returns whether the container is empty (equivalent to size() == 0, but might be faster)
v1.max_size()	Returns the maximum number of elements possible
v1.capacity()	Returns the maximum possible number of elements without reallocation
v1.reserve()	Enlarges capacity, if not enough yet
v1 == v2	Returns whether v1 is equal to v2
v1 != v2	Returns whether v1 is not equal to v2

Table 2. Assignments

Operation	Effect
v1 = v2	Assigns all elements of v2 to v1
v1.assign(n elem)	Assigns n copies of element elem
v1.assign(beg, end)	Assigns the elements of the range [beg, end]
v1.swap(v2)	Swaps the data of v1 and v2
swap(v1, v2)	global function (same as v1,swap(v2))

Table 3. Element access

Operation	Effect
v.at(idx)	Returns the element with index idx (throws range error exception if idx is out of range)
v[idx]	Returns the element with index idx (no range checking)
v.front()	Returns the first element (no check whether a first element exists)
v.back()	Returns the last element(no check whether a last element exits)

Table 4. Inserting and removing elements

Operation	Effect
v.insert(pos, elem)	Inserts at iterator position "pos" a copy of "elem" and returns the position of the new element
v.insert(pos, n, elem)	Inserts at iterator position "pos" "n" copies of "elem" (returns nothing)
v.insert(pos,beg,end)	Inserts at iterator position "pos" a copy of all elements of the range [beg, end] (returns nothing)
v.push_back(elem)	Appends a copy of element at the end
v.pop_back()	Removes the last element (does not return it)
v.erase(pos)	Removes the element at iterator position "pos" and returns the position of the next element
v.erase(beg, end)	Removes all elements of the of the range [beg,end] and returns the position of the next element
v.resize(num)	Changes the number of elements to num(if size() grows, new elements are created by their default constructor)
v.resize(num, elem)	Changes the number of elements to num(if size() grows, new elements are copies of elem)
v.clear()	Removes all elements (makes the container empty)

Table 5. Iterator functions

Operation	Effect
v.begin()	Returns a random access iterator for the first element
v.end()	Returns a random access iterator for the position after the last element
v.rbegin()	Returns a reverse iterator for the first element of a reverse iteration
v.rend()	Returns a reverse iterator for the position after the last element of a reverse iteration

Example:

```
//==================================================================
// Example Program
// Traversing through the vector elements using an vector iterators
//==================================================================
#include <iostream> #include <vector> using namespace std; int main ()
{
vector<int> myVector; //Creating an empty integer vector named myVector
//Using a for loop to insert 5 elements in the vector. The elements 0 through
4 will be inserted in the vector.
for (int i = 0; i < 5; i++)
{
myVector.push_back(i); //this statement inserts the value I in the //vector
}
vector<int>::iterator iter; //declaring a vector iterator of the type int
//The following statement prints the string "myVector contains:"; cout << "my-
Vector contains:";
//The for loop is used to traverse through the vector starting from the first
//element to the last. myVector.begin() points to the first element of the //
vector. myVector.end() points to the position after the last element.
for (iter = myVector.begin(); iter < myVector.end(); iter++)
{
cout << " " << *iter;
}
cout << endl;
return 0;
}
```

This C++ program illustrates how to explore a vector's items using an iterator.

Initially, a vector called myVector that is empty is constructed. Next, five items (0 through 4) are inserted into the vector using the push back() function using a for loop.

Next, an int-type vector iterator iter is defined. An iterator is an object that points to a container element and may be used to traverse the container's elements.

Then, a for loop is used to move from the first to the last member of the vector.The iterator returned by myVector.begin() points to the vector's first element, while the iterator returned by myVector.end() points to the location after the vector's last member.

The *iter syntax is used inside the loop to dereference the iterator and acquire the value of the element to which it refers. The value of the element is then output using the cout command.

Finally, the program outputs a newline and returns 0 to signal a successful conclusion.

This program shows how to use iterators to get the items in a vector and look at them.

Example:

```
#include <iostream>
#include <vector>
#include<string>
using namespace std;
int main()
{
vector<string> heroes;
heroes.push_back("Wolverine");
heroes.push_back("Storm");
heroes.push_back("Jean Grey");
heroes.push_back("The Beast");
heroes.push_back("Gambit");
heroes.push_back("Magneto");
for (string hero: heroes)
cout << hero << endl;
cout << "There are " << heroes.size() << " heroes in the list.\n";
cout << heroes[2] << endl;
cout << heroes.at(2) << endl;
system("pause");
return 0;
}
```

This is a C++ program that uses the standard library's iostream, vector, and string headers.

The application constructs an originally empty vector of strings named heroes. The push back() technique is then used to add six strings to the vector.

With the cout command, the for loop iterates through each string in the heroes vector and outputs it to the console. The endl command appends a newline character to each line's end.

After printing all of the heroes, the size() function is used to print the total number of heroes in the vector. The third hero in the vector is then printed using both the [] and at() operations.

The system("pause") command is used to halt the program before its exit, allowing the user to observe the output before the console window closes. The return 0 statement at the conclusion of main() notifies the operating system that the program has properly completed execution.

3.16 Using Algorithms

The STL specifies a set of techniques that let you handle container items using iterators. There are algorithms for typical tasks like searching, randomizing, and sorting. These algorithms are your innate arsenal of adaptability and effectiveness. By using them, you may eliminate the tedious work of manipulating container parts in a standard STL manner, allowing you to concentrate on designing your games. The strength of these algorithms is that they are general; the same approach may be used to containers of various kinds.

3.16.1 Preparing to Use Algorithms

To enable the usage of STL algorithms, I have included a file containing their definitions. #integrate <algorithm>

All STL components reside in the std namespace, as you well know. I may refer to algorithms without prefixing them with std::.

use namespace std;

3.16.2 Using the find() Algorithm

After showing the score vector's contents, I ask the user for a value to enter in the score variable. Then I use the find() technique to seek the vector's value:

iter = find(point.start(), point.end(), point); The STL find() method examines a range of given elements in a container for a value. It returns an iterator that refers to the first element that matches the criteria. If no match is discovered, an iterator at the end of the range is returned. You must provide an iterator for the start point, an iterator for the end point, and a value to search. The algorithm searches between the start and end iterators but does not include the start iterator. To locate the whole vector, I gave Scores.begin() and Scores.end() as the first and second parameters, respectively. I supplied the point as the third parameter while searching for a user-entered value.

Then I check if the value point is found:

```
if(iter != scores.end())
{
}
else
{
}
cout << "Score found.\n";
cout << "Score not found.\n";
```

Remember, iter will reference the first occurrence of the point in the vector, if the value is found. So as long as iter is not equal to score.end(), I know that the point was found and I print a message saying so. Otherwise iter will be equal to score.end() and I know the score is not found.

3.16.3 Using the random_shuffle() Algorithm

Next, I will construct the random shuffle() technique to randomize the scores. Similar to when I produce a unique random number, I initialize the random number generator prior to using the random shuffle() method to ensure that the order of the scores is unique each time I run the program.

```
srand(static_cast<unsigned int>(time(0)));
```

Next, I randomly rank the scores.

```
random_shuffle(scores.begin(), scores.end());
```

The random_shuffle() method shuffles a sequence's elements. As an iterator, you must provide the beginning and end of the string to be shuffled. In this instance, I passed the Scores.begin() and Scores. end(). These two iterators indicate that I want to shuffle all partition elements. Thus, the points contain the same information, but in a random arrangement. The scores are then shown to indicate that the randomization is effective.

3.16.4 Using the sort() Algorithm

I then arrange the scores. sort (point.start(), point.end());

The sort() method arranges array members in ascending order. As an iterator, you must provide the beginning and end points of the series to be sorted. I passed the iterators returned by Scores.begin() and Scores.end() in this instance (). These two iterators indicate that I want to sort all partitioned items. Thus, the point includes the points in ascending order.

I then present scores to illustrate that the sorting was successful.

3.16.5 Understanding Vector Performance

Vectors, like other STL containers, give game developers complex methods to manipulate data, but this sophistication might come at the sacrifice of speed. And if there is one thing that game developers are obsessed about, it is performance. Vectors and other STL containers, however, are incredibly efficient. They have been used in PC and console games previously released. Nevertheless, these containers have strengths and limitations; a game programmer must understand the performance characteristics of several kinds of containers to choose the most appropriate one for a given task.

3.16.6 Examining Vector Growth

Even though vectors expand as needed, each vector has a defined size. When a new element is added to a vector that exceeds its existing size, the computer reallocates memory and may transfer all the vector's elements into a new memory block. get it. This may result in diminished performance.

The most important thing to think about when figuring out how well a program works is whether you should care. For instance, vector memory reallocation may not occur at the program's performance-critical section. In this instance, it is safe to disregard the reassignment cost. Additionally, the reassignment overhead might be minor for tiny vectors, so you can safely disregard it. If you need further control over when these memory reallocations occur, you have that ability.

3.16.7 Using the capacity() Member Function

The vector member function capacity() returns the capacity of a vector, i.e. the number of elements a vector can hold before the program has to reallocate more memory to it. The capacity of a vector is not the same as its size (the number of elements a vector currently contains). Here is a piece of code to help you understand this point:

```
cout << "Creating a 10 element vector to hold scores.\n";
vector<int> scores(10, 0); //initialize all 10 elements to 0 cout << "Vector
size is:" << scores.size() << endl;
cout << "Vector capacity is:" << scores.capacity() << endl;
cout << "Adding a score.\n";
scores.push_back(0); / /memory is reallocated to accommodate growth cout <<
"Vector size is:" << scores.size() << endl;
cout << "Vector capacity is:" << scores.capacity() << endl;
```

This code immediately after declaring and initializing the vector states that both its size and capacity are 10. Nonetheless, after adding an element, the code indicates that the vector's size is 11, when its capacity is 20. This is because the capacity of a vector doubles whenever new memory is reallocated to it. When a new score is added, the memory is reallocated and the vector's capacity increases from 10 to 20.

Use reserve member()

The reserve() member function expands a vector's capacity to the number specified as an argument. Reserve() enables you to determine when more memory is allocated. Here's an illustration:

```
cout << "Creating a list of scores.\n";
vector<int> scores(10, 0); //initialize all 10 elements to 0 cout << "Vector
size is:" << scores.size() << endl;
cout << "Vector capacity is:" << scores.capacity() << endl; cout << "Reserving
more memory.\n";
scores.reserve(20); //reserve memory for 10 additional elements cout << "Vec-
tor size is:" << scores.size() << endl;
cout << "Vector capacity is:" << scores.capacity() << endl;
```

This code, immediately after declaring and initializing the vector, states that both its size and capacity are 10. Yet, after reserving memory for a further 10 items, the code consistently returns the vector's size as 10, despite its capacity being 20. You may postpone delayed memory reallocation by using reserve() to preserve the vector's capacity, if sufficient for your requirements. choice.

3.16.8 Examining Element Insertion and Deletion

The push_back() and pop_back() member functions of a vector are very effective for inserting or deleting elements from the vector's tail. When inserting or deleting elements from the vector somewhere other than the beginning or end, additional operations may be needed to accommodate the insertion or deletion of the element. Although adding or removing items in the midst of a small vector has no cost, doing so with a big vector (say, millions of elements) might lead significant performance decreases.

The list is a sequence container provided by the STL that enables for fast insertion and deletion operations on sequences of any size. Keep in mind that there isn't just one magic box that can solve all your storage woes. Even though vectors are very malleable and the most popular STL container, there are cases when another container might be preferable.

3.16.9 Examining Other STL Containers

The STL specifies many varieties of containers, often classified as either sequential or associative. Values stored in sequential containers may be retrieved in sequence, but those in associative containers can be retrieved using keys. One kind of sequential container is the vector.

In what ways might various containers be utilized? Take, for example, a web-based, turn-based strategic game. A sequential container may be used to organize a group of players into a selectable list. On the other hand, you may utilize federated containers to receive data on a random player by querying for some kind of unique identifier, such as the player's IP address. A container adapter, which may be used with any of the sequence containers, is also defined in the STL. Common data types in computers are represented by container adapters.

Table 6. STL containers

Container	Type	Description
Deque	Sequential	Double-ended queue
List	Sequential	Linear list
Map	Associative	Collection of key/value pairs in which each key may be associated with exactly one value.
Multimap	Associative	Collection of key/value pairs in which each key may be associated with more than one value.
Multiset	Associative	Collection in which each element is not necessarily unique.
Priority-queue	Adapter	Priority queue
Queue	Adapter	Queue
Set	Associative	Collection in which each element is unique.
Stack	Adapter	Stack
vector	Sequential	Dynamic array

Example:

Note: In class, we used vector<string> heroes { "Wolverine", "Storm", "Jean Grey", "The Beast", "Gambit" }; If you are using an older version of C++, use push_back() to add elements as in the example below.

```
#include <iostream>
#include <vector>
#include<string>
using namespace std;
int main()
{
//Only in Newer Versions: vector<string> heroes { "Wolverine", "Storm", "Jean
Grey", "The Beast", "Gambit" };
vector<string> heroes;
heroes.push_back("Wolverine");
heroes.push_back("Storm");
heroes.push_back("Jean Grey");
heroes.push_back("The Beast");
heroes.push_back("Gambit");
heroes.push_back("Magneto");
for (string hero: heroes)
cout << hero << endl;
cout << "There are " << heroes.size() << " heroes in the list.\n";
cout << heroes[2] << endl;
cout << heroes.at(2) << endl;
system("pause");
return 0;
}
```

This is a C++ program that uses the standard library's iostream, vector, and string headers.

The application constructs an originally empty vector of strings named heroes. The push_back() technique is then used to add six strings to the vector.

With the cout command, the for loop iterates through each string in the heroes vector and outputs it to the console. The endl command appends a newline character to each line's end.

After printing all of the heroes, the size() function is used to print the total number of heroes in the vector. The third hero in the vector is then printed using both the [] and at() operations.

The system("pause") command is used to halt the program before its exit, allowing the user to observe the output before the console window closes. The return 0 statement at the conclusion of main() notifies the operating system that the program has properly completed execution.

In addition, the program has a note that says in future versions of C++, values can be added to the heroes vector using braces instead of push_back().

Advanced Practice Exercises With Answers

1. **Example 1: Dynamic Array Manipulation:**
    - **Objective:** Create a dynamic array and implement functions to insert, delete, and search for elements.

```
#include <iostream>
#include <algorithm> // For copy
using namespace std;
class DynamicArray {
    int* arr;
    int capacity;
    int current;
public:
    DynamicArray(): capacity(5), current(0) {
        arr = new int[capacity];
    }
    void insert(int data) {
        if (current == capacity) {
            int* temp = new int[2 * capacity];
            for (int i = 0; i < capacity; i++) {
                temp[i] = arr[i];
            }
            delete[] arr;
            capacity *= 2;
            arr = temp;
        }
        arr[current] = data;
        current++;
    }
    void remove(int index) {
        if (index < current) {
            for (int i = index; i < current - 1; i++) {
                arr[i] = arr[i + 1];
            }
            current--;
        }
    }
    int search(int data) {
        for (int i = 0; i < current; i++) {
            if (arr[i] == data) return i;
        }
        return -1; // Not found
    }
    ~DynamicArray() {
        delete[] arr;
    }
};
```

Explanation:

This C++ program defines a simple implementation of a dynamic array class, named **DynamicArray**. Here's how it works:

Key Components:

- **Dynamic Memory Allocation**: The class uses dynamic memory allocation to manage its storage. This allows the array to resize itself when needed, increasing its capacity to hold more elements.
- **Private Member Variables**:
- **int* arr**: A pointer to an integer array, serving as the underlying storage of the dynamic array.
- **int capacity**: Stores the total capacity of the array, i.e., how many elements it can currently hold.
- **int current**: Tracks the current number of elements in the array.

Core Methods:

- **Constructor (DynamicArray)**: Initializes the dynamic array with a predefined capacity (5) and sets the current size to 0. It allocates memory for the array based on the initial capacity.
- **insert(int data)**: Adds a new element to the array. If the array is full (**current == capacity**), it doubles the capacity, creates a new array with the updated capacity, copies existing elements to the new array, deletes the old array, and then adds the new element.
- **remove(int index)**: Removes the element at the specified index. It shifts all elements after the removed element one position to the left to fill the gap. This method doesn't reduce the capacity of the array.
- **search(int data)**: Searches for the given data in the array. If found, it returns the index of the first occurrence of the data; otherwise, it returns -1.
- **Destructor (~DynamicArray)**: Deallocates the dynamically allocated memory to prevent memory leaks.

Explanation:

- The dynamic array starts with a fixed capacity but can grow as more elements are inserted. This behavior mimics the functionality of C++ **std::vector** but with a simplified implementation.
- The **insert** method intelligently manages memory by checking if there's enough space for a new element and expanding the array if necessary. This ensures that the array can always accommodate new data.
- The **remove** method ensures the continuity of the array elements by shifting subsequent elements one position back, effectively deleting the element at the given index.
- The **search** function allows for simple lookup operations, demonstrating how basic search algorithms can be integrated into custom data structures.
- Memory management is a critical aspect of this class. The destructor ensures that the allocated memory is released when an instance of **DynamicArray** is destroyed, highlighting the importance of resource management in C++.

This class serves as an educational tool to understand dynamic memory management, class design, and basic algorithm implementation in C++. While it demonstrates key concepts, it lacks many features and optimizations of standard library containers like **std::vector**.

2. **Example 2: 2D Array Spiral Traversal:**
   - **Objective:** Given a 2D array, write a function to print its elements in a spiral order.

```
#include <iostream>
#include <vector>
using namespace std;
void spiralPrint(int m, int n, vector<vector<int>> a) {
    int i, k = 0, l = 0;
    while (k < m && l < n) {
        for (i = l; i < n; ++i) cout << a[k][i] << " ";
        k++;
        for (i = k; i < m; ++i) cout << a[i][n - 1] << " ";
        n--;
        if (k < m) {
            for (i = n - 1; i >= l; --i) cout << a[m - 1][i] << " ";
            m--;
        }
        if (l < n) {
            for (i = m - 1; i >= k; --i) cout << a[i][l] << " ";
            l++;
        }
    }
}

int main() {
    vector<vector<int>> a = { {1, 2, 3, 4},
                              {5, 6, 7, 8},
                              {9, 10, 11, 12},
                              {13, 14, 15, 16} };
    spiralPrint(4, 4, a);
    return 0;
}
```

Explanation:

This C++ program prints the elements of a 2D vector in a spiral order. Here's a detailed explanation of how it works:

Key Components:

- **Header Files**: Includes **<iostream>** for input/output operations and **<vector>** for using the vector container.
- **The spiralPrint Function**:
- Parameters: **m** and **n** represent the number of rows and columns, respectively, and **a** is the 2D vector to be printed.
- Variables: **k** and **l** mark the starting row and column indexes, and **i** is used as a loop counter.

- The function uses four loops in a while loop that runs as long as there are rows (**k < m**) and columns (**l < n**) left to traverse.
- **First Loop**: Prints the first row from the remaining rows.
- **Second Loop**: Prints the last column from the remaining columns.
- **Third Loop**: Prints the last row from the remaining rows (if any rows are left).
- **Fourth Loop**: Prints the first column from the remaining columns (if any columns are left).
- After each of these steps, it updates the indices (**k**, **l**, **m**, **n**) to narrow down the matrix boundaries and prepare for the next layer of the spiral.

Algorithm Explanation

- The algorithm systematically reduces the size of the 2D vector boundary after completing a round of printing in each direction (right, down, left, up) until all elements are printed in a spiral order.
- This method effectively simulates peeling off the outer layers of the matrix sequentially, ensuring that each element is printed exactly once.

Key Concepts Illustrated

- **Nested Loops**: Demonstrates the use of multiple nested loops to iterate over a 2D data structure in a complex pattern.
- **Boundary Conditions**: Showcases how to manage boundary conditions in a matrix to implement a specific traversal order.
- **2D Vectors**: Uses 2D vectors for storing and accessing matrix data, highlighting the versatility of vectors in C++ for handling multidimensional arrays.

This example is practical in scenarios where matrix data needs to be processed or displayed in a non-traditional order, such as in graphical applications, data visualization, or game development.

3. **Example 3: Vector of Tuples Sorting:**
    - **Objective:** Given a **vector** of **tuple<int, string, float>**, sort it based on the floating-point value in ascending order.

```
#include <algorithm>
#include <iostream>
#include <tuple>
#include <vector>
using namespace std;
int main() {
    vector<tuple<int, string, float>> vec = { {1, “Apple”, 2.9f}, {2, “Ba-
nana”, 0.5f}, {3, “Cherry”, 1.5f} };
    sort(vec.begin(), vec.end(), [](const auto& a, const auto& b) {
        return get<2>(a) < get<2>(b);
        });
    for (auto& [id, fruit, price]: vec) {
```

```
        cout << id << " " << fruit << " " << price << endl;
    }
    return 0;
}
```

Explanation:

This C++ program sorts a vector of tuples based on the floating-point value (price) contained in each tuple. Here's how it works:

Key Components:

- **Header Files**: Includes **<algorithm>** for the **sort** function, **<iostream>** for input/output operations, **<tuple>** for using tuples, and **<vector>** for using the vector container.
- **The main Function**:
- Initializes a **vector** of **tuple<int, string, float>** named **vec**, where each tuple represents an item with an integer ID, a string name (fruit), and a float price.
- Calls the **sort** function to sort the vector. The sorting criterion is provided by a lambda function that compares the third element (price) of the tuples.
- **get<2>(a)** and **get<2>(b)** are used to access the third element (price) of tuples **a** and **b**, respectively.
- The lambda function returns **true** if the price of tuple **a** is less than the price of tuple **b**, ensuring the vector is sorted in ascending order of price.
- Uses a range-based **for** loop with structured binding (**auto& [id, fruit, price]**) to iterate through the sorted vector and print the ID, fruit name, and price of each item.

Algorithm Explanation

- The program demonstrates how to use tuples to store a collection of heterogeneous data types and then sort a vector of such tuples based on one of the tuple elements.
- The lambda function used in the **sort** call provides a custom comparator, which is a common technique for sorting data according to a specific criterion that is not the default sorting behavior.

Key Concepts Illustrated

- **Tuples**: Showcases the use of tuples in C++ to store and manipulate collections of mixed data types.
- **Sorting with Custom Comparator**: Illustrates sorting a vector using a lambda function as a custom comparator, allowing for flexible sorting criteria.
- **Structured Bindings**: Uses C++17 structured bindings in the range-based **for** loop for easy access to tuple elements, enhancing code readability.

This example is useful in scenarios where data needs to be sorted based on one of several attributes, such as sorting database records by a specific field, and highlights modern C++ features for concise and expressive code.

4. **Example 4: Matrix Rotation:**
    - **Objective:** Rotate a square matrix by 90 degrees clockwise.

```
#include <iostream>
#include <vector>
using namespace std;
void rotate(vector<vector<int>>& matrix) {
    int n = matrix.size();
    for (int i = 0; i < n / 2; ++i) {
        for (int j = i; j < n - i - 1; ++j) {
            int temp = matrix[i][j];
            matrix[i][j] = matrix[n - j - 1][i];
            matrix[n - j - 1][i] = matrix[n - i - 1][n - j - 1];
            matrix[n - i - 1][n - j - 1] = matrix[j][n - i - 1];
            matrix[j][n - i - 1] = temp;
        }
    }
}

int main() {
    vector<vector<int>> matrix = { {1, 2, 3},
                                   {4, 5, 6},
                                   {7, 8, 9} };
    rotate(matrix);
    for (auto& row: matrix) {
        for (int elem: row) cout << elem << " ";
        cout << endl;
    }
    return 0;
}
```

Explanation:

This C++ program demonstrates a function to rotate a square matrix by 90 degrees clockwise. Here's how it works:

Key Components:

- **Header Files**: The program includes **<iostream>** for input and output operations and **<vector>** for using the vector container.
- **The rotate Function**:
- Takes a reference to a 2D vector **matrix** as its argument, allowing it to modify the matrix in place.
- The outer loop runs from 0 to **n/2** (half the matrix's size), ensuring that it rotates the matrix layer by layer from the outermost layer to the innermost layer.
- The inner loop runs from the current outer index **i** to **n - i - 1**, which iterates over each element in the current layer.

- Within the inner loop, it performs a four-way swap between the elements at the current position, the position 90 degrees clockwise, the position 180 degrees clockwise, and the position 270 degrees clockwise, effectively rotating the layer by 90 degrees.
- **The main Function**:
- Initializes a **matrix** with 3x3 elements.
- Calls the **rotate** function to rotate the matrix.
- Uses a nested loop to print the rotated matrix, demonstrating the result.

Algorithm Explanation

- The algorithm divides the matrix into layers, rotating each layer individually.
- For each element in a layer, it calculates the positions of the element and its three corresponding positions in the 90-degree rotation. It then performs a cyclic swap among these four elements.
- This approach ensures that all elements are moved to their correct positions in a single pass, making the rotation efficient.

Key Concepts Illustrated

- **2D Vectors**: Utilizes 2D vectors to represent a matrix, showcasing how to perform operations on 2D data structures.
- **In-Place Modification**: The matrix is rotated in place, meaning no additional matrix is created for the rotation operation, which optimizes memory usage.
- **Layer-by-Layer Rotation**: Demonstrates a methodical approach to solving a complex problem by breaking it down into simpler, manageable tasks (rotating the matrix layer by layer).

This example serves as an excellent demonstration of manipulating 2D vectors (matrices) in C++ and illustrates an elegant solution to a common problem encountered in graphics programming, game development, and other fields where matrix manipulation is essential.

5. **Example 5: Implementing Vector from Scratch:**
    - **Objective:** Implement a simplified version of the **vector** class that supports dynamic resizing.

```
#include <iostream>
using namespace std;
template<typename T>
class SimpleVector {
private:
    T* arr;
    size_t capacity;
    size_t current;
public:
    SimpleVector(): arr(new T[1]), capacity(1), current(0) {}
    void push(T data) {
        if (current == capacity) {
```

```
            T* temp = new T[2 * capacity];
            for (size_t i = 0; i < capacity; i++) {
                temp[i] = arr[i];
            }
            delete[] arr;
            capacity *= 2;
            arr = temp;
        }
        arr[current] = data;
        current++;
    }
    void pop() {
        if (current > 0) current--;
    }
    T& operator[](size_t index) {
        if (index < current) return arr[index];
        else throw out_of_range("Index out of range");
    }
    size_t size() const { return current; }
    size_t getCapacity() const { return capacity; }
    ~SimpleVector() { delete[] arr; }
};
int main() {
    SimpleVector<int> vec;
    vec.push(10);
    vec.push(20);
    cout << "Element at index 1: " << vec[1] << endl;
    cout << "Vector size: " << vec.size() << ", capacity: " << vec.getCapac-
ity() << endl;
    return 0;
}
```

Explanation:

This C++ program demonstrates the implementation of a simplified version of a dynamic array, akin to the standard **std::vector**. Here's a detailed breakdown:

Key Components

- **Template Class SimpleVector**: Defined with a template type **T**, allowing it to store elements of any data type.
- **Private Member Variables**:
- **T* arr**: A pointer to an array that stores the elements.
- **size_t capacity**: The total capacity of the array.
- **size_t current**: The current number of elements in the array.

- **Constructor**:
- Initializes the **arr** pointer to a dynamically allocated array of size 1.
- Sets **capacity** to 1 and **current** (number of elements) to 0.
- **push Method**:
- Adds an element to the vector. If the current number of elements equals the capacity, it allocates a new array of double the current capacity, copies the elements to the new array, deletes the old array, and updates **arr** to point to the new array.
- **pop Method**:
- Reduces the **current** count by one, effectively removing the last element. It does not actually delete the element or reduce the capacity.
- **operator[] Overload**:
- Provides access to elements by their index. It throws an **out_of_range** exception if the index is beyond the current number of elements.
- **Accessors**:
- **size**: Returns the number of elements in the vector.
- **getCapacity**: Returns the current capacity of the vector.
- **Destructor**:
- Releases the dynamically allocated memory to prevent memory leaks.

The main Function:

- Demonstrates creating a **SimpleVector<int>**, adding elements to it, accessing an element by index, and displaying the vector's size and capacity.

Algorithm Explanation

- The dynamic resizing algorithm allows the **SimpleVector** to grow as needed. When the internal array reaches its capacity and a new element is added, the capacity is doubled, which offers a good balance between memory usage and the number of reallocations required.
- The doubling strategy ensures that the amortized time complexity of the **push** operation remains constant.

Key Concepts Illustrated

- **Dynamic Array Implementation**: Showcases a basic implementation of a dynamic array that automatically resizes as elements are added.
- **Template Programming**: Utilizes templates to create a generic container that can hold elements of any type.
- **Resource Management**: Demonstrates proper memory management in C++ by manually allocating and deallocating memory in a class.
- **Operator Overloading**: Overloads the subscript operator [] to provide easy access to elements.

This **SimpleVector** class offers a foundational look into how dynamic containers like **std::vector** might be implemented, highlighting important concepts in C++ programming such as memory management, template classes, and operator overloading.

6. **Example 6: Vector Deduplication:**
   - **Objective:** Given a sorted **vector**, remove all duplicates in place, returning the new length of the vector.

```
#include <iostream>
#include <vector>
using namespace std;
int removeDuplicates(vector<int>& nums) {
    int len = 0;
    for (int i = 0; i < nums.size(); i++) {
        if (i == 0 || nums[i] != nums[i - 1]) {
            nums[len++] = nums[i];
        }
    }
    return len;
}
int main() {
    vector<int> nums = { 1, 1, 2, 2, 3, 4, 4 };
    int newLength = removeDuplicates(nums);
    for (int i = 0; i < newLength; ++i) {
        cout << nums[i] << " ";
    }
    return 0;
}
```

Explanation:

This C++ program is designed to remove duplicates from a sorted vector and return the new length of the vector after duplicates have been removed. Here's a breakdown of how it operates:

Key Components

- **Header Files**: It includes **<iostream>** for basic input and output operations, and **<vector>** for using the vector container.
- **The removeDuplicates Function**:
- Takes a reference to a vector of integers (**nums**) as its argument. This reference allows the function to modify the vector in place.
- It initializes a variable **len** to track the length of the vector after duplicates are removed.
- Iterates over each element in the vector. If an element is not a duplicate (i.e., it's the first element or different from the previous one), it's copied to the **nums[len]** position, and **len** is incremented.
- Returns the new length of the vector after duplicates have been removed.

The main Function:

- Initializes a vector **nums** with a sample set of integers, which includes duplicates.
- Calls the **removeDuplicates** function with **nums** and stores the returned new length in **newLength**.
- Iterates over the modified vector up to **newLength** and prints each element, effectively showing the vector without duplicates.

Algorithm Explanation:

- The algorithm relies on the vector being sorted, as it only checks the current element against the previous one to determine if it's a duplicate.
- By iterating through the vector and only copying non-duplicate elements to the front of the vector, it compacts the vector to contain only unique elements at the beginning.
- The function maintains the order of elements and does not require any extra space for a temporary vector, achieving in-place removal of duplicates.

Key Concepts Illustrated:

- **Vector Manipulation**: Demonstrates modifying a vector in place, including iterating over vector elements and changing the vector's contents based on specific conditions.
- **In-Place Algorithm**: The algorithm efficiently modifies the vector without needing additional memory for a second vector, showcasing an in-place technique for solving the problem.

This example serves as a practical demonstration of handling common data cleanup tasks, such as removing duplicates from a collection, which is a frequent requirement in data processing and manipulation scenarios.

7. **Example 7: 3D Array Flattening:**
    - **Objective:** Flatten a 3D array into a 1D vector.

```
#include <iostream>
#include <vector>
using namespace std;
int main() {
    vector<vector<vector<int>>> array3D = { {{1, 2}, {3, 4}}, {{5, 6}, {7, 8}}
};
    vector<int> flatArray;
    for (const auto& twoD: array3D) {
        for (const auto& oneD: twoD) {
            for (int elem: oneD) {
                flatArray.push_back(elem);
            }
        }
    }
```

```
    for (int elem: flatArray) {
        cout << elem << " ";
    }
    return 0;
}
```

Explanation:

This C++ program demonstrates how to flatten a 3-dimensional vector into a 1-dimensional vector, effectively transforming a complex nested structure into a simple linear sequence. Here's a detailed breakdown:

Key Components:

- **Header Files**: **<iostream>** for input/output operations and **<vector>** to use the vector container.
- **3D Vector Initialization**: A 3-dimensional vector **array3D** is initialized with integer elements. This vector represents a 3D array, with its structure indicated by the nested curly braces. It's essentially an array of arrays of arrays.
- **Flattening Process**:
- A flat vector **flatArray** is declared to hold the result of the flattening operation.
- Three nested loops iterate over each dimension of the 3D vector. The outermost loop iterates through the 2D arrays within **array3D**, the middle loop iterates through the 1D arrays within each 2D array, and the innermost loop iterates through the integers within each 1D array.
- Inside the innermost loop, each element encountered is added to **flatArray** using **push_back**.
- **Output**: The contents of the flattened **flatArray** are printed to the console, displaying a linear sequence of all the elements originally present in the 3D vector.

Key Concepts Illustrated:

- **Nested Loop Iteration**: The use of nested loops to navigate through the layers of a multi-dimensional vector.
- **Vector Manipulation**: Demonstrates the creation and manipulation of both 3-dimensional and 1-dimensional vectors, including initializing multi-dimensional vectors with nested braces and using **push_back** to add elements to a vector.
- **Data Structure Transformation**: Showcases an algorithm for transforming a complex nested data structure into a simpler, flat structure. This is a common task in data processing where multi-dimensional data needs to be linearized for analysis or storage.

This example highlights the flexibility of vectors in C++ to represent multi-dimensional arrays and the ease with which they can be manipulated to suit various data processing needs.

8. **Example 8: Vector to 2D Array Conversion:**

    - **Objective:** Convert a **vector** of integers into a 2D array of given dimensions.

```
#include <iostream>
#include <vector>
using namespace std;

vector<vector<int>> convertTo2DArray(const vector<int>& vec, int rows, int
cols) {
    vector<vector<int>> result(rows, vector<int>(cols));
    for (int i = 0; i < vec.size(); ++i) {
        result[i / cols][i % cols] = vec[i];
    }
    return result;
}

int main() {
    vector<int> vec = { 1, 2, 3, 4, 5, 6 };
    auto array2D = convertTo2DArray(vec, 2, 3);
    for (const auto& row: array2D) {
        for (int elem: row) {
            cout << elem << " ";
        }
        cout << "\n";
    }
    return 0;
}
```

Explanation:

This C++ program demonstrates how to convert a flat **vector<int>** into a 2-dimensional vector, effectively mimicking a 2D array's behavior. Here's a detailed explanation:

Key Components:

- **Header Files**: **<iostream>** for input/output operations, and **<vector>** to utilize the vector container.
- **The convertTo2DArray Function**:
- Accepts a constant reference to a vector of integers (**vec**) and two integers representing the desired number of rows and columns (**rows** and **cols**, respectively) for the 2D array.
- Initializes a 2D vector (**result**) with dimensions **rows x cols**, filled with default values (0s).
- Iterates over the input vector, placing each element into the correct position in the 2D vector based on its index. The row index is calculated by dividing the current index by the number of columns (**i / cols**), and the column index by taking the remainder of the division (**i % cols**).
- Returns the filled 2D vector.

The main Function:

- Initializes a **vector<int>** (**vec**) with a sequence of integers.

- Calls **convertTo2DArray** with **vec** and the desired dimensions (**2 rows x 3 columns**) to reshape the flat vector into a 2D vector.
- Iterates over the resulting 2D vector, printing each element to demonstrate the conversion result.

Algorithm Explanation:

- The conversion process involves mapping a linear sequence of elements (the input vector) into a matrix-like structure (the 2D vector). This is achieved by computing the target row and column for each element based on its index in the flat vector, utilizing integer division and modulus operations.
- This approach ensures that elements are distributed row-wise in the resulting 2D vector, filling up rows one after another until all elements from the input vector are placed.

Key Concepts Illustrated:

- **Vector Manipulation**: The program showcases how to work with both 1-dimensional and 2-dimensional vectors, including their initialization and access patterns.
- **Algorithmic Thinking**: Demonstrates a straightforward method to reshape data structures, a common task in data processing and manipulation tasks.

This example is practical for scenarios where a flat data collection needs to be structured into a more complex form for processing, visualization, or other computational purposes. It highlights the versatility of vectors in C++ and how they can be used to implement dynamic arrays and matrices.

9. **Example 9: Binary Search on Rotated Sorted Vector:**
    - **Objective:** Perform a binary search on a rotated sorted **vector** to find a given element.

```
#include <iostream>
#include <vector>
using namespace std;

int search(vector<int>& nums, int target) {
    int lo = 0, hi = nums.size() - 1;
    while (lo <= hi) {
        int mid = lo + (hi - lo) / 2;
        if (nums[mid] == target) return mid;
        if (nums[lo] <= nums[mid]) {
            if (target >= nums[lo] && target < nums[mid]) hi = mid - 1;
            else lo = mid + 1;
        }
        else {
            if (target > nums[mid] && target <= nums[hi]) lo = mid + 1;
            else hi = mid - 1;
        }
```

```
    }
    return -1;
}

int main() {
    vector<int> nums = { 4, 5, 6, 7, 0, 1, 2 };
    int target = 0;
    cout << "Index of " << target << ": " << search(nums, target) << endl;
    return 0;
}
```

Explanation:

This C++ program implements a search function to find the index of a target value in a rotated sorted vector and demonstrates its use. Here's a breakdown of the program's components and logic:

Key Components:

- **Header Files**: **<iostream>** for input/output operations and **<vector>** to use the vector container.
- **The search Function**:
- Takes a reference to a vector of integers (**nums**) and an integer (**target**) as parameters.
- The function performs a binary search to find the target's index in the rotated sorted vector.
- It uses two pointers (**lo** and **hi**) to keep track of the current search range within the vector.
- The binary search is modified to handle the rotation by dividing the search space into two segments at the midpoint and determining which segment is properly sorted.
- Depending on whether the target is within the sorted segment, it narrows down the search range to the segment where the target must lie.
- Continues the search until the target is found or the search range is exhausted.
- Returns the index of the target if found; otherwise, returns **-1**.

Algorithm Explanation:

- The vector is sorted but rotated at some pivot. The **search** function checks the midpoint of the current search range to determine if the left or right half is sorted correctly.
- It then checks if the target is within the sorted half of the range. If so, it narrows down the search to that half. If not, it searches in the other half.
- This process is repeated until the target is found or the search range is exhausted.

The main Function:

- Initializes a vector **nums** with a rotated sorted sequence of integers.
- Specifies a **target** value to search for within the vector.
- Calls the **search** function with **nums** and **target** as arguments and stores the result in a variable.
- Outputs the index of the target value if it's found within the vector.

Key Concepts Illustrated:

- **Binary Search**: The **search** function illustrates an adapted binary search algorithm that accounts for the vector's rotation, showcasing how binary search can be modified to work under different constraints.
- **Vector Manipulation**: Demonstrates passing a vector by reference to a function and working with its elements.
- **Conditional Logic**: Uses if-else statements to determine which half of the vector to search based on the arrangement of elements.

This program effectively demonstrates how to perform a binary search in a rotated sorted vector, a common problem in algorithmic challenges and technical interviews.

10. **Example 10: Vector Shuffling Algorithm:**
    - **Objective:** Implement the Fisher-Yates shuffle algorithm to randomly shuffle elements in a **vector**.

```
#include <iostream>
#include <vector>
#include <random>
#include <algorithm>
using namespace std;

void shuffle(vector<int>& nums) {
    random_device rd;
    mt19937 g(rd());
    for (int i = nums.size() - 1; i > 0; --i) {
        uniform_int_distribution<> dis(0, i);
        int j = dis(g);
        swap(nums[i], nums[j]);
    }
}

int main() {

    vector<int> nums = { 1, 2, 3, 4, 5, 6, 7, 8, 9, 10 };
    cout << "Original vector:\n";
    for (int num: nums) {
        cout << num << " ";
    }
    cout << "\nShuffled vector:\n";
    shuffle(nums);
    for (int num: nums) {
        cout << num << " ";
```

```
    }
    cout << endl;
    return 0;
}
```

Explanation:

This C++ program demonstrates a simple yet effective way to shuffle the elements of a **vector<int>** randomly. Here's a breakdown of how the program works:

Header Files:

- **<iostream>**: For input and output operations.
- **<vector>**: To use the vector container.
- **<random>**: For generating random numbers.
- **<algorithm>**: Provides the **swap()** function used in the shuffling algorithm.

The shuffle Function:

- It takes a reference to a vector of integers as its parameter.
- **random_device** and **mt19937** are used to create a high-quality random number generator.
- A loop iterates backward through the vector from the last element to the first.
- For each element at position **i**, it generates a random index **j** between **0** and **i** (inclusive).
- The current element **nums[i]** is swapped with the element at the randomly chosen index **nums[j]**.
- This approach ensures that each element has an equal probability of ending up in any position in the vector, achieving a fair shuffle.

The main Function:

- Defines and initializes a vector **nums** with integers from 1 to 10.
- Prints the original vector to the console.
- Calls the **shuffle** function to randomly shuffle the elements of the vector.
- Prints the shuffled vector to demonstrate the result of the shuffling.

Key Concepts Illustrated:

- **Random Number Generation**: The use of **random_device** as a seed and **mt19937** (a Mersenne Twister engine) to generate high-quality random numbers.
- **Uniform Distribution**: **uniform_int_distribution<>** ensures that all integers within the specified range have an equal probability of being chosen.
- **Vector Manipulation**: Demonstrates passing vectors by reference to functions and iterating over them.
- **Algorithm Usage**: The use of **swap()** to exchange the values of two elements in the vector.

This example encapsulates several important C++ programming concepts, such as working with STL containers like vectors, generating random numbers, and applying algorithms, all of which are fundamental in creating efficient and effective C++ programs.

SUMMARY

In this chapter, we delve into the foundational concepts and advanced techniques associated with arrays and vectors in C++, offering readers a comprehensive understanding of these essential data structures. The chapter is meticulously structured to guide readers from the basics of array usage to the dynamic capabilities of vectors, along with practical insights into common problems and their solutions.

The journey begins with an exploration of arrays, starting from their definition and initialization to accessing individual elements. Readers learn how to efficiently traverse arrays using loops, a fundamental skill for manipulating and processing stored data. The discussion extends to multidimensional arrays, shedding light on creating, initializing, and accessing elements in 2D and 3D arrays. This segment equips readers with the knowledge to handle complex data structures, often used in mathematical computations and image processing.

Transitioning from the static nature of arrays, the chapter introduces vectors - the dynamic arrays of C++. Vectors provide a flexible and powerful alternative to arrays, supporting automatic resizing, and offering a suite of member functions for managing elements. The section on vectors covers their definition, initialization, and methods for adding or removing elements, alongside techniques for accessing and modifying individual items.

Building upon the basics, the chapter delves into vector algorithms. This part highlights the utility of the vector class in implementing common algorithms like searching and sorting. Readers learn to leverage these algorithms to manipulate vector contents efficiently, demonstrating the versatility and power of vectors in algorithmic problem-solving.

Addressing common challenges, the chapter concludes with a discussion on typical array and vector issues such as out-of-bounds errors, memory allocation errors, and performance considerations. Through practical advice and strategies, readers are equipped to avoid these pitfalls, enhancing the reliability and efficiency of their C++ programs.

Overall, this chapter serves as a vital resource for understanding and mastering arrays and vectors in C++, from their fundamental principles to advanced applications and troubleshooting. It lays a solid foundation for readers to harness these data structures in developing sophisticated and efficient C++ applications.

Multiple Choice

1. What is the primary difference between an array and a vector in C++?
    a. Arrays are fixed-size, while vectors can grow and shrink dynamically.
    b. Arrays can store different data types, while vectors can only store one data type.
    c. Arrays are more efficient for small data sets, while vectors are more efficient for large data sets.
    d. Arrays and vectors are identical data structures.

2. Which of the following is a valid way to declare an array in C++?
    a. int myArray[5]
    b. array myArray = [5]
    c. myArray<int> = {5}
    d. myArray<int>(5)
3. What is the correct syntax for accessing the third element of an array named myArray in C++?
    a. myArray(2)
    b. myArray[3]
    c. myArray[2]
    d. myArray.third()
4. What is the correct syntax for declaring a vector that can hold 10 integers in C++?
    a. vector<int>(10)
    b. vector<int> myVector[10]
    c. vector myVector = {10}
    d. vector<int> myVector(10)
5. What is the main advantage of using a vector instead of an array in C++?
    a. Vectors are more efficient than arrays.
    b. Vectors can store more data than arrays.
    c. Vectors can be resized dynamically at runtime.
    d. Vectors have a smaller memory footprint than arrays.
6. Which of the following is a valid way to add an element to the end of a vector named myVector in C++?
    a. myVector.add(5)
    b. myVector.append(5)
    c. myVector.push_back(5)
    d. myVector.insert(5)
7. What is the correct syntax for accessing the fifth element of a vector named myVector in C++?
    a. myVector(4)
    b. myVector[5]
    c. myVector[4]
    d. myVector.fifth()
8. What is the correct way to remove the last element from a vector named myVector in C++?
    a. myVector.pop()
    b. myVector.remove(-1)
    c. myVector.erase(myVector.end() - 1)
    d. myVector.delete_back()
9. What is the maximum number of elements that can be stored in an array in C++?
    a. 100
    b. 1000
    c. 10,000
    d. There is no maximum, but it depends on available memory.

10. Which of the following is a valid way to declare a 2-dimensional array with 3 rows and 4 columns in C++?
    a. int myArray[3][4]
    b. array myArray = {3, 4}
    c. myArray<int>(3, 4)
    d. myArray<int>[3][4]

Exercise

Write a C++ programs for the following questions:

1- Write a C++ program to declare an array of integers with size 5, initialize it with the values {2, 4, 6, 8, 10}, and print the values using a for loop.
2- Write a C++ program that uses a while loop to read integers from the user and store them in an array until the user enters a negative number. Then print the array in reverse order.
3- Write a C++ program to declare a vector of strings, add the values "apple", "banana", "orange", and "grape" to it, and print the values using a for-each loop.
4- Write a C++ program to declare a vector of integers, add the values 2, 4, 6, 8, and 10 to it, and print the values using a for loop.
5- Write a C++ program that reads integers from the user and stores them in a vector until the user enters a negative number. Then print the sum of the values in the vector.
6- Write a C++ program that declares an array of integers with size 10 and initializes it with random values between 1 and 100. Then, find the minimum and maximum values in the array and print them.
7- Write a C++ program to declare a vector of integers, add the values 1 to 10 to it, and then remove the values 3, 5, and 7. Finally, print the values in the vector using a for-each loop.
8- Write a C++ program that declares two arrays of integers with size 5, initializes them with different values, and then merges them into a new array. Finally, print the values in the new array.
9- Write a C++ program to declare a vector of strings and sort it in alphabetical order using the sort function from the algorithm library. Finally, print the sorted vector.
10- Write a C++ program that reads integers from the user and stores them in a vector until the user enters a duplicate number. Then print the index of the first occurrence of the duplicate number in the vector.
11- Write a program that rotates a 2D vector (matrix) 90 degrees clockwise. The matrix should be represented as a vector of vectors.
12- Implement your own vector class, supporting basic functionalities like push_back, pop_back, and dynamic resizing.
13- Develop a program to find all unique elements in a vector of integers. The solution should optimize both space and time complexity.
14- Create a two-way map (bi-directional map) where you can search by key to get a value and also search by value to get keys, using vectors.
15- Write a program to represent a sparse matrix using vectors. Implement functionalities to add a new element and to display the matrix.
16- Write a C++ program, given a collection of intervals represented as pairs in a vector, merge all overlapping intervals.

17- Write a C++ program, consider a matrix where each row and column is sorted in ascending order. Write a program to find the kth smallest element in the matrix.
18- Write a C++ program,, using arrays, implement a circular buffer that supports read and write operations efficiently, handling buffer overflows gracefully.
19- Write a program using a vector as a stack to check for balanced parentheses in a given string of characters.
20- Write a C++ program, implement an algorithm to shuffle an array of integers. Ensure that each permutation of the array is equally likely.

Chapter 4
Functions

ABSTRACT

Chapter 4 delves into the heart of modular programming in C++: functions. Starting with an introduction, it establishes the significance of functions in the realm of programming. The chapter systematically dissects the nuances of function prototypes and underscores the importance of function signatures and argument coercion. By elaborating on the intricacies of argument promotion, the reader gains a profound understanding of the subtleties in function calls. A categorization of functions based on return type and argument passing offers clarity and depth to the topic. The chapter elucidates the pivotal concept of scope, supported by a practical "Yes or No" program example. A deep dive into references and the distinct differences between pass-by-value and pass-by-reference paves the way for more advanced topics. Highlights include the exploration of default arguments, the power of function overloading, and the magic of recursion juxtaposed against iteration. The discussion on storage classes, with an emphasis on static storage, reinforces understanding.

4.1 INTRODUCTION

Functions, which are also called **methods** or **procedures** in other programming languages, let the programmer break up a program's tasks into separate parts that can run on their own. Every program you've developed has used functions. Sometimes known as **user-defined** functions or **programmer-defined functions,** the statements in the function bodies are written just once, repeated in many places, and concealed from other functions.

There are several reasons to modularize a program using functions. One is the divide-and-conquer strategy, which makes software development more manageable by developing programs from tiny, straightforward components. The reusability of software functions as building blocks for the creation of new programs, which is another aspect. In older programs, for instance, we did not need to declare how to read a line of text from the keyboard. The getline function of the string> header file is how C++ provides this functionality. Avoiding code redundancy is a third incentive. In addition, separating a program into logical functions makes it simpler to debug and maintain.

DOI: 10.4018/979-8-3693-2007-5.ch004

NOTE: To make software easier to reuse, each function should only be used for a single, well-defined task, and the name of the function should make it clear what it does. These functions make it simpler to develop, test, debug, and maintain applications.

A function that does just one duty is simpler to test and debug than a function that performs several functions.

When a function is run, it either makes something happen or gives control back to the person who called it.This program's structure is comparable to the hierarchical method of management. A manager (similar to the calling function) instructs an employee (similar to the called function) to complete a job and report back (i.e., return) the results. The manager function is unaware of how the worker function completes its assigned responsibilities. Unbeknownst to the employer, the employee may also perform other employee functions. This concealment of implementation specifics improves software engineering excellence.

We have created classes that include basic functions with no more than one argument. Often, functions need many pieces of information to fulfill their duties. Now we will examine functions with numerous arguments.

Each parameter (sometimes referred to as a "**formal parameter"**) in the function specification must have one argument in the function call.

Transfer control back to the caller.

There are three methods to restore control to the initial execution point of a function. If the function does not return a value (i.e., it has a void return type), **control returns** when the program reaches the function-ending right brace or when the statement is executed. Return;.

If the function does return a result, the statement return expression; evaluates expression and returns the value of expression to the caller.

4.2 FUNCTION PROTOTYPES AND ARGUMENT COERCION

A function prototype, which is also called a "**function declaration**," tells the compiler the name of the function, the type of data it returns, the number of parameters it expects to get, the types of those parameters, and the order in which it expects to get parameters of the same type.

In C++, function prototypes are used to declare a function prior to its definition. A function prototype informs the compiler of the return type, name, and argument list of the function. This information is used by the compiler to verify that the right amount and kinds of arguments are given to the function during function calls.

For instance:

```
int add(int a, int b);
```

This is the function prototype for the "add" function, which takes two integers as input and returns an integer.

Coercion of function arguments is the automated conversion of an argument to the data type required by the function. For instance, if a function expects a double argument but is supplied with an int parameter, the int value will be immediately transformed to a double before being sent to the function. The term for this is type coercion.

This is an example of Argument Coercion:

```
void printSquare(double x) {
std::cout << x * x << std::endl;
}
int main() {
int i = 5;
printSquare(i); // argument is automatically converted to double
return 0;
}
```

In this example, the printSquare(double x) function expects a double argument, but the main function passes the function an int value. Before being provided to the method, the int value I is automatically transformed to double. This permits the function to operate successfully even if the input supplied to it is not of the appropriate data type.

Developers must be aware that argument coercion might result in unexpected behavior and loss of accuracy if the provided argument is of a different type than anticipated, and they should use it with care.

4.3 FUNCTION SIGNATURES

The section of a function prototype including the function's name and the types of its parameters is referred to as the **function signature**. The return type is not specified in the function signature. Functions within the same scope must have distinct signatures. The function's scope is the portion of a program in which it is known and accessible.

In C++, a function's signature is the combination of its name and the types of its arguments. It is used to uniquely identify a function and verify function call compatibility. Consider the following two functions:

```
int add(int a, int b);
double add(double a, double b);
```

The function signatures for these two functions are:

```
int add(int, int);
double add(double, double);
```

As can be seen, the function signature consists of the return type, function name, and argument types.

In C++, functions are overloaded using function signatures. Function overloading permits the creation of numerous functions with the same name and distinct arguments. The function signature is used by the compiler to decide which function to call depending on its inputs.

Here's another example:

```
void print(std::string s);
void print(int x);
```

The function signatures for these two functions are:

```
void print(std::string);
void print(int);
```

In this example, both functions have the same name but take different kinds of arguments. The first function accepts a std::string parameter, while the second accepts an int parameter. When the function print is used, the compiler will examine the types of the supplied arguments and call the corresponding function.

In C++, function signatures don't list the names of the arguments; they only list the types of the arguments. This means that two functions with the same number and types of parameters, but different names are considered to have the same signature.

In C++, function signatures are needed to find and call functions, as well as for function overloading, templates, and other related features.

4.4 ARGUMENT COERCION

Argument coercion, i.e., forcing **arguments** to the right types defined by the parameter declarations, is a fundamental aspect of function prototypes. A program may, for instance, call a function with an integer parameter, even if the function prototype demands a double argument; the function will still run appropriately.

In C++, argument coercion, also known as type casting, is the conversion of one data type to another. This may be accomplished directly with casting operators or implicitly using type promotion and type conversion.

The following casting operators may be used for explicit type casting:

```
static_cast<type> (expression) - used for safe conversions between related
types, such as converting a derived class to a base class.
dynamic_cast<type> (expression) - used for safe conversions between related
types, and also performs runtime type checking.
reinterpret_cast<type> (expression) - used for conversions between unrelated
types, such as converting a pointer to an integer.
const_cast<type> (expression) - used for modifying the constness of a vari-
able.
For example, if you want to convert a floating - point number to an integer,
you can use the static_cast<int> (expression) operator:
float x = 3.14;
int y = static_cast<int> (x); // y will be 3
```

In C++, implicit type casting is also possible through type promotion and type conversion. Expressions automatically convert smaller data types (such as char or short) to bigger ones (such as int) using type promotion. For instance:

```
short x = 3;
int y = x + 2; // x is promoted to int before the addition
```

Type conversion is the automated conversion of types in function calls and assignments. It is also known as type coercion. For instance, the string argument str is implicitly transformed to a boolean before being supplied to the function foo in the following code:

```
void foo(bool b) { /* ... */ }
string str = "true";
foo(str); // str is implicitly converted to bool before the call
```

Noting that both explicit and implicit type casting might result in unexpected behavior and loss of accuracy if not handled with care, it is recommended to use them with caution and test the consequences.

4.5 ARGUMENT PROMOTION RULES

Before a function is called, the compiler may transform argument values that do not match exactly to the parameter types in the function prototype to the correct type. These conversions occur according to the promotion rules of C++. The promotion rules provide instructions on how to convert between data types without losing any information. It is possible to convert an int to a double without altering its value. But when a double is converted to an int, the fractional portion of the double value is truncated. Keep in mind that double variables may store far larger values than int variables, thus the data loss may be substantial. When converting big integer types to tiny integer types (e.g., long to short), signed to unsigned, or unsigned to signed, values may also be adjusted.

Expressions having values of two or more data types are subject to the promotion rules; such expressions are also known as mixed-type expressions. In a mixed-type expression, the type of each value is promoted to the “highest” type in the expression (actually, a temporary version of each value is created and used for the expression; the original values remain unchanged). When the type of a function argument does not match the parameter type given in the function specification or prototype, promotion also happens.

Changing values to basic types with fewer capabilities might result in erroneous values. Thus, a value may only be transformed to a lower fundamental type by explicitly assigning it to a variable of a lower type (in which case, certain compilers would generate a warning) or by using the cast operator.

Argument promotion (or type promotion) is the automated translation of smaller data types (such as char, short, or float) to bigger data types (such as int, long, or double) in expressions in C++. The C++ standard specifies a set of criteria for determining the promoted type of an expression based on its promoted arguments. The basic rules for argument promotion are:

char, signed char, and unsigned char are promoted to int.short is promoted to int.

float is promoted to double.

For example, if you have the following code:

```
char c = 'a';
short s = 2;
float f = 3.14;
int i = c + s + f;
```

c's value is promoted to int, s's value is already an int, and f's value is promoted to double. The promoted types are then added, and the resulting value is assigned to i.

Importantly, the argument promotion rules only apply to expressions. They have no effect on the types of variables or arguments given to functions. For instance, a char variable sent as an argument to a function will not be converted to an int.

Also, argument promotion rules have no effect on how the program works, though the accuracy and range of variables may vary. For instance, if a variable of type float is promoted to type double, its accuracy and range will increase, but it may also lead to unexpected behavior if the variable is used in a situation where precision is crucial.

In conclusion, argument promotion is an automated conversion procedure that happens in C++ to transform smaller data types into bigger ones in expressions based on a set of criteria stated by the C++ standard. It may alter the accuracy and range of the variable, but the program's behavior stays the same.

4.5.1 Examples

A function in C++ is a piece of code that performs a specified purpose and may be called several times inside a program. Typically, functions are used to structure and make code more understandable and reusable.

The following are examples of function declarations and how to invoke them:

```
// A function that takes no arguments and returns no value
void printHello() {
cout << "Hello, World!" << endl;
}
// A function that takes no arguments and returns no value
void printHello() {
cout << "Hello, World!" << endl;
}
// Call the function
printHello(); // Outputs "Hello, World!"
// A function that takes an integer argument and returns an integer
int add(int x, int y) {
return x + y;
}
// Call the function
int result = add(3, 5); // result will be 8
// A function that takes two strings and returns a new string
string concatenate(string a, string b) {
return a + b;
```

```
}
// Call the function
string newString = concatenate("Hello, ", "World!"); // newString will be
"Hello, World!"
```

More Examples

Write a program to display three exponents four and six exponents five.

A- Write a C++ program to calculate the exponent number without using functions.

B- Write a C++ program to calculate the exponent number by using function.

A: Without using functions we need to use repetition structure twice; one for the first case 3^4 and second for 5^6.

```
#include <iostream>
using namespace std;
void main() {
int threeExpFour = 1;
for (int i = 0; i < 4; i = i + 1)
{
threeExpFour = threeExpFour * 3;
}
cout << "3^4 is " << threeExpFour << endl;
int sixExpFive = 1;
for (int i = 0; i < 5; i = i + 1)
{
sixExpFive = sixExpFive * 6;
}
cout << "6^5 is " << sixExpFive << endl;
system ("pause");
}
```

B: Declare function raiseToPower to find the exponent values.

```
#include <iostream>
using namespace std;
int raiseToPower(int base, int exponent) {
int result = 1;
for (int i = 0; i < exponent; i = i + 1) {
result = result * base;
}
return result;
}
void main() {
cout<< raiseToPower(3, 4);
```

```
cout << "3^4 is " << threeExpFour << endl;
int sixSeven = raiseToPower(6,7);
cout << "6^7 is " << sixSeven << endl;
system("pause");
}
```

4.6 FUNCTION TYPES BASED ON THE RETURN TYPE AND PASSING ARGUMENTS

1. No return and no passing arguments
2. No return with passing arguments
3. Return and no passing arguments
4. Return and with passing arguments

In C++, functions are categorized according to their return type and the number and type of arguments they accept. The following are frequent kinds of functions based on the above criteria:

Void functions: These are functions without a return value. They are declared using the void keyword and without a return clause. For instance:

```
void printHello()
{
cout << "Hello, World!" << endl;
}
```

Functions that return a value: These are functions that return a particular value type. They may be of any data type, including **integer**, **float**, **string**, etc. For instance:

```
int add(int x, int y)
{
return x + y;
}
```

Functions that take no arguments: These are functions that do not take any arguments. They are called without any parameters. For example:

```
void printToday()
{
cout << "Today is " << __DATE__ << endl;
}
```

Functions that take arguments: These are functions that take one or more arguments of any type. The type and number of arguments must be specified in the function declaration. For example:

```
string concatenate(string a, string b)
{
return a + b;
}
```

Functions that take a variable number of arguments: These are functions that take a variable number of arguments. In C++, this can be achieved using the **...** operator (or "ellipsis") and the **va_list**, **va_start**, **va_arg**, and **va_end** macros. For example:

```
void printNumbers(int count, ...)
{
va_list args; va_start(args, count);
for (int i = 0; i < count; i++)
{
int num = va_arg(args, int);
cout << num << " ";
}
va_end(args);
}
```

C++ functions may be categorized according to their return type and the number and kind of arguments they accept. Common sorts of functions include void functions, functions that return a value, functions that accept no arguments, functions that accept arguments, and functions that accept an arbitrary amount of parameters.

More Examples

1- C++ program demonstrates Function types based on the return type and passing arguments.

```
#include<iostream>
using namespace std;
//Function Types based on the return types and the passing arguments
// Display 1() and Display2() functions don't return any value, return type
void.
void Display1();
void Display2(int);
// Display 3() and Display 4() functions return integer.
int Display3();
int Display4(int y);
int main()
{
Display1();
Display2(20);
int result = Display3();
```

```
int result2 = Display4(50);
system("pause");
return 0;
}
void Display1()
{
cout << "void Display1()"<<endl;
}
void Display2(int x)
{
cout << "void Display2(int x)" << endl;
}
int Display3()
{
cout << "int Display3()" << endl;
return 10;
}
int Display4(int y)
{
cout << "int Display4(int y)" << endl;
return 30;
}
```

Display 1 and Display 2 functions not returning any value, they are just for local calculations and printing messages.

Display 3 and Display 4 return values, so we need to prepare variables with the same return type from the main program to hold the results.

2- Write a program to display the results for 2 integers.

```
#include<iostream>
using namespace std;
int sum(int x, int y);
void main()
{
int result = sum(20, 30);
cout << "result = " << result << endl;
system("pause");
}
int sum(int x, int y)
{
return (x + y);
}
```

This is a C++ program that uses the sum function to compute the sum of two integers. The following is a summary of the program:

1- This line contains the program's input/output stream library. This library includes input and output functions for C++, such as "cout" and "cin."
2- This line defines the use of the standard namespace by the application. This enables us to use standard C++ functions and variables without prefixing them with "std::."
3-This line defines the "sum" function, which accepts two integer parameters and returns an integer result. This section defines the function.
4- This is the program's primary function. The "void" keyword indicates that the function does not return a value. In this function, an integer variable named "result" is declared and assigned the value returned by the "sum" function when called with the parameters 20 and 30. The result is then sent to the console through the "cout" function.
5- This line outputs to the console the text "result = " followed by the value of the "result" variable. The "endl" keyword appends a new line character to the output's last line.
6- This line use the "system" function to stop the program and wait for the user to hit a key before terminating the program. This is often used to keep the console window open after program execution has concluded.
7- Function accepts two integer parameters, sums them, and returns the resulting integer value.

3- Write a program to display the value

```
#include <iostream>
using namespace std;
void displayValue(int);
int main()
{
displayValue(2017);
system("pause");
return 0;
}
void displayValue(int year) {
cout << "The year is " << year << endl;
}
```

This C++ program creates a function named "displayValue" that accepts an integer argument and outputs a console message with the argument's value. The main function then calls this function with the input 2017 as its argument. The software then utilizes the "system" function to halt the program prior to exiting.

The "#include iostream>" directive incorporates the standard input/output library into the program, which offers input/output functions such as "cout" and "cin."

The "using namespace std;" phrase states that the application is using the standard namespace, allowing the usage of standard C++ functions and variables without the "std::" prefix.

The "void displayValue(int year)" declaration specifies the "displayValue" function, which accepts the "year" integer parameter. It utilizes the "cout" function to output a message to the console with the "year" argument's value.

The "displayValue" method is called in the "main" function with the input 2017 to output "The year is 2017" to the console. The "system" function is then used to stop the program and wait for the user to hit a key before terminating the application. Finally, the function returns 0 to signify that the program has properly finished.

4- Write a program to display the ATM bank menu

```
#include<iostream>
using namespace std;
void menu();
int main()
{
menu();
system("pause");
return 0;
}
void menu()
{
int input;
do
{
cout << " ATM Menu\n ***************\n
1-Deposite\n 2- Withdraw\n 3- CheckBalance\n 4- Exit\n\n ";
cout << "Please make selection\n";
cin >> input;
switch (input)
{
case 1:
cout << " 1- Deposite\n";
break;
case 2:
cout << " 2- Withdraw\n";
break;
case 3:
cout << " 3- CheckBalance\n";
break;
case 4:
cout << " 4- Exit\n";
break;
default:
cout << " Please enter different value\n";
```

```
}
} while (input != 4);
}
```

This C++ software creates a function named “menu” that presents a rudimentary ATM menu to the user and then executes the user’s selection using a switch statement. The main function invokes the “menu” function, followed by the “system” function to halt the application before exiting.

The “#includeiostream>” directive incorporates the standard input/output library into the program, which offers input/output functions such as “cout” and “cin.”

The “using namespace std;” phrase states that the application is using the standard namespace, allowing the usage of standard C++ functions and variables without the “std::” prefix.

The “void menu()” declaration specifies the “menu” function, which uses the “cout” function to show a rudimentary ATM menu to the user. The “cin” function is then used to read the user’s selection into the “input” variable, and a switch statement is used to perform the appropriate action depending on the user’s selection.

The “menu” function, which shows the menu and enables the user to make a selection, is called from the “main” function. The “system” function is then used to stop the program and wait for the user to hit a key before terminating the application. Finally, the function returns 0 to signify that the program has properly finished.

Figure 1. Menu function

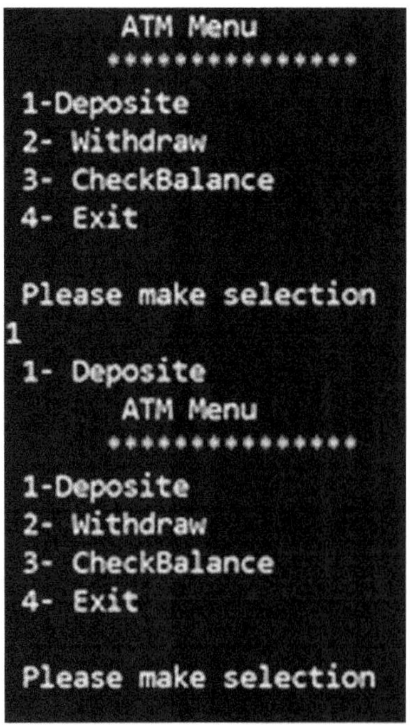

4.7 SCOPE RULES

Its scope is the area of the program where an identifier may be utilized. For instance, when a local variable is declared in a block, it may only be accessed inside that block and blocks that are nested within it. This section describes four identifier scopes: **function scope**, **file scope**, **block scope**, and **function-prototype scope**.

The file scope of an identifier defined outside of any function or class. From the time it is defined until the conclusion of the file, this identifier is "known" by all functions. File scope applies to global variables, function declarations, and function prototypes put outside of a function.

Identifiers specified inside a block have scope within that block. Block scope starts with the declaration of an identifier and ends with the closing right brace () of the block in which the declaration occurs. Local variables and function arguments, which are likewise local variables of the function, both have block scope. Any block may include declarations of variables. When blocks are nested when an outer block identification has the same name as an inner block identifier, the outer block identifier is "hidden" until the inner block finishes. During execution in the inner block, the inner block observes the value of its own local identifier rather than the value of the similarly named identifier in the outer block. Even though they exist from the moment the program starts execution, local variables declared static nevertheless have block scope. The period of storage has no effect on the scope of an identifier.

Labels are the only identifiers having function scope (identifiers preceded by a colon, such as start:). Labels may be used anywhere inside a function, but cannot be referred outside of the function body. In goto statements, labels are used.

Identifiers used in a function prototype's argument list are the only ones having function prototype scope. As previously stated, function prototypes do not need names in the argument list; just types are necessary. The compiler disregards names appearing in the argument list of a function prototype. Identifiers used in a function prototype may be reused without ambiguity elsewhere in the program. In a single prototype, an identifier may only be used once.

The section of a C++ program where variables and functions may be accessible is referred to as the function's scope. The location where a variable or function is defined and declared determines its scope.

- Variables specified inside a function are available only within that function. They are referred to as local variables.
- Variables declared outside of functions are available throughout the whole of the code. They are referred to as global variables.
- A function declared inside another function is available only within the scope of its enclosing function. They are referred to as nested functions.
- A function created outside of any function is available throughout the whole of the program. They are referred to as global functions.

For example:

```
int global_var = 5; // global variable
void func1()
{
int local_var = 10; // local variable
```

```
cout << global_var << endl; // Outputs 5
cout << local_var << endl; // Outputs 10
}
void func2()
{
cout << global_var << endl; // Outputs 5 //
cout << local_var; // Error: local_var is not defined in this scope
}
int main()
{
func1();
func2();
return 0;
}
```

The variable **global var** is declared outside of any function in this example, allowing it to be accessible across the whole program. **local var** is only accessible inside the function **func1(),** since it is declared within that function.

Functions also adhere to the same scope rules, such as:

```
void outerFunc()
{
void innerFunc()
{ // nested function
cout << "Inside innerFunc" << endl;
}
innerFunc(); // call innerFunc
}
void globalFunc()
{
cout << "Inside globalFunc" << endl;
}
int main()
{
outerFunc();
globalFunc();
// innerFunc(); // Error: innerFunc is not defined in this scope
return 0;
}
```

In this example, **innerFunc** is declared inside **outerFunc**, so it can only be accessible within the scope of **outerFunc. globalFunc**, on the other hand, is defined outside of any function, so it may be used across the whole program.

In conclusion, function scope specifies where in a program a variable or function may be accessed. Variables and functions declared inside a function are available exclusively within that function, but variables and functions defined outside of any function are accessible across the whole of the program. The scope of a variable or function is determined by where it is defined and declared, and it is essential to keep this in mind while programming in C++.

4.8 INTRODUCING THE YES OR NO PROGRAM

The Yes or No software presents the user with common gaming-related questions. First, the application prompts the user for a yes or no response. The application then becomes more detailed by asking whether the user want to save his game. Again, the program's findings are unremarkable, but their execution is intriguing. Each inquiry is presented by a distinct function that interacts with the main function ().

```
// Yes or No
// Demonstrates return values and parameters #include <iostream>
#include <string> using namespace std;
char askYesNo1();
char askYesNo2(string question);
int main()
{
char answer1 = askYesNo1();
cout << "Thanks for answering: " << answer1 << "\n\n";
char answer2 = askYesNo2("Do you wish to save your game?"); cout << "Thanks
for answering: " << answer2 << "\n";
return 0;
}
//Each question is asked by a separate function, and information is passed be-
tween these functions and main()
char askYesNo1()
{
char response1;
do
{
cout << "Please enter 'y' or 'n': "; cin >> response1;
} while (response1 != 'y' && response1 != 'n'); return response1;
}
char askYesNo2(string question)
{
char response2;
do
{
cout << question << " (y/n): "; cin >> response2;
```

```
} while (response2 != 'y' && response2 != 'n'); return response2;
}
```

This C++ application illustrates the usage of function return values and arguments. The program specifies two functions, "askYesNo1" and "askYesNo2", which ask the user a yes or no question and return the user's answer to the function that called them.

These two functions are called by the main function, which then displays the return values to the user. The user is requested to submit a "y" or "n" answer on the initial call to "askYesNo1" without any parameters. A string argument is supplied to the method on the second call to "askYesNo2" in order to tailor the question that is posed.

The "char" data type is used to represent the user's answer, and a do-while loop is used to check the user's input and guarantee that they enter either "y" or "n".

The "cout" function is used to show messages to the user, whereas "cin" is used to receive the user's console input. The function returns the user's answer to the calling function, which displays a message to the user based on this value.

4.9 REFERENCES AND REFERENCE PARAMETERS

In many programming languages, there are two methods to provide parameters to functions: **pass-by-value** and **pass-by-reference**. When an argument is supplied by value, a duplicate of its value is created and passed to the called function (on the function call stack). Modifications to the copy have no effect on the value of the original variable in the caller. This eliminates the unintentional side effects that impede the creation of proper and dependable software systems to such a large extent. Each parameter supplied in this chapter's programs to this point has been passed by value.

4.9.1 Pass-By-Value

When a function is called with an argument in C++, the function receives the argument's value. This is referred to as "pass by value," and it indicates that the function gets a copy of the argument's value as opposed to a reference to the original. Any modifications made to the argument inside the function will have no effect on the parameter's value outside of the function. The following are instances of C++ pass by value functions:

```
void increment(int x) {
x++;
}
int main() {
int a = 5;
increment(a);
cout << a << endl; // Outputs "5"
return 0;
}
```

This C++ program illustrates the notion of passing function parameters by value. The program creates a function called "increment" that accepts the input "x" as an integer. The function increases "x" by 1 without returning a value. The main function declares and initializes the integer variable "a" with the value 5. The main function then calls increment with the input "a". Nevertheless, the parameter is supplied by value, which implies that a copy of the value of "a" rather than the original variable is sent to the function. When the "increment" function increases the value of "x", it has no effect on the value of "a" inside the main function. The program displays the unchanged value of "a" to the console, proving that the "increment" function had no effect on "a's" value.

In this example, increment accepts an integer parameter x and increases its value by 1. Nonetheless, since the function use the pass-by-value mechanism, the value of an in the main function will stay unaltered.

```
void swap(int x, int y) {
int temp = x;
x = y;
y = temp;
}
int main() {
int a = 5, b = 10;
swap(a, b);
return 0;
}
```

This C++ program illustrates the notion and constraints of passing function parameters by value. The program creates a "swap" function that accepts two integer inputs "x" and "y". Using the temporary variable "temp," the function exchanges the values of "x" and "y." However, the function returns no value. The main function declares and initializes two integer variables, a and b, with the values 5 and 10, respectively. The main function then invokes the swap function with "a" and "b" as parameters. Nevertheless, the parameters are supplied by value, which implies that the function receives a copy of the values of "a" and "b" rather than the original variables. Consequently, the "swap" function does not alter the values of "a" and "b" in the main function when it swaps the values of "x" and "y." This indicates that the "swap" function did not alter the values of "a" and "b."

More Examples

/*1- pass-by-value: When an argument is passed by value, a copy of the argument's value is made and passed (on the function call stack) to the called function. Changes to the copy do not affect the original variable's value in the caller*/

//Examples for passing parameters by Value

Example 1: Passing 3 arguments (a, b, and c) by values to duplicate function. The function not accessing the original values in memory. The duplicate function can change variable values just within the function scope without touching the original values.

```
#include <iostream>
using namespace std;
```

```
void duplicate(int a, int b, int c)
{
a *= 2;
b *= 2;
c *= 2;
cout << a << "\n" << b << "\n"<<c << "\n";
}
void main()
{
int x = 1, y = 3, z = 7;
duplicate(x, y, z);
cout << "x=" << x << ", y=" << y << ", z=" << z << endl;
system("pause");
}
```

This C++ program illustrates the notion and constraints of passing function parameters by value. The program constructs a duplicate function with three integer arguments “a”, “b”, and “c”. Each of these parameters is multiplied by 2 and the resultant values are returned to the terminal. The main function creates and initializes three integer variables named “x”, “y”, and “z” with the values 1, 3, and 7, respectively. The main function then invokes the duplicate function with the parameters “x”, “y”, and “z”. Nevertheless, the inputs are supplied by value, which implies that the function receives a copy of the values of “x”, “y”, and “z” rather than the original variables. Consequently, the “duplicate” function has no effect on the values of “x”, “y”, and “z” in the main function when it multiplies “a”, “b”, and “c” by 2. The values of “x”, “y”, and “z” are then printed to the console to demonstrate that the “duplicate” function did not alter the values of these variables. The application then waits for the user to touch a key before utilizing the “system” function to leave.

Example 2: C++ program to display the value for X variable before and after passByValue call and how the call affecting the X value.

```
#include<iostream>
using namespace std;
void passByValue(int x)
{
cout << "x from inside the function = " << x << endl;
x++;
cout << "x from inside the function = " << x << endl;
}
void main()
{
int x = 5;
cout << " X from the main = " << x << endl;
passByValue(x);
cout << "X from the main =" << x << endl;
```

```
system("pause");
}
```

This program illustrates the C++ idea of passing function parameters by value.

The passByValue() method increases the integer input x by 1. The integer variable x is defined and initialized to 5 in the main() method. The value of x is then written to the console, and the passByValue() method is called with x as its argument.

The function prints the value of x, increments it by 1, and then prints it again. Nevertheless, this modification changes just the local copy of x inside the function and has no effect on x's original value in the main() function. The value of x is reported again in the main() function after the function call to validate that it has not been altered by the function.

4.9.2 Pass-By-Reference

This section presents reference parameters, the first of two pass-by-reference mechanisms provided by C++. Using pass-by-reference, the caller grants the called function immediate access to the caller's data and the power to alter that data if the called function so chooses.

A reference parameter is an alias for the function argument it represents. To indicate that a function parameter is provided by reference, simply append an ampersand (&) to the type of the parameter in the function prototype; use the same approach when stating the parameter's type in the function header. the following declaration in a function header is an example:

when read from right to left, int& count is pronounced "count is an int reference." Just provide the variable's name in the function call to pass it by reference. Then, referencing the variable by its parameter name inside the body of the called function corresponds to the original variable in the calling function, which may be updated directly by the called function. The function prototype and header must always coincide.

When a function is called in C++ with an argument, the parameter's value may also be supplied via reference. This indicates that the function gets a reference to the original argument, as opposed to a duplicate of its value. Any modifications made to the argument inside the function will have an effect on the parameter's value outside of the function. In order to pass an argument by reference in C++, the & operator may be used in the function definition. The following are instances of pass by reference functions in C++:

```
void increment(int& x) {
x++;
}
int main() {
int a = 5;
increment(a);
cout << a << endl; // Outputs "6"
return 0;
}
```

This program defines the increment function, which accepts an integer reference as an argument, increases the value of the referenced variable by one, and returns nothing. Then, inside the main function, the variable an is declared and initialized with the value 5. The increment function is called with an as its parameter, therefore an is supplied as a reference to the function. During the increment function, the referenced variable's value is increased by 1. Then, the main function outputs the current value of a, which is 6.

```
void swap(int& x, int& y) {
int temp = x;
x = y;
y = temp;
}
int main() {
int a = 5, b = 10;
swap(a, b);
return 0;
}
```

This program defines the "swap" function, which accepts two integer parameters by reference using the '&' symbol. The function swaps the two parameters' values.

In the main function, the numbers 5 and 10 are assigned to the integer variables a and b, respectively. The "swap" function is then run with the inputs a and b. The function swaps the values of a and b, resulting in a having the value 10 and b having the value 5. Nevertheless, because the function does not provide any output, the software does not produce any console output.

More Examples:

```
/*2- pass-by-reference: With pass-by-reference, the caller gives the called
function the ability
to access the caller's data directly, and to modify that data if the called
function chooses to
do so. */
// passing parameters by reference
```

Example 1: Passing 3 arguments (a, b, and c) by references to duplicate function. The function can access the original values in memory. The duplicate function can change values.

```
#include<iostream>
using namespace std;
void duplicate(int& a, int& b, int& c)
{
a *= 2;
b *= 2;
c *= 2;
}
```

```
void main()
{
int x = 1, y = 3, z = 7;
duplicate(x, y, z);
cout << "x=" << x << ", y=" << y << ", z=" << z << endl;
system ("pause");
}
```

This C++ program introduces a duplicate() method that accepts three integer arguments given by reference using the ampersand (&). Each of the three integer arguments is multiplied by 2 by the function. The duplicate() method is called with the three integer variables x, y, and z by the main function. When these variables are provided by reference, the duplicate() method modifies their values. Using cout, the main function then outputs the modified values of x, y, and z. Lastly, the software awaits a key input from the user before terminating utilizing system ("pause").

Example 2: Passing 2 arguments (x and y) by reference to the update function. The function can access the original values in memory. The update function can change values.

```
#include <iostream>
using namespace std;
int update (int &, int &);
void main()
{
int x = 10, y = 20;
cout << " x= " << x << "y= " << y << "\n";
int result = update(x, y);
cout << " Pass by value for the function call " << "result = " << result <<
endl;
cout << " From the main values are: x= " << x << " y= " << y << "\n";
system("pause");
}
int update (int& x, int& y)
{
x= 100, y = 200;
int r = 0;
cout << " From the update fun values are: x= " << x << " y= " << y << "\n";
r = x + y;
return r;
}
```

This program illustrates the C++ pass-by-reference concept. The update function accepts two integer arguments by reference (int& x and int& y), which indicates that any modifications made to these variables inside the function will have an effect on the original variables in the main function.

The variables x and y are initialized to 10 and 20, respectively, in the main function. These two variables are sent to the update function, and the return value is saved in the result variable. The update function modifies the values of x and y to 100 and 200, respectively, and returns the total of x and y.

Once the update function returns, the main function prints the values of x, y, and result. As x and y were supplied to the update method via reference, their corresponding values were updated to 100 and 200. Thus, the output of the main function indicates that x = 100 and y = 200. The main function also prints the return result of the update function (i.e., the sum of x and y), which is 300.

Example 3: Passing one argument (x) by reference to PassByValue function. The function can access the original values in memory. The PassByValue function can change the value.

```
#include<iostream>
using namespace std;
void PassByValue(int &x)
{
cout << "x from inside the function = " << x << endl;
x++;
cout << "x from inside the function = " << x<< endl;
}
void main()
{
int x = 5;
cout << " X from the main = " << x << endl;
PassByValue(x);
cout << "X from the main =" << x << endl;
system("pause");
}
```

This code shows the use of a function argument that is passed by reference. The function PassByValue accepts a reference to an integer argument x and increases it by one. The value of x is supplied using the & symbol as a reference.

In the main function, the number 5 is assigned to the integer variable x. The PassByValue method is then run with the input x. The function increases x by one and returns its new value. The value of x is shown by the main function after the function call. Due to the fact that x is provided by reference, its value is modified inside the function and mirrored in the main function, with the result being 6.

4.9.3 Function With Array Parameter

Arrays may be sent as arguments to functions in C++, just like any other data type. The array argument is supplied by reference to the function, thus any changes made to the array inside the method will be mirrored outside the function as well. Here are some instances of array-accepting function parameters:

```
// A function that takes an array and its size and prints all its elements
void printArray(int arr[], int size) {
for (int i = 0; i < size; i++) {
```

```
cout << arr[i] << " ";
}
cout << endl;
}
int main() {
int arr[] = { 1, 2, 3, 4, 5 };
int size = sizeof(arr) / sizeof(arr[0]);
printArray(arr, size); // Outputs "1 2 3 4 5"
return 0;
}
```

The code constructs a method called printArray that accepts an array of integers and its size as inputs, and then uses a for loop to print each array member. The main function declares an integer array with some starting values, determines the array's size using the sizeof operator, and then uses the printArray function to display the array's members. The program's output consists of array members separated by a space.

```
// A function that takes an array and its size and returns the sum of all its
elements
int sumArray(int arr[], int size) {
int sum = 0;
for (int i = 0; i < size; i++) {
sum += arr[i];
}
return sum;
}
int main() {
int arr[] = { 1, 2, 3, 4, 5 };
int size = sizeof(arr) / sizeof(arr[0]);
int total = sumArray(arr, size); // total will be 15
cout << total << endl;
return 0;
}
```

The code implements a sumArray function that accepts an integer array and its size as inputs and returns the sum of the array's members. It does this by initializing a variable sum to 0 and then using a for loop to add each array member to the sum as it traverses the array. The function then returns the total.

In the function main(), an integer array is defined, populated with some values, and its size is determined. The array and its size are then sent as inputs to the sumArray function, and the resultant sum is saved in a variable named total. The total variable is then sent to the console.

```
// A function that takes a 2D array, its number of rows and columns and prints
all its elements
void print2DArray(int arr[][3], int rows, int cols) {
```

```
for (int i = 0; i < rows; i++) {
for (int j = 0; j < cols; j++) {
cout << arr[i][j] << " ";
}
cout << endl;
}
}
int main() {
int arr[][3] = { {1, 2, 3}, {4, 5, 6}, {7, 8, 9} };
int rows = 3;
int cols = 3;
print2DArray(arr, rows, cols);
return 0;
}
/* Outputs:
1 2 3
4 5 6
7 8 9
*/
```

The code provides a function print2DArray that, when given a 2D array arr and its dimensions rows and cols, outputs all of the array's items. The method iterates over each row and column of the array using two nested loops and outputs each element followed by a space. This function writes a new line at the end of each row.

The main method defines and initializes the 3x3-dimensional array arr with integer values. The rows and cols variables are set to 3, and the print2DArray function is used with the inputs arr, rows, and cols. The program's output will consist of the components of arr printed in rows and columns.

Note that when giving arrays to a function, the array's size must also be supplied as an argument so that the function knows how many items are included in the array. The sizeof operator may be used to determine the size of an array.

4.10 DEFAULT ARGUMENTS

It is not unusual for a software to repeatedly execute a function with the same parameter argument value. In such situations, the programmer might declare that the parameter has a **default argument**, or a default value that will be provided to the parameter. When a program omits an argument for a parameter with a default argument in a function call, the compiler rewrites the function call to include the argument's default value.

Default arguments must be the last (rightmost) arguments in the parameter list of a function. If an omitted argument is not the rightmost argument in the argument list when calling a function with two or more default parameters, then all arguments to the right of that argument must likewise be omitted. The default parameters must be supplied at the first occurrence of the function name, often in the function prototype. The default parameters should be supplied in the function header if the function prototype is missing since the function definition also acts as the prototype. Expressions of any kind, including constants, global variables, and function calls, may serve as default values. You may also utilize default parameters with inline functions.

A default argument in C++ is a value that is automatically supplied to a function parameter if no value is provided when the function is called. In the function declaration, default arguments may be given by setting a value to the parameter. The following are instances of C++ methods using default arguments:

```
void printNumbers(int a, int b = 0, int c = 0) {
cout << a << " " << b << " " << c << endl;
}
int main() {
printNumbers(1); // Outputs "1 0 0"
printNumbers(1, 2); // Outputs "1 2 0"
printNumbers(1, 2, 3); // Outputs "1 2 3"
return 0;
}
```

This code provides a function named printNumbers that accepts three integer arguments named a, b, and c. If no value is specified for b and c, their default values are 0.

printNumbers is called three times with distinct arguments inside the main function. When printNumbers is used with a single input, the default values for b and c are 0. When it is invoked with two parameters, the default value for c is 0. When called with three arguments, the values given for all three parameters will be used.

With the cout command, the function outputs all three arguments in each instance, separated by spaces.

```
int add(int x, int y = 1) {
return x + y;
}
int main() {
cout << add(1) << endl; // Outputs "2"
cout << add(1, 2) << endl; // Outputs "3"
return 0;
}
```

This code defines the add function, which accepts two integer parameters and returns their total. The second parameter has a default value of 1, therefore if just one argument is supplied when the function is called, the second argument is considered to be 1.

The add function is called twice in the main function: once with one parameter (1) and once with two arguments (2). (1 and 2). Because the default value of the second parameter is 1, the result of the first call is 2 and the output of the second call is 3. (since both arguments are explicitly provided).

It is important to remember that default arguments must be specified in the function declaration from right to left, meaning that default arguments cannot be used in the middle of the function declaration, but only on the right side. If a function has a default argument in the middle, then all the arguments on the right must also have default values.

More Examples:

```
// default values in functions
#include <iostream>
using namespace std;
int divide(int a, int b = 2)
{
int r;
r = a / b;
return (r);
}
void main()
{
cout << divide(12) << '\n';
cout << divide(20, 4) << '\n';
system("pause");
}
```

This code explains the usage of a function's default argument. a and b are the two integer arguments for the division function. If b is not specified when the function is called, its default value is 2. The function returns the division result of a by b.

The division function is called twice in the main function, once with one parameter and once with two arguments. The value of b is set to 2 and the function returns the result of dividing a by 2 when called with a single parameter. When the function is used with two inputs, it returns the result of dividing a by b. The output is sent to the console using the cout function.

4.11 FUNCTION OVERLOADING

C++ permits the definition of several functions with the same name, so long as these functions have distinct sets of arguments (at least as far as the parameter types or the number of parameters or the order of the parameter types are concerned). This feature is known as function overloading. The C++ compiler determines the correct function based on the number, types, and order of the call's parameters when an overloaded function is invoked. Often, function overloading is used to construct many functions with the same name that execute comparable operations on distinct data types. Several functions in the math library, for example, support multiple numeric data types.

```
// overloading functions
#include <iostream>
using namespace std;
void operate(int a, int b)
{
cout<< (a*b);
}
```

```
void operate(double a, double b)
{
cout<<(a* b);
}
void main()
{
int x = 5, y = 2;
double n = 5.0, m = 2.3;
operate(x, y);
cout << "\n";
operate(n, m);
cout << "\n";
system("pause");
}
```

The code is an example of function overloading in C++. Two functions with the same name, "operate," but distinct arguments are specified. The first function accepts two integers, whereas the second function accepts two doubles.

x and y are defined as integers and initialized to 5 and 2, respectively, in the main function. n and m are also specified as doubles and initialized to 5.0 and 2.3, respectively.

The function operate is called twice with different arguments in the main function. It is called the first time with two integers and the second time with two doubles. The result will be the product of the two input parameters.

4.12 RECURSION

A **recursive function** is a function that directly or indirectly invokes itself. Recursive problem-solving strategies share a number of characteristics. Calling a recursive function to solve a problem. The function truly only understands how to tackle the simplest cases, or **base case (s).** If the function is invoked with a base case, it produces a simple result. If the function is invoked with a more sophisticated issue, it will often partition the problem into two conceptual parts: one that the function can handle and one that it cannot. For recursion to be practical, the final component must resemble the original issue, but be significantly simpler or smaller. This is referred to as a **recursive call** and is also known as the **recursion phase.** The function launches a new copy of itself to work on the smaller issue. Often, the recursion stage contains the term return, since its result will be merged with the piece of the issue that the function has solved to generate a solution that will be returned to the original caller, presumably main.

The recursion step runs while the initial function call is still active, i.e. it has not yet completed running. The recursion stage might result in several further recursive calls, as the function continues to divide each new sub-problem into two conceptual components. Each time the function calls itself with a somewhat simplified form of the original issue, this succession of smaller and smaller problems must finally converge on the base case for the recursion to eventually stop. At that point, the function identifies the base case and returns a result to the previous copy of the function, followed by a series of returns up the line until the original function call gives the ultimate result to main.

Using recursive functions to solve problems that can be broken into similar subproblems. Recursive functions are very useful for addressing issues with a recurring or intrinsically recursive structure, such as traversing a tree or calculating the factorial. The following are examples of recursive C++ functions:

```
int factorial(int n) {
if (n == 0) return 1;
return n * factorial(n - 1);
}
int main() {
cout << factorial(5) << endl; // Outputs "120"
return 0;
}
```

The code provides a factorial function that accepts an integer n as input and returns the factorial of n. The recursion's base case occurs when n equals 0, in which case the function returns 1. If not, the function multiplies n by the result of executing factorial(n-1) which recursively calculates the factorial of n-1. The main function calls factorial with 5 as an argument and outputs 120.

```
void printNumbers(int n) {
if (n == 0) return;
cout << n << " ";
printNumbers(n - 1);
}
int main() {
printNumbers(5); // Outputs "5 4 3 2 1 "
return 0;
}
```

The program creates the recursive function printNumbers(), which accepts an integer parameter n. The function displays n, decrements n by 1, and then runs itself recursively with n's new value. The function terminates when n equals 0.

In the main() function, the printNumbers(5) command is invoked, prompting the program to print the numbers 5, 4, 3, 2, and 1 sequentially before terminating.

Importantly, recursive functions must include a base case that finally terminates the recursion; otherwise, the recursion would continue endlessly and cause a stack overflow problem.

4.12.1 Recursion vs. Iteration

Iteration and recursion are both dependent on a control statement. Iteration employs a structure of repetition, whereas recursion employs a framework of selection. Iteration and recursion are both forms of repetition: Iteration employs a repeating structure directly, while recursion accomplishes repetition through repeated function calls. Both iteration and recursion need a termination test: Iteration ends when the condition for loop continuation fails; recursion ends when a base case is identified. Iteration with counter-controlled repetition and recursion both approach completion in a progressive manner: Iteration updates a counter until the counter reaches a value that causes the loop-continuation condition to fail; recursion generates progressively simplified variants of the original issue until the base case is reached.

Both infinite repetition and recursion are possible: An endless loop happens if the loop-continuation condition never becomes false; an infinite recursion arises if the recursion step does not decrease the issue during each recursive call in a way that converges on the base case.

Recursion has several drawbacks. It frequently employs the mechanism and, hence, the burden of function calls. This may be costly in terms of both CPU time and memory space. Each recursive call creates a new copy of the function (really, simply the function's variables), which might take a significant amount of memory. Iteration often happens inside a function, eliminating the need for repeated function calls and unnecessary memory allocation.

More Examples:

```
//*A recursive function is a function that calls itself, either directly, or
indirectly_ Recursivity is the
//property that functions have to be called by themselves. It is useful for
some tasks, such as sorting elements,
//or calculating the factorial of numbers. For example, in order to obtain the
factorial of a number (n!) the mathematical
//formula would be:__n! = n * (n-1) * (n-2) * (n-3) ... * 1 _More concretely,
// 5! (factorial of 5) would be:__5! = 5 * 4 * 3 * 2 * 1 = 120 _And a recur-
sive function to calculate this in C++ could be:*/
// factorial calculator
#include <iostream>
using namespace std;
int factorial(int a)
{
if (a > 1)
return (a * factorial(a - 1));
else return 1;
}
void main()
{
int number = 5;
cout << number << "! = " << factorial(number) << endl;
system("pause");
}
```

This software uses recursion to determine the factorial of an integer. The factorial() function accepts an integer argument and returns the number's factorial. When an equals 1, the function returns 1. This is the fundamental case of the recursion. If not, the function multiplies a by the result of running factorial() with the argument a-1. The main function sets the value of a variable to 5, calls factorial(number) to compute the factorial of 5, and then returns the result. Since 5! (5 factorial) is equivalent to 120, the result would be "5! = 120."

//*A recursive function is a function that calls itself, either directly, or indirectly_ Recursivity is the property that functions have to be called by themselves. It is useful for some tasks, such as sorting elements, or calculating the factorial of numbers. For example, in order to obtain the factorial of a number (n!) the mathematical

```
//formula would be:__n! = n * (n-1) * (n-2) * (n-3) ... * 1 _More concretely,
// 5! (factorial of 5) would be:__5! = 5 * 4 * 3 * 2 * 1 = 120 _And a recur-
sive function to calculate this in C++ could be:*/
//
//
// factorial calculator
#include <iostream>
using namespace std;
long factorial(int a)
{
if (a > 1)
return (a * factorial(a - 1));
else return 1;
}
void main()
{
int number = 3;
cout << number << "! = " << factorial(number)<<endl;
system ("pause");
}
```

This code provides a factorial function that accepts an integer parameter a and calculates its factorial recursively. If the input is more than one, the if statement multiplies it by the result of executing factorial with a-1. If an is less than or equal to 1, the method returns 1.

The main function declares and initializes an integer variable with the value 3. Then, it executes the factorial function with number as its parameter and outputs number! = factorial (number). Before ending, the software waits for the user to touch a key.

4.12.2 So Why Choose Recursion?

Each issue solvable recursively may also be solved iteratively (non-recursively). A recursive technique is often preferred over an iterative approach when the recursive approach replicates the issue more naturally and produces a program that is simpler to comprehend and debug. An further argument to choose a recursive solution is because an iterative solution is not obvious.

4.13 STORAGE CLASSES

Variable names in the programs you have seen so far are represented by identifiers. Variable properties include name, type, size, and value. In reality, each identifier in a program has additional properties, such as **storage class**, **scope**, and **linkage**.

Five storage-class specifiers are available in C++: auto, register, extern, mutable, and static. This section addresses auto, register, extern, and static storage-class specifiers.

Class of Storage, Scope, and Connection

The storage class of an identifier controls how long that identifier lives in memory. Some identifiers persist temporarily, while others are constantly produced and deleted during the duration of a program's execution. This section examines static and automated storage classes.

The scope of an identifier indicates where it may be referenced inside a program. Certain identifiers may be referenced throughout a program, whereas others can only be referenced from specific sections.

The linkage of an identifier controls whether it is solely known in the source file where it is declared or across many files that are compiled and then linked together. The storage-class specifier of an identifier helps define its storage class and linkage.

Storage Classifications

The storage-class specifiers may be divided into two classes: automated and static. Declaring variables of the automatic storage class using the keywords auto and register. These variables are generated when the program enters the block in which they are defined, exist while the block is active, and are removed when the program departs the block.

Local Variables

A local variable is a variable defined inside a function or block. Local variables are only available inside the defined scope and are discarded when the scope is quit. Here's an example of a local variable in C++:

```
void printHello() {
int x = 5; // local variable
cout << "Hello, World! " << x << endl;
}
int main() {
printHello();
// cout << x; // Error: x is not defined in this scope
return 0;
}
```

The program creates the printHello() method that outputs a message and the local variable x with the value 5. The main() method then invokes the printHello() function. A commented-out line attempts to access x outside of its scope, which would result in an error.

A local variable is a variable declared inside a function that can only be accessed within the scope of that function. In this instance, the variable x is declared inside the printHello() function and cannot be accessed outside of it.

Note that local variables are different from global variables, which are declared outside of any function and have a global scope, allowing access from anywhere in the program.

Automatic storage class may only be used for local variables inside a function. Local variables and parameters are often of the automatic storage kind. The storage class specifier auto specifies variables as belonging to the automatic storage class. For instance, the following declaration specifies that the double variables x and y are local variables of automatic storage class and exist only inside the closest pair of enclosing curly braces within the body of the function where the definition appears:

```
auto double x, y;
```

Local variables are by default of the automatic storage type, hence the term auto is seldom used. Variables with automatic storage class will be referred to as automatic variables for the duration of the book.

Example:

```
//*Scopes (local & Global variables)_block scope*/
// inner block scopes
#include <iostream>
using namespace std;
void main()
{
int x = 10;
int y = 20;
{
int x; // ok, inner scope.
x = 50; // sets value to inner x
y = 50; // sets value to (outer) y
cout << "inner block:\n";
cout << "x: " << x << '\n';
cout << "y: " << y << '\n';
}
cout << "outer block:\n";
cout << "x: " << x << '\n';
cout << "y: " << y << '\n';
system("pause");
}
```

This code illustrates the variable scope notion in C++. In the main function, the variables x and y are assigned respective values of 10 and 20. Then, using curly brackets, an inner block is formed, and a new variable, x, is declared inside the inner block. This is permitted because the inner block has a distinct scope than the outer block, and variables in the outer block cannot be accessed from inside the inner block.

The value of x is set to 50 inside the inner block, which modifies the value of the inner x variable. The value of y is also set to 50 within the inner block, which modifies the value of the outer y variable since it is in the same scope as the outer block.

The outer block continues processing after the inner block is exited, and the values of x and y are written both within and outside the inner block to indicate that the values of the variables have changed solely inside their respective scopes.

Using NameSpace

A namespace is a container in C++ that contains identifiers (such as variable names, function names, and class names) and makes them accessible for usage in your program. Namespaces are used to avoid name collisions and organize code. A namespace scope is the portion of a program from which identifiers specified in a namespace may be accessible.

This is an example of namespace scope use in C++:

```
#include <iostream>
using namespace std;
namespace MyNamespace {
int x = 5;
void printHello() {
cout << "Hello, World! " << x << endl;
}
}
int main() {
cout << MyNamespace::x << endl; // Outputs "5"
MyNamespace::printHello(); // Outputs "Hello, World! 5"
return 0;
}
```

This code explains namespace use in C++. The MyNamespace namespace is constructed, including the variable x with the value 5 and the method printHello(), which prints a message to the terminal along with the value of the x variable. The x variable is accessed in the main() method using the namespace notation MyNamespace::x, and the printHello() function is invoked using MyNamespace::printHello() (). This enables the usage of the same names in several namespaces without conflict.

Notably, you may also use the using directive to import all identifiers from a namespace into the current scope, as follows:

```
#include <iostream>
namespace MyNamespace {
int x = 5;
void printHello() {
cout << "Hello, World! " << x << endl;
}
}
using namespace MyNamespace;
int main() {
cout << x << endl; // Outputs "5"
printHello(); // Outputs "Hello, World! 5"
return 0;
}
```

This code explains namespace use in C++. The code establishes a namespace named MyNamespace that includes the variable x initialized to 5 and the method printHello() that emits "Hello, World!" along with the value of x. In the main function, the using directive is used to bring all the names from the MyNamespace namespace into scope, allowing immediate access to the variable x and the method printHello() without the need to declare the namespace. The program then prints the value of x and executes the printHello() method, which both use variables and functions from the MyNamespace namespace.

In this situation, the scope resolution operator:: is not required to access identifiers from the MyNamespace namespace.

A namespace scope is the region of a program where the identifiers defined in a namespace can be accessed. Namespaces are used to avoid naming conflicts and organize code.

Example:

```
// using namespace example
#include <iostream>
using namespace std;
namespace first
{
int x = 5;
}
namespace second
{
double x = 3.1416;
}
void main()
{
{
using namespace first;
cout << x << '\n';
}
{
using namespace second;
cout << x << '\n';
}
system("pause");
}
```

This application shows the usage of C++ namespaces. First and second namespaces, each having a variable x, are defined by the program. The main function then employs the using directive to designate which namespace following code blocks should use.

The first code block's using directive says that the first namespace should be utilized, therefore the cout statement outputs the value of first::x (which is 5).

The second code block uses the second namespace, as specified by the using directive, thus the cout statement outputs the value of second::x (3,1416) to the console.

The application then utilizes a system feature to halt the console output so the user may see the findings.

Register Variables

Typically, data is put into registers in the machine-language version of a program for calculations and other processing.

A compiler may disregard register declarations. For instance, there may not be enough registers available for the compiler to use. The following definition advises that the integer variable counter be placed in one of the computer's registers; counter is initialized to 1 regardless of whether the compiler performs this:

register int counter =1 ;

Register may only be used with local variables and function arguments.

4.14 STATIC STORAGE CLASS

The keywords extern and static define identifiers for variables and functions belonging to the static storage type. Variables of the static-storage-class exist from the moment program execution starts and persist for the length of the program. Storage for a variable of type static-storage is allocated when the program starts execution. Such a variable is initialized once upon encountering its declaration. Like with other functions, the name of the function exists prior to program execution for functions. Despite the fact that variable and function names exist from the beginning of program execution, this does not imply that these identifiers may be utilized throughout the program.

Identifiers with Class of Static Storage

External identifiers (such as **global variables** and global function names) and local variables declared with the storage class specifier static are the two forms of identifiers with static storage class. Create global variables by declaring variables outside of any class or function definition. Global variables maintain their values during the program's execution. Any function that follows their declarations or definitions in the source file may access global variables and global functions.

Unlike automatic variables, static local variables preserve their values when the function returns to its caller. The next time the function is invoked, the static local variable is evaluated.

Variables store the values they held when the last function was executed. The sentence below defines the local variable count to be static and initialized to 1:

```
static int count = 1;
```

All numeric variables of the static storage class are initialized to zero if they are not explicitly initialized by the programmer; nevertheless, it is recommended that all variables be explicitly initialized.

The static keyword is used to define static variables, functions, and class members. The term static has several meanings based on its context of usage.

A static variable is a shared variable across all instances of a class or function. Its value is only initialized once and is saved in static storage. The value of the static variable is preserved between function calls.

```
#include <iostream>
using namespace std;
void func() {
static int x = 0; // static variable
```

```
x++;
cout << x << endl;
}
int main() {
func(); // Outputs "1"
func(); // Outputs "2"
func(); // Outputs "3"
return 0;
}
```

In this code, the static variable x is initialized to 0 before func() is declared. x is increased by 1 and its value is sent to the console using cout whenever func() is executed. The static keyword in this situation indicates that the value of x is maintained between invocations of func ().

When main() is invoked, func() is called three times consecutively, causing the console to report 1, 2, and 3. If x were not specified as static, its value would be reset to 0 each time func() was invoked, resulting in the output of 1, 1, and 1.

A static function is a function that is shared by all instances of a class and has no access to non-static class members. It can only access static class members.

```
class MyClass {
static int x;
public:
static void setX(int value) {
x = value;
}
static int getX() {
return x;
}
};
int MyClass::x = 0; // static variable
int main() {
MyClass::setX(5);
cout << MyClass::getX() << endl; // Outputs "5"
return 0;
}
```

The code establishes a class named MyClass that has a static integer variable named x. The setX and getX methods are also static, meaning they may be used without instantiating an instance of the MyClass class.

The setX method is used in the main function to set the value of x to 5, and then the getX method is invoked to obtain the value of x, which is printed to the console.

Outside of the class declaration, the static variable x is initialized to 0 and is shared by all instances of the MyClass class.

4.15 TEMPLATE FUNCTION

Several data types may be accommodated using a template function. With templates, one may design general functions that can be used with many sorts of data without having to write individual functions for each type. The template keyword is followed by angle brackets > that hold the template type argument to define a template (s).

Here is a template function example in C++:

```
template <typename T>
T add(T a, T b) {
return a + b;
}
int main() {
cout << add(1, 2) << endl; // Outputs "3"
cout << add(1.5, 2.5) << endl; // Outputs "4"
return 0;
}
```

This demonstrates a C++ function template. The template specifies an add function that accepts two parameters of the same type T and returns the result. The function is compatible with all types that support the + operator, including int, double, and any user-defined type that overloads the + operator.

The add function is called twice with distinct types in the main function: once with integers and once with doubles. The function automatically determines the kinds of the arguments based on the types of the given values. With the cout command, the output of each call is shown on the console.

It is essential to remember that when you call a template function, the compiler will produce a particular version of the function based on the kinds of parameters supplied to it at the call site. This process is known as template instantiation.

Example:

```
// function template
#include <iostream>
using namespace std;
template <class T> T sum(T a, T b)
{
T result;
result = a + b;
return result;
}
void main()
{
int i = 5, L = 6, k;
double f = 2.0, g = 0.5, h;
k = sum<int>(i, L);
h = sum<double>(f, g);
```

```
cout << k << "\n"; cout << h << "\n";
system("pause");
}
```

This application shows the use of a C++ function template. The template function sum returns the sum of two inputs of the same data type T. The function accepts parameters of several data types, including int, double, float, etc.

In the main function, two int and double variables are defined and given values. The sum function is called twice with these variables as inputs, the first time with I and L and the second time with f and g. The resulting values are allocated to the variables k and h before being reported to the console using the cout command. Before terminating, the application waits to await human input.

Advanced Practice Exercises With Answers

Example 1: Custom Math Library

Objective: Demonstrate how to declare, define, and call functions in C++ for basic arithmetic operations.

```
#include <iostream>
using namespace std;

// Function declarations
double add(double a, double b);
double subtract(double a, double b);
double multiply(double a, double b);
double divide(double a, double b);

int main() {
    // Function calls
    cout << "Addition: " << add(5, 3) << endl;
    cout << "Subtraction: " << subtract(5, 3) << endl;
    cout << "Multiplication: " << multiply(5, 3) << endl;
    cout << "Division: " << divide(5, 3) << endl;
    return 0;
}

// Function definitions
double add(double a, double b) { return a + b; }
double subtract(double a, double b) { return a - b; }
double multiply(double a, double b) { return a * b; }
double divide(double a, double b) { return b != 0 ? a / b: 0; }
```

Explanation:

This C++ program defines a simple calculator that performs basic arithmetic operations: addition, subtraction, multiplication, and division. It demonstrates function declarations, function calls, and function definitions. Here's a breakdown of how the program works:

Function Declarations:

Before the **main** function, the program declares four functions: **add**, **subtract**, **multiply**, and **divide**. Each function takes two **double** arguments (**a** and **b**) and returns a **double**. These declarations tell the compiler about the existence and signature of these functions, allowing them to be called before they are defined.

Main Function:

- The **main** function contains calls to each of the arithmetic functions with **5** and **3** as arguments.
- It outputs the results of these operations to the console using **cout**.

Function Definitions:

After the **main** function, the program provides the definitions for the previously declared functions:

- **add**: Returns the sum of **a** and **b**.
- **subtract**: Returns the result of subtracting **b** from **a**.
- **multiply**: Returns the product of **a** and **b**.
- **divide**: Returns the result of dividing **a** by **b**. It includes a check to avoid division by zero, returning **0** if **b** is **0**.

Output:
Addition: 8
Subtraction: 2
Multiplication: 15
Division: 1.66667

Key Concepts Illustrated:

- **Function Declaration and Definition**: The program separates the declaration of functions (informing the compiler about the function's existence) from their definition (providing the actual implementation).
- **Arithmetic Operations**: The implementation of basic arithmetic operations as separate functions.
- **Handling Division by Zero**: The **divide** function demonstrates a simple error-checking mechanism to prevent division by zero, a common issue in arithmetic operations.

This example serves as a basic introduction to functions in C++, illustrating how to organize code into reusable blocks that perform specific tasks, improving readability and maintainability.

Program 2: Inline Square Function

Objective: Demonstrate the use and benefits of inline functions in C++.

```
#include <iostream>
using namespace std;

// Inline function declaration and definition
inline double square(double x) { return x * x; }

int main() {
    double number = 4.0;
    // Inline function call
    cout << "Square of " << number << " is " << square(number) << "." << endl;
    return 0;
}
```

Explanation:

This C++ program demonstrates the use of an inline function to calculate the square of a number. Inline functions are a feature in C++ that instructs the compiler to insert the complete body of the function wherever the function is called, rather than using a traditional function call. This can potentially reduce the overhead of a function call, especially in small, frequently called functions. Here's how the program works:

Inline Function square:

- Defined with the **inline** keyword before the function return type, suggesting to the compiler that the function body should be expanded inline where the function is called.
- Takes a single argument **x** of type **double** and returns the square of **x** (i.e., **x * x**).

Main Function:

- Initializes a **double** variable **number** with the value **4.0**.
- Calls the **square** function with **number** as its argument and prints the result.
- The **square** function is called inline, meaning the expression **x * x** replaces the function call in the compiled code, which in this context calculates **4.0 * 4.0**.

Output:

csharpCopy code

Square of 4 is 16.

Key Concepts Illustrated:

- **Inline Functions**: Intended to optimize performance by eliminating the overhead associated with function calls. They are most beneficial for small, frequently used functions.
- **Function Calls**: The process of executing a function by passing control and parameters (if any) from a caller to a function for execution and then returning the control back to the caller.
- **Compilation and Optimization**: The compiler decides whether to inline a function based on various factors, including the function's complexity and the specific optimizations enabled during

compilation. Despite the **inline** keyword, the compiler might choose not to inline a function if it determines inlining wouldn't be beneficial.

This example effectively showcases the simplicity and potential performance benefits of inline functions for small, straightforward operations like calculating the square of a number.

Program 3: Recursive Function - Factorial

Objective: Show how to write a recursive function to calculate the factorial of a number.

```
#include <iostream>
using namespace std;

// Recursive function declaration and definition
unsigned long long factorial(unsigned int n) {
    if (n == 0) return 1; // Base case
    else return n * factorial(n - 1); // Recursive case
}

int main() {
    unsigned int number = 5;
    cout << "Factorial of " << number << " is " << factorial(number) << "." <<
endl;
    return 0;
}
```

Explanation:

This C++ program calculates the factorial of a number using recursion, illustrating how a function can call itself to solve a problem in smaller increments. Here's a detailed explanation:

Recursive Function factorial:

- **Base Case**: When **n** is 0, the function returns 1. This is a critical aspect of recursion, providing a condition under which the function will stop calling itself, thus preventing infinite recursion.
- **Recursive Case**: For any other value of **n**, the function returns **n** multiplied by the result of calling itself with **n - 1**. This effectively breaks down the factorial calculation into smaller problems (e.g., **5 * factorial(4)**, **4 * factorial(3)**, etc.) until it reaches the base case.

Main Function:

- An unsigned integer **number** is initialized with the value 5, representing the number for which the factorial is to be calculated.
- The program then calls the **factorial** function with **number** as an argument and outputs the result.

- The use of an **unsigned int** for **number** and **unsigned long long** for the return type of **factorial** ensures that the program can handle large factorial values without negative overflow, although it's still limited by the maximum value that **unsigned long long** can hold.

Output:
For the input value of 5, the output of the program will be:
Factorial of 5 is 120.
Key Concepts Illustrated:

- **Recursion**: The process by which a function calls itself directly or indirectly. It's a powerful tool for solving problems that can be divided into similar sub-problems.
- **Base Case**: Essential for stopping recursion. Without it, the function would call itself indefinitely, leading to a stack overflow error.
- **Factorial Calculation**: An example of a problem well-suited for recursion since each step of the calculation depends on the result of the previous step, down to the base case of **factorial(0)**.

This program demonstrates recursion's elegance and simplicity for problems like factorial calculation, where each step's complexity is reduced until a simple, known result is reached.

Program 4: Function Templates for Swapping

Objective: Illustrate the use of function templates to create a generic swapping mechanism.

```
#include <iostream>
using namespace std;

// Function template declaration and definition
template <typename T>
void swapValues(T& a, T& b) {
    T temp = a;
    a = b;
    b = temp;
}

int main() {
    int i = 10, j = 20;
    cout << "Before swap: i = " << i << ", j = " << j << endl;
    swapValues(i, j);
    cout << "After swap: i = " << i << ", j = " << j << endl;
    return 0;
}
```

Explanation:

This C++ program illustrates the use of a template function to swap the values of two variables. Function templates are a powerful feature in C++ that allow you to write a single function that can operate on different data types. Here's how this program works:

Function Template for swapValues:

- **Template Declaration**: The program begins with the declaration of a template function **swapValues** using the **template** keyword followed by a type parameter **T** within angle brackets. **T** serves as a placeholder that will be replaced by a concrete data type when the function is instantiated.
- **Function Definition**: The **swapValues** function takes two references (**T&**) as parameters, allowing the function to modify the variables passed to it directly. It uses a temporary variable **temp** of type **T** to hold the value of **a** while **a** is assigned the value of **b**, and then **b** is assigned the value stored in **temp**. This effectively swaps the values of **a** and **b**.

Main Function:

- The **main** function demonstrates the usage of the **swapValues** template function with two integer variables, **i** and **j**, initialized to 10 and 20, respectively.
- Before the swap operation, the initial values of **i** and **j** are printed to the console.
- The **swapValues** function is called with **i** and **j** as arguments. Since **i** and **j** are integers, the template parameter **T** is deduced to be **int**, and the compiler generates an instantiation of the **swapValues** function for integer arguments.
- After the swap operation, the updated values of **i** and **j** are printed, showing that their values have been exchanged.
- The program ends with the values of **i** and **j** swapped, demonstrating the flexibility and utility of template functions in performing operations on various data types using a single function definition.

Output:

Before swap: i = 10, j = 20

After swap: i = 20, j = 10

This example highlights the power of C++ template functions to write generic, type-independent code that can operate on various data types, making the code more reusable and reducing duplication.

Program 5: Function Overloading - Area Calculation

Objective: Use function overloading to calculate the area of different geometric shapes (circle and rectangle).

```
#include <iostream>
using namespace std;

// Function overloading for area calculation
double area(double radius) {
    return 3.14159 * radius * radius; // Circle area
```

```
}

double area(double length, double width) {
    return length * width; // Rectangle area
}

int main() {
    cout << "Area of circle (radius = 5): " << area(5) << endl;
    cout << "Area of rectangle (length = 4, width = 5): " << area(4, 5) <<
endl;
    return 0;
}
```

This C++ program demonstrates the concept of function overloading, which allows multiple functions to have the same name but different parameters. The program includes two overloaded versions of the **area** function: one that calculates the area of a circle given its radius and another that calculates the area of a rectangle given its length and width.

Function Overloading Explained

- **double area(double radius)**: This version of the **area** function calculates the area of a circle. It takes a single **double** parameter representing the radius of the circle. The area of the circle is calculated using the formula πr^2, where π is approximated as 3.14159.
- **double area(double length, double width)**: This version calculates the area of a rectangle. It takes two **double** parameters representing the length and width of the rectangle, respectively. The area of the rectangle is calculated using the formula length × width.

Main Function:

- The **main** function demonstrates the use of both overloaded versions of the **area** function:
- First, it calls the circle version of **area** with a radius of **5**, and prints the calculated area of the circle.
- Next, it calls the rectangle version of **area** with a length of **4** and a width of **5**, and prints the calculated area of the rectangle.

Output:

- The program outputs the area of a circle with a radius of 5 units and the area of a rectangle with length 4 units and width 5 units. The use of function overloading makes it possible to use a single function name (**area**) for different area calculations, improving code readability and organization.

Key Concepts Illustrated:

- **Function Overloading**: The ability to have multiple functions with the same name in the same scope, differentiated by their parameter lists. The correct function to be called is determined at compile time based on the arguments passed to the function.
- **Code Readability and Reusability**: Function overloading allows similar operations that apply to different types or numbers of arguments to be grouped under a single function name, making the code more readable and easier to manage.

This example effectively showcases how function overloading can be used in C++ to create more intuitive and flexible interfaces for performing similar operations on different types of data or configurations.

Program 6: Pass-By-Reference vs. Pass-By-Value

Objective: Demonstrate the difference between passing parameters by value and by reference

```
#include <iostream>
using namespace std;

void incrementByValue(int value) {
    value += 1;
}

void incrementByReference(int& value) {
    value += 1;
}

int main() {
    int a = 5;
    incrementByValue(a);
    cout << "After incrementByValue: " << a << endl; // Output: 5
    incrementByReference(a);
    cout << "After incrementByReference: " << a << endl; // Output: 6
    return 0;
}
```

Explanation

This C++ program demonstrates the difference between passing parameters by value and by reference. It defines two functions, **incrementByValue** and **incrementByReference**, each intending to increment the provided argument by 1. The main distinction between these functions is how they receive their argument, affecting the original variable passed from the **main** function.

Function Explanations:

- **incrementByValue(int value)**: This function takes an integer argument by value, meaning it works with a copy of the original value passed to it. When **value** is incremented inside the function, only the copy is modified, leaving the original variable in the calling environment unchanged. This is why the value of **a** remains **5** after **incrementByValue** is called.
- **incrementByReference(int& value)**: In contrast, this function accepts its argument by reference, using **&** next to the parameter type. It directly works on the original variable passed from the caller. As a result, when **value** is incremented inside this function, the change is reflected in the original variable **a** in the **main** function, updating its value to **6**.

Main Function:

- An integer **a** is initialized with the value **5**.
- **incrementByValue(a)** is called first, intending to increase **a** by 1. However, since the argument is passed by value, **a** remains unchanged, demonstrating that changes made to the parameter within the function do not affect the original variable.
- **incrementByReference(a)** is then called, successfully incrementing **a** by 1, as the function operates directly on the memory address of **a**. This shows that passing by reference allows functions to modify the original variable.

Key Concepts Illustrated

- **Pass-By-Value**: A method of parameter passing where a copy of the argument is made. Modifications to the parameter within the function do not affect the original argument.
- **Pass-By-Reference**: A method of parameter passing where the function receives a reference to the argument. Changes to the parameter within the function directly modify the original argument.

This example clearly illustrates how the choice between pass-by-value and pass-by-reference impacts the ability of functions to modify the original variables passed to them, a fundamental concept in C++ programming that affects both function design and usage.

Program 7: Default Arguments - Greeting Message

Objective: Illustrate how to use default arguments in functions for customizable greeting messages.

```
#include <iostream>
using namespace std;

void greet(string name, string message = "Hello") {
    cout << message << ", " << name << "!" << endl;
}

int main() {
```

```
    greet("Alice");
    greet("Bob", "Good morning");
    return 0;
}
```

Explanation:

This C++ program demonstrates the use of default arguments in function parameters. It defines a function **greet** that takes two parameters: a **string** named **name** and a **string** named **message**, with "Hello" set as the default value for **message**. The program then calls this function twice in the **main** function, showcasing both the use of the default message and a custom message.

Function Explanation:

- **greet Function**: This function prints a greeting message to the console. The **message** parameter has a default value of "Hello", which means that if the **greet** function is called without specifying a message, "Hello" will be used. The function concatenates the message, a comma, the name, and an exclamation mark to form the greeting, which is then printed to the console.

main Function:

- In the first call to **greet**, it is passed only one argument, "Alice". Since the second parameter (**message**) is not provided, the default value "Hello" is used. The output of this call will be "Hello, Alice!".
- In the second call, **greet** is provided with both parameters: "Bob" for **name** and "Good morning" for **message**. Therefore, the function uses the provided message instead of the default. The output of this call will be "Good morning, Bob!".

Key Concepts Illustrated:

- **Default Arguments**: The program showcases how default arguments can be used to provide default values for function parameters. This feature allows functions to be called with fewer arguments than they are defined to accept, making the functions more flexible and easier to use in various contexts.
- **Function Overloading (implicitly via default arguments)**: While not function overloading in the traditional sense (where multiple functions have the same name but different parameter lists), the use of default arguments allows a single function definition to act like multiple overloads. In this case, **greet** can be called either with one argument or with two, behaving differently based on the number of arguments provided.

This simple yet effective example serves as an excellent demonstration of how default arguments can enhance function flexibility and usability in C++.

Program 8: Recursive vs. Iterative - Fibonacci Sequence

Objective: Compare recursive and iterative approaches to calculating the nth Fibonacci number.

```
#include <iostream>
using namespace std;

// Recursive Fibonacci
int fibonacciRecursive(int n) {
    if (n <= 1) return n;
    return fibonacciRecursive(n - 1) + fibonacciRecursive(n - 2);
}

// Iterative Fibonacci
int fibonacciIterative(int n) {
    if (n <= 1) return n;
    int a = 0, b = 1, sum;
    for (int i = 2; i <= n; i++) {
        sum = a + b;
        a = b;
        b = sum;
    }
    return b;
}

int main() {
    int term = 10;
    cout << "Recursive Fibonacci (" << term << "): " <<
fibonacciRecursive(term) << endl;
    cout << "Iterative Fibonacci (" << term << "): " <<
fibonacciIterative(term) << endl;
    return 0;
}
```

Explanation:

This C++ program provides two different implementations for calculating the nth Fibonacci number: a recursive approach and an iterative approach. Both methods are defined to showcase their differences in logic and performance.

Recursive Fibonacci

- The recursive version, **fibonacciRecursive**, takes an integer **n** as its argument.
- It checks if **n** is less than or equal to 1, in which case **n** itself is returned, as the first two Fibonacci numbers are defined as 0 and 1.
- For all other cases, it returns the sum of the two preceding numbers in the sequence by calling itself with **n-1** and **n-2**.
- This implementation demonstrates recursion, where a function calls itself to break down the problem into smaller instances.

Iterative Fibonacci

- The iterative version, **fibonacciIterative**, also accepts an integer **n**.
- It similarly checks if **n** is less than or equal to 1, returning **n** directly for these base cases.
- For higher values of **n**, it initializes two variables, **a** and **b**, to represent the first two Fibonacci numbers. A **sum** variable is used to store the sum of **a** and **b**, representing the next Fibonacci number.
- A for-loop iterates from 2 to **n**, updating **a** and **b** in each iteration to move through the Fibonacci sequence until the nth number is calculated.
- This method highlights an iterative approach, utilizing loops to achieve the result without the overhead of recursive function calls.

Main Function

- The **main** function tests both the recursive and iterative implementations by calculating the 10th Fibonacci number with each method.
- It outputs the results of both calculations, showing the same result obtained through two different approaches.

Discussion

- This program effectively demonstrates two fundamental programming techniques for solving the same problem. The recursive method is elegant and closely matches the mathematical definition of the Fibonacci sequence but can be less efficient for large values of **n** due to repeated calculations and greater function call overhead. The iterative approach is typically more efficient, especially for large **n**, as it avoids the overhead of recursive calls and uses a simple loop to reach the result.

Choosing between these two approaches depends on the specific requirements of the problem at hand, including considerations for readability, performance, and the limitations of recursion depth.

Program 9: Inline Functions - Performance Comparison

Objective: Demonstrate the use of inline functions to potentially increase performance by comparing execution time with a non-inline version of the same function.

```
#include <iostream>
#include <chrono>
using namespace std;

// Inline function
inline long long inlineSum(long long n) {
    return n * (n + 1) / 2;
}
```

```
// Non-inline function
long long nonInlineSum(long long n) {
    return n * (n + 1) / 2;
}

int main() {
    auto startInline = chrono::high_resolution_clock::now();
    cout << "Inline sum: " << inlineSum(1000000) << endl;
    auto stopInline = chrono::high_resolution_clock::now();
    auto durationInline = chrono::duration_cast<chrono::microseconds>(stopInli
ne - startInline);

    auto startNonInline = chrono::high_resolution_clock::now();
    cout << "Non-inline sum: " << nonInlineSum(1000000) << endl;
    auto stopNonInline = chrono::high_resolution_clock::now();
    auto durationNonInline = chrono::duration_cast<chrono::microseconds>(stopN
onInline - startNonInline);

    cout << "Inline function duration: " << durationInline.count() << " micro-
seconds" << endl;
    cout << "Non-inline function duration: " << durationNonInline.count() << "
microseconds" << endl;

    return 0;
}
```

Explanation:

This C++ program is designed to compare the execution time of an inline function versus a non-inline function. Both functions perform the same task of calculating the sum of all integers from 1 to n, where n is a large number, in this case, 1,000,000. The goal is to observe any performance differences between using inline and non-inline functions for the same calculation. Here's a detailed breakdown:

Functions:

- **Inline Function inlineSum**: Defined with the **inline** keyword, suggesting to the compiler that it should attempt to embed the function's code at each point of call to reduce the function call overhead.
- **Non-inline Function nonInlineSum**: A regular function without the **inline** keyword. It will be called in the usual manner, which involves the overhead of a function call each time it is used.

Main Function:

- **Timing the Inline Function**:
- A high-resolution clock (**chrono::high_resolution_clock**) is used to capture the start time before calling **inlineSum**.

- After calling **inlineSum** with **n = 1,000,000**, the stop time is captured.
- The duration of the inline function call is calculated by subtracting the start time from the stop time and converting the result to microseconds.
- **Timing the Non-inline Function**:
- Similarly, the program captures start and stop times around the call to **nonInlineSum** with the same argument (**n = 1,000,000**).
- The duration for the non-inline function call is calculated in the same manner as for the inline function.

Output:

- The program prints the result of the sum calculation for both the inline and non-inline function calls to ensure both functions perform the same calculation and to verify correctness.
- It then prints the execution duration in microseconds for both the inline and non-inline function calls.

Observations:

- This program illustrates how inline functions can potentially offer performance benefits by eliminating the overhead associated with regular function calls. However, the actual performance gain depends on various factors, including the compiler's optimization capabilities and the complexity of the function being inlined.
- For simple functions like the sum calculation presented here, inline functions can lead to noticeable performance improvements. For more complex functions, the benefits of inlining might be less clear and depend on the specific context and compiler optimizations.

It's important to note that the **inline** keyword is more of a suggestion than a command. The compiler ultimately decides whether to inline a function based on its internal heuristics and optimization criteria.

Program 10: Using Function Templates for Generic Operations

Objective: Create a function template to perform a generic comparison operation between two values of any type (where comparison is valid).

```
#include <iostream>
using namespace std;

// Function template for comparison
template <typename T>
T max(T a, T b) {
    return a > b ? a: b;
}

int main() {
```

```
    cout << "Max of 5 and 10: " << max(5, 10) << endl;
    cout << "Max of 5.5 and 2.3: " << max(5.5, 2.3) << endl;
    cout << "Max of 'a' and 'z': " << max('a', 'z') << endl;

    return 0;
}
```

Explanation:

This C++ program showcases the use of function templates to create a generic **max** function that can compare two values of any type (as long as the comparison operation is defined for that type). Here's a breakdown of how the program works:

1. **Function Template Declaration**:
    - The program begins by declaring a function template **max** using the **template** keyword followed by a type parameter **T** in angle brackets. **T** represents a placeholder for any data type.
    - The **max** function takes two parameters **a** and **b** of type **T**. It returns a value of type **T**.
    - Inside the function, a ternary operator (**?:**) is used to compare **a** and **b**. If **a** is greater than **b**, **a** is returned; otherwise, **b** is returned.
2. **Main Function**:
    - In the **main** function, the **max** template function is called three times with different types of arguments to demonstrate its versatility:
    - First, it's called with two integers, **5** and **10**.
    - Next, it's called with two floating-point numbers, **5.5** and **2.3**.
    - Finally, it's called with two characters, **'a'** and **'z'**.
3. **Output**:
    - For each call, the program outputs the larger of the two values compared. This illustrates that the **max** function template can work seamlessly across different data types, thanks to the power of C++ templates.

This example effectively demonstrates how function templates enable writing flexible, generic code that can operate on various data types, enhancing code reusability and maintainability.

SUMMARY

Chapter 4, titled "Functions," embarks on a comprehensive journey into the realm of modular programming in C++, emphasizing the critical role of functions. This chapter begins with an introduction that underscores the significance of functions in enhancing code modularity, reusability, and clarity, setting the stage for a detailed exploration of this fundamental programming concept.

The narrative progresses to cover function prototypes and argument coercion, introducing the concept of function prototypes as a way to inform the compiler about a function's return type, name, and parameter types. It delves into the nuances of argument coercion, where C++ automatically adjusts argument types to match function parameter types, and discusses function signatures, which are crucial for identifying functions, especially in the context of overloading.

As the chapter unfolds, it meticulously categorizes functions based on their return type and the method of passing arguments, whether by value or by reference, providing a clear understanding of different function behaviors. The concept of scope is explored in depth, using practical examples to demonstrate how variable visibility is managed within a program.

A significant portion of the chapter is dedicated to discussing the distinctions between passing arguments by value and by reference. This discussion highlights how references can be used to avoid unnecessary data copying and allow functions to modify the values of passed arguments. The introduction of default arguments is presented as a means to enhance function flexibility by making some parameters optional.

The power of function overloading is also examined, showcasing how C++ allows multiple functions with the same name to exist, provided they differ in their parameter types or numbers. The chapter then ventures into the intricacies of recursion, comparing it with iteration to highlight scenarios where recursion might offer a more natural or elegant solution to certain problems.

Furthermore, the chapter addresses storage classes, with a focus on the static storage class, offering insights into how variable lifetimes and visibility are crucial for managing states across function calls.

In summary, Chapter 4 provides an in-depth analysis of functions in C++, from their syntax and semantics to their profound impact on programming practices. Through detailed explanations and practical examples, the chapter equips readers with a solid understanding of how to effectively utilize functions in C++, paving the way for mastering more advanced programming concepts.

Multiple Choice

a. In C++, program components are referred to as_____________ and_____________.
b. Invoking a function with a(n)___________________.
c. a(n) denotes a variable that is only known within the function in which it is defined ______________________.
d. The______________ statement inside the called function returns the expression's value to the calling function. This keyword is used in a function header to indicate that a function does not return a value or has no arguments.
e. This keyword __________________is used in a function header to indicate that a function does not return a value or has no arguments.
f. The ________________of an identifier is the section of a program where it may be utilized.
g. There are three methods to return control from a function to its caller:_________,__________ and_________.
h. A(n)________________ enables the compiler to verify the number, types, and order of a function's arguments.
i. The________ function generates random numbers.
j. Function______________is used to establish the random number seed for a program's randomization.
k. The storage-class specifiers k____________,________, and ________are changeable.

Exercises

1- Write a function that accepts input two numbers and returns their total. Test the function by invoking it with different arguments and displaying the output.

2- Write a function that accepts an array of integers and its size and returns the array's biggest member. Test the function by invoking it with various arrays and seeing the output.
3- Write a function that accepts a string as input and returns the string's vowel count. Test the function by invoking it with various string arguments and reporting the output.
4- Develop a recursive function that accepts an integer as input and returns that number's factorial. Test the function by invoking it with various parameters and displaying the output.
5- Write a function that accepts a string and a character as input and returns the character's occurrence count inside the string. Test the function by invoking it with various parameters and displaying the output.
6- Write a function that accepts as input a two-dimensional array and its dimensions and outputs the array's items in spiral order. Test the function by invoking it with various arrays and seeing the output.
7- Develop a template function that accepts two arguments of any type and returns the greater of the two. Test the function by invoking it with inputs and types of varying kinds (e.g., int, double, string).
8- Bank Account Mini Project

NOTE: Minimum requirement to qualify for grading: 1) Code must be properly indented, modularized and follows the best practices.

Accounting Task (A bank account has methods to deposit, withdraw, and check the balance.)

1. There are three primary variables in the program: accountBalance, accountName, and accountNum. Choose suitable data formats for these variables
2. initializes the accountName using the provided option. Random values are assigned to the member variables accountBalance and accountNum (No need to use rand function).
3. The application will have member features with the names menu, withdraw, and deposit.

The withdraw function verifies that adequate funds are available for withdrawal. If true, the balance is decreased by the specified amount; otherwise, an appropriate message indicating insufficient money is shown along with the current balance.

The deposit feature increases the balance by the deposit amount and shows the new balance.

These menu items will be included in the menu function: Check Balance, Deposit Amount, Withdrawal Amount, Exit. Use the proper messages for each choice picked and then call the appropriate function to complete the process.

Output:

Welcome to the Bank Account program

Here is your Initial Account Information:

Account for: Sarah

Account #: 13579

Balance: $1200

****

Menu

****

1. Check Balance
2. Deposit Amount

3. Withdraw Amount
4. Exit

Please make a selection: 8
ERROR: Invalid choice. Please try again !!!
****
Menu
****

1. Check Balance
2. Deposit Amount
3. Withdraw Amount
4. Exit

Please make a selection: 1
Here is the account Information:
Account for: Sarah
Account #: 13579
Balance: $1200
****
Menu
****

1. Check Balance
2. Deposit Amount
3. Withdraw Amount
4. Exit

Please make a selection: 2
Enter the amount you want to deposit: 50
Depositing $50 to Acc# 13579
Your new balance is now $1250

9- Write a C++ function prototype for a function named **transform**, which takes an integer array and its size as arguments and returns void. Implement this function to double the value of each element in the array.

10- Demonstrate argument coercion by defining a function **printNumber** that takes a float argument but is called with an integer. Observe how C++ coerces the integer to a float.

11- Create two functions with the same name **process** but different signatures—one that takes an integer and another that takes a double. Demonstrate function overloading by calling both versions from **main**().

12- Write a program that defines a global variable and a local variable with the same name in a function. Inside the function, use both the global and the local variable to demonstrate the scope rules.

13- Illustrate the difference between pass-by-value and pass-by-reference by writing two functions that attempt to modify an argument, one with a value parameter and the other with a reference parameter.
14- Define a function **greet** that takes two arguments: a string name and an integer representing the number of times to print the greeting. Make the second argument a default parameter with the value **1**.
15- Write overloaded functions named **sum** that compute the sum of two numbers. The functions should be capable of handling integer, double, and float pairs, respectively.
16- Implement a recursive function **factorial** that calculates the factorial of a given number. Compare its execution time with an iterative version of the same functionality.
17- Write a program that uses a static variable within a function to keep track of how many times the function has been called.
18- Write a recursive and an iterative version of a function that calculates the nth Fibonacci number. Discuss the advantages and disadvantages of each approach in terms of performance and readability.
19- Create a function that returns the address of a local static variable. Call this function multiple times from **main()** and observe the behavior.
20- Overload a function **printPattern** in two ways: one that takes an integer **n** and prints a pattern of **n** asterisks, and another that recursively prints a pattern of asterisks decreasing from **n** to 1.

Chapter 5
Pointers

ABSTRACT

Chapter 5 delves deep into one of the foundational and powerful concepts in C++: pointers. The chapter embarks with an enlightening introduction, elucidating the importance and utility of pointers in programming. Readers are guided through pointer variable declaration, initialization, and are introduced to pivotal pointer operations. The nuances of pointer arithmetic and expressions unfold, paving the way for a detailed discussion on pass-by-reference mechanisms with pointers. A significant focus is given to the interplay of 'const' with pointers, elaborating on varying degrees of pointer and data constancy. The chapter then demystifies the intricate relationship between pointers and arrays, leading into the intriguing world of arrays of pointers and function pointers. The 'sizeOf' operator's interaction with pointers is explored. Practical applications emerge through bubble sort and selection sort examples utilizing pass-by-reference. Closing the chapter is an engaging segment on pointer-based string processing.

5.1 INTRODUCTION

A pointer is basically a variable that is used to hold the value of the memory address of another variable. It can be thought of as a "handle" to a specific location in memory, allowing the programmer to directly access and manipulate the value stored at that location. Pointers can be used to create more efficient and powerful programs by allowing direct manipulation of memory, passing function arguments by reference, creating dynamic data structures, and more.

We can declare a pointer by putting an asterisk (*) before the variable, with the type of the variable it points to following the asterisk. For example, a pointer to an integer would be declared as int* ptr; The & operator is used to get the memory address of a variable, and the * operator is used to dereference a pointer and access the value stored at the memory location it points to.

It's important to note that when working with pointers, it's necessary to be careful to not create memory leaks by not freeing up the memory once it's no longer needed. C++11 introduced smart pointers, which are a type of pointer that automatically manages the memory they point to; they are safer than raw pointers.

Pointers are the most powerful features of C++.

DOI: 10.4018/979-8-3693-2007-5.ch005

5.2 POINTER VARIABLE DECLARATION AND INITIALIZATION

In C++, a pointer variable is declared by putting an asterisk (*) in front of the variable name, followed by the type of the variable to which it points. For example, a pointer to an integer would be declared as int* ptr; Once declared, a pointer variable can be initialized with the memory address of another variable using the & operator.

Here are some examples of pointer variable declaration and initialization in C++:

Declaring and initializing a pointer to an integer

int x = 5;

int* ptr = &x; // ptr is a pointer to an integer and is initialized with the address of x

In this example, ptr is a pointer to an integer and is initialized with the address of variable x using the& operator.

Declaring and initializing a pointer to a character:

char c = 'A';

char* ptr = &c; // ptr is a pointer to a character and is initialized with the address of c

Declaring and initializing a pointer to a dynamically allocated memory:

int* ptr = new int; // ptr is a pointer to an integer and is initialized with the address of dynamically allocated memory

*ptr = 5;

It's important to note that when a pointer is declared and initialized with the address of a variable, it points to the memory location of that variable, and any change made through the pointer will reflect the change in the original variable. Also, when a pointer points to a dynamically allocated memory, it's the responsibility of the programmer to free the memory when it's no longer needed to avoid memory leaks.

Pointers Are Variables That Contain Memory Addresses as Their Values

int y = 5; //declares an ordinary variable called y int *yPtr; //declares a pointer variable called yPtr

int* yPtr = &y; //creates a pointer yPtr that points to the variable y.

y-- Returns the value of the variable

yPtr-- Returns the address of the variable it points to.

* yPtr -- Returns the value of the variable it points to.

The *** operator**, is commonly referred to as the **indirection operator** or **dereferencing operator**

The **& operator** is commonly referred to as the address of **the operator** or **referencing operator.**

The & (ampersand), read as "the address of", when associated with a variable, returns the memory address of the variable.

A pointer can be initialized to either 0 or NULL. A pointer with the value 0 or NULL is known as a null pointer and points to nothing. The iostream> header file and several other standard library header files define the symbolic constant NULL, which stands in for the value 0.

Initializing a pointer to NULL is equivalent to initializing a pointer to 0. 0 is the only integer value that can be explicitly assigned to a pointer variable without first casting the integer to a pointer type.

5.3 POINTER OPERATORS

There are several pointer operators that are used to manipulate pointers and the memory they point to. These operators are:

The & operator: This operator is used to get the memory address of a variable. For example:

```
int x = 5;
int* ptr = &x; // ptr holds the address of x
```

The* operator: This operator is used to dereference a pointer and access the value stored at the memory location it points to.It is also known as the indirection operator. For example:

```
int x = 5;
int* ptr = &x;
*ptr = 10; // x is now 10
```

The[] operator: This operator is used to access elements of an array through a pointer. It is a shorthand for* (ptr + i).For example:

```
int arr[5] = { 1, 2, 3, 4, 5 };
int* ptr = arr;
cout << ptr[2]; // Outputs "3"
```

The++and --operators: These operators are used to increment or decrement a pointer, respectively. For example:

```
int arr[5] = { 1, 2, 3, 4, 5 };
int* ptr = arr;
ptr++; // ptr now points to the second element of the array
```

These are the most commonly used pointer operators in C++. It's important to note that the * operator has a different meaning when used in a pointer declaration and when used to dereference a pointer. Also, care must be taken when using these operators to avoid accessing memory that is out of bounds or has already been freed to avoid errors such as memory leaks or segmentation faults.

5.3.1 Pointer Arithmetic

On pointers, multiple arithmetic operations can be conducted. One can increment (++) or decrement (--) a pointer, add an integer to a pointer (+ or +=), subtract an integer from a pointer (- or -=), or subtract one pointer from another.

Assume that the array int v[5] has been declared and that its first element is located at memory address 3000. Consider vPtr to have been initialized to point to v[0] (i.e., the value of vPtr is 3000).

Note that either of the following statements can be used to set vPtr to point to array v, since the name of an array is the same as the address of its first element:

```
int* vPtr = v;
int* vPtr = &v[0];
```

According to standard arithmetic, the sum of 3000 and 2 is 3002. This is not typically the case when performing pointer arithmetic. When adding or subtracting an integer from a pointer, the pointer is not merely incremented or decremented by the integer but by the integer multiplied by the size of the object to which the pointer refers. The quantity of bytes depends on the data nature of the object. For instance, the assertion

```
vPtr += 2;
```

Assuming an int is contained in four bytes of memory, the result would be 3008 (3000 + 2 * 4). Within the array v, vPtr now points to v[2].

If vPtr had been raised to 3016, which is the address of v[4, the statement would have run.

```
vPtr -= 4;
```

would reset vPtr to 3000, the array's beginning. The increment (++) and decrement (--) operators can be used to increment or decrement a pointer by one. Each of the statements advances the pointer to the following array element.

Each statement decrements the pointer so that it points to the previous array element.

```
--vPtr;
vPtr--;
```

Variables that refer to the same array can be subtracted from each other. If vPtr contains the location 3000 and v2Ptr contains the address 3008, for instance, the statement.

```
x = v2Ptr - vPtr;
```

assigns the number of array elements from vPtr to v2P to x.

Pointer math is useless here unless it is done on a pointer that points to an array. We can't assume that two variables of the same type are next to each other in memory unless they are next to each other in an array.

NOTA: It is a logical error to subtract or compare two pointers that do not refer to elements of the same array.

When both pointers are of the same type, they can be assigned to one another. Otherwise, a cast operator must be used to convert the pointer value on the right of the assignment to the pointer type on the left. The exception to this norm is the void pointer (i.e., void *), which can represent any pointer type. All pointer types can be assigned without casting to a pointer of type void *. However, a pointer of type void * cannot be explicitly assigned to a pointer of another type; it must first be cast to the appropriate pointer type.

A pointer of type void * cannot be dereferenced. On a machine with four-byte integers, the compiler "knows" that a pointer to int refers to four bytes of memory, whereas a pointer to void simply contains a memory address for an undefined data type. The compiler is unaware of the precise number of bytes to which the pointer refers and the data type. To determine the number of bytes to be dereferenced for a particular pointer, the compiler must know the data type. For a pointer to void, this number cannot be determined from the type.

Comparing pointers is possible using equality and relational operators. Unless the pointers point to members of the same array, comparisons with relational operators are irrelevant. Pointer comparisons evaluate the stored addresses of the pointers. A comparison of two pointers pointing to the same array could reveal, for instance, that one pointer points to an array element with a higher index than the other. Commonly, pointer comparison is used to determine if a pointer is 0 (i.e., the pointer is a null pointer; it does not point to anything).

5.3.2 Pointer Expressions

Pointer expressions are expressions that involve one or more pointers. These expressions are used to manipulate memory and perform arithmetic operations on pointers.

Here are some examples of pointer expressions in C++:

Pointer arithmetic:

```
int arr[5] = { 1, 2, 3, 4, 5 };
int* ptr = arr;
ptr = ptr + 2; // ptr now points to the third element of the array
cout << *ptr; // Outputs "3"
```

In this case, the address of the first item in the array arr is given to the pointer ptr. The expression ptr + 2 performs pointer arithmetic and increments the pointer, which means it now points to the third element in the array. Dereferencing the pointer *ptr gives the value of the element it points to, which is 3 in this case.

Pointer comparison:

```
int arr[5] = { 1, 2, 3, 4, 5 };
int* p1 = arr;
int* p2 = &arr[3];
if (p1 < p2) {
cout << "p1 points to a lower memory location than p2";
}
```

In this example, the pointers p1 and p2 are initialized with the addresses of the first and fourth elements of the array, respectively. The expression p1 < p2 compares the memory addresses stored in the pointers and returns true if the address stored in p1 is lower than the address stored in p2.

Pointer subtraction:

```
int arr[5] = { 1, 2, 3, 4, 5 };
int* p1 = arr;
int* p2 = &arr[3];
```

```
int distance = p2 - p1;
cout << distance; // Outputs "3"
```

In this example, the pointers p1 and p2 are initialized with the addresses of the first and fourth elements of the array, respectively. The expression p2 - p1 performs pointer subtraction, which returns the number of elements between the two pointers.

These are just a few examples of pointer expressions in C++. Pointers can be used in many other ways and combinations, such as pointer to pointer, pointer to function, and more. It's important to note that when working with pointers, it's necessary to be careful to not create memory leaks by not freeing up the memory once it's no longer needed and to not access memory that is out of bounds or already freed to avoid errors such as memory leaks or segmentation faults.

5.4 PASS_BY_REFERENCE WITH POINTERS

Passing variables by reference allows a function to directly access and manipulate the original variable, instead of working with a copy. This can be achieved in C++ by passing a pointer to the variable as a function argument. This method is called pass by reference with pointers.

Here's an example of passing a variable by reference with pointers:

```
void swap(int* x, int* y) {
int temp = *x;
*x = *y;
*y = temp;
}
int main() {
int a = 5, b = 10;
swap(&a, &b); // passing variables a and b by reference using pointers
cout << "a: " << a << " b: " << b; // Outputs "a: 10 b: 5"
return 0;
}
```

In this example, the swap function accepts two pointers to integers as arguments. Inside the function, the values at the memory locations pointed to by the pointers are swapped. Since the pointers are passed by reference, the changes made to the values at those memory locations are reflected in the original variables a and b.

Passing by reference with pointers also allows a function to return multiple values. Here is an example of how to return multiple values from a function using pointers:

```
void divide(int x, int y, int* quotient, int* remainder) {
*quotient = x / y;
*remainder = x % y;
}
int main() {
```

```
int a = 10, b = 3;
int quotient, remainder;
divide(a, b, &quotient, &remainder);
cout << "Quotient: " << quotient << " Remainder: " << remainder; // Outputs
"Quotient: 3 Remainder: 1"
return 0;
}
```

In this example, the divide function accepts two integers and two pointers as arguments. It calculates the quotient and remainder of dividing the first argument by the second and stores the values at the memory locations pointed to by the pointers.

It's important to remember that in C++, pass by reference with pointers is less safe than pass by reference with references. This is because there is no way to find null pointers when passing them as function arguments, which can cause errors like segmentation faults.

5.5 USING CONST WITH POINTERS

Using the const keyword with a pointer in C++ makes it impossible to change the value stored in the memory location that the pointer points to.This can be useful for protecting important data and preventing accidental modification.

Here are some examples of using const with pointers in C++:

Declaring a constant pointer:

```
int x = 5;
const int* ptr = &x; // ptr is a pointer to a constant integer
*ptr = 10; // Compile-time error: cannot modify value pointed to by a const
pointer
```

In this example, the pointer ptr is declared as a pointer to a constant integer, meaning that the value stored at the memory location pointed to by ptr cannot be modified. If you try to change the value of x through the pointer, it will cause a compile-time error.

Declaring a pointer to a constant:

```
int x = 5;
int* const ptr = &x; // ptr is a constant pointer to an integer
ptr = &x; // Compile-time error: cannot change the value of a const pointer
```

In this example, the pointer ptr is declared as a constant pointer to an integer. This means that the memory location that ptr points to cannot be changed. If you try to make the pointer point to another location, it will cause a compile-time error.

Declaring a pointer to a constant and a constant pointer:

```
int x = 5;
const int* const ptr = &x; // ptr is a constant pointer to a constant integer
*ptr = 10; // Compile-time error: cannot modify value pointed to by a const
pointer
ptr = &x; // Compile-time error: cannot change the value of a const pointer
```

In this example, the pointer ptr is declared as a constant pointer to a constant integer. This means that both the value stored at the memory location pointed to by ptr and the value pointed to by ptr are always the same.

Don't forget that the const qualifier lets the programmer tell the compiler that the value of a variable should not be changed.

NOTICE: If the value of a parameter can't change in the body of a function to which it is passed, it must be declared "const" to prevent this from happening by accident.

If you try to change a const value, the compiler will either give you a warning or an error.

5.5.1 Nonconstant Pointer to Nonconstant Data

A nonconstant pointer grants the greatest access to nonconstant data.

The data can be modified via the dereferenced pointer, which can also be modified to point to other data. The declaration of a pointer to non-constant data does not include the keyword const. This pointer can be used to receive a string terminated by a null character within a function that modifies the pointer's value to process (and possibly modify) each character in the string.

5.5.2 Nonconstant Pointer to Constant Data

A nonconstant pointer to constant data is a pointer that can be modified to point to any data item of the appropriate type but cannot modify the data it points to. This pointer could be used to pass an array argument to a function that will process each array element, but the data should not be modified.

5.5.3 Constant Pointer to Nonconstant Data

A constant pointer to nonconstant data is a pointer that always points to the same memory location. The data at that memory location can be changed using the pointer. The default format for an array identifier A name for an array is a constant pointer to the array's beginning. All of the array's data can be accessed and modified using the array's name and subscripting. A constant pointer to nonconstant data can be used to pass an array as an argument to a function that uses array subscript notation to access array elements. Const-declared pointers must be initialized at the time they are declared. (If the pointer is a function parameter, it is initialized with the passed-in pointer).

5.5.4 Constant Pointer to Constant Data

A constant pointer to constant data provides the lowest level of access privilege. Such a pointer always points to the same location in memory, and the data at that location cannot be modified using the pointer.

This is how an array should be passed to a function that only receives it and does not modify it, using array subscript notation.

5.6 THE RELATIONSHIP BETWEEN POINTERS AND ARRAYS

Pointers and arrays have a close relationship. In fact, an array can be thought of as a constant pointer to its first element. This means that when an array is passed to a function, it is passed by reference (as a pointer), and when an array is indexed, it is dereferenced like a pointer.

Here are some examples of the relationship between pointers and arrays in C++:

Array name as a pointer:

```
int arr[5] = { 1, 2, 3, 4, 5 };
int* ptr = arr; // arr is a constant pointer to the first element of the array
cout << *ptr; // Outputs "1"
```

In this example, the array arr is assigned to the pointer ptr. The array name arr is actually a constant pointer to the first element of the array, so ptr points to the first element of the array.

Array indexing as pointer dereferencing:

```
int arr[5] = { 1, 2, 3, 4, 5 };
cout << arr[2]; // Outputs "3"
cout << *(arr + 2); // Outputs "3"
```

In this case, you can get to the array's elements using either the array indexing notation arr[2] or the pointer dereferencing notation *(arr + 2).Both notations access the same memory location and return the same value.

Array passed as a pointer to a function:

```
void printArray(int* arr, int size) {
for (int i = 0; i < size; i++) {
cout << arr[i] << " ";
}
}
int main() {
int arr[5] = { 1, 2, 3, 4, 5 };
printArray(arr, 5); // Outputs "1 2 3 4 5"
return 0;
}
```

In this example, the array arr is passed as an argument to the function printArray. The function accepts a pointer to an integer and the size of the array. Inside the function, the elements of the array are accessed using the array indexing notation arr[i] which is possible because the array is passed as a pointer.

It's important to note that although arrays and pointers are related, there are some important differences between them.

5.7 ARRAY OF POINTERS

In C++, an array of pointers is an array that stores the memory addresses of other variables. This can be useful in situations where an array of variables is needed but the number of elements is not known beforehand.

Here's an example of an array of pointers in C++:

```
int x = 5, y = 10, z = 15;
int* arr[3] = { &x, &y, &z };
cout << *arr[0] << " " << *arr[1] << " " << *arr[2]; // Outputs "5 10 15"
```

In this example, arr is an array of pointers to integers, and it stores the memory addresses of variables x, y, and z. The elements of the array are accessed by dereferencing the pointer using the * operator, which returns the value stored at the memory location pointed to by the pointer.

Another example could be an array of pointers to functions:

```
int add(int a, int b) { return a + b; }
int subtract(int a, int b) { return a - b; }
int multiply(int a, int b) { return a * b; }
int (*operations[3])(int, int) = { add, subtract, multiply };
cout << operations[0](3, 4) << " " << operations[1](3, 4) << " " << opera-
tions[2](3, 4); // Outputs "7 -1 12"
```

In this example, operations is an array of pointers to functions that take two integers as arguments and return an integer. The elements of the array are accessed by calling the function through the pointer, which returns the result of the function.

It's important to note that when working with arrays of pointers, it's necessary to be careful to not create memory leaks by not freeing up the memory once it's no longer needed and to not access memory that is out of bounds or already freed to avoid errors such as memory leaks or segment.

Note: Array names cannot be modified in arithmetic expressions because array names are constant pointers.

```
int arr[5] equals 1,2,3,4,5;
arr++; /throws an exception: C2105: '++' requires l-value
```

Arrays may contain identifiers. A prevalent application of this data structure is to create an array of pointer-based strings, also known as a string array. In C++, a string is effectively a pointer to its first character, so each element in an array of strings is merely a pointer to the first character of a string. Consider the string array suit declaration that could be beneficial for representing a deck of cards:

```
const char *suit[4] = "Hearts," "Diamonds," "Clubs," and "Spades";
```

The suit[4] portion of the declaration identifies a four-element array. Const char * indicates that each element of an array suit is of type "pointer to char constant data." The array must contain the values "hearts,", "diamonds,", "clubs,", and "Spades". Each is stored in memory as a null-terminated string of characters that is one character longer than the number of characters between the quotation marks. The lengths of the four sequences are seven, nine, six, and seven characters, respectively (including their terminating null characters).

Although it appears that these strings are being stored in the suit array, only pointers are stored there. Each pointer corresponds to the first character of its respective string. Thus, despite its fixed capacity, the suit array provides access to character strings of any length. This flexibility exemplifies the robust data-structuring capabilities of C++.

The suit threads could be placed in a two-dimensional array, where each row corresponds to a suit and each column corresponds to a letter of a suit name. This data structure must have the same number of columns per row as the greatest string.

Because most strings are shorter than the longest string, a lot of memory is wasted when a lot of strings are stored. In the following section, we use arrays of strings to aid in depicting a deck of cards.

5.8 FUNCTION POINTERS

Function pointers are pointers that point to a function. Function pointers can be used to store the address of a function and call it later, which can be useful in situations where a function needs to be passed as an argument to another function or a function needs to be selected at runtime based on certain conditions.

Here's an example of using a function pointer in C++:

```
int add(int a, int b) { return a + b; }
int subtract(int a, int b) { return a - b; }
int multiply(int a, int b) { return a * b; }
int divide(int a, int b) { return a / b; }
int main() {
int (*operation)(int, int); // declares a function pointer
int a = 10, b = 5;
operation = add; // assigns the address of the add function to the function
pointer
cout << operation(a, b) << endl; // Outputs "15"
operation = subtract;
cout << operation(a, b) << endl; // Outputs "5"
operation = multiply;
cout << operation(a, b) << endl; // Outputs "50"
operation = divide;
cout << operation(a, b) << endl; // Outputs "2"
return 0;
}
```

In this example, the function pointer operation is declared, and four functions are defined. The function pointer is assigned the address of one of the functions, and then the function is called by dereferencing the function pointer. This way, we can change the operation that is being performed by the program at runtime.

Function pointers can also be used to pass a function as an argument to another function. Here is an example of passing a function pointer as an argument to another function:

```
int perform_operation(int a, int b, int (*operation)(int, int)) {
return operation(a, b);
}
int main() {
int a = 10, b = 5;
cout << perform_operation(a, b, add) << endl; // Outputs "15"
cout << perform_operation(a, b, subtract) << end
}
```

The code specifies a function named "perform operation" that accepts three arguments: two integers, "a" and "b," representing the operands, and a pointer to a function that accepts two integers as arguments and returns an integer indicating the outcome of the operation.

The perform operation function returns the result of calling the function indicated by the "operation" parameter with the two integer parameters "a" and "b.".

Two integer variables, "a" and "b," are declared and initialized with the values 10 and 5, respectively, in the main function. The "add" and "subtract" function pointers are given as the third parameter of two separate calls to the "perform operation" function. The console displays the results of the two function calls.

Based on the function pointer supplied to "perform operation", the result of the first call is 15 (the sum of 10 and 5), whereas the result of the second call is 5. (the result of subtracting 5 from 10).

Notice that the "add" and "subtract" functions are not declared in your code and must be written elsewhere.

5.9 POINTERS AND SIZE OF OPERATOR

In C++, you can use the sizeof operator to find out how big a variable or data type is. When used with pointers, the sizeof operator gives back the size of the variable that the pointer points to, not the size of the memory location that the pointer points to.

Here's an example of using the sizeof operator with a pointer in C++:

```
int x = 5;
int* ptr = &x;
cout << sizeof(ptr) << endl; // Outputs "4" or "8" depending on the platform
```

The sizeof operator is used in this example to find out how big the pointer variable ptr is. The output will be the size of the pointer in bytes, which is 4 bytes on a 32-bit platform and 8 bytes on a 64-bit platform.

It's important to note that the sizeof operator doesn't work on pointer expressions; it only works on pointer variables. Here's an example:

```
int arr[] = { 1, 2, 3, 4, 5 };
cout << sizeof(arr + 2); // Outputs "4" or "8" depending on the platform
```

In this case, the sizeof operator is used on a pointer expression, arr + 2 which is a pointer to the third element of the array. The output will be the size of the pointer in bytes, not the size of the memory location pointed to by the pointer. To get the size of the memory location pointed to by the pointer, you can use sizeof(*(arr+2)).

In addition to that, when working with pointers and arrays, it's important to keep in mind that the sizeof operator returns the size of the entire array, not the number of elements.

In summary, when using the sizeof operator with pointers, it will return the size of the pointer variable in bytes, not the size of the memory location pointed to by the pointer. To get the size of the memory location pointed to by the pointer, you can use sizeof(*pointer).

5.10 BUBBLE SORT USING PASS-BY-REFERENCE

The bubble sort algorithm is a simple sorting algorithm that repeatedly steps through the list to be sorted, compares each pair of adjacent items, and swaps them if they are in the wrong order. Bubble sort is less efficient than other sorting algorithms like quicksort, merge sort, and heapsort.

Here is an example of implementing the bubble sort algorithm using pass-by-reference in C++:

```
void bubbleSort(int* arr, int size) {
for (int i = 0; i < size - 1; i++) {
for (int j = 0; j < size - i - 1; j++) {
if (arr[j] > arr[j + 1]) {
int temp = arr[j];
arr[j] = arr[j + 1];
arr[j + 1] = temp;
}
}
}
}
int main() {
int arr[] = { 5, 1, 4, 2, 8 };
int size = sizeof(arr) / sizeof(arr[0]);
bubbleSort(arr, size);
for (int i = 0; i < size; i++) {
cout << arr[i] << " ";
```

```
}
// Outputs "1 2 4 5 8"
return 0;
}
```

In this example, the function bubbleSort takes a pointer to an integer array and its size as arguments and sorts the array using the bubble sort algorithm. The function uses two loops inside of each other to step through the array and swap any adjacent elements that are out of place.

The bubbleSort function sorts the array in place and doesn't create a new copy; it modifies the original array, so it uses pass-by-reference.

It's important to note that the bubble sort algorithm's time complexity is O(n^2) which makes it inefficient for large arrays, and other sorting algorithms like quicksort, merge sort, and heapsort are more efficient and faster.

5.11 SELECTION SORT USING PASS-BY-REFERENCE

The selection sort algorithm is a simple way to sort things. It finds the least important element in the part of the array that isn't sorted and swaps it with the first unsorted element.

Here's an example of implementing the selection sort algorithm using pass-by-reference in C++:

```
void selectionSort(int* arr, int size) {
for (int i = 0; i < size - 1; i++) {
int min_index = i;
for (int j = i + 1; j < size; j++) {
if (arr[j] < arr[min_index]) {
min_index = j;
}
}
int temp = arr[min_index];
arr[min_index] = arr[i];
arr[i] = temp;
}
}
int main() {
int arr[] = { 5, 1, 4, 2, 8 };
int size = sizeof(arr) / sizeof(arr[0]);
selectionSort(arr, size);
for (int i = 0; i < size; i++) {
cout << arr[i] << " ";
}
// Outputs "1 2 4 5 8"
return 0;
}
```

In this example, the function selectionSort takes a pointer to an integer array and its size as arguments and sorts the array using the selection sort algorithm. The function uses two nested loops to repeatedly find the minimum element from the unsorted part of the array and swap it with the first element of the unsorted part.

The selectionSort function sorts the array in place and doesn't create a new copy; it modifies the original array, so it uses pass-by-reference.

It's important to note that the selection sort algorithm's time complexity is O(n^2) which makes it inefficient for large arrays, and other sorting algorithms like quicksort, merge sort, and heapsort are more efficient and faster.

5.12 POINTER-BASED STRING PROCESSING

Strings can be processed using pointers. Pointer-based string processing allows for direct manipulation of the memory locations holding the characters of a string, which can be useful in situations where string manipulation is required.

Here's an example of using pointers to process a string in C++:

```
#include <iostream>
#include <cstring>
using namespace std;
int main() {
char str[] = "Hello, World!";
char* ptr = str;
while (*ptr != '\0') {
cout << *ptr;
ptr++;
}
cout << endl;
// Outputs "Hello, World!"
return 0;
}
```

In this example, the address of the first character in the string str is given to the pointer ptr. The pointer is then used to go through the characters of the string one by one by dereferencing the pointer and increasing it at each iteration. This way, we can print every character of the string one by one.

Another example is how to copy a string using pointers:

```
char source[] = "Hello, World!";
char destination[20];
char* src_ptr = source;
char* dest_ptr = destination;
while (*src_ptr != '\0') {
*dest_ptr = *src_ptr;
```

```
dest_ptr++;
src_ptr++;
}
*dest_ptr = '\0';
cout << destination;
// Outputs "Hello, World!"
```

In this example, two pointers, src_ptr and dest_ptr, are declared, one pointing to the source string and the other to the destination string. Then we copy each character of the source string to the destination string by dereferencing the source pointer, copying the character to the destination pointer, and incrementing both pointers at each iteration. And finally, we add the null-terminator \0 at the end of the destination string to indicate the end of the string.

It's important to note that when using pointers to manipulate strings, it's essential to be careful not to go out of bounds or to forget to add the null-terminator to the end of the string, to avoid errors such as buffer overflow.

Characters are the fundamental components of C++ source code. Every program consists of a string of characters that, when put together meaningfully, the compiler interprets as a set of instructions used to carry out a task.A program may contain constant character strings. A character constant is an integer value enclosed in single quotation marks and representing a single character. The value of a character constant is the integer value of the character within the character set of the machine. For instance, 'z' represents the integer value of the character z (122 in the ASCII character set; see Appendix B), and 'n' represents the integer value of the character newline (10 in the ASCII character set).

A string is a sequence of characters that is regarded as a unit. A string may contain letters, numbers, and special characters, including +, -, *, /, and $. In C++, string literals or string constants are enclosed in double quotation marks.

```
"John Q. Doe" (a given name),
"9999 Main Street" (a street address),
"Maynard, Massachusetts" (a city and state)
"John Q. Doe" (a given name),
```

In C++, a string based on a pointer is an array of characters that ends with the null character ('0'), which indicates where the string ends in memory. The first character of a string is referenced by a pointer. The value of a string is its first character's address. In C++, it is appropriate to state that a string is a constant pointer that points to the first character of the string. In this regard, strings are comparable to arrays, as the name of an array is also a pointer to its first element.

A string literal can be used as an initializer when declaring a character array or a variable of type char *.The assertions

```
char color[] = "blue";
const char *colorPtr = "blue";
```

Each variable is initialized with the string "blue." The first declaration creates a five-element array named color with the values 'b', 'l', 'u', 'e', and '0'. The second declaration creates the pointer variable colorPtr, which points somewhere in memory to the letter b in the string "blue" (which ends in '0'). String literals have a static storage type (they exist for the duration of the application) and a static storage class.

If the same string literal is used more than once in a program, it might be shared or it might not. In addition, string literals in C++ cannot have their characters altered.

The declaration char color[] = "blue"; could also be written as char color[] = "blue".

```
char color[] = { 'b', 'l', 'u', 'e', '\0' };
```

When you tell a character array to hold a string, it has to be big enough to hold both the string and the null character that ends it. The number of initializers in the initializer list determines the size of the array.This is what the above declaration does.

Through stream extraction with Cin, a string can be read into a character array. The following statement, for example, can be used to read a string into the character array:

```
cin >> word;
```

The user-entered string is stored in Word. The foregoing statement reads characters until it encounters either a white-space character or an end-of-file indicator. Note that the string length should not exceed 19 characters to accommodate the terminating null character. The setw stream manipulator ensures that the string read into words does not exceed the array's capacity. For instance, the assertion

```
cin >> setw(20) >> word;
```

Indicates that Cin should only read up to 19 characters into the array word and use the 20th array location to store the null character that ends the string. The setw stream manipulator only pertains to the next input value. If more than 19 characters are inputted, they are not kept in Word but are instead read in and can be stored in another variable.

In certain circumstances, it is desirable to submit a full line of text into an array. For this purpose, C++ provides the cin.getline function in the iostream header file. The cin.getline function requires three arguments: a character array to retain the line of text, a length, and a delimiter character. Specifically, the program segment

```
char sentence[80];
cin.getline(sentence, 80, '\n');
```

Declares an 80-character array sentence and extracts a line of text from the keyboard into it. When the delimiter character 'n' is encountered, when the end-of-file indicator is entered, or when the number of characters read thus far is one less than the length specified in the second parameter, the function ceases reading characters. (The final character in an array is reserved for the null terminator character.) The delimiter character is read and discarded if encountered. The default value of the third argument to cin.getline is 'n,' so the preceding function call could have been written as follows:

```
cin.getline(sentence, 80);
#include <iostream>
```

```
using namespace std;
int main()
{
int vals[] = { 4, 7, 11 };
int* valptr = vals;
valptr++; // points at 7
cout << *valptr << endl;
valptr--; // now points to 4
cout << *valptr << endl;
cout << *(valptr + 2) << endl; // prints 11
valptr = vals; // points to 4
valptr += 2; // points to 11;
cout << *valptr << endl;
cout << valptr - vals << endl; // number of ints between valptr and vals
system("pause");
return 0;
}
```

This C++ code shows the usage of array indexing and pointers.

The preprocessor command "#include iostream>" incorporates the standard input/output library. The expression "using namespace std;" enables the usage of standard C++ library functions and objects without the "std::" prefix.

The "int main()" function is the program's entry point. The array "vals" is defined and initialized with the values 4, 7, and 11 inside the main method. Declare and initialize a pointer variable called "valptr" to refer to the first entry of the "vals" array.

The "valptr++;" expression moves the pointer to the second entry in the "vals" array, which has the value 7.The instruction "cout *valptr endl;" outputs the value that the pointer pointed to, which is 7.

The "valptr—;" instruction decreases the pointer to the first member of the "vals" array, which has a value of 4.The instruction "cout *valptr endl;" outputs the value that the pointer pointed to, which is 4.

"cout *(valptr + 2) endl;" outputs the value of the third member of the array "vals," which is 11. Dereferencing the pointer after adding 2 to it is how you achieve this.

"valptr = vals;" resets the pointer to the first member of the array "vals," which has a value of 4. The "valptr += 2;" instruction moves the pointer to the third entry in the "vals" array, which is where the value is stored.11. The instruction "cout *valptr endl;" outputs the value that the pointer pointed to, which is 11.

This statement shows the number of integers between the pointer "valptr" and the array "vals."This is done by taking the difference between the memory address of the "vals" array and the "valptr" pointer and dividing it by the size of an integer.There are two integers between the "valptr" pointer and the "vals" array, so the output in this case is 2.

The phrase "system("pause");" stops the program so that the output may be seen prior to program termination. The "return 0;" sentence signifies that the program has been properly finished.

Example

```
#include <iostream>
#include <cstring>
using namespace std;
void reverseString(char* str) {
int len = strlen(str);
char* start = str;
char* end = str + len - 1;
while (start < end) {
char temp = *start;
*start = *end;
*end = temp;
start++;
end--;
}
}
int countVowels(char* str) {
int count = 0;
char* ptr = str;
while (*ptr != '\0') {
if (*ptr == 'a' || *ptr == 'e' || *ptr == 'i' || *ptr == 'o' || *ptr == 'u' ||
*ptr == 'A' || *ptr == 'E' || *ptr == 'I' || *ptr == 'O' || *ptr == 'U') {
count++;
}
ptr++;
}
return count;
}
int main() {
char str[] = "Hello, World!";
// Reversing the string
reverseString(str);
cout << "Reversed String: " << str << endl;
// Outputs "!dlroW, olleH"
// Counting the number of vowels in the string
int vowel_count = countVowels(str);
cout << "Number of vowels: " << vowel_count << endl;
// Outputs "3"
return 0;
}
```

This C++ code shows how to use pointers and functions to turn a string upside down and count how many vowels it has.

The preprocessor command "#include iostream>" incorporates the standard input/output library. The "#include cstring>" directive incorporates the C string library, which offers string manipulation capabilities.

"using namespace std;" lets you use functions and objects from the standard C++ library without the "std::" prefix.

The "reverseString" method accepts a character array reference and reverses the order of the array's characters. This is performed by use two pointers, "start" and "end", which point to the array's first and final characters, respectively. The function then swaps the characters at the two points and advances them toward the center until they meet.

The "countVowels" function counts the number of vowels in a character array given its reference. This is achieved via a while loop that iterates over each character in the array using the "ptr" reference. If the letter is a vowel, the function will increase the "count" counter.

The "main" function initializes the "str" character array with the string "Hello, World!" The "reverseString" function is used to reverse the order of the characters in the "str" array, and "cout" is used to output the result to the console.

The "countVowels" function is used to determine the number of vowels in the "str" array, and "cout" is used to report the result to the console. The "return 0;" sentence signifies that the program has been properly finished.

This sample illustrates how pointers and functions are used to alter strings in C++.

ADVANCED PRACTICE EXERCISES WITH ANSWERS

1. Initialize and Manipulate Integer via Pointer

Objective: Practice basic pointer operations by declaring, initializing, and manipulating an integer value through a pointer.

```
#include <iostream>
int main() {
    int value = 5;
    int* ptr = &value;
    std::cout << "Original value: " << *ptr << std::endl;
    *ptr = 10;
    std::cout << "Modified value: " << *ptr << std::endl;
    return 0;
}
```

Explanation:

This C++ program illustrates a fundamental concept of pointers: modifying the value of a variable through its memory address. It does this in a concise and clear manner. Here's an explanation of how the program operates:

Overview of the Program:

1. **Variable Declaration**: The program begins by declaring an integer variable **value** and initializes it to **5**.
2. **Pointer Initialization**: Next, a pointer variable **ptr** is declared and initialized with the address of **value** using the address-of operator (**&**). This means **ptr** now holds the memory address where the integer **value** is stored.
3. **Dereferencing and Outputting Original Value**: The program then outputs the original value of **value** by dereferencing **ptr** (using ***ptr**) within a **std::cout** statement. Dereferencing **ptr** yields the value stored at the memory address it points to, which is **5**.
4. **Modifying Value Through Pointer**: The value of **value** is then changed to **10** by dereferencing **ptr** and assigning a new value (***ptr = 10;**). This operation modifies the value stored at the memory location to which **ptr** points, effectively changing the value of **value**.
5. **Outputting Modified Value**: Finally, the program outputs the modified value of **value** again by dereferencing **ptr**. This time, the output will be **10**, reflecting the change made through the pointer.

Key Concepts Demonstrated:

- **Pointer Declaration and Use**: The program shows how to declare a pointer and use it to store the address of a variable. This is fundamental for understanding memory management and manipulation in C++.
- **Dereferencing a Pointer**: By using the dereference operator (*) on **ptr**, the program accesses and modifies the value stored in the memory location pointed to by **ptr**. This demonstrates how pointers can be used to directly interact with memory locations.
- **Modifying Variable Values Using Pointers**: The alteration of **value** through ***ptr** illustrates how pointers can be used to change variable values without directly referencing the variable by name after its address is assigned to a pointer.

Output:
Original value: 5
Modified value: 10
Practical Use:
Understanding and using pointers is crucial in C++ for direct memory access and manipulation, which is essential for various programming tasks, including dynamic memory management, implementing data structures (like linked lists and trees), and interfacing with low-level system resources. This program serves as a basic introduction to these concepts.

2. Array Traversal Using Pointer Arithmetic

Objective: Utilize pointer arithmetic to traverse and print elements of an integer array.

```
#include <iostream>
int main() {
    int arr[] = { 10, 20, 30, 40, 50 };
    int* ptr = arr;
    for (int i = 0; i < 5; ++i) {
```

```
        std::cout << *(ptr + i) << " ";
    }
    return 0;
}
```

Explanation:

This C++ program demonstrates how to iterate over and print the elements of an array using a pointer. It's a concise example of pointer arithmetic and array access in C++. Here's a breakdown of how it works:

Program Overview

- An integer array **arr** is declared and initialized with five elements: **{10, 20, 30, 40, 50}**.
- A pointer **ptr** is then initialized to point to the first element of the array **arr**. This is done by simply assigning **arr** to **ptr**, as the name of an array acts as a pointer to its first element in C++.
- The program uses a **for** loop to iterate over the array. However, instead of using array subscript notation (**arr[i]**), it uses pointer arithmetic to access each element: ***(ptr + i)**. This expression adds **i** to the pointer (effectively moving it **i** positions forward in the array) and then dereferences the pointer to access the value at that position.
- Inside the loop, the value pointed to by **ptr + i** is printed to the console, followed by a space.

Key Concepts Illustrated

- **Pointer to Array**: The pointer **ptr** is used to store the address of the first element of the array. This showcases how arrays and pointers are closely related in C++.
- **Pointer Arithmetic**: The expression **ptr + i** demonstrates pointer arithmetic, where adding an integer value to a pointer moves the pointer forward by that many elements in the array. Since **ptr** points to an **int**, adding **i** to **ptr** moves the pointer **i * sizeof(int)** bytes forward in memory.
- **Dereferencing Pointers**: The dereference operator * is used to access the value that **ptr + i** points to. This operator is essential for working with pointers, as it allows you to access or modify the data at the memory address stored in the pointer.

Output

The program outputs the elements of the array **arr** in order:

10 20 30 40 50

Practical Use

Understanding how to access array elements using pointers and pointer arithmetic is fundamental in C++ and C programming. It allows for more flexible and potentially efficient code, especially in contexts where direct memory manipulation is necessary or preferred. This approach is widely used in low-level programming, algorithms that require direct manipulation of memory addresses, and in interfacing with hardware or other software systems where memory addresses are important.

3. Implementing Pass-By-Reference Using Pointers

Objective: Demonstrate the use of pointers to swap two integers by reference.

```
#include <iostream>
void swap(int* a, int* b) {
    int temp = *a;
    *a = *b;
    *b = temp;
}
int main() {
    int x = 1, y = 2;
    swap(&x, &y);
    std::cout << "x: " << x << ", y: " << y << std::endl;
    return 0;
}
```

Explanation:

This C++ program demonstrates a simple yet fundamental operation in computer programming: swapping the values of two variables. It does so by using pointers to directly modify the values of the variables passed to it. Here's a step-by-step breakdown of how the program works:

Function: swap

- **Purpose**: Swaps the values of two integers.
- **Parameters**:
- **int* a**: A pointer to the first integer.
- **int* b**: A pointer to the second integer.
- **Process**:
- A temporary variable **temp** is used to store the value pointed to by **a**.
- The value pointed to by **a** is then replaced with the value pointed to by **b**.
- Finally, the value pointed to by **b** is replaced with the value stored in **temp**, effectively swapping the values of the two integers.

Main Function

- Two integer variables, **x** and **y**, are declared and initialized to **1** and **2**, respectively.
- The **swap** function is called with the addresses of **x** and **y** (**&x** and **&y**) as arguments. This passes pointers to **x** and **y** to the function, allowing it to modify their values directly.
- After the swap operation, the new values of **x** and **y** are printed to the console, showing that their values have been successfully swapped.

Output

The program outputs the swapped values of **x** and **y**:

x: 2, y: 1

Key Concepts Illustrated

- **Pointer Parameters**: The **swap** function takes pointers as parameters, enabling it to modify the values of the variables passed to it directly. This is a common use case for pointers in functions—allowing functions to modify the actual arguments passed to them, rather than working on copies.
- **Passing by Address**: The addresses of **x** and **y** are passed to the **swap** function (**&x** and **&y**). This technique is known as "passing by address," and it's a way to achieve "pass-by-reference" semantics in C++.
- **Value Swapping**: Swapping values is a basic operation that is widely used in various algorithms, especially sorting algorithms. This program provides a clear and concise implementation of this operation using pointers.

Practical Use

Understanding how to swap two values is essential for programming, especially in algorithms where rearranging elements is required. The approach used in this program, involving pointers, is particularly relevant in C and C++, where direct memory manipulation is a common practice.

4. Using const with Pointers

Objective: Explore the use of **const** in different pointer contexts for data protection.

```
#include <iostream>
int main() {
    int value = 5;
    const int* ptrToConst = &value; // Pointer to const data
    int* const constPtr = &value; // Const pointer to data
    // *ptrToConst = 10; // Error: modification of const location
    value = 10; // Allowed: Direct modification
    // constPtr = &value; // Error: constPtr cannot be reassigned
    *constPtr = 15; // Allowed: Modifying data through const pointer
    return 0;
}
```

This C++ program illustrates two different ways of using **const** with pointers, demonstrating how it affects the mutability of both the pointer itself and the data it points to. Let's dissect its components and functionality:

Main Concepts Demonstrated

1. **Pointer to Constant Data**: **const int* ptrToConst = &value;**
    - This declaration creates a pointer that points to a constant integer. It means that the integer value **ptrToConst** points to cannot be changed through this pointer. However, the pointer itself (**ptrToConst**) can point to different addresses.

- Attempting to modify the data pointed to by **ptrToConst** (e.g., ***ptrToConst = 10;**) would result in a compilation error because the pointer is to **const** data, which cannot be altered via the pointer.

2. **Constant Pointer to Data**: **int* const constPtr = &value;**
   - This declaration creates a constant pointer to an integer. The constant nature of the pointer means that the address it holds cannot be changed; **constPtr** will always point to the same **int** variable. However, the data at the address it points to can be modified.
   - Attempting to reassign **constPtr** to point to a different address (e.g., **constPtr = &value;**) would result in a compilation error because **constPtr** is a constant pointer.

Code Walkthrough

- **Initial Setup**: An integer variable **value** is declared and initialized to 5.
- **Pointer to Constant Data**: A pointer **ptrToConst** is initialized to point to **value**. The **const** keyword indicates that **ptrToConst** cannot be used to alter the integer it points to.
- **Constant Pointer to Data**: Another pointer **constPtr** is also initialized to point to **value**. This time, the **const** keyword is positioned after the asterisk, making **constPtr** itself constant, not the data it points to.
- **Modification Attempts**:
- The program includes commented-out lines to illustrate what operations are not allowed due to the **const** restrictions:
- Modifying **value** through **ptrToConst** is disallowed because **ptrToConst** points to constant data.
- Changing where **constPtr** points is disallowed because **constPtr** is a constant pointer.
- However, directly modifying **value** or modifying it through **constPtr** is allowed. **value = 10;** directly changes **value**, and ***constPtr = 15;** modifies **value** through the constant pointer, which is permitted because the constness of **constPtr** applies only to the pointer itself, not the data it points to.

Key Takeaways

- The placement of **const** in a pointer declaration is crucial. It determines whether the pointer is to constant data (**const int***), making the pointed-to data read-only, or whether the pointer itself is constant (**int* const**), making the pointer's target immutable.
- This code snippet is a concise demonstration of understanding and applying **const** correctly in pointer declarations to control data and pointer mutability in C++. It underscores the importance of **const** correctness in C++ programming, a best practice that enhances code safety by preventing unintended modifications.

5. Pointer-Array Relationship

Objective: Illustrate the relationship between arrays and pointers by printing array elements using a pointer.

```
#include <iostream>
int main() {
    int arr[] = { 1, 2, 3, 4, 5 };
```

```
    int* ptr = arr;
    for (int i = 0; i < 5; ++i) {
        std::cout << *(ptr++) << " "; // Increment pointer to move through ar-
ray
    }
    return 0;
}
```

Explanation:

This C++ program demonstrates a simple yet effective use of pointers to iterate over and print the elements of an integer array. Here's how it works in detail:

Program Overview

- An integer array **arr** is defined with five elements: {1, 2, 3, 4, 5}.
- A pointer **ptr** is declared and initialized to point to the first element of the array **arr**.
- A **for** loop is used to iterate over the array. Instead of accessing array elements using array indexing, the program uses the pointer **ptr**.
- Inside the loop, the program prints the value pointed to by **ptr** and then increments **ptr** (using **ptr++**). This increment operation moves the pointer to the next element in the array.
- By incrementing **ptr** within the **std::cout** statement, the program efficiently traverses the array without the need for an index variable.

Key Concepts Illustrated

- **Pointer Initialization**: The pointer **ptr** is initialized to point to the first element of the array **arr** by simply assigning it the array's name. In C++, the array name can be used as a pointer to its first element.
- **Pointer Dereferencing**: The program uses the dereference operator (*) to access the value of the element that **ptr** points to. This is how it accesses each element of the array to print it.
- **Pointer Arithmetic**: The use of **ptr++** demonstrates pointer arithmetic. In this context, incrementing a pointer moves it to point to the next element of the array. This is possible because pointers in C++ know the size of the data type they point to, and adding one to a pointer actually adds the size of the data type (in this case, the size of an **int**) to the address stored in the pointer.
- **Efficient Array Traversal**: This approach to array traversal is a classic example of pointer arithmetic's utility in C++. It allows for concise and efficient iteration over an array without the need for a separate index variable.

Output

The program outputs the elements of the array **arr** in order:

1 2 3 4 5

CONCLUSION

This program serves as a clear example of the power and simplicity of using pointers for array manipulation in C++. By combining pointer initialization, dereferencing, and arithmetic, it illustrates an alternative to traditional indexed array access, showcasing pointers' role in efficient data manipulation within C++ programs.

6. Sorting with Pointers

Objective: Implement bubble sort using pointers to sort an array of integers.

```
#include <iostream>
void bubbleSort(int* arr, int size) {
    for (int i = 0; i < size - 1; ++i) {
        for (int j = 0; j < size - i - 1; ++j) {
            if (*(arr + j) > *(arr + j + 1)) {
                int temp = *(arr + j);
                *(arr + j) = *(arr + j + 1);
                *(arr + j + 1) = temp;
            }
        }
    }
}
int main() {
    int arr[] = { 5, 1, 4, 2, 8 };
    bubbleSort(arr, 5);
    for (int i = 0; i < 5; ++i) {
        std::cout << arr[i] << " ";
    }
    return 0;
}
```

Explanation:

This C++ program implements the Bubble Sort algorithm to sort an array of integers in ascending order. It provides a clear demonstration of using pointers for direct manipulation of array elements. Here's a detailed explanation:

Bubble Sort Algorithm

The Bubble Sort algorithm is a simple sorting algorithm that repeatedly steps through the list, compares adjacent elements, and swaps them if they are in the wrong order. The pass through the list is repeated until the list is sorted. It is named for the way smaller elements "bubble" to the top of the list (beginning of the array) as the sorting process goes on.

Function: bubbleSort

- **Purpose**: Sorts an array of integers in ascending order.
- **Parameters**:
- **int* arr**: A pointer to the first element of the array to be sorted. The function expects a pointer because arrays decay to pointers when passed to functions, allowing the function to modify the array in place.
- **int size**: The number of elements in the array.
- **Process**:
- The function uses two nested **for** loops to implement the Bubble Sort algorithm.
- The outer loop runs **size - 1** times, ensuring that each element is moved to its correct position.
- The inner loop performs the comparisons and swaps if necessary. It iterates up to **size - i - 1** on each pass to avoid comparing elements that have already been placed in their final position.
- Pointer arithmetic (***(arr + j)**) is used to access and modify the elements of the array directly. If the current element is greater than the next element, they are swapped.

Main Function

- An integer array **arr** is declared and initialized with 5 integers.
- The **bubbleSort** function is called with **arr** and its size (5) as arguments. Since the array is passed by reference (implicitly converted to a pointer to its first element), the function sorts the original array in place.
- After sorting, a **for** loop iterates through the sorted array, printing each element to demonstrate the result of the sorting operation.

Output

The program outputs the elements of the array in sorted order:

1 2 4 5 8

Key Concepts Illustrated

- **Pointer Arithmetic and Array Manipulation**: The use of pointers to directly access and modify array elements is a fundamental aspect of C and C++ programming. This program illustrates how to perform these operations within the context of a sorting algorithm.
- **In-place Modification**: The array is sorted in place, demonstrating efficient use of memory by modifying the existing array rather than creating a new one.
- **Algorithm Implementation**: It provides a practical example of implementing a well-known sorting algorithm in C++, showcasing algorithmic thinking alongside language-specific features.

Conclusion

This program is a straightforward demonstration of applying pointer arithmetic and algorithmic concepts in C++ to sort an array in place. It reinforces understanding of pointers, arrays, and basic sorting algorithms in C++.

7. Function Pointers for Conditional Execution

Objective: Use function pointers to execute one of two functions based on user input.

```
#include <iostream>
void greetMorning() {
    std::cout << "Good morning!" << std::endl;
}
void greetEvening() {
    std::cout << "Good evening!" << std::endl;
}
int main() {
    void (*greetFunction)() = nullptr;
    char timeOfDay;
    std::cout << "Enter 'm' for morning or 'e' for evening: ";
    std::cin >> timeOfDay;
    if (timeOfDay == 'm') greetFunction = &greetMorning;
    else if (timeOfDay == 'e') greetFunction = &greetEvening;
    if (greetFunction) greetFunction();
    return 0;
}
```

Explanation:

This C++ program showcases how to dynamically select and invoke functions based on user input, using function pointers. Here's a detailed breakdown of its components and functionality:

Structure of the Program:

- **Function Definitions**: Two functions, **greetMorning** and **greetEvening**, are defined at the beginning of the program. Each prints a greeting appropriate for the time of day when called.
- **Main Function**:
- **Function Pointer Declaration**: A function pointer, **greetFunction**, is declared and initialized to **nullptr**. This pointer is designed to point to functions that return **void** and take no parameters.
- **User Input**: The program prompts the user to enter 'm' for morning or 'e' for evening and reads the input into the **timeOfDay** variable.
- **Function Pointer Assignment**: Depending on the user's input, **greetFunction** is assigned the address of either **greetMorning** or **greetEvening**. This assignment is done using the address-of operator (**&**) to get the function's address.
- **Function Invocation**: If **greetFunction** is not **nullptr** (indicating valid input and successful assignment), the function it points to is invoked using **greetFunction()**. This calls either **greetMorning** or **greetEvening** based on the earlier assignment.

Key Concepts Illustrated:

- **Function Pointers**: The program demonstrates the use of function pointers as variables that can store the address of a function. This feature allows for the dynamic selection and invocation of functions at runtime.

- **Conditional Logic**: By using a simple **if-else** statement based on user input, the program shows how to conditionally execute different code paths. In this case, the path is the invocation of different functions.
- **User Interaction**: It uses basic console I/O operations (**std::cout** for output and **std::cin** for input) to interact with the user, guiding the program's behavior based on user choices.

Practical Use

This example is particularly useful for illustrating the concept of callbacks or event-driven programming in a simplified form. Function pointers allow for a high degree of flexibility and modularity by enabling functions to be passed as arguments, stored in variables, or called conditionally. This technique is widely used in various programming paradigms, including GUI programming, where actions are performed in response to user events (e.g., button clicks).

Conclusion

The program efficiently demonstrates a practical application of function pointers in C++, enabling dynamic function invocation based on runtime conditions. It serves as a clear example of how C++ allows for flexible and powerful manipulation of functions as first-class objects through the use of pointers.

8. Dynamic Execution Paths with Function Pointers

Objective: Implement a menu system that uses function pointers to invoke different functions based on user selection.

```
#include <iostream>
#include <vector>
void option1() { std::cout << "Executing Option 1\n"; }
void option2() { std::cout << "Executing Option 2\n"; }
int main() {
    std::vector<void(*)()> options = { option1, option2 };
    int choice;
    std::cout << "Enter option number (1 or 2): ";
    std::cin >> choice;
    if (choice >= 1 && choice <= options.size()) {
        (*options[choice - 1])();
    }
    else {
        std::cout << "Invalid option\n";
    }
    return 0;
}
```

This C++ program demonstrates the use of function pointers stored within a **std::vector** to dynamically execute functions based on user input. Here's how it functions in detail:

Key Components

- **Header Inclusion**: The program includes **<iostream>** for standard input/output operations and **<vector>** for using the **std::vector** container.
- **Function Declarations**: Two functions, **option1** and **option2**, are declared and defined to print messages indicating their execution. These functions have no parameters and return void.
- **Main Function**:
- A **std::vector** named **options** is initialized with function pointers to **option1** and **option2**. The vector stores pointers to functions returning void and taking no parameters (**void(*)()**).
- The program prompts the user to enter a choice (1 or 2) to select which function to execute.
- User input is read into the **choice** variable.
- A conditional check ensures the entered choice is within the valid range (1 or 2, corresponding to the vector's indices 0 and 1). The program then executes the function corresponding to the user's choice by dereferencing the function pointer stored in the vector at the appropriate index (**choice - 1** to adjust for 0-based indexing) and invoking it.
- If the user enters an invalid option, the program outputs "Invalid option".

Program Flow:

1. **Function Execution Based on User Choice**: Depending on the user's input, either **option1** or **option2** is executed. This demonstrates a simple way of implementing a menu system where different functionalities can be triggered based on user input.
2. **Use of Function Pointers**: The program showcases how function pointers can be stored, managed, and invoked dynamically. This is particularly useful for scenarios where the exact function to be called is determined at runtime.
3. **Error Handling for Invalid Input**: The program includes basic error handling for out-of-range input, demonstrating a simple validation mechanism.

Practical Application:

This example is particularly useful for creating modular and extensible programs where the functionality might need to be selected dynamically at runtime. It exemplifies a fundamental technique for implementing command dispatchers, menu systems, or callback mechanisms, making the code more organized and flexible.

Conclusion

By utilizing function pointers within a **std::vector**, the program effectively decouples the execution logic from the decision-making process, illustrating a powerful concept in C++ programming that facilitates dynamic function invocation based on runtime conditions.

9. Pointer-Based String Reversal

Objective: Reverse a string in-place using pointers.

```
#include <iostream>
#include <cstring>
void reverseString(char* str) {
    char* end = str + std::strlen(str) - 1;
    while (str < end) {
        char temp = *str;
        *str++ = *end;
        *end-- = temp;
    }
}
int main() {
    char str[] = "Hello  World!";
    std::cout << "Original string: " << str << std::endl;
    reverseString(str);
    std::cout << "Reversed string: " << str << std::endl;
    return 0;
}
```

Explanation:

This C++ program reverses a given string in place using pointers. It showcases efficient string manipulation techniques, employing pointer arithmetic for traversing and modifying the string directly. Here's a breakdown of how the code works:

Key Components

- **Header Inclusion**: The program includes **<iostream>** for input and output operations, allowing it to print strings to the console. It also includes **<cstring>** for access to the **std::strlen** function, which is used to determine the length of the string.
- **reverseString Function**:
- **Purpose**: Reverses the characters of the string in place.
- **Parameter**: Accepts a **char* str**, which is a pointer to the first character of the string to be reversed.
- The function calculates the pointer to the last character of the string (**end**) by adding the length of the string (found using **std::strlen(str)**) to **str** and then subtracting one to adjust for the zero-based index.
- It uses a **while** loop to swap characters at the **str** and **end** pointers, moving towards the center of the string. The loop continues as long as the **str** pointer is before the **end** pointer.
- Within the loop, it performs a swap using a temporary **char** variable (**temp**), incrementing the **str** pointer and decrementing the **end** pointer after each swap to move towards the middle of the string.

Main Function Flow:

- **String Declaration**: Defines a **char** array **str[]** with the content "Hello World!", which is the string to be reversed.
- **Original String Output**: Prints the original string to the console to show the string before reversal.
- **String Reversal**: Calls the **reverseString** function, passing the array **str** as an argument. Since arrays decay to pointers when passed to functions, the function receives a pointer to the first element of the array.
- **Reversed String Output**: Prints the reversed string to the console to demonstrate the result of the in-place reversal.

Program Output

Original string: Hello World!
Reversed string: !dlroW olleH

Key Concepts Illustrated

- **In-Place Modification**: The program efficiently reverses the string without needing additional storage, demonstrating in-place data manipulation.
- **Pointer Arithmetic**: Uses pointer arithmetic (**str + std::strlen(str) - 1**) to navigate through the string and perform operations based on pointer locations.
- **String Manipulation**: Provides a clear example of manipulating C-style strings (**char** arrays) directly with pointers, a common practice in lower-level C and C++ programming.

Practical Use

This example is useful for understanding how strings can be manipulated at a low level in C and C++, showcasing fundamental concepts like pointers and memory management. While higher-level string manipulation is more common in modern C++ through the **std::string** class, understanding these basics remains valuable, especially for performance-critical applications and interfacing with C libraries or legacy code.

10. Implementing Bubble Sort and Selection Sort Using Pointers

Objective: Utilize pointers to implement both bubble sort and selection sort algorithms for an array of integers. Allow the user to choose which sorting algorithm to apply.

```
#include <iostream>

void bubbleSort(int* arr, int n) {
    for (int i = 0; i < n - 1; i++) {
        for (int j = 0; j < n - i - 1; j++) {
            if (*(arr + j) > *(arr + j + 1)) {
                int temp = *(arr + j);
                *(arr + j) = *(arr + j + 1);
```

```
                *(arr + j + 1) = temp;
            }
        }
    }
}

void selectionSort(int* arr, int n) {
    for (int i = 0; i < n - 1; i++) {
        int minIdx = i;
        for (int j = i + 1; j < n; j++) {
            if (*(arr + j) < *(arr + minIdx)) {
                minIdx = j;
            }
        }
        if (minIdx != i) {
            int temp = *(arr + i);
            *(arr + i) = *(arr + minIdx);
            *(arr + minIdx) = temp;
        }
    }
}

int main() {
    int arr[] = { 64, 34, 25, 12, 22, 11, 90 };
    int n = sizeof(arr) / sizeof(arr[0]);
    int choice;

    std::cout << "Select Sorting Algorithm:\n1. Bubble Sort\n2. Selection
Sort\nChoice: ";
    std::cin >> choice;

    if (choice == 1) {
        bubbleSort(arr, n);
        std::cout << "Array sorted using Bubble Sort:\n";
    }
    else if (choice == 2) {
        selectionSort(arr, n);
        std::cout << "Array sorted using Selection Sort:\n";
    }
    else {
        std::cout << "Invalid choice.\n";
        return 1;
    }
```

```
    for (int i = 0; i < n; i++) {
        std::cout << arr[i] << " ";
    }
    std::cout << std::endl;
    return 0;
}
```

Explanation:

This C++ code provides a hands-on demonstration of implementing and using two sorting algorithms, Bubble Sort and Selection Sort. Users are given the choice to select which algorithm they wish to apply to sort an integer array. The program exemplifies the use of pointers for direct memory manipulation, and dynamic execution based on user input. Here's an exploration of the code's components and functionality without direct code snippets:

Program Structure

1. **Header Inclusion**: The program begins by including the **<iostream>** header, enabling it to perform input and output operations.
2. **Bubble Sort Implementation**: A function named **bubbleSort** is defined, taking a pointer to an integer array and the size of the array as arguments. The Bubble Sort algorithm iteratively compares and swaps adjacent elements if they are in the wrong order, ensuring that after each pass through the array, the next largest element is moved to its correct position.
3. **Selection Sort Implementation**: Another function, **selectionSort**, is provided, which also takes a pointer to an integer array and its size. This algorithm selects the minimum element from the unsorted portion of the array and swaps it with the element at the current position, progressively sorting the array from the beginning.
4. **Main Function Execution Flow**:
    - An integer array is declared and initialized with a set of values.
    - The program calculates the array's size.
    - It prompts the user to choose between the Bubble Sort (**1**) and Selection Sort (**2**) algorithms via console input.
    - Based on the user's choice, the corresponding sorting function is called with the array and its size as parameters.
    - After sorting, the program iterates through the array, printing each element to display the sorted result.

Key Concepts Illustrated

- **Dynamic Sorting Choice**: The code showcases how to provide dynamic execution paths based on user input, allowing for flexible program behavior.
- **Pointer Arithmetic in Array Manipulation**: Both sorting functions utilize pointer arithmetic to access and modify the array elements, illustrating an efficient way to handle arrays in C++.
- **Sorting Algorithms**: By implementing two basic sorting algorithms, the program serves as a practical example of algorithmic thinking and optimization.

- **Efficient Memory Usage**: The sorting is performed in-place, demonstrating efficient use of memory by manipulating the original array without the need for additional arrays or data structures.

Practical Application

The program is a concise and effective educational tool, illustrating not just the theoretical underpinnings of Bubble Sort and Selection Sort algorithms but also their practical implementation in C++. It highlights important C++ programming concepts such as pointer manipulation, dynamic user input handling, and in-place array sorting. This example is particularly useful for learners and educators in computer science and programming courses, providing a clear comparison between two fundamental sorting techniques and demonstrating essential C++ features.

SUMMARY

- **Pointer Variable Declaration and Initialization**: The chapter kicks off by demystifying how to declare and initialize pointer variables, providing the groundwork for understanding how pointers are used to store memory addresses.
- **Pointer Operations**: Readers are introduced to essential pointer operations, including dereferencing and address-of operations, which are pivotal for manipulating the data pointers refer to.
- **Pointer Arithmetic and Expressions**: This section unravels the nuances of performing arithmetic on pointers, illustrating how to navigate through memory locations efficiently.
- **Pass-By-Reference with Pointers**: An in-depth discussion on using pointers to achieve pass-by-reference semantics in functions, allowing for more flexible and efficient manipulation of function arguments.
- **Using const with Pointers**: The chapter elaborates on various constancy degrees when using pointers, such as nonconstant pointers to nonconstant data, nonconstant pointers to constant data, constant pointers to nonconstant data, and constant pointers to constant data, shedding light on maintaining data integrity and function predictability.
- **The Relationship Between Pointers and Arrays**: It uncovers the intrinsic link between pointers and arrays, explaining how pointers can be used to traverse and manipulate arrays.
- **Array of Pointers**: This topic explores arrays that store pointers, further extending the versatility of pointers in managing collections of memory addresses.
- **Function Pointers**: A fascinating dive into function pointers, demonstrating how pointers can be used to invoke functions, enabling dynamic execution paths and callback mechanisms.
- **Pointers and sizeof Operator**: Discusses how the **sizeof** operator interacts with pointers, providing insights into memory management and data structure alignments.
- **Sorting Algorithms Using Pass-By-Reference**: Practical applications of pointers are showcased through examples of bubble sort and selection sort algorithms, illustrating how pointers enable efficient data manipulation by reference.
- **Pointer-Based String Processing**: The chapter concludes with a segment on processing strings using pointers, emphasizing pointers' role in string manipulation and character array traversal.

Multiple Choice

Q1: Pointers are variables that contain__________

Q2: Pointers may be assigned which of the following values?

a. Any integer values.
b. An address.
c. NULL.
d. Both (b) and (c).

Q3: What does the following assertion assert?

integer *countPtr, number;

a. Two int variables.
b. One int variable and one int pointer.
c. Two pointers to ints.
d. The statement is invalid.

Q4: Three of the four expressions listed below have the same value. Which one of the following expressions has a different value than the others?

a. *&ptr
b. &*ptr
c. *ptr
d. ptr

Q5: The following is the least privilege principle:

a. A nonconstant pointer to nonconstant data.
b. A nonconstant pointer to constant data.
c. A constant pointer to nonconstant data.
d. A constant pointer to constant data.

Q6: Which of the following operations can accept a pointer as an operand?

a. ++
b. *=
c. %
d. /

Q7: Given that k is an array of integers beginning at location 2000, kPtr is a pointer to k, and each integer occupies 4 bytes of memory, determine where kPtr + 3 points

a. 2003
b. 2006
c. 2012
d. 2024

Q8: Which expression refers to the address of array element 3 if t is an array and tPtr is a pointer to that array?

a. *(tPtr + 3)
b. tPtr[3]
c. &t[3]
d. *(t + 3)

Exercises

1. Declare a double variable called weight and initialize it to 128.4.
   - Create a pointer named weightPtr and point it to the variable weight.
   - Display the value directly using the variable itself.
   - Display the address directly using the address of the operator.
2. Modify the previous assignment by adding the following lines of code:
   - Set the value of the variable weight to 149.3
   - Repeat steps 3 through 6.
   - Now set *weightPointer to 173.8
   - Repeat steps 3 through 6.
3. Create an array named myArray of size 10 and using an initializer list set it with random values. Create a pointer to the array named myArrayPtr. Display the elements of the array using the pointer. (Hint use a for loop and pointer arithmetic)
4. Write a program that declares an array of integers, and then uses pointers to print the elements of the array in reverse order.
5. Write a program that takes two integer pointers as arguments and swaps the values they point to.
6. Write a program that declares a string, and then uses pointers to copy the string to a new location in memory.
7. Write a program that takes a character pointer as an argument, and then uses the
8. Write a program that takes two character pointers as arguments, and then uses the pointers to compare the two strings. If the strings are equal, the program should print "Strings are equal", otherwise it should print "Strings are not equal".
9. Write a program that declares an array of integers, and then uses a pointer to find the minimum and maximum elements of the array.
10. Write a program that uses a pointer to dynamically allocate memory for an array of integers, and then uses the pointer to initialize the array with user-specified values.
11. Write a program that takes a character pointer as an argument, and then uses the pointer to convert the string to uppercase.
12. Write a program that takes a character pointer as an argument, and then uses the pointer to count the number of words in the string.
13. Write a program that takes a character pointer as an argument, and then uses the pointer to reverse the string.
14. Write a C++ program that declares an integer variable, **a**, initialized to 5. Create a pointer **p** that points to **a**. Use the pointer to print **a**'s value, then change **a**'s value to 10 using the pointer and print the new value.
15. Given an array of integers **arr[]** = {10, 20, 30, 40, 50}, write a program that uses pointer arithmetic to traverse the array and print each element's value.
16. Implement a C++ function that swaps the values of two integer variables using pointers. Demonstrate this functionality in **main()** by swapping two variables.
17. Write a program that demonstrates the use of a nonconstant pointer to constant data and a constant pointer to nonconstant data, highlighting the difference in their usage.
18. Create an array of pointers to integers. Initialize this array with the addresses of five different integers. Then, use this array of pointers to print the values of the integers.

19. Implement two sorting algorithms: bubble sort and selection sort. Create a function pointer that can point to either of these sorting functions. Use this function pointer to call each sorting algorithm on an array of integers.
20. Write a program that reverses a string in place using pointers. The program should define a function that takes a character array (C-style string) as an argument and reverses the string without using any standard library functions.

Chapter 6
File Processing

ABSTRACT

Chapter 6 provides a comprehensive exploration of file processing in C++. It commences with an enlightening introduction, setting the tone for the intricate world of file operations. A deep dive into data hierarchy establishes a foundational understanding of organized data storage. Practical segments on appending data to files, whether it be characters or whole lines, are provided with illustrative examples. The chapter introduces the utility of the getline function for formatted input and delves into manipulating both input and output streams. As the chapter progresses, readers are shown the methods to create files and write data into them, followed by techniques to efficiently read from files. The concept of a file position pointer is introduced, allowing for intricate file manipulations. Essential to any file operation, the chapter concludes by highlighting the importance of recognizing exceptions and strategies for robust error handling. With hands-on exercises, readers are ensured a holistic understanding of file processing in C++.

6.1 INTRODUCTION

File stream is a C++ feature that enables you to read from and write to the file system of your computer. This is accomplished via the use of input and output streams, which are objects that may be used to conduct input and output operations on files.

A file stream object is an instance of a C++ Standard Template Library (STL) class that lets you read from or write to a file, such as fstream, ifstream, or ofstream. The location where a file stream object is created and initialized determines its scope.

Data is written to a file using ofstream (output file stream). It provides many member functions for opening, writing to, and closing a file. For instance, the open() function can be used to open a file, the write() function can be used to write data to the file, and the close() function may be used to shut the file.

A file is read using ifstream (input file stream). It has the same member functions as ofstream, but it is used for reading rather than writing.

fstream (file stream) is a combination of ofstream and ifstream that may be used to read and write to a file.

DOI: 10.4018/979-8-3693-2007-5.ch006

This is an example of writing data to a file using an ofstream object:

```
#include <fstream>
using namespace std;
int main() {
ofstream outFile; // Create an ofstream object
outFile.open("example.txt"); // Open the file for writing
outFile << "Writing to a file in C++ is easy!" << endl; // Write data to the
file
outFile.close(); // Close the file
return 0;
}
```

In this example, an ofstream object is created, and the open() method is used to open the "example. txt" file for writing. The operator is then used to write data to the file, and the file is closed using the close() function.

```
Similarly, the ifstream object may be used to read from a file.
#include <fstream>
#include <string>
using namespace std;
int main() {
ifstream inFile; // Create an ifstream object
inFile.open("example.txt"); // Open the file for reading
string line;
while (getline(inFile, line)) { // Read the file line by line
cout << line << endl;
}
inFile.close(); // Close the file
return 0;
}
```

In this example, an ifstream object is created, and the open() method is used to read from the file "example.txt." The file is then read using the getline() method, which reads a single line of text from the file, and closed with the close() function.

Note that when you open a file, you must use the is open() method to find out if the action to open the file was successful.

This is an example of global scope file processing:

```
#include <fstream>
ofstream outFile; // Global scope
int main() {
outFile.open("output.txt");
outFile << "Writing to a file at the global scope." << endl;
```

```
outFile.close();
return 0;
}
```

This example defines the file stream object outFile at the global level so that it may be used across the whole program.

The following is an example of file processing inside a function:

```
#include <fstream>
void writeToFile(string fileName, string message) {
ofstream outFile; // Local scope
outFile.open(fileName);
outFile << message << endl;
outFile.close();
}
int main() {
writeToFile("output.txt", "Writing to a file within a function.");
return 0;
}
```

In this example, the file stream object outFile is declared inside the method writeToFile. Its scope is limited to the function, so it can't be used outside of the function.

It's important to remember that file stream objects must always be closed when they're done being used. Otherwise, memory leaks and other problems could happen.

Where file stream objects are declared and set up determines where they can be used to work with files.

6.2 DATA HIERARCHY

Data hierarchy is the way that pieces of data are put together in a structured way so that they look like a tree. Each level of the hierarchy is made up of data pieces that are related to each other based on their characteristics. Here are a few C++ examples of data hierarchy:

- The smallest unit of data in C++ is the bit. A bit may have the value 0 or 1.
- Byte: A collection of 8 bits. The smallest accessible unit of memory in C++ is the byte.
- A field is a named data unit containing one or more bytes. Fields are used to represent certain data types, such as integers, floating-point numbers, characters, and strings.
- Record: A collection of fields that together reflect a single entity. A record may, for instance, represent a person, a product, or an order.
- A collection of linked documents. With files, it is possible to store and manage data over an extended period of time.
- A collection of connected data files large volumes of data are stored, managed, and retrieved using databases.

Data hierarchy is important in C++ because it makes it easier to organize data in a way that makes sense and makes it easier to keep track of and process. It also contributes to the maintenance of data integrity and consistency.

6.3 APPENDING TO A FILE WITH EXAMPLES

Using the fstream library, appending to a file in C++ is possible. The following is an example of appending text to a file:

```
#include <iostream>
#include <fstream>
int main() {
// Open the file in append mode
std::ofstream file("example.txt", std::ios::app);
if (file.is_open()) {
// Write some text to the file
file << "This is some appended text.\n";
// Close the file
file.close();
std::cout << "Text has been appended to the file." << std::endl;
}
else {
std::cout << "Unable to open file for appending." << std::endl;
}
return 0;
}
```

In this example, the ofstream object is formed with the filename "example.txt" and the append mode flag std::ios::app. The text is then written to the file using the operator, and the close() function is used to close the file.

When you open a file in append mode, everything you write after that will be added to the end.If you want to replace what's already in the file, open it in truncate mode (std::ios::trunc).

On the first two lines, you'll find the standard input-output stream library and the file stream library.

The main method then generates an output file stream object called file, which opens the "example.txt" file in append mode.

If the file is opened successfully, the program uses the put and print operators to add an exclamation mark and a new line to the file's end.

The software then closes the file and prints a message that says if the file was successfully added or not.

If the file cannot be opened to append, the application will print a notice stating that it was unable to open the file.

6.4 APPENDING CHARACTERS AND LINES

In C++, to append characters or lines is to add new characters or lines to the end of an existing text file. The following demonstrates how to add characters or lines to a file:

```
#include <iostream>
#include <fstream>
int main() {
// Open the file in append mode
std::ofstream file("example.txt", std::ios::app);
if (file.is_open()) {
// Append a single character to the end of the file
file.put('!');
// Append a new line to the end of the file
file << "\nThis is a new line.";
// Close the file
file.close();
std::cout << "Text has been appended to the file." << std::endl;
}
else {
std::cout << "Unable to open file for appending." << std::endl;
}
return 0;
}
```

The put() function is used in this example to add a single character ('!') to the end of the file. The operator is used to attach a new line and some text to the file's conclusion.

Note that when adding text to a file, it is essential to verify that the file is opened in the right mode (std::ios::app) and closed appropriately after the operation is complete.

This code demonstrates how to add text to an existing file in C++.

On the first two lines, you'll find the standard input-output stream library and the file stream library.

The main method then generates an output file stream object called file, which opens the "example.txt" file in append mode.

If the file is opened successfully, the program uses the put and print operators to add an exclamation mark and a new line to the file's end.

The software then closes the file and prints a message that says if the file was successfully added or not.

If the file cannot be opened to append, the application will print a notice stating that it was unable to open the file.

6.5 FORMATTING WITH GETLINE

Formatting using getline() in C++ involves reading a line of text from a file and parsing it into separate fields or tokens depending on a particular delimiter or separator. Here is an example of how to format text from a file using the getline() function:

Say we have a text file called "example.txt" that contains the following:

John Smith,30,Male

Mary Johnson,25,Female

We can use getline() to read each line of text from the file and stringstream to parse each line into separate fields depending on the comma delimiter. This is the code:

```
#include <iostream>
#include <fstream>
#include <sstream>
#include <string>
int main() {
std::ifstream file("example.txt");
if (file.is_open()) {
std::string line;
// Read each line from the file
while (std::getline(file, line)) {
std::stringstream ss(line);
std::string name, age, gender;
// Parse the line into individual fields based on the comma separator
std::getline(ss, name, ',');
std::getline(ss, age, ',');
std::getline(ss, gender);
// Output the formatted fields
std::cout << "Name: " << name << std::endl;
std::cout << "Age: " << age << std::endl;
std::cout << "Gender: " << gender << std::endl;
}
// Close the file
file.close();
}
else {
std::cout << "Unable to open file." << std::endl;
}
return 0;
}
```

In this example, we read each line of text using getline from the "example.txt" file (). Next, a stringstream object is made so that each line can be split into separate fields based on where the comma delimiter is.Again, we use getline() to read each field from the stringstream object, and then we send the prepared fields to the console.

This code demonstrates how to get data from a file using the C++ programming language.

The standard input-output stream library, file stream library, string stream library, and string library comprise the first four lines.

The main method then generates an input file stream object called file, which opens the "example.txt" file.

If the file is successfully opened, each line is read using the std::getline() method, which retrieves a line of text from a file stream and puts it in a string object called line.

The software then constructs a string stream object called ss, whose input source is the line string.

Using the comma separator, the SS object parses the line text into distinct fields. The std::getline() method is used once again to extract each field from the SS object and save it in distinct string objects titled name, age, and gender.

Output:
Name: John Smith
Age: 30
Gender: Male
Name: Mary Johnson
Age: 25
Gender: Female

6.6 MANIPULATING INPUT AND OUTPUT

Setting precision, padding, and alignment are examples of manipulating input and output in C++. The following is an example of manipulating input and output in C++:

```
#include <iostream>
#include <iomanip>
int main() {
double number = 123.456789;
// Set output precision to 2 decimal places
std::cout << std::fixed << std::setprecision(2);
std::cout << "Number: " << number << std::endl;
// Set output field width and padding with zeros
std::cout << std::setw(10) << std::setfill('0') << "123" << std::endl;
// Set output field alignment
std::cout << std::left << std::setw(10) << "Left aligned" << std::endl;
std::cout << std::right << std::setw(10) << "Right aligned" << std::endl;
return 0;
}
```

In this example, we output a double number after setting the output precision to 2 decimal places using std::fixed and setprecision(). We then produce a string after setting the output field width to 10 characters and padding with zeros using std::setw() and std::setfill(). We output two additional strings after setting the output field alignment to left or right using std::left and std::right.

This code demonstrates how to format output in the computer language C++.

The input-output manipulator library and the standard input-output stream library are on the first two lines.

The main function then creates the number variable with the value 123.456789.

The program uses the std::fixed and std::setprecision() manipulators to set the output precision to 2 decimal places and the std::cout stream object to output the number variable.

Using the std::setw() and std::setfill() manipulators, the output field width is set to 10 characters, and the string "123" is padded with zeros.

The program then uses the std::left and std::right manipulators to align the output field to the left and right, respectively. It then outputs two strings with a field width of 10 characters: "Left aligned" and "Right aligned."

At the end of each line, the std::endl manipulator outputs a newline character.

Output:

Number: 123.46

0000000123

Left aligned

Right aligned

Manipulating input and output using file streams in C++ refers to altering the format and presentation of data while reading or writing a file. Here is an example of manipulating file input and output streams in C++:

```
#include <iostream>
#include <fstream>
#include <iomanip>
int main() {
// Open the file in output mode
std::ofstream outfile("example.txt");
if (outfile.is_open()) {
// Set output precision to 2 decimal places
outfile << std::fixed << std::setprecision(2);
outfile << "Number: " << 123.456789 << std::endl;
// Set output field width and padding with zeros
outfile << std::setw(10) << std::setfill('0') << "123" << std::endl;
// Set output field alignment
outfile << std::left << std::setw(15) << "Left aligned" << std::endl;
outfile << std::right << std::setw(15) << "Right aligned" << std::endl;
// Close the file
outfile.close();
std::cout << "Data has been written to the file." << std::endl;
}
else {
std::cout << "Unable to open file for writing." << std::endl;
```

```
}
// Open the file in input mode
std::ifstream infile("example.txt");
if (infile.is_open()) {
std::string line;
// Read each line from the file and output to the console
while (std::getline(infile, line)) {
std::cout << line << std::endl;
}
// Close the file
infile.close();
}
else {
std::cout << "Unable to open file for reading." << std::endl;
}
return 0;
}
```

In this example, "example.txt" is opened in output mode, and formatted data is written to it using std::ofstream. Like in the last example, we set the output accuracy, field width, padding, and alignment. The file is then closed, and a message is printed to the console.

The same file is then opened in input mode using std::ifstream, and each line of text is read using std::getline (). Each line is sent to the console. This application displays C++ Standard Library input/output file operations.

In the main function, std::ofstream is used to open the "example.txt" file in output mode. The program then checks that the file was opened correctly and writes data to it using different formatting options, such as output precision, field width, fill character, and alignment.Finally, the file is closed, and a message confirming that the data has been written to the file is shown on the terminal.

Next, std::ifstream is used to open the same file in input mode. Again, the software verifies that the file was properly opened before reading each line using std::getline. Using std::cout, each line is then displayed to the console. Finally, the file is closed, and a message indicating whether the file was successfully opened for reading is sent to the terminal.

Overall, this program demonstrates the basics of writing and reading data to and from a file using the C++ Standard Library, as well as how to use various formatting options when writing data to a file.

Output:

Data has been written to the file.

Number: 123.46

0000000123

Left aligned

Right aligned

6.7 CREATE FILE AND WRITE INTO A FILE

Creating a file and writing to it are two basic C++ procedures that are used often in software development.

When you make a file, you need to make a file object, which is usually done with the ofstream class. After a file object has been created, it may be opened using the open method with the file's name and path. When the file has been opened, you may write data to it using different ofstream class methods.

When writing to a file, the ofstream class is used to write data to the file. You can add data to a file or write binary data using other methods, such as the operator or the write method.

Creating a file and writing to it are basic C++ tasks that are used a lot when making software.

6.7.1 Create File

File streams are used for reading from and writing to files in C++. The following code demonstrates how to construct a file stream in C++:

```
#include <iostream>
#include <fstream>
int main() {
// Create an output file stream
std::ofstream outfile("example.txt");
if (outfile.is_open()) {
outfile << "This is an example file." << std::endl;
outfile << "It contains some text." << std::endl;
outfile.close();
std::cout << "Data has been written to the file." << std::endl;
}
else {
std::cout << "Unable to open file for writing." << std::endl;
}
// Create an input file stream
std::ifstream infile("example.txt");
if (infile.is_open()) {
std::string line;
while (std::getline(infile, line)) {
std::cout << line << std::endl;
}
infile.close();
}
else {
std::cout << "Unable to open file for reading." << std::endl;
}
return 0;
}
```

In this example, std::ofstream is used to construct an output file stream. The constructor of the std::ofstream object receives the name of the file to which we want to write ("example.txt"). Then, some text is written to the file using the operator, and the file is closed using the close() method.

Next, an input file stream is created using std::ifstream. The std::ifstream object's constructor receives the filename ("example.txt") from which we want to read. We use std::getline() to read each line of text from the file and std::cout to print it to the console.

The code explains how to read and write data to and from a file using C++ file streams.

It begins by establishing an output file stream object and opening the "example.txt" file. The software sends two lines of text to the file using the output stream operator "" and then closes the file if the file was successfully opened. If the file cannot be opened, an error message is shown on the console.

Then, the program makes an input file stream object and uses it to open the same file ("example.txt"). If the file is successfully opened, each line is read using the getline() method and shown on the console. If the file cannot be opened, an error message is shown on the console.

The program concludes by returning 0 to signify successful completion.

Output:

Data has been written to the file.

This is an example file.

It contains some text.

6.7.2 Write Into File

File streams are used for reading from and writing to files in C++. The following is an example of writing into a file stream in C++:

```
#include <iostream>
#include <fstream>
int main() {
// Create an output file stream
std::ofstream outfile("example.txt");
if (outfile.is_open()) {
outfile << "This is an example file." << std::endl;
outfile << "It contains some text." << std::endl;
outfile.close();
std::cout << "Data has been written to the file." << std::endl;
}
else {
std::cout << "Unable to open file for writing." << std::endl;
}
return 0;
}
```

In this example, std::ofstream is used to construct an output file stream. The constructor of the std::ofstream object receives the name of the file to which we want to write ("example.txt"). Then, some text is written to the file using the operator, and the file is closed using the close() method.

This software generates an output file stream and writes data to the "example.txt" file. The file stream is constructed using the std::ofstream class, with the file name supplied as a constructor argument.

If the file stream is open, the program writes some data to the file using the output operator. It sends two lines of text to the file, followed by a line-termination character (std::endl), and then closes the file stream. If the file stream cannot be opened for writing, an error message is shown on the console. The software then returns 0 to signify successful completion.

Output:

Data has been written to the file.

This will create a new text file called "example.txt" in the same directory as your program and append the two lines of text to it. If the file already exists, the text is added to its end.

6.8 READ FROM THE FILE

File streams are used for reading from and writing to files in C++. The following is an example of reading from a file stream in C++:

```
#include <iostream>
#include <fstream>
int main() {
// Create an input file stream
std::ifstream infile("example.txt");
if (infile.is_open()) {
std::string line;
while (std::getline(infile, line)) {
std::cout << line << std::endl;
}
infile.close();
}
else {
std::cout << "Unable to open file for reading." << std::endl;
}
return 0;
}
```

In this example, std::ifstream is used to build an input file stream. The std::ifstream object's constructor receives the filename ("example.txt") from which we want to read. We use std::getline() to read each line of text from the file and std::cout to print it to the console.

This C++ code reads information from the "example.txt" file.

Initially, the class ifstream is used to build the input file stream object infile. The procedure then verifies that the file was successfully opened using the is open() method of the ifstream class. If the file is open, each line is read using the getline() function and sent to the console using the std::cout statement if the file is open. The file is finally closed using the close() function of the ifstream class.

If the file cannot be opened, an error message is printed to the terminal. The function returns 0 upon completion, signifying success.

Output:

This is an example file.

It contains some text.

This will read the example.txt file in the same directory as your application and print each line to the console. If the file cannot be opened or does not exist, an error message will be shown.

6.9 A FILE POSITION POINTER

In C++, a file position pointer specifies the current location inside a file that is being read or written. This pointer maintains the current byte offset inside the file and may be moved using the seekg() and seekp() methods.

Here is an example of how to shift the file location pointer using seekg() and seekp():

```
#include <iostream>
#include <fstream>
int main() {
std::ofstream outfile("example.txt");
// Write some data to the file
outfile << "This is the first line.\n";
outfile << "This is the second line.\n";
outfile << "This is the third line.\n";
outfile << "This is the fourth line.\n";
outfile.close();
std::ifstream infile("example.txt");
// Move the file position pointer to the beginning of the third line
infile.seekg(2, std::ios::beg); // The third line starts at byte 2
std::string line;
std::getline(infile, line);
std::cout << "Third line: " << line << std::endl;
// Move the file position pointer to the end of the second line
infile.seekg(18, std::ios::beg); // The second line ends at byte 18
std::getline(infile, line);
std::cout << "Second line: " << line << std::endl;
infile.close();
return 0;
}
```

In this example, an output file stream is created using std::ofstream, and data is written to the file.

Next, we use std::ifstream to make an input file stream and seekg () to change the file position pointer. By giving 2 as the offset argument and std::ios::beg as the reference point parameter, we move the pointer to the beginning of the third line.The third line is then read using std::getline() and printed to the console.

We then moved the file position pointer to the end of the second line by giving 18 as the offset and std::ios::beg as the reference point.The second line is then read using std::getline() and printed to the console.

This application illustrates file placement using input and output file streams in C++. The application generates an output file stream and sends some data to the "example.txt" file. The application then starts an input file stream and uses the seekg() function to advance the file position pointer to certain locations inside the file.

In this case, the software moves the file position pointer to the beginning of the third line and uses the std::getline function () to read the line.The file position pointer is then moved to the end of the second line, and that line is also read. The application ends after closing the input file stream.

This app shows how to use file placement to read specific parts of a file. This is useful when working with large files or when you only need to read certain parts.

Eventually, the input file stream is closed.

Output:

Third line: This is the third line.

Second line: This is the second line.

This will advance the file position pointer to particular places inside the file and begin reading from there. It is handy for random data access inside a file.

6.10 RECOGNIZING EXCEPTIONS

When an error occurs when reading from or writing to a file, file streams in C++ might raise exceptions. Here is an example of how to identify and handle file stream exceptions:

```
#include <iostream>
#include <fstream>
#include <string>
int main() {
try {
// Create an input file stream
std::ifstream infile("example.txt");
if (!infile) {
throw std::runtime_error("Unable to open file for reading.");
}
std::string line;
while (std::getline(infile, line)) {
std::cout << line << std::endl;
}
infile.close();
}
catch (const std::exception & ex) {
std::cerr << "Exception: " << ex.what() << std::endl;
}
```

```
return 0;
}
```

This program reads the file “example.txt” and sends each line to the terminal.A try-catch block is used for exception management in the application. If an exception is encountered when trying to open or read the file, the catch block will capture it and output an error message to the console. The application contains C++ header files for input/output operations and textual manipulation.

In this example, std::ifstream is used to build an input file stream. If the file cannot be opened, a std::runtime error exception is thrown with a descriptive error message.

A try block is used to enclose code that may throw an exception, and a catch block is used to handle the exception if it is thrown. In this case, we grab a reference to a std::exception and use std::cerr to send out the error message.

Output:

Unable to open the file for reading.

Exception: Unable to open the file for reading.

This will capture the exception and report it to the console. If the file can be successfully opened and read, the function inside the try block will run properly and not raise an error.

6.11 HANDLING ERRORS

By reading from or writing to a file in C++, file streams might encounter problems. Here is an example of handling file stream error conditions in C++:

```
#include <iostream>
#include <fstream>
#include <stdexcept>
int main() {
try {
// Create an output file stream
std::ofstream outfile("example.txt");
if (!outfile) {
throw std::runtime_error("Unable to open file for writing.");
}
outfile << "This is some text that we want to write to the file." << std::endl;
if (outfile.fail()) {
throw std::runtime_error("Error writing to file.");
}
outfile.close();
// Create an input file stream
std::ifstream infile("example.txt");
if (!infile) {
throw std::runtime_error("Unable to open file for reading.");
}
```

```
std::string line;
while (std::getline(infile, line)) {
std::cout << line << std::endl;
}
infile.close();
}
catch (const std::exception & ex) {
std::cerr << "Exception: " << ex.what() << std::endl;
}
return 0;
}
```

In this example, we use std::ofstream to construct an output file stream and then test if the file can be opened for writing. If the file cannot be opened, a std::runtime error exception is thrown with a descriptive error message.

We write some text to the file using the operator and then use the fail() function to see if the write operation was successful. If the write operation fails, another std::runtime error exception is thrown.

We then generate an input file stream using std::ifstream after closing the output file stream. Checking if the file can be opened for reading, we then read each line of text using std::getline ().

A try block is used to enclose code that may throw an exception, and a catch block is used to handle the exception if it is thrown. In this case, we grab a reference to a std::exception and use std::cerr to send out the error message.

This C++ application illustrates the use of file streams and exception handling. After the creation of an output file stream, the application writes text to the file. It then determines if an error occurred when writing to the file and throws a runtime error if one did. After shutting down the output file stream, the software establishes an input file stream and then reads the file's contents. It determines if an error occurred when reading from the file and throws a runtime error if one did. Lastly, the software captures any thrown exceptions and displays an error message.

Output:

This is some text that we want to write to the file.

This will capture any exceptions that occur when reading or writing to the file and show them on the console. If the file actions are successful, the code inside the try block will run normally and not raise an exception.

Advanced Practice Exercises With Answers

1. Dynamic Log File Creation and Writing

Exercise: Create a C++ program that dynamically generates log file names based on the current date and writes log messages to it.

Objective: To practice using **<chrono>** and **<iomanip>** for generating dynamic log file names based on the current date, and to write log messages to this file.

Solution Outline:

- Use **<chrono>** and **<iomanip>** to get the current date.
- Format the date to create a unique log file name.
- Use **std::ofstream** to open and write messages to the file.

```
#include <chrono>
#include <fstream>
#include <iomanip>
#include <sstream>

int main() {
    auto now = std::chrono::system_clock::now();
    std::time_t t = std::chrono::system_clock::to_time_t(now);
    std::tm tm = *std::localtime(&t);

    std::ostringstream oss;
    oss << std::put_time(&tm, "%Y-%m-%d-%H-%M-%S") << "-log.txt";
    std::string filename = oss.str();

    std::ofstream logfile(filename, std::ios::app);a
    logfile << "Log message" << std::endl;
}
```

Explanation:

This C++ program demonstrates how to create a log file with a timestamp in its name and append a log message to it. It's a straightforward example of using C++'s **<chrono>**, **<fstream>**, and **<iomanip>** libraries for dealing with time, file I/O, and data formatting. Let's go through each part of the program:

Key Components:

- **<chrono>**: Provides classes and functions to work with dates, times, and durations. The program uses it to get the current time.
- **<fstream>**: For file stream operations, allowing the program to write to files. Here, it's used to open (or create if it doesn't exist) a log file and append a message to it.
- **<iomanip>**: Contains I/O manipulators that can modify the input/output stream. It's used here with **std::put_time** to format the time into a human-readable string.
- **<sstream>**: Provides string stream classes. **std::ostringstream** is used to build the file name with the formatted timestamp.

Program Flow:

1. **Get the Current Time**: The program uses **std::chrono::system_clock::now()** to capture the current time point.

2. **Convert Time Point to time_t**: It converts the time point to **std::time_t** using **std::chrono::system_clock::to_time_t(now)**, which represents the time in seconds since the Unix epoch (00:00, Jan 1, 1970).
3. **Convert time_t to std::tm**: It converts the **std::time_t** object to a **std::tm** structure representing calendar time, broken down into its components (year, month, day, etc.).
4. **Format the Timestamp and Create Filename**: Using **std::put_time**, it formats the **std::tm** object into a string representing the local time in the format **YYYY-MM-DD-HH-MM-SS**. This formatted string is then used to construct a file name, appending **"-log.txt"** to it.
5. **Create/Open and Write to the Log File**: It opens (or creates if it doesn't exist) a file with the generated name in append mode (**std::ios::app**). It then writes "Log message" followed by a newline to the file.

Note:

There's a typo at the end of the line initializing **std::ofstream logfile(filename, std::ios::app);**. The character **a** after the semicolon is likely an unintended addition and should be removed for the code to compile successfully.

Considerations

- **File Naming**: The use of a timestamp in the file name ensures that each execution of the program within a unique second generates a new log file, making this pattern suitable for applications that require timestamped logs for each run.
- **Time Zone**: The program uses **std::localtime**, which converts the **std::time_t** value to the local time zone. For logging purposes, especially in distributed systems, consider the implications of time zone differences.
- **Error Handling**: The program does not include error handling for file operations. In a complete application, you should check if the file has been successfully opened before attempting to write to it.

This program offers a basic yet practical demonstration of creating time-stamped log files in C++, which can be particularly useful for debugging, monitoring, or tracking events over time in software applications.

2. Secure File Appending

Exercise: Write a program that appends user input to a file securely, ensuring that input ending with a specific keyword doesn't get written to the file.

Objective: To enhance file security by appending user input to a file, excluding inputs that terminate with a specified keyword.

Solution Outline

- Read user input in a loop.
- Check if the input ends with the specified keyword. If it does, break from the loop.

- Otherwise, append the input to the file.

```
#include <iostream>
#include <fstream>
#include <string>

int main() {
    std::ofstream file("secure_append.txt", std::ios::app);
    std::string input;
    while (getline(std::cin, input) && input != "end") {
        file << input << std::endl;
    }
}
```

Explanation

This C++ program is designed to append text to a file named "secure_append.txt" continuously. It reads input from the user through the console until the user types "end", signaling the program to stop. Here's a breakdown of how it operates:

Key Components

- **<iostream>**: Included for input and output operations. Here, it's used to read from the standard input (**std::cin**) and print to the standard output.
- **<fstream>**: For handling file operations. The program uses **std::ofstream** to open and write to the file.
- **<string>**: To work with strings in C++. The program reads input into a **std::string** variable.

Program Flow

1. **Open the File**: The program opens "secure_append.txt" for writing with the append mode (**std::ios::app**) enabled. This mode ensures that new data is added to the end of the file without overwriting existing content.
2. **Read and Append Loop**:
    - It enters a loop that continuously reads lines of text from the user via **std::cin**.
    - Each line of text is stored in the **std::string input**.
    - The loop condition checks if the input is not "end". If the input is "end", the loop terminates, effectively ending the program.
    - For every input that is not "end", the program appends the input to "secure_append.txt", followed by a newline character to keep each entry on a separate line.
3. **Loop Termination**: When the user types "end", the condition in the while loop evaluates to false, breaking the loop. The program then naturally reaches its end, and the **std::ofstream file** object goes out of scope and is automatically closed.

Considerations

- **No Explicit File Closure**: The program does not explicitly call **close()** on the **std::ofstream file** object because the destructor of **std::ofstream** automatically closes the file when the object is destroyed (i.e., when it goes out of scope at the end of **main**).
- **Error Handling**: This program does not include error handling for file operations. In a more robust implementation, you might want to verify that the file has been successfully opened for appending before attempting to write to it.
- **Efficiency**: Opening a file in append mode for each line might be less efficient than other methods for frequent writes. However, since this program keeps the file open and appends to it in a loop, it mitigates this concern.

Example Usage

When you run this program, it waits for user input. You can type any text and press Enter to append it to “secure_append.txt”. When you’re done, typing “end” stops the program. Each line you entered will be on its own line in “secure_append.txt”.

3. Custom Text File Encryption and Decryption

Exercise: Implement a simple encryption algorithm to write encrypted data to a file and then read and decrypt it.

Objective: To apply a simple character shift algorithm for encrypting and decrypting file contents.

Solution Outline

- For encryption, shift each character by a fixed number before writing to the file.
- For decryption, read the file and reverse the shift on each character.

```
#include <fstream>
#include <string>

void encryptDecrypt(std::string inputFile, std::string outputFile, int key,
bool encrypt) {
    std::ifstream input(inputFile);
    std::ofstream output(outputFile);
    char ch;
    while (input.get(ch)) {
        char shifted = encrypt ? ch + key: ch - key;
        output.put(shifted);
    }
}

int main() {
```

```
    encryptDecrypt("original.txt", "encrypted.txt", 3, true); // Encrypt
    encryptDecrypt("encrypted.txt", "decrypted.txt", 3, false); // Decrypt
}
```

Explanation

This C++ program provides a basic implementation of a character shift-based encryption and decryption mechanism. The **encryptDecrypt** function reads characters from an input file, applies a shift to the ASCII value of each character (based on a provided key), and writes the result to an output file. This approach can encrypt a file's contents by shifting characters forward and decrypt by shifting back. Here's a breakdown of its components:

Key Components

- **<fstream>**: For handling file operations. It uses **std::ifstream** to read from the source file and **std::ofstream** to write to the destination file.
- **<string>**: To handle the file names passed to the **encryptDecrypt** function as **std::string**.
- **encryptDecrypt Function**:
- **Parameters**:
- **std::string inputFile**: The path to the input file.
- **std::string outputFile**: The path to the output file where the result will be saved.
- **int key**: The number of characters to shift for encryption or decryption.
- **bool encrypt**: A boolean flag indicating whether to encrypt or decrypt. True for encryption, false for decryption.
- **Process**:
- Opens the input file for reading and the output file for writing.
- Reads each character from the input file, applies the character shift (based on the **key** and the **encrypt** flag), and writes the shifted character to the output file.
- The character shift is a simple addition or subtraction of the ASCII value of the character by the **key** value. For encryption, the key is added to the character's ASCII value. For decryption, the key is subtracted.

Main Function

- Calls **encryptDecrypt** twice:
- First, to encrypt the contents of "original.txt" using a key of 3 and saves the result in "encrypted.txt".
- Then, to decrypt "encrypted.txt" back to its original form, saving the result in "decrypted.txt".

Limitations and Considerations

- **Security**: This encryption method (known as a Caesar cipher when the shift is uniform across all characters) is very basic and not secure by modern standards. It's easily broken with frequency analysis or brute force if the key is small.

- **Character Encoding**: The program directly shifts character ASCII values, which may not behave well with non-ASCII characters (e.g., characters in UTF-8 files that are outside the standard ASCII range).
- **Error Handling**: The program lacks error handling for file operations. It does not check if the input file exists or if the files have been successfully opened for reading/writing.
- **Binary Files**: While this code works for text files, it can technically be applied to binary files as well. However, shifting bytes in binary files could render them unusable, as the file structure and format could be compromised.

Usage Scenario

This simple encryption/decryption utility could be used for educational purposes to demonstrate the concept of symmetric key encryption and the importance of secure encryption methods. For any serious application, more robust and secure encryption methods provided by established cryptographic libraries should be used.

4. Efficient Line-by-Line File Copier

Exercise: Create a program that copies a large text file line by line to another file, reporting progress every 100 lines.

Objective: To develop a program for copying files line by line with progress reporting.

Solution Outline:

- Use **std::getline** to read and **std::ofstream** to write lines.
- After every 100 lines copied, output a progress message.

```
#include <fstream>
#include <iostream>
#include <string>

int main() {
    std::ifstream source("source.txt");
    std::ofstream dest("destination.txt");
    std::string line;
    int lineCount = 0;
    while (getline(source, line)) {
        dest << line << std::endl;
        if (++lineCount % 100 == 0) {
            std::cout << lineCount << " lines copied." << std::endl;
        }
    }
}
```

Explanation

This C++ program demonstrates a simple file copy operation with progress reporting. It reads the content of a source file line by line and writes each line to a destination file. Additionally, it prints a message to the console every 100 lines copied, indicating progress. Here's how it operates:

Key Components

- **<fstream>**: The header included for file stream operations, allowing the program to read from (**std::ifstream**) and write to (**std::ofstream**) files.
- **<iostream>**: Included for console output operations, used here to report the progress of the file copying process.
- **<string>**: Provides the **std::string** class, which is used for storing lines read from the source file.

Program Flow

1. **Open the Source File**: An **std::ifstream** object named **source** is created and opened with **"source.txt"** as its input. This file is expected to exist in the same directory as the program or the specified path.
2. **Open the Destination File**: An **std::ofstream** object named **dest** is created for the output, associated with **"destination.txt"**. This file will be created if it doesn't exist or overwritten if it does.
3. **Read and Write Loop**:
   - The program enters a loop that continues as long as there are lines to read from the source file.
   - Each line read is immediately written to the destination file, followed by a newline to maintain the original file's structure.
   - The variable **lineCount** is incremented for each line processed.
4. **Progress Reporting**:
   - After writing each line, the program checks if the current **lineCount** is a multiple of 100 using the modulo operator (%).
   - If so, it prints a message to the console reporting the number of lines copied so far.
5. **End of File**:
   - The loop terminates when there are no more lines to read from the source file, indicating the end of the file has been reached.
   - The **source** and **dest** file streams are automatically closed when they go out of scope (as the program exits the **main** function).

Example Usage

If "source.txt" contains text, running this program will create or overwrite "destination.txt" with the exact content of "source.txt". For every 100 lines copied, it reports the progress, e.g., "100 lines copied." This process continues until the entire content of "source.txt" has been successfully copied to "destination.txt".

Considerations

- **Error Handling**: This program does not explicitly handle errors, such as if "source.txt" does not exist or if there's an issue opening "destination.txt" for writing. Adding error checking after opening the files would make the program more robust.
- **Efficiency**: For very large files, consider buffering the writes or using more sophisticated methods to enhance performance.
- **Feedback Mechanism**: The progress is reported to the console, which is useful for long-running copy operations to provide feedback to the user.

5. File Data Analyzer

Exercise: Develop a program that reads a CSV file and calculates the sum and average of numeric values in each column.

Objective: To parse CSV files for calculating and reporting sums and averages of numerical data.

Solution Outline

- Parse each line using **std::getline** and a **std::stringstream**.
- Sum values per column and calculate averages at the end.

```
#include <fstream>
#include <iostream>
#include <sstream>
#include <vector>

int main() {
    std::ifstream file("data.csv");
    std::string line;
    std::vector<double> sums;
    int rowCount = 0;

    while (getline(file, line)) {
        std::istringstream iss(line);
        std::string value;
        int columnIndex = 0;
        while (getline(iss, value, ',')) {
            double num = std::stod(value);
            if (rowCount == 0) sums.push_back(num);
            else sums[columnIndex] += num;
            columnIndex++;
        }
        rowCount++;
    }
```

```
    for (double sum: sums) {
        std::cout << "Average: " << sum / rowCount << std::endl;
    }
}
```

Explanation

This C++ program is designed to read numeric data from a CSV file and calculate the average of each column. It illustrates the use of standard C++ libraries for file and string manipulation, as well as techniques for processing delimited text files. Here's a breakdown of its operation:

Key Components:

- **<fstream>**: For handling file input operations. The program uses an **std::ifstream** object to read from the file.
- **<iostream>**: For outputting results to the console.
- **<sstream>**: Utilized to parse each line of the file. **std::istringstream** is used to separate values within a line based on commas.
- **<vector>**: To dynamically store the sums of each column as the file is read. This allows for flexible handling of an unknown number of columns.

Process Flow

1. **Opening the File**: The program attempts to open "data.csv" for reading. If the file doesn't exist or cannot be opened, the program will terminate without executing the main loop.
2. **Reading the File Line by Line**: The program reads the file line by line using **std::getline**. Each line is expected to represent a row of data in the CSV file.
3. **Parsing Each Line**: For each line, an **std::istringstream** is used to separate the line into individual values based on the comma delimiter. This effectively splits a CSV row into its component cells.
4. **Calculating Column Sums**: Each value is converted from a string to a double using **std::stod** and added to the corresponding column's sum. The program dynamically expands the **sums** vector to match the number of columns encountered in the first row. For subsequent rows, it simply adds to the existing sums.
5. **Counting Rows**: The number of rows is tracked with **rowCount** to calculate the average later.
6. **Calculating and Printing Averages**: Once all lines have been processed, the program iterates over the **sums** vector, dividing each column's sum by the total number of rows (**rowCount**) to find the average. Each column's average is then printed to the console.

Example Usage and Output

Given a CSV file named "data.csv" with the following content:

```
1.0,2.0,3.0
4.0,5.0,6.0
7.0,8.0,9.0
```

The program will output:

```
Average: 4
Average: 5
Average: 6
```

This indicates that it has successfully calculated the average of each column.

Considerations

- **Error Handling**: The program assumes that every value in the CSV is a valid double. In practice, you might want to add error handling for cases where **std::stod** throws an exception due to invalid input.
- **Efficiency**: For very large CSV files, memory and performance considerations might require more sophisticated approaches, such as processing the file in chunks.
- **CSV Format Assumptions**: The program assumes a simple CSV format without quoted fields or escaped commas. More complex CSV files would require a more robust parsing strategy.

6. File Position Bookmarking

Exercise: Write a program that allows the user to bookmark a position in a text file and jump back to it later.

Objective: Enable users to bookmark a position in a text file to easily return to it later.

Solution Outline

- Use **std::fstream** and its **tellg** and **seekg** methods to mark and return to positions.

```
#include <fstream>
#include <iostream>

int main() {
    std::fstream file("example.txt", std::ios::in | std::ios::out);
    std::streampos bookmark;

    // Assuming the user wants to bookmark the beginning of the file
    bookmark = file.tellg();

    // Do some operations in between
    file.seekg(0, std::ios::end);
```

```
    std::cout << "End of the file reached." << std::endl;

    // Jump back to the bookmarked position
    file.seekg(bookmark);

    // Continue reading or writing from the bookmarked position
    std::string line;
    std::getline(file, line);
    std::cout << "Reading from bookmark: " << line << std::endl;

    file.close();
    return 0;
}
```

Explanation

This C++ program demonstrates how to use a file stream to read from and write to a file while illustrating the concept of bookmarking a position within a file for later access. The program specifically showcases how to mark a position in the file, perform operations that change the current position, and then return to the bookmarked position to continue operations from there. Here's a step-by-step explanation:

Key Components and Steps:

1. **Open the File**: The program opens "example.txt" for both input and output operations using **std::fstream** with the mode **std::ios::in | std::ios::out**. This allows the program to both read from and write to the file.
2. **Bookmarking the Position**: It bookmarks the current position in the file using **file.tellg()**, which returns the current position of the file pointer for input operations. The position is stored in the **bookmark** variable. Initially, this is at the beginning of the file.
3. **Moving to the End of the File**: The program then uses **file.seekg(0, std::ios::end)** to move the file pointer to the end of the file, effectively skipping over all content. It outputs a message indicating that the end of the file has been reached.
4. **Returning to the Bookmarked Position**: The file pointer is moved back to the bookmarked position using **file.seekg(bookmark)**. This demonstrates how you can return to a specific part of a file after performing other operations.
5. **Reading from the Bookmark**: Immediately after returning to the bookmarked position, the program attempts to read a line from the file using **std::getline(file, line)** and prints the line. Since the bookmark was at the beginning of the file, it reads the first line.
6. **Closing the File**: Finally, the file is closed using **file.close()**.

Concepts Illustrated

- **File Positioning**: The use of **tellg()** to get the current file position and **seekg()** to move to a specific position within the file. This is useful for complex file operations where you need to navigate to different parts of a file.
- **Reading and Writing Files**: Opening a file for both reading and writing and performing these operations sequentially.
- **Stream Positions**: Demonstrates the manipulation of stream positions (**std::streampos**) to bookmark and return to specific locations within a file.

Use Case

This technique is particularly useful in scenarios where you need to process or analyze specific parts of a file while retaining the ability to return to the starting point or another significant position. Examples include parsing files with headers or metadata at the beginning, processing large datasets where multiple passes are required, or implementing complex file modifications that require referencing earlier parts of the file.

The simplicity of the program highlights the flexibility and power of C++ file streams for sophisticated file manipulation tasks, making it a valuable tool for a wide range of applications involving file processing.

7. Exception-Proof File Reader

Exercise: Implement a robust file reader that handles all potential exceptions and reports them to the user without crashing.

Objective: Develop a file reader that gracefully handles exceptions, ensuring robust operation.

Solution Outline

- Encapsulate file operations in try-catch blocks.
- Catch and handle specific exceptions, providing meaningful error messages.

```
#include <fstream>
#include <iostream>
#include <string>

void robustFileReader(const std::string& fileName) {
    std::ifstream file;
    try {
        file.open(fileName);
        if (!file.is_open()) {
            throw std::runtime_error("File cannot be opened.");
        }
        std::string line;
```

```
        while (std::getline(file, line)) {
            std::cout << line << std::endl;
        }
    }
    catch (const std::exception& e) {
        std::cerr << "Error: " << e.what() << std::endl;
    }
}

int main() {
    robustFileReader("example.txt");
    return 0;
}
```

Explanation

This C++ program is a demonstration of how to implement a robust file reader function, **robustFileReader**, which is designed to read and print the contents of a specified file line by line. It includes error handling to manage scenarios where the file cannot be opened or other issues arise. Here's a breakdown of how it works:

Key Components

- **<fstream>**: This header is included to allow for file stream operations, specifically for reading from files using **std::ifstream**.
- **<iostream>**: Included for input-output operations. It's used here to print file contents to the console and report errors.
- **<string>**: This header is used because the program deals with strings for both file names and the contents being read.

The robustFileReader Function

- **Purpose**: To safely open and read a file specified by **fileName**, printing its contents line by line to the console. It is designed to be robust against exceptions, such as failing to open the file.
- **Parameters**:
- **const std::string& fileName**: The name (and possibly path) of the file to be read.
- **Process**:
- Attempts to open the specified file using an **std::ifstream** object.
- If the file cannot be opened, it throws a **std::runtime_error**, which is immediately caught by a catch block designed to handle **std::exceptions**.
- If the file is successfully opened, it reads the file line by line using **std::getline** inside a while loop, printing each line to the console.
- **Error Handling**:

- Uses a try-catch block to catch and report exceptions. This ensures that if an error occurs (e.g., the file does not exist or cannot be opened for some reason), the program will not crash but instead print a descriptive error message.

Main Function

- Simply calls **robustFileReader** with **"example.txt"** as its argument, demonstrating how to use the function to read a file.

Key Concepts Illustrated

- **Exception Handling in File Operations**: The program showcases how to make file reading operations more reliable by using exceptions to catch and handle errors gracefully.
- **Input Stream and Line-by-Line Reading**: Demonstrates efficient reading of file content using **std::getline** to process a file line by line, which is memory-efficient and straightforward.
- **Robust Programming Practices**: Emphasizes the importance of anticipating and managing potential runtime errors, particularly in operations like file IO, which are dependent on external resources that may not always be in the expected state.

Use Case

This example is particularly useful in scenarios where reading file content is a common operation, and the robustness of the application is crucial. It provides a template for handling file IO operations safely, ensuring that the application can gracefully handle issues such as missing files or permission errors.

8. Batch File Renamer

Exercise: Create a program that renames all files in a directory based on a pattern specified by the user.
Objective: Allow users to rename all files in a directory according to a specified pattern.

Solution Outline

- Use **<filesystem>** to iterate over files in a directory.
- For each file, construct a new name based on the user's pattern and rename the file.

```
#include <filesystem>
#include <iostream>
#include <string>

namespace fs = std::filesystem;

void batchRename(const fs::path& dirPath, const std::string& newNamePattern) {
    try {
        int counter = 1;
```

```
        for (auto& entry: fs::directory_iterator(dirPath)) {
            if (entry.is_regular_file()) {
                fs::path newFileName = newNamePattern + std::to_
string(counter++) + entry.path().extension().string();
                fs::rename(entry.path(), dirPath / newFileName);
            }
        }
    }
    catch (const fs::filesystem_error& e) {
        std::cerr << "Error: " << e.what() << std::endl;
    }
}

int main() {
    batchRename("./testDir", "NewFile_");
    return 0;
}
```

Explanation

This C++ program demonstrates how to batch rename files in a specified directory using the C++17 **<filesystem>** library. It's designed to rename all regular files in the directory to a new name pattern followed by a sequence number, preserving their file extensions. Here's a detailed explanation:

Includes and Namespace

- **<filesystem>**: Used for accessing and manipulating file systems. This program uses it to iterate through directory contents, check if entries are regular files, and rename them.
- **<iostream>**: For reporting errors to the console.
- **<string>**: For handling string operations, including constructing new file names.
- **namespace fs = std::filesystem;**: Creates an alias for **std::filesystem** to simplify code and improve readability.

The batchRename Function

- **Purpose**: Renames all regular files in a given directory to a specified new name pattern, appending a unique sequence number to each.
- **Parameters**:
- **const fs::path& dirPath**: The path of the directory whose files are to be renamed.
- **const std::string& newNamePattern**: The new name pattern to apply to each file.
- **Process**:
- Iterates over the contents of the specified directory using **fs::directory_iterator**.
- For each entry, it checks if it is a regular file. If so, it constructs a new file name using the provided pattern and a counter to ensure uniqueness. The original file extension is preserved.

- Renames the file to the new name using **fs::rename**.
- **Error Handling**:
- Catches and reports filesystem-related errors using a try-catch block.

Main Function

- Calls **batchRename** with the path to the directory (**"./testDir"**) to be processed and the new file name pattern (**"NewFile_"**).

Key Concepts Demonstrated

- **Filesystem Library Usage**: Shows practical use of the **<filesystem>** library for real-world tasks like batch renaming files, including directory traversal and file renaming.
- **Error Handling**: Demonstrates handling exceptions that may arise from filesystem operations, ensuring the program can report errors gracefully without crashing.
- **String Manipulation and File Extensions**: Illustrates handling file names and extensions carefully to ensure that the new file names are constructed correctly without losing their extensions.

Use Case

This program can be particularly useful for organizing files in a directory, such as photos from a camera, documents from a download folder, or any scenario where uniform file naming is desired. By using a sequence number, it ensures that file names are unique and sorted in the order they were processed.

Limitations and Considerations

- If the program is run multiple times on the same directory, it will rename all files again, overwriting the previously renamed files because the counter resets on each run.
- Files are processed in the order they are returned by the directory iterator, which may not necessarily be alphabetical or creation order.

9. Filesystem Space Reporter

Exercise: Develop a program that analyzes disk usage by files in a directory and reports the top 5 largest files.

Objective: Analyze and report the largest files in a directory, helping in disk space management.

Solution Outline:

- Traverse the directory, collecting file sizes.
- Sort the files by size and report the top 5.

```
#include <filesystem>
#include <vector>
#include <algorithm>
#include <iostream>

namespace fs = std::filesystem;

void reportLargestFiles(const fs::path& dirPath, size_t topN) {
    std::vector<std::pair<fs::path, fs::file_size_type>> fileSizes;

    for (const auto& entry: fs::directory_iterator(dirPath)) {
        if (entry.is_regular_file()) {
            fileSizes.emplace_back(entry.path(), entry.file_size());
        }
    }

    std::sort(fileSizes.begin(), fileSizes.end(), [](const auto& a, const
auto& b) {
        return a.second > b.second;
        });

    for (size_t i = 0; i < topN && i < fileSizes.size(); ++i) {
        std::cout << "File: " << fileSizes[i].first << ", Size: " <<
fileSizes[i].second << " bytes\n";
    }
}

int main() {
    reportLargestFiles("./", 5);
    return 0;
}
```

Explanation

This C++ program utilizes the **<filesystem>** library to scan a directory and report the largest files within it. It showcases modern C++17 filesystem operations and standard algorithms for sorting and processing data. Here's a detailed explanation of how it works:

Includes and Namespace

- **<filesystem>**: Used for directory and file manipulation. The program operates on paths, iterates through directory contents, and retrieves file sizes using functionalities provided by this module.
- **<vector> and <algorithm>**: Support storing file paths and sizes in a container and sorting them based on file size.

- **<iostream>**: For outputting the results to the console.
- **namespace fs = std::filesystem;**: Creates an alias **fs** for the **std::filesystem** namespace to simplify code and improve readability.

The reportLargestFiles Function

- **Purpose**: To find and report the top N largest files in a specified directory.
- **Parameters**:
- **const fs::path& dirPath**: The directory path to scan.
- **size_t topN**: The number of largest files to report.
- **Process**:
- It iterates over all entries in the specified directory using **fs::directory_iterator**.
- For each entry, it checks if it's a regular file. If so, it adds the file's path and size to a vector of pairs.
- The vector is then sorted in descending order of file size.
- Finally, it prints the paths and sizes of the top N largest files.

Main Function

- Calls **reportLargestFiles** with the current directory **"./"** and requests the top 5 largest files to be reported.

Key Concepts Demonstrated

- **Filesystem Operations**: The use of the **<filesystem>** library to interact with the file system in a platform-independent manner.
- **Directory Iteration**: How to iterate through the contents of a directory and perform actions based on the type of each entry (e.g., filtering regular files).
- **Data Sorting**: Employing the **<algorithm>** library's **std::sort** function with a custom comparator to order files by size.
- **Lambda Expressions**: The use of a lambda for the custom comparator in the sort operation, showcasing the power and flexibility of lambdas in C++.
- **Modern C++ Practices**: This program exemplifies modern C++ idioms, including the use of auto type deduction, range-based for loops, and the filesystem library introduced in C++17.

Example Output

The output will list the top 5 largest files in the current directory, displaying each file's path and size in bytes. The specific output will depend on the directory's contents where the program is executed.

This program is a practical tool for filesystem analysis, useful for tasks like cleaning up disk space or simply understanding the distribution of file sizes within a directory.

10. Concurrent Log File Writer

Exercise: Write a multithreaded logger that allows concurrent writes to a log file without data corruption.

Objective: Implement a logger that supports concurrent writes from multiple threads without data loss or corruption.

Solution Outline:

- Use **<thread>** for multithreading and **<mutex>** to lock the file for writing.
- Ensure each thread safely appends a log message to the file.

```
#include <fstream>
#include <mutex>
#include <thread>
#include <vector>

std::mutex logMutex;

void logMessage(const std::string& message) {
    std::lock_guard<std::mutex> guard(logMutex);
    std::ofstream logFile("log.txt", std::ios::app);
    logFile << message << std::endl;
}

void worker(int id) {
    logMessage("Worker " + std::to_string(id) + " started.");
}

int main() {
    std::vector<std::thread> workers;
    for (int i = 0; i < 5; ++i) {
        workers.emplace_back(worker, i);
    }
    for (auto& t: workers) {
        t.join();
    }
    return 0;
}
```

Explanation

This C++ program is designed to demonstrate concurrent logging to a file using multiple threads, ensuring thread safety with a mutex. Here's a breakdown of its components and functionality:

Includes and Global Mutex Declaration

- **<fstream>**: For file stream operations, enabling writing to files.
- **<mutex>**: Provides mutex classes for managing locks, ensuring that only one thread writes to the log file at a time.
- **<thread>**: For working with threads, allowing concurrent operations.
- **<vector>**: To store multiple threads.
- **std::mutex logMutex;**: A global mutex used to synchronize access to the log file, preventing data corruption or loss.

The logMessage Function

- Wraps file writing operations in a mutex lock to ensure that only one thread can execute the block at any given time, preventing concurrent access to the log file which could lead to race conditions.
- **std::lock_guard<std::mutex> guard(logMutex);**: Automatically locks the mutex upon creation and unlocks it when the guard object goes out of scope (when the function ends).
- Opens "log.txt" in append mode (**std::ios::app**) and writes the provided message followed by a newline.

The Worker Function

- Represents a task that might be executed by multiple threads concurrently.
- Calls **logMessage**, passing a string that includes the worker's ID to indicate which worker has started.

The Main Function

- Initializes a vector of **std::thread** objects, representing the worker threads.
- Loops to create 5 worker threads, each executing the **worker** function with a unique ID.
- After creating the threads, it loops again using **join** on each thread to wait for all threads to finish executing before the program exits. This ensures that the main thread (the execution flow of **main**) waits for all worker threads to complete their tasks before terminating.

Key Concepts Demonstrated

- **Concurrency**: The program shows how to perform tasks in parallel using threads, a core aspect of modern C++ for efficient computing.
- **Thread Safety**: It illustrates the necessity of synchronizing access to shared resources (in this case, a file) in a multi-threaded environment to prevent data inconsistency.
- **Resource Management**: The use of RAII (Resource Acquisition Is Initialization) pattern through **std::lock_guard** to manage mutex locks automatically, reducing the risk of deadlock.

Use Case

This approach can be utilized in applications that require logging from multiple components running in parallel, ensuring that log entries are not lost or intermixed due to concurrent writes.

SUMMARY

Chapter 6 dives into the essentials of file processing in C++, covering the complete cycle of creating, writing, appending, reading, and managing files, along with handling the associated data and errors. This comprehensive guide starts with an introduction to file processing, emphasizing its importance in storing and retrieving data persistently.

The chapter progresses to explain the data hierarchy, setting the stage for understanding how data is structured and managed in file operations. It then delves into practical aspects, beginning with appending data to files. Through examples, it illustrates how to add characters and lines to existing files without overwriting the current content, an essential skill for updating files dynamically.

Formatting input and output is covered next, highlighting the use of the **getline** function for reading lines from a file, a crucial technique for processing text data efficiently. The chapter continues with a deep dive into manipulating input and output streams, offering insights into the advanced management of file data, enhancing the flexibility and control programmers have over file interactions.

In sections 6.7 to 6.7.2, the focus shifts to creating new files and writing data into them. This part provides a step-by-step guide on initializing files and populating them with data, a fundamental task for persisting information across sessions.

Reading from files is thoroughly explored next, presenting methods to retrieve and process data stored in files, a key operation for most applications that rely on external data sources.

The concept of a file position pointer is introduced, explaining how to navigate within files to read or write data at specific locations, thereby adding another layer of control over file manipulation.

As with any operations that involve external resources, recognizing and handling exceptions and errors is critical. Sections 6.10 and 6.11 tackle recognizing exceptions and handling errors in file processing, equipping readers with the knowledge to build robust applications capable of dealing with anomalies in file operations gracefully.

Concluding with exercises, the chapter reinforces learning through practical application, allowing readers to apply concepts covered in real-world scenarios. This ensures a deep, hands-on understanding of file processing in C++, making it a valuable resource for both beginners and experienced programmers looking to refine their file manipulation skills.

Multiple Choice

The following are multiple-choice questions pertaining to file streams in C++:

1- What is the name of the C++ header file used for file stream operations?

a) <iostream>
b) <fstream>
c)< stdio.h>
d) <string>

Response: b) <fstream>

2- In which of the following modes may a file be opened in input mode?

a) std::ios::in
b) std::ios::out
c) std::ios::app
d) std::ios::binary

Answer: a) std::ios::in

3- Which function is used to write data to a file?

a) std::cin
b) std::cout
c) std::getline()
d) std::ofstream::write()

Answer: d) std::ofstream::write()

4- Which of the functions listed below is used to read data from a file?

a) std::cin
b) std::cout
c) std::getline()
d) std::ifstream::read()

Answer: d) std::ifstream::read()

5- Which of the following functions is used to determine if a file has been opened successfully?

a) std::ifstream::fail()
b) std::ifstream::good()
c) std::ifstream::eof()
d) std::ifstream::bad()

Answer: b) std::ifstream::good()

6- Which mode is used by default to open a file in C++ file streams?

a) std::ios::in
b) std::ios::out
c) std::ios::app
d) std::ios::binary

Answer: b) std::ios::out

7- Which function is used to relocate the file location pointer?

a) std::ofstream::seekp()
b) std::ifstream::seekg()
c) std::fstream::seekp()
d) std::fstream::seekg()

Answer: d) std::fstream::seekg()

8- Which of the functions listed below is used to close a file stream?

a) std::fstream::close()
b) std::ifstream::close()
c) std::ofstream::close()
d) All of the above

Answer: d) All of the above

9- Which mode is used to open a file in binary mode?

a) std::ios::in
b) std::ios::out
c) std::ios::app
d) std::ios::binary

Answer: d) std::ios::binary

10- Which of the following functions is used to get the current file position pointer location?

a) std::ofstream::tellp()
b) std::ifstream::tellg()
c) std::fstream::tellp()
d) std::fstream::tellg()

Answer: d) std::fstream::tellg()

Exercises

1- Write a C++ application that will create a file and insert text into it.
2- Write a C++ application to open and read the contents of an existing file.
3- Write a C++ application to add text to an existing file that is already open.
4- Write a C++ application to count the amount of text file lines.
5- Count the amount of words in a text file using a C++ application.
6- Count the number of characters in a text file using a C++ application.
7- Copy the contents of one text file to another using a C++ application.
8- Write a C++ application that would read a file and replace every instance of a certain term with another one.
9- Write a C++ program that creates a file and writes the numbers 1 to 100 into it, each on a new line. Then, open the same file to append the numbers 101 to 200.
10- Implement a C++ function that takes a file path and a character as arguments and counts the occurrence of the given character in the file.
11- Develop a C++ program that reads a text file line by line and writes each line to a new file in reverse order.
12- Create a C++ utility that copies a file's contents to another file, excluding any lines that contain a specific word provided by the user.

13- Write a C++ program that opens a file and displays the longest and shortest lines along with their lengths.

14- Design a C++ program that uses file position pointers to insert a string into a specific position in a file without overwriting the existing content.

15- Implement a C++ program that reads a CSV file and finds the average of numbers in each column, writing the results to a new file.

16- Develop a C++ function that takes a filename as input and returns a map of each word encountered in the file to its frequency count.

17- Create a C++ program that reads a file containing a list of names and addresses, formats them nicely, and writes them to a new file. Use getline to read input and format output using IO manipulators.

18- Write a C++ program that serializes a list of student objects (containing id, name, and grade) to a file and then deserializes it back into student objects.

19- Develop a C++ program that monitors a log file in real-time. Whenever a new line is added to the log file, print the new line to the console. Hint: Consider using file position pointers to remember where you left off.

20- Implement a robust C++ file processor that reads from a file and writes to another file while handling all possible file-related exceptions and errors gracefully, logging errors to a separate file without crashing.

Chapter 7
Classes and Objects

ABSTRACT

Chapter 7 offers a meticulous exploration of the cornerstone of C++: classes and objects, ushering readers into the object-oriented paradigm. It commences with foundational topics on classes, their data members, and member functions. A thorough introduction to object-oriented analysis and design (OOAD) and the historical development of the unified modeling language (UML) creates a framework for understanding modern software design. As readers progress, the chapter unfolds the nuances of defining classes, with a UML representation of a sample class 'GradeCourse'. Emphasis is placed on software engineering principles, encompassing set and get functions, constructors, and destructors. The crucial concept of encapsulation is elucidated with detailed discussions on header files, source files, and client files. This chapter delves deep into advanced topics such as constructors (default and overloaded), destructors, static members, operator overloading, and the significance of the 'this' pointer.

7.1 INTRODUCTION

Human thought is object-based. People, animals, plants, automobiles, airplanes, buildings, computers, and so on may be observed everywhere in the actual world.

Occasionally, we separate items into two categories: living and nonliving. Animated objects are "living" in the sense that they move and perform actions. On the contrary, inanimate objects do not move on their own. Yet, both sorts of objects have some characteristics. They all possess characteristics (such as size, shape, color, and weight) and display behaviors (e.g., a ball rolls, bounces, inflates, and deflates; a baby cries, sleeps, crawls, walks, and blinks; a car accelerates, brakes, and turns; a towel absorbs water). We will investigate the properties and behavior of software objects.

Humans gain knowledge about existing items by analyzing their characteristics and watching their behavior. Various items might have similar characteristics and display comparable actions. For instance, comparisons may be drawn between infants and adults, as well as between humans and chimpanzees.

Object-oriented design (OOD) represents software in a language comparable to that used to describe physical things. It makes use of class associations, in which things of a specific class, such as a class of vehicles, share similar properties; for example, automobiles, trucks, little red wagons, and roller skates

DOI: 10.4018/979-8-3693-2007-5.ch007

all share many similarities. OOD exploits inheritance relationships, in which new classes of objects are formed by absorbing properties of current classes and adding their own unique traits. Objects of the class "convertible" have all the features of the more general class "automobile," but their roof may be raised and lowered.

Object-oriented design offers a natural and straightforward perspective on the software design process, namely modeling things by their properties, actions, and interrelationships, exactly as we describe real-world objects. OOD also simulates inter-object communication. Objects interact via messages in the same way that people do (e.g., a sergeant instructs a soldier to stand at attention). A bank account object may receive a message instructing it to reduce its balance by a specified amount due to a client withdrawal.

OOD encapsulates (wraps) properties and operations (behaviors) in objects. An object's properties and actions are linked in a way that can't be separated. Things have the property of concealing information. This implies that objects may know how to communicate with one another via well-defined interfaces, but they are often not permitted to know how other objects are implemented. Instead, implementation details are typically concealed within the objects themselves. As long as we know how to operate the accelerator pedal, the brake pedal, the steering wheel, etc., we can drive a car efficiently without understanding the internal workings of engines, gearboxes, brakes, and exhaust systems. As we shall see, information concealment is important for excellent software engineering.

Object-oriented languages like C++ are prevalent. Programming in such a language is referred to as object-oriented programming (OOP), and it allows computer programmers to implement an object-oriented design as a functional software system. On the other side, procedural languages like C tend to result in action-oriented programming. In C, the function is the fundamental programming unit. The programming unit in C++ is the class, from which objects are ultimately instantiated (an OOP term for "created"). Classes in C++ include data and methods that implement operations and characteristics, respectively.

The focus of C programmers is on writing functions. Programmers organize activities that execute a common job into functions and then organize functions into programs. Despite the significance of data in C, it is believed that data exists largely to assist the operations performed by functions. The verbs in a system specification assist the C programmer in determining the collection of functions that will collaborate to create the system.

7.2 CLASSES, DATA MEMBERS AND MEMBER FUNCTIONS

Classes, which are **user-defined types**, are the focus of a C++ programmer's efforts. Each class includes both data and a collection of methods that alter that data and provide client services (i.e., other classes or functions that use the class). **Data members** are the components of a class that contain data. For instance, a bank account may include a number and a balance. Member functions refer to the **function components** of a class (typically called **methods** in other object-oriented programming languages such as Java). A bank account class, for instance, may have member methods to make a deposit (raising the balance), make a withdrawal (decreasing the balance), and query the current balance. Built-in types (and other user-defined kinds) serve as "building blocks" for the creation of additional user-defined types (classes). The nouns in a system specification assist the C++ programmer in identifying the collection of classes from which the system's objects are derived and implemented.

Classes are to things what house plans are to buildings. A class is a "blueprint" for constructing objects of the class. Just as several homes may be constructed from a single blueprint, multiple objects can be instantiated (created) from a single class. You cannot prepare meals in a blueprint's kitchen, but you can cook meals in a house's kitchen. You cannot sleep in a blueprint's bedroom, but you can sleep in a house's bedroom.

Classes can establish connections with one another. In an object-oriented design of a bank, for instance, the "bank teller" class must link to other classes, such as the "customer," "cash drawer," and "safe" classes. These connections are known as **associations**.

Packaging software as classes enables reuse of the classes by future software systems. Class groups are frequently packaged as reusable components. Much as realtors frequently cite "location, location, location" as the three most influential variables on the price of real estate, software developers frequently cite "reuse, reuse, reuse" as the three most influential aspects on the future of software development. Classes can be used to define custom data types. A class is the blueprint for an object, and an instance of a class is an object.

Classes may have data members, which are variables that hold data, and member functions, which are connected with an instance of a class.

Here is an example of a simple class definition in C++ that has data members and member functions:

```
class FirstClass {
public:
int x;
float y;
string name;
void printData() {
cout << "x: " << x << endl;
cout << "y: " << y << endl;
cout << "name: " << name << endl;
}
void setData(int a, float b, string c) {
x = a;
y = b;
name = c;
}
};
```

In this example, FirstClass is the name of the class, and it has three data members: x, which is an integer; y, which is a float; and name, which is a string. It also has two member functions: printData(), which prints the values of the data members to the console, and setData(int a, float b, string c), which sets the values of the data members to the given parameters.

To create an instance of the class, you can use the following syntax:

```
FirstClass classObj;
```

You can access the data membersand member functions of the class using the dot operator (.):

```
classObj.setData(5, 3.14, "John Doe");
```

classObj.printData(); //It's also possible to create constructor and destructor for class.

```
class FirstClass {
public:
int x;
float y;
string name;
FirstClass(int a, float b, string c) {
x = a;
y = b;
name = c;
}
~FirstClass() {
cout << "destructor called";
}
void printData() {
cout << "x: " << x << endl;
cout << "y: " << y << endl;
cout << "name: " << name << endl;
}
};
```

You can create object of class with passing parameter:

```
FirstClass classObj(5, 3.14, "John Doe");
classObj.printData();
```

This is just a simple example of how to define a class in C++ with data members and member functions, and there are many more features and capabilities that classes can provide, such as inheritance and polymorphism.

7.3 INTRODUCTION TO OBJECT-ORIENTED ANALYSIS AND DESIGN (OOAD)

You will soon be developing C++ apps. How will the code for your programs be created?

Like many novice programmers, you may simply turn on your computer and begin typing. This strategy may work for tiny projects, but what if you were tasked with developing a multiplayer game with all the bells and whistles? Or suppose you were offered to join a team of one thousand game developers creating the next generation of strategic games. For such huge and intricate tasks, it would be impossible to just begin developing programs.

To generate the most effective solutions, you should adhere to a methodical procedure for assessing your project's requirements (i.e., understanding what the system is intended to perform) and producing a **design** that meets them (i.e., deciding how the system should do it). Before developing code, you should follow this procedure and thoroughly evaluate the design (or have your design reviewed by other software professionals). This procedure is called object-oriented analysis and design (OOAD) if it involves evaluating and developing your system from an **object-oriented perspective.** Programmers with extensive experience are aware that analysis and design may save many hours by preventing the need to abandon a poorly planned system development strategy in the middle of its execution, therefore potentially squandering a substantial amount of time, money, and effort.

OOAD is the generic term for the procedure of studying an issue and creating a solution strategy. Minor issues, such as those mentioned in the preceding chapters, do not necessitate an entire OOAD procedure. Before developing C++ code, it may be necessary to write **pseudocode**, an informal text-based method of describing computer logic. It is not a programming language, but we may use it as a sort of blueprint to assist our code writing.

When the scale of issues and groups of people attempting to solve them grows, OOAD approaches soon become more suitable than pseudocode. Ideally, a group should agree on a clearly defined procedure for problem-solving and a standardized method for conveying the findings of that process. Widespread adoption of a common graphical language for expressing the outcomes of any OOAD process has occurred despite the existence of several distinct OOAD methods. This language, known as the Unified Modeling Language (UML), was created in the mid-1990s by Grady Booch, James Rumbaugh, and Ivar Jacobson, three software methodologists.

7.4 HISTORY OF THE UML

In the 1980s, a growing number of firms started constructing their applications using OOP, and a demand arose for a standardized OOAD methodology. Several methodologists, including Booch, Rumbaugh, and Jacobson, independently developed and advocated distinct techniques to meet this need. Each procedure used its own notation or "language" (in the form of graphical diagrams) to communicate the outcomes of research and design.

By the beginning of the 1990s, several organizations and even divisions within the same company were using their own procedures and notations. Also, these companies want to use technological solutions that will help them do their work better. It was tough for software companies to create tools for so many procedures. Obviously, standardized nomenclature and procedures were required.

James Rumbaugh joined Grady Booch at Rational Software Company (now a subsidiary of IBM) in 1994, and the two started to work on unifying their popular procedures. Ivar Jacobson quickly joined their ranks. In 1996, the group published early versions of the UML and solicited comments from the software engineering community. Around the same time, the Object Management GroupTM (OMGTM) solicited proposals for a standard modeling language. The Object Management Group (OMG) (www.omg.org) is a non-profit organization that promotes the standardization of object-oriented technologies by publishing guidelines and specifications such as the Unified Modeling Language (UML). Numerous companies, including HP, IBM, Microsoft, Oracle, and Rational Software, have previously acknowledged the necessity for a standardized modeling language. In response to the OMG's call for proposals, these firms established UML Partners, the consortium that designed and submitted UML version 1.1 to the OMG. In 1997, the OMG approved the idea and took responsibility for the UML's ongoing maintenance and modification. The OMG published UML version 1.5 in March 2003. Version 2 of the UML, which had been accepted and was in the process of being completed at the time of this publication, represents the first significant upgrade to the standard since version 1.1 was released in 1997. Several publications, modeling tools, and industry professionals already use UML version 2, so we teach vocabulary and notation for UML version 2 throughout this course.

7.4.1 What Is the UML?

Nowadays, the Unified Modeling Language is the most popular graphical representation approach for modeling object-oriented systems. It has in fact harmonized the several prevalent notational systems. As we do throughout this book, system designers employ language (in the form of diagrams) to represent their systems.

The UML's adaptability is an appealing characteristic. The UML is **extendable** (i.e., it may be augmented with new features) and independent of any specific OOAD method. UML modelers are allowed to create systems using a variety of approaches, but all developers may now describe their ideas using a common set of graphical notations.

UML is a complicated and feature-rich graphical programming language. Learning this will help you create efficient software designs for your capstone project.

7.5 INTRODUCTION TO CLASSES AND OBJECTS

Encapsulation, inheritance, and polymorphism (or generic functionality) are three features of modern OO languages that make it easier and better for programmers to make programs.

Related topics involve objects, classes, and data abstraction.

Abstraction in the object-oriented world generalizes the characteristics and behaviors of an item. Example: Automobile.

Encapsulation hides how an object works from other objects. This makes the object work like a black box.Example: The functionality of the brake is hidden.

Inheritance is a way to form new classes using classes that have already been defined. Inheritance is employed to help reuse existing code with little or no modification. Example: animal, tiger.

Polymorphism refers to the ability to execute different operations in response to the same message. Example: Movement in various types of animals such as frogs, birds, snakes, fish, etc.

Classes and Objects

Assume you wish to drive an automobile and accelerate it by depressing the accelerator pedal. What must occur before you can do this? Yet, before you can drive a vehicle, it must first be designed and constructed. Typically, a car's design starts with engineering drawings, comparable to home plans. These illustrations depict the accelerator pedal that the driver will use to accelerate the vehicle. In a way, the accelerator pedal "reveals" the complicated mechanics that accelerate the vehicle, just as the brake pedal "reveals" the mechanisms that slow the vehicle, the steering wheel "reveals" the systems that turn the vehicle, etc. By employing the accelerator pedal, the brake pedal, the steering wheel, the transmission shifting mechanism, and other user-friendly "interfaces" to the automobile's complicated internal processes, this allows persons with little or no understanding of how cars are constructed to drive a car with relative ease.

Unfortunately, you cannot drive the engineering plans of a vehicle; the automobile must be constructed from the technical drawings that describe it before it can be driven. A finished automobile will feature a real accelerator pedal to increase speed. But, this is not sufficient; the vehicle will not accelerate on its own; thus, the driver must push the accelerator pedal to get the vehicle to speed up.

A program's task execution needs a function (such as main). The function specifies the processes through which the job is carried out. The function conceals from its user the complexity of the tasks it accomplishes, just as the accelerator pedal of a car conceals from the driver the complexity of the systems that cause the vehicle to accelerate. In C++, we begin by building a class to house a function, similar to how an automobile's technical blueprints include the design of an accelerator pedal. A function that is associated with a class is known as a member function.

In a class, one or more member functions are provided to accomplish the class's duties. Similar to how you cannot "drive" a vehicle designed by engineers, you cannot "drive" a class. In the same way that someone must construct a vehicle from its engineering drawings before it can be driven, you must create an object of a class before you can instruct a computer to do the duties described by the class. This is one of the reasons why C++ is considered an object-oriented programming language. Notice that, just as several automobiles can be constructed from the same technical design, multiple objects may be constructed from the same class. So classes provide data abstraction and data encapsulation. While driving a vehicle, pushing the gas pedal gives a signal to the automobile to complete a task, which is to accelerate. Likewise, when you send messages to an object, each message is referred to as a member-function call and instructs a member function of the object to carry out its purpose. Often, this is referred to as requesting a service from an object. In addition to its capabilities, an automobile has several qualities, such as its color, number of doors, quantity of gasoline in its tank, current speed, and total kilometers traveled (as shown by the odometer). Similar to the car's capabilities, these characteristics are shown in its engineering diagrams as part of its design. These characteristics are always related to a vehicle's operation. Every automobile has unique characteristics. For instance, each vehicle knows how much gas is in its own tank but not that of other vehicles. Similarly, an object's properties accompany the object when it is utilized in a program. These properties are defined as part of the class of the object. A class is created using the keyword class. A class can contain private as well as public members. By default, all items defined in a class are private. When the members are declared private, only the members of the class can access them, not any other part of your program.

This is one way that encapsulation works. If you keep some pieces of data private, you can tightly control who can see them. Additionally, you have the option to define private functions that only other class members can call.

To make parts of a class public (i.e., accessible to other parts of your program), you must declare them after the public keyword.

All other functions in your program can use any variables or functions that you define after the public specifier.

Most of the time, your program will use the public functions of a class to get to its private members.

General form of a class definition:

```
class class_name
{
```

```
private: (optional)
private data and functions
public:
public data and functions
}object_list;
```

Note: You cannot initialize the variables inside the class declaration. Variables can be initialized using constructors.

7.6 DEFINING A CLASS WITH A MEMBER FUNCTION

The GradeCourse class specification includes the displayMessage member method, which shows a message on the screen. Remember that a class is analogous to a blueprint, therefore we must create an instance of the GradeCourse class and run its displayMessage member function to show the welcome message.

Class is the first keyword in the class definition, followed by the class name GradeCourse. By tradition, the name of a user-defined class starts with a capital letter, and for clarity, each successive word in the class name also begins with a capital letter. Since the arrangement of uppercase and lowercase letters mimics the shape of a camel, this capitalization style is commonly referred to as camel case.

GradeCourse
+ displayMessage()
GradeCourse
-courseName: String
+setCourseName(name: String) +getCourseName(): String +displayMessage()

The body of each class is contained by left and right braces ({and}). The end of the class definition is a semicolon.

Remember that the function main is always called when a program is executed. The majority of functions are not called automatically. As you shall see shortly, you must explicitly invoke the member function displayMessage for it to execute.

The term for the keyword public is access specifier. The member function follows the access specifier public: to signal that it is "accessible to the public," i.e., it may be called by other functions in the program and by member functions of other classes. Specifiers of access are always followed by a colon (:).

Each function in a program performs a job and may return a value after it completes its work. For instance, a function may conduct a computation and then return the result. You must specify a return type when defining a function in order to specify the type of value that the function will return once its work is complete. The term void to the left of the function name displayMessage indicates the return type of the function. displayMessage will do a job but will not return (i.e., give back) any data to its calling function (in this case, main, as we'll see in a minute).

displayMessage is the name of the member function that precedes the return type. According to tradition, function names begin with a lowercase letter, and all following words begin with capital letters. The parenthesis after the name of the member function indicate that it is a function. A pair of empty parenthesis indicates that this member function needs no more data to complete its purpose.

```
#include <iostream>
#include <string>
//OOPs concept -- Object Oriented Programming
//Class is a blueprint.
//Classes encapsulate state and behavior
//data abstraction
class GradeCourse
{
private:
public:
GradeCourse()
{}
void displayMessage()
{
std::cout << "Welcome to Grade Book" << std::endl;
}
};
int main()
{
//All objects have their own copy of member variables
//and share a pointer to the member functions
GradeCourse gbObj;
gbObj.displayMessage();
GradeCourse newGBObj;
newGBObj.displayMessage();
return 0; //indicates successful completion
}
```

The body of a function comprises the statements that carry out its purpose. In this instance, the member function displayMessage consists of a single statement that outputs "Welcome to the Grade Book!" When this statement runs, the function's duty is complete.

7.6.1 UML Class Diagram for Class GradeCourse

Programmers use the Unified Modeling Language (UML) to model their object-oriented systems in a consistent way. In the UML, each class is represented in a class diagram as a three-compartment rectangle. The following diagram is a UML class diagram for the GradeCourse class. The name of the class is centered horizontally and in boldface font on the top container. The center section includes the class's attributes, which correspond to C++'s data members. The section in the center is empty since the version of class GradeCourse lacks properties. The compartment at the bottom includes the class's operations, which equate to member functions in C++. The UML models operations by listing the operation's name in parenthesis. The single member function of the GradeCourse class is displayMessage; hence, the bottom compartment lists one action with this name. The parentheses after displayMessage in the class diagram are empty, exactly as they are in the member function's header, since the displayMessage member function does not need extra parameters to accomplish its duties. The plus symbol (+) before the operation name indicates that displayMessage is a public operation in the UML (equivalent to a public member function in C++).

The UML shows data members as attributes by giving the name of the attribute, a colon, and the type of attribute.In C++, data members are private; hence, the class diagram displays a negative sign (-) before the attribute's name. In UML, the negative sign corresponds to the private access specifier in C++. The UML specifies the return type of an operation by inserting a colon and the return type after the operation's name and between the parentheses. Class GradeCourse's member function getCourseName returns a string in C++; hence, the class diagram depicts a String return type in the UML. Noting that setCourseName and displayMessage do not return values (i.e., they return void), the UML class diagram does not define a return type after the parenthesis of these actions. When a function returns no value, the UML does not utilize the void keyword like C++ does. Class diagrams in UML are widely used to describe class properties and actions. Class Diagram in UML

7.6.2 Member function:

A member function definition need not be placed inside the class definition. If you want to put it outside the class definition, you need to put the prototype for the function inside the class.

To implement a function that is a member of a class, you must tell the compiler to which class the function belongs by qualifying the function name with the class name.

The:: is called the scope resolution operator.

Defining a member function with a parameter

Member functions are functions that are associated with an instance of a class. They can have parameters, which are used to pass data into the function. Here is an example of a class with a member function that has a parameter:

```
class FirstClass {
public:
int x;
float y;
string name;
void setData(int a, float b, string c) {
x = a;
y = b;
name = c;
```

```
}
};
```

In this example, the class FirstClass has a member function called setData(int a, float b, string c), which takes three parameters: an integer a, a float b, and a string c. These parameters are used to set the values of the data members x, y, and name.

You can call this member function on an instance of the class like this:

```
FirstClass classObj;
classObj.setData(5, 3.14, "John Doe");
```

It's also possible to define member functions with default values, which means if the value of the parameter is not passed while calling the function, it will take the default value.

```
class FirstClass {
public:
int x;
float y;
string name;
void setData(int a = 0, float b = 0.0, string c = "") {
x = a;
y = b;
name = c;
}
};
```

You can call this member function on an instance of the class and can pass any number of parameters:

```
FirstClass classObj;
classObj.setData(5);
classObj.setData(5, 3.14);
classObj.setData(5, 3.14, "John Doe");
```

These are just a few examples of how to define a member function with parameters in C++. Keep in mind that member functions can also return values and have different access levels, such as private or protected.

In our automobile example, we explained that depressing the gas pedal sends a signal to the car to accelerate. Yet, how quickly should the automobile accelerate? As you are aware, the deeper you push the accelerator pedal, the quicker the vehicle accelerates. So, the communication to the vehicle comprises both the job to be performed and any extra information that will assist the vehicle in doing the task. This extra information is referred to as a parameter, and its value helps the automobile calculate how quickly to accelerate. Similarly, a member function may need extra data in the form of one or more arguments in order to complete its work. A function call provides argument values for each of the function's parameters.

Variables defined in the body of a function definition are known as local variables and may only be utilized from the line of their declaration to the line immediately after the closing right brace (}). Local variables must be defined prior to their usage inside a function. A local variable cannot be accessed outside of the defined function. When a function exits, its local variable values are lost.

Typically, a class includes one or more member functions that alter the characteristics of a specific instance of the class. Variables represent attributes in a class specification. These variables are referred to as data members and are defined inside the class declaration but outside the member-function definitions. Each object of a class has its own memory copy of its attributes. This section offers an example of a GradeCourse class that includes a courseName data member to reflect a GradeCourse object's course name.

GradeCourse Class With a Data Member, a Set Function, and a Get Function

Access Specifiers, Private and Public

The majority of data member declarations follow the access-specification label private:. Private, like public, is an access specifier. Variables or functions specified after the private access specifier (and before the next access specifier) are available exclusively to the class's member functions. Hence, the data member courseName can only be accessed through the member methods setCourseName, getCourseName, and displayMessage of the class GradeCourse. Since the data member courseName is private, it cannot be accessed by functions outside the class (such as main) or by functions belonging to other classes in the program. At these program locations, attempting to access the data member courseName using an expression such as myGradeCourse.courseName would result in a compilation error.

The default access for class members is private, so all class members after the class header and before the first access specifier are private by default.Repetition of the access specifiers public and private is unnecessary and might be misleading.

The practice of declaring data members as private is known as data hiding. When a software program instantiates (creates) an object of the class GradeCourse, the data member courseName is encapsulated (hidden) and can only be accessed by member functions of the object's class. setCourseName and getCourseName are member methods of the GradeCourse class that directly alter the data member courseName (and displayMessage could do so if necessary).

```
setCourseName and getCourseName are member functions.
```

The member function setCourseName doesn't return any data when it's done, so its return type is "void."The member function accepts one parameter representing the course name it will receive as an argument.

```
#include <iostream>
#include <string>
class GradeCourse
{
public:
GradeCourse()
```

```
{
setCourseName("C++");
//if set methods are not present then we initialize
//member variables as follow:
//courseName = "C++" //NOT best practice
}
//Validate data and store information in member variables
void setCourseName(std::string name)
{
courseName = name;
}
//Retrieve information from the member variables
std::string getCourseName()
{
return courseName;
}
void displayMessage()
{
std::cout << "Welcome to " <<getCourseName() << std::endl;
}
private:
std::string courseName;
};
int main()
{
//All objects have their own copy of member variables
//and share a pointer to the member functions
GradeCourse gbObj;
gbObj.displayMessage();
gbObj.setCourseName("C Plus Plus");
GradeCourse newGBObj;
newGBObj.displayMessage();
std::string cName;
std::cout << "Please enter a course name: ";
std::cin >> cName;
newGBObj.setCourseName (cName);
gbObj.displayMessage();
newGBObj.displayMessage();
return 0; //indicates successful completion
}
```

getCourseName is a member function that returns the courseName of a GradeCourse object. The member function's argument list is empty, indicating that it does not need any extra data to complete its purpose. The function's return type is specified as a string. When a function that specifies a return type other than void is called and its purpose is completed, the function provides a result to its calling function. For instance, when you visit an automated teller machine (ATM) and request your account balance, you anticipate that the ATM will provide a figure that corresponds to your account balance. Similarly, when a statement uses the GradeCourse object's member function getCourseName, the statement anticipates receiving the GradeCourse's course name (in this example, a string, as defined by the method's return type).

7.7 SOFTWARE ENGINEERING WITH SET AND GET FUNCTIONS CONSTRUCTORS DESTRUCTORS

Only functions that are also members of a class can alter members of that class who have private data. So every class or function that calls an object's member functions from outside the object invokes the class's public member functions to request the class's services.

specific instances of the class. This is why the lines in function main invoke the GradeCourse object's member methods setCourseName, getCourseName, and displayMessage. Classes often have public member methods that enable customers to set or acquire the values of private data members. The names of these member functions do not need to begin with set or get, although it is a popular naming practice. In this example, the member function that changes the value of the courseName data member is named setCourseName, and the member function that retrieves the courseName data member's value is named getCourseName. Remember that set functions are sometimes referred to as mutators (because they modify values), and get functions are also referred to as accessors (because they access values).

Even though these member functions have direct access to the private data, they should use the set and get methods of a class to change the private data of the class.

7.7.1Member Function displayMessage

The member function displayMessage doesn't return any data when it's done, so its return type is "void."As the function receives no arguments, its parameter list is empty.

7.7.2 Testing Class GradeCourse

The main function makes one object of class GradeCourse called myGradeCourse and calls each of its member functions.Main also shows the initial course name by using the getCourseName method of the object. Notice that the first line of output does not include a course name since the object's courseName data member (a string) is initially empty by default. The first value of a string is the so-called empty string, which contains no characters. A blank screen is shown when an empty string is presented. The main then requests a course name from the user.

By calling the getline method, the user-entered course name is given to the local string variable nameOfCourse. When the member function setCourseName is called, the value of the argument is moved to the name of the parameter. Then, the value of the argument is allocated to the data member courseName. The function call for the object uses myGradeCourse's displayMessage member function to display the welcome message containing the course name.

GradeCourse
-courseName: String
+setCourseName(name: String) +getCourseName(): String +displayMessage()

UML Class Diagram

7.8 ENCAPSULATION

For reusability, a class in a separate file. If client code is aware of how a class is implemented, its developer may create client code based on the class's implementation information. If the implementation of a class changes, the class's client should not be required to update. Hiding the class's implementation details makes it simpler to modify the class's implementation while limiting or, ideally, eliminating client code modifications.

When our classes are correctly packed, other programmers around the world may be able to use them. This is one of the benefits of generating class definitions.

7.8.1 Header Files (.h)

When making an object-oriented C++ program, it's common to put source code that can be used more than once (like a class) in a file called a "header file" that ends in ".h."Programs use #include preprocessor directives to include header files and leverage reusable program components, such as type strings given by the C++ Standard Library and user-defined types such as class Game. This file should include the definition of the class.

7.8.2: Separating Interface From Implementation - Source Files (.cpp)

Convention dictates that member-function definitions be put in a source-code file with the same base class.name (for example, Game) as the class's header file, but with a.cpp suffix.. Since the interface of the class is part of the class definition in the Game.h header file, the source files must have access to this file and be #include in it.

7.8.3 Client File

To use the class, the client code must merely understand its interface and be able to connect its object code. Since the class interface is part of the class definition in the Game.h header file, the client-code developer must have access to this file and #include it in the client's source code. The compiler utilizes the class definition in Game.h to verify that the main function properly generates and manipulates objects of type Game when the client code is generated.

7.8 CONSTRUCTORS

A constructor is a special function that is a member of a class and that has the same name as the class. It is called when an object is created. Notice that the constructor has no return type. In C++, constructors do not return values and, therefore, have no return type. (Not even void may be specified.) An object's constructor is called when the object is created. This means that it is called when the object's declaration is executed.

For global objects, the constructor is called when the program begins execution, prior to the call to main. For local objects, the constructor is called each time the object declaration is encountered. A constructor can have parameters. This allows you to give member variables program defined initial values when an object is created. You do this bypassing arguments to an object's constructor.

Constructors are special member functions that are called automatically when an object of a class is created. They are used to initialize the data members of the class. Constructors have the same name as the class and do not have a return type (not even void).

7.8.1: A Default Constructor vs. an Overloaded Constructor

A default constructor is one that is made by the compiler automatically if no other constructors are defined in the class.It typically initializes the class's member variables to their default values.

A programmer-defined overloaded constructor is one that has different parameters than the default constructor.This lets the programmer set the member variables of the class to certain values when an object is made.

Here is an example of a class with a default constructor and an overloaded constructor in C++:

```
class FirstClass {
public:
// Default constructor
FirstClass() {
// Initialize member variables to default values
x = 0;
y = 0;
}
// Overloaded constructor
FirstClass(int x, int y) {
// Initialize member variables to specific values
x = x;
y = y;
}
private:
int x;
int y;
};
```

In this example, the member variables x and y are set to 0 by the default constructor, but the overloaded constructor lets the user set them to different values when a new object of the class is made.

You can use the default constructor when you don't need to initialize the member variable with any specific value, and you can use the overloaded constructor when you want to initialize the member variable with a specific value.

Here is an example of a simple class with a constructor:

```
class FirstClass {
public:
int x;
float y;
string name;
FirstClass(int a, float b, string c) {
x = a;
y = b;
name = c;
}
};
```

In this example, FirstClass is the name of the class, and it has a constructor FirstClass(int a, float b, string c) which takes three parameters: an integer a, a float b, and a string c.These parameters are used to initialize the values of the data members x, y, and name.

You can create an instance of the classand initialize the data members in one step like this:

```
FirstClass classObj(5, 3.14, "John Doe");
```

It's also possible to define a constructor with no parameter, called as default constructor

```
class FirstClass {
public:
int x;
float y;
string name;
FirstClass() {
x = 0;
y = 0.0;
name = "";
}
};
```

You can create an instance of the classand initialize the data members with default value in one step like this:

```
FirstClass classObj;
```

It's also possible to define multiple constructors with different number of parameters, which is called as constructor overloading.

FirstClass
-x: int -y: float -name: String
+ FirstClass() + FirstClass(x: int, y: float) + FirstClass(x: int, y: float, c:string)

```
class FirstClass {
public:
int x;
float y;
string name;
FirstClass() {
x = 0;
y = 0.0;
name = "";
}
FirstClass(int a, float b) {
x = a;
y = b;
name = "";
}
FirstClass(int a, float b, string c) {
x = a;
y = b;
name = c;
}
};
```

You can create an instance of the classand initialize the data members with different number of parameters in one step like this:

```
FirstClass classObj;
FirstClass classObj1(5, 3.14);
FirstClass classObj2(5, 3.14, "John Doe");
```

In C++, constructors are an important part of class definition, as they provide a way to initialize the data members of an object when it is create.

7.8.2 Overloaded Constructor With Default Arguments

In C++, you can give "default arguments" to the arguments of an overloaded constructor. This means that the arguments will have the same value.This means that the user can use the overloaded constructor to create an object without giving all of the arguments. In that case, the default values will be used for the missing arguments.

Here is an example of a class with an overloaded constructor that has default arguments:

```
class FirstClass {
public:
// Overloaded constructor with default arguments
FirstClass(int x = 0, int y = 0) {
// Initialize member variables to specific values
x = x;
y = y;
}
private:
int x;
int y;
};
```

In this example, the overloaded constructor has two parameters, x and y, and both have default values of 0. This means that if the user creates an object of the class and only provides a value for x, y will be set to 0, and if the user doesn't provide any values, both x and y will be set to 0.

Here is an example of how to use the overloaded constructor:

```
FirstClass obj1; // Creates an object with x=0, y=0 (default values used)
FirstClass obj2(5); // Creates an object with x=5, y=0 (default value used for
y)
FirstClass obj3(5, 7); // Creates an object with x=5, y=7 (no default value
used)
```

It's important to know that when a constructor has default arguments, the compiler will automatically make a default constructor for the class that calls the overloaded constructor with the default arguments. So in the above example, if we don't define a default constructor, the compiler will automatically define it for us, and calling it will create an object with x=0, y=0. Also, it is important to note that the default argument should be at the end of the argument list.

Example

```
//*************************************************************
//This file contains the declaration of the GradeCourse class.
//The class acts like a blue print and is used to create
//complex data types.
```

```
//***********************************************************
//<> indicate that the file exists in the standard library
#include <iostream> //input output stream
#include <string>
using namespace std;
#ifndef GRADE_Course_H
#define GRADE_Course_H
class GradeCourse
{
private:
string courseName; //MEMBER VARIABLE
int numOfStud; //Member variable
public:
// OVERLOADED CONSTRUCTOR WITH DEFAULT ARGS
GradeCourse(string cName = "DirectX", int nos = 100);
void setCourseName(string name);
string getCourseName(); //ACCESS FUNCTION
void setNumOfStud(int xyz);
int getNumOfStud(); //ACCESS FUNCTION
void displayMessage(); //ACCESS FUNCTION
};
#endif
//***********************************************************
//This file contain the implementation of all the function
//prototypes specified in the GradeCourse class declared inside
//GradeCourse.h file
//***********************************************************
#include "GradeCourse.h" //"" that the file is in the current project
//NOTE: Same code works for overloaded constructor and
//overloaded constructor with default arguments
//
GradeCourse::GradeCourse(std::string cName, int nos)
{
cout << "Creating object..." << endl;
setCourseName(cName);
setNumOfStud (nos);
}
//set function is used to stores information from the local
//variable name into the member variable courseName
void GradeCourse::setCourseName(std::string name)
{
courseName = name;
}
//get function is used to retrieve information from the
```

```
//member variable courseName
string GradeCourse::getCourseName()
{
return courseName;
}
void GradeCourse::setNumOfStud(int studs)
{
if (studs < 0)
{
studs = 0;
}
else if(studs > 60)
{
studs = 60;
}
numOfStud = studs;
}
int GradeCourse::getNumOfStud()
{
//numOfStud = 7;
return numOfStud;
}
void GradeCourse::displayMessage()
{
cout << "Welcome to " << getCourseName() << endl;
cout << "Num of Students are " << getNumOfStud() << endl;
}
//*************************************************************
//This file contains main function which is the entry point
//for program execution. Once the object is instantiated
//in main, we can invoke all the members using the object name,
// the dot operator and member name.
//*************************************************************
#include "GradeCourse.h"
#include "GradeCourse.h"
#include <ctime>
#include <vector>
using namespace std;
void main()
{
GradeCourse gbObj("C++", 45); //invokes the overloaded constructor
gbObj.displayMessage();
system ("pause");
}
```

The above example defines a class GradeCourse which acts as a blueprint for creating complex data types. The class contains two private member variables courseName and numOfStud, and four public member functions: GradeCourse() - an overloaded constructor with default arguments, setCourseName() - sets the value of the courseName member variable, getCourseName() - returns the value of the courseName member variable, setNumOfStud() - sets the value of the numOfStud member variable, getNumOfStud() - returns the value of the numOfStud member variable, and displayMessage() - displays a welcome message along with the courseName and numOfStud member variables.

The implementation of the GradeCourse class is spread across two files: GradeCourse.h and GradeCourse.cpp. The GradeCourse.h file contains the declaration of the GradeCourse class and its member functions, while the GradeCourse.cpp file contains the implementation of the GradeCourse class member functions.

The main() function creates an instance of the GradeCourse class by invoking the overloaded constructor with the arguments "C++" and 45. The displayMessage() function is then called on the created object to display a welcome message along with the courseName and numOfStud member variables. Finally, the system("pause") function is called to pause the execution of the program until the user presses a key.

7.9 DESTRUCTORS

The complement of the constructor is the destructor. In many circumstances, an object will need to perform some action or series of actions when it is destroyed. Local objects are created when their block is entered, and destroyed when the block is left. Global objects are destroyed when the program terminates. There are many reasons why a destructor may be needed. For example, an object may need to deallocate memory that it had previously allocated. In C++, it is the destructor that handles deactivation. The destructor has the same name as the constructor, but the destructor's name is preceded by ~. Like constructors, destructors do not have return types.

Constructors and destructors are automatically invoked by the compiler. The sequence of these function calls is determined by the order in which execution enters and exits the scopes in which the objects are created. In general, destructor calls are made in the opposite order as constructor calls; however, the storage classes of objects might vary the sequence of destructor calls.

Objects declared in global scope have their constructors called before any other function (including main) in that file is run. However, the order of global object constructor execution across files is not guaranteed.When the main exits, the associated destructors are invoked. Function exit terminates a program instantly and does not perform automated object destructors. When an input error is discovered or when a file to be processed by the program cannot be opened, the function is often used to halt the application. Similar to function exit, function abort terminates the program instantly without enabling the destructors of any objects to be executed. Typically, the **abort** function is used to signify an abnormal program termination. When execution reaches the place where an automated local object is declared, the constructor for that object is invoked. When execution exits the object's scope (i.e., when the block in which the object was declared has completed running), the relevant destructor is invoked. Automatic objects' constructors and destructors are invoked whenever execution enters and exits the object's scope. Automatic objects' destructors are not invoked if the program stops with a call to function **exit** or function **abort**. The constructor for a **static** local object is called just once, when execution first reaches the place where the object is specified. The matching destructor is executed when the **main** exit or function exit is invoked. The destruction of global and static items occurs in the reverse order of their creation. **Static** object destructors are not invoked if the program quits with an abort function call. Each CreateAndDestroy object has an integer (objectID) and a string (message) that are used to identify the object in the program's output.

In C++, destructors are special member functions that are called automatically when an object of a class is destroyed. They are used to get rid of an object's resources and take care of other cleanup tasks.

Here is an example of a simple class with a destructor:

```
class FirstClass {
public:
int x;
float y;
string name;
~FirstClass() {
cout << "Object is being destroyed" << endl;
}
};
```

In this example, FirstClass is the name of the class, and it has a destructor ~FirstClass() which does not take any parameter and does not return anything. Inside the destructor, it will print the message "Object is being destroyed" when the object is destroyed.

When an object goes out of scope or when it is deleted explicitly with the keyword delete, the destructor will be called.

```
{
FirstClass classObj;
}
// The destructor is called when the object classObj goes out of scope
FirstClass* classObj = new FirstClass();
delete classObj;
// The destructor is called when the object is deleted explicitly
Destructor are also useful when freeing resources like memory and file handles.
class MyFile {
private:
string m_fileName;
ofstream m_file;
public:
MyFile(string fileName): m_fileName(fileName) {
m_file.open(fileName, ios::out);
}
~MyFile() {
m_file.close();
}
};
```

In this example, MyFile is the name of the class which takes a string parameter as filename, it opens the file in the constructor and closes it in the destructor.

Destructors are important when working with classes that manage resources, such as memory, file handles, and network connections. They provide a way to release those resources when the object is destroyed, avoiding resource leaks.

7.10 PREPROCESSOR WRAPPER

A preprocessor wrapper is an essential C++ software engineering concept used in header files to prevent the header code from being included multiple times in the same source code file. These preprocessor directives eliminate multiple-definition problems since a class may only be declared once.

The class definition is contained in the preprocessor wrapper shown below. The class definition is enclosed in the following **preprocessor wrapper**:

```
// prevent multiple inclusions of header file
#ifndef TIME_H
#define TIME_H
   ...
#endif
```

As bigger programs are constructed, further definitions and declarations will be inserted in header files. If the term TIME H has been defined, the accompanying preprocessor wrapper prevents the code between #ifndef ("if not defined") and #endif from being included. If the header was not previously included in a file, the #define directive defines the name TIME H and includes the header file statements. If the header file has already been included, TIME H is already declared, and the header file is not included again. Efforts to include a header file several times (inadvertently) are common in big applications with many header files that may contain further header files. [Note: The typical format for the symbolic constant name in preprocessor directives is the header file's name in uppercase with an underscore in place of the period.]

A preprocessor wrapper is a piece of code that lets you decide whether or not to compile a block of code based on a predefined macro.

Here is an example of a simple preprocessor wrapper:

```
#define DEBUG 1
#if DEBUG
#define debug_print(x) cout << x << endl;
#else
#define debug_print(x)
#endif
int main() {
int x = 5;
debug_print(x); // will print x if DEBUG is set to 1, otherwise does nothing
```

```
return 0;
}
```

In this example, the #define directive is used to define a macro called DEBUG with a value of 1. The #if and #else preprocessor directives are used to create a wrapper around the debug_print macro. If DEBUG is defined as 1, the debug_print macro will expand to the code that prints the value of x to the console. If DEBUG is not defined or is defined as 0, the debug_print macro will expand to an empty statement, and the code inside the macro will not be executed.

Another common use of preprocessor wrappers is to include or exclude code based on the platform or the compiler being used. Here is an example:

```
#ifdef _WIN32
// code specific to Windows
#else
// code for other platforms
#endif
```

In this example, the #ifdef preprocessor directive checks whether the _WIN32 macro is defined.If it is defined, the code inside the first block will be included in the compilation and the second block will be excluded.If it is not defined, the second block will be included and the first block will be excluded.

Wrapper Preprocessor can also be used to include header files.

```
#ifdef _WIN32
#include <Windows.h>
#else
#include <unistd.h>
#endif
```

In this example, the #include directive is used to include the <Windows.h> header file on Windows platforms and the <unistd.h> header file on other platforms.

Preprocessor wrappers are a powerful tool that can be used to decide whether or not to compile code based on macros that have already been set up. They are commonly used for debugging, platform-specific code, and to include header files.

Example

```
//************************************************************
//This file contains the declaration of the GradeCourse class.
//The class acts like a blue print and is used to create
//complex data types.
//************************************************************
//<> indicate that the file exists in the standard library
#include <iostream> //input output stream
#include <string>
```

```
using namespace std;
#ifndef GRADE_Course_H
#define GRADE_Course_H
class GradeCourse
{
private:
string courseName; //MEMBER VARIABLE
int numOfStud; //Member variable
public:
// OVERLOADED CONSTRUCTOR WITH DEFAULT ARGS
GradeCourse(string cName = "DirectX", int nos = 100);
void setCourseName(string name);
string getCourseName(); //ACCESS FUNCTION
void setNumOfStud(int xyz);
int getNumOfStud(); //ACCESS FUNCTION
void displayMessage(); //ACCESS FUNCTION
};
#endif
//************************************************************
//This file contain the implementation of all the function
//prototypes specified in the GradeCourse class declared inside
//GradeCourse.h file
//************************************************************
#include "GradeCourse.h" //"" that the file is in the current project
//NOTE: Same code works for overloaded constructor and
//overloaded constructor with default arguments
//
GradeCourse::GradeCourse(std::string cName, int nos)
{
cout << "Creating object..." << endl;
setCourseName(cName);
setNumOfStud (nos);
}
//set function is used to stores information from the local
//variable name into the member variable courseName
void GradeCourse::setCourseName(std::string name)
{
courseName = name;
}
//get function is used to retrieve information from the
//member variable courseName
string GradeCourse::getCourseName()
{
return courseName;
```

```
}
void GradeCourse::setNumOfStud(int studs)
{
if (studs < 0)
{
studs = 0;
}
else if(studs > 60)
{
studs = 60;
}
numOfStud = studs;
}
int GradeCourse::getNumOfStud()
{
//numOfStud = 7;
return numOfStud;
}
void GradeCourse::displayMessage()
{
cout << "Welcome to " << getCourseName() << endl;
cout << "Num of Students are " << getNumOfStud() << endl;
}
//**********************************************************
//This file contains main function which is the entry point
//for program execution. Once the object is instantiated
//in main, we can invoke all the members using the object name,
// the dot operator and member name.
//**********************************************************
#include "GradeCourse.h"
#include "GradeCourse.h"
#include <ctime>
#include <vector>
using namespace std;
void main()
{
GradeCourse gbObj("C++", 45); //invokes the overloaded constructor
gbObj.displayMessage();
system ("pause");
}
```

In this example, a header guard is used to prevent multiple definitions of the GradeCourse class in the same program.

When a header file is added to a program, the #include directive is changed to the contents of the header file by the preprocessor.If the same header file is included multiple times in the same program, it can lead to multiple definitions of the same class, which causes a compilation error.

The header guards #ifndef GRADE_Course_H and #define GRADE_COURSE_H ensure that the contents of the header file are included only once in the program. If the header file has already been included, the preprocessor skips the contents between #ifndef and #endif. If it has not been included yet, it defines the constant GRADE_COURSE_H and includes the contents of the file.

This code defines a C++ class called “GradeCourse” that contains a private member variable called “courseName” of type string and another private member variable called “numOfStud” of type int. The class has four public member functions, including an overloaded constructor that takes two arguments (the course name and the number of students) and sets the member variables accordingly.

The other public member functions include setCourseName(), getCourseName(), setNumOfStud(), and getNumOfStud(). The set functions are used to store information in the corresponding member variables, while the get functions are used to retrieve information from the member variables.

Lastly, the main() function creates an object of the GradeCourse class by passing the name of the course and the number of students to the constructor. It then calls the displayMessage() function to write a welcome message to the console.

7.11 DEFINING MEMBER FUNCTIONS OUTSIDE THE CLASS DEFINITION; CLASS SCOPE

Even if a member function declared in a class definition is defined outside of that class definition and “tied” to the class using the binary scope resolution operator, that member function stays within the scope of the class. This means that its name is only known to other members of the class unless it is called using an object of the class, a reference to an object of the class, a pointer to an object of the class, or the binary scope resolution operator.

If a member function is defined in the body of a class declaration, the C++ compiler tries to inline its calls.With the explicit keyword inline, member functions declared outside of a class declaration may be inlined. Note that the compiler may choose not to inline any function.

In the class header, you should only list the most basic and stable member functions, which are those whose implementations are not likely to change.

Member functions of a class can be defined both inside and outside the class definition. When a member function is defined inside the class definition, it’s called an inline function. When a member function is defined outside the class definition, it’s called an out-of-line function.

Here is an example of defining a member function inside the class definition:

```
class FirstClass {
public:
FirstClass(int x): x(x) {}
int getX() { return x; }
private:
int x;
};
```

In this example, the getX member function is defined inside the class definition and is an inline function. Here is an example of defining a member function outside the class definition:

```
class FirstClass {
public:
FirstClass(int x): x(x) {}
int getX();
private:
int x;
};
int FirstClass::getX() {
return x;
}
```

In this example, the getX member function is defined outside the class definition. The implementation of the member function is in a separate source file, while the declaration of the member function is in the header file. The scope resolution operator:: is used to indicate that the getX function is a member of the FirstClass class.

When a member function is defined outside of the class, it can access the private members of the class, but the function name must be qualified by the class name and the scope resolution operator. To access the private members of the class, you can use this pointer, which is a pointer to the current object.

Here's an example:

```
class FirstClass {
public:
FirstClass(int x): x(x) {}
void incrementX();
private:
int x;
};
void FirstClass::incrementX() {
this->x++;
}
```

In this example, the incrementX member function is defined outside the class and use this pointer to access the private member x and increment it.

It's also possible to use friend function to allow a non-member function to access the private members of a class. Here's an example:

```
class FirstClass {
public:
FirstClass(int x): x(x) {}
friend void increment(FirstClass& obj);
private:
```

```
int x;
};
void increment(FirstClass& obj) {
obj.x++;
}
```

In this example, the increment function is defined as a friend function of the FirstClass class, which means it has access to the private members of the class, in this case x.

It's important to note that defining member functions outside the class definition can make the code more modular and easier to maintain, as the implementation details are separated from the interface.

7.11.1 Member Functions vs. Global Functions

It is interesting to note that the member functions take no arguments This is due to the fact that these member functions know implicitly that they must print the data members of the Time object for which they were requested. This may make member function calls in procedural programming more succinct than ordinary function calls.

Member functions are functions that are associated with a class and have access to the private members of the class, while global functions are functions that are not associated with any class and do not have access to the private members of a class.

Here is an example of a member function:

```
class FirstClass {
public:
FirstClass(int x): x(x) {}
int getX() { return x; }
private:
int x;
};
```

In this example, the getX member function is a member of the FirstClass class and has access to the private member x.

Here is an example of a global function:

```
void incrementX(FirstClass& obj) {
obj.x++;
}
```

In this example, the incrementX function is not a member of any class and does not have access to the private members of the FirstClass class. It takes a reference to a FirstClass object as an argument and increments its x member.

Here is an example of how the two functions would be used:

```
FirstClass obj(5);
cout << obj.getX() << endl; // prints 5
incrementX(obj);
cout << obj.getX() << endl; // prints 6
```

In this example, the getX member function is used to get the value of the private member x of the FirstClass object, while the incrementX global function is used to increment the value of x.

It's important to note that global functions do not have access to the private members of a class, so they must use the public interface of the class to interact with its objects. On the other hand, member functions have direct access to the private members of the class, which makes them more efficient and easier to use, but can make the class harder to maintain and test, as the implementation details are tightly coupled with the interface.

7.11.2 Object Size

People who aren't familiar with object-oriented programming might think that because an object has data members and member methods, it must be pretty big.Theoretically, it is true that a programmer may think of objects as carrying data and functions (and our discussion has definitely strengthened this point of view), but physically, this is not the case.Objects are much smaller than if they also had member functions, since they just carry data. When sizeof is applied to a class name or an object of that class, just the size of the class's data members will be reported. The compiler generates a single copy of the member functions distinct from all class objects. All class objects share this single copy.

Obviously, each object needs its own copy of the class's data since the data might differ across instances. The function code is immutable (also known as reentrant code or a pure method) and may thus be shared by all instances of a class. The size of an object depends on the data members and the implementation of the class. The size of an object can be determined using the sizeof operator.

Here is an example of how to determine the size of an object:

```
class FirstClass {
public:
int x;
double y;
};
int main() {
FirstClass obj;
cout << sizeof(obj) << endl; // prints size of the object in bytes
return 0;
}
```

In this example, the FirstClass class has two data members, an int and a double. The sizeof operator is used to determine the size of the object, which will depend on the size of an int and a double on the specific platform.

It's crucial to keep in mind that the alignment of the data members can also affect the size of an object. Alignment refers to the way data is arranged in memory, and can affect the size of an object if the data members are not naturally aligned.

Here is an example of how alignment can affect the size of an object:

```
class FirstClass {
public:
char c;
int x;
};
int main() {
FirstClass obj;
cout << sizeof(obj) << endl; // prints size of the object in bytes
return 0;
}
```

In this example, the FirstClass class has a char and an int data members. The sizeof operator is used to determine the size of the object. On most platforms, an int is 4 bytes and a char is 1 byte, but due to alignment, the size of the object might be 8 bytes.

It's also important to note that any virtual functions and virtual tables that the class may have will have an impact on the size of an object. If a class has virtual functions, it will have a virtual table pointer (vptr) to store the addresses of the virtual functions, which increases the size of the object.

7.11.3 Class Scope and Accessing Class Members

The scope of a class includes its data members (variables listed in the class declaration) and member functions (functions listed in the class definition). At **file scope**, nonmember functions are defined.

Within the scope of a class, members are instantly available to all member functions of that class and may be referred to by name. Public class members are accessed outside of a class's scope through one of the handles on an object: an object name, a reference to an object, or a pointer to an object. The interface (i.e., the member functions) available to the client is determined by the type of the object, reference, or pointer.

Class member functions may be overloaded, but only by other class member functions. To overload a member function, just supply a prototype for each version of the overloaded function in the class definition and a separate function definition for each version.

Variables that are set up inside a member function have block scope, which means they can only be used inside that function.If a member function declares a variable with the same name as a class-scope variable, the block-scope variable hides the class-scope variable.You can get back to such a hidden variable by adding the class name and the scope resolution operator (::) to the variable name.With the unary scope resolution operator, you may access hidden global variables.

To get to an object's members, you need to put the object's name or a reference to the object before the dot member selection operator (.). To get to an object's members, the arrow member selection operator (->) must come before a pointer to the object.

7.11.4 Access Functions and Utility Functions

Access functions may show or read data. Access functions are also often used to test the truth or falsehood of conditions; these functions are generally referred to as **predicate functions**. An example of a predicate function would be the isEmpty function for any container class, such as a linked list, stack, or queue. Before trying to read another item from the container object, a program may verify isEmpty.

The isFull predicate function can be used to check a container-class object to see if there is no more room.isAM and isPM are useful predicate methods for our Time class.

Utility functions are private member functions that help the public member functions of a class work. It is not part of a class's public interface. Clients of a class are not meant to utilize utility functions.

7.12 DEFAULT MEMBER WISE ASSIGNMENT

The assignment operator (=) may be used to assign the same type of object to another object. Each data member of the object to the right of the assignment operator is separately assigned to the corresponding data member of the object to the left of the assignment operator. [Beware: Using **member-wise assignment** with a class whose data members include references to dynamically allocated memory might create severe issues.]

Objects may be supplied as parameters to functions and returned from functions. Pass-by-value is used for such passing and returning; by default, a copy of the object is sent or returned. In such situations, C++ generates a new object and uses a copy constructor to copy the values of the old object into the new objectg; by default, a copy of the object is sent or returned. In such situations, C++ generates a new object and uses a copy constructor to copy the values of the old object into the new object. The compiler offers a **copy constructor** by default for each class that copies each member of the old object into the corresponding member of the new object. Copy constructors, like member-wise assignment, may pose significant issues when used with a class whose data members include references to dynamically allocated memory.

7.13 CONST (CONSTANT) OBJECTS AND CONST MEMBER FUNCTIONS

Certain items must be modified, whereas others do not. The programmer may use the term const to indicate that an object cannot be modified and that any effort to do so should result in a compilation fault. The expression

const Time noon(12, 0, 0);

defines and initializes a const object of type Time named noon with the value 12 noon.

By declaring an object as const, the concept of least privilege is enforced. Efforts to change the object are detected at compile time as opposed to producing issues during execution. Const use is essential to class design, program design, and coding.

Const variables and object declarations may enhance performance. Compilers that optimize variables cannot perform some optimizations on constants that can be done on constants. Compilers for C++ prohibit calling member functions on const objects unless the member functions are likewise declared const. Even for obtain member methods that do not affect the object, this holds true. Furthermore, the compiler prohibits member functions marked as const from modifying the object. Const is specified in both the prototype and the definition of a function.

Constructors and destructors, each of which normally alters objects, face an intriguing dilemma. Constructors and destructors are prohibited from using the const declaration. A constructor must be permitted to change an object in order for the object to be correctly initialized. Prior to the system reclaiming an object's memory, a destructor must be able to complete its termination housekeeping duties.

```
// Time class definition with const member functions.
// Member functions defined in Time.cpp.
# include <iostream>
#ifndef TIME_H
#define TIME_H
class Time
{
public:
Time(int, int, int); // default constructor
// set functions
void setTime(int, int, int); // set time
void set_Hour(int); // set hour
void set_Minutes(int); // set minute
void set_Second(int); // set second
// get functions (normally declared const)
int get_Hour() const; // return hour
int get_Minutes() const; // return minute
int get_Second() const; // return second
// print functions (normally declared const)
void printUniversal() const; // print universal time
void printStandard() ;
private:
int hour; // 0 - 23 (24-hour clock format)
int minute; // 0 - 59
int second; // 0 - 59
}; // end class Time
#endif
```

Initializing a const Data Member with a Member Initializer

Const data members and reference data members must be initialized using member initializer syntax.

In this example, the parameters c and I of the constructor are used to set up count and increment. You'll notice that commas separate the various initializers for member variables.Note also that the member initializer list runs before the constructor's body.

Const objects cannot be updated by assignment; thus, they must be initialized. When a class's data member is declared const, a member initializer must be used to provide the constructor with the initial value of the data member. The same applies to references.

7.14 COMPOSITION: OBJECTS AS MEMBERS OF CLASSES

Why not add a Time object as a member of the AlarmClock class, given that an AlarmClock object has to know when it should sound its alarm? Such a skill is known as composition and is also known as having a connection. A class may have as members objects of other classes. The object's constructor is automatically invoked upon creation. Before, we learned how to send parameters to the constructor of an object generated in the main function.

This section shows how member initializers let the constructor of an object send parameters to the constructors of member objects.Member objects are created in the order that they are defined in the class declaration, not in the order that they are listed in the constructor's member initializer list, and before their host class objects.

Class date and class Employees are used to illustrate items as members of other objects. Employee's class definition includes the private data members firstName, lastName, birthDate, and hireDate. birthDate and hireDate are constant Date objects, which include the private data members month, day, and year. The header of the Employee constructor states that it gets four arguments (first, last, dateOfBirth and dateOfHire). The first two constructor arguments are used to initialize the character arrays firstName and lastName. The last two arguments are provided to the Date class constructor through member initializers. In the header, the colon (:) separates the member initializers from the parameter list. The member initializers provide the employee constructor arguments that are supplied to the member Date objects' constructors. dateOfBirth is supplied to the birth object as a parameter. Date's constructor and the dateOfHire argument are supplied to hireDate's constructor. Again, initializers for members are separated by commas. When you examine the class Date, you will find that it lacks a constructor that accepts an argument of type Date.

Example 1:

```
// Time class definition with const member functions.
// Member functions defined in Time.cpp.
# include <iostream>
#ifndef TIME_H
#define TIME_H
class Time
{
public:
Time(int, int, int); // default constructor
// set functions
void setTime(int, int, int); // set time
void set_Hour(int); // set hour
void set_Minutes(int); // set minute
void set_Second(int); // set second
// get functions (normally declared const)
int get_Hour() const; // return hour
int get_Minutes() const; // return minute
int get_Second() const; // return second
// print functions (normally declared const)
```

```
void printUniversal() const; // print universal time
void printStandard() ;
private:
int hour; // 0 - 23 (24-hour clock format)
int minute; // 0 - 59
int second; // 0 - 59
}; // end class Time
#endif
// Time class member-function definitions.
#include <iostream>
#include <iomanip>
#include <stdexcept>
#include "TIME.h" // include definition of class Time
using namespace std;
// constructor function to initialize private data;
// calls member function setTime to set variables;
// default values are 0 (see class definition)
Time::Time(int hour, int minute, int second)
{
setTime(hour, minute, second);
} // end Time constructor
// set hour, minute and second values
void Time::setTime(int hour, int minute, int second)
{
set_Hour(hour);
set_Minutes(minute);
set_Second(second);
} // end function setTime
// set hour value
void Time::set_Hour(int h)
{
if (h >= 0 && h < 24)
hour = h;
else
cout<<"hour must be 0-23";
} // end function set_Hour
// set minute value
void Time::set_Minutes(int m)
{
if (m >= 0 && m < 60)
minute = m;
else
cout<<"minute must be 0-59";
} // end function set_Minutes
```

```
// set second value
void Time::set_Second(int s)
{
if (s >= 0 && s < 60)
second = s;
else
cout<<"second must be 0-59";
} // end function set_Second
// return hour value
int Time::get_Hour() const // get functions should be const
{
return hour;
} // end function get_Hour
// return minute value
int Time::get_Minutes() const
{
return minute;
} // end function get_Minutes
// return second value
int Time::get_Second() const
{
return second;
} // end function get_Second
// print Time in universal-time format (HH:MM:SS)
void Time::printUniversal() const
{
cout << setfill('0')<<setw(2) << hour << ":"
<< setw(2) << minute << ":" << setw(2) << second<<endl;
} // end function printUniversal
// print Time in standard-time format (HH:MM:SS AM or PM)
void Time::printStandard() // note lack of const declaration
{
cout << ((hour == 0 || hour == 12) ? 12: hour % 12)
<< ":" << setfill('0') << setw(2) << minute
<< ":" << setw(2) << second << (hour < 12 ? " PM": " AM")<<endl;
} // end function printStandard
// Attempting to access a const object with non-const member functions.
#include "TIME.h" // include Time class definition
void main()
{
Time wakeUp(6, 45, 0); // non-constant object
const Time noon(12, 0, 0); // constant object
// OBJECT MEMBER FUNCTION
wakeUp.set_Hour(18); // non-const non-const
```

```
//noon.set_Hour(12); // const non-const
wakeUp.get_Hour(); // non-const const
noon.get_Minutes(); // const const
noon.printUniversal(); // const const
wakeUp.printStandard(); // const non-const
system("pause");
} // end main
```

The above code defines a class named "Time", which represents time in hours, minutes, and seconds. It contains three private integer variables (hour, minute, and second) and several public member functions to set and get these variables. Additionally, it has two print functions, one that prints the time in universal time format (HH:MM:SS) and another that prints it in standard time format (HH:MM:SS AM or PM).

The code also demonstrates the use of const member functions. In the main function, an object named "wakeUp" is created using the default constructor, which is not a constant. Another object named "noon" is created using a constructor that takes three arguments, and this object is marked as constant using the const keyword. The main function then calls several member functions on these objects, some of which are non-constant and some of which are constants. The code demonstrates that non-constant member functions cannot be called on constant objects, but constant member functions can be called on both constant and non-constant objects.

Example 2:

```
/*
Const Member Variables
*/
#include <iostream>
#include <string>
using namespace std;
#ifndef BOSS_H
#define BOSS_H
class Boss
{
private:
int attack;
int health;
const int MAX; //CONSTANT VARIABLE
public:
Boss();
Boss(int cValue);
Boss(int aValue, int hValue, int cValue);
void displayBoss(); //non-static
};
#endif
#include "Boss.h"
//Constant variables can ONLY be initialized using MEMBER INITIALIZER list as
```

```
follows
//non-const member variables can ALSO be initialized using member initializer
list,
//note that attack and health are non-const member variables
Boss::Boss(): MAX(50)/*, attack(20), health(200)*/
{
cout << "Inside Boss constructor" << endl;
attack = 20; //valid initialization since attack is non-const member variable
health = 200;//valid initialization since health is non-const member variable
//MAX = 50; //Will not work bcoz this is a const variable
}
//NOTE: non-const member variables can also be initialized using member ini-
tializer list,
Boss::Boss(int cValue):MAX(cValue)
{
cout << "Inside Boss constructor" << endl;
attack = 20;
health = 200;
}
Boss::Boss(int aValue, int hValue, int cValue): MAX(cValue)/*, attack(aValue),
health(hValue)*/
{
cout << "Inside Overloaded constructor" << endl;
//MAX = 100; //ERROR: CONST VARIABLE CANNOT BE INITIALIZED INSIDE THE CON-
STRUCTOR
attack = aValue; //Correct since this is a non-const variable
health = hValue; //Correct since this is a non-const variable
}
void Boss::displayBoss()
{
cout<<"\n\nDisplay Function for Boss class: " << endl;
cout<<"Attack: "<<attack<<endl;
cout<<"Health: "<<health<<endl;
cout << "Const variable MAX = " << MAX << endl;
}
#include "Boss.h"
#include <ctime>
int main()
{
Boss bossObj;
bossObj.displayBoss();
Boss newBossObj(22575);
newBossObj.displayBoss();
Boss overBossObj(85, 2000, 65535);
```

```
overBossObj.displayBoss();
system("pause");
return 0;
}
```

In the above code, const member variables are used to declare a constant variable, MAX, inside the Boss class. The const keyword is used to specify that the value of the variable cannot be changed after initialization. Since the MAX variable is declared as const, it can only be initialized using a member initializer list in the constructor. This means that we cannot change the value of MAX after it has been initialized.

In the Boss class constructor, the member initializer list is used to set up the MAX variable.But you can also set up non-const member variables like attack and health by using the member initializer list or the constructor body.

The code also includes an example of creating objects of the Boss class and calling the displayBoss() function to display the values of the member variables, including the MAX constant variable.

7.15 FRIEND FUNCTIONS AND FRIEND CLASSES

A **friend** function of a class is defined outside the class's scope but has access to the class's **private** (and **public**) members. Classes or individual functions may be defined as friends of another class. Friend functions may improve efficiency. This section demonstrates mechanically how the friend function works.

To designate a function as a friend of a class, use the term friend before the function prototype in the class specification. Place a declaration of the form friend class ClassTwo in the definition of class ClassOne to declare all member functions of class ClassTwo as friends of class ClassOne.

```
friend class ClassTwo;
```

Note: While friend function prototypes exist in the class declaration, friend functions are not member functions. [Friend declarations are not affected by the ideas of private, protected, and public member access; therefore, they may be inserted anywhere inside a class definition.

Friendship is not earned, but given. Hence, for class B to be a friend of class A, class A must state clearly that class B is a friend. Also, the friendship relation is neither symmetric nor transitive; that is, if class A is a friend of class B and class B is a friend of class C, you cannot infer that class B is a friend of class A (again, because friendship is not symmetric), that class C is a friend of class B (also because friendship is not symmetric), or that class A is a friend of class C (because friendship is not transitive).

7.15.1 Modifying a Class's Private Data With a Friend Function

A mechanical example in which we construct the buddy function setX to set the class Count's private data member x Notice that, by tradition, the friend declaration occurs first in the class definition, even before the public member functions. Remember, this declaration of a buddy might exist anywhere inside the class.

The method setX is an independent C-style function; it is not a member function of the Count class. As a result, when setX is called for object counter, it takes counter as an argument rather than a handle (such as the object's name) to call the function, as in

```
counter. setX(8);
```

As previously said, this is a mechanical example of using friend construction. The method setX should often be defined as a member function of the class Count. Moreover, it would be desirable to divide the program into three files:

- A header file (e.g., Count.h) that defines the Count class and includes the prototype of the setX friend function.
- A file containing the definitions of class Count's member functions and the definition of buddy function setX (e.g., Count.cpp).
- A test program (such as main.cpp) containing the main.

7.15.2 Erroneously Attempting to Modify a Private Member With a Non-Friend Function

The application illustrates the error messages generated by the compiler when the non-friend function cannot be resolved. SetX modifies the private data member x.

It is possible to designate overloaded functions as a class's buddies. Any overloaded function intended to be a friend must be expressly defined as a friend in the class's definition.

Example 1:

```
// Friends can access private members of a class.
#include <iostream>
using namespace std;
// Count class definition
class Count
{
friend void setX(Count &, int); // friend declaration
public:
// constructor
Count()
: x(0) // initialize x to 0
{
// empty body
} // end constructor Count
// output x
void print() const
{
cout << x << endl;
} // end function print
```

```
private:
int x; // data member
}; // end class Count
// function setX can modify private data of Count
// because setX is declared as a friend of Count (line 9)
void setX(Count &c, int val)
{
c.x = val; // allowed because setX is a friend of Count
} // end function setX
void main()
{
Count counter; // create Count objectg
cout << "counter.x after instantiation: ";
counter.print();
setX(counter, 8); // set x using a friend function
cout << "counter.x after call to setX friend function: ";
counter.print();
system("pause");
} // end main
```

In C++, a friend function is a function that is not a member of a class but has access to the private members of the class. In the given code, the function **setX** is declared as a friend of the **Count** class, which means it can access the private member **x** of the **Count** class. The **setX** function takes a **Count** object and an integer value as parameters and sets the value of **x** to the integer value passed as a parameter.

The **main** function creates a **Count** object and initializes its **x** member to 0. It then calls the **setX** function, passing the **counter** object and the value 8. The **setX** function sets the value of **x** to 8 using friend access. Finally, the **main** function prints the value of **x** after the call to the **setX** function.

Using the friend function can be useful in cases where a function needs access to private data of members of a class but is not a member function of that class. However, overuse of friend functions can make it difficult to maintain the encapsulation of the class.

Example 2:

```
#include <iostream>
using namespace std;
class FirstClass
{
friend void displayClassInfo(FirstClass *obj); //will access to all the pri-
vate information
//friend class SomeClass;
public:
//member functions
FirstClass (int value = 0);
void display();
private:
```

```
//member variables
int totalPlayers;
//private member functions
int getTotalPlayers();
void setTotalPlayers(int total);
};
#include "FirstClass.h"
FirstClass::FirstClass(int total)
{
setTotalPlayers(total);
}
void FirstClass::setTotalPlayers(int total)
{
if(total >50)
{
total = 50;
}
totalPlayers = total;
}
int FirstClass::getTotalPlayers()
{
return totalPlayers;
}
void FirstClass::display()
{
cout<<"Total Players: "<<getTotalPlayers()<<endl;
}
#include "FirstClass.h"
//Global function
//void displayClassInfo(FirstClass *obj);
void main()
{
FirstClass mcObj;
mcObj.display();
displayClassInfo(&mcObj);
system("pause");
}
void displayClassInfo(FirstClass *obj)
{
cout<<"Inside Global function"<<endl;
obj->setTotalPlayers(5);
cout<<"Total no of players are: "<<endl;
obj->display();
}
```

In this code, the concept of friend functions in C++ is demonstrated. A friend function is a function that is not a member of a class but has access to the private members of that class. In this code, the class FirstClass has a private member function called getTotalPlayers() and a private member variable called totalPlayers. The class also has a friend function, displayClassInfo() that has access to these private members.

The totalPlayers variable is set up by the FirstClass constructor using the setTotalPlayers() function. This function checks to see if the value is greater than 50 and, if it is, limits it to 50.The display() function simply outputs the current value of totalPlayers.

The main() function creates an object of FirstClass and calls its display() function, which outputs the value of totalPlayers. Then, it calls the friend function displayClassInfo() and passes a pointer to the object. The displayClassInfo() function calls setTotalPlayers() to set a new value for totalPlayers and then calls display() to output the new value.

In this case, the reason for using friend functions is to give a global function that can access and change private members of FirstClass.

7.16 USING THE THIS POINTER

We've seen that an object's member functions can change the object's data. How do member functions choose which data members of an object to manipulate? With a pointer named this (a C++ keyword), every object has access to its own address. The size of the operation on an object does not reflect the amount of memory it uses.

This pointer is instead given (by the compiler) as an implicit parameter to each non-static member function of the object. To access their data members and member functions, objects utilize this pointer either implicitly (as we have done so far) or explicitly.

The type of this pointer depends on the type of the object and the consistency declaration of the member function where it is used.In a nonconstant Employee class member function, for instance, the type of this reference is Employee * const (a constant pointer to a nonconstant Employee object). The data type of this reference in a constant Employee class member function is const Employee * const (a constant pointer to a constant Employee object).

The first example in this section demonstrates both explicit and implicit usage of this pointer; later in this chapter, we demonstrate more significant and sophisticated uses of it.

7.16.1 Implicitly and Explicitly Using the this Pointer to Access an Object's Data Members

The implicit and explicit usage of the this pointer to allow a Test class member function to output the Test object's private data x.

As an example, the member function print prints x by utilizing the this reference implicitly and specifying just the data member's name. Then, print employs two distinct notations to access x via the this pointer: the arrow operator (->) and the dot operator (.) off the dereferenced this pointer.

Observe the parenthesis around *this when the dot member selection operator is used (.). Since the dot operator has greater precedence than the * operator, parentheses are necessary. Without the parentheses, the expression *this.x would be evaluated as if it were enclosed in parenthesis as *(this.x), which would result in a compilation error as the dot operator cannot be used with a pointer. The this pointer may be used to prevent an object from being allocated to itself.

7.16.2 Dynamic Memory Management With Operators new and delete

In C++, programmers can control how much memory is used and how much is freed up for any built-in or user-defined data type. This is referred to as **dynamic memory management**, and it is accomplished via the operators new and delete. Remember that class Employee" employs two 25-character arrays to represent an employee's first and last names. When declaring these arrays as data members, the Employee class definition must specify the number of elements in each array, as the size of the data members determines the amount of memory required to hold each Employee object.

As was already said, names with less than 24 characters may waste space in these arrays.In addition, names longer than 24 characters must be shortened to fit in these arrays of fixed size.

Wouldn't it be great if we could use arrays with exactly the number of items required to hold the first and last names of an employee? This is exactly what dynamic memory management enables us to achieve. If we replace the array data elements firstName and lastName with pointers to char, we can use the new operator to dynamically reserve (**allocate**) the precise amount of memory necessary to store each name at execution time. Dynamically allocating memory in this manner results in the creation of an array (or any other built-in or user-defined type) in the free store (also called the heap), a section of memory given to each program for storing objects produced at execution time. After the memory for an array has been allocated in the free store, it may be accessed by pointing a pointer to the array's first element. After the array is no longer required, we may return the memory to the **free store** by using the delete operator to **deallocate** (i.e., release) the memory, which can then be utilized by subsequent new operations.

First, the new and delete operators are used to allocate memory on the fly for storing objects, fundamental types, and arrays.Consider the following statement and declaration:

```
Time *timePtr;
timePtr = new Time;
```

The new operator gives an object of type Time the right amount of storage space, runs the object's default constructor to set it up, and returns a pointer of the type given to the right of the new operator, in this case a Time *.Remember that new may be used to allocate dynamically any basic or class type (such as int or double). If new can't find enough memory space for the object, it "throws an exception" to let you know there's a problem.

Use the delete operator as shown to get rid of a dynamically allocated object and free up its space:

```
delete timePtr;
```

This statement first executes the destructor for the object pointed to by timePtr, then deallocates the memory associated with the object. Following the previous line, the system may reuse the RAM to allocate more objects.

Note: If dynamically allocated memory is not released when it is no longer required, the system may run out of memory prematurely. This is often referred to as a "memory leak."

In C++, you can give an initializer to a new variable of type fundamental, as in

```
double *ptr = new double(3.14159);
```

which sets the first value of a newly created double to 3.14159 and gives the result to ptr as a pointer. The same syntax may be used to pass a comma-separated list of constructor parameters to an object.

```
Time *timePtr = new Time (12, 45, 0);
```

For example, set the first value of a new Time object to 12:45 PM and set the reference to timePtr. As previously mentioned, the new operator may be used to dynamically allocate arrays. A 10-element integer array, for instance, can be created and assigned to grades. Array as follows:

```
int *gradesArray = new int [10];
```

declares and gives gradesArray a reference to the first integer in a 10-element array that is built on the fly. Remember that a constant integral expression must be used to give the size of an array that is made during compilation. Still, the size of an array that is created on the fly can be set by any expression that can be evaluated at runtime and returns an integer. When an array of objects is created on the fly, the programmer cannot give each object its own constructor parameters. Instead, default constructors are used to initialize each item in the array. Use

```
delete [] gradesArray;
```

to destroy the dynamically allocated array to which gradesArray points. The accompanying statement deallocates the array to which gradesArray points. If the address in the previous statement corresponds to an array of objects, the statement calls the destructor for each item in the array before deallocating the memory. If the above sentence does not have square brackets ([]) and grades, the assertion is incorrect. If Array is linked to an array of objects, only the first object would receive a call to its destructor.

When working with arrays of objects, using delete instead of delete [] could cause logic problems at run time.To guarantee that each item in the array receives a destructor function, memory created as an array must always be deleted using the operator delete []. Similarly, memory allocated as an individual element should always be deleted using operator delete.

Developing and sustaining dynamic data structures necessitates dynamic memory allocation, which enables a program to acquire more memory at runtime in order to accommodate new nodes. When this memory is no longer required by the software, it can be freed so that it can be utilized in the future to allocate additional objects.

The limit for dynamic memory allocation could be as big as the amount of physical memory on the computer or the amount of virtual memory on a virtual memory system.Often, the restrictions are substantially lower since memory must be shared among several processes.

The new operator takes as a parameter the type of the object that will be created on the fly and gives back a pointer to an object of that type.

```
Node *newPtr = new Node(10); / /create Node with data 10.
```

allots sizeof(Node) bytes, executes the Node constructor, and assigns the address of the new Node object to newPtr. If there is no accessible memory, new will throw a bad alloc error. The number 10 is supplied to the node constructor, which sets the data member's value to 10.

The delete operator invokes the node destructor and frees up memory created with new. Memory is returned to the system so that it may be repurposed at a later time. To clear memory allocated dynamically by the preceding new, use the

```
delete newPtr;
```

Note that newPtr itself is not erased; rather, the space newPtr links to is deleted. If the pointer newPtr has a value of 0, the last statement has no effect. It is OK to remove a null pointer.

Examples 1:

```
// Using the this pointer to refer to object members.
#include <iostream>
using namespace std;
class Test
{
public:
Test(int = 0); // default constructor
void print() const;
private:
int x;
}; // end class Test
// constructor
Test::Test(int value)
: x(value) // initialize x to value
{
// empty body
} // end constructor Test
// print x using implicit and explicit this pointers;
// the parentheses around *this are required
void Test::print() const
{
// implicitly use the this pointer to access the member x
cout << " x = " << x;
// explicitly use the this pointer and the arrow operator
// to access the member x
cout << "\n this->x = " << this->x;
// explicitly use the dereferenced this pointer and
// the dot operator to access the member x
cout << "\n(*this).x = " << (*this).x << endl;
```

```
} // end function print
void main()
{
Test testObject(12); // instantiate and initialize testObject
testObject.print();
system("pause");
} // end main
```

This is a pointer in C++ to the object that is running a member function right now.It can be used to access the object's member variables and methods. In this code, the print() member function of the Test class uses this pointer to access the x member variable in three different ways.

First, the x member variable is accessed implicitly using the x identifier. This is equivalent to writing this->x, where this is a pointer to the current object.

Second, the x member variable is directly accessed by using the this pointer and the arrow (->) operator. This is equivalent to the first method.

Lastly, the x member variable is directly accessed using this pointer that has been dereferenced and the dot (.) operator. This is equivalent to writing (*this).x.

The output of the print() function shows the value of the x member variable using all three methods, which should all print the same value.

Example 2:

```
//************************************************************
//This file contains the declaration of the GradeCourse class.
//The class acts like a blue print and is used to create
//complex data types.
//************************************************************
//<> indicate that the file exists in the standard library
#include <iostream> //input output stream
#include <string>
using namespace std;
#ifndef GRADE_Course_H
#define GRADE_Course _H
class GradeCourse
{
private:
string courseName; //MEMBER VARIABLE
int numOfStud; //Member variable
//bool win;
public:
// OVERLOADED CONSTRUCTOR WITH DEFAULT ARGS
GradeCourse(string cName = "DirectX", int nos = 100);
~GradeCourse();
void setCourseName(string courseName);
string getCourseName()const; //ACCESS FUNCTION
```

```
void setNumOfStud(int xyz);
int getNumOfStud()const; //ACCESS FUNCTION
//bool isWin(); //PREDICATE FUNCTION --return true or false value
void displayMessage()const; //ACCESS FUNCTION
};
#endif
//*********************************************************
//This file contain the implementation of all the function
//prototypes specified in the GradeCourse class declared inside
//GradeCourse.h file
//*********************************************************
#include "GradeCourse.h" //"" that the file is in the current project
//NOTE: Same code works for overloaded constructor and
//overloaded constructor with default arguments
//
GradeCourse::GradeCourse(std::string cName, int nos)
{
cout << "Creating object..." << endl;
setCourseName(cName);
setNumOfStud (nos);
}
GradeCourse::~GradeCourse()
{
cout << "Destructor called." << endl;
system("pause");
}
//set function is used to stores information from the local
//variable name into the member variable courseName
void GradeCourse::setCourseName(std::string courseName)
{
this->courseName = courseName;
}
//get function is used to retrieve information from the
//member variable courseName
string GradeCourse::getCourseName()const
{
return courseName;
}
void GradeCourse::setNumOfStud(int studs)
{
if (studs < 0)
{
studs = 0;
}
```

```
else if(studs > 60)
{
studs = 60;
}
numOfStud = studs;
}
int GradeCourse::getNumOfStud()const
{
//numOfStud = 7;
return numOfStud;
}
void GradeCourse::displayMessage()const
{
cout << "Welcome to " << getCourseName() << endl;
cout << "Num of Students are " << getNumOfStud() << endl;
}
//*************************************************************
//This file contains main function which is the entry point
//for program execution. Once the object is instantiated
//in main, we can invoke all the members using the object name,
// the dot operator and member name.
//*************************************************************
#include "GradeCourse.h"
#include "GradeCourse.h"
#include <ctime>
#include <vector>
using namespace std;
int main()
{
const GradeCourse gbObj;
gbObj.displayMessage();
//This will not work coz u cannot modify const data
//gbObj.setNumOfStud(5); //This will not work for const objects
//cout << endl;
//const GradeCourse overGBObj("XYZ", 12);
//overGBObj.setNumOfStud(5);//This will not work for const objects
//overGBObj.displayMessage();
system("Pause");
return 0;
}
```

The declaration and implementation of the GradeCourse class, which is used to make complex data types, are shown in this example.

The declaration of the GradeCourse class includes two private member variables: courseName of type string and numOfStud of type int. The class also includes an overloaded constructor that takes in two arguments and a destructor. The class has four member functions: setCourseName(), getCourseName(), setNumOfStud(), and getNumOfStud(), which are used to set and get the values of the private member variables. The class also has a displayMessage() function that prints out the values of the private member variables.

The definition of the overloaded constructor and destructor is part of the implementation of the GradeCourse class.The definitions of the member functions setCourseName(), getCourseName(), setNumOfStud(), getNumOfStud(), and displayMessage() are also part of the implementation.

Using the default constructor, the main() function makes a new object of the GradeCourse class and calls its displayMessage() function. It also shows that the private member variables can't be changed by the member functions if the object is declared as "const." Finally, the program waits for a key press before exiting.

Example 3:

```
/*
DYNAMIC MEMORY ALLOCATION
*/
#include <iostream>
#include <string>
using namespace std;
#ifndef BOSS_H
#define BOSS_H
class Boss
{
private:
//These pointers will be allocated memory later
int *attackPtr; //variable declaration at runtime
int *healthPtr; //variable declaration at runtime
public:
Boss();//non-static
Boss(int aValue, int hValue);//non-static
~Boss();//non-static
void setAttack(int aValue);//non-static
int getAttack();
void setHealth(int hValue);//non-static
int getHealth();
void displayBoss(); //non-static
};
#endif
#include "Boss.h"
Boss::Boss()
{
cout << "Inside Boss constructor" << endl;
```

```
//allocate memory to the member variables
attackPtr = new int; //these variables are already declared in .h file
healthPtr = new int;
////if set function are not available --initialization is done as follows
//*attackPtr = 20;
//*healthPtr = 100;
//Initialization using set function
setAttack(20);
setHealth(100);
}
Boss::Boss(int aValue, int hValue)
{
cout << "Inside Overloaded constructor" << endl;
//allocate memory to the member variables
attackPtr = new int;
healthPtr = new int;
////if set function are not available --initialization is done as follows
//*attackPtr = aValue;
//*healthPtr = hValue;
//Initialization using set function
setAttack(aValue);
setHealth(hValue);
}
Boss::~Boss()
{
cout << "Deleting memory allocated..." << endl;
delete attackPtr;
delete healthPtr;
}
void Boss::setAttack(int aValue)
{
*attackPtr = aValue;
//oR
//attackPtr = &aValue;
}
int Boss::getAttack()
{
return *attackPtr;
}
void Boss::setHealth(int hValue)
{
*healthPtr = hValue;
}
int Boss::getHealth()
```

```
{
return *healthPtr;
}
void Boss::displayBoss()
{
cout<<"\nDisplay Function for Boss class: " << endl;
////The following code can be used if there is no get function
//cout << "Boss's attack strength is " << *attackPtr << endl;
//cout << "Boss's health is " << *healthPtr << endl;
////The following code is used when there is get function
cout << "Boss's attack strength is " << getAttack() << endl;
cout << "Boss's health is " << getHealth() << endl;
}
#include "Boss.h"
#include <ctime>
void main()
{
//********Object creation at RUN time************
//Invoking default constructor at RUN time
Boss *runtimePtr = new Boss;
runtimePtr->displayBoss();
(*runtimePtr).displayBoss();
delete runtimePtr; //This can be placed anywhere in this function
runtimePtr = NULL; //GOOD programming practice to avoid runtime errors
//The display function will be called only if the pointer resides in the memo-
ry
if(runtimePtr != NULL)
{
runtimePtr->displayBoss();
}
cout << endl;
//Invoking overloaded constructor at RUN time
Boss *overRTPtr = new Boss(35, 200);
overRTPtr->displayBoss();
delete overRTPtr;
overRTPtr = NULL;
cout << endl;
/*********Object creation at COMPILE time************
Invoking default constructor at compile time*/
//Boss compileTimeObj;
//compileTimeObj.displayBoss();
//
//cout << endl;
////Invoking overloaded constructor at compile time
```

```
//Boss overCTObj(8, 800);
//overCTObj.displayBoss();
//cout << endl;
system("pause");
}
```

The above program demonstrates dynamic memory allocation using pointers. The program defines a Boss class that has two private member variables, attackPtr and healthPtr, which are pointers to int types. The class also has constructors, destructors, and member functions that allow the user to set and get the values of these member variables and display them.

In the main function, the program demonstrates object creation at runtime and compile time. The default constructor is called using the new operator at runtime to allocate memory to the Boss object, and the overloaded constructor is also called at runtime with user-defined values for attack and health variables. After the objects are created, their member functions are called to display the values of the attack and health variables, and then the memory allocated to the objects is released using the delete operator.

The program also shows good programming practice by setting the pointer to NULL after deleting the object to avoid any runtime errors. Finally, the program uses the system("pause") command to pause the console window so that the user can view the output before the window closes.

7.17 STATIC CLASS MEMBERS

There is a significant exception to the rule that every object of a class has its own copy of all the class's data members. In some cases, all class objects should share just one instance of a variable.A **static data member** is employed for these and other purposes. This kind of variable conveys "class-wide" information (i.e., a property of the class shared by all instances, as opposed to a property of a single instance of the class). Static members are declared with the term static.

Static data members of a class have class scope, even though they may appear to be global variables. Moreover, static members may be marked as public, private, or protected. By default, a fundamental-type static data member is initialized to 0. If you desire a different beginning value, you can initialize a static data member only once. A const static data member of int or enum type can be initialized in the class declaration. However, all other static data members must be specified outside the file scope (i.e., outside the class definition's body) and can only be initialized in those definitions. Note that static data members of class types (i.e., static member objects) whose default constructors are called do not need to be initialized.

Most of the time, you can get to private and protected static members of a class through public member functions of the class or through friends.Static members of a class exist even if there are no instances of that class.If there are no instances of the class, you can still access a public static class member by adding the class name and the binary scope resolution operator (::) to the member's name.

The public static class members of a class can also be accessed via any object of that class using the object's name, the dot operator, and the member's name. To access a private or protected static class member when there are no objects of the class, create a public static member function and call it by prefixing its name with the class name and the binary scope resolution operator.

[NOTE: Even if there are no instances of a class, its static data members and static member functions still exist and can be used.]

If a member function doesn't use non-static data members or non-static member functions, it should be marked as static. A static member function does not have this reference, unlike non-static member functions, because static data members and static member functions exist independently of any instances of a class. When a static member function is used, there may be no instances of its class in memory, so this reference must belong to a specific instance of the class.

Example:

```
/*
Static Members
*/
#include <iostream>
#include <string>
using namespace std;
#ifndef BOSS_H
#define BOSS_H
class Boss
{
private:
int attack;
int health;
//static members belong to class
public:
Boss();
//Boss(int cValue);
//Boss(int aValue, int hValue, int cValue);
void displayBoss(); //non-static
static void displayStaticVar(); //static
static int bossCount; //declaration of static member variable
};
#endif
#include "Boss.h"
////initialization -- Notice that this is not inside a member function
int Boss::bossCount = 0;
//Constant variables are initialized using member initializer list as follows
Boss::Boss()
{
cout << "Inside Boss constructor" << endl;
attack = 20;
health = 200;
//This is a good place to increment because we cannot explicitly
//call the constructor
++bossCount; //increment the static variable
```

```
}
//Boss::Boss(int cValue):MAX(cValue)
//{
// cout << "Inside Boss constructor" << endl;
// attack = 20;
// health = 200;
//
// //This is a good place to increment because we cannot explicitly
// //call the constructor
// ++bossCount; //increment the static variable
//}
//Boss::Boss(int aValue, int hValue, int cValue):attack(aValue),
health(hValue), MAX(cValue)
//{
// cout << "Inside Overloaded constructor" << endl;
// //MAX = 100; //ERROR: CONST VARIABLE CANNOT BE INITIALIZED INSIDE THE CON-
STRUCTOR
// //attack = 4; //Correct since this is a non-const variable
// ++bossCount; //increment the static variable
//}
void Boss::displayBoss()
{
cout<<"\n\nDisplay Function for Boss class: " << endl;
cout<<"Attack: "<<attack<<endl;
cout<<"Health: "<<health<<endl;
//cout << "Const variable MAX = " << MAX << endl;
//STATIC VARIABLE inside a non-static member function
//cout << "Number of objects created are: " << bossCount << endl;
//static member function call
displayStaticVar();
}
//STATIC MEMBER FUNCTION CANNOT HANDLE NON-STATIC INFO
void Boss::displayStaticVar()
{
//displayBoss(); //NON-STATIC -- ERROR
//STATIC VARIABLE inside a STATIC member function
cout << "Number of objects created are: " << bossCount << endl;
}
#include "Boss.h"
#include <ctime>
void main()
{
Boss bossObj;
bossObj.displayBoss();
```

```
//cout << "Boss Count: " << bossObj.bossCount << endl;
Boss newBossObj;
newBossObj.displayBoss();
//cout << "Boss Count: " << Boss::bossCount << endl;
Boss::displayStaticVar();
bossObj.displayStaticVar();
system("pause");
}
```

The above code is an example of how to use static members in a C++ class.

Static members are shared by all objects in the class and are stored in a common memory location. They are not associated with any particular object in the class.

The class Boss has two private non-static members, attack and health, and two static members: the static member function displayStaticVar() and the static member variable bossCount.

The bossCount variable is declared as static inside the class definition but is initialized outside of it using the scope resolution operator:: in the following line: int Boss::bossCount = 0; This sets the initial value of bossCount to zero.

The Boss constructor increments the bossCount variable. Since bossCount is static, it is shared by all objects of the class, and the bossCount value will increase by one each time a new object of the class is created.

The displayStaticVar() function shows the current value of the bossCount variable. It is a static member function.Note that a static member function can only access static members of the class; it cannot access non-static members of the class.

The displayBoss() function is a non-static member function of the Boss class that shows an object's attack and health values.It also calls the static member function displayStaticVar() to display the bossCount value.

In the main() function, two objects of the Boss class are created, and the displayBoss() function is called for each object to display their attack and health values as well as the current value of the bossCount variable. The static member function displayStaticVar() is also called twice to display the same value.

7.17 OPERATOR OVERLOADING

C++ permits programmers to overload the majority of operators to make them context-sensitive. Based on the context (namely, the kinds of operands), the compiler creates the appropriate code. Although operator overloading seems like an uncommon skill, most programmers routinely employ it. The C++ language itself, for instance, overloads the addition operator (+) and the subtraction operator (-). (-). Depending on the context, these operators behave differently in integer arithmetic, floating-point arithmetic, and pointer arithmetic.

7.17.1 Fundamentals of Operator Overloading

Programmers can utilize core data types and define new data types in C++. The fundamental types are compatible with C++'s extensive set of operators. Operators provide programmers with a simple syntax for describing operations on fundamental-type objects.

Programmers may also utilize operators with user-defined types. Although C++ does not permit the creation of new operators, it does let the majority of current operators to be overloaded such that, when used with objects, they have the right meaning. This is a formidable ability. An operator is overloaded by defining a non-static member function or global function with the keyword operator followed by the symbol for the operator being overloaded. For instance, the addition operator (+) may be overloaded using the function name operator+. When operators are overloaded as member functions, they must be non-static, as they must be invoked on an instance of the class and operate on that instance.

To be used on class objects, an operator must be overloaded with three exceptions. Operator overloading is not automatic; functions must be written to follow the desired procedures. Sometimes these functions are better implemented as member functions; occasionally they are best implemented as standalone functions. They are better as friend functions, however, they can occasionally be created as global functions that are not friends.

To use an operator on class objects, that operator must be overloaded with three exceptions.

- Assignment operator (=)
  - May be used with every class to perform memberwise assignment between objects
- Address operator (&)
  - Returns address of object
- Comma operator (,)
  - Evaluates expression to its left then the expression to its right
  - Returns the value of the expression to its right

Overloading provides concise notation

```
object2 = object1.add(object2);
vs.
object2 = object2 + object1;
```

Operator notation is frequently more comprehensible and familiar to programmers. An operator is overloaded by defining a non-static member function or global function with the keyword operator followed by the symbol for the operator to be overloaded. When operators are overloaded as member functions, they must be non-static, as they must be invoked on an instance of the class and operate on that instance.

7.17.2 Restrictions on Operator Overloading

We cannot change:

- Precedence of operator (order of evaluation)

  - Use parentheses to force order of operators
- Associativity (left-to-right or right-to-left)
- "arity" - Number of operands
  - e.g., & is unary, can only act on one operand
- How operators act on built-in data types (i.e., cannot change integer addition)
- Cannot create new operators; only existing operators can be overloaded
- Operators must be overloaded explicitly
- Overloading + and = does not overload +=
- Operator ?: cannot be overloaded

Overloading an assignment operator and an addition operator to allow statements like

```
object2 = object2 + object1;
```

does not imply that the += operator is also overloaded to allow statements such as

```
object2 += object1;
```

Such behavior can be achieved only by explicitly overloading operator += for that class.

7.17.3 Operator Functions as Class Members vs. Global Functions

Operator functions can be either member functions or global functions. Member functions are often paired with global functions to improve performance. Member functions implicitly utilize this pointer to access one of their class object parameters (the left operand for binary operators). In a global function call, the arguments for both operands of a binary operator must be specified explicitly. When an operator function is implemented as a member function, the following occurs: The leftmost object must be of the same class as the operator function.

- Use this keyword to implicitly get the left operand argument.
- Operators (), [], -> or any assignment operator must be overloaded as a class member function.
- Operator member functions of a specific class are called when
  - The left operand of the binary operator is of this class.
  - A single operand of the unary operator is of this class.
- as global functions
  - Need parameters for both operands.
  - Can have an object of a different class than the operator.
  - Can a friend access private or protected data?

If an operator function is implemented as a member function, the first (or only) operand must be an object (or a reference to an object) of the operator's class.

If the left operand must be an object of a different class or a basic type, this operator function must be made as a global function. A global operator function can be made a friend of a class if it needs direct access to private or protected members of that class.

7.17.4 Overloaded Stream Insertion and Stream Extraction Operators Are Overloaded as Global Functions

The operator is another example of a C++ operator that does more than one thing. It can be used as both the stream insertion operator and the bitwise left-shift operator. Also overloaded is >>, which serves as both the stream extraction operator and the bitwise right-shift operator.

In an expression with a left operand of type ostream &, the overloaded stream insertion operator () is used, just like in cout classObject.To use the operator in this fashion, when the right operand is a user-defined class object, it must be overloaded as a global function. To qualify as a member function, the operator must belong to the Ostream class. This is not feasible for user-defined classes, as modifying C++ Standard Library classes is prohibited.

Similarly, when the overloaded stream extraction operator (>>) is used in an expression where the left operand is of type istream &, as in cin >> classObject, and the right operand is an object of a user-defined class, it must also be a global function. In addition, each of these overloaded operator functions may require access to the private data members of the class object being produced or input; hence, for performance reasons, these overloaded operator methods can be declared buddy functions of the class.

You can use an operator as a global, non-friend function. If the function needs to access a class's private or protected data, it must use the set and get methods on the class's public interface. The overhead of calling these functions could slow down performance, so they can be put inline to improve efficiency. In an expression where the left operand is of type ostream &, the overloaded stream insertion operator (<<) is utilized.

The function operator<< accepts 2 arguments: a reference to ostream and the appropriate data type.

==

Function prototype to be included in the class definition is:

==

```
friend ostream& operator<<(ostream&, const ClassName&);
friend istream& operator>>(istream&, ClassName&);
//----------------------------------------------------------------
// ClassClassPlayer.h This contains the class definition.
//----------------------------------------------------------------
#include <iostream>
#include <string>
#include <ctime>
using namespace std;
class ClassPlayer
{
// Function prototypesOverloaded insertion and
// extration operators. Note that the left
// parameter is a reference to object of the output/input
// streams and the right parameter is a reference
// to an object of a user defined datatype
```

```
friend ostream& operator<<(ostream&, const ClassPlayer&);
friend istream& operator>>(istream&, ClassPlayer&);
private:
string playerName; //stores the name of the player
int playerScore; //stores the player's score
};
//-----------------------------------------------------------------
// ClassPlayer.cpp
//-----------------------------------------------------------------
#include "ClassPlayer.h"
ostream& operator<<(ostream& output, const ClassPlayer& player)
{
output << "Name is: " << player.playerName << "Score is: "
<< player.playerScore << endl;
return output;
}
istream& operator>>(istream& input, ClassPlayer& player)
{
input >> player.playerName;
input >> player.playerScore;
return input;
}
//-----------------------------------------------------------------
// Main.cpp
//-----------------------------------------------------------------
#include "ClassPlayer.h"
int main()
{
ClassPlayer player;
cout << "Please enter your name and score separated by spaces: ";
//Notice that we are able to use the name of the object
//directly without using any member functions.
cin >> player;
cout << "You entered: " << endl;
//Notice that we are able to use the name of the object
//directly without using any member functions.
cout << player;
}
```

Operator overloading in C++ lets user-defined types or objects change how operators like +, -, *, /, etc. work.One such example of operator overloading is overloading the insertion (<<) and extraction (>>) operators. The operator<< is used for output, and the operator>> is used for input.

In the given code, the insertion and extraction operators are overloaded as friend functions in the class ClassPlayer.The operator<< takes two parameters, an output stream and a constant reference to the Player object, and returns a reference to the output stream. The operator>> takes two parameters, an input stream and a reference to the Player object, and returns a reference to the input stream.

The overloaded operators are defined outside the class in the ClassPlayer.cpp file. In the main function, an object of the ClassPlayer class is created, and the overloaded >> operator is used to input the player name and score. Then the overloaded << operator is used to output the player name and score.

7.17.5 Overloading Binary Operators

A binary operator may be overloaded as a non-static member function with one parameter or as a global function with two arguments (one of the arguments must be a class object or a class object reference).

```
==============================================================
```

Function prototype to be included in the class definition for overloading the + and = = operator as a *member function* is:

```
==============================================================
ClassName operator+(const ClassName& right) const;
bool operator==(const ClassName& right) const;
========================================================================
```

Function prototype to be included in the class definition for overloading the + and = = operator as a *global function* is:

```
========================================================================
friend ClassName operator+(const ClassName& left, const ClassName& right);
friend bool operator==(const ClassName& left, const ClassName& right);
//---------------------------------------------------------------
// BinaryOperator.h
// In this program the binary operators + and == are overloaded
// as member functions
//---------------------------------------------------------------
#include <iostream>
#include <string>
using namespace std;
class BinaryOperator
{
//Overloaded insertion and extraction operators
friend ostream& operator<<(ostream&, const BinaryOperator&);
friend istream& operator>>(istream&, BinaryOperator&);
public:
BinaryOperator(string = "", int = 0); //constructor
//Overloaded + operator
BinaryOperator operator+(const BinaryOperator&) const;
```

```
//Overloaded == operator
bool operator==(const BinaryOperator&) const;
//Get Function
string getName();
private:
//Member variables
int playerScore;
string playerName;
};
//-------------------------------------------------------------------
// BianryOperator.cpp
//-------------------------------------------------------------------
#include "BinaryOperator.h"
BinaryOperator::BinaryOperator(string name, int score)
{
playerName = name;
playerScore = score;
}
string BinaryOperator::getName()
{
//returns the contents of the member variable playerName
return playerName;
}
BinaryOperator BinaryOperator::operator+(const BinaryOperator& right) const
{
BinaryOperator temp; //create a temp object to store the result
//adding the score of the current object and the score of the
// object right and storing in temp object
temp.playerScore = playerScore + right.playerScore;
temp.playerName = ""; //setting the name of the temp obj to null
return temp; //return temp object
}
bool BinaryOperator::operator ==(const BinaryOperator& right) const
{
//tests if the player score of the object rigth is same as
// score of the current object
if (right.playerScore == playerScore)
{
return true; // returns true if scores are same
}
else
{
return false; // returns false if scores are not same
}
```

```
}
//---------------------------------------------------------------------
// Main.cpp
//---------------------------------------------------------------------
#include "BinaryOperator.h"
int main()
{
// create an object called alien and assign name and score
BinaryOperator alien("Zork", 250);
// create an object called cowBoy and assign name and score
BinaryOperator cowBoy("Buffalo Bill", 540);
// Notice that we are using the + operator directly to add the
// contents of 2 objects and display them. This is not
// possible if we did not overload the + operator and the
// << operator
cout << "Total score of alien and cowboy is: " << alien + cowBoy << endl;
// Notice that we are using the == operator directly to
// check the contents of 2 objects. This is not possible if
// we did not overload the == operator
if (alien == cowBoy)
{
cout << alien.getName() << " And " << cowBoy.getName() << " have same scores"
<< endl;
}
else
{
cout << alien.getName() << " And " << cowBoy.getName() << " do not have same
scores" << endl;
}
cout << "\nEnter new score for cowBoy: ";
// Notice that we are using the >> operator directly to get the
// score for cowBoy object. This is not possible if we did not
// overload the >> operator
cin >> cowBoy;
cout << "\nYou have entered: " << cowBoy << endl;
if (alien == cowBoy)
{
cout << alien.getName() << " And " << cowBoy.getName() << " have same scores"
<< endl;
}
else
{
cout << alien.getName() << " And " << cowBoy.getName() << " do not have same
scores" << endl;
```

```
}
return 0;
}
ostream& operator<<(ostream& output, const BinaryOperator& object)
{
output << object.playerScore; // storing the score in the output
return output; //returning the output object
}
istream& operator>>(istream& input, BinaryOperator& object)
{
input >> object.playerScore; //gets the score stored
return input;
}
```

This code demonstrates operator overloading in C++. Specifically, it shows how to overload the + and == operators as member functions of a class and as global functions.

The class used in this example is called BinaryOperator. It has two member variables: playerScore and playerName. The constructor initializes these variables, and the getName member function returns the value of playerName.

The + operator is overloaded as a member function of the BinaryOperator class. It takes a const BinaryOperator& object as its argument and returns a BinaryOperator object. Inside the function, a temporary BinaryOperator object called temp is created to store the result. The playerScore of the current object and the playerScore of the right-hand side object are added together and stored in the temporary object's playerScore variable. The playerName of the temporary object is set to an empty string, and the temporary object is returned.

The == operator is also overloaded as a member function of the BinaryOperator class. It takes a const BinaryOperator& object as its argument and returns a bool value. Inside the function, it checks whether the playerScore of the right-hand side object is equal to the playerScore of the current object. If they are equal, the function returns true. Otherwise, it returns false.

In addition to overloading these operators as member functions, they are also overloaded as global functions using the friend keyword. The + operator takes two const BinaryOperator& objects as its arguments and returns a BinaryOperator object. The implementation is similar to the member function implementation, but it is defined outside the class definition. The == operator is similarly defined as a global function.

Finally, the << and >> operators are also overloaded as global functions using the friend keyword. These functions allow for the insertion and extraction of BinaryOperator objects to and from input and output streams, respectively.

The main function makes two BinaryOperator objects and shows how the overloaded + and == operators can be used to add the scores of the two objects and compare them, respectively.It also shows how the overloaded >> operator can be used to read in a new score for one of the objects and how the << operator can be used to output the object's score.

7.17.6 Overloading Unary Operator

The process of overloading unary operators is like that of binary operators. In case of unary the operand is only one. Therefore, to overload the unary class:

1. If the operator function is a member of class, it has no parameters
2. If the operator is a non- member (friend), it has one parameter.

Overloading ++ and --

It is possible to overload both the prefix and postfix versions of the increment and decrement operators. We will examine how the compiler differentiates between the prefix and postfix versions of the increment and decrement operators. To overload the increment operator to support both prefix and postfix increment usage, each overloaded operator function must have a unique signature so the compiler can know which version of ++ is meant. The prefix versions are precisely as overloaded as any other prefix unary operator.

==

Function prototype to be included in the class definition for overloading the ++ prefix and postfix operators as member functions ==

```
ClassName& operator++(); // prefix ++ operator
ClassName operator++ (int) //postfix ++ operator
==============================================================
```

Function prototype to be included in the class definition for overloading the ++ prefix and postfix operators as global functions ==

```
ClassName& operator++ (ClassName&); // prefix ++ operator
ClassName operator++ (ClassName&, int) //postfix ++ operator
```

The compiler may distinguish between the prefix and postfix increment operator functions by using the integer parameter that is often provided as 0, which is strictly a "dummy value."

7.18 COMPOSITION

Composition is a way to relate two classes in C++, where one class (the "composing" class) contains an instance of another class (the "composed" class) as a member variable. This allows the composing class to use the functionality of the composed class and is often used to implement the "has-a" relationship between classes.

Here is an example of a class FirstClass that composes an instance of the class OtherClass:

```
class OtherClass {
public:
void print() {
std::cout << "OtherClass" << std::endl;
}
};
class FirstClass {
public:
FirstClass() {
// Initialize the composed object
m_other = OtherClass();
}
void doSomething() {
// Use the functionality of the composed class
m_other.print();
}
private:
OtherClass m_other;
};
```

In this example, the class FirstClass has an instance of OtherClass as a member variable, and it can use the functionality of OtherClass by calling its methods.

Here is an example of how to use the class FirstClass:

```
FirstClass obj;
obj.doSomething(); // Output: "OtherClass"
```

This shows that the FirstClass object "has an" instance of OtherClass and can use it's functionality by calling print() method of OtherClass.

This is just a basic example of composition, and it can be used for more complex classes, for example, a car class that composes an engine, wheels, and other parts.

It's worth noting that composition should be used when you want to reuse the functionality of a class and when the lifetime of composed class is dependent on the composing class.

Example:

```
#include <iostream>
#include <string>
using namespace std;
#ifndef CAR_H
#define CAR_H
class Car
{
```

```
private:
string color;
string model;
public:
Car();
void displayCarDetails();
};
#endif
/*
Composition
*/
#include "Car.h"
//class Car; //Forward declaration
#ifndef BOSS_H
#define BOSS_H
class Boss
{
private:
int attack;
int health;
public:
Car bCar; //Car object -- Composition
Boss();
void displayBoss();
//void driveCar(Car bossCar); //Aggregation
};
#endif
#include "Car.h"
#include <iostream>
using namespace std;
Car::Car()
{
cout << "Inside Car Constructor" << endl;
color = "Black";
model = "Hummer";
}
void Car::displayCarDetails()
{
cout << "\nInside Display function for car: " << endl;
cout << "Color of car is " << color << endl;
cout << "Car model is " << model << endl;
}
#include "Boss.h"
Boss::Boss() //member initializer list
```

```
{
cout << "Inside Boss constructor" << endl;
attack = 20;
health = 200;
}
void Boss::displayBoss()
{
cout<<"\n\nDisplay Function for Boss class: " << endl;
cout<<"Attack: "<<attack<<endl;
cout<<"Health: "<<health<<endl;
cout << "Boss drives: "<< endl;
bCar.displayCarDetails();
}
#include "Boss.h"
#include "Car.h"
int main()
{
Boss obg ;
obg.displayBoss();
system("pause");
return 0;
}
```

This code demonstrates the concepts of composition and member initializer lists in C++.

The code starts by including the standard library headers iostream and string, and then using the std namespace. It then defines a class Car with two private member variables, color and model, a public default constructor, and a function displayCarDetails() that displays the color and model of the car. The class also uses the include guards #ifndef and #define to prevent multiple inclusions of the header file.

Next, the code defines a class Boss with two private member variables, attack and health, and a public member variable bCar of type Car. This is an example of composition, where a class Boss contains an object of another class Car. The class Boss also has a default constructor and a function displayBoss() that displays the attack and health of the boss and calls the displayCarDetails() function of the Car object.

The code then defines the member functions of the Car and Boss classes. The Car constructor initializes the color and model variables, and the displayCarDetails() function displays their values. The Boss constructor uses member initializer list syntax to initialize the attack and health variables. The displayBoss() function displays the attack and health of the boss, and calls the displayCarDetails() function of the Car object to display its color and model.

Finally, the code includes the Boss and Car headers, creates an object of the Boss class, and calls its displayBoss() function to display the boss and the car details. The system("pause") function is used to pause the output console window to view the output.

In summary, this code demonstrates how to use composition in C++ to create complex classes that contain other objects and how to use member initializer list syntax to initialize class member variables in the constructor.

7.19 VIRTUAL DESTRUCTOR

A virtual destructor is a destructor that is declared as virtual in a base class. This allows the correct derived class destructor to be called when a base class pointer or reference points to an object of a derived class.

Here is an example of a class MyBase with a virtual destructor:

```
class MyBase {
public:
virtual ~MyBase() {
std::cout << "MyBase destructor" << std::endl;
}
};
class MyDerived: public MyBase {
public:
~MyDerived() {
std::cout << "MyDerived destructor" << std::endl;
}
};
```

In this example, the destructor of MyBase is declared as virtual, which means that when a pointer or reference of type MyBase points to an object of type MyDerived, the destructor of MyDerived will be called.

Here is an example of how to use the class MyBaseand MyDerived:

```
MyBase * ptr = new MyDerived();
delete ptr;
// Output: MyDerived destructor
// MyBase destructor
```

As you see, in the above example, the derived destructor is called before the base destructor. This is because the virtual destructor of the base class ensures that the derived class destructor will be called before the base class destructor.

It's important to note that if the base class destructor is not virtual, the base class destructor will be called instead of the derived class destructor when using a pointer or reference to the base class. This can cause resource leaks and other problems if the derived class has allocated resources that need to be freed up in its destructor.

Things to note about classes:

- The class declaration must end with a semicolon.
- The public and private members are grouped. It is generally considered a good idea to put the public members first, but that is not a C++ requirement.
- The class's constructor function must have the same name as the class, and no return type (not even *void*).

- In general, member functions that do not change any of the data members of the class hold should be declared *const.*
- A class can contain members with **static** data. Every instance of the class will include its own copy of each of the non-static data members, but there will only be one copy of each static data member for the whole class.
- Only static data members can be initialized as part of the class declaration. The class's constructor function(s) initialize other data members.

Once an object of a class is created (instantiated), you can access the public members of that class using the dot(.) operator.

ADVANCED PRACTICE EXERCISES FOR CHAPTER 7 ON CLASSES AND OBJECTS IN C++

Exercise 1: Implementing Class Basics

- **Task**: Define a C++ class **Rectangle** that encapsulates the attributes **length** and **width** (as doubles) and provides member functions to calculate the area and perimeter.
- **Answer**:

```
#include <iostream>
#include <algorithm> // For std::max

class Rectangle {
private:
    double length;
    double width;

public:
    // Default constructor
    Rectangle(): length(0), width(0) {}

    // Parameterized constructor
    Rectangle(double l, double w): length(std::max(l, 0.0)), width(std::max(w,
0.0)) {}

    // Setters for length and width that ensure values are non-negative
    void setLength(double l) {
        length = std::max(l, 0.0);
    }

    void setWidth(double w) {
        width = std::max(w, 0.0);
```

```
    }

    // Getters for length and width
    double getLength() const {
        return length;
    }

    double getWidth() const {
        return width;
    }

    // Member function to calculate the area
    double area() const {
        return length * width;
    }

    // Member function to calculate the perimeter
    double perimeter() const {
        return 2 * (length + width);
    }

    // Function to display the rectangle's details
    void display() const {
        std::cout << "Rectangle details:\n"
            << "Length = " << length << ", Width = " << width << "\n"
            << "Area = " << area() << ", Perimeter = " << perimeter() <<
std::endl;
    }
};

int main() {
    // Create a rectangle with positive dimensions
    Rectangle rect(4.5, 2.3);

    // Display the details of the rectangle
    rect.display();

    // Attempt to set the length and width to negative values, which will be
corrected to 0.0
    rect.setLength(-5.0);
    rect.setWidth(-3.0);

    std::cout << "After attempting to set negative dimensions:" << std::endl;
    rect.display();
```

```
    return 0;
}
```

Explanation

This C++ program demonstrates a class **Rectangle** that encapsulates the properties of a geometric rectangle and includes several key features of object-oriented programming: encapsulation, constructor overloading, member functions for data validation, and a utility function for displaying object state.

Key Components and Their Functions:

- **Encapsulation**: The **length** and **width** properties are declared as **private**, meaning they can only be accessed and modified by member functions of the **Rectangle** class. This encapsulation protects the rectangle's state from invalid modifications.
- **Default Constructor**: Initializes a new instance of **Rectangle** with both **length** and **width** set to **0.0**. This ensures that a **Rectangle** object cannot have negative dimensions right from its creation without explicit initialization.
- **Parameterized Constructor**: Allows initializing a new **Rectangle** object with specific **length** and **width** values. The **std::max** function ensures that these values are not negative by comparing the provided arguments with **0.0** and selecting the maximum, effectively preventing negative dimensions.
- **Setters (setLength and setWidth)**: These member functions provide a controlled way to modify the dimensions of a **Rectangle** object after it has been created. They use **std::max** to prevent the assignment of negative values, thereby enforcing the invariant that **length** and **width** must be non-negative.
- **Getters (getLength and getWidth)**: These **const** member functions provide read-only access to the **length** and **width** properties, allowing the rest of the program to inspect but not modify these values directly.
- **Area Calculation (area)**: This **const** member function calculates and returns the area of the rectangle by multiplying **length** by **width**.
- **Perimeter Calculation (perimeter)**: Similar to **area**, this **const** member function calculates and returns the perimeter of the rectangle using the formula **2 * (length + width)**.
- **Display (display)**: A utility function that prints the dimensions, area, and perimeter of the rectangle to the console. This function demonstrates how an object can report its own state in a human-readable format.

Main Function

- Initializes a **Rectangle** object named **rect** using the parameterized constructor with positive dimensions (**4.5** by **2.3**). It then displays these dimensions, along with the calculated area and perimeter.
- Attempts to set **rect**'s **length** and **width** to negative values using the setter functions. Due to the validation logic in these functions, the dimensions are corrected to **0.0**.

- Displays the rectangle's details again, showing the effect of the attempted (but invalidated) dimension changes. The output demonstrates that the rectangle's dimensions remain non-negative, as enforced by the class's design.

Conclusion

This program is a concise illustration of fundamental object-oriented principles in action. By using encapsulation, constructors, validation through setter functions, and utility methods, it defines a robust and reusable **Rectangle** class. The class ensures its instances always represent valid rectangles by enforcing non-negative dimensions, illustrating the power of encapsulation and validation in maintaining object integrity.

Exercise 2: Utilizing Constructors and Destructors

- **Task**: Enhance the **Rectangle** class by adding a constructor to initialize **length** and **width** and a destructor that prints a message when an object is destroyed.
- **Answer**:

```
#include <iostream>
#include <algorithm> // For std::max

class Rectangle {
private:
    double length;
    double width;

public:
    // Default constructor
    Rectangle(): length(1.0), width(1.0) {}

    // Parameterized constructor
    Rectangle(double l, double w) {
        setDimensions(l, w);
    }

    // Setters for length and width
    void setDimensions(double l, double w) {
        length = std::max(0.0, l); // Prevent negative values
        width = std::max(0.0, w);  // Prevent negative values
    }

    // Getter for area
    double area() const {
        return length * width;
```

```
    }

    // Getter for perimeter
    double perimeter() const {
        return 2 * (length + width);
    }

    // Display function for showing dimensions, area, and perimeter
    void display() const {
        std::cout << "Rectangle: \n"
            << "Length = " << length << ", Width = " << width << "\n"
            << "Area = " << area() << ", Perimeter = " << perimeter() <<
std::endl;
    }
};

int main() {
    Rectangle rect1; // Uses default constructor
    Rectangle rect2(4.5, 2.3); // Uses parameterized constructor

    std::cout << "Using the default constructor:" << std::endl;
    rect1.display();

    std::cout << "\nUsing the parameterized constructor with positive values:"
<< std::endl;
    rect2.display();

    // Attempting to set negative dimensions
    rect1.setDimensions(-5.0, -3.0);
    std::cout << "\nAfter attempting to set negative dimensions:" << std::endl;
    rect1.display();

    return 0;
}
```

Explanation

This C++ code defines a **Rectangle** class to model rectangles, allowing for calculation of their area and perimeter. It demonstrates fundamental object-oriented programming concepts such as encapsulation, constructors, member functions, and data validation. Here's an explanation of its components and functionality:

The Rectangle Class

- **Private Members**: The class keeps **length** and **width** as private data members, ensuring that these properties can only be modified through the class's public member functions, thus maintaining control over the rectangle's state.
- **Default Constructor**: Initializes a rectangle object with both **length** and **width** set to **1.0**. This provides a sensible default state for the rectangle.
- **Parameterized Constructor**: Allows the creation of a rectangle with specified **length** and **width**. It utilizes the **setDimensions** member function to assign these values, ensuring any negative inputs are corrected to **0.0**, thus preventing invalid rectangle dimensions.
- **setDimensions Member Function**: This function sets the **length** and **width** of the rectangle, using **std::max** to ensure that negative values are corrected to **0.0**. This validation guards against invalid geometric states.
- **area Member Function**: Computes and returns the area of the rectangle by multiplying **length** by **width**.
- **perimeter Member Function**: Computes and returns the perimeter of the rectangle as **2 * (length + width)**.
- **display Member Function**: A utility function that prints the rectangle's dimensions, area, and perimeter to the standard output. This is useful for demonstrating the rectangle's state at various points in the program.

The main Function

- **rect1 Initialization**: A **Rectangle** object, **rect1**, is default-constructed, meaning its dimensions are set to **1.0** by **1.0**. The **display** function is then called to show these default values along with the calculated area and perimeter.
- **rect2 Initialization**: Another **Rectangle** object, **rect2**, is created with specified dimensions (**4.5** by **2.3**) using the parameterized constructor. The **display** function is called to output **rect2**'s dimensions, area, and perimeter, demonstrating how specified values are used.
- **Negative Dimensions Handling**: The code attempts to set **rect1**'s dimensions to negative values using the **setDimensions** function. Due to the validation within **setDimensions**, these negative values are corrected to **0.0**. The subsequent call to **display** shows that **rect1** now has dimensions **0.0** by **0.0**, demonstrating the effectiveness of the validation logic.

Key Concepts Illustrated

- **Encapsulation**: By keeping **length** and **width** private and manipulating them through public member functions, the **Rectangle** class ensures that its internal state remains valid and consistent.
- **Constructor Overloading**: The class defines both a default and a parameterized constructor, showcasing how constructors can be overloaded to initialize objects in different ways based on the provided arguments.
- **Data Validation**: The **setDimensions** function exemplifies how a class can validate and correct its input data to maintain a valid state, in this case, ensuring rectangle dimensions are non-negative.

- **Utility Functions**: The **display** function highlights how classes can include utility functions to perform common tasks related to the object's state, such as reporting its properties and calculated values.

This program is a straightforward example of encapsulating geometric calculations within a class structure, utilizing constructors for object initialization, and applying data validation to ensure object integrity.

Exercise 3: Encapsulation With Set and Get Functions

- **Task**: Implement **set** and **get** functions for both **length** and **width** in the **Rectangle** class, ensuring negative values cannot be assigned.
- **Answer**:

```
#include <iostream>

class Rectangle {
private:
    double length;
    double width;

public:
    // Constructor with default values for length and width
    Rectangle(double l = 0.0, double w = 0.0) {
        setLength(l);
        setWidth(w);
    }

    // Set function for length
    void setLength(double l) {
        length = (l > 0.0) ? l: 0.0;
    }

    // Set function for width
    void setWidth(double w) {
        width = (w > 0.0) ? w: 0.0;
    }

    // Get function for length
    double getLength() const {
        return length;
    }

    // Get function for width
    double getWidth() const {
```

```
        return width;
    }

    // Function to calculate area
    double area() const {
        return length * width;
    }
};

int main() {
    Rectangle rect;

    // Setting length and width to positive values
    rect.setLength(5.0);
    rect.setWidth(3.0);
    std::cout << "Rectangle with positive values:\n";
    std::cout << "Length: " << rect.getLength() << ", Width: " << rect.get-
Width();
    std::cout << ", Area: " << rect.area() << std::endl;

    // Attempting to set length and width to negative values
    rect.setLength(-5.0);
    rect.setWidth(-3.0);
    std::cout << "Rectangle after attempting to set negative values:\n";
    std::cout << "Length: " << rect.getLength() << ", Width: " << rect.get-
Width();
    std::cout << ", Area: " << rect.area() << std::endl;

    return 0;
}
```

Explanation

This C++ program defines a **Rectangle** class with encapsulated properties **length** and **width**, ensuring that these dimensions cannot be negative. The class provides public set and get functions for both dimensions and a method to calculate the area of the rectangle. Here's an explanation of its components and functionality:

The Rectangle Class

- **Private Members**: The class maintains two private data members, **length** and **width**, to store the dimensions of a rectangle.
- **Constructor**: The constructor initializes **length** and **width** with provided values, defaulting to **0.0** if no values are given or if negative values are provided. This initialization is performed through

the **setLength** and **setWidth** member functions to apply the validation logic contained within them.

- **Set Functions**: **setLength** and **setWidth** are public member functions that allow external code to set the dimensions of a rectangle. These functions include validation to ensure that **length** and **width** are non-negative, assigning a value of **0.0** if a negative value is provided.
- **Get Functions**: **getLength** and **getWidth** provide read-only access to the rectangle's dimensions. These functions are marked **const** to indicate that they do not modify the object state.
- **Area Calculation**: The **area** member function calculates and returns the rectangle's area by multiplying **length** by **width**. This function is also **const**, showing that it doesn't change any member variables.

Main Function

- **Rectangle Initialization**: A **Rectangle** object named **rect** is default-constructed. Since no arguments are provided, its dimensions are initialized to **0.0** by the constructor.
- **Setting Positive Values**: The program first sets the rectangle's dimensions to positive values (**5.0** for length and **3.0** for width) using the **setLength** and **setWidth** functions. It then prints these values along with the calculated area.
- **Setting Negative Values**: The program attempts to set the rectangle's dimensions to negative values using the same set functions. Due to the validation in the set functions, these attempts result in the dimensions being set to **0.0** instead. The program prints the dimensions (which remain at the positive values previously set) and the calculated area again to demonstrate the effect of the validation.

Output Explanation

The output of the program demonstrates the encapsulation and validation logic in action:

- The first part shows the rectangle's dimensions and area after setting positive values for **length** and **width**.
- The second part attempts to set negative values, but due to the validation logic in the set functions, the dimensions remain unchanged, and the calculated area reflects the positive values previously set.

This program exemplifies basic object-oriented programming principles in C++, such as encapsulation (using private members and public accessor functions) and the importance of input validation to maintain the integrity of an object's state.

Exercise 4: Operator Overloading

- **Task**: Overload the + operator to add the areas of two **Rectangle** objects.
- **Answer**:

```
Ex#include <iostream>

class Rectangle {
private:
    double length;
    double width;

public:
    // Constructor to initialize the length and width of the rectangle
    Rectangle(double l = 0, double w = 0): length(l), width(w) {}

    // Member function to calculate the area of the rectangle
    double area() const {
        return length * width;
    }

    // Overload the + operator as a friend function
    friend double operator+(const Rectangle& a, const Rectangle& b);
};

// Definition of the overloaded + operator
double operator+(const Rectangle& a, const Rectangle& b) {
    // The operator returns the sum of the areas of two rectangles
    return a.area() + b.area();
}

int main() {
    // Create two Rectangle objects
    Rectangle rect1(4.0, 5.0);
    Rectangle rect2(2.5, 3.0);

    // Use the overloaded + operator to add the areas of rect1 and rect2
    double totalArea = rect1 + rect2;

    // Output the result
    std::cout << "Total area of the two rectangles: " << totalArea <<
std::endl;

    return 0;
}
planation:
```

To complete the task of overloading the + operator to add the areas of two **Rectangle** objects, we will define a **Rectangle** class with length and width as attributes. We will implement a member function to calculate the area of a rectangle and then overload the + operator to add the areas of two rectangles. This operator will be implemented as a friend function to allow it access to the private members of **Rectangle**.

In this program:

- The **Rectangle** class defines rectangles with a constructor to initialize their dimensions and a method to calculate their area.
- The + operator is overloaded to add the areas of two **Rectangle** objects. This is done using a friend function to ensure it has access to the private attributes of the **Rectangle** class.
- In the **main** function, two **Rectangle** objects are created, and their areas are added using the overloaded + operator. The total area is then printed to the console.

This example demonstrates how operator overloading can be used to perform operations directly on objects in a way that is intuitive and natural to the problem domain.

Exercise 5: Static Members

- **Task**: Add a static member to the **Rectangle** class to count the number of **Rectangle** objects created.
- **Answer**:

```
#include <iostream>

class Rectangle {
public:
    static int count;
    double length;
    double width;

    Rectangle(double l, double w): length(l > 0 ? l: 0), width(w > 0 ? w: 0) {
        ++count;
    }

    ~Rectangle() {
        --count;
    }

    double area() const {
        return length * width;
    }
};

int Rectangle::count = 0;
```

```
int main() {
    Rectangle rect1(4.5, 2.5);
    Rectangle rect2(3.5, 1.5);
    std::cout << "Total Rectangles: " << Rectangle::count << std::endl;
    return 0;
}
```

Explanation

This C++ code defines a **Rectangle** class that calculates the area of a rectangle, tracks the number of **Rectangle** instances created, and decrements this count upon their destruction. Here's a detailed explanation:

The Rectangle Class

- **Static Member count**: This static integer variable keeps track of the number of **Rectangle** instances that exist at any given time. Being static, this variable is shared across all instances of the **Rectangle** class.
- **Member Variables length and width**: These represent the dimensions of a rectangle. They are initialized to non-negative values, ensuring that the rectangle's dimensions are always valid.
- **Constructor**: The constructor initializes **length** and **width** with positive values, defaulting to **0** if negative values are provided. It also increments the static **count** variable by **1** for each new **Rectangle** instance created, reflecting the creation of a new rectangle.
- **Destructor**: When a **Rectangle** object is destroyed, the destructor decrements the static **count** variable by **1**, indicating that there's one fewer instance of the class.
- **Member Function area()**: This function calculates and returns the area of the rectangle using the formula **length * width**.

Static Member Initialization

- Outside the class definition, **Rectangle::count** is initialized to **0**. This sets up the initial count of **Rectangle** instances before any objects are created.

The main Function

- Two **Rectangle** objects, **rect1** and **rect2**, are created with specified dimensions. This results in the constructor being called twice, incrementing **Rectangle::count** to **2**.
- The program then prints the total number of **Rectangle** instances, which is expected to be **2** at this point, showing the effectiveness of the static member variable **count** in tracking the number of instances.
- After the **main** function scope ends, **rect1** and **rect2** go out of scope and are destroyed, invoking the destructor for each object. However, the effect of the destructors on **Rectangle::count** is not observed within the output of this program since it prints the count before the program ends.

Output

```
mathematical
Total Rectangles: 2
```

This output confirms that two instances of the **Rectangle** class were successfully created and counted.

Key Concepts Illustrated

- **Static Members**: Demonstrates how a static member variable can be used to track class-wide state, in this case, the number of class instances.
- **Class Constructors and Destructors**: Shows how constructors can initialize object state and how destructors can clean up when an object's lifetime ends.
- **Member Initialization**: Uses an initializer list in the constructor to ensure that **length** and **width** are set to valid (non-negative) values.
- **Encapsulation**: Although this example does not encapsulate the **length** and **width** members (as they are public), it demonstrates how methods can control access to the internal state (e.g., ensuring non-negative dimensions and calculating the area).

This example is a straightforward illustration of using static members in conjunction with constructors and destructors to manage and track resources or state across all instances of a class in C++.

Exercise 6: Using the this Pointer

- **Task**: Modify the set functions in the **Rectangle** class to return ***this** to allow method chaining.
- **Answer**:

```
#include <iostream>

class Rectangle {
public:
    double length;
    double width;

    Rectangle& setLength(double l) {
        length = l > 0 ? l: 0;
        return *this;
    }

    Rectangle& setWidth(double w) {
        width = w > 0 ? w: 0;
        return *this;
    }
```

```
    double area() const {
        return length * width;
    }
};

int main() {
    Rectangle rect;
    rect.setLength(5.0).setWidth(3.0);
    std::cout << "Area of rectangle: " << rect.area() << std::endl;
    return 0;
}
```

Explanation

This C++ code demonstrates a simple implementation of a **Rectangle** class that allows method chaining for setting its dimensions. Here's a breakdown of its key components and how it operates:

The Rectangle Class

- **Public Members**: The class defines two public data members, **length** and **width**, representing the dimensions of a rectangle.
- **setLength Method**: This method sets the **length** of the rectangle. It takes a **double** parameter **l** and assigns it to **length** if **l** is greater than **0**; otherwise, it assigns **0** to **length**. It returns a reference to the current instance (***this**), allowing for method chaining.
- **setWidth Method**: Similar to **setLength**, this method sets the **width** of the rectangle. It also performs a check to ensure that **width** is set to a positive value or **0** if the input is non-positive. It returns a reference to the current instance, enabling method chaining.
- **area Method**: This **const** member function calculates and returns the area of the rectangle by multiplying **length** by **width**.

The main Function

- An instance of the **Rectangle** class named **rect** is default-constructed. Since there's no explicit constructor defined, C++ generates a default constructor for **Rectangle**, which initializes **rect**.
- Method chaining is used to set the dimensions of **rect**. The call **rect.setLength(5.0).setWidth(3.0)** first sets the length to **5.0**. Since **setLength** returns a reference to **rect**, **setWidth(3.0)** is immediately called on the same object, setting the width to **3.0**.
- The **area** of **rect** is calculated and printed to the console. Given the dimensions **5.0** by **3.0**, the output will be:

mathematical
Area of rectangle: 15

Key Concepts Illustrated

- **Method Chaining**: By returning a reference to the current instance (***this**), methods like **setLength** and **setWidth** can be called in a chain. This is a common design pattern that enhances readability and conciseness.
- **Input Validation**: The methods **setLength** and **setWidth** ensure that the rectangle's dimensions are non-negative, demonstrating a simple form of input validation.
- **Encapsulation**: Although the **length** and **width** members are public in this example, the methods for setting these values encapsulate the logic for maintaining valid state (non-negative dimensions), which is a fundamental principle of object-oriented programming.
- **Const-Correctness**: The **area** method is marked as **const**, indicating that it does not modify any member variables of the **Rectangle** class. This is an example of const-correctness, a practice that enhances code safety and clarity regarding which methods alter the state of an object.

This code snippet is a straightforward example of encapsulation, method chaining, and validation in a class design, showcasing effective practices in C++ object-oriented programming.

Exercise 7: Friend Functions

- **Task**: Implement a friend function for the **Rectangle** class that compares the area of two rectangles and prints which one is larger.
- **Answer**:

```
#include <iostream>

class Rectangle {
public:
    double length;
    double width;

    Rectangle(double l = 0, double w = 0): length(l), width(w) {}

    double area() const {
        return length * width;
    }

    friend void compareArea(const Rectangle& a, const Rectangle& b);
};

void compareArea(const Rectangle& a, const Rectangle& b) {
    if (a.area() > b.area()) std::cout << "Rectangle A is larger\n";
    else if (b.area() > a.area()) std::cout << "Rectangle B is larger\n";
    else std::cout << "Rectangles are equal in size\n";
}
```

```
int main() {
    Rectangle rectA(4, 5);
    Rectangle rectB(3, 6);
    compareArea(rectA, rectB);
    return 0;
}
```

Explanation

This C++ code defines a **Rectangle** class, a friend function **compareArea**, and uses these in the **main** function to compare the areas of two **Rectangle** objects. Here's a detailed breakdown:

The Rectangle Class

- **Attributes**: The class has two public attributes, **length** and **width**, representing the dimensions of a rectangle.
- **Constructor**: The **Rectangle** constructor initializes an object with given **length** and **width** values. If no values are provided, it defaults to **0** for both dimensions.
- **Area Calculation**: The member function **area()** calculates the rectangle's area (**length * width**) and returns it.
- **Friend Function Declaration**: The **compareArea** function is declared as a friend of the **Rectangle** class, allowing it to access private and protected members directly. This is necessary because **compareArea** needs to access the **area()** member function of **Rectangle** instances.

The compareArea Function

- Defined outside the **Rectangle** class, this function takes two **Rectangle** objects as parameters and compares their areas.
- It uses the **area()** function of each rectangle to determine which one is larger or if they are equal in size and prints a message to the standard output accordingly.
- Being a friend function, **compareArea** can access the private **area()** function of **Rectangle** objects directly, despite **area()** being a public member function. Friend functions are more commonly needed for accessing private or protected data.

The main Function

- Two **Rectangle** objects, **rectA** and **rectB**, are created with specified dimensions.
- The **compareArea** function is then called with **rectA** and **rectB** as arguments to compare their areas and output the result.

Output Explanation

- Depending on the dimensions of the rectangles provided to **rectA** and **rectB**, the program will print which rectangle is larger based on area or if they are equal in size.
- For **rectA(4, 5)** and **rectB(3, 6)**, the areas are **20** and **18** respectively, so the output will be:

C++ code

Rectangle A is larger

This is because **rectA** has a larger area (**20**) compared to **rectB** (**18**).

Key Concepts Illustrated

- **Classes and Objects**: The **Rectangle** class encapsulates the properties and behaviors of a rectangle, and objects of this class represent individual rectangles.
- **Constructor Initialization List**: The **Rectangle** constructor uses an initialization list to set the **length** and **width** of a rectangle.
- **Friend Functions**: **compareArea** is a friend function to the **Rectangle** class, showcasing how functions outside a class can be granted access to the class's private and protected members.
- **Conditional Logic**: The program uses if-else statements to compare values and control flow based on the comparison results.
- **Operator Overloading**: While not explicitly demonstrated in this example, the concept of friend functions is often used in conjunction with operator overloading, allowing external functions to work intimately with class data.

This code serves as a concise example of how to model simple geometrical shapes in C++ and compare them using object-oriented programming principles.

Exercise 8: Implementing Composition

- **Task**: Create a class **House** that contains **Rectangle** objects representing rooms.
- **Answer**:

```
#include <iostream>
#include <vector>

class Rectangle {
public:
    double length;
    double width;

    Rectangle(double l = 0, double w = 0): length(l), width(w) {}

    double area() const {
        return length * width;
    }
};
```

```
class House {
    std::vector<Rectangle> rooms;
public:
    void addRoom(const Rectangle& room) {
        rooms.push_back(room);
    }

    double totalArea() const {
        double total = 0;
        for (const auto& room: rooms) total += room.area();
        return total;
    }
};

int main() {
    House myHouse;
    myHouse.addRoom(Rectangle(10, 10));
    myHouse.addRoom(Rectangle(5, 5));
    std::cout << "Total house area: " << myHouse.totalArea() << std::endl;
    return 0;
}
```

Explanation

This C++ code defines a simple system to calculate the total area of a **House** by summing up the areas of its constituent **Rectangle** objects, representing rooms. Here's a breakdown of its components and functionality:

1. **The Rectangle Class**:
    - Defines a geometric rectangle with **length** and **width** as its properties.
    - The constructor **Rectangle(double l = 0, double w = 0)** initializes a **Rectangle** object with the provided **length** and **width**, defaulting to **0** if no values are given.
    - The **area()** member function calculates and returns the area of the rectangle (**length * width**).
2. **The House Class**:
    - Represents a house that contains multiple rooms, with each room modeled as a **Rectangle** object.
    - Uses a **std::vector<Rectangle>** to store the list of rooms within the house.
    - The **addRoom(const Rectangle& room)** member function adds a new **Rectangle** object to the **rooms** vector, effectively adding a new room to the house.
    - The **totalArea() const** member function iterates over all **Rectangle** objects in the **rooms** vector, summing up their areas to calculate the total area of the house. This is done using a range-based for loop and the **Rectangle::area()** function.

3. **Main Function**:
   - A **House** object named **myHouse** is created.
   - Two **Rectangle** objects representing rooms, one with dimensions **10x10** and another with **5x5**, are added to **myHouse** using the **addRoom()** function.
   - The total area of **myHouse** is calculated using the **totalArea()** function and printed to the console.
4. **Output**:
   - The program prints the total area of the house to the standard output. Given the dimensions of the rooms added, the output will be:

mathematical

Total house area: 125

This result is obtained by summing the areas of the two rectangles: **10 * 10 + 5 * 5 = 100 + 25 = 125**.

Key Concepts Illustrated

- **Composition**: The **House** class is composed of **Rectangle** objects, demonstrating the "has-a" relationship. This is a fundamental concept in object-oriented design, where complex objects are constructed from simpler ones.
- **Encapsulation**: Both classes encapsulate their data (**length**, **width**, and **rooms**) and behavior (**area()** and **totalArea()**) within well-defined interfaces. This promotes modularity and information hiding.
- **Use of Standard Template Library (STL)**: The program uses **std::vector**, a dynamic array from the C++ Standard Template Library, to manage a collection of **Rectangle** objects. This showcases how C++ STL facilitates managing dynamic collections of objects.

Overall, this code provides a clear example of how object-oriented programming principles can be applied in C++ to model real-world entities and their interactions.

Exercise 9: Virtual Destructors

- **Task**: Explain why a base class destructor should be virtual when using polymorphism.
- **Answer**: A base class destructor should be virtual to ensure that the destructor of the derived class is called when an object is deleted through a base class pointer, preventing resource leaks and undefined behavior.

```
#include <iostream>

class Base {
public:
    virtual ~Base() {
        std::cout << "Base destructor\n";
    }
};
```

```
class Derived: public Base {
public:
    ~Derived() {
        std::cout << "Derived destructor\n";
    }
};

int main() {
    Base* ptr = new Derived();
    delete ptr;
    return 0;
}
// Output:
// Derived destructor
// Base destructor
```

Explanation

This C++ code snippet illustrates several key object-oriented programming concepts, including inheritance, polymorphism, and the importance of virtual destructors.

1. **Inheritance**:
   - The **Derived** class is defined as inheriting from the **Base** class, making **Derived** a subclass of **Base**. This relationship allows objects of **Derived** to be treated as objects of **Base**, enabling polymorphism.
2. **Virtual Destructor**:
   - The **Base** class declares a virtual destructor. This is crucial in a class hierarchy, especially when dealing with polymorphism. The virtual destructor ensures that the destructor of the derived class (**Derived**) is called first, followed by the base class (**Base**) destructor when an object of the derived class is deleted through a base class pointer.
   - Without the virtual keyword, if a derived class object is deleted through a base class pointer, only the base class's destructor would be called, potentially leading to resource leaks if the derived class allocates resources (like dynamic memory).
3. **Dynamic Polymorphism**:
   - In the **main** function, a pointer of type **Base*** (**ptr**) is used to dynamically allocate an object of **Derived**. This demonstrates polymorphism, where a base class pointer refers to a derived class object.
   - When **delete ptr;** is executed, it triggers the destructor sequence. Because the base class destructor is virtual, C++ correctly identifies that **ptr** actually points to a **Derived** object and thus calls **Derived**'s destructor first.
4. **Destructor Sequence**:
   - The output of the program:

Derived destructor
Base destructor
indicates that the **Derived** class destructor is called first, performing any cleanup specific to **Derived**. Once **Derived**'s destructor completes, the **Base** class destructor is automatically called to perform any additional cleanup. This order ensures that resources are released in the opposite order of their allocation, following the "stack unwinding" principle, which is crucial for resource management in C++.

5. **Memory Management**:
    - Dynamic memory allocated with **new** is released with **delete**, preventing memory leaks. The use of virtual destructors guarantees that the appropriate destructors are called, ensuring proper resource cleanup.

In summary, this code is a concise demonstration of how virtual destructors are essential for safe and predictable resource management in polymorphic class hierarchies in C++.

Exercise 10: Advanced UML Diagram Interpretation

- **Task**: Given a UML diagram of a class hierarchy involving **Vehicle**, **Car**, and **Bike**, implement the classes in C++ adhering to the diagram's specifications.
- **Answer**: Implementation will vary based on the specific UML diagram provided. The key is to correctly interpret the relationships (inheritance, composition, etc.) and class members (attributes, operations) defined in the UML.

Case

```
#include <iostream>

class Vehicle {
public:
    virtual void display() const = 0;
    virtual ~Vehicle() {}
};

class Car: public Vehicle {
public:
    void display() const override {
        std::cout << "Car\n";
    }
};

class Bike: public Vehicle {
public:
    void display() const override {
        std::cout << "Bike\n";
```

```
    }
};

int main() {
    Vehicle* v1 = new Car();
    Vehicle* v2 = new Bike();

    v1->display();
    v2->display();

    delete v1;
    delete v2;

    return 0;
}
```

Explanation

This C++ code snippet demonstrates the use of polymorphism, inheritance, and virtual functions, which are key concepts in object-oriented programming (OOP). Here's a breakdown of its functionality:

1. **Abstract Base Class with Virtual Functions**:
   - The **Vehicle** class is an abstract base class, indicated by the pure virtual function **display()** (**= 0;**). This means **Vehicle** cannot be instantiated directly.
   - It declares a virtual destructor, which is essential when using polymorphism to ensure that derived class destructors are called correctly when an object is deleted through a pointer to the base class.
2. **Derived Classes**:
   - **Car** and **Bike** are derived classes that inherit from **Vehicle**. They provide specific implementations for the **display()** function, overriding the pure virtual function in the base class. This is marked with the **override** keyword for clarity and additional safety checks by the compiler.
3. **Polymorphism**:
   - In the **main()** function, pointers to **Vehicle** (**v1** and **v2**) are used to instantiate **Car** and **Bike** objects, respectively. This is polymorphism in action: a base class pointer is used to refer to objects of its derived classes.
   - When **display()** is called on these pointers, the program determines at runtime which implementation of the function to execute based on the actual object type (**Car** or **Bike**). This is known as dynamic polymorphism or runtime polymorphism, enabled by virtual functions.
4. **Memory Management**:
   - Dynamically allocated memory for **v1** and **v2** (using **new**) is properly released using **delete**. This calls the destructor of the derived class (**Car** or **Bike**) and, because the base class destructor is virtual, ensures that any resources are correctly cleaned up, preventing memory leaks.

5. **Output**:
   - The program outputs:

Car Bike

This is the result of calling the **display()** function on the **Car** and **Bike** objects, which prints their respective messages to the standard output.

In summary, this code exemplifies how abstract classes, virtual functions, and polymorphism can be used together to create flexible and extensible programs in C++.

Case Study

Creating a comprehensive real-world application that encapsulates the concepts from Chapter 7 of an advanced C++ programming guide requires a blend of multiple features like classes and objects, encapsulation, constructor and destructor utilization, and more. For this purpose, we will design a simple yet advanced Book Management System using C++. This system will incorporate a variety of classes, inheritance, friend functions, and other C++ advanced features. The application will allow users to add, view, and search for books in the system.

Book Management System

Objective: Develop a console-based book management system that allows adding new books, listing all books, and searching for a book by title.

Concepts Used:

- Classes and Objects
- Encapsulation
- Static Members
- Friend Functions
- Operator Overloading
- Virtual Destructors

Classes:

1. **Book**: Basic class representing a book with attributes like title, author, and ISBN.
2. **BookManager**: Manages a collection of books with functionalities to add, list, and search books.
3. **Logger**: A utility class to log system operations, demonstrating friend functions and static members.

```
#include <iostream>
#include <vector>
#include <string>
#include <algorithm>

// Forward declaration
class Logger;
```

```
class Book {
    std::string title;
    std::string author;
    std::string isbn;

public:
    Book(std::string title, std::string author, std::string isbn):
title(title), author(author), isbn(isbn) {}

    friend class Logger; // Allows Logger to access private members of Book

    // Getter methods
    std::string getTitle() const { return title; }
    std::string getAuthor() const { return author; }
    std::string getISBN() const { return isbn; }

    // Method to display book details
    void display() const {
        std::cout << "Title: " << title << ", Author: " << author << ", ISBN:
" << isbn << std::endl;
    }

    // Operator overloading for comparison (used in search)
    bool operator==(const std::string& searchTitle) const {
        return title == searchTitle;
    }
};

class BookManager {
    std::vector<Book> books;

public:
    void addBook(const Book& book) {
        books.push_back(book);
        Logger::log("Book added: " + book.getTitle());
    }

    void listBooks() const {
        for (const auto& book: books) {
            book.display();
        }
    }
```

```
    void searchBook(const std::string& title) const {
        auto it = std::find(books.begin(), books.end(), title);
        if (it != books.end()) {
            std::cout << "Book found:\n";
            it->display();
        }
        else {
            std::cout << "Book not found.\n";
        }
    }
};

class Logger {
    static int logCount;

public:
    static void log(const std::string& message) {
        std::cout << "[Log " << ++logCount << "]: " << message << std::endl;
    }
};

int Logger::logCount = 0;

int main() {
    BookManager manager;
    manager.addBook(Book("The C++ Programming Language", "Bjarne Stroustrup",
"1234567890"));
    manager.addBook(Book("Effective Modern C++", "Scott Meyers",
"0987654321"));

    std::cout << "\nListing all books:\n";
    manager.listBooks();

    std::cout << "\nSearching for 'Effective Modern C++':\n";
    manager.searchBook("Effective Modern C++");

    return 0;
}
```

This application demonstrates the use of classes to model real-world entities, encapsulation to protect data integrity, static members to maintain a log count, and friend classes to grant special access privileges. Additionally, it employs operator overloading to simplify the search functionality, illustrating how these advanced C++ features can be seamlessly integrated to build a practical and functional system.

SUMMARY

Chapter 7 serves as a comprehensive guide into the realm of classes and objects in C++, offering a foundational step into the object-oriented programming paradigm. This exploration begins with an introduction to classes, their data members, and member functions, setting the stage for a deeper dive into Object-Oriented Analysis and Design (OOAD) and the development and application of the Unified Modeling Language (UML). The chapter meticulously guides readers through the process of defining classes, highlighted by the UML representation of the 'GradeCourse' class as a prime example.

The narrative progresses to emphasize core software engineering principles, detailing the implementation and significance of set and get functions, constructors (both default and overloaded), destructors, and the crucial concept of encapsulation. Through a careful examination of header files, source files, and client files, the chapter illuminates the intricacies of encapsulating data and functionality within a class, thereby fostering a robust understanding of this fundamental object-oriented principle.

Advancing into more sophisticated topics, the chapter explores the dynamics of static members, the utility and application of operator overloading, and the pivotal role of the 'this' pointer in accessing object data members. Real-world scenarios of composition, the use of friend functions, and the subtleties of operator overloading are presented through practical examples, enriching the reader's learning experience.

The chapter concludes by addressing advanced concepts such as static members, the nuances of operator overloading, and the importance of virtual destructors. Each section is designed to not only impart theoretical knowledge but also to challenge the reader through comprehensive exercises, including multiple-choice questions, ensuring a thorough grasp of the material.

Overall, Chapter 7 stands as an invaluable resource for software developers aiming to master advanced C++ programming techniques. It not only broadens the reader's understanding of object-oriented programming concepts but also equips them with the skills necessary to design and develop high-quality software applications using modern C++ practices.

Exercises

Fill in the blanks in each of the following:

a. Each parameter in a function header should specify both a(n) _________ and a(n).
b. ___________________ in the object oriented world generalizes the characteristics and behaviors of an item.
c. ___________________ conceals the functional details of an object from other objects, i.e., the object operates as a black box.
d. ___________________ is a way to form new classes using classes that have already been defined.
e. ___________________ refers to the ability of executing different operations in response to the same message.
f. The ___________ in a system specification help the C++ programmer determine the set of classes to implement the system.
g. The _______ or ______________ ______________ ____________ is now the most widely used graphical representation scheme for modeling object-oriented systems.
h. _______________ must be used to initialize constant members of a class.

i. The keyword _______________ specifies that an object or variable is not modifiable after it is initialized.
j. If a member initializer is not provided for a member object of a class, the object's _______________ is called.

Multiple Choice

1. C++ functions other than main are executed:
   a) Before main executes.
   b) After main completes execution.
   c) When they are explicitly called by another function.
   d) Never.
2. Calling a member function of an object requires which item?
   a) The dot operator.
   b) Open and close braces.
   c) The class name.
   d) None of the above.
3. In the UML, the top compartment of the rectangle modeling a class contains:
   a) The class's name.
   b) The class's attributes.
   c) The class's behaviors.
   d) All of the above.
4. Attributes of a class are also known as:
   a) Constructors.
   b) Local variables.
   c) Data members.
   d) Classes.
5. What type of member functions allow a client of a class to assign values to private data members?
   a) *Client* member functions.
   b) *Get* member functions.
   c) *Set* member functions.
   d) None of the above.
   e)
6. A default constructor has how many parameters?
   a) 0.
   b) 1.
   c) 2.
   d) Variable number.
   e)
7. A constructor can specify the return type:
   a) int.
   b) string.
   c) void.
   d) A constructor cannot specify a return type.

8. The compiler will implicitly create a default constructor if:
   a) The class does not contain any data members.
   b) The programmer specifically requests that the compiler do so.
   c) The class does not define any constructors.
   d) The class already defines a default constructor.
9. A header file is typically given the filename extension:
   a) .h
   b) .hdr
   c) .header
   d) .cpp
10. In the source-code file containing a class's member function definitions, each member function definition must be tied to the class definition by preceding the member function name with the class name and::, which is known as the:
    a) Member definition linker.
    b) Class implementation connector.
    c) Source code resolver.
    d) Binary scope resolution operator.

Exercises

1- Create a class called "Person" with private attributes "name" and "age" (both strings), and public member functions "getName()", "setName(string)", "getAge()", "setAge(string)", and "display()". "display()" should print out the name and age of the person in the format "Name: [name], Age: [age]".

2- Overload the "+" operator for the "Person" class to combine two people's names into one. The resulting Person object should have the combined name and an age of 0.

3- Add a constructor and destructor to the "Person" class. The constructor should take in a name and age and set them as the attributes of the Person object. The destructor should print out a message saying that the object is being destroyed.

4- Create a friend function called "printPersonAge" that takes a "Person" object and prints out their age.

5- Add the "getName()" and "getAge()" member functions as const member functions.

6- Add a static member function to the "Person" class called "displayPersonCount()" that prints out the number of "Person" objects that have been created.

7- Add a private const member variable to the "Person" class called "BIRTH_YEAR" with a value of 2000.

8- Add a private static member variable to the "Person" class called "personCount" that keeps track of the number of "Person" objects that have been created. Increment this variable in the constructor and decrement it in the destructor.

9- Class Design and Encapsulation: Given a class Vehicle with private attributes for make, model, and year, write a complete class definition including parameterized constructor, accessors (getters), and mutators (setters) following encapsulation principles. How would you ensure the year is within a reasonable range (e.g., 1900 to the current year)?

10- Constructor Overloading and Delegation: Implement two overloaded constructors for a Matrix class representing a 2D matrix. The first constructor should create a matrix given rows and columns with all elements initialized to 0, and the second should allow initializing the matrix with a std::vector of std::vectors. Demonstrate constructor delegation if applicable.

11- Destructor and Resource Management: Design a class FileHandler that opens a file in its constructor and closes it in its destructor. Explain how this class would manage resource allocation and deallocation, particularly how it adheres to RAII (Resource Acquisition Is Initialization) principles.
12- Static Members Usage: Add a static data member to the Book class to track the total number of books created. Write a static member function that returns this count. Discuss how static members are shared across objects and their typical use cases.
13- Friend Functions Real-world Application: Provide a real-world scenario where using a friend function would be beneficial. Implement a simple class Account and a friend function transferAmount that allows transferring funds from one account to another, bypassing encapsulation. Discuss the implications of using friend functions in terms of encapsulation and design principles.
14- Operator Overloading for Custom Data Types: Implement operator overloading in the Fraction class to support addition (+), subtraction (-), and equality (==) operators. Ensure that the operations return a new Fraction object with the result of the operation.
15- The this Pointer Utility: In a class Chain, demonstrate the use of the this pointer to enable method chaining. Specifically, implement set functions for different attributes that return *this.
16- Implementing Composition in Classes: Design a Library class that contains a collection of Book objects. Implement methods in the Library class to add a book to the collection and to list all books. Discuss how composition relates to the "has-a" relationship in object-oriented design.
17- Virtual Destructors and Polymorphism: Explain the significance of declaring destructors as virtual in base classes when dealing with inheritance and polymorphism. Provide an example with a base class Shape and derived classes Circle and Square to illustrate your explanation.
18- Advanced UML Diagram Interpretation for C++ Class Implementation: Given a UML class diagram that includes a Person base class and two derived classes Employee and Customer with multiple attributes, methods, and relationships (aggregation, composition, inheritance), write the corresponding C++ code that accurately represents the diagram. Discuss any assumptions or design decisions made during the implementation.

Chapter 8
OOP Inheritance and Polymorphism

ABSTRACT

Chapter 8 embarks on a detailed journey into the heart of object-oriented programming (OOP) by focusing on inheritance and polymorphism. It begins with an introductory discourse, highlighting the advantages of the OOP paradigm, and establishing a foundation with concepts like class hierarchy. The relationship between base and derived classes is elucidated, with focus given to access control specifiers, discussing their advantages and drawbacks. This sets the stage for understanding inheritance in depth, emphasizing the significance of constructors and destructors within derived classes. Public, protected, and private inheritance are examined meticulously. Polymorphism, one of the pillars of OOP, is expounded upon, with distinctions drawn between static and dynamic binding. Further, the chapter demystifies complex relationships among objects in inheritance, assignments between base and derived classes, and touches upon critical topics like overloading, virtual functions, pure virtual functions, abstract classes, and virtual destructors.

8.1 INTRODUCTION

Using inheritance, a programmer can build a class that takes the data and behaviors of the current class and improves them with new features. An is-a notation illustrates inheritance. An object of a derived class may also be regarded as an object of its parent class in an is-a relationship. For instance, consider a car. It is a vehicle, so any property and behavior of a vehicle are also properties of a car.

Inheritance and polymorphism are two of the most important ideas in object-oriented programming (OOP). They help programmers make code that can be used again and again and is easy to maintain. Polymorphism lets a single function or operator work on multiple types of data. Inheritance lets a new class take on the properties and methods of an existing class. Together, these concepts enable developers to create complex and powerful object-oriented programs.

Inheritance: Inheritance is how a new class can get the properties and methods of an existing class. The current class is called a base class, and the new class is called a derived class. The derived class inherits all the properties and methods of the base class and can also add new properties and methods of its own. This allows for code reusability and makes it easy to create new classes that share common functionality.

DOI: 10.4018/979-8-3693-2007-5.ch008

Polymorphism: Polymorphism is the ability of a single function or operator to operate on multiple types of data. In C++, polymorphism is implemented using virtual functions and function overriding. Virtual functions are functions that can be overridden by derived classes, which allows for runtime polymorphism, where the behavior of a function can change based on the type of object it is called on.

Virtual and Override: In C++, virtual functions are those that derived classes can override. In order to indicate that a function should be virtual, the keyword **virtual** is used before the function declaration.

The keyword override is used to show that a function in a derived class is meant to replace a virtual function in the base class. This is useful for catching errors such as accidental mis-matching of function signatures.

8.1.1 OOP Principle Advantages

Software reusability helps save a lot of time while developing the program. Furthermore, reusability reduces the number of times the software must be tested, so it can be thoroughly tested only once. This improves the probability of success.

Developers can pass on the members of one class to another instead of creating new data members and functions.

Programmers can choose to have a new class use the data members and member functions of an existing class instead of making new data members and member functions. The first class is known as the **base class (also called the super class or parent class)**, and the latter is referred to as the **derived class (also called the subclass or child class).**

A derived class stands for a more focused collection of items. A derived class typically includes both new behaviors and behaviors that were inherited from the parent class.

8.1.2 Class Hierarchy

Class hierarchy is a way of organizing classes in a logical and meaningful way by creating a parent-child relationship between classes. This allows for code reusability, maintainability, and encapsulation.

In C++, class hierarchy is set up through inheritance. A new class can take the properties and methods of an existing class, making a parent-child relationship between classes. The current class is referred to as the parent class, and the new class is known as a derived class.

Example:

```
class Shape {
public:
    double area() {
return 0;
}
};

class Rectangle: public Shape {
private:
    double length, breadth;
public:
```

```
    Rectangle(double b, double l): breadth(b), length(h) {}
    double area() { return breadth * length; }
};
class Square: public Rectangle {
public:
    Square(double side): Rectangle(side, side) {}
};
```

In this example, the base class is Shape, and the classes Rectangle and Square are the two that are derived. The class Rectangle inherits the properties and methods of the class Shape, and the class Square inherits the properties and methods of the class Rectangle.

This creates a class hierarchy, where the class Shape is at the top and the classes Rectangle and Square are below it. The classes Rectangle and Square share common functionality, but they can also have unique functionality of their own.

In this example, the class Square is a special type of rectangle, so it makes sense for it to inherit from the Rectangle class. The class Square is derived from the Rectangle class, and it uses the properties and methods of the Rectangle class. It can also add any new properties and methods if needed.

This class hierarchy lets you reuse code because you can define common functionality in the base class and share it with all derived classes. It also lets you hide implementation details in the base class and only show the derived classes the properties and methods they need.

In C++, it's also possible to create multiple levels of inheritance, where a derived class can also be a base class for another derived class, creating a more complex class hierarchy.

A **direct base class** is the base class whose properties are directly inherited by a derived class.

An **indirect base class** is the class that inherits the properties from the derived class of another base class, i.e., from two or more levels in the **class hierarchy**.

With single inheritance, a class takes the properties only from a single base class.

Due to multiple inheritance, there are multiple base classes for one derived class. Multiple inheritance can be complicated and prone to errors.

The base class contains all the common data members and functions declared. Developers only need to update the parent class when any improvements are required for these common features. Then the derived classes automatically inherit the new code. Without inheritance, modifications would have to be made to every source code file that includes a duplicate of the code.

Abstraction

Abstraction is a fundamental concept of object-oriented programming (OOP) that allows developers to focus on the essential features of an object, while hiding its implementation details. It is the process of hiding the implementation details of an object and only exposing its essential features to the user.

In C++, abstraction is implemented using classes and objects. A class defines the properties and methods of an object, while an object is an instance of a class. The properties and methods of a class are the essential features of an object, while the implementation details of a class are hidden from the user.

Example:

```
class Shape {
public:
virtual double area() = 0;
};
class Rectangle: public Shape {
private:
double breadth, length;
public:
Rectangle(double b, double l): breadth(b), length(l) {}
double area() { return breadth * length; }
};
int main() {
Shape* s = new Rectangle(10, 5);
cout << s->area();
return 0;
}
```

In this example, the class Shape is an abstract class, which is a class that cannot be instantiated and is meant to be subclassed.

Abstraction, focuses on sharing among objects in the system

"is-a" vs. "has-a"

The **is-a** relationship represents inheritance. An object of a derived class may also be regarded as an object of its base class in an is-a relationship. Example: Cabbage is a vegetable, so any properties and behaviors of a vegetable are also properties of a cabbage.

The **has-a** relationship represents composition. In a has-a relationship, an object contains one or more objects of other classes as members. Example: A car *has a gear*. A car includes many components; it has a brake pedal, a transmission, and many other components.

8.2 Base Classes and Derived Classes

An object of one class is frequently also an object of another. For example, in geometry, the shape of a rectangle is a quadrilateral (as are squares, parallelograms, and trapezoids). So, in C++, class Quadrilateral's properties are inherited by class Rectangle. Here, class Rectangle is a derived class, and class Quadrilateral is called the base class. Although there are different kinds of quadrilaterals, a quadrilateral is not necessarily a square. Other shapes like the parallelogram are also called quadrilaterals.

The object set of a base class has generally more objects than the object set represented by any of its derived classes because any object of a derived class is an object of its base class, and one base class can have any number of derived classes. For instance, all vehicles, such as automobiles, trucks, boats, airplanes, motorcycles, and so forth, are represented by the basic class Vehicle. The derived class Car, in comparison, depicts a more constrained collection of all cars.

Inheritance relationships resemble tree-like hierarchical structures. A base class and its derived classes are related to one another hierarchically. Although classes can exist separately, they become associated with other classes once they are used in inheritance connections. A class can become both a parent class that shares its members with other classes and a derived class that inherits members from other classes.

Inheritance is how a new class can take on the properties and methods of an existing class, making a parent-child relationship between classes.The existing class is known as the base class, and the new class is known as the derived class.

The derived class gets all of the base class's properties and methods, and it can also add its own properties and methods.This allows for code reuse, as common functionality can be defined in the base class and shared by all derived classes.

In order to support polymorphism, the base class can also define virtual functions that the derived class can override.

Example:

```
class Shape {
public:
double area() { return 0; }
};
class Rectangle: public Shape {
private:
double width, height;
public:
Rectangle(double w, double h): width(w), height(h) {}
double area() { return width * height; }
};
class Circle: public Shape {
double radius;
public:
Circle(double r): radius(r) {}
double area() { return 3.14159 * radius * radius; }
};
```

In this example, the class Shape is the base class and it defines an area() method with a default implementation. The classes Rectangle and Circle are derived classes and they inherit the area() method from the base class Shape. They also provide their own implementation of the area() method.

Deriving from Base Class

A derived class automatically contains all the members of the base class with some restrictions. The only members of a base class that are not inherited by a derived class are:

1. Constructors
2. Copy Constructors
3. Destructors
4. Overloaded Assignment Operators

This is because the derived class requires having its own copies of the above.

8.3 ACCESS CONTROL SPECIFIERS

Access control specifiers are used to define the accessibility of class members (properties and methods) to other parts of the program. There are three main access control specifiers in C++:

Private

This is the default access mode for C++ classes. Only members of that class can access the members declared as private. Usually, data shared by members of a class should be kept private. This enables data hiding.

Public

Outside programs, functions, and classes can access the publicly declared members. Usually the functions are declared as public. Public functions can be used to set the value of private data members.

Protected

These members are not accessible outside the class. However, these members are accessible through its derived class.

By default, class members are private.

Example:

```
class MyClass {
public:
int public_var;
void public_method();
private:
int private_var;
void private_method();
protected:
int protected_var;
void protected_method();
};
```

In this example, the public_var and public_method can be accessed from anywhere in the program, while the private_var and private_method can only be accessed from within the class MyClass and the protected_var and protected_method can be accessed from within the class MyClass and its derived classes.

The idea of access control specifiers in C++ is to enforce the encapsulation principle of object-oriented programming by allowing the developer to hide the implementation details of a class and only expose the necessary properties and methods to the user.

Example:

```
class MyClass {
public:
int public_var;
void public_method() {
cout << "This is a public method" << endl;
}
private:
int private_var;
void private_method() {
cout << "This is a private method" << endl;
}
protected:
int protected_var;
void protected_method() {
cout << "This is a protected method" << endl;
}
};
int main() {
MyClass obj;
obj.public_var = 10; //Accessible
obj.public_method(); //Accessible
obj.private_var = 5; //Not accessible (compilation error)
obj.private_method(); //Not accessible (compilation error)
obj.protected_var = 20; //Not accessible (compilation error)
obj.protected_method(); //Not accessible (compilation error)
return 0;
}
```

In this example, MyClass has 3 members: public_var, private_var, and protected_var, and 3 methods: public_method, private_method, and protected_method.

In the main function, we create an object called MyClass. The public variable and method can be accessed from anywhere in the program, as they are public. The private variable and method can't be accessed from outside the class, as they are private. The protected variable and method can't be accessed from outside the class and derived classes, as they are protected.

Controlling Access Under Inheritance

If the data in the base class is under the private access specifier, A derived class's member functions cannot access it. To enable a derived class to be able to access the members of a base class, we can declare those as protected in the base class.

8.3.1 Advantages and Disadvantages of Private Accessor

The main advantage of using the private access control specifier in C++ is that it allows for the encapsulation of the implementation details of a class. By making class members private, the developer can ensure that these members can only be accessed and modified by the class itself and not by other parts of the program. This helps to prevent accidental or intentional modification of these members and ensures that the class behaves as expected.

Additionally, private members can also be used to hide implementation details that are not relevant to the user and thus make the class easier to understand and use.

One of the main disadvantages of using the private access control specifier is that it can make it difficult to extend or modify a class, as private members cannot be accessed or modified by other parts of the program. This can make it difficult to add new functionality to a class or fix bugs.

Another disadvantage of using the private access control specifier is that it can make it difficult to test a class, as private members cannot be accessed from outside the class. This can make it difficult to write unit tests for a class or verify its behavior.

Overall, it is important to use the private access control specifier judiciously, as it can provide important benefits in terms of encapsulation and maintainability but can also introduce limitations in terms of extensibility and testability.

8.3.2 Advantages and Disadvantages of Protected

By inheriting protected data members, we can get to the members right away without having to make extra calls to set or get member methods. This slightly improves efficiency. But it is usually better to use private data members to encourage good software architecture and let the compiler take care of making sure the code is efficient. This means that the code will be easier to maintain, modify, and debug.

There are two main disadvantages of using protected data members. Firstly, setting the value of the private data member of the base-class does not require the use of a member method on the object of the derived class. Thereby, an invalid value can easily be assigned to the protected data member by a derived-class object, hence making the object inconsistent.

The second issue with protected data members is that it is more common for derived-class member methods to be designed in a way that they rely on the base-class implementation. Derived classes shouldn't rely on the base-class code but rather just the base-class utilities (i.e., public member functions). If the base class has protected data elements, we might have to change all classes that are based on that base class if the code in the base class changes. Software in this situation is said to be unstable or brittle because even a minor change to the parent class can "break" the implementation of derived classes.

8.3.3 Advantages and Disadvantages of Public

The main advantage of using the public access control specifier in C++ is that it allows for full access to class members from anywhere in the program. This makes it easy for other parts of the program to access and use the functionality provided by the class.

Additionally, public access also allows for easy extension and modification of a class. By making class members public, other parts of the program can access and modify them, making it easy to add new functionality or fix bugs.

Another advantage of the public access control specifier is that it makes it easy to test a class, as public members can be accessed from outside the class. This makes it easy to write unit tests for a class or verify its behavior.

One of the main disadvantages of using the public access control specifier is that it can make it difficult to encapsulate the implementation details of a class. By making class members public, other parts of the program can access and modify them, which can lead to accidental or intentional modification of these members and cause the class to behave unexpectedly.

Another disadvantage of using the public access control specifier is that it can make it difficult to understand and use a class, as the implementation details are exposed to the user. This can make the class harder to understand and use, especially for users who are not familiar with the class's implementation details.

Overall, it is important to use public access control specifications judiciously, as they can provide important benefits in terms of accessibility and extensibility but can also introduce limitations in terms of encapsulation and understandability.

8.4 RELATIONSHIP BETWEEN BASE CLASSES AND DERIVED CLASSES

The relationship between base classes and derived classes is known as inheritance. Inheritance allows a derived class to inherit the properties and methods of a base class, making it easier to reuse and extend existing code.

A base class is one from which one or more derived classes are made.A derived class is a class that inherits properties and methods from one or more base classes.

The basic syntax for deriving a class from a base class is to use the operator and the base class name like this:

```
class DerivedClass: public BaseClass {
// properties and methods of the derived class
};
```

For example, consider a base class called Shapeand a derived class called Rectangle.The Shape class has a method called calculateArea which is inherited by the Rectangle class:

```
class Shape {
public:
virtual double calculateArea() = 0;
};
class Rectangle: public Shape {
public:
double width;
double height;
double calculateArea() {
return width * height;
```

```
}
};
```

In this example, the Rectangle class inherits the calculateArea method from the Shape class. The Rectangle class can also have its own properties and methods that are specific to rectangles, such as width and height.

8.4.1 Using #include to Pass the Base Class Header File to the Derived Class Header File

When a derived class is based on a base class, the #include preprocessor directive must be used to include the base class header file in the derived class header file.This lets the compiler see the declarations of the base class members that the derived class will inherit, like properties and methods.

Here is an example of a base class header file called BaseClass.h and a derived class header file called DerivedClass.h:

```
//------------------------------------------------------------
// Filename: BaseClass.h
// Base class definition
//------------------------------------------------------------
#pragma once
class BaseClass {
public:
int base_var;
void base_method();
};
//------------------------------------------------------------
// Filename: DerivedClass.h
// Derived class definition
//------------------------------------------------------------
#pragma once
#include "BaseClass.h"
class DerivedClass: public BaseClass {
public:
int derived_var;
void derived_method();
};
```

In this case, the #include preprocessor directive is used to add the BaseClass.h header file to the DerivedClass.h header file.Since the DerivedClass class is based on the BaseClass, this lets the compiler get to the declarations of the base_var and base_method members.

It is good practice to use the #pragma once preprocessor directive at the top of each header file.

The base class's header file is included using #include in the header file of the derived class. This step is required mainly for three reasons. First, we must let the compiler know about the existence of the base class.

The second reason is that a class's specification tells us how big an entity of that class is.If a client program wants the compiler to set aside the right amount of memory for an object, it must #include the class description. While implementing inheritance, the data members declared in its class definition and the data members inherited from its direct and indirect base classes decide the derived-class object's size.

The last reason is that the compiler can see how well the derived class uses the parts of the parent class that it inherited.

```
//------------------------------------------------------------
// Filename: Boss.h
// Base class definition
//------------------------------------------------------------
#ifndef BOSS_H
#define BOSS_H
#include <iostream>
using namespace std;
class Boss
{
public:
Boss();
~Boss();
void setDamage(int att);
int getDamage();
void displayAttack();
private:
int damage;
};
#endif
//------------------------------------------------------------
// Filename: BigBoss.h
// Derived class definition
//------------------------------------------------------------
#ifndef BIGBOSS_H
#define BIGBOSS_H
#include "Boss.h"
//public inheritance of Boss class - BigBoss class automatically inherits
// all the public and protected members of the Boss class
class BigBoss: public Boss
{
public:
BigBoss();
~BigBoss();
```

```
void setDamageMultiplier(int dm);
int getDamageMultiplier();
void specialAttack();
private:
int damageMultiplier;
};
#endif
//------------------------------------------------------------
// Filename: Boss.cpp
// Base class implementation
//------------------------------------------------------------
#include "Boss.h"
Boss::Boss()
{
cout << "Boss Constructor Called !" << endl;
setDamage(10);
}
Boss::~Boss()
{
cout << "Boss Destructor Called !" << endl;
}
void Boss::setDamage(int att)
{
damage = att;
}
int Boss::getDamage()
{
return damage;
}
void Boss::displayAttack()
{
cout << "Attack causes " << getDamage() << " damage" << endl;
}
//------------------------------------------------------------
// Filename: BigBoss.cpp
// Derived class implementation
//------------------------------------------------------------
#include "BigBoss.h"
BigBoss::BigBoss()
{
cout << "Big Boss Constructor Called !" << endl;
setDamageMultiplier(3);
}
BigBoss::~BigBoss()
```

```
{
cout << "Big Boss Destructor Called !" << endl;
}
void BigBoss::setDamageMultiplier(int dm)
{
damageMultiplier = dm;
}
int BigBoss::getDamageMultiplier()
{
return damageMultiplier;
}
void BigBoss::specialAttack()
{
cout << "Special Attack causes " << getDamageMultiplier() * getDamage() << "
damage" << endl;
}
//----------------------------------------------------------
// Filename: Main.cpp
// Main Function
//----------------------------------------------------------
#include "Boss.h"
#include "BigBoss.h"
int main()
{
cout << "Boss: " << endl;
Boss boss; //creating an object of the base class Boss
boss.displayAttack();
cout << endl << endl;
cout << "Big Boss" << endl;
BigBoss bb; //creating an object of the derived class BigBoss
bb.displayAttack(); //boss
bb.specialAttack(); //bigboss
cout << endl << endl;
return 0;
}
```

This C++ code defines two classes, Boss and BigBoss, to show inheritance, polymorphism, and how to make an object.

The basic class Boss contains a private data member named damage that represents the amount of damage an attack does. It consists of a default constructor, a destructor, and three member functions: setDamage(), getDamage(), and displayAttack(). The setDamage() method sets the damage data member, the getDamage() function retrieves the damage data member, and the displayAttack() function displays the amount of damage an attack causes.

BigBoss is the class that openly inherits from the Boss class. It also includes three member functions: setDamageMultiplier(), getDamageMultiplier(), and specialAttack()tDamageMultiplier(), getDamageMultiplier(), and specialAttack(). The setDamageMultiplier() function sets the damageMultiplier data member, the getDamageMultiplier() function returns the damageMultiplier data member, and the specialAttack() function overrides the displayAttack() function of the Boss class and displays the damage caused by a special attack, which is the product of the damageMultiplier and damage data members.

The Main() method creates new instances of both types and calls their member functions, displayAttack() and specialAttack(), respectively. It shows polymorphism by invoking the overridden specialAttack() method on the derived BigBoss class object. The displayAttack() method is inherited from the Boss class and hence works identically in both instances.

Initializing Data Members

In C++, it is necessary that a derived-class constructor call its base-class constructor to initialize the data members that are inherited from the base class. There is a chance of encountering a compilation error when a derived-class constructor calls any of its base-class constructors with inconsistent arguments. In a derived-class constructor, a default constructor is called when initializing member objects and invoking base-class constructors explicitly in the member initializer list stops duplicate initialization, and then data members are modified again in the derived-class constructor's body.

```
//-----------------------------------------------------------
// Filename: Boss.h
// Base class definition
//-----------------------------------------------------------
#ifndef BOSS_H
#define BOSS_H
#include <iostream>
using namespace std;
class Boss
{
public:
Boss(int damageValue);
~Boss();
void setDamage(int att);
int getDamage();
void displayAttack();
private:
int damage;
};
//-----------------------------------------------------------
// Derived class definition
//public inheritance of Boss class - BigBoss class automatically inherits
// all the public and protected members of the Boss class
//-----------------------------------------------------------
```

```
class BigBoss: public Boss
{
public:
BigBoss(int damage, int damageMultiplierValue);
~BigBoss();
void setDamageMultiplier(int dm);
int getDamageMultiplier();
void specialAttack();
private:
int damageMultiplier;
};
#endif
//----------------------------------------------------------
// Filename: Boss.cpp
// Base class implementation
//----------------------------------------------------------
#include "Boss.h"
Boss::Boss(int damageValue)
{
cout << "Boss Constructor Called !" << endl;
setDamage(damageValue);
}
Boss::~Boss()
{
cout << "Boss Destructor Called !" << endl;
}
void Boss::setDamage(int damageValue)
{
damage = damageValue;
}
int Boss::getDamage()
{
return damage;
}
void Boss::displayAttack()
{
cout << "Attack causes " << getDamage() << " damage" << endl;
}
//----------------------------------------------------------
// Derived class implementation
//----------------------------------------------------------
BigBoss::BigBoss(int damage, int damageMultiplierValue): Boss(damage)
{
cout << "Big Boss Constructor Called !" << endl;
```

```
setDamageMultiplier(damageMultiplierValue);
}
BigBoss::~BigBoss()
{
cout << "Big Boss Destructor Called !" << endl;
}
void BigBoss::setDamageMultiplier(int dm)
{
damageMultiplier = dm;
}
int BigBoss::getDamageMultiplier()
{
return damageMultiplier;
}
void BigBoss::specialAttack()
{
cout << "Special Attack causes " << getDamageMultiplier() * getDamage() << "
damage" << endl;
}
//---------------------------------------------------------
// Filename: Main.cpp
// Main Function
//---------------------------------------------------------
#include "Boss.h"
int main()
{
cout << "Boss: " << endl;
Boss boss(25); //creating an object of the base class Boss
boss.displayAttack();
cout << endl << endl;
cout << "Big Boss" << endl;
BigBoss bb(50, 2); //creating an object of the derived class BigBoss
bb.displayAttack(); //boss
bb.specialAttack(); //bigboss
cout << endl << endl;
return 0;
}
```

The BigBoss class inherits from the Boss class in this C++ example of inheritance. Class Boss is the basic class, whereas class BigBoss is the derived class.

The constructor of the Boss class sets the damage value, and when the object is destroyed, the destructor sends out a message.In addition, it provides a function to set the damage value, a method to receive the damage value, and a function to show the attack.

The BigBoss class has a constructor that invokes the Boss class's constructor. When the object is destroyed, it also has a destructor that prints a message. It provides functions to set the value of damageMultiplier, obtain the value of damageMultiplier, and execute a specific attack.

The main function generates instances of each class and invokes their appropriate methods. The method begins by creating an instance of the Boss class, setting its damage amount, and displaying its attack. The method then creates an instance of the BigBoss class, sets its damage and damageMultiplier values, and shows both its normal and special attacks.

8.5 CONSTRUCTOR AND DESTRUCTORS IN DERIVED CLASSES

When a derived-class object is created, a series of constructor calls begin. The derived-class constructor first calls the constructor of its direct base class, either explicitly (through a base-class member initializer) or implicitly (by calling the base class's default constructor), before starting to work on its own tasks. The base-class constructor must call the constructor of the class that is next in the chain, and so on, if the base class is descended from another class. The constructor of the class at the bottom of the hierarchy, whose body completes execution first, is the last constructor invoked in this sequence. The content of the initial derived-class constructor is the last to execute. The base-class data elements that the derived-class object inherits are initialized by each base-class constructor.

The software invokes the destructor of a derived-class object when it is destroyed. This starts a series of destructor calls in which the members of the classes, the direct and indirect base classes, and the derived class destructors all execute in the opposite sequence to the constructors' execution. The destructor of a derived-class object executes its function when it is called, at which point it calls the destructor of the parent class below it in the hierarchy. Up until the ultimate base class at the summit of the hierarchy is invoked, this procedure is repeated. The item is then deleted from memory.

Derived classes do not borrow from base class constructors, destructors, or excessive assignment operators. Although they cannot invoke base-class constructors, destructors, or extended assignment operators, derived-class constructors, destructors, and assignment operators can.

Constructors and destructors are special member functions that are used to initialize and clean up objects of a class, respectively. When a derived class is inherited from a base class, the constructors and destructors of the base class are also inherited by the derived class.

The derived class can also have its own constructors and destructors, which can be used to set up and clean up its own members as well as the members it inherited from the base class.

Here is an example of a base class with a constructor and a destructor and a derived class with its own constructor and destructor:

```
class BaseClass{
public:
int base_var;
BaseClass() {
base_var = 0;
cout << "BaseClass constructor called" << endl;
}
~BaseClass() {
```

```
cout << "BaseClass destructor called" << endl;
}
};
class DerivedClass: public BaseClass {
public:
int derived_var;
DerivedClass() {
derived_var = 0;
cout << "DerivedClass constructor called" << endl;
}
~DerivedClass() {
cout << "DerivedClass destructor called" << endl;
}
};
int main() {
DerivedClass* d = new DerivedClass(); // calls both BaseClass and DerivedClass
constructors
delete d; // calls both DerivedClass and BaseClass destructors
return 0;
}
```

This code demonstrates inheritance in C++. DerivedClass is a child class, whereas BaseClass is a parent class. The DerivedClass inherits directly from the BaseClass.

In the main function, the new keyword is used to make a pointer to the DerivedClass object. This dynamically allocates memory for the DerivedClass object.The constructor of DerivedClass is invoked, and the derived var is initialized. As DerivedClass is a subclass of BaseClass, the BaseClass constructor is also invoked, which initializes the base variable.

When delete is called, DerivedClass's destructor is invoked first, followed by BaseClass's destructor. This is because the destructor of a derived class is invoked before its base class's destructor.

In general, when an object of a derived class is created, the base class's constructor is called before the derived class's constructor, and when the object is destroyed, the derived class's destructor is called before the base class's destructor.

8.6 PUBLIC, PROTECTED, AND PRIVATE INHERITANCE

A parent class may be inherited through public, protected, or private inheritance when a class is derived from it. Protected inheritance and private inheritance should only be used under very specific circumstances, and we generally use public inheritance in this book.

If you don't tell the compiler how to access a base class, it will think it's private.

Public members of the base class become public members of the derived class, and protected members of the base class become protected members of the derived class when a class is derived from a public base class. The public and protected members of the base class can be called to get to the private members of the base class, which are never directly accessible from derived classes.

```
// Inherit from Base publicly
class Pub: public Base
{
};
```

Public inheritance is a type of inheritance where the members of the base class are accessible to the derived class and to the code that uses the derived class. This means that the derived class can access the public and protected members of the base class directly, and the code that uses the derived class can access the public members of the base class through the derived class.

Here is an example of a base class called Shape and a derived class called Rectangle that uses public inheritance:

```
class Shape {
public:
double width;
double height;
double calculateArea() {
return width * height;
}
};
class Rectangle: public Shape {
public:
Rectangle(double w, double h) {
width = w;
height = h;
}
};
int main() {
Rectangle r(5, 10);
cout << "Area of the rectangle: " << r.calculateArea() << endl;
return 0;
}
```

In this example, the Rectangle class is derived from the Shape class using the public keyword. This means that the Rectangle class can directly access the width, height, and calculateArea members of the Shape class.The main function makes an object of the Rectangle class and then uses the Shape class's calculateArea method to figure out how big the rectangle is.

It is also possible to override the base class methods or add new methods or properties in the derived class; the derived class can also access the protected members of the base class as well, and it can also access the public members of the base class as well.

When a class inherits from a protected base class, the public and protected members of the base class become protected members of the derived class.

```
// Inherit from Base protectedly
class Pro: protected Base
{
};
```

Protected inheritance is a type of inheritance where the members of the base class are accessible to the derived class but not to the code that uses the derived class. This means that the derived class can access the protected and public members of the base class directly, but the code that uses the derived class can only access the public members of the base class through the derived class.

Here is an example of a base class called Shape and a derived class called Rectangle that use protected inheritance:

```
class Shape {
protected:
double width;
double height;
double calculateArea() {
return width * height;
}
};
class Rectangle: protected Shape {
public:
double getArea() {
return calculateArea();
}
Rectangle(double b, double l) {
breadth = b;
length = l;
}
};
int main() {
Rectangle r(5, 10);
cout << "Area of the rectangle: " << r.getArea() << endl;
return 0;
}
```

In this example, the Rectangle class is derived from the Shape class using the protected keyword, which means that the Rectangle class can access the width, height, and calculateArea members of the Shape class directly, but the main function can only access the getArea method, which is a public member of the Rectangle class.

It is a good practice to use protected inheritance when the derived class is an implementation detail of the base class and should not be used directly by the code that uses the base class.

Also, it is possible to access the protected members of the base class from the derived class, but it is not possible to access them from outside the derived class, even if the derived class object is being passed as a parameter or being returned from a function.

When a private base class is derived from, the public and protected members of the private base class become private members (like utility methods) of the derived class.

```
// Inherit from Base privately
class Pri: private Base
{
};
class Def: Base // Defaults to private inheritance
{
};
```

Private inheritance is a type of inheritance in which the members of the base class are not available to the derived class or the code that uses the derived class, unless explicit type casting is used. This means that the derived class can access the private members of the base class only by casting a pointer or a reference to the base class.

Here is an example of a base class called Shape and a derived class called Rectangle that uses private inheritance:

```
class Shape {
private:
double width;
double height;
double calculateArea() {
return width * height;
}
};
class Rectangle: private Shape {
public:
double getArea() {
Shape* s = this;
return s->calculateArea();
}
Rectangle(double w, double h) {
Shape* s = this;
s->width = w;
s->height = h;
}
};
int main() {
Rectangle r(5, 10);
cout << "Area of the rectangle: " << r.getArea() << endl;
```

```
return 0;
}
```

In this example, the private keyword is used to make the Rectangle class come from the Shape class. This means that the Rectangle class can't directly access the width, height, and calculateArea members of the Shape class. Instead, it must use explicit type casting.

It is a good practice to use private inheritance when you want to reuse the implementation of a base class but don't want to expose the public interface of the base class to the code that uses the derived class.

Also, you can't access the private members of the base class from the derived class or from outside the derived class, unless you use explicit type casting. This is true even if the derived class object is being passed as a parameter or returned from a function.

IS-a relationships do not include private and protected inheritance.

Figure 1.

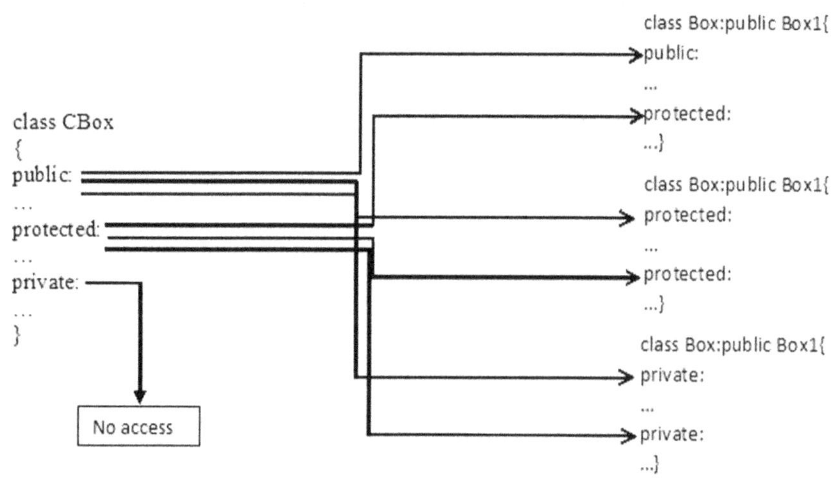

8.7 POLYMORPHISM

Instead of "programming in the specific," polymorphism allows us to "program in the general." Polymorphism makes it possible to write programs that handle objects of classes that are in the same class hierarchy as if they were all objects of the hierarchy's base class in particular.

Considering the following example of polymorphism:

Example: A vehicle hierarchy

- Base class: Vehicle
  - function move is present in every derived class.
- Different vehicle objects are maintained as a vector of vehicle pointers.
- Program issues a common message (move) to each vehicle
- The proper function gets invoked.

- A boat will move by water.
- A bike will move by road.
- An airplane will move by flying.

With polymorphism, a single function can result in a variety of outcomes based on the class of the object on which it is called. The programmer now has a huge range of creative options.

When a program calls a virtual function using a vehicle-based base class pointer or reference, polymorphism takes place. C++ automatically (i.e., at runtime) selects the appropriate function for the class from which the object was created.

A modified class object may be used in the same way as a parent class object. This makes possible a number of intriguing changes. The compiler permits this even though the derived-class objects are of various kinds because each derived-class object is an object of its parent class. A base-class object, however, cannot be treated as an object of any of its derived classes. Errors can occur when a base-class object is treated as a(n) derived-class object.

Whenever you create a base class and a derived class with the same function name and compile them, the call to the base class function is set once and for all by the compiler as the version defined in the base class. The compiler will have no knowledge that any other derived class function with the same name exists. This is called **static resolution** of the function call since the function call is fixed before the program is executed. This is also sometimes called **early binding** because the particular base class function chosen is bound to the call during the compilation of the program.

The **dynamic linkage,** or **late binding,** resolves this issue and ensures that the correct function is called. Events that need to happen at runtime are referred to as late binding. When a function call is late bound, the location of the function being called isn't known until the application has finished running. An entity that is late bound is a virtual function.

C++ supports polymorphism using virtual functions. The same rules that apply to calling member functions also apply to virtual functions. However, the capacity to enable run-time polymorphism is what makes a virtual function intriguing. It informs the algorithm that static linkage is not desired for this procedure. You want to base the procedure that will be executed at any particular moment in the program on the type of object for which it is intended.

In base classes, the term virtual is added before the function prototype to define virtual functions. They allow inherited classes to appropriately modify functions. When a function is made virtual, it stays that way throughout the structure.

Polymorphism is a feature of the language that allows objects of different classes to be treated as objects of a common base class. This allows a single function or operator to work with multiple types of objects without the need for explicit type checking or type casting.

There are two types of polymorphism in C++: compile-time polymorphism and run-time polymorphism.

Static polymorphism, which is what compile-time polymorphism is also called, is made possible by function overloading and operator overloading.Function overloading allows multiple methods with the same name to be defined if they have different parameter lists. Operator overloading allows operators to be redefined for different types.

Here is an example of function overloading in C++:

```
void print(int x) {
cout << x << endl;
```

```
}
void print(string stri) {
cout << stri << endl;
}
int main() {
print(stri);
print("Hello World");
return 0;
}
```

In this example, the print function is overloaded to accept both an int and a string parameter, allowing it to be used with different types of objects.

Run-time polymorphism, also called dynamic polymorphism, is done by using virtual functions and pointers or references to base classes.A virtual function is a member function that is marked as "virtual" in the base class. This lets it be changed in the classes that inherit from it.

Here is an example of run-time polymorphism in C++:

```
#include <iostream>
using namespace std;
class Shape {
public:
virtual double getArea() = 0;
};
class Rectangle: public Shape {
private:
double breadth;
double length;
public:
Rectangle(double b, double l) {
breadth = b;
length = l;
}
double getArea() {
return breadth * length;
}
};
class Circle: public Shape {
private:
double radius;
public:
Circle(double r) {
radius = r;
}
double getArea() {
```

```
return 3.14159 * radius * radius;
}
};
int main() {
Shape* shape1 = new Rectangle(4, 5);
Shape* shape2 = new Circle(3);
cout << "Area of rectangle: " << shape1->getArea() << endl;
cout << "Area of circle: " << shape2->getArea() << endl;
return 0;
}
```

In this example, the class Shape is an abstract base class that defines the pure virtual function getArea(). The classes Rectangle and Circle are derived from Shape, and they both override the getArea() function to provide their own implementation.

In the main() function, we create two pointers of type Shape and assign them a rectangle object and a circle object, respectively. When we call the getArea() function through these pointers, the correct implementation for the actual object is called at run-time, which is polymorphism.

output:

Area of rectangle: 20

Area of circle: 28.27431

8.7.1 Static Binding

Static binding, also known as compile-time binding, occurs when the type of an object is determined at compile time. In C++, this is usually done through the use of function overloading and operator overloading.

For example, consider the following code:

```
class Shape {
public:
virtual double getArea() = 0;
};
class Rectangle: public Shape {
private:
double width, height;
public:
Rectangle(double w, double h): width(w), height(h) {}
double getArea() { return width * height; }
};
class Circle: public Shape {
private:
double rad;
public:
Circle(double r): rad(r) {}
```

```
double getArea() { return 3.14159 * rad * rad; }
};
void printArea(Shape& s) {
cout << "Area: " << s.getArea() << endl;
}
int main() {
Rectangle r(5, 10);
Circle c(2);
printArea(r);
printArea(c);
return 0;
}
```

In this code, the function printArea() takes a reference to a Shape object. The type of the object passed to printArea() is determined at compile time based on the type of the object being passed.

Another example of static binding in C++ is the use of overloaded operators. For example, consider the following code:

```
class Complex {
private:
double real, imag;
public:
Complex(double r, double i): real(r), imag(i) {}
Complex operator+(const Complex& other) {
return Complex(real + other.real, imag + other.imag);
}
};
int main() {
Complex c1(1, 2), c2(3, 4);
Complex c3 = c1 + c2;
return 0;
}
```

In this code, the operator + is overloaded for the Complex class. The type of the objects being passed to the operator is determined at compile time, allowing the correct version of the operator to be called.

In both examples, the type of the object is determined at compile time, hence the term static binding.

8.7.2 Dynamic Binding

Dynamic binding, which is also called "run-time binding," is when an object's type is determined at run time. In C++, this is usually done through the use of virtual functions.

For example, consider the following code:

```
class Shape {
public:
virtual double getArea() = 0;
};
class Rectangle: public Shape {
private:
double width, height;
public:
Rectangle(double w, double h): width(w), height(h) {}
double getArea() { return width * height; }
};
class Circle: public Shape {
private:
double radius;
public:
Circle(double r): radius(r) {}
double getArea() { return 3.14159 * radius * radius; }
};
void printArea(Shape& s) {
cout << "Area: " << s.getArea() << endl;
}
int main() {
Shape* fig[2];
fig[0] = new Rectangle(5, 10);
fig[1] = new Circle(2);
for (int i = 0; i < 2; i++) {
printArea(*fig[i]);
}
return 0;
}
```

In this code, the printArea() function takes a reference to a Shape object. However, the objects passed to printArea() are actually pointers to Rectangleand Circle objects. Because the getArea() function is declared as virtual, the correct version of the function that is invoked depends on the object called at run-time rather than the type of the pointer.

Another example of dynamic binding in C++ is the use of virtual destructors.For example, consider the following code:

```
class Shape {
public:
virtual ~Shape() {}
};
class Rectangle: public Shape {
public:
```

```
~Rectangle() { cout << "Rectangle destructor" << endl; }
};
class Circle: public Shape {
public:
~Circle() { cout << "Circle destructor" << endl; }
};
int main() {
Shape* s1 = new Rectangle();
Shape* s2 = new Circle();
delete s1;
delete s2;
return 0;
}
```

Here, the Shape class has a virtual destructor. When s1 and s2 are deleted, the correct destructor for the actual type of the object is called at run-time, rather than the type of the pointer.

In both examples, the type of the object is determined at run-time, hence the term dynamic binding. Dynamic binding occurs only on pointer and reference handles.

```
//---------------------------------------------------------------
// Animal Class. This is the Base class.
//---------------------------------------------------------------
class Animals
{
public:
Animal(const string& type);
virtual string move(); // Notice keyword virtual
string getAnimalType();
void setAnimalType(string type);
private:
string animalType;
};
//---------------------------------------------------------------
// Fish Class. This is the Derived class. This inherits from the
// base class Animal.
//---------------------------------------------------------------
class Fish: public Animals
{
public:
Fish(const string& type);
string move();//keyword virtual can also be used here but is optional, but
should be used if its derived classes needs to override this funtion
};
//---------------------------------------------------------------
```

```
// Frog Class. This is the Derived class. This inherits from the
// base class Animal.
//------------------------------------------------------------------
class Frog: public Animals
{
public:
Frog(const string& type);
string move();
};
//------------------------------------------------------------------
// Bird Class. This is the Derived class. This inherits from the
// base class Animal.
//------------------------------------------------------------------
class Bird: public Animals
{
public:
Bird(const string& type);
string move();
};
//-----------------------------------------------------------------------
// Implementation File
//-----------------------------------------------------------------------
Animals::Animal(const string& type)
{
// Indirect initialization using the set function
setAnimalType(type);
}
void Animals::setAnimalType(const std::string type)
{
animalType = type; // sets the member variable with new value
}
string Animals::getAnimalType()
{
return animalType; // returns the value of the member variable
}
string Animals::move()
{
// returns the animal type along with a string
return getAnimalType() + " Walks";
}
//invokes the base class constructor Animal
Fish::Fish(const std::string& type): Animals(type)
{ }
string Fish::move()
```

```
{
// returns the animal type along with a string
return getAnimalType() + " Swims";
}
//invokes the base class constructor Animal
Frog::Frog(const string& type): Animals(type)
{}
string Frog::move()
{
// returns the animal type along with a string
return getAnimalType() + " Leaps";
}
//invokes the base class constructor Animal
Bird::Bird(const std::string& type): Animals(type)
{}
string Bird::move()
{
// returns the animal type along with a string
return getAnimalType() + " Flies";
}
//---------------------------------------------------------------------
// Client File
//---------------------------------------------------------------------
int main()
{
// Instantiation of the Class object, Here we are creating 3 new // Animal
objects dynamically of the type Fish, Bird, Frog. This // is possible because
these are a type of Animal
Animals* animals[] =
{
//dynamically allocates memory to 3 new objects
new Fish("Fish"),
new Bird("Bird"),
new Frog("Frog")
};
for (int i = 0; i < 3; i++)
{
cout << animals[i]->move() << endl;
delete animals[i];
}
return 0;
}
```

This demonstrates inheritance in C++. Fish, Frog, and Bird are derived classes of the Animals base class. The derived classes inherit the parent class's attributes and methods. move() and getAnimalType are member methods of the basic class (). The move() method has a virtual declaration, allowing derived classes to alter its implementation.

Each derived class implements the move() method independently. Each derived class' implementation of the move() method produces a string describing how the animal moves.

In the main function, an array of Animal references is generated, and objects of the derived classes are instantiated. The move() method is then invoked on each item, and the result is reported. Lastly, memory allocated dynamically is released using delete.

8.8 RELATIONSHIPS AMONG OBJECTS IN AN INHERITANCE

Objects can have relationships with each other through inheritance. Inheritance is a mechanism that allows one class to inherit properties and methods from another. This allows for code reuse and a more organized and efficient codebase.

Here is an example of inheritance in C++:

```
class Shape {
public:
int x, y;
void move(int dx, int dy) {
x += dx;
y += dy;
}
};
class Rectangle: public Shape {
public:
int width, height;
int area() {
return width * height;
}
};
```

In this example, the Rectangle class inherits from the Shape class. This means that objects of the Rectangle class have access to the x, y, and move() properties and methods from the Shape class, in addition to their own properties and methods.

You can also use the keyword private or protected as the access level to make the inheritance private or protected, which limits who can see the inherited members.

```
class Shape {
private:
int x, y;
public:
```

```
void move(int dx, int dy) {
x += dx;
y += dy;
}
};
class Rectangle: private Shape {
public:
int width, height;
int area() {
return width * height;
}
};
```

In this case, members in Rectangle class can only access the inherited members from Shape but the other classes can't.

Another relationship between objects is composition, also known as has - a relationship.A class "has-a" another class object as a member.

```
class Engine {
};
class Car {
private:
Engine engine;
};
```

In this example, a car has an engine object, so the Car class is composed of an Engine object.

8.9 ALLOWED ASSIGNMENTS BETWEEN BASE-CLASS AND DERIVED-CLASS OBJECTS AND POINTERS

Assignment between base-class and derived-class objects and pointers is allowed under certain conditions.

Assignments between objects:

A derived-class object can be assigned to a variable of its base class, if the base class has a virtual destructor.

```
class Shape {
public:
virtual ~Shape() {}
};
class Rectangle: public Shape {
};
Shape s;
Rectangle r;
s = r; // this is allowed
```

Assignments between pointers:

A pointer to a derived - class object can be assigned to a pointer of its base class, if the base class has a virtual destructor.

```
class Shape {
public:
virtual ~Shape() {}
};
class Rectangle: public Shape {
};
Shape* s;
Rectangle* r;
s = r; // this is allowed
```

A pointer to a base - class object can be assigned to a pointer of its derived class with a explicit cast.

```
Shape * s;
Rectangle* r;
r = static_cast<Rectangle*>(s); // this is allowed
```

A base - class reference can be assigned to a derived - class reference, if the base class has a virtual destructor.

```
class Shape {
public:
virtual ~Shape() {}
};
class Rectangle: public Shape {
};
Shape& s;
Rectangle& r;
r = s; // this is allowed
```

However, it is important to note that reverse assignments are not allowed; that is, a derived-class object cannot be assigned to a variable of its base class, and a pointer to a base-class object cannot be assigned to a pointer of its derived class, unless with explicit casting.

Also, if the base class does not have a virtual destructor, the assignments might lead to undefined behavior.

In addition, it is important to be aware of the slicing problem, which occurs when a derived-class object is assigned to a variable of its base class. This can lead to loss of data, as only the base-class members are copied.

Base-class objects are also derived-class objects, but they are not the same thing. Even though they can sometimes be regarded as base-class objects, derived-class objects Given that the derived class includes every member of the parent class, this relationship makes sense. Although the derived class may contain extra members that are exclusive to the derived class, base-class objects cannot be handled as if they were derived-class objects. Because of this, pointing a derived-class reference at a base-class object requires an explicit cast and would leave the base-class object's derived-class-only elements undefined.

There are four ways to aim base - class pointersand derived - class pointers at base - class objectsand derived - class objects:

1. Aiming a base - class pointer at a base - class object is straight forward.Calls made off the base - class pointer simply invoke base - class functionality.

```
// Pointing the base class pointer to base class object
animalPtr = &animalObj;
```

2. It's less complicated to direct a derived-class pointer at a derived-class object. Calls made off the derived - class pointer simply invoke derived - class functionality.

```
// Pointing the derived class pointer to derived class
// object
birdPtr = &birdObj;
```

Because a derived-class object is an object of its parent class, pointing a base-class pointer at one is secure. But you can only use this pointer to invoke base-class member functions. If the author attempts to refer to the single member of a derived class using the base class pointer, the machine produces an error. To avoid this mistake, the coder must change the base-class pointer into a derived-class pointer. The derived-class pointer can then be used to access the complete functionality of the derived-class object. Downcasting, however, is a technique that might be harmful.

```
// Downcasting:
// Base class pointer aimed at derived class object
// Can invoke only base class functions
animalPtr = &birdObj;
```

3. Aiming a derived - class pointer at a base - class object generates a compilation error.The is - a relationship applies only from a derived class to its direct and indirect base classes, and not vice versa.A base - class object does not contain the derived - class - only members that can be invoked off a derived - class pointer.

```
// Derived class pointer aimed at base class object
birdPtr = &animalObj; // WILL THROW ERROR !!!
```

8.10 VIRTUAL FUNCTIONS

Virtual functions are a mechanism that allows for dynamic binding of function calls. This means that the function that is called is determined at runtime, rather than at compile time.

Here is an example of a virtual function in C++:

```
class Shapes {
public:
virtual void drawing() {
cout << "constructing a shape" << endl;
}
};
class Rectangle: public Shapes {
public:
void drawing() {
cout << "constructing a rectangle" << endl;
}
};
class Circle: public Shapes {
public:
void drawing() {
cout << "constructing a circle" << endl;
}
};
```

In this example, the draw() function is declared as virtual in the Shape class. This means that when a Shape object is created, the draw() function that is called is determined at runtime, based on the actual type of the object.

```
Shape* shape = new Rectangle();
shape->draw(); // this will call the draw function of Rectangle
shape = new Circle();
shape->draw(); // this will call the draw function of Circle
```

The virtual function mechanism makes the codebase more flexible and expandable, since new derived classes can be added to the program without having to change the existing code.

Another important point is that, if a base class function is declared as virtual, all the overridden functions in derived classes must also be declared as virtual, otherwise the function calls in the derived class objects will be bound to the base class function and not the overridden one.

It's also worth noting that virtual functions can have a performance cost, as the program needs to check the actual type of the object at runtime. So, it's important to only use virtual functions when they are truly necessary.

8.11 DIFFERENCES BETWEEN OVERLOADING AND VIRTUAL FUNCTIONS

It might seem like function overloading and rewriting a virtual function in a class that is derived are similar. However, the two processes are distinctly different:

- A new virtual function must have the exact same type, number, and return type, while an overloaded function must vary in type and/or number of arguments. (In fact, if you change either the number or type of parameters when redefining a virtual function, it will simply become an overloaded function, and its virtual nature is lost.)
- It is mandatory for virtual functions to be class members.
- Constructors cannot be virtual, while destructors can.

The word "overriding" is used to define the redefinition of virtual functions due to the variations between overloaded functions and redefined virtual functions.

In terms of transmission, virtual tasks are arranged hierarchically.

When a derived class does not replace a virtual function, the parent class's method is used.

8.12 PURE VIRTUAL FUNCTIONS

In some cases, when a virtual function is defined in the base class, it has no useful purpose to carry out. Because a basic class frequently does not adequately define a complete class by itself, this situation frequently arises. It only provides a basic collection of member methods and variables, with the rest being provided by the derived class.

The inference is that if a virtual function of a master class serves no purpose, any derived class must replace this function. This will happen because C++ allows pure virtual functions.

```
virtual type func-name (parameter-list) = 0;
```

The most important part of this declaration is setting the function's value to 0.

Any class that is derived from the base class must override a virtual method that has been made pure. So, making a virtual function pure is a way to make sure that a class that derives from it will define itself.

A pure virtual function lacks a definition but does have a prototype. utilized when a default implementation is unnecessary.

"=0" is referred to as a clean specifier. Pure virtual functions do not supply implementations. Every concretely derived class must substitute concrete iterations of all base-class pure virtual methods. In contrast to a pure virtual function, which does not provide an implementation and necessitates that the derived class modify the function, a virtual function has an implementation and gives the derived class the option to do so (for that derived class to be concrete; otherwise, the derived class remains abstract). A perfect virtual class is one that has only virtual functions and cannot be created. Its subcategories, however, can.

Pure virtual functions are a mechanism that allows for the creation of abstract classes. Other classes can inherit from an abstract class, but they cannot create it.A pure virtual function is a virtual function that the derived class must implement because the base class does not have an implementation of it.

Here is an example of a pure virtual function in C++:

```
class Shape {
public:
virtual void draw() = 0;
};
class Rectangle: public Shape {
public:
void draw() {
cout << "Drawing a rectangle" << endl;
}
};
class Circle: public Shape {
public:
void draw() {
cout << "Drawing a circle" << endl;
}
};
```

In this example, the Shape class is an abstract class because it contains a pure virtual function, the draw() function. This means that the Shape class cannot be instantiated, and any object that is created must be of a derived class that implements the draw() function.

```
Shape* shape = new Rectangle();
shape->draw(); // this will call the draw function of Rectangle
shape = new Circle();
shape->draw(); // this will call the draw function of Circle
```

Pure virtual functions are useful when a base class defines an interface that must be implemented by derived classes, but the base class does not provide an implementation for the interface. This allows for the creation of a common interface that can be used by different derived classes, each with their own implementation.

A class containing one or more pure virtual functions is called abstract class, you cannot create an instance of an abstract class and if you try to do so, you'll get a compile time error.

Shape shape; // this will give a compile time error

It's also worth noting that, if a derived class does not implement all the pure virtual functions of its base class, it will also become an abstract class and cannot be instantiated.

8.13 ABSTRACT CLASSES

A class is considered abstract if it has ***at least one pure*** virtual function. An abstract class cannot have any objects made because it is an incomplete type and includes at least one method for which there is no body. As a result, generic classes only exist to be copied.

Abstract classes are useful in a number of situations because a programmer never has to make an object for them. We refer to these as abstract base classes because they are only used as base classes. No generic class instances may be created. Concrete classes are those from which things can be created.

A class that includes one or more pure virtual functions is said to be abstract. An abstract class cannot be instantiated but can be inherited by other classes. The derived classes must implement the pure virtual functions in order to be instantiated.

Here is an example of an abstract class in C++:

```
class Shape {
public:
virtual void draw() = 0;
};
class Rectangle: public Shape {
public:
void draw() {
cout << "Drawing a rectangle" << endl;
}
};
class Circle: public Shape {
public:
void draw() {
cout << "Drawing a circle" << endl;
}
};
```

In this example, the Shape class is an abstract class because it contains a pure virtual function, the draw() function. This means that the Shape class cannot be instantiated, and any object that is created must be of a derived class that implements the draw() function.

```
Shape* shape = new Rectangle();
shape->draw(); // this will call the draw function of Rectangle
shape = new Circle();
shape->draw(); // this will call the draw function of Circle
```

An abstract class is useful when a base class defines an interface that must be implemented by derived classes, but the base class does not provide an implementation for the interface. This allows for the creation of a common interface that can be used by different derived classes, each with their own implementation.

```
Shape shape; // this will give a compile time error
```

It's also worth noting that, if a derived class does not implement all the pure virtual functions of its base class, it will also become an abstract class and cannot be instantiated.

```
class Triangle: public Shape {
// no implementation for draw function
};
Triangle t; // this will give a compile time error
```

In this example, the class Triangle is an abstract class because it does not implement the pure virtual function draw() defined in the base class Shape. Thus, it cannot be instantiated.

Example:

```
//======================================================================
// Creature.h
// Abstract Class -- Cannot instantiate an object of this class
//======================================================================
#include <iostream>
using namespace std;
class Creature
{
public:
Creature(int health = 100); // Default constructor
void setHealth(int health);
int getHealth();
virtual void displayHealth();
//abstract function -- does not contain any code
// Notice that it is assigned a value of 0
virtual void greet() = 0;
private:
int health;
};
//======================================================================
// Griffin.h
// Concrete class -- instantiation of objects is possible, i.e,
// It is possible to create an object of this type. //=======================
==============================================
class Griffin: public Creature
{
public:
Griffin(int health = 200);
//concrete function -- contains code
virtual void greet();
```

```
};
//==================================================================
// Creature.cpp
//==================================================================
#include "Creature.h"
Creature::Creature(int health)
{
setHealth(health);
}
void Creature::setHealth(int health)
{
this->health = health;
}
int Creature::getHealth()
{
return health;
}
void Creature::displayHealth()
{
cout << "Health: " << getHealth() << endl;
}
//==================================================================
// Griffin.cpp
//==================================================================
#include "Griffin.h"
//calling the base class constructor
Griffin::Griffin(int health):Creature(health)
{}
void Griffin::greet()
{
cout << "Hello, I am the Griffin!!!" << endl;
}
//==================================================================
// Main.cpp
//==================================================================
#include "Creature.h"
#include "Griffin.h"
int main()
{
Griffin* opinicus = new Griffin();
opinicus->greet();
opinicus->displayHealth();
cout << endl;
Creature* pCreature = new Griffin();
```

```
cout << "Displaying the greeting of the creature: " << endl;
pCreature->greet();
cout << endl;
pCreature->displayHealth();
return 0;
}
```

This C++ source code illustrates abstract classes and inheritance. The code constructs an abstract class, Creature, that cannot be created due to the presence of a pure virtual function, welcome (). Griffin is a class that derives from Creature and implements the welcome() method.

The Creature class has a default constructor and member methods for setting health, getting health, and showing health.The constructor of the Griffin class calls the constructor of the base class and implements the welcome() method.

The welcome() and displayHealth() procedures are run by the main() method, and a reference to a Griffin object of type Creature is created. To show polymorphism, the welcome() and displayHealth() methods are called via the pointer.

8.14 VIRTUAL DESTRUCTORS

When processing objects in a class hierarchy that are dynamically assigned, polymorphism can lead to issues. Nonvirtual destructors, or destructors that are not defined with the term virtual, have been seen up to this point. The C++ standard states that the behavior is undefined if a derived-class object with a nonvirtual destructor is expressly destroyed by using the delete operator on a base-class reference to the object.

Making a virtual destructor in the parent class (a destructor that is defined with the keyword virtual) is the straightforward answer to this issue. Despite the fact that they do not share the same name as the base-class destructor, this renders all derived-class destructors virtual. Now, the destructor for the right class is triggered based on the object to which the base-class pointer points if an object in the hierarchy is specifically deleted by using the delete operator on a base-class reference. It's essential for the destructors of both the derived class and base class to run because when an object of a derived class is deleted, the object's base-class component is also destroyed. Following the derived-class destructor, the base-class destructor runs immediately.

A virtual destructor is a destructor that is declared as virtual in a base class. This lets objects of derived classes be deleted in the right way when they have a pointer or reference to the base class.

Here is an example of a virtual destructor in C++:

```
class Shape {
public:
virtual ~Shape() {
cout << "Deleting Shape" << endl;
}
};
class Rectangle: public Shape {
```

```
public:
~Rectangle() {
cout << "Deleting Rectangle" << endl;
}
};
class Circle: public Shape {
public:
~Circle() {
cout << "Deleting Circle" << endl;
}
};
```

In this example, the Shape class has a virtual destructor, which means that when a Rectangle or Circle object is deleted through a pointer or reference to the Shape class, the derived class's destructor will be called first and then the base class's destructor will be called.

```
Shape* shape = new Rectangle();
delete shape; // this will call the destructor of Rectangle then Shape
shape = new Circle();
delete shape; // this will call the destructor of Circle then Shape
```

Without a virtual destructor, when an object is deleted through a pointer or reference to the base class, only the base class's destructor will be called. This can cause memory leaks and other problems if the derived class uses resources that aren't freed by the base class's destructor.

It's worth noting that, if a class has a virtual function, it's generally a good practice to make its destructor virtual as well, to ensure proper destruction of objects of derived classes.

Also, it's important to note that the destructor is not inherited; if a derived class does not declare its own destructor, the base class's destructor will be called, whether it's virtual or not.

Example:

```
//=====================================================================
// This program shows the working of the virtual destructor
//=====================================================================
class Boss
{
public:
Boss(int damage = 10);
// constructors cannot be virtual only destructors can be
// virtual used deallocate any memory reserved when calling
// calling the functions from the base class
virtual ~Boss();
void setDamage(int att);
int getDamage();
virtual void displayAttack();
```

```
private:
int* damagePtr;
};
class BigBoss: public Boss
{
public:
BigBoss(int multiplier = 3);
virtual ~BigBoss();
void setDamageMultiplier(int dm);
int getDamageMultiplier();
virtual void displayAttack();
private:
int* damageMultiplierPtr;
};
//==================================================================
// Implementation
//==================================================================
#include "Boss.h"
Boss::Boss(int damage)
{
cout << "Boss Constructor called" << endl;
setDamage(damage);
}
Boss::~Boss()
{
cout << "Boss Destructor: Removing the corruptedptr" << endl;
delete damagePtr;
damagePtr = NULL;
}
void Boss::setDamage(int att)
{
damagePtr = new int(att);
}
int Boss::getDamage()
{
return *damagePtr;
}
void Boss::displayAttack()
{
cout << "Attack causes " << getDamage()
<< " damage points" << endl << endl;
}
BigBoss::BigBoss(int multiplier)
{
```

```
cout << "Big Boss Constructor called" << endl << endl;
setDamageMultiplier(multiplier);
}
BigBoss::~BigBoss()
{
cout << "BigBoss Destructor: Deleting the damageMultiplierPtr"
<< endl;
delete damageMultiplierPtr;
damageMultiplierPtr = NULL;
}
void BigBoss::setDamageMultiplier(int dm)
{
damageMultiplierPtr = new int(dm);
}
int BigBoss::getDamageMultiplier()
{
return *damageMultiplierPtr;
}
void BigBoss::displayAttack()
{
cout << "Special Attack causes "
<< getDamageMultiplier() * getDamage()
<< " damage points" << endl << endl;
}
//====================================================================
// Client
//====================================================================
int main()
{
// Dynamically creates a pointer
Boss* pBadGuy = new BigBoss();
pBadGuy->displayAttack();
// Deleting the pointer
delete pBadGuy;
pBadGuy = NULL;
return 0;
}
```

This program explains how a virtual destructor in C++ works. A virtual destructor is a destructor that is declared as virtual in the base class and offers a means for ensuring that the destructors of both the base and derived classes are invoked in the right sequence when an object is removed through a reference to a base class. There are two classes in this program: boss and large boss. BigBoss derives from the term Boss.

The Boss class has the methods constructor, virtual destructor, setDamage, getDamage, and displayAttack. BigBoss is a subclass of Boss that includes the constructor, virtual destructor, setDamageMultiplier, getDamageMultiplier, and displayAttack methods. The setDamageMultiplier function modifies BigBoss's damage multiplier.

In the implementation part, the Boss constructor initializes the damagePtr and the destructor frees the damagePtr memory. The setDamage method sets the damage value, whereas the getDamage function retrieves it. The function displayAttack shows the damage produced by an assault. In a similar fashion, the BigBoss constructor initializes the damageMultiplierPtr and the destructor frees the memory allocated for the damageMultiplierPtr. getDamageMultiplier returns the damage multiplier, which is set by the setDamageMultiplier function. The displayAttack function shows the damage produced by the BigBoss's special assault.

In the client part, the main method produces a Boss pointer on the fly and passes it to a BigBoss object.

It then invokes the displayAttack method to show the attack's damage. The software then deletes the pointer using the delete operator and sets it to the value NULL.

This application shows how virtual destructors make sure that base class and derived class destructors are run in the right order when an object is deleted using a base class reference.

ADVANCED PRACTICE EXERCISES WITH ANSWERS

Example 1: Demonstrating Constructors and Destructors in Inheritance

Objective: To understand how constructors and destructors are invoked in a class hierarchy.

```
#include <iostream>

class Base {
public:
    Base() { std::cout << "Base Constructor\n"; }
    virtual ~Base() { std::cout << "Base Destructor\n"; }
};

class Derived: public Base {
public:
    Derived() { std::cout << "Derived Constructor\n"; }
    ~Derived() override { std::cout << "Derived Destructor\n"; }
};

int main() {
    std::cout << "Creating Derived Object:\n";
    Derived d;
    std::cout << "Exiting main()\n";
    return 0;
}
```

Explanation:

This C++ code snippet demonstrates the principles of inheritance, particularly focusing on constructors and destructors, and how virtual destructors play a crucial role in a class hierarchy. Here's a step-by-step breakdown of what happens when the program runs:

Class Definitions and Constructors/Destructors

- **Base Class**:
- The constructor prints **"Base Constructor\n"** when an object of **Base** (or any derived class) is instantiated.
- The destructor is declared **virtual** and prints **"Base Destructor\n"** upon object destruction. Making the destructor virtual ensures that the destructor of the derived class is called first if an object of a derived class is deleted through a pointer to **Base**.
- **Derived Class**:
- Inherits from **Base**. Its constructor prints **"Derived Constructor\n"**, indicating it has been instantiated.
- Overrides the base class destructor (although using **override** is optional for destructors) and prints **"Derived Destructor\n"** upon destruction.

Main Function Execution

1. **Creating Derived Object**:
    - The message **"Creating Derived Object:\n"** is printed.
    - When the **Derived** object **d** is instantiated, the **Base** constructor is called first (due to inheritance), printing **"Base Constructor\n"**, followed by the **Derived** constructor, which prints **"Derived Constructor\n"**.
2. **Exiting main()**:
    - The message **"Exiting main()\n"** is printed. This indicates the scope of the **Derived** object **d** is about to end, triggering the destruction process.
    - Since **d** is a local object, its lifetime is bound to the scope it is defined in (in this case, the **main** function). When the scope ends, **d** is destroyed.
3. **Object Destruction**:
    - The destructors are called in the reverse order of the constructors. First, the **Derived** destructor is called, printing **"Derived Destructor\n"**, followed by the **Base** destructor, printing **"Base Destructor\n"**. This ensures that any resources allocated by **Derived** and then **Base** during construction are properly released in the opposite order during destruction.

Output

```
The output of the program will be:
Creating Derived Object:
Base Constructor
Derived Constructor
Exiting main()
```

```
Derived Destructor
Base Destructor
```

Key Concepts Illustrated

- **Constructor and Destructor Order**: In a class hierarchy, base class constructors are called before derived class constructors during object creation, and derived class destructors are called before base class destructors during object destruction.
- **Virtual Destructors**: Essential in class hierarchies to ensure proper cleanup if a derived class object is deleted through a base class pointer. While not demonstrated directly in this snippet (since destruction is done without polymorphism), the practice of declaring base class destructors as virtual is critical for scenarios involving dynamic polymorphism.

This example neatly encapsulates the lifecycle of objects in C++ with inheritance, from creation to destruction, highlighting the importance of constructor and destructor order and the role of virtual destructors in ensuring resources are properly managed.

Example 2: Polymorphism With Virtual Functions

Objective: To demonstrate polymorphism and the effect of virtual functions.

```
#include <iostream>

class Animal {
public:
    virtual void speak() const { std::cout << "This animal speaks an unknown
language.\n"; }
    virtual ~Animal() = default;
};

class Dog: public Animal {
public:
    void speak() const override { std::cout << "Dog barks.\n"; }
};

class Cat: public Animal {
public:
    void speak() const override { std::cout << "Cat meows.\n"; }
};

void promptAnimalToSpeak(const Animal& animal) {
    animal.speak();
}
```

```
int main() {
    Dog dog;
    Cat cat;
    std::cout << "Prompting the animals to speak:\n";
    promptAnimalToSpeak(dog);
    promptAnimalToSpeak(cat);
    return 0;
}
```

Explanation:

This C++ code demonstrates the use of polymorphism, virtual functions, and inheritance in the context of a simple class hierarchy involving animals. The program defines a base class **Animal** and two derived classes, **Dog** and **Cat**, each overriding the **speak** method to produce animal-specific sounds. Let's dive into the details:

Classes and Inheritance

- **Animal (Base Class)**:
- Contains a virtual method **speak** that prints a generic message. This method serves as a placeholder to be overridden by derived classes, allowing them to specify their own implementations.
- Includes a virtual destructor, which is a good practice when designing base classes intended for inheritance, especially when dynamic memory allocation is involved or when using polymorphism. The **= default** specifier indicates that the compiler should generate the default implementation for the destructor.
- **Dog (Derived Class)**:
- Inherits from **Animal** and overrides the **speak** method to print "Dog barks." This demonstrates polymorphism, where **Dog** provides its specific behavior for the **speak** method.
- **Cat (Derived Class)**:
- Similar to **Dog**, it inherits from **Animal** and overrides the **speak** method, but prints "Cat meows." again illustrating polymorphism.

Polymorphism in Action

- The function **promptAnimalToSpeak** takes a reference to an **Animal** as its parameter and calls the **speak** method on the passed-in animal. Due to polymorphism and the use of virtual functions, the correct **speak** method is called at runtime based on the actual type of the object passed (either **Dog** or **Cat**), despite the function parameter being of type **Animal**.

Main Function

- Creates instances of **Dog** and **Cat**.
- Outputs an introductory message.
- Calls **promptAnimalToSpeak** with the **dog** and **cat** instances. Thanks to dynamic binding, the appropriate **speak** methods for **Dog** and **Cat** are invoked, demonstrating polymorphism.

Output

Prompting the animals to speak:
    Dog barks.
    Cat meows.

Key Takeaways

- **Virtual Functions and Polymorphism**: This example showcases how virtual functions enable polymorphism in C++. Derived classes can override a base class's virtual functions to provide specific implementations, which are then correctly invoked even when using base class references or pointers.
- **Good Practices**: Using a virtual destructor in the base class ensures that destructors of derived classes are called correctly when an object is deleted through a base class pointer, avoiding resource leaks.
- **Usage of References for Polymorphism**: The example also highlights that polymorphism isn't limited to pointers. It works with references as well, allowing functions to operate on base class references and automatically use the derived class's implementation of a virtual function.

This concise example efficiently encapsulates key OOP concepts, making it a valuable learning resource for understanding inheritance and polymorphism in C++.

Example 3: Public vs. Protected vs. Private Inheritance

Objective: To demonstrate the effects of public, protected, and private inheritance on member visibility.

```
#include <iostream>
class Base {
public:
    int publicVar = 1;
protected:
    int protectedVar = 2;
private:
    int privateVar = 3;
};

class PublicDerived: public Base {};
class ProtectedDerived: protected Base {};
class PrivateDerived: private Base {};

int main() {
    PublicDerived pd;
    std::cout << "PublicDerived publicVar: " << pd.publicVar << std::endl; //
Accessible
```

```
    // ProtectedDerived pd2;
    // std::cout << pd2.publicVar << std::endl; // Not accessible

    // PrivateDerived pd3;
    // std::cout << pd3.publicVar << std::endl; // Not accessible
}
```

Explanation:

This C++ code snippet illustrates the effects of different inheritance modes (**public**, **protected**, and **private**) on member access from outside the class. Let's dissect the example and understand each part:

Base Class Definition

The **Base** class defines three variables with different access specifiers:

- **publicVar** is public and can be accessed from anywhere.
- **protectedVar** is protected and can only be accessed within the class itself, its derived classes, and friend classes/functions.
- **privateVar** is private and can be accessed only within the **Base** class.

Derived Classes

Three derived classes are defined with different types of inheritance:

- **PublicDerived** inherits publicly from **Base**. Members inherited from **Base** retain their original access levels.
- **ProtectedDerived** inherits **Base** under **protected** access. Public and protected members of **Base** become protected in **ProtectedDerived**.
- **PrivateDerived** inherits **Base** under **private** access. Both public and protected members of **Base** become private in **PrivateDerived**.

Main Function Analysis

- **Accessing publicVar through PublicDerived**: Since **PublicDerived** inherits from **Base** publicly, **publicVar** remains public in **PublicDerived**, and can be accessed from an object of **PublicDerived**. The line printing **publicVar** for **PublicDerived** works as expected.
- **Accessing publicVar through ProtectedDerived**: The commented-out section illustrates an attempt to access **publicVar** through an object of **ProtectedDerived**. This access is invalid because, with protected inheritance, **publicVar** becomes protected in **ProtectedDerived**, making it inaccessible from outside the class.
- **Accessing publicVar through PrivateDerived**: Similar to **ProtectedDerived**, attempting to access **publicVar** through an object of **PrivateDerived** is also invalid. In private inheritance, **publicVar** becomes private in **PrivateDerived**, hence it's not accessible from outside the class.

Key Takeaways

- **Public Inheritance** is the most permissive, keeping the access levels of base class members unchanged in the derived class.
- **Protected Inheritance** restricts access more than public inheritance by making public and protected members of the base class protected in the derived class.
- **Private Inheritance** is the most restrictive, converting all inherited members (public and protected) to private in the derived class.

Output

The only un-commented, valid line in **main()** will output:

```
PublicDerived publicVar: 1
```

This output demonstrates that public inheritance allows access to public members of the base class from outside the derived class, reflecting the direct effects of inheritance access modifiers on member accessibility in C++.

Example 4: Static Binding vs. Dynamic Binding

Objective: Illustrate static and dynamic binding in C++.

```
#include <iostream>
class Base {
public:
    void staticBindFunc() { std::cout << "Base staticBindFunc\n"; }
    virtual void dynamicBindFunc() { std::cout << "Base dynamicBindFunc\n"; }
};

class Derived: public Base {
public:
    void staticBindFunc() { std::cout << "Derived staticBindFunc\n"; }
    void dynamicBindFunc() override { std::cout << "Derived dynamicBindFunc\n";
}
};

int main() {
    Base* basePtr = new Derived();

    // Static Binding
    basePtr->Base::staticBindFunc(); // Calls Base's version

    // Dynamic Binding
```

```
    basePtr->dynamicBindFunc(); // Calls Derived's version due to virtual
function

    delete basePtr;
}
```

Explanation:

This C++ code snippet is an excellent demonstration of the difference between static and dynamic binding in the context of inheritance and polymorphism. Let's break down how it works:

Base and Derived Classes

- **Base Class**: Defines two functions, **staticBindFunc()** and **dynamicBindFunc()**. While **staticBindFunc()** is a regular member function, **dynamicBindFunc()** is marked as **virtual**, indicating it's intended for use with dynamic binding, allowing derived classes to provide a specific implementation.
- **Derived Class**: Inherits from **Base** and provides its own implementations for both **staticBindFunc()** and **dynamicBindFunc()**. The override of **dynamicBindFunc()** is explicitly marked with the **override** keyword, signaling that this function overrides a virtual function in the base class.

Main Function

- **Dynamic Allocation**: A **Base** class pointer named **basePtr** is dynamically allocated an instance of **Derived**. This setup is used to demonstrate polymorphism, where a base class pointer can point to a derived class object.
- **Static Binding**: The code explicitly calls **Base::staticBindFunc()** using the base class pointer **basePtr**. This call is statically bound at compile time to the **Base** class's version of **staticBindFunc()**, ignoring the fact that **basePtr** actually points to a **Derived** object. Static binding means the function to call is determined at compile time based on the type of the pointer, not the type of the object it points to.
- **Dynamic Binding**: When calling **dynamicBindFunc()** on **basePtr**, dynamic binding occurs. Because **dynamicBindFunc()** is a virtual function and **basePtr** points to a **Derived** object, the **Derived** class's version of the function is executed. Dynamic binding (or late binding) means the function to call is determined at runtime based on the actual type of the object pointed to by the pointer.

Cleanup

- The dynamically allocated object is deleted to free up the allocated memory.

Output

Base staticBindFunc

Derived dynamicBindFunc

This output illustrates the key concepts:

- **Static Binding**: Directly calling a function on a class (even through a derived class pointer using the class's scope resolution) bypasses polymorphism and always executes that class's version of the function.
- **Dynamic Binding**: Virtual functions allow C++ to use the object's runtime type to determine which function to execute, leading to the derived class's implementation being used when called through a base pointer or reference.

This snippet effectively highlights the distinction between static and dynamic binding in C++, showcasing the powerful capabilities of polymorphism through virtual functions.

Example 5: Virtual Function and Override

Objective: Show how to correctly override a base class's virtual function.

```
#include <iostream>
class Animal {
public:
    virtual void sound() { std::cout << "Animal makes a sound.\n"; }
};

class Dog: public Animal {
public:
    void sound() override { std::cout << "Dog barks.\n"; }
};

int main() {
    Animal* myPet = new Dog();
    myPet->sound();
    delete myPet;
}
```

Explanation:

This C++ code snippet is a straightforward example of polymorphism, a core concept in object-oriented programming. It demonstrates how polymorphism allows methods to be invoked on objects of different types through a base class pointer. Here's a detailed breakdown:

Components:

- **Animal Class (Base Class)**:
- Contains a virtual function **sound()** that prints a generic message indicating that an animal makes a sound. The **virtual** keyword indicates that this function can be overridden by derived classes.
- **Dog Class (Derived Class)**:
- Inherits from the **Animal** class.

- Overrides the **sound()** function to provide a specific implementation for a dog, printing a message that a dog barks.

Main Function

- An **Animal** pointer named **myPet** is dynamically allocated as a **Dog** object using **new**. This is a demonstration of upcasting, where a derived class object is assigned to a base class pointer.
- The **sound()** method is called on the **myPet** pointer. Due to polymorphism and the fact that **sound()** is a virtual function in the base class (**Animal**), the overridden version in the **Dog** class is invoked, printing "Dog barks.\n".
- The dynamically allocated **Dog** object is then deleted, freeing the allocated memory.

Output

Dog barks.

Key Concepts Illustrated

- **Polymorphism**: The ability of different class objects to be treated as objects of their base class but still invoke their own versions of the base class methods. Polymorphism is what allows **myPet->sound()** to call the **Dog** class's **sound()** method, even though **myPet** is an **Animal***.
- **Virtual Functions**: A function declared as **virtual** in a base class and overridden in a derived class enables polymorphism. When a virtual function is called on a base pointer or reference that points to a derived object, the derived class's version of the function is invoked.
- **Dynamic Memory Allocation**: The use of **new** to dynamically allocate memory for a **Dog** object and **delete** to free that memory. It's crucial in C++ to match every **new** with a **delete** to prevent memory leaks.
- **Object Lifetime Management**: When **delete myPet;** is executed, the destructor for **Dog** (implicitly defined here) and then **Animal** (also implicitly defined) is called, ensuring proper cleanup of resources associated with the **Dog** object.

This example encapsulates the essence of using virtual functions to achieve runtime polymorphism, a fundamental mechanism in C++ that allows for more flexible and dynamic code behavior.

Example 6: Abstract Class and Pure Virtual Function

Objective: Demonstrate the use of an abstract class and pure virtual function.

```
#include <iostream>
class Shape {
public:
    virtual double area() const = 0; // Pure virtual function makes Shape an
abstract class
};
```

```
class Circle: public Shape {
    double radius;
public:
    Circle(double r): radius(r) {}
    double area() const override { return 3.14 * radius * radius; }
};

int main() {
    Shape* shape = new Circle(5);
    std::cout << "Area: " << shape->area() << std::endl;
    delete shape;
}
```

Explanation:

This C++ code snippet showcases the use of abstract classes and virtual functions to implement polymorphism, focusing on a simple hierarchy of shapes. Here's how it works:

Abstract Base Class: Shape

- **Purpose**: Serves as a base class for different kinds of shapes. It defines a common interface for all shapes.
- **Pure Virtual Function**: The **area** function is declared as a pure virtual function (**= 0**) in the **Shape** class. This means the **Shape** class cannot be instantiated on its own (making it an abstract class) and forces derived classes to provide their own implementation of the **area** method.

Derived Class: Circle

- **Inheritance**: Inherits from the **Shape** class, making it a concrete class that must implement the **area** method.
- **Constructor**: Accepts a **double** representing the radius of the circle and initializes the **radius** member variable with it.
- **Area Calculation**: Overrides the **area** method from **Shape** to provide a specific implementation for calculating the area of a circle using the formula $A=\pi r$^2. The value of π is approximated as **3.14**.

Main Function

- **Polymorphism**: Demonstrates polymorphic behavior by allocating a **Circle** object on the heap and assigning its address to a pointer of type **Shape***. This is possible because **Circle** is derived from **Shape**.
- **Area Calculation**: Calls the **area** method on the **Shape** pointer, which dynamically binds to the **Circle**'s override of the **area** method at runtime, ensuring the correct calculation based on the object's actual type.

- **Memory Management**: The allocated **Circle** object is deleted at the end of **main** to free the allocated memory.

Output

Area: 78.5

This output results from calculating the area of a circle with a radius of **5** using the provided implementation (A=3.14×5^2).

Key Concepts Illustrated

- **Abstract Classes and Pure Virtual Functions**: The code demonstrates how to define an abstract base class (**Shape**) with a pure virtual function (**area**) to establish a common interface for derived classes.
- **Polymorphism**: The use of a base class pointer to refer to a derived class object and the virtual function mechanism allow for polymorphic behavior, where the derived class method is called through a base class reference or pointer.
- **Dynamic Memory Management**: The example also touches on dynamic memory allocation and deallocation using **new** and **delete**, highlighting the importance of freeing allocated resources to avoid memory leaks.

This pattern is fundamental in C++ for creating flexible and reusable components, especially when dealing with a hierarchy of objects that share a common interface but have different implementations.

Example 7: Virtual Destructor

Objective: Highlight the importance of virtual destructors in base classes.

```
#include <iostream>
class Base {
public:
    Base() { std::cout << "Base Constructor\n"; }
    virtual ~Base() { std::cout << "Base Destructor\n"; }
};

class Derived: public Base {
public:
    Derived() { std::cout << "Derived Constructor\n"; }
    ~Derived() { std::cout << "Derived Destructor\n"; }
};

int main() {
    Base* b = new Derived();
```

```
    delete b;
}
```

Explanation:

This C++ code snippet demonstrates the use of polymorphism, particularly through virtual destructors, in a base and derived class relationship. Here's a detailed breakdown:

Code Explanation

- **Base Class**: Defines a constructor and a virtual destructor. The constructor prints a message when an object of type **Base** (or any class derived from **Base**) is created. The destructor is marked **virtual**, which is crucial for ensuring that the derived class's destructor is called when an object is deleted through a pointer to **Base**.
- **Derived Class**: Inherits from **Base**. It defines its own constructor and destructor, which also print messages. The destructor does not need to be explicitly marked **virtual** because the base class's destructor is virtual. This ensures that the destructor chaining happens correctly, starting from the most derived class's destructor to the base class's destructor.

main Function

- A pointer to **Base** named **b** is created and initialized with an instance of **Derived** using **new**. This dynamic allocation and the use of a base pointer to refer to a derived object is a common use case for polymorphism.
- When **delete b;** is executed, it triggers the destructor chain. Because the destructor in the **Base** class is declared **virtual**, C++ correctly calls the **Derived** class's destructor first, followed by the **Base** class's destructor.

Output

Base Constructor
Derived Constructor
Derived Destructor
Base Destructor

Key Takeaways

- **Constructor Call Order**: When constructing an object of a derived class, the base class's constructor is called first, followed by the derived class's constructor. This ensures that all parts of the object are properly initialized before the derived class's constructor logic is executed.
- **Destructor Call Order**: Destructors are called in the reverse order of constructors. First, the derived class's destructor is executed to clean up the resources allocated by the derived class. Then, the base class's destructor is called. Marking the base class destructor as **virtual** ensures that the derived class's destructor is called even when the object is deleted through a pointer to the base class.

- **Virtual Destructor Importance**: The virtual destructor in the base class is essential for proper resource management in polymorphic base/derived class hierarchies. Without it, if an object of a derived class is deleted through a pointer to the base class, only the base class's destructor would be called, potentially leading to resource leaks if the derived class acquires resources that need explicit release in its destructor.

This code snippet serves as a concise example of how virtual destructors enable safe polymorphic behavior, ensuring that resources are correctly managed and that destructors of both base and derived classes are called as expected in polymorphic situations.

Example 8: Overloading and Virtual Functions

Objective: Contrast overloading a function within a class vs. overriding a virtual function in a derived class.

```
#include <iostream>
class Base {
public:
    virtual void greet() { std::cout << "Hello from Base\n"; }
};

class Derived: public Base {
public:
    void greet() override { std::cout << "Hello from Derived\n"; }
    void greet(std::string msg) { std::cout << msg << " from Derived\n"; } //
Overloading
};

int main() {
    Derived d;
    d.greet(); // Calls overridden method
    d.greet("Hi"); // Calls overloaded method
}
```

Explanation:

This C++ code illustrates two fundamental Object-Oriented Programming (OOP) concepts: method overriding and method overloading, within the context of class inheritance.

Breakdown

- **Base Class**: Contains a single virtual function **greet()**, which prints a greeting message to the console. The use of the **virtual** keyword indicates that this function can be overridden by derived classes, enabling polymorphism.
- **Derived Class**: Inherits from the **Base** class and demonstrates both overriding and overloading:

- **Overriding**: Implements its own version of the **greet()** function, as indicated by the **override** keyword. This version outputs a different message, showcasing runtime polymorphism. When a **Derived** object calls **greet()**, it uses this overridden version rather than the **Base** class's version.
- **Overloading**: Introduces a new version of **greet()** that accepts a **std::string** parameter, allowing the same function name (**greet**) to be used for different purposes. This demonstrates compile-time polymorphism, where the function to be called is determined based on the arguments provided.

Main Function

- Creates an instance of the **Derived** class named **d**.
- Calls **d.greet()** without any arguments, which invokes the overridden **greet()** method in the **Derived** class, printing "Hello from Derived\n".
- Calls **d.greet("Hi")** with a string argument, which invokes the overloaded **greet(std::string msg)** method in the **Derived** class, printing "Hi from Derived\n".

Key Concepts

- **Method Overriding** is a feature of polymorphism that allows a derived class to provide a specific implementation of a function that is already defined in its base class. This mechanism is used to change the behavior of a function in the derived class while preserving its interface.
- **Method Overloading** allows multiple functions in the same scope to have the same name but different parameters. It's a form of compile-time polymorphism where the called function is determined by the number and type of arguments passed.

Output

```
Hello from Derived
Hi from Derived
```

This code snippet effectively demonstrates how inheritance coupled with method overriding and overloading can be utilized in C++ to create flexible and powerful class hierarchies. Through these mechanisms, derived classes can extend and customize the behavior of base classes in a type-safe manner, enhancing reusability and readability.

Example 9: Multiple Inheritance

Objective: Demonstrate the use of multiple inheritance in C++.

```
#include <iostream>
class Printer {
public:
    void print() { std::cout << "Printing...\n"; }
};
```

```
class Scanner {
public:
    void scan() { std::cout << "Scanning...\n"; }
};

class MultiFunctionDevice: public Printer, public Scanner {};

int main() {
    MultiFunctionDevice mfd;
    mfd.print();
    mfd.scan();
```

Explanation

This C++ code snippet illustrates a simple example of multiple inheritance, where a class (**MultiFunctionDevice**) inherits functionalities from more than one base class (**Printer** and **Scanner**). The example showcases how a derived class can aggregate and utilize features from multiple base classes, mimicking a real-world multifunction device that can both print and scan.

Breakdown of the Code

- **Printer Class**: A simple class with a public member function **print()** that outputs a message indicating a printing action.
- **Scanner Class**: Another simple class with a public member function **scan()** that outputs a message indicating a scanning action.
- **MultiFunctionDevice Class**: Inherits publicly from both **Printer** and **Scanner** classes. This class doesn't add any new members or functionalities of its own. Instead, it inherits all the public members of **Printer** and **Scanner**, making it capable of performing both printing and scanning actions.
- **Main Function**:
- An instance of **MultiFunctionDevice** named **mfd** is created.
- **mfd.print()**: Calls the **print()** method inherited from the **Printer** class, which outputs **"Printing...\n"**.
- **mfd.scan()**: Calls the **scan()** method inherited from the **Scanner** class, which outputs **"Scanning...\n"**.

Key Concepts Illustrated

- **Multiple Inheritance**: This code demonstrates multiple inheritance, a feature of C++ that allows a class to inherit from more than one base class. **MultiFunctionDevice** serves as a practical example, combining functionalities from both **Printer** and **Scanner**.
- **Code Reusability**: The example illustrates how multiple inheritance can be used to reuse code across different classes. Instead of redefining printing and scanning functionalities within **MultiFunctionDevice**, it simply inherits them from **Printer** and **Scanner**, respectively.

- **Simplifying Complex Relationships**: Multiple inheritance can be a powerful tool for modeling complex relationships in software. It allows developers to create modular classes that encapsulate specific behaviors (**Printer** and **Scanner**) and then combine those behaviors in more complex classes (**MultiFunctionDevice**).

Considerations

While multiple inheritance can be very useful, it also comes with complexities, such as the diamond problem, where a class inherits from two classes that both inherit from a common base class. This can lead to ambiguity and issues with data duplication. However, this simple example does not encounter such issues since **Printer** and **Scanner** are unrelated and do not share a common base class.

Conclusion

This code snippet effectively demonstrates how multiple inheritance allows a class to inherit and utilize functionalities from more than one base class, enabling the creation of versatile and modular designs in C++ applications.

Example 10: Protected Inheritance

Objective: Demonstrate the effects of protected inheritance on member access.

```
#include <iostream>
class Base {
public:
    void sayHello() const { std::cout << "Hello from Base\n"; }
};

class Derived: protected Base {};

int main() {
    Derived d;
    // d.sayHello(); // Error: sayHello is protected within Derived
    return 0;
}
```

Explanation

This C++ code snippet demonstrates the use of protected inheritance and its impact on access control. The **Derived** class inherits from the **Base** class using protected inheritance. Let's break down the key components and explain the behavior:

Code Analysis

- **Base Class**: A simple class with a public member function **sayHello()** that outputs a greeting message. Since **sayHello()** is public in **Base**, it can be accessed by any code that can access **Base** objects.
- **Derived Class**: Inherits from **Base** using the **protected** keyword. This means all public and protected members of **Base** (which includes **sayHello()**) become protected members of **Derived**. Protected members of a class are accessible within the class itself, in derived classes, but not from outside code.

Main Function

- An instance of **Derived**, named **d**, is created.
- The commented-out line **d.sayHello();** attempts to call the **sayHello()** function through a **Derived** object. However, this will result in a compilation error because **sayHello()** is inherited as a protected member of **Derived** due to protected inheritance. Protected members cannot be accessed through instances of the class or its derived classes from outside the class.

Protected Inheritance Implications

- **Protected Inheritance** is less common than public inheritance and is typically used when the derived class represents a specialized form of the base class but only within the implementation of a class hierarchy (i.e., it needs access to the base class's protected and public members, but those members should not be exposed to the users of the derived class).
- It restricts the accessibility of the inherited members more than public inheritance but less than private inheritance, balancing encapsulation and accessibility for derived classes.

Expected Behavior and Output

- Since the **d.sayHello();** line is commented out, this program produces no output. If the line were uncommented, it would not compile due to the access violation explained above.

Conclusion

Protected inheritance is a nuanced feature of C++ that controls the visibility and accessibility of base class members in derived classes. It is particularly useful when you need to restrict access to inherited functionality from outside the class hierarchy while still allowing derived classes to use and override that functionality. This example clearly illustrates how protected inheritance affects member access, making **Base** class public members behave as protected members within **Derived**, thus restricting their direct access through **Derived** instances.

Example 11: Private Inheritance

Objective: Showcase how private inheritance affects member access

```
#include <iostream>
class Base {
public:
    void sayHello() const { std::cout << "Hello from Base\n"; }
};

class Derived: private Base {
public:
    using Base::sayHello; // Make sayHello publicly accessible through Derived
};

int main() {
    Derived d;
    d.sayHello(); // Works due to using declaration
    return 0;
}
```

Explanation

This C++ code demonstrates an interesting use of inheritance access control and the **using** directive within class definitions. Here's how it works:

Overview

- **Base Class**: Defines a simple member function **sayHello()** that prints a greeting message to the console indicating it's from the **Base** class.
- **Derived Class**: Inherits from the **Base** class privately, which means all public and protected members of **Base** become private members of **Derived**. However, the **Derived** class uses a **using** directive to change the access level of the **Base::sayHello** method, making it publicly accessible through **Derived** instances.
- **Main Function**: Creates an instance of **Derived** and calls **sayHello()** on it. Despite **Derived** inheriting from **Base** privately, the **using** declaration within **Derived** makes this call valid and successful.

Key Concepts

- **Private Inheritance**: When a class inherits from another class using the **private** keyword, all the base class's public and protected members are treated as private within the derived class. This means they can't be accessed using derived class instances, although the derived class itself can access them internally.
- **Using Declaration**: The **using** directive in the **Derived** class redeclares **Base::sayHello** within **Derived**'s scope. This effectively changes its access level to public within the context of **Derived**, allowing it to be called through instances of **Derived**. It's a technique to selectively expose or change the accessibility of inherited members.

Code Behavior

- The main function successfully calls **d.sayHello()**, where **d** is an instance of **Derived**. This works as intended because of the **using** directive in the **Derived** class that makes **Base::sayHello** accessible as if it were a public member of **Derived**.

Output

The output of this program will be:
Hello from Base

Usage and Implications

- **Selective Exposure**: This pattern can be used to selectively expose or hide base class functionality in derived classes. It allows developers to create a controlled interface to the functionality inherited from base classes, especially useful in complex inheritance hierarchies or when implementing adapters and wrappers.
- **Encapsulation and Abstraction**: Despite private inheritance generally being used to express a "has-a" or "implemented-in-terms-of" relationship rather than an "is-a" relationship, the **using** directive provides a way to carefully expose inherited functionality, maintaining encapsulation while offering a tailored interface to class users.

This example underscores the flexibility of C++ in managing class interfaces and inheritance, showcasing how access levels can be manipulated to design class hierarchies with specific behavior and access patterns.

Example 12: Static Binding

Objective: Illustrate static binding with a non-virtual function call.

```
#include <iostream>
class Base {
public:
    void sayHello() const { std::cout << "Hello from Base\n"; }
};

class Derived: public Base {
public:
    void sayHello() const { std::cout << "Hello from Derived\n"; }
};

int main() {
    Base* b = new Derived();
    b->sayHello(); // Calls Base::sayHello due to static binding
```

```
    delete b;
    return 0;
}
```

Explanation

This C++ code demonstrates the concept of static binding, which is a key feature of C++ when dealing with inheritance and method calls on base class pointers or references that point to derived class objects. Here's a detailed breakdown:

Key Components

- **Base Class**:
- Contains a non-virtual member function **sayHello()** that outputs "Hello from Base".
- **Derived Class**:
- Inherits from the **Base** class and overrides the **sayHello()** function to output "Hello from Derived". Note that in this context, "override" means providing a new implementation, but C++ treats this specific case as "hiding" rather than overriding due to the lack of the **virtual** keyword in the base class method.

main Function

- Dynamically allocates a **Derived** class object on the heap and assigns its address to a pointer **b** of type **Base***. This demonstrates polymorphism where a base class pointer is used to refer to a derived class object.
- Calls **sayHello()** on the **Base*** pointer. Since the **sayHello()** method in the **Base** class is not marked as **virtual**, the call resolves to **Base::sayHello()** at compile time. This is known as static binding (or early binding) because the method to be called is determined during compilation rather than at runtime.
- The dynamically allocated object is then deleted to free the memory.

Output

Hello From Base

This output shows that the **Base::sayHello()** method is called, despite **b** pointing to an object of type **Derived**. This is because, in C++, if a method in the base class is not declared as **virtual**, the method call is resolved at compile time based on the type of the pointer or reference, not the actual type of the object it points to or references.

Importance of Virtual Functions for Polymorphism

The key takeaway from this example is the importance of declaring methods as **virtual** in the base class to enable dynamic binding (also known as late binding), which is a cornerstone of runtime polymorphism in C++. If the **sayHello()** method in the **Base** class were declared as **virtual**, calling **b->sayHello()** would have resulted in **Derived::sayHello()** being called, demonstrating dynamic dispatch based on the actual object type at runtime.

Example 13: Dynamic Binding

Objective: Demonstrate dynamic binding with virtual functions.

```
#include <iostream>
class Base {
public:
    virtual void sayHello() const { std::cout << "Hello from Base\n"; }
};

class Derived: public Base {
public:
    void sayHello() const override { std::cout << "Hello from Derived\n"; }
};

int main() {
    Base* b = new Derived();
    b->sayHello(); // Calls Derived::sayHello due to dynamic binding
    delete b;
    return 0;
}
```

Explanation

This C++ code exemplifies the use of polymorphism, specifically runtime polymorphism or dynamic binding, through the use of virtual functions and inheritance. Here's a breakdown of how the code operates:

Code Components

- **Base Class**:
- Contains a public virtual function named **sayHello** that prints **"Hello from Base\n"** to the standard output. The use of the **virtual** keyword here is crucial; it indicates that the function can be overridden by derived classes and that the version of the function to be called will be determined at runtime based on the actual type of the object that the **Base** pointer refers to.
- **Derived Class**:
- Inherits from the **Base** class and overrides the **sayHello** method. The **override** keyword is used to explicitly state that this function is intended to override a virtual function from the base class. This version of **sayHello** prints **"Hello from Derived\n"**.
- **Main Function**:

- A pointer of type **Base*** named **b** is dynamically allocated and initialized to point to an instance of **Derived**. This demonstrates polymorphism; although **b** is a pointer to **Base**, it actually points to an instance of **Derived**.
- **b->sayHello();** is called. Due to dynamic binding (enabled by the **virtual** function mechanism), the call is resolved to **Derived::sayHello**, and **"Hello from Derived\n"** is printed.
- The dynamically allocated **Derived** object is then deleted to prevent memory leaks.

Key Concepts Illustrated

- **Polymorphism**: The ability of a base class pointer (or reference) to refer to objects of derived classes and to call overridden functions based on the actual type of the object, not the type of the pointer.
- **Dynamic Binding**: The process of determining which overridden function to call at runtime. Dynamic binding allows C++ programs to use pointers or references to base class types to invoke methods on derived class objects, choosing the correct method based on the actual object's type.
- **Virtual Functions**: Declaring a member function as **virtual** in the base class tells the compiler to support dynamic binding for that function. It means the function is expected to be overridden in derived classes, and the version of the function that gets executed will be determined at runtime.
- **Memory Management**: The program dynamically allocates memory for a **Derived** object but uses a **Base** pointer to manage it. It's important to delete dynamically allocated objects to free the memory when they are no longer needed. Notably, because **sayHello** is a virtual function, **Base** should also have a virtual destructor to ensure the correct destructor is called when an object is deleted through a base class pointer, preventing resource leaks. However, adding a virtual destructor is not shown in this snippet but is a best practice for such scenarios.

Conclusion

This code snippet clearly demonstrates the principles of runtime polymorphism in C++, showing how virtual functions enable dynamic method dispatch. It allows derived class methods to be called through base class pointers or references, making it a powerful feature for designing flexible and reusable code in object-oriented programming.

Example 14: Overloading vs. Overriding

Objective: Show the difference between method overloading and overriding.

```
#include <iostream>
class Base {
public:
    virtual void greet() { std::cout << "Hello from Base\n"; }
    void greet(std::string name) { std::cout << "Hello, " << name << " from 
Base\n"; }
};
```

```
class Derived: public Base {
public:
    void greet() override { std::cout << "Hello from Derived\n"; } // Overrid-
ing
};

int main() {
    Derived d;
    d.greet(); // Calls overridden greet()
    d.greet("World"); // Calls Base::greet(std::string), demonstrating over-
loading
    return 0;
}
```

Explanation

This C++ code snippet illustrates several key object-oriented programming concepts: inheritance, method overriding, and method overloading within the context of a class hierarchy. Here's a detailed explanation of how it works:

Code Breakdown

- **Base Class**:
- The **Base** class defines two versions of the **greet** method. The first version is a parameterless method marked as **virtual**, which allows it to be overridden by derived classes. The second version is an overloaded method that takes a **std::string** parameter named **name** and is not marked as **virtual**, hence it cannot be overridden but can be overloaded.
- **Derived Class**:
- Inherits publicly from the **Base** class, meaning all public and protected members of **Base** are accessible in **Derived**.
- Overrides the **greet** method from the **Base** class (the parameterless one) to provide its own implementation. This is indicated by the **override** keyword, which enforces that the method is overriding a **virtual** method from the base class.
- Does not redefine or overload the **greet(std::string name)** method, so the version from the **Base** class is inherited as-is.

main Function

- Creates an instance of the **Derived** class named **d**.
- Calls **d.greet()**, which invokes the overridden version in the **Derived** class, outputting **"Hello from Derived\n"**.
- Calls **d.greet("World")**, which, since there's no overload for **greet** that takes a string in the **Derived** class, falls back to the **Base** class's version of **greet(std::string name)**, outputting **"Hello, World from Base\n"**.

Key Concepts Illustrated

- **Inheritance**: The **Derived** class inherits methods and properties from the **Base** class, demonstrating a fundamental principle of object-oriented programming.
- **Overriding (Polymorphism)**: By using the **override** keyword, the **Derived** class provides its own implementation for a method defined in the **Base** class (**greet()**), showcasing runtime polymorphism. This is where the method to execute is determined at runtime based on the object's actual type, not the type of the reference or pointer that points to the object.
- **Overloading**: The **Base** class demonstrates method overloading, where two methods share the same name (**greet**) but have different parameters (one takes no parameters, and the other takes a **std::string**). Overloading is resolved at compile time based on the method signature used in the call.

Output:

The program produces the following output:

C++

Hello from Derived

Hello, World from Base

This output reflects the dynamic dispatch mechanism of C++ (selecting the overridden **greet** method in **Derived**) and the static linkage for overloaded methods (falling back to the **Base** class's **greet(std::string name)** method since it is not overridden or overloaded in **Derived**).

Example 15: Using #include for Base Class Inclusion

Objective: Understand how to include a base class header in a derived class header.

```
// Base.h
#ifndef BASE_H
#define BASE_H
class Base {
public:
    void show() { /* Implementation */ }
};
#endif

// Derived.h
#include "Base.h"
class Derived: public Base {
    // Derived class implementation
};

// Note: This example is split across files to illustrate the concept.
```

Explanation

The provided code snippet demonstrates the use of header files to define class hierarchies in C++. It's split into two parts, representing two separate header files: **Base.h** and **Derived.h**. This example illustrates how to establish an inheritance relationship between two classes across different files, a common practice in C++ development for organizing code and managing dependencies.

Base.h

The **Base.h** file declares and defines a class named **Base**. It starts with an include guard, which prevents multiple inclusions of the header file, a situation that could lead to compilation errors. The include guard consists of three parts:

- **#ifndef BASE_H** checks if **BASE_H** has not been defined yet.
- **#define BASE_H** defines **BASE_H** if it hasn't been defined already.
- **#endif** ends the include guard.

The **Base** class has a public member function **show()**, which is intended to be implemented within the class definition. The use of **/* Implementation */** suggests that the actual code is omitted for brevity.

Derived.h

The **Derived.h** file shows how to include the **Base.h** header to utilize the **Base** class. By including **Base.h**, the **Derived** class can inherit from **Base**, allowing it to reuse the **Base** class's interface and implementation.

- The **#include "Base.h"** directive includes the contents of **Base.h** at this point in **Derived.h**. This makes the definition of **Base** available to **Derived**, enabling inheritance.
- The **Derived** class is then declared to publicly inherit from **Base** using the syntax **class Derived: public Base**. This means all public and protected members of **Base** are accessible to **Derived** and any instances of **Derived**.

Note on Compilation

- When compiling a project that uses these header files, both **Base.h** and **Derived.h** would need to be included in the respective source files (***.cpp**) where instances of **Base** or **Derived** are created or used.
- It's essential that **Base.h** is included before **Derived.h** wherever **Derived** objects are used or declared, directly or indirectly. The direct inclusion in **Derived.h** ensures this order is maintained automatically for **Derived** objects.

Practical Usage

Splitting class definitions across header files in this manner promotes modularity, reusability, and maintainability in larger projects. It allows classes to be developed, tested, and modified independently, as long as their interfaces remain consistent. This approach is particularly useful in large projects, libraries, and frameworks where clear separation of concerns and dependencies is crucial.

SUMMARY

Chapter 8 delves into the intricate world of Object-Oriented Programming (OOP), focusing primarily on inheritance and polymorphism—two fundamental pillars that underpin the OOP paradigm. The chapter kicks off with an introduction to the advantages of OOP and the concept of class hierarchy, laying the groundwork for a deeper exploration of how classes relate to one another through inheritance. It thoroughly discusses the roles and implications of access control specifiers (private, protected, and public) and how they govern the accessibility of class members. The narrative progresses to dissect the dynamics between base and derived classes, emphasizing the critical roles of constructors and destructors within inherited class structures. Different forms of inheritance—public, protected, and private—are meticulously analyzed to understand their distinct impacts on code structure and accessibility.

Polymorphism is another cornerstone concept elaborated upon in this chapter, distinguishing between static and dynamic binding and elucidating their roles in enabling flexible and dynamic code behavior. The chapter further explores the complex relationships among objects in an inheritance hierarchy, permissible assignments between base-class and derived-class objects and pointers, thereby enhancing the reader's understanding of object compatibility and assignment semantics in OOP.

Advanced topics such as overloading, virtual functions, pure virtual functions, abstract classes, and virtual destructors are also covered. These concepts are pivotal for designing flexible, reusable, and maintainable code in software development. The chapter not only demystifies these advanced OOP principles but also reinforces learning through exercises, fill-in-the-blank statements, and multiple-choice questions, ensuring a comprehensive grasp of inheritance and polymorphism in object-oriented design and programming.

Fill in the Blanks in Each of the Following Statements

a. ______________________ is a type of software reuse where new classes take the information and actions of older classes and add new features to them.
b. The ______________________ members of a base class can only be viewed in the specification of the base class or in the descriptions of derived classes.
c. An object of a derived class may also be regarded as an object of its parent class in a (n) _______________ relationship.
d. When class has one or more objects of the other classes, the relationship called ______________________.
e. Everywhere the program has a reference to an object of a base class or an object of one of its derived classes, the program can reach the ________________ members of that base class.
f. Members of a basic class with protected access enjoy security on par with those with public and ________________ access.
g. C++ supports ________________, which means the derived class can inherit from many base classes.

h. The base class's _______________ is called implicitly or explicitly when an object of a derived class is created in order to perform the necessary initialization of the base-class data members in the derived-class object.
i. The private members of the base class become _______________ members of the derived class, and the base class's public members become _______________ members, when a class derives from a base class with public inheritance.
j. When a class is derived from a base class with protected inheritance, the base class's protected members become _______________ members of the derived class, and its public members become _______________ members..
k. Treating a base-class object as a(n) ________ can cause errors.
l. A class is a(n) _________ class if it has at least one pure virtual function.
m. Classes that may be used to create objects are known as _______ classes.
n. ________ entails calling virtual methods on base-class and derived-class objects using a base-class pointer or reference..
o. Overridable functions are declared using keyword _________ .

It is known as ________ to cast a base-class pointer to a derived-class pointer.
Indicate the truth or falsity of each of the following statements. If untrue, why not?

a. Derived classes do not receive base-class operators.
b. Inheritance is used to create a has-a connection.
c. The Brakes and SteeringWheel classes have an is-a connection with the Vehicle class.
d. Transfer promotes the usage of tested, top-notch software.
e. The destructors are triggered in the opposite sequence of the constructors when an object of a derived class is killed.
f. Pure virtual functions must be defined for each virtual function in an abstract parent class..
g. Referring to a derived-class object with a base-class handle is dangerous.
h. A class is made abstract by declaring that class virtual.
i. In order for a derived class to be considered a concrete class, it must implement any pure virtual functions that the parent class specifies.

Multiple Choice

1. Select the wrong statement.
   a. The attributes and actions of a derived class can differ from those of its parent class.
   b. Other derived classes may use a derived class as their basis.
   c. There may be several parent classes for some descendant classes.
   d. Typically, base classes are more specialized than derived classes.
2. Choose the alternative that doesn't include C++'s version of inheritance?
   a. public.
   b. private.
   c. static.
   d. protected.

3. Is-a relationship indicate.
   a. Composition.
   b. Inheritance.
   c. Information Hiding.
   d. A friend.
4. Which of the following most likely serves as a foundation class for the other three?
   a. automobile.
   b. convertible.
   c. miniVan.
   d. sedan.
5. Which of the following is not an excellent illustration of a hierarchy that is apt to be represented by inheritance?
   a. Airplanes.
   b. Geometric shapes.
   c. Animals.
   d. Prime numbers.
6. Writing the following would designate class subClass as a secretly derivate class of superClass:
   a. class subclass: private superClass
   b. class subclass:: private superClass
   c. class subclass < private superClass >
   d. class subclass inherits private superclass
7. The access variables are listed below in order of least to most restriction:
   a. protected, private, public
   b. private, protected, public
   c. private, public, protected
   d. protected, public, private
8. Considering that the class BasePlus-CommissionEmployee derives from class Point, the constructor specification for the class begins with the following,

```
BasePlusMarketingEmployee::BasePlusMarketingEmployee(string first,
string last, string ssn, double sales, double rate, double salary)
: MarketingStudent(first, last, ssn, sales, rate)
```

The second line:
   a. Invokes the MarketingStudent constructor with arguments.
   b. Causes a compiler error.
   c. is not required since the MarketingStudent constructor is invoked immediately.
   d. Indicates inheritance.
9. Which of the following is not a drawback of copying code from one class into another class using the "copy-and-paste" method?
   a. Mistakes have a tendency to propagate..
   b. It is time consuming.
   c. Code upkeep becomes a nightmare as a result of the system being forced to maintain numerous physical versions of the code.

   d. The "copy-and-paste" method has the drawbacks listed above.

10. When should base class members be declared protected?
    a. When all customers ought to have access to these individuals.
    b. when only the member methods of this parent class use these members.
    c. When other customers other than derived classes (and pals) should not have access to these members.
    d. Never use the restricted access that was provided.
11. The _________ constructor initializes the _________ members when an instance of a derived class is created.
    a. Base class, base class.
    b. Derived class, base class.
    c. Base class, derived class.
    d. Derived class, public.
12. Let's say class A descends from basic class B. When an object of type A is created and then destroyed, what sequence will their constructors and destructors be called?
    a. A constructor, B constructor, B destructor, A destructor.
    b. B constructor, A constructor, B destructor, A destructor.
    c. B constructor, A constructor, A destructor, B destructor.
    d. A constructor, B constructor, A destructor, B destructor.
13. Which inheritance models involve is-a connections?
    a. All inheritance ties are is-a links.
    b. Only public and private.
    c. Only public and protected.
    d. Only public.
14. When a class derives from a protected base class, the public members of the base class become _______ and the protected members of the base class become _________, correct?
    a. protected, private
    b. public, private
    c. protected, protected
    d. public, protected
15. Implement Polymorphism by:
    a. Member functions.
    b. virtual functions and dynamic binding.
    c. inline functions.
    d. Non-virtual functions.
16. Which of the following is not a member function that Fish, Frog, and Bird should take from parent class Animal and then provide their own definitions for, so that the function call can be executed polymorphically?
    a. eat
    b. sleep
    c. move
    d. flapWings

17. HourlyWorker is a derived class from Employee and has a non-virtual print method that has been modified. Will the result of the two print function calls be the same given the ensuing statements?

```
HourlyWorker h;
Employee *ePtr = &h;
ePtr->print();
ePtr->Employee::print();
```

  a. Yes.
  b. Yes, if print is a static function.
  c. No.
  d. depends on the print function implementation.

18. Which of the following assignments would be a compilation error?
  a. giving a base-class reference the location of a base-class object.
  b. giving a derived-class reference the base-class object's location.
  c. giving a base-class reference the location of an object of a derived class.
  d. giving a derived-class reference the location of an object of that class.

19. When all of the objects in a class that is descended from a single parent class must draw themselves, the draw() method is most likely to be defined.:
  a. private
  b. virtual
  c. protected
  d. friend

20. virtual functions must:
  a. Be overridden in every derived class.
  b. every descendant class to contain a virtual declaration.
  c. be a basic class virtual declaration.
  d. have a consistent execution across all related classes..

21. In relation to virtual functions, which of the following assertions is untrue?
  a. They enable the software to choose the appropriate version during execution.
  b. Depending on the names on which the methods are called, they can use either static or dynamic binding.
  c. Up the inheritance chain, they do not stay imaginary.
  d. You can dial them by using the dot operator.

22. The line:

```
virtual double earnings() const = 0;
appears in a class definition. You cannot deduce that:
```

  a. This function will be overridden by all classes that immediately descend from this class.
  b. It is a vague class, this one.
  c. This class's tangible descendants will all have an earnings method.
  d. Probably, other classes will use this class as their parent class.

23. Abstract classes:
    a. only one clean virtual function at most.
    b. Depending on the rights that have been established, objects may be instantiated from them.
    c. cannot have derived classes that are generic,
    d. defined,but the coder has no intention of creating any items from them.
24. A virtual function and a clean virtual function are primarily distinguished by:
    a. The return type.
    b. The member access specifier.
    c. that there cannot be an instance of a pure virtual function.
    d. The location in the class.
25. Which of the following is not allowed?
    a. Objects of abstract classes.
    b. A single abstract class that contains numerous pure virtual methods.
    c. pointers to abstract classes.
    d. Arrays of pointers to abstract classes.
26. The following class declaration cannot be used as an abstract class due to what error?

```
class Shapes
{
public:
virtual double print() const;
double area() const { return length * breadth; }
private:
double length;
double breadth;
};
```

    a. There are no pure virtual functions.
    b. There is a non-virtual function.
    c. A public function has access to private variables.
    d. No error, it is good abstract class.
27. virtual destructors are ought to be used in which scenario:
    a. In the parent class, the constructor is virtual.
    b. A base-class reference to a derived-class entity is deleted..
    c. delete is used on a derived-class object.
    d. A virtual constructor can be found in either the parent class or child class..

EXERCISES

1- Case Study:

```
Base Class:
class Creature
```

```
{
public:
Creature(string newName);
void setName(string name);
string getName();
void setHealth(short health);
short getHealth();
void setDamage(short damage);
short getDamage();
void attack();
protected:
string creatureName;
short creatureHealth;
short creatureDamage;
};
Derived Class:
class Monster
{
public:
Monster(string name);
private:
static const short claws = 2;
};
```

CREATURE CLASS INSTRUCTIONS

Constructor

1. Write default or oveloaded cnstructor and inside the constructor body, ctreate int damage randrom number between 1 and 5.
2. Call setName function to Initialize the creature's name.
3. Call sethealth funation to set the health to 100.
4. Call setDamage function to initialize the damage by passing the generated random damage as its argument.

Setter and Getter Functions

1. For these functions, use appropriate code for them. The functions should have valid return types, class names and parameters

Attack Function

Print the following information:

1- Object's name.
2- Object's strength.
3- Use proper messages for the overall losses.

Monster Class Instructions

Constructor:

1. Initialize the Monster class member variable by Calling the base class constructor.
2. Declear two variables named damage and totalDamage in the constructor body.
3. Set the Monster's actual damage variable.
4. Use totalDamage to store the claws's damage plus the actual damage
5. Use the setDamage and pass the totalDamage as its argument.
6. Print the total damage and the actual damage.

Main

1. Create an object for the Creature class.
2. using Creature object, call the attack function.
3. Create an object for the Monster class.
4. Using Monster object, call the attack function.

2- Write a C++ program that demonstrates simple inheritance by creating a base class Shape with a method draw() and a derived class Circle that overrides the draw() method.
3- Create a C++ program that illustrates the difference between public, protected, and private inheritance by creating a base class Vehicle and three derived classes each using a different type of inheritance.
4- Implement runtime polymorphism in C++ using a base class pointer to call a virtual function in both the base class and a derived class.
5- Design a base class Animal with a virtual function speak() and derived classes Dog and Cat that override speak(). Demonstrate polymorphic behavior by invoking speak() on a collection of Animal pointers that point to Dog and Cat objects.
6- Write a C++ program with a function clone() in a base class Cloneable as a pure virtual function. Derive classes CloneableInt and CloneableString that implement clone(). The clone() method should return a copy of the object.
7- Create an abstract class Writer with a pure virtual function write(std::string message). Derive classes Printer and Screen to implement write(std::string message) method. Instantiate Printer and Screen objects and call write() on them.
8- Explain, with a C++ example, how virtual destructors are used and why they are important in a class hierarchy involving base and derived classes.
9- Demonstrate function overriding in C++ by creating a base class with a virtual function perform() and a derived class that overrides perform(). Call perform() on an object of the derived class through a base class pointer.
10- Illustrate the concept of "slicing" in C++ and how it can be avoided when dealing with base and derived class objects.

11- Implement an interface in C++ using an abstract class with only pure virtual functions. Create two classes that implement this interface and demonstrate their usage.
12- Show how access specifiers affect inheritance in C++ by creating a base class with public, protected, and private members and deriving a class from it. Try accessing these members from the derived class.
13- Using C++, create a base class File with a virtual function open(). Derive two classes TextFile and BinaryFile from File, each providing their own implementation of open().
14- Write a C++ program that uses dynamic casting to safely convert a base class pointer to a derived class pointer in a class hierarchy with virtual functions.
15- Design a class hierarchy in C++ representing different types of employees in a company. Use virtual functions to calculate the salary of each type of employee.
16- Explain with a C++ example how multiple inheritance can be implemented and discuss potential issues that might arise from using multiple inheritance.
17- Create a C++ program that demonstrates the use of override and final specifiers in a class hierarchy involving virtual function overriding.
18- Illustrate, with a C++ example, the difference between static and dynamic binding using virtual and non-virtual functions.
19- Develop a C++ program that showcases how to implement and use a pure virtual destructor in an abstract base class.
20- Write a C++ program that demonstrates object slicing and how to prevent it using pointers or references to base class objects.

Chapter 9
Advanced C++ Programming Techniques

ABSTRACT

This chapter delves into the sophisticated facets of modern C++ programming, aiming to equip developers with the knowledge and skills necessary to leverage advanced features and best practices in their software development endeavors. It begins with an introduction to the significance of modern C++ practices and an overview of the advanced features that have been introduced in recent versions of the C++ standard. In summary, this chapter serves as a comprehensive guide to advanced C++ programming techniques, from theoretical concepts to practical applications, offering valuable insights into modern C++ practices and how they can be applied to develop high-quality, efficient, and scalable applications.

CHAPTER SCOPE

This chapter aims to provide an in-depth exploration of advanced C++ programming techniques, focusing on both the theoretical underpinnings and practical applications of modern C++ features. It is designed to bridge the gap between foundational C++ programming knowledge and the proficient use of C++'s advanced capabilities in complex software development projects. The scope of this chapter encompasses a comprehensive examination of contemporary C++ features, integration with key frameworks and libraries, and the demonstration of these concepts through practical case studies.

Theoretical Foundations and Language Features

The chapter begins by laying the groundwork with an overview of the advanced features introduced in recent C++ standards, emphasizing the importance of adopting modern C++ practices for efficient software development. It then delves into specific language features that are pivotal to mastering advanced C++, including:

- **Lambda Expressions**: Detailed coverage of syntax, uses, and the benefits of lambda expressions, facilitating concise and functional-style programming.

DOI: 10.4018/979-8-3693-2007-5.ch009

- **Move Semantics**: An exploration of move semantics to optimize resource management and performance, including practical guidance on implementing move constructors and move assignment operators.
- **Smart Pointers**: Comprehensive discussion on types of smart pointers (unique_ptr, shared_ptr, weak_ptr), their role in automatic resource management, and best practices for their use.
- **Type Deduction**: Insight into the use of auto and decltype for simplifying code and improving readability and maintainability.
- **Constexpr and Compile-Time Functions**: How to leverage constexpr for performing computations at compile time, reducing runtime overhead.
- **Variadic Templates and Template Metaprogramming**: Techniques for creating flexible functions and classes, and an introduction to the power of compile-time computations and type manipulations with template metaprogramming.

Integration With Frameworks and Libraries

Recognizing the importance of frameworks and libraries in extending the capabilities of C++ for application development, this chapter provides an overview of how C++ integrates with several key technologies, including:

- **GUI Development with Qt**: Basics of creating user interfaces and applications with Qt.
- **Game Development with SDL**: Introduction to using SDL for game development, focusing on creating graphics, handling user input, and managing audio.
- **Network Programming with Boost.Asio**: Techniques for asynchronous network programming using Boost.Asio.
- **Numerical Computations with Eigen**: Utilizing Eigen for efficient matrix operations and linear algebra computations.
- **Web Development with CPPRESTSDK**: Building web services and clients using CPPRESTSDK.

Practical Applications and Case Studies

To illustrate the real-world applicability of the discussed advanced C++ features, this chapter includes several case studies and examples of practical applications, such as:

- **Cross-Platform GUI Application Development**: Demonstrating the design and development of a cross-platform GUI application using Qt.
- **Optimizing a 2D Game Engine**: Strategies for developing and optimizing a game engine with SDL.
- **High-Performance Web Server Creation**: Building a concurrent web server using Boost.Asio for high-performance networking.
- **Engineering Applications with Eigen**: Implementing efficient solutions for engineering problems using matrix operations and linear algebra with Eigen.
- **RESTful Web Services Design and Deployment**: Designing and deploying scalable and efficient web services with CPPRESTSDK.

9.1 INTRODUCTION

In the evolving landscape of software development, C++ continues to stand as a cornerstone language, renowned for its power, versatility, and performance. As we delve into the advanced territories of C++, the language unveils a plethora of features and practices that, when adeptly harnessed, can elevate the quality, efficiency, and scalability of software projects to unprecedented levels. Chapter 9, "Advanced C++ Programming Techniques," is meticulously crafted to guide experienced developers through the intricate nuances of modern C++ programming, shedding light on the language's latest features, best practices, and their practical applications in real-world scenarios.

This chapter embarks on a journey through the modern features of C++, starting with an insightful discussion on the significance of adopting contemporary C++ practices in software development. The introduction sets the stage for an in-depth exploration of advanced C++ features that have been introduced or standardized in recent C++ updates, emphasizing their critical role in modern software development.

Section 1 of the chapter is dedicated to unraveling modern C++ language features, beginning with the expressive power of lambda expressions. It guides the reader through the nuances of move semantics, a pivotal feature for optimizing resource management, and navigates the complexities of smart pointers, which are instrumental in automatic resource management. The section further demystifies type deduction, delves into the realm of compile-time functions with constexpr, introduces the flexibility offered by variadic templates, and culminates with a deep dive into the art of template metaprogramming.

Transitioning from language features to practical applications, Section 2 explores the integration of C++ with various frameworks and libraries, showcasing the language's adaptability across different domains of software development. From GUI development with Qt and game development with SDL to network programming with Boost.Asio, numerical computations with Eigen, and web development with CPPRESTSDK, this section illustrates how C++ remains at the forefront of innovation, enabling developers to build cutting-edge applications.

In Section 3, the chapter brings theory into practice through a series of case studies and practical applications. Each case study, from building a cross-platform GUI application to deploying RESTful web services, serves as a testament to the power and flexibility of advanced C++ programming techniques. These real-world examples not only provide a practical perspective on the application of advanced C++ features but also offer insights into overcoming development challenges and adopting best practices for successful project outcomes.

As we navigate through Chapter 9, our objective is to arm developers with the knowledge and skills necessary to leverage advanced C++ features effectively, thereby enhancing the quality, performance, and maintainability of their software projects. Whether you are looking to deepen your understanding of modern C++ features, integrate C++ with various development frameworks, or explore practical applications of the language, this chapter serves as your comprehensive guide to mastering advanced C++ programming techniques.

9.1 Section 1: Modern C++ Language Features

9.1.1 Lambda Expressions: Syntax, Uses, and Benefits

Lambda expressions, introduced in C++11, are a succinct way to write anonymous functions within C++ code. They enable developers to write in-line functions that can capture variables from their surrounding scope, making them highly useful for short snippets of code for callbacks, sorting, or any scenario where a quick, one-off function is needed.

Lambda expressions are one of the most powerful features introduced in modern C++. They allow you to write anonymous functions directly where they are needed, often as arguments to other functions or for defining custom, one-off operations without the overhead of formally defining a function.

The syntax of a lambda expression is composed of several parts:

- **Capture Clause**: Defined by square brackets [], it specifies which variables from the surrounding scope are available inside the lambda, and how (by value or by reference).
- **Parameter List**: Enclosed in parentheses (), it defines the parameters passed to the lambda, similar to parameters in regular functions.
- **Mutable Specification**: Optionally, the **mutable** keyword allows the lambda to modify the values of the captured variables.
- **Return Type**: Specified using the arrow **->** followed by a type, it defines the return type of the lambda. It is optional if the return type can be unambiguously inferred by the compiler.
- **Function Body**: Enclosed in braces **{}**, it contains the code to be executed when the lambda is invoked.

Lambdas are particularly useful in algorithms, event handling, and situations requiring small, simple functions. They improve code readability and maintainability by keeping related logic close together.

Examples

Example 1: Capturing local variables by value.

```
#include <iostream>
int main() {
    int x = 10;
    auto print = [x]() { std::cout << x << std::endl; };
    print();  // Outputs: 10
    return 0;
}
```

This lambda expression captures the local variable **x** by value and prints it. The capture by value ensures that the lambda uses a copy of **x** at the point where the lambda was defined.

Example 2: Using lambdas with the Standard Library's **std::sort**.

```
#include <vector>
#include <algorithm>
#include <iostream>

int main() {
    std::vector<int> v = { 4, 1, 3, 5, 2 };
    std::sort(v.begin(), v.end(), [](int a, int b) { return a < b; });
    for (auto i: v) std::cout << i << ' ';  // Outputs: 1 2 3 4 5
```

```
    return 0;
}
```

A lambda is used to define the sorting criterion directly inline, making the code concise and easy to understand.

Practice

Practice 1: Write a lambda expression that captures a local **int** variable by reference and increments it.

Practice 2: Create a lambda expression to count how many strings in a **std::vector<std::string>** have more than 5 characters.

Solution

Solution to Practice 1:

```
int x = 0;
auto increment = [&x]() { ++x; };
increment();
// x is now 1
```

This lambda captures the variable **x** by reference and increments it. The change is reflected in the original variable **x** because it is captured by reference.

Solution to Practice 2

```
std::vector<std::string> words = { "hello", "world", "C++", "lambda", "expres-
sions" };
auto count = std::count_if(words.begin(), words.end(), [](const std::string&
word) {
    return word.length() > 5;
    });
// count will hold the number of strings with more than 5 characters
```

This lambda is used with **std::count_if** to count strings longer than 5 characters in a vector.

9.1.2 Understanding and Applying Move Semantics

Move semantics, introduced in C++11, allow developers to efficiently transfer resources from temporary objects to others, reducing unnecessary copying. This is achieved through r-value references and the **std::move** function, enhancing performance, especially for classes managing dynamic memory.

Move semantics are a fundamental optimization technique in modern C++. Before C++11, objects were copied even if they were temporary and would be destroyed shortly after. Move semantics allow these temporary objects to “transfer” their resources to another object, avoiding costly deep copies.

The key components of move semantics are:

- **R-value References (&&)**: Unlike l-value references, which refer to a persistent object, r-value references bind to temporary objects (r-values). They allow functions to detect whether their arguments are temporaries.
- **Move Constructor and Move Assignment Operator**: These special member functions take r-value references as parameters and "move" the resources from the source to the destination, leaving the source in a valid but unspecified state.

Applying move semantics can dramatically improve performance for classes that manage their own memory, like containers or strings, by eliminating unnecessary copies.

Examples

Example 1: Basic illustration of move semantics.

```
#include <iostream>
#include <vector>

class MovableClass {
public:
    std::vector<int> data;

    // Move constructor
    MovableClass(MovableClass&& other) noexcept: data(std::move(other.data)) {
        std::cout << "Moved!\n";
    }

    // Constructor
    MovableClass(int n): data(n) { }
};

int main() {
    MovableClass a(10); // Regular constructor
    MovableClass b(std::move(a)); // Move constructor is called

    return 0;
}
```

This example demonstrates a move constructor in action. When **b** is initialized with **std::move(a)**, the data ownership is transferred from **a** to **b**, avoiding copying the vector.

Example 2: Using **std::move** with the Standard Library.

```
#include <string>
#include <iostream>
int main() {
std::string str1 = "Hello, World!";
std::string str2 = std::move(str1); // Move str1 into str2
```

```
std::cout << "str1: " << str1 << "\n"; // str1 is in a moved-from state
std::cout << "str2: " << str2 << "\n"; // str2 contains the "Hello, World!"
data
return 0;
}
```

After the move, **str1** is empty because its contents have been transferred to **str2**, demonstrating the efficiency of move semantics.

Practice

Practice 1: Implement a move assignment operator for a class that manages a dynamic array.

Practice 2: Use **std::move** to transfer the ownership of a **std::unique_ptr** from one variable to another.

Solution

Solution to Practice 1:

```
class ArrayWrapper {
private:
    int* data;
    size_t size;

public:
    // Constructor
    ArrayWrapper(size_t size): size(size), data(new int[size]) {}

    // Move assignment operator
    ArrayWrapper& operator=(ArrayWrapper&& other) noexcept {
        if (this != &other) {
            delete[] data; // Free existing resource
            data = other.data; // Transfer ownership
            size = other.size;
            other.data = nullptr; // Leave other in a valid state
            other.size = 0;
        }
        return *this;
    }

    // Destructor
    ~ArrayWrapper() {
        delete[] data;
    }
};
```

Solution to Practice 2:

```
#include <memory>
#include <iostream>

int main() {
    std::unique_ptr<int> ptr1 = std::make_unique<int>(10);
    std::unique_ptr<int> ptr2 = std::move(ptr1); // Transfer ownership

    std::cout << "ptr1: " << (ptr1 ? "Not null": "null") << "\n";
    std::cout << "ptr2: " << *ptr2 << "\n";

    return 0;
}
```

After the move, **ptr1** becomes **null** because its ownership of the heap-allocated integer is transferred to **ptr2**.

9.1.3 Smart Pointers for Automatic Resource Management

C++ is a powerful programming language that offers a wide range of features, including direct memory management. While this provides great flexibility, it also introduces the risk of memory leaks and dangling pointers if resources are not properly managed. To address these challenges, C++ introduced smart pointers, which are wrapper classes that automatically manage the lifetime of dynamically allocated objects.

Smart pointers are an integral part of modern C++ programming, as they provide a safer and more efficient way to handle resources. They ensure that objects are properly deleted when they are no longer needed, thus preventing memory leaks. Additionally, smart pointers can help to avoid common pitfalls such as double deletion and invalid pointer access.

There are three main types of smart pointers in the C++ Standard Library:

1. **std::unique_ptr**: This is a lightweight smart pointer that owns a dynamically allocated object exclusively. It ensures that there is only one **unique_ptr** pointing to any given object at any time. When the **unique_ptr** goes out of scope, it automatically deletes the object it owns.
2. **std::shared_ptr**: This smart pointer allows multiple **shared_ptr** instances to own the same object. It uses reference counting to keep track of how many **shared_ptr** instances are pointing to the same object. When the last **shared_ptr** pointing to an object is destroyed or reset, the object is automatically deleted.
3. **std::weak_ptr**: This is used in conjunction with **shared_ptr** to prevent circular references that can lead to memory leaks. A **weak_ptr** does not contribute to the reference count of a **shared_ptr**, but it can be used to check whether the object it points to is still alive.

In this guide, we will explore the concepts and usage of smart pointers in C++, providing examples and best practices to help you effectively manage resources in your C++ applications.

9.1.3.1 Unique_ptr, Shared_ptr, and Weak_ptr

unique_ptr, **shared_ptr**, and **weak_ptr** are smart pointers provided by the C++ Standard Library to manage dynamic memory with automatic storage duration. These smart pointers help prevent memory leaks by ensuring proper memory deallocation.

Detailed Explanation

Smart pointers are a key component of modern C++ for safe memory management. They encapsulate raw pointers, automatically managing the lifetime of the object being pointed to.

- **unique_ptr**: Owns and manages another object through a raw pointer and disposes of that object when the **unique_ptr** goes out of scope. It supports only one owner of the underlying pointer, making it lightweight but strict in ownership semantics.
- **shared_ptr**: Allows multiple **shared_ptr** instances to share ownership of a single object. The object is destroyed when the last surviving **shared_ptr** owning it is destroyed or reset. It uses reference counting to keep track of how many **shared_ptr** instances own the object.
- **weak_ptr**: Complements **shared_ptr** by holding a non-owning reference to an object that is managed by **shared_ptr**. It is used to break circular references between **shared_ptr** instances.

Using these smart pointers helps prevent memory leaks and dangling pointers, making resource management safer and more intuitive.

Examples

Example 1: Using **unique_ptr** for exclusive ownership.

```
#include <memory>
#include <iostream>

class MyClass {
public:
    MyClass() { std::cout << "MyClass created\n"; }
    ~MyClass() { std::cout << "MyClass destroyed\n"; }
};

int main() {
    std::unique_ptr<MyClass> myUniquePtr = std::make_unique<MyClass>();
    // Output: MyClass created
    // No need to manually delete; destructor called automatically when out of
scope
    return 0;
    // Output: MyClass destroyed
}
```

Example 2: Sharing an object between **shared_ptr**s.

```
#include <memory>
#include <iostream>

int main() {
    std::shared_ptr<int> shared1 = std::make_shared<int>(100);
    std::shared_ptr<int> shared2 = shared1; // Both share ownership of the in-
teger

    std::cout << "shared1: " << *shared1 << "\n";
    std::cout << "shared2: " << *shared2 << "\n";
    std::cout << "use_count: " << shared1.use_count() << "\n"; // Outputs 2
    return 0;
}
```

Example 3: Using **weak_ptr** to access data without owning it.

```
#include <memory>
#include <iostream>

int main() {
    std::shared_ptr<int> shared = std::make_shared<int>(100);
    std::weak_ptr<int> weak = shared;

    std::cout << "shared use_count: " << shared.use_count() << "\n"; // Out-
puts 1
    if (auto tmp = weak.lock()) { // Creates a shared_ptr if the object exists
        std::cout << "Value: " << *tmp << "\n"; // Safe to access
    }
    else {
        std::cout << "The object has been destroyed.\n";
    }
    return 0;
}
```

Practice

Practice 1: Write a function that takes a **unique_ptr<int>** as an argument and prints its value.

Practice 2: Create two **shared_ptr<int>** instances sharing the same underlying integer, modify the integer using one instance, and print its value using the other.

Solution

Solution to Practice 1:

```
#include <memory>
#include <iostream>
void printUniquePtrValue(const std::unique_ptr<int>& ptr) {
```

```
    if (ptr) {
        std::cout << *ptr << "\n";
    }
    else {
        std::cout << "Pointer is null.\n";
    }
}

int main() {
    std::unique_ptr<int> ptr = std::make_unique<int>(10);
    printUniquePtrValue(ptr);
    // Output: 10
    return 0;
}
```

Solution to Practice 2:

```
#include <memory>
#include <iostream>

int main() {
    std::shared_ptr<int> shared1 = std::make_shared<int>(20);
    std::shared_ptr<int> shared2 = shared1; // Share ownership

    *shared1 = 30; // Modify through shared1
    std::cout << "shared2 points to: " << *shared2 << "\n"; // Access through
shared2
    // Output: shared2 points to: 30
    return 0;
}
```

9.1.3.2 Smart Pointer Best Practices

Smart pointers in C++ manage dynamic memory allocation and deallocation, simplifying memory management and preventing memory leaks. Understanding and applying best practices for using **unique_ptr**, **shared_ptr**, and **weak_ptr** can significantly enhance the safety and efficiency of C++ programs.

Smart pointers are wrappers around raw pointers, providing automatic memory management and additional safety features. Each type of smart pointer (**unique_ptr**, **shared_ptr**, **weak_ptr**) serves different memory management needs. Best practices ensure their effective and correct use:

- **Prefer unique_ptr for exclusive ownership**: Use **unique_ptr** when the memory referenced by the pointer should not be shared or transferred without transferring ownership.

- **Use shared_ptr for shared ownership**: When an object's lifetime should be extended across multiple owners, use **shared_ptr**. Be mindful of circular references, as they can prevent proper resource deallocation.
- **Utilize weak_ptr to break circular references**: **weak_ptr** allows access to an object that is owned by one or more **shared_ptr**s without owning it, which is crucial for breaking circular references that can lead to memory leaks.
- **Avoid mixing raw and smart pointers**: Consistently use smart pointers to manage memory. Mixing raw and smart pointers can lead to confusion about ownership and memory management responsibilities.
- **Transfer ownership with std::move when necessary**: To transfer ownership of a resource managed by a **unique_ptr**, use **std::move**. This makes intentions clear and avoids accidental copies.
- **Use make_unique and make_shared to create smart pointers**: These functions provide a safer, exception-safe way to allocate memory and instantiate smart pointers.

By following these guidelines, developers can leverage the full potential of smart pointers for safer and more reliable C++ code.

Examples

Example 1: Using **unique_ptr** for exclusive ownership and transferring ownership.

```
#include <memory>
#include <iostream>

std::unique_ptr<int> createUniqueInt() {
    return std::make_unique<int>(10);
}

int main() {
    auto myUniquePtr = createUniqueInt();
    auto newOwner = std::move(myUniquePtr); // Transfer ownership
    if (!myUniquePtr) {
        std::cout << "Ownership transferred.\n";
    }
    // Use newOwner...
}
```

This example demonstrates creating a **unique_ptr** and transferring its ownership with **std::move**, illustrating exclusive ownership and safe transfer of resources.

Example 2: Avoiding circular references with **weak_ptr**.

```
#include <memory>
#include <iostream>

class B; // Forward declaration
```

```
class A {
public:
    std::shared_ptr<B> bPtr;
    ~A() { std::cout << "A destroyed\n"; }
};

class B {
public:
    std::weak_ptr<A> aPtr; // Use weak_ptr to avoid circular reference
    ~B() { std::cout << "B destroyed\n"; }
};

int main() {
    auto a = std::make_shared<A>();
    auto b = std::make_shared<B>();
    a->bPtr = b;
    b->aPtr = a;

    // Without weak_ptr, A and B would never be destroyed.
}
```

This code snippet shows how **weak_ptr** can prevent memory leaks by breaking a circular reference between two shared objects.

Practice

Practice 1: Create a function that returns a **shared_ptr** to a dynamically allocated object and demonstrate sharing its ownership with another **shared_ptr**.

Practice 2: Write code that demonstrates the use of **weak_ptr** to access an object owned by a **shared_ptr** without taking ownership.

Solution

Solution to Practice 1:

```
#include <memory>
#include <iostream>

std::shared_ptr<int> createSharedInt() {
    return std::make_shared<int>(42);
}

int main() {
    auto shared1 = createSharedInt();
    std::shared_ptr<int> shared2 = shared1; // Share ownership
    std::cout << "shared1: " << *shared1 << ", shared2: " << *shared2 << "\n";
    std::cout << "use_count: " << shared1.use_count() << "\n"; // Outputs 2
}
```

Solution to Practice 2:

```
#include <memory>
#include <iostream>

int main() {
    auto shared = std::make_shared<int>(100);
    std::weak_ptr<int> weak = shared;

    if (auto sharedCopy = weak.lock()) { // Temporarily acquire ownership
        std::cout << "Value: " << *sharedCopy << "\n";
        // sharedCopy is destroyed, releasing ownership
    }
    else {
        std::cout << "The shared_ptr no longer exists.\n";
    }
}
```

9.1.4 Type Deduction With Auto and Decltype

In C++, **auto** and **decltype** are type deduction features that simplify the syntax by allowing the compiler to automatically deduce the type of a variable or expression. **auto** is used for deducing the type of variables at initialization, while **decltype** is used to deduce the type of an expression or variable without initializing it.

Type deduction with **auto** and **decltype** enhances code readability and maintainability by reducing the verbosity associated with explicitly typed declarations, especially with complex types like iterators or function pointers. These features also aid in generic programming by making code more adaptable to changes.

- **auto**: Automatically deduces the type of a variable from its initializer. It is particularly useful in loop constructs and when dealing with types that are difficult to express manually, like lambda expressions or iterators.
- **decltype**: Evaluates the type of a given expression or variable but does not instantiate it. Useful for declaring variables meant to have the same type as expressions or function returns, particularly in template and metaprogramming contexts.

Together, **auto** and **decltype** provide powerful tools for writing cleaner, more flexible C++ code.
Examples
Example 1: Using **auto** for variable type deduction.

```
#include <iostream>
#include <vector>

int main() {
```

```
    auto num = 5; // num is deduced to be int
    auto pi = 3.14159; // pi is deduced to be double

    std::vector<int> vec = { 1, 2, 3, 4, 5 };
    for (auto it = vec.begin(); it != vec.end(); ++it) {
        std::cout << *it << " "; // it is deduced to be
std::vector<int>::iterator
    }
    return 0;
}
```

Example 2: Using **decltype** to declare variables of the same type.

```
#include <iostream>

int main() {
    int x = 5;
    decltype(x) y = 10; // y is of the same type as x, i.e., int

    std::cout << "y: " << y << std::endl;

    const int& xRef = x;
    decltype(xRef) yRef = y; // yRef is of type const int&

    return 0;
}
```

Practice

Practice 1: Use **auto** to simplify the declaration of a loop iterator over a **std::map<std::string, int>**.

Practice 2: Use **decltype** to create a new variable that has the same type as the result of adding two integers.

Solution

Solution to Practice 1:

```
#include <iostream>
#include <map>
#include <string>

int main() {
    std::map<std::string, int> ageMap = { {"Alice", 30}, {"Bob", 25}, {"Char-
lie", 35} };

    for (auto it = ageMap.begin(); it != ageMap.end(); ++it) {
        std::cout << it->first << " is " << it->second << " years old.\n";
```

```
    }
    return 0;
}
```

Solution to Practice 2:

```
#include <iostream>

int main() {
    int a = 5, b = 10;
    decltype(a + b) sum = a + b; // sum is deduced to be int

    std::cout << "Sum: " << sum << std::endl;
    return 0;
}
```

9.1.5 Writing Compile-Time Functions With Constexpr

constexpr specifies that the value of a variable or the return value of a function can be evaluated at compile time. This feature, introduced in C++11 and expanded in later standards, enables more efficient and safer code by performing computations during compilation rather than at runtime.

The **constexpr** specifier is used to declare variables and functions that can be evaluated at compile time, leading to optimizations that can significantly reduce runtime overhead for constant expressions. For a function to be **constexpr**, its return type and all parameter types must be literal types, and the function body must contain a single return statement in C++11 (this restriction is relaxed in later standards).

Using **constexpr** allows the compiler to check expressions at compile time, ensuring that values meet certain criteria before the program runs, which can be especially useful for initializing constants and evaluating constant expressions.

- **constexpr Variables**: Can be used to define compile-time constants.
- **constexpr Functions**: Enable compile-time function execution if the arguments are known at compile time, but can also be executed at runtime if the arguments are only known then.

constexpr plays a crucial role in template metaprogramming and in the development of compile-time algorithms, enhancing both performance and reliability of C++ applications.

Examples

Example 1: **constexpr** Variable

```
#include <iostream>

constexpr int factorial(int n) {
    return n <= 1 ? 1: n * factorial(n - 1);
}
```

```
int main() {
    constexpr int val = factorial(5); // Compile-time evaluation
    std::cout << "Factorial of 5 is " << val << std::endl; // Outputs 120
    return 0;
}
```

Example 2: **constexpr** Function

```
#include <iostream>

constexpr double square(double x) {
    return x * x;
}

int main() {
    double radius = 4.5;
    constexpr double area = square(10.0); // Compile-time evaluation
    double dynamicArea = square(radius); // Runtime evaluation
    std::cout << "Area of circle with radius 10 is " << area << std::endl;
    std::cout << "Area of circle with radius " << radius << " is " << dynami-
cArea << std::endl;
    return 0;
}
```

Practice

Practice 1: Implement a **constexpr** function that calculates the nth Fibonacci number.

Practice 2: Write a **constexpr** function that checks whether a given integer is prime.

Solution

Solution to Practice 1:

```
#include <iostream>

constexpr int fibonacci(int n) {
    return n <= 1 ? n: fibonacci(n - 1) + fibonacci(n - 2);
}

int main() {
    constexpr int fib10 = fibonacci(10); // Compile-time
    std::cout << "10th Fibonacci number is " << fib10 << std::endl; // Outputs
55
    return 0;
}
```

Solution to Practice 2:

```
#include <iostream>

constexpr bool isPrime(int num, int div = 2) {
    return (div * div > num) ? true: (num % div == 0 ? false: isPrime(num, div
+ 1));
}

int main() {
    constexpr bool primeCheck = isPrime(11); // Compile-time
    std::cout << "Is 11 prime? " << (primeCheck ? "Yes": "No") << std::endl;
// Outputs Yes
    return 0;
}
```

9.1.6 Implementing Flexible Functions With Variadic Templates

Variadic templates in C++ allow functions, classes, and structs to accept an arbitrary number of template arguments. This feature, introduced in C++11, enables the creation of highly flexible and reusable code components that can handle any number of arguments of any type.

Variadic templates leverage a special syntax using ellipsis (**...**) to denote that the template can take any number of arguments. This powerful feature is utilized to write generic functions or classes that can operate on a varied number of parameters without overloading or specifying each case explicitly.

The core concept revolves around template parameter packs and function parameter packs, which can be expanded in different contexts to process each argument. Variadic templates are especially useful for designing generic libraries, template metaprogramming, and creating tuple-like data structures.

- **Function Templates**: Allow writing functions that can accept a variable number of arguments of different types.
- **Class Templates**: Enable the definition of classes that can be parameterized with a flexible number of types.

Understanding and applying variadic templates can significantly reduce code duplication and increase the flexibility of C++ applications.

Examples

Example 1: Variadic Template Function to Print Arguments

```
#include <iostream>

template<typename T>
void print(T arg) {
    std::cout << arg << std::endl; // Base case
}

template<typename T, typename... Args>
```

```
void print(T firstArg, Args... args) {
    std::cout << firstArg << ", ";
    print(args...); // Recursive unpacking
}

int main() {
    print(1, 2.5, "three", '4');
    // Output: 1, 2.5, three, 4
    return 0;
}
```

Example 2: Variadic Template Class to Implement a Tuple

```
template<typename... Values>
class Tuple;

template<>
class Tuple<> { // Base case: empty tuple
};

template<typename Head, typename... Tail>
class Tuple<Head, Tail...> {
private:
    Head head;
    Tuple<Tail...> tail;

public:
    Tuple(Head h, Tail... t): head(h), tail(Tuple<Tail...>(t...)) {}

    // Accessor methods omitted for brevity
};

int main() {
    Tuple<int, double, std::string> myTuple(1, 2.0, "three");
    // A tuple containing an int, a double, and a string
    return 0;
}
```

Practice

Practice 1: Implement a variadic template function that sums up a variable number of arguments.

Practice 2: Create a variadic template class **Box** that can hold any number of values of any types and provides a method to print all of them.

Solution

Solution to Practice 1:

```
#include <iostream>

template<typename T>
T sum(T t) {
    return t; // Base case
}

template<typename T, typename... Args>
T sum(T first, Args... args) {
    return first + sum(args...); // Recursive summing
}

int main() {
    auto total = sum(1, 2, 3, 4.5);
    std::cout << "Sum: " << total << std::endl; // Outputs 10.5
    return 0;
}
```

Solution to Practice 2:

```
#include <iostream>
#include <sstream>

template<typename... Values>
class Box;

template<>
class Box<> { // Base case: empty box
public:
    void print() const {
        std::cout << "Empty box" << std::endl;
    }
};

template<typename Head, typename... Tail>
class Box<Head, Tail...> {
private:
    Head head;
    Box<Tail...> tail;

public:
    Box(Head h, Tail... t): head(h), tail(Box<Tail...>(t...)) {}

    void print() const {
```

```
        std::stringstream ss;
        ss << head;
        std::cout << ss.str() << ", ";
        tail.print();
    }
};

int main() {
    Box<int, double, std::string> myBox(1, 2.0, "three");
    myBox.print(); // Outputs: 1, 2, three,
    return 0;
}
```

9.1.7 Exploring Template Metaprogramming and Metaprogramming Techniques

Template metaprogramming (TMP) in C++ is a technique that leverages the compiler's template instantiation mechanisms to perform computations at compile time, generating optimized code tailored to specific tasks. TMP enables the creation of programs that can manipulate other programs or themselves, offering powerful compile-time computation, code introspection, and automatic code generation capabilities.

Template metaprogramming utilizes templates to execute algorithms during the compilation process, thus reducing runtime overhead and enhancing the performance of applications. TMP can be used for a variety of tasks, such as optimizing code, generating custom data structures, and implementing compile-time conditionals and loops.

Key concepts in TMP include:

- **Compile-time computation**: Performing calculations at compile time to reduce runtime costs.
- **Type traits**: Inspecting and transforming type properties to make decisions at compile time.
- **SFINAE (Substitution Failure Is Not An Error)**: A language feature that allows the creation of fallback template instantiations when certain conditions are not met.
- **Expression templates**: Delaying the evaluation of expressions to runtime to enable optimizations like loop fusion and lazy evaluation.

TMP requires a deep understanding of C++ templates and a different mindset, as it blurs the line between programming and meta-programming, allowing programmers to write more expressive and efficient code.

Examples

Example 1: Compile-time Factorial Calculation

```
template<int N>
struct Factorial {
    static const int value = N * Factorial<N - 1>::value;
};

template<>
```

```
struct Factorial<0> { // Base case
    static const int value = 1;
};

int main() {
    int fact5 = Factorial<5>::value; // Compile-time calculation
    // fact5 is 120
    return 0;
}
```

Example 2: Type Traits to Check for Type Properties

```
#include <iostream>
#include <type_traits>

template<typename T>
void print_is_integral() {
    if (std::is_integral<T>::value) {
        std::cout << "Integral type\n";
    }
    else {
        std::cout << "Not an integral type\n";
    }
}

int main() {
    print_is_integral<int>(); // Outputs: Integral type
    print_is_integral<float>(); // Outputs: Not an integral type
    return 0;
}
```

Practice

Practice 1: Implement a compile-time power function that calculates the power of a number raised to an exponent, both provided at compile time.

Practice 2: Use type traits to create a compile-time function that determines if a type is a pointer.

Solution

Solution to Practice 1:

```
template<int Base, int Exponent>
struct Power {
    static const int value = Base * Power<Base, Exponent - 1>::value;
};

template<int Base>
```

```
struct Power<Base, 0> { // Base case
    static const int value = 1;
};

int main() {
    constexpr int result = Power<2, 3>::value; // 2^3 = 8
    // result is 8
    return 0;
}
```

Solution to Practice 2:

```
#include <iostream>
#include <type_traits>

template<typename T>
void check_is_pointer() {
    if (std::is_pointer<T>::value) {
        std::cout << "Is a pointer\n";
    }
    else {
        std::cout << "Is not a pointer\n";
    }
}

int main() {
    check_is_pointer<int*>(); // Outputs: Is a pointer
    check_is_pointer<int>(); // Outputs: Is not a pointer
    return 0;
}
```

9.2 Section 2: Integration With Frameworks and Libraries

In modern software development, leveraging existing frameworks and libraries is essential for building robust and efficient applications. These tools provide pre-built functionalities that can significantly reduce development time and effort. In the context of C++ programming, there are several powerful frameworks and libraries that cater to various domains, from graphical user interface (GUI) development to game development, network programming, numerical computations, and web development.

GUI development is a critical aspect of many applications, and Qt is a cross-platform framework widely used for this purpose. It provides a comprehensive set of tools and components that simplify the design and implementation of user interfaces. With support for various platforms, including Windows, macOS, Linux, and mobile operating systems, Qt allows developers to write code once and deploy it across multiple platforms.

Game development is another area where C++ shines, and the Simple DirectMedia Layer (SDL) is a popular library for this purpose. SDL provides low-level access to audio, keyboard, mouse, joystick, and graphics hardware, making it suitable for developing both 2D and 3D games. It offers a simple interface for rendering graphics, handling user input, and managing game loops.

Network programming is essential for many applications, and Boost.Asio is a library that offers a consistent asynchronous model for this task. Part of the Boost C++ Libraries, Boost.Asio provides a high-level interface for handling network connections, timers, and other I/O operations. It allows for the establishment of TCP and UDP connections, the performance of asynchronous I/O operations, and the management of concurrent tasks in network applications.

Numerical computations are crucial in scientific computing, computer graphics, and machine learning applications. The Eigen library is a high-performance C++ library for linear algebra, matrix, and vector operations. It supports various matrix operations, solving linear systems, and eigenvalue problems, making it a valuable tool for numerical computations.

Web development is increasingly important, and CPPRESTSDK, also known as the C++ REST SDK, is a library for building web services and clients. It provides a modern asynchronous API for HTTP client and server functionality, JSON parsing, and other web-related tasks. With CPPRESTSDK, developers can create RESTful web services, handle HTTP requests and responses, and interact with web APIs.

By integrating these frameworks and libraries into your C++ projects, you can take advantage of their powerful features to build high-performance and scalable applications across various domains.

9.2.1 GUI Development With Qt: An Introduction

Qt is a free and open-source widget toolkit for creating graphical user interfaces (GUIs) as well as cross-platform applications that run on various software and hardware platforms with little or no change in the underlying codebase. Qt supports various platforms, including Windows, macOS, Linux, and mobile operating systems.

Qt provides developers with a comprehensive set of tools and libraries for building GUI applications. It uses C++ as its primary programming language, supplemented by QML (Qt Modeling Language) for designing user interfaces. Key features of Qt include signals and slots for communication between objects, a wide range of pre-built widgets for creating complex user interfaces, and the Qt Creator IDE for development.

The framework supports the Model-View-Controller (MVC) and Model-View-ViewModel (MVVM) design patterns, facilitating the separation of data, business logic, and presentation layers. This separation enhances code maintainability and allows developers to focus on individual aspects of the application development.

Learning objectives:

- Understand the basics of Qt and its application in GUI development.
- Familiarize with Qt Creator IDE and its features.
- Learn how to create simple GUI applications using widgets.
- Explore the signals and slots mechanism for event-driven programming in Qt.

Examples

Example 1: Creating a Simple Qt Widget Application

```
#include <QApplication>
#include <QPushButton>

int main(int argc, char** argv) {
    QApplication app(argc, argv);

    QPushButton button("Hello, Qt!");
    button.show();

    return app.exec();
}
```

This example demonstrates creating a basic Qt application with a single button. The application uses **QApplication** and **QPushButton** from the Qt Widgets module.

Example 2: Connecting a Button Click Signal to a Slot

```
#include <QApplication>
#include <QPushButton>
#include <QMessageBox>

int main(int argc, char** argv) {
    QApplication app(argc, argv);
    QPushButton button("Click Me!");

    QObject::connect(&button, &QPushButton::clicked, []() {
        QMessageBox::information(nullptr, "Message", "Button Clicked!");
        });

    button.show();
    return app.exec();
}
```

This example shows how to connect the clicked signal of a button to a lambda slot that displays a message box. It illustrates the signals and slots mechanism in Qt.

Practice

Practice 1: Create a Qt application with a main window containing two buttons: "Greet" and "Close". The "Greet" button should display "Hello, World!" in a message box when clicked, and the "Close" button should close the application.

Practice 2: Extend the application from Practice 1 by adding a text input field. Modify the "Greet" button functionality to display the text entered in the input field instead of "Hello, World!".

Solution

Solution to Practice 1:

```
#include <QApplication>
#include <QMainWindow>
#include <QPushButton>
#include <QMessageBox>
#include <QHBoxLayout>
#include <QWidget>

int main(int argc, char** argv) {
    QApplication app(argc, argv);
    QMainWindow mainWindow;

    QWidget centralWidget;
    QHBoxLayout layout;

    QPushButton greetButton("Greet");
    QPushButton closeButton("Close");

    layout.addWidget(&greetButton);
    layout.addWidget(&closeButton);
    centralWidget.setLayout(&layout);

    mainWindow.setCentralWidget(&centralWidget);

    QObject::connect(&greetButton, &QPushButton::clicked, []() {
        QMessageBox::information(nullptr, "Greeting", "Hello, World!");
        });
    QObject::connect(&closeButton, &QPushButton::clicked, [&]() {
        mainWindow.close();
        });

    mainWindow.show();
    return app.exec();
}
```

Solution to Practice 2:

```
// Include necessary headers
#include <QLineEdit>

// Add a QLineEdit member to the layout
QLineEdit inputField;
layout.addWidget(&inputField);

// Modify the greetButton's lambda to use inputField's text
```

```
QObject::connect(&greetButton, &QPushButton::clicked, [&]() {
    QMessageBox::information(nullptr, "Greeting", "Hello, " + inputField.
text() + "!");
    });
```

9.2.2 Game Development Essentials With SDL

Simple DirectMedia Layer (SDL) is a cross-platform development library designed to provide low-level access to audio, keyboard, mouse, joystick, and graphics hardware via OpenGL and Direct3D. It is used by video playback software, emulators, and popular games as a foundation for building complex software that requires direct control of hardware resources.

SDL provides an efficient framework for managing windows, rendering graphics, handling input events, and playing audio, making it a popular choice for game development and multimedia applications. SDL abstracts away the complexities of directly interfacing with different operating systems and hardware, enabling developers to write code that's portable across multiple platforms without significant changes.

Key features of SDL include:

- **Graphics Rendering**: SDL provides functions to create and manage windows and rendering contexts, draw shapes, and handle textures and sprites.
- **Input Handling**: SDL supports input from keyboards, mice, and game controllers, allowing for comprehensive control mechanisms in games.
- **Audio Management**: It offers facilities to load, play, and manipulate audio files, essential for creating immersive game experiences.
- **Cross-Platform Development**: SDL supports Windows, Mac OS X, Linux, iOS, and Android, facilitating the development of applications that can run on a wide range of devices.

Learning objectives:

- Understand the architecture and main components of SDL.
- Learn how to set up an SDL development environment.
- Create simple SDL applications that can handle user input and render basic graphics.
- Explore SDL's capabilities for audio playback and input handling.

Examples

Example 1: Initializing SDL and Creating a Window

```
#include <SDL.h>
#include <stdio.h>

int main(int argc, char* argv[]) {
    SDL_Init(SDL_INIT_VIDEO); // Initialize SDL2

    // Create an application window with the following settings:
    SDL_Window* window = SDL_CreateWindow(
```

```
        "SDL Tutorial",                    // window title
        SDL_WINDOWPOS_UNDEFINED,           // initial x position
        SDL_WINDOWPOS_UNDEFINED,           // initial y position
        640,                               // width, in pixels
        480,                               // height, in pixels
        SDL_WINDOW_OPENGL                  // flags - see below
    );

    // Check that the window was successfully created
    if (window == NULL) {
        // In the case that the window could not be made...
        printf("Could not create window: %s\n", SDL_GetError());
        return 1;
    }

    // The window is open: enter program loop (see SDL_PollEvent)
    SDL_Delay(3000);  // Pause execution for 3000 milliseconds, for example

    // Close and destroy the window
    SDL_DestroyWindow(window);

    // Clean up
    SDL_Quit();
    return 0;
}
```

Example 2: Handling Keyboard Input

```
#include <SDL.h>
#include <stdbool.h>

int main(void) {
    SDL_Init(SDL_INIT_VIDEO);
    SDL_Window* window = SDL_CreateWindow("Input Handling", SDL_WINDOWPOS_UN-
DEFINED, SDL_WINDOWPOS_UNDEFINED, 640, 480, 0);
    SDL_Renderer* renderer = SDL_CreateRenderer(window, -1, 0);

    bool running = true;
    SDL_Event event;

    while (running) {
        while (SDL_PollEvent(&event)) {
            if (event.type == SDL_QUIT) {
                running = false;
```

```
            }
            else if (event.type == SDL_KEYDOWN) {
                switch (event.key.keysym.sym) {
                case SDLK_ESCAPE:
                    running = false;
                    break;
                    // Add more key case handlers as needed
                }
            }
        }

        SDL_RenderClear(renderer);
        // Add rendering code here
        SDL_RenderPresent(renderer);
    }

    SDL_DestroyRenderer(renderer);
    SDL_DestroyWindow(window);
    SDL_Quit();
    return 0;
}
```

Practice

Practice 1: Set up an SDL project and create a window that closes when the user presses the escape key.

Practice 2: Extend the SDL window application to draw a rectangle that moves across the screen when the arrow keys are pressed.

Solution

Solution to Practice 1:

The solution involves initializing SDL, creating a window, and setting up an event loop that listens for the SDL_QUIT event and the escape key press to exit the application. This is demonstrated in the provided Example 2 with the addition of a case for SDLK_ESCAPE in the event handling section.

Solution to Practice 2:

```
#include <SDL.h>
#include <stdbool.h>

int main(void) {
    SDL_Init(SDL_INIT_VIDEO);
    SDL_Window* window = SDL_CreateWindow("Moving Rectangle", SDL_WINDOWPOS_
UNDEFINED, SDL_WINDOWPOS_UNDEFINED, 640, 480, 0);
    SDL_Renderer* renderer = SDL_CreateRenderer(window, -1, SDL_RENDERER_AC-
CELERATED);

    bool running = true;
```

```
    SDL_Event event;
    SDL_Rect rect = { 320, 240, 50, 50 }; // Initial position

    while (running) {
        while (SDL_PollEvent(&event)) {
            if (event.type == SDL_QUIT) {
                running = false;
            }
            else if (event.type == SDL_KEYDOWN) {
                switch (event.key.keysym.sym) {
                case SDLK_ESCAPE:
                    running = false;
                    break;
                case SDLK_UP:
                    rect.y -= 5;
                    break;
                case SDLK_DOWN:
                    rect.y += 5;
                    break;
                case SDLK_LEFT:
                    rect.x -= 5;
                    break;
                case SDLK_RIGHT:
                    rect.x += 5;
                    break;
                }
            }
        }

        SDL_SetRenderDrawColor(renderer, 0, 0, 0, SDL_ALPHA_OPAQUE); // Black
background
        SDL_RenderClear(renderer);
        SDL_SetRenderDrawColor(renderer, 255, 255, 255, SDL_ALPHA_OPAQUE); //
White rectangle
        SDL_RenderFillRect(renderer, &rect);
        SDL_RenderPresent(renderer);
    }

    SDL_DestroyRenderer(renderer);
    SDL_DestroyWindow(window);
    SDL_Quit();
    return 0;
}
```

This solution demonstrates handling keyboard inputs to move a rectangle drawn on the window, showcasing basic animation and input management in SDL.

9.2.3 Network Programming With Boost.Asio

Boost.Asio is a cross-platform C++ library for network and low-level I/O programming that provides developers with a consistent asynchronous model. It offers a high-level abstraction over various networking APIs and protocols like TCP, UDP, and SSL, making it a powerful tool for building scalable and performant network applications.

Boost.Asio simplifies the complex details of socket programming and asynchronous I/O operations. It enables developers to write efficient network programs in C++ without delving into the intricacies of platform-specific APIs. The library is part of the Boost set of C++ libraries and can be used independently of other Boost libraries.

Key features of Boost.Asio include:

- **Asynchronous and Synchronous Operations**: Offers both asynchronous (non-blocking) and synchronous (blocking) operations, allowing developers to choose the best approach based on their application needs.
- **Scalable Networking Solutions**: Supports the Reactor and Proactor design patterns, enabling the development of scalable network applications that can handle thousands of simultaneous connections.
- **Timer and I/O Objects**: Provides timer objects for asynchronous waits and I/O objects for network sockets and serial ports, facilitating complex I/O management and event-driven programming.
- **Error Handling**: Incorporates a robust error handling mechanism that works seamlessly with C++ exception handling.

Learning objectives:

- Gain an understanding of basic networking concepts and the Boost.Asio library's architecture.
- Learn how to set up a simple TCP/UDP server and client using Boost.Asio.
- Explore asynchronous programming patterns and error handling in networked applications.
- Develop skills to create efficient and scalable network programs.

Examples

Example 1: Creating a TCP Echo Server with Boost.Asio

```
#include <boost/asio.hpp>
#include <iostream>

using boost::asio::ip::tcp;

int main() {
    try {
        boost::asio::io_context io_context;
```

```
        tcp::acceptor acceptor(io_context, tcp::endpoint(tcp::v4(), 1234));

        while (true) {
            tcp::socket socket(io_context);
            acceptor.accept(socket);

            std::string message = "Hello from Boost.Asio TCP server!";
            boost::system::error_code ignored_error;
            boost::asio::write(socket, boost::asio::buffer(message), ignored_
error);
        }
    }
    catch (std::exception& e) {
        std::cerr << e.what() << std::endl;
    }

    return 0;
}
```

Example 2: Asynchronous TCP Client with Boost.Asio

```
#include <boost/asio.hpp>
#include <boost/array.hpp>
#include <iostream>

using boost::asio::ip::tcp;

void read_handler(const boost::system::error_code& ec, std::size_t bytes_
transferred) {
    // Handler code here
}

int main() {
    try {
        boost::asio::io_context io_context;
        tcp::resolver resolver(io_context);
        auto endpoints = resolver.resolve("example.com", "daytime");
        tcp::socket socket(io_context);
        boost::asio::connect(socket, endpoints);

        boost::array<char, 128> buf;
        boost::system::error_code error;

        socket.async_read_some(boost::asio::buffer(buf), read_handler);
```

```
        io_context.run();
    }
    catch (std::exception& e) {
        std::cerr << e.what() << std::endl;
    }

    return 0;
}
```

Practice

Practice 1: Implement a Boost.Asio application that connects to a TCP server and sends a simple "ping" message, then receives and prints the server's response.

Practice 2: Extend the TCP server from Example 1 to handle multiple clients asynchronously, responding to each with a unique message.

Solution

Solution to Practice 1:

```
#include <boost/asio.hpp>
#include <iostream>

using boost::asio::ip::tcp;

int main() {
    try {
        boost::asio::io_context io_context;
        tcp::resolver resolver(io_context);
        auto endpoints = resolver.resolve("localhost", "1234");
        tcp::socket socket(io_context);
        boost::asio::connect(socket, endpoints);

        std::string msg = "ping";
        socket.write_some(boost::asio::buffer(msg));

        char reply[1024];
        size_t reply_length = socket.read_some(boost::asio::buffer(reply));
        std::cout << "Reply is: ";
        std::cout.write(reply, reply_length);
        std::cout << "\n";
    }
    catch (std::exception& e) {
        std::cerr << "Exception: " << e.what() << "\n";
    }
```

```
    return 0;
}
```

Solution to Practice 2:

Implementing an asynchronous server that handles multiple clients requires significant modifications to the basic server example, including setting up an asynchronous accept operation with a handler that processes incoming connections and initiates asynchronous read/write operations for each connected client. Due to the complexity and length of a proper solution, which would involve defining multiple classes and handlers for managing connections and data transfers, a comprehensive code example exceeds the scope of this response.

9.2.4 Numerical Computations Using the Eigen Library

Eigen is a high-level C++ library for linear algebra, matrix and vector operations, numerical solvers, and related algorithms. Designed for efficiency, flexibility, and ease of use, Eigen is widely employed in both academic and industry projects for tasks ranging from simple vector arithmetic to complex matrix decompositions and solving systems of linear equations.

Eigen provides a comprehensive set of tools for performing various numerical computations, which are essential in many fields of science and engineering. The library uses template metaprogramming techniques, enabling it to offer high performance alongside ease of integration into C++ projects.

Key aspects of Eigen include:

- **Matrix and Vector Arithmetic**: Supports all basic matrix and vector operations, including addition, subtraction, scalar multiplication, and more.
- **Linear Algebra**: Offers functions for matrix decompositions, eigenvalues/eigenvectors, and solving linear systems.
- **Geometry**: Contains classes and functions for performing operations related to geometry, such as transformations and rotations.
- **Interoperability**: Designed to work well with standard C++ arrays and the STL, making it easy to integrate with existing codebases.

Learning objectives:

- Understand the basics of the Eigen library and how it can be used for numerical computations.
- Learn to perform matrix and vector operations using Eigen.
- Explore Eigen's capabilities for solving systems of linear equations and performing decompositions.
- Discover how Eigen can be applied to real-world numerical problems.

Examples

Example 1: Basic Vector Operations

```
#include <Eigen/Dense>
#include <iostream>
```

```
int main() {
    Eigen::Vector3d v(1.0, 2.0, 3.0);
    Eigen::Vector3d w(1.0, 0.0, 0.0);

    // Vector addition
    Eigen::Vector3d result = v + w;

    std::cout << "Result of v + w:\n" << result << std::endl;
    // Output: Result of v + w: [2, 2, 3]

    return 0;
}
```

Example 2: Solving a System of Linear Equations

```
#include <Eigen/Dense>
#include <iostream>

int main() {
    Eigen::Matrix3f A;
    Eigen::Vector3f b;
    A << 1, 2, 3,
        4, 5, 6,
        7, 8, 10;
    b << 3, 3, 4;

    Eigen::Vector3f x = A.colPivHouseholderQr().solve(b);
    std::cout << "Solution of Ax = b:\n" << x << std::endl;
    // Output: Solution of Ax = b: [1, -1, 1]

    return 0;
}
```

Practice

Practice 1: Create a 4x4 matrix and a 4-element vector. Perform a matrix-vector multiplication and print the result.

Practice 2: Use Eigen to find the eigenvalues of a 3x3 matrix.

Solution

Solution to Practice 1:

```
#include <Eigen/Dense>
#include <iostream>

int main() {
```

```
    Eigen::Matrix4d M;
    Eigen::Vector4d v;
    M << 1, 2, 3, 4,
        5, 6, 7, 8,
        9, 10, 11, 12,
        13, 14, 15, 16;
    v << 1, 2, 3, 4;

    Eigen::Vector4d result = M * v;
    std::cout << "Result of M * v:\n" << result << std::endl;
    // Expected output: Result of M * v: [30, 70, 110, 150]

    return 0;
}
```

Solution to Practice 2:

```
#include <Eigen/Dense>
#include <iostream>

int main() {
    Eigen::Matrix3d A;
    A << 1, 2, 1,
        6, -1, 0,
        -1, 2, 1;

    Eigen::EigenSolver<Eigen::Matrix3d> solver(A);
    std::cout << "The eigenvalues of A are:\n" << solver.eigenvalues() <<
std::endl;
    // Outputs the eigenvalues of matrix A

    return 0;
}
```

9.2.5 Web Development Techniques With CPPRESTSDK

The C++ REST SDK, also known as CPPRESTSDK or Casablanca, is an open-source, cross-platform library that aims to simplify the consumption and production of HTTP services. It provides developers with a modern asynchronous API for accessing RESTful services from C++ applications, supporting tasks such as making HTTP requests, working with JSON data, and implementing OAuth authentication.

CPPRESTSDK encapsulates the complexity of HTTP communication and data manipulation through a set of high-level classes and functions, making web development in C++ both feasible and efficient. The library is designed around asynchronous operations, leveraging modern C++ features like futures and lambdas to handle network responses without blocking the main thread.

Key features of CPPRESTSDK include:

- **HTTP Client and Server**: Facilitates sending HTTP requests and building RESTful services.
- **JSON**: Offers comprehensive support for parsing, generating, and manipulating JSON data.
- **URI Handling**: Provides utilities for constructing and parsing URIs.
- **Asynchronous Programming**: Uses the PPL (Parallel Patterns Library) to handle asynchronous operations, allowing for non-blocking I/O operations.

Learning objectives:

- Understand the architecture and components of the CPPRESTSDK library.
- Learn how to perform HTTP GET and POST requests using CPPRESTSDK.
- Manipulate JSON data for sending and receiving complex data structures.
- Implement basic web services and clients for RESTful applications.

Examples

Example 1: Making an HTTP GET Request

```
#include <cpprest/http_client.h>
#include <iostream>

using namespace web::http;
using namespace web::http::client;

int main() {
    http_client client(U("http://httpbin.org/get"));

    client.request(methods::GET).then([](http_response response) {
        if (response.status_code() == status_codes::OK) {
            std::wcout << response.to_string() << std::endl;
        }
        }).wait();

        return 0;
}
```

Example 2: Parsing JSON Data from an HTTP Response

```
#include <cpprest/http_client.h>
#include <cpprest/json.h>
#include <iostream>

using namespace web::http;
using namespace web::http::client;
```

```
using namespace web::json;

int main() {
    http_client client(U("http://httpbin.org/get"));

    client.request(methods::GET).then([](http_response response) ->
pplx::task<json::value> {
        if (response.status_code() == status_codes::OK) {
            return response.extract_json();
        }
        return pplx::task_from_result(json::value());
        }).then([](json::value jsonObject) {
            std::wcout << U("Origin IP: ") << jsonObject[U("origin")].as_
string() << std::endl;
            }).wait();

            return 0;
}
```

Practice

Practice 1: Use CPPRESTSDK to create a simple HTTP client that sends a POST request to http://httpbin.org/post with JSON data and prints the response.

Practice 2: Implement a simple RESTful web service using CPPRESTSDK that listens on localhost and responds with a JSON object containing a greeting message when accessed.

Solution

Solution to Practice 1:

```
#include <cpprest/http_client.h>
#include <cpprest/json.h>
#include <iostream>

using namespace web::http;
using namespace web::http::client;
using namespace web::json;

int main() {
    http_client client(U("http://httpbin.org/post"));
    json::value postData;
    postData[U("name")] = json::value::string(U("CPPRESTSDK User"));

    client.request(methods::POST, U(""), postData.serialize(), U("application/
json")).then([](http_response response) {
        if (response.status_code() == status_codes::OK) {
            std::wcout << response.to_string() << std::endl;
```

```
        }
        }).wait();

        return 0;
}
```

Solution to Practice 2:

```
#include <cpprest/http_listener.h>
#include <cpprest/json.h>
#include <iostream>

using namespace web;
using namespace web::http;
using namespace web::http::experimental::listener;

void handleGet(http_request request) {
    json::value response_data;
    response_data[U("message")] = json::value::string(U("Hello from CPPREST-
SDK!"));

    request.reply(status_codes::OK, response_data);
}

int main() {
    http_listener listener(U("http://localhost:8080"));

    listener.support(methods::GET, handleGet);

    try {
        listener
            .open()
            .then([&listener]() { std::wcout << U("Starting to listen at ") <<
listener.uri().to_string() << std::endl; })
            .wait();

        std::wcout << U("Press ENTER to exit.") << std::endl;
        std::wstring line;
        std::getline(std::wcin, line);
    }
    catch (const std::exception& e) {
        std::cerr << "An error occurred: " << e.what() << std::endl;
    }
```

```
    return 0;
}
```

9.3 Section 3: Practical Applications and Case Studies

The versatility of C++ allows for its application in a wide range of practical scenarios. This section explores some of these practical applications through case studies, demonstrating the real-world utility of C++ in various domains.

Building a cross-platform GUI application is a common requirement in software development. By leveraging frameworks like Qt, developers can create applications that run seamlessly on different operating systems. A case study in this area might explore the design and development process of a cross-platform application, highlighting the challenges and solutions encountered in ensuring compatibility across platforms.

Developing and optimizing a 2D game engine is another practical application of C++. A case study in this context could delve into the architecture of a game engine, focusing on the optimization techniques employed to achieve smooth performance. This might include discussions on efficient rendering, physics simulations, and resource management.

Creating a high-performance web server is a critical task in the era of the internet. C++ can be used to develop web servers that handle high volumes of traffic with low latency. A case study on this topic might examine the implementation details of a web server, including the use of asynchronous I/O operations and multi-threading to enhance performance.

Implementing efficient matrix operations is crucial in engineering applications, where numerical computations are often at the core of problem-solving. A case study in this area could focus on the use of libraries like Eigen to perform matrix operations efficiently. It might explore the challenges of dealing with large datasets and the strategies employed to optimize computations for speed and accuracy.

Designing and deploying RESTful web services is a vital aspect of modern web development. C++ can be utilized to create scalable and performant web services. A case study on this topic might cover the design principles of RESTful architecture, the implementation of endpoints using CPPRESTSDK, and the considerations for security and scalability in a production environment.

These case studies highlight the practical applications of C++ in various domains, showcasing its adaptability and efficiency in solving real-world problems. By examining these examples, developers can gain insights into the best practices and techniques for leveraging C++ in their projects.

9.3.1 Building a Cross-Platform GUI Application

Creating a cross-platform GUI application involves designing and developing an application that can run on multiple operating systems (such as Windows, macOS, Linux) with a graphical user interface that remains consistent across platforms. This approach maximizes code reuse, reduces development time, and ensures a uniform user experience.

Cross-platform GUI development requires a framework that abstracts away the differences between operating systems, providing a unified API for window creation, event handling, drawing operations, and common controls like buttons, text fields, and sliders. Popular frameworks include Qt, wxWidgets, and GTK+. Each offers tools and libraries to facilitate the development of applications that compile and run on various platforms.

Key considerations for building a cross-platform GUI application include:

- **Choosing the Right Framework**: Factors include language support, licensing, community and documentation, and the range of supported platforms.
- **Design and Usability**: Designing a user interface that looks and feels natural on all platforms while adhering to user interface guidelines of each.
- **Testing and Deployment**: Testing the application on all target platforms to ensure consistent behavior and appearance, and using appropriate packaging and deployment strategies.

Learning objectives:

- Gain familiarity with a cross-platform GUI framework (e.g., Qt).
- Understand the basics of GUI application architecture, including event-driven programming.
- Learn to design and implement a basic cross-platform GUI.
- Explore strategies for testing and deploying cross-platform GUI applications.

Examples

Since Qt is one of the most popular frameworks for cross-platform GUI application development, the examples will focus on Qt.

Example 1: Basic Qt Application

```
#include <QApplication>
#include <QPushButton>

int main(int argc, char** argv) {
    QApplication app(argc, argv);

    QPushButton button("Hello, World!");
    button.show();

    return app.exec();
}
```

This simple Qt application creates a window with a single button. The **QApplication** class manages application-wide resources and settings. **QPushButton** creates a clickable button.

Example 2: Handling Button Clicks

```
#include <QApplication>
#include <QPushButton>
#include <QMessageBox>

int main(int argc, char** argv) {
    QApplication app(argc, argv);
    QPushButton button("Click Me");
```

```
    QObject::connect(&button, &QPushButton::clicked, []() {
        QMessageBox::information(nullptr, "Clicked", "You clicked the but-
ton!");
        });

    button.show();
    return app.exec();
}
```

This example demonstrates connecting a button's **clicked** signal to a slot using a lambda function, which displays a message box when the button is clicked.

Practice

Practice 1: Create a Qt application that opens a main window with the title "My First Application", containing a label that says "Welcome to Qt".

Practice 2: Extend the application from Practice 1 by adding two buttons, "OK" and "Cancel". Connect these buttons to slots that print messages to the console when clicked.

Solution

Solution to Practice 1:

```
#include <QApplication>
#include <QLabel>
#include <QMainWindow>

int main(int argc, char** argv) {
    QApplication app(argc, argv);
    QMainWindow window;
    window.setWindowTitle("My First Application");

    QLabel* label = new QLabel("Welcome to Qt", &window);
    window.setCentralWidget(label);

    window.show();
    return app.exec();
}
```

Solution to Practice 2:

```
#include <QApplication>
#include <QLabel>
#include <QMainWindow>
#include <QPushButton>
#include <QWidget>
#include <QHBoxLayout>
```

```
#include <iostream>

int main(int argc, char** argv) {
    QApplication app(argc, argv);
    QMainWindow window;
    window.setWindowTitle("My First Application");

    QWidget* centralWidget = new QWidget();
    QHBoxLayout* layout = new QHBoxLayout();

    QLabel* label = new QLabel("Welcome to Qt");
    layout->addWidget(label);

    QPushButton* okButton = new QPushButton("OK");
    QPushButton* cancelButton = new QPushButton("Cancel");
    layout->addWidget(okButton);
    layout->addWidget(cancelButton);

    QObject::connect(okButton, &QPushButton::clicked, []() {
        std::cout << "OK button clicked" << std::endl;
        });
    QObject::connect(cancelButton, &QPushButton::clicked, []() {
        std::cout << "Cancel button clicked" << std::endl;
        });

    centralWidget->setLayout(layout);
    window.setCentralWidget(centralWidget);

    window.show();
    return app.exec();
}
```

9.3.2 Developing and Optimizing a 2D Game Engine

A 2D game engine is a software framework designed for the creation and development of 2D games. It provides developers with a set of tools and functionalities such as rendering, physics, animation, and asset management, which are essential for building interactive and engaging 2D games. Developing an efficient and flexible game engine requires a deep understanding of game mechanics, optimization techniques, and software design principles.

The core components of a 2D game engine typically include:

- **Rendering System**: Manages the drawing of textures, sprites, and animations on the screen.
- **Physics Engine**: Handles collision detection, object movement, and simulates physical interactions within the game world.

- **Audio System**: Manages game sounds, including background music and sound effects.
- **Input Management**: Processes input from the user through various devices such as keyboards, mice, or gamepads.
- **Scene Management**: Organizes game levels, transitions, and entities within the game.
- **Asset Management**: Efficiently loads and manages game assets like images, sounds, and other resources.

Optimizing a 2D game engine involves improving its performance and reducing resource consumption without compromising the game's quality. Techniques include minimizing CPU and GPU workload, optimizing data structures, and efficient memory management.

Learning objectives:

- Understand the architecture and key components of a 2D game engine.
- Learn to implement basic rendering, physics, and input management systems.
- Explore optimization strategies for enhancing engine performance.
- Develop skills for creating flexible and reusable game engine components.

Examples

Example 1: Basic Rendering Loop

```
void GameEngine::render() {
    while (gameRunning) {
        clearScreen();
        for (const auto& entity: entities) {
            draw(entity);
        }
        presentScreen();
    }
}
```

This pseudo-code illustrates a simple rendering loop where each entity in the game is drawn to the screen every frame.

Example 2: Basic Collision Detection

```
bool checkCollision(const Entity& a, const Entity& b) {
    // Simple AABB collision detection
    return (a.x < b.x + b.width &&
        a.x + a.width > b.x &&
        a.y < b.y + b.height &&
        a.y + a.height > b.y);
}
```

This pseudo-code demonstrates a basic Axis-Aligned Bounding Box (AABB) collision detection between two entities.

Practice

Practice 1: Implement a simple sprite rendering function that draws an image at a specified position on the screen.

Practice 2: Create a basic physics system that allows entities to move based on velocity and checks for collisions between them.

Solution

Solution to Practice 1:

Given the variety of programming languages and graphics libraries, a specific code example may vary. Here's a conceptual approach using a hypothetical graphics library:

```
void drawSprite(const Sprite& sprite, int x, int y) {
    graphicsLibrary.draw(sprite.image, x, y);
}
```

Solution to Practice 2:

This pseudo-code outlines a basic physics update and collision check for a list of entities:

```
void updatePhysics(std::vector<Entity>& entities) {
    for (auto& entity: entities) {
        entity.x += entity.velocityX;
        entity.y += entity.velocityY;
        for (const auto& other: entities) {
            if (&entity != &other && checkCollision(entity, other)) {
                handleCollision(entity, other);
            }
        }
    }
}
```

9.3.3 Creating a High-Performance Web Server

A high-performance web server in C++ is engineered to efficiently manage a vast number of client requests with minimal response time. It involves leveraging C++'s capabilities for low-level network handling, optimizing concurrency through modern C++ concurrency models, and minimizing resource consumption, all while upholding stringent security standards.

Developing a high-performance web server in C++ demands a solid grasp of networking protocols, concurrent programming, optimization strategies, and security practices. C++ offers the speed and low-level system access necessary for fine-tuned control over these aspects, making it an ideal choice for building robust web servers.

Key aspects include:

- **Networking Protocols**: Deep understanding of TCP/IP, HTTP/HTTPS, and SSL/TLS for secure data transmission.

- **Concurrency Models**: Effective use of C++11 and beyond threading, async patterns, and event-driven programming to handle multiple client connections concurrently.
- **Optimization Techniques**: Techniques like efficient memory management, algorithmic optimizations, and leveraging C++ standard library features for performance gains.
- **Security Practices**: Implementing SSL/TLS for encrypted communication, validating and sanitizing user input to prevent common web vulnerabilities.

Learning objectives:

- Master the use of C++ for implementing low-level network communication.
- Apply modern C++ concurrency features for efficient multi-client handling.
- Employ optimization techniques specific to C++ for enhanced server performance.
- Incorporate security measures to safeguard against common web threats.

Examples

Example 1: Basic HTTP Server Setup in C++

A simplified example using POSIX sockets:

```
#include <sys/socket.h>
#include <netinet/in.h>
#include <unistd.h>
#include <cstring>
#include <iostream>

void startServer(int port) {
    int server_fd, new_socket;
    struct sockaddr_in address;
    int opt = 1;
    int addrlen = sizeof(address);
    char buffer[1024] = { 0 };
    char* hello = "HTTP/1.1 200 OK\nContent-Type: text/plain\n\nHello, world!";

    // Creating socket file descriptor
    if ((server_fd = socket(AF_INET, SOCK_STREAM, 0)) == 0) {
        perror("socket failed");
        exit(EXIT_FAILURE);
    }

    // Forcefully attaching socket to the port
    if (setsockopt(server_fd, SOL_SOCKET, SO_REUSEADDR | SO_REUSEPORT, &opt,
sizeof(opt))) {
        perror("setsockopt");
        exit(EXIT_FAILURE);
    }
```

```
    address.sin_family = AF_INET;
    address.sin_addr.s_addr = INADDR_ANY;
    address.sin_port = htons(port);

    // Binding socket to the port
    if (bind(server_fd, (struct sockaddr*)&address, sizeof(address)) < 0) {
        perror("bind failed");
        exit(EXIT_FAILURE);
    }
    if (listen(server_fd, 3) < 0) {
        perror("listen");
        exit(EXIT_FAILURE);
    }
    if ((new_socket = accept(server_fd, (struct sockaddr*)&address,
(socklen_t*)&addrlen)) < 0) {
        perror("accept");
        exit(EXIT_FAILURE);
    }
    read(new_socket, buffer, 1024);
    send(new_socket, hello, strlen(hello), 0);
    close(new_socket);
}

int main() {
    startServer(8080);
    return 0;
}
```

Example 2: Simple Thread Pool Implementation in C++

Utilizing C++11 **<thread>**, **<vector>**, and **<queue>**:

```
#include <vector>
#include <queue>
#include <thread>
#include <functional>
#include <mutex>
#include <condition_variable>

class ThreadPool {
public:
    ThreadPool(size_t threads): stop(false) {
        for (size_t i = 0; i < threads; ++i)
            workers.emplace_back([this] {
```

```
            while (true) {
                std::function<void()> task;

                {
                    std::unique_lock<std::mutex> lock(this->queue_mutex);
                    this->condition.wait(lock, [this] { return this->stop ||
!this->tasks.empty(); });
                    if (this->stop && this->tasks.empty())
                        return;
                    task = std::move(this->tasks.front());
                    this->tasks.pop();
                }

                task();
            }
                });
    }

    ~ThreadPool() {
        {
            std::unique_lock<std::mutex> lock(queue_mutex);
            stop = true;
        }
        condition.notify_all();
        for (std::thread& worker: workers)
            worker.join();
    }

    template<class F, class... Args>
    auto enqueue(F&& f, Args&&... args)
        -> std::future<typename std::result_of<F(Args...)>::type> {
        using return_type = typename std::result_of<F(Args...)>::type;

        auto task = std::make_shared< std::packaged_task<return_type()> >(
            std::bind(std::forward<F>(f), std::forward<Args>(args)...)
       );

        std::future<return_type> res = task->get_future();
        {
            std::unique_lock<std::mutex> lock(queue_mutex);

            if (stop)
                throw std::runtime_error("enqueue on stopped ThreadPool");
```

```
            tasks.emplace([task]() { (*task)(); });
        }
        condition.notify_one();
        return res;
    }

private:
    std::vector< std::thread > workers;
    std::queue< std::function<void()> > tasks;

    std::mutex queue_mutex;
    std::condition_variable condition;
    bool stop;
};
```

Practice

Practice 1: Extend the basic HTTP server example to handle HTTP GET requests by serving a simple HTML page stored on the server.

Practice 2: Implement a function using the thread pool that processes incoming HTTP requests and logs them to a file asynchronously.

Solution

Solution to Practice 1:

```
// Assuming startServer function from Example 1
void handleGETRequest(int socket) {
    const char* htmlContent = "HTTP/1.1 200 OK\nContent-Type: text/html\n\
n<!DOCTYPE html><html><body><h1>Welcome to My C++ Web Server</h1></body></
html>";
    send(socket, htmlContent, strlen(htmlContent), 0);
}

// Inside the while loop of startServer, replace the send call with:
handleGETRequest(new_socket);
```

Solution to Practice 2:

```
#include <fstream>
#include <iostream>

void logRequest(const std::string& request) {
    std::ofstream logFile("requests.log", std::ios::app);
    if (logFile.is_open()) {
        logFile << request << std::endl;
        logFile.close();
```

```
    }
    else {
        std::cerr << "Failed to open log file." << std::endl;
    }
}

// Assuming ThreadPool class from Example 2
// Inside your request handling function, use:
threadPool.enqueue(logRequest, "Received a request: " + requestDetails);
```

9.3.4 Implementing Efficient Matrix Operations for Engineering Applications

Efficient matrix operations are crucial in engineering applications for tasks such as simulations, optimizations, and solving systems of linear equations. Implementing these operations in C++ allows for high-performance computations, taking advantage of C++'s speed and lower-level control over hardware resources.

Matrix operations, including addition, multiplication, inversion, and determinant calculation, are foundational in various engineering fields. In C++, these can be efficiently implemented using libraries like Eigen or Armadillo, or by manually optimizing algorithms to leverage hardware capabilities such as SIMD instructions and multi-threading.

Key considerations for implementing efficient matrix operations include:

- **Data Structures**: Choosing the right data structure for matrix representation (e.g., array, vector, or custom structures) to facilitate cache-friendly access patterns.
- **Algorithm Optimization**: Applying mathematical techniques to reduce computational complexity, such as Strassen's algorithm for matrix multiplication.
- **Parallel Computing**: Utilizing multi-threading and vectorization to perform matrix operations concurrently across multiple cores or using GPU acceleration.

Learning objectives:

- Understand how to represent matrices in C++ and perform basic operations.
- Explore advanced algorithms for efficient matrix computations.
- Learn to leverage C++'s concurrency features for parallel matrix operations.
- Apply optimization techniques to improve performance for engineering applications.

Examples

Example 1: Basic Matrix Addition Using Vectors

```
#include <vector>
#include <iostream>

typedef std::vector<std::vector<double>> Matrix;
```

```
Matrix addMatrices(const Matrix& A, const Matrix& B) {
    Matrix result = A; // Assuming A and B are of the same size
    for (size_t i = 0; i < A.size(); ++i) {
        for (size_t j = 0; j < A[i].size(); ++j) {
            result[i][j] += B[i][j];
        }
    }
    return result;
}

void printMatrix(const Matrix& matrix) {
    for (const auto& row: matrix) {
        for (const auto& elem: row) {
            std::cout << elem << " ";
        }
        std::cout << "\n";
    }
}

int main() {
    Matrix A = { {1, 2}, {3, 4} };
    Matrix B = { {5, 6}, {7, 8} };

    Matrix result = addMatrices(A, B);
    printMatrix(result);

    return 0;
}
```

Example 2: Parallel Matrix Multiplication

For the sake of brevity, this example outlines the concept. Real-world implementation would involve using threads or parallel algorithms.

```
#include <thread>
#include <vector>

// Simplified example function to demonstrate concept
void multiplyRowByColumn(const Matrix& A, const Matrix& B, Matrix& result,
size_t row, size_t col) {
    // Assuming matrices are correctly sized
    for (size_t k = 0; k < A[0].size(); ++k) {
        result[row][col] += A[row][k] * B[k][col];
    }
```

```
}

void parallelMatrixMultiply(const Matrix& A, const Matrix& B, Matrix& result)
{
    std::vector<std::thread> threads;

    for (size_t i = 0; i < A.size(); ++i) {
        for (size_t j = 0; j < B[0].size(); ++j) {
            threads.emplace_back(multiplyRowByColumn, std::cref(A),
std::cref(B), std::ref(result), i, j);
        }
    }

    for (auto& thread: threads) {
        thread.join();
    }
}
```

Practice

Practice 1: Implement a function in C++ to calculate the transpose of a matrix.

Practice 2: Write a C++ program that performs matrix inversion using the Gauss-Jordan elimination method.

Solution

Solution to Practice 1:

```
Matrix transposeMatrix(const Matrix& matrix) {
    size_t rows = matrix.size();
    size_t cols = matrix[0].size();
    Matrix transposed(cols, std::vector<double>(rows));

    for (size_t i = 0; i < rows; ++i) {
        for (size_t j = 0; j < cols; ++j) {
            transposed[j][i] = matrix[i][j];
        }
    }
    return transposed;
}
```

Solution to Practice 2:

The Gauss-Jordan method for matrix inversion is complex and involves multiple steps, including forming the augmented matrix, applying partial pivoting, and performing row operations to achieve the reduced row echelon form. Due to the complexity, a detailed implementation is beyond the scope of this brief example. However, libraries like Eigen provide functions to perform matrix inversion efficiently.

9.3.5 Designing and Deploying RESTful Web Services

RESTful web services in C++ involve creating server applications that adhere to the principles of Representational State Transfer (REST) architecture. These services provide a standardized approach for performing CRUD operations (Create, Read, Update, Delete) over HTTP, making them essential for web, mobile, and distributed application development.

Developing RESTful web services in C++ requires an understanding of HTTP methods, status codes, and the concept of resources. C++ frameworks like CppRestSDK (also known as Casablanca) offer comprehensive support for building RESTful services, including JSON serialization/deserialization, URI manipulation, and asynchronous request handling.

Key aspects include:

- **HTTP Methods and Status Codes**: Using GET, POST, PUT, DELETE, etc., appropriately and responding with correct HTTP status codes.
- **Resource Identification**: Designing URL endpoints that logically represent resources and their relationships.
- **Request and Response Handling**: Efficiently processing incoming requests and generating responses with necessary headers and body content.
- **Serialization and Deserialization**: Converting between in-memory data structures and JSON/XML representations for network communication.

Learning objectives:

- Learn to set up and configure a RESTful web service using a C++ framework.
- Understand how to handle different HTTP methods and produce corresponding responses.
- Explore the serialization and deserialization of data formats like JSON and XML.
- Implement security best practices for RESTful web services.
- Deploy a C++ RESTful web service on a server and test its functionality.

Examples

Example 1: Basic HTTP GET Handler with CppRestSDK

```
#include <cpprest/http_listener.h>
#include <cpprest/json.h>
using namespace web;
using namespace web::http;
using namespace web::http::experimental::listener;

void handleGet(http_request request) {
    json::value response_data;
    response_data[U("message")] = json::value::string(U("Hello, World!"));

    request.reply(status_codes::OK, response_data);
}
```

```
int main() {
    http_listener listener(U("http://localhost:8080/hello"));
    listener.support(methods::GET, handleGet);

    try {
        listener
            .open()
            .then([&listener]() {std::cout << "Starting to listen at: " <<
listener.uri().to_string() << std::endl; })
            .wait();

        std::string line;
        std::getline(std::cin, line);
    }
    catch (const std::exception& e) {
        std::cerr << "An error occurred: " << e.what() << std::endl;
    }

    return 0;
}
```

Example 2: Handling POST Requests to Create a Resource

```
void handlePost(http_request request) {
    request
        .extract_json()
        .then([](json::value request_data) {
        std::cout << "Received request: " << request_data.serialize() <<
std::endl;

        // Assume we create a resource here and generate a new ID
        json::value response_data;
        response_data[U("id")] = json::value::number(1); // Example ID

        return response_data;
            })
        .then([request](json::value response_data) {
                request.reply(status_codes::Created, response_data);
            })
                .wait();
}
```

Practice

Practice 1: Create a RESTful endpoint for retrieving a list of items using CppRestSDK. The items can be statically defined in your application.

Practice 2: Extend your RESTful service to support adding a new item to the list via a POST request. Ensure the item's details are extracted from the request body.

Solution

Solution to Practice 1:

```
#include <cpprest/http_listener.h>
#include <cpprest/json.h>
using namespace web;
using namespace web::http;
using namespace web::http::experimental::listener;

std::vector<json::value> items = { json::value::string(U("Item 1")),
json::value::string(U("Item 2")) };

void handleGetItems(http_request request) {
    json::value response_data;
    response_data[U("items")] = json::value::array(items);

    request.reply(status_codes::OK, response_data);
}

int main() {
    http_listener listener(U("http://localhost:8080/items"));
    listener.support(methods::GET, handleGetItems);
    // Listener setup and open code...
    return 0;
}
```

Solution to Practice 2:

```
void handlePostItem(http_request request) {
    request
        .extract_json()
        .then([](json::value request_data) {
        items.push_back(request_data[U("newItem")]); // Assuming "newItem" key
exists
        return json::value::object({ {U("success"), json::value::boolean(true)}
});
            })
        .then([request](json::value response_data) {
                request.reply(status_codes::Created, response_data);
            })
```

```
                  .wait();
}

// Inside main, add support for POST method
listener.support(methods::POST, handlePostItem);
```

Advanced Practice Exercises With Answers

Exercise 1: Lambda Expressions and Algorithms

- **Task**: Write a C++ program using lambda expressions to sort a **std::vector<std::pair<int, std::string>>** first by the integer value in ascending order, and then by the string length in descending order, using the STL sort algorithm.
- **Answer**:

```
#include <algorithm>
#include <iostream>
#include <string>
#include <vector>
#include <utility>

int main() {
    std::vector<std::pair<int, std::string>> vec = { {2, "banana"}, {1, "ap-
ple"}, {1, "grape"}, {2, "pear"} };

    std::sort(vec.begin(), vec.end(), [](const auto& a, const auto& b) {
        return a.first < b.first || (a.first == b.first && a.second.size() >
b.second.size());
        });

    for (const auto& [num, fruit]: vec) {
        std::cout << num << ": " << fruit << "\n";
    }
}
```

Explanation:

This C++ code demonstrates sorting a vector of pairs using a custom sorting criterion with a lambda function. It then prints the sorted pairs to the standard output. Let's break down the code and its functionality:

Key Components

- **Standard Library Headers**: The code includes headers for **algorithm**, **iostream**, **string**, **vector**, and **utility**. These provide access to standard functions and classes used in the program, such as **std::sort**, **std::vector**, **std::pair**, and standard input/output operations.
- **Vector of Pairs**: A **std::vector** named **vec** is defined, containing elements of type **std::pair<int, std::string>**. Each pair holds an integer and a string, representing some data and its associated label (for example, a count and a fruit name).
- **Sorting with std::sort**: The **std::sort** algorithm is used to sort **vec**. Sorting begins from **vec.begin()** to **vec.end()**, encompassing the entire vector. The third argument to **std::sort** is a lambda function that defines the sorting criterion.
- **Lambda Function for Sorting**: The lambda takes two pairs (**a** and **b**) as its parameters and returns **true** if **a** should come before **b** in the sorted sequence. The sorting criterion is twofold:
    1. **Primary Criterion**: Pairs are first compared based on their **first** element (the integer), with smaller integers coming first.
    2. **Secondary Criterion**: If the **first** elements are equal, pairs are then compared based on the size of their **second** element (the string), with longer strings coming before shorter ones. This is achieved using **a.second.size() > b.second.size()**.
- **Range-based For Loop**: After sorting, a range-based for loop iterates over **vec**, destructuring each **std::pair** into **num** (the integer) and **fruit** (the string). The structured binding declaration (**const auto& [num, fruit]**) provides a concise way to access the elements of each pair.
- **Output**: For each pair in the sorted **vec**, the loop prints the integer and string to the console, formatted as "**num**: **fruit**\n".

Output Explanation

Given the initial vector and the specified sorting criteria, the output will be sorted primarily by the integer value and secondarily by the string length when integers are equal. The expected output is:

```
makefile
1: apple
1: grape
2: pear
2: banana
```

- The pairs with **1** as their first element come first, sorted alphabetically by their second element since their first elements are equal and no secondary sort criterion is applied.
- The pairs with **2** as their first element come next. Although "banana" is alphabetically before "pear", "pear" is placed before "banana" because "banana" has a longer string length, which is the secondary sorting criterion when the first elements are equal.

This program demonstrates how to use **std::sort** with a custom sorting criterion to organize complex data structures in C++, showcasing the power and flexibility of lambda expressions and the utility of the Standard Template Library (STL).

Exercise 2: Utilizing Move Semantics

- **Task**: Implement a class **Buffer** that encapsulates a dynamic array of integers, demonstrating the use of move semantics to efficiently pass **Buffer** objects.
- **Answer**:

```
#include <iostream>
#include <algorithm>

class Buffer {
    int* data;
    size_t size;

public:
    Buffer(size_t size): size(size), data(new int[size]) {}

    // Move constructor
    Buffer(Buffer&& other) noexcept: data(other.data), size(other.size) {
        other.data = nullptr;
        other.size = 0;
    }

    // Move assignment operator
    Buffer& operator=(Buffer&& other) noexcept {
        if (this != &other) {
            delete[] data;
            data = other.data;
            size = other.size;
            other.data = nullptr;
            other.size = 0;
        }
        return *this;
    }

    ~Buffer() { delete[] data; }

    // Example function to use the buffer
    void fill(int value) {
        std::fill_n(data, size, value);
    }

    void print() const {
        for (size_t i = 0; i < size; ++i) std::cout << data[i] << " ";
        std::cout << "\n";
```

```
    }
};
```

Explanation:

This C++ code defines a class named **Buffer** that encapsulates dynamic memory management for an array of integers. It demonstrates modern C++ memory management techniques, including move semantics, to efficiently handle resources during object copy and assignment operations. Here's a breakdown of its key components and functionality:

Buffer Class

- **Private Members**: **data** is a pointer to an array of integers, and **size** holds the number of elements in that array.
- **Constructor**: Allocates dynamic memory for the **data** array based on the provided **size**. This establishes the **Buffer** object's size and allocates the corresponding memory for its data.
- **Move Constructor**: Implements move semantics, allowing the efficient transfer of resources from one **Buffer** object to another temporary object (**other**). The constructor takes the resources (memory and size) from **other**, and then sets **other**'s data pointer to **nullptr** and its size to **0**, leaving the moved-from object in a valid but empty state. Marked **noexcept** to indicate it does not throw exceptions, which is important for certain STL container optimizations.
- **Move Assignment Operator**: Also implements move semantics for assignment. It first releases the current object's resources (if any) by deleting **data**, then transfers **other**'s resources to the current object in the same manner as the move constructor. It also ensures self-assignment does not cause issues by checking if **this** is not the same as the address of **other**. Finally, it returns a reference to ***this** to allow chaining of assignment operations. Also marked **noexcept**.
- **Destructor**: Releases the dynamically allocated memory to prevent memory leaks. This is crucial for classes that manage resources to ensure proper cleanup.
- **fill Function**: Fills the **Buffer** with a specified integer value using the standard algorithm **std::fill_n**, which sets **size** elements of **data** to the given **value**.
- **print Function**: Outputs the contents of the **Buffer** to the standard output. Iterates over each element in **data** and prints it, demonstrating how to access and use the managed resources.

Key Concepts Illustrated

- **Resource Management**: The class demonstrates how to responsibly manage dynamic memory in C++, allocating in the constructor and deallocating in the destructor to adhere to RAII (Resource Acquisition Is Initialization) principles.
- **Move Semantics**: By implementing a move constructor and move assignment operator, the class can transfer resources from temporary objects or objects that are about to be destroyed, minimizing unnecessary copying and dynamic memory allocation. This is particularly useful for performance-critical applications and when the object is used in contexts that involve copying or assigning objects, such as resizing a **std::vector**.

- **Noexcept**: The move operations are marked **noexcept** to improve their usability with the standard library and to enable certain optimizations, such as those performed by **std::vector** when reallocating memory.

This **Buffer** class is a simplified example but encapsulates many of the best practices for managing resources in C++, showcasing the efficiency gains possible with move semantics and the importance of careful resource management in destructor to avoid leaks.

Exercise 3: Smart Pointers for Resource Management

- **Task**: Create a simple factory function that returns a **std::unique_ptr** to an array of integers and demonstrates automatic cleanup.
- **Answer**:

```
#include <iostream>
#include <memory>

std::unique_ptr<int[]> createArray(size_t size, int initialValue) {
    std::unique_ptr<int[]> arr(new int[size]);
    for (size_t i = 0; i < size; ++i) arr[i] = initialValue;
    return arr;
}

int main() {
    auto arr = createArray(5, 42);
    for (size_t i = 0; i < 5; ++i) std::cout << arr[i] << " ";
}
```

Explanation:

This C++ code snippet demonstrates the use of smart pointers, specifically **std::unique_ptr**, for dynamic memory management. It defines a function **createArray** that creates and initializes an array of integers to a specified value, then returns this array encapsulated in a **std::unique_ptr**. Here's a breakdown of how it works:

Key Components

- **#include <iostream>**: Includes the standard I/O stream library to enable input and output operations, such as printing to the console.
- **#include <memory>**: Includes the memory header from the C++ Standard Library, which provides utilities for dynamic memory management, including smart pointers like **std::unique_ptr**.
- **std::unique_ptr<int[]>**: This is a smart pointer specifically designed to manage dynamic arrays. **std::unique_ptr** automatically deletes the associated memory when the **std::unique_ptr** goes out of scope, preventing memory leaks. The use of **int[]** as the template argument indicates that it's managing an array of integers.

- **createArray Function**:
- **Purpose**: Creates a dynamic array of integers, initializes all elements to a given value (**initialValue**), and then returns this array encapsulated in a **std::unique_ptr**.
- **Parameters**: Takes the size of the array (**size**) and the initial value to set each element (**initialValue**).
- **Process**: Allocates a new array of integers of the specified **size** using **new int[size]** and wraps this raw pointer in a **std::unique_ptr<int[]>** to ensure automatic memory management. It then initializes each element of the array to **initialValue** using a for loop.
- **Return Value**: Returns the **std::unique_ptr<int[]>** managing the newly created and initialized array.
- **main Function**:
- **Array Creation**: Calls **createArray** to create and initialize an array of **5** integers, each set to **42**, and receives the **std::unique_ptr<int[]>** managing this array.
- **Output**: Iterates over the array using a for loop and prints each integer to the console followed by a space.

How It Works

When **createArray(5, 42)** is called, it dynamically allocates an array of 5 integers, sets each element to 42, and then returns a **std::unique_ptr<int[]>** pointing to this array. This smart pointer takes ownership of the array, ensuring that the memory is automatically deallocated when the pointer (named **arr** in **main**) goes out of scope, thereby avoiding memory leaks.

Output

The output of the program will be:

```
42 42 42 42 42
```

This output demonstrates that the array has been successfully created, initialized, and accessed through the **std::unique_ptr**. The program showcases an effective way to manage dynamic arrays in moder

Exercise 4: Type Deduction With auto and decltype

- **Task**: Write a function template **swapAny** that swaps the values of any two given variables using **auto** and **decltype**.
- **Answer**:

```
#include <iostream>

template<typename T1, typename T2>
void swapAny(T1& a, T2& b) {
    auto temp = a;
    a = b;
    b = temp;
```

```
}

int main() {
    int x = 10;
    double y = 20.5;
    swapAny(x, y);
    std::cout << "x: " << x << ", y: " << y << std::endl;
}
```

Explanation:

This C++ code snippet demonstrates a template function named **swapAny** designed to swap the values of two variables. However, it's important to note an issue with type compatibility in this specific implementation. Let's break down the code:

Key Components

- **Template Function**: **swapAny** is a function template that takes two parameters, **a** and **b**, whose types are specified as template arguments **T1** and **T2**, respectively. This means the function can accept arguments of different types.
- **Swapping Logic**: Inside **swapAny**, a temporary variable **temp** of type **auto** is used to hold the value of **a** before **a** is assigned the value of **b**. Then, **b** is assigned the value stored in **temp**, effectively swapping the values of **a** and **b**.
- **Main Function**: Demonstrates the use of **swapAny** by attempting to swap an **int** variable **x** with value **10** and a **double** variable **y** with value **20.5**.

Issues and Explanation

- **Type Mismatch and Precision Loss**: While the function **swapAny** is designed to accept two variables of potentially different types, directly swapping an **int** and a **double** can lead to unintended behavior due to type conversion. When **a = b;** is executed with **a** being an **int** and **b** a **double**, the value of **b** is implicitly converted to an **int** before assignment, potentially resulting in precision loss. Similarly, when assigning the **int** value to **b**, which is a **double**, the integer is converted to a **double**.
- **Outcome**: After calling **swapAny(x, y);**, **x** will try to take the value of **y**, but since **x** is an **int**, it can only store the integer part of **y**, which is **20**. Conversely, **y** will take the value of **x**, which is **10**, but stored as a **double**, so **y** becomes **10.0**.
- **Printed Output**: The output of the program will be:

```
x: 20, y: 10
```

This reflects the integer part of **y**'s original value being assigned to **x**, and **x**'s original value being assigned to **y**.

Important Considerations

- **Template Function for Swapping**: While template functions are powerful for creating generic and reusable code, the specific task of swapping values of different types requires careful consideration of type conversions and potential precision loss.
- **Type-Safe Swapping**: For type-safe operations, it's generally recommended to use **swapAny** with variables of the same type to avoid implicit conversions. Alternatively, handling type conversion explicitly inside the function or using specialized functions/templates for different type pairs can mitigate issues.

This example illustrates the flexibility of template functions in C++ but also highlights the need for careful handling of type conversions and the potential for loss of precision when dealing with different data types.

Exercise 5: Writing constexpr Functions

- **Task**: Implement a **constexpr** function in C++ that calculates and returns the area of a circle given its radius.
- **Answer**:

```
#include <iostream>

constexpr double pi() { return 3.14159265358979323846; }

constexpr double areaOfCircle(double radius) {
    return pi() * radius * radius;
}

int main() {
    constexpr double area = areaOfCircle(5);
    std::cout << "Area: " << area << std::endl;
}
```

Explanation:

This C++ code demonstrates the use of **constexpr** functions for compile-time computation. It calculates the area of a circle given a radius and outputs the result. Here's a detailed explanation of its components and how it works:

Key Components:

- **#include <iostream>**: This line includes the standard I/O header file that allows the program to perform input and output operations, such as printing to the console.

- **constexpr Keyword**: Used to define expressions or functions that can be evaluated at compile time. This keyword ensures that the function or value is constant and, if possible, computed at compile time, leading to optimized runtime performance.
- **pi Function**: A **constexpr** function that returns the value of π (pi). Since π is a constant value, marking this function as **constexpr** allows its value to be computed at compile time when used in constant expressions.
- **areaOfCircle Function**: Another **constexpr** function that calculates the area of a circle using the formula πr^2, where r is the radius of the circle. Because this function is **constexpr** and it only uses **constexpr** operations and values, the compiler will attempt to compute the area at compile time if the radius provided is a constant expression.

Program Flow

1. **Calculation of Area**: In the **main** function, **areaOfCircle(5)** is called with **5** as the radius. Since **5** is a compile-time constant and **areaOfCircle** is a **constexpr** function, the compiler computes the area of the circle during compilation rather than at runtime. The computed area is then assigned to the **constexpr double area**.
2. **Output**: The program prints the calculated area to the console. Given the radius of **5**, the output will display the area of the circle using the pre-calculated value of π provided by the **pi()** function.

Output:

```
makefile
Area: 78.5398
```

This output represents the area of a circle with a radius of **5**, calculated using the formula πr^2 with π approximated as **3.14159265358979323846**.

Importance

The use of **constexpr** functions and values is a powerful feature introduced in C++11 and expanded in later standards. It allows certain computations to be moved from runtime to compile time, reducing runtime overhead and potentially leading to more efficient code. In this example, the area of the circle is calculated at compile time, demonstrating how **constexpr** can be used for compile-time calculations in C++.

Exercise 6: Implementing Flexible Functions With Variadic Templates

- **Task**: Create a variadic template function **printAll** that prints all its arguments separated by commas.
- **Answer**:

```
#include <iostream>

template<typename T>
void printAll(const T& value) {
    std::cout << value << std::endl;
}

template<typename T, typename... Args>
void printAll(const T& first, const Args&... args) {
    std::cout << first << ", ";
    printAll(args...);
}

int main() {
    printAll(1, 2.5, "three", '4');
}
```

Explanation:

This C++ code demonstrates the use of variadic templates and template recursion to print a variable number of arguments of different types. It showcases how templates can be utilized to create functions that can accept any number of parameters with varying data types. Here's a breakdown of its components and how it works:

Key Components

- **Variadic Template Function printAll**:
- The code defines two overloaded functions named **printAll**.
- The first **printAll** function is a base case for the recursion, which takes a single argument of any type **T** and prints it to the standard output. This function is called when there's only one argument left to print, effectively ending the recursion.
- The second **printAll** function is a variadic template that can take an arbitrary number of arguments. It uses template parameter packing (**typename... Args**) to accept any number of additional arguments **args...** of potentially varying types. It prints the first argument followed by a comma and then recursively calls itself with the rest of the arguments (**args...**). This recursion continues until only one argument is left, at which point the first **printAll** function is called.
- **Main Function**:
- Calls **printAll** with four arguments of different types (**int**, **double**, **const char***, and **char**), demonstrating the function's ability to handle multiple types and numbers of arguments.
- The variadic **printAll** function is invoked, printing each argument followed by a comma (except for the last argument, which is handled by the base case **printAll** function and does not have a comma following it).

How It Works

1. When **printAll(1, 2.5, "three", '4')** is called in **main**, the variadic version of **printAll** is invoked with these four arguments.
2. **printAll** prints the first argument (**1**) and a comma, then recursively calls itself with the remaining arguments (**2.5, "three", '4'**).
3. This process repeats, with each recursive call printing the next argument and a comma, then passing the remaining arguments to the next recursive call.
4. When the final argument (**'4'**) is reached, the recursion base case (the single-parameter **printAll**) is called, printing the last argument without a trailing comma.
5. The recursion ends, and the program has printed all provided arguments to the standard output, separated by commas.

Output:

```
1, 2.5, three, 4
```

This output demonstrates the variadic template function's ability to accept and process a variable number of arguments of different types, showcasing the flexibility and power of C++ templates for generic programming tasks.

Exercise 7: Exploring Template Metaprogramming Techniques

- **Task**: Use template metaprogramming to create a compile-time structure that calculates the sum of a sequence of integers.
- **Answer**:

```
#include <iostream>

template<int... nums> struct Sum;

template<int first, int... rest>
struct Sum<first, rest...> {
    static const int value = first + Sum<rest...>::value;
};

template<>
struct Sum<> {
    static const int value = 0;
};

int main() {
    std::cout << "Sum: " << Sum<1, 2, 3, 4, 5>::value << std::endl;
}
```

Explanation:

This C++ code demonstrates a compile-time computation using template metaprogramming. Specifically, it calculates the sum of a sequence of integers provided as template parameters. Here's a detailed explanation of how it works:

Key Components

- **Variadic Template Struct Sum**: The core of this technique is the **Sum** template struct, which uses variadic templates to accept an arbitrary number of integer template parameters. Variadic templates are a feature that allows templates to accept an arbitrary number of template arguments, making them ideal for operations on sequences of values.
- **Partial Specialization for Sum**: The **Sum** struct is partially specialized for a case where there is at least one integer (**first**) followed by zero or more integers (**rest...**). In this specialization, **value** is a static constant integer that represents the sum of **first** and the sum of the rest of the integers. It calculates this sum recursively by deferring the computation of the sum of **rest...** to another instantiation of **Sum**.
- **Base Case for Recursion (Sum<>)**: A full specialization of the **Sum** struct with no template arguments acts as the base case for the recursion. It defines **value** as **0**, effectively ending the recursive summation when there are no more numbers to add.

How It Works:

1. **Recursive Summation**: When **Sum<1, 2, 3, 4, 5>::value** is accessed, the compiler instantiates the **Sum** struct for the provided sequence of numbers. The computation of **value** involves recursive instantiation of **Sum** with progressively fewer numbers, accumulating their sum:
    - **Sum<1, 2, 3, 4, 5>::value** computes **1 + Sum<2, 3, 4, 5>::value**
    - **Sum<2, 3, 4, 5>::value** computes **2 + Sum<3, 4, 5>::value**
    - This process continues until **Sum<>** is instantiated, which provides the base case with a value of **0**.
2. **Compile-time Evaluation**: Because all the operations involved in computing **value** are constant expressions and the values are known at compile time, the entire computation is performed during compilation. The result is a compile-time constant.
3. **Output**: The program prints the sum of the numbers, which is calculated to be **15** for the sequence **1, 2, 3, 4, 5**.

Output:

```
makefile
Sum: 15
```

This output confirms that the compile-time calculation of the sum of the provided sequence of numbers was successful.

Importance

This code illustrates the power of template metaprogramming in C++ for performing computations at compile time, which can lead to highly optimized code. Techniques like this are used in various contexts within C++ programming, including optimization, static configuration, and implementing compile-time checks and algorithms.

Exercise 8: GUI Development With Qt

- **Task**: Design a Qt GUI application with a QMainWindow that has a QPushButton. When clicked, the button should close the application.
- **Answer**: Please refer to Qt documentation or tutorials for setting up a Qt project, as the solution requires setting up a Qt project and using Qt-specific classes and methods, which are not represented in plain C++ code.

```
#include <QApplication>
#include <QMainWindow>
#include <QPushButton>

int main(int argc, char* argv[]) {
    QApplication app(argc, argv);

    QMainWindow window;
    window.setWindowTitle("Qt Application");

    QPushButton* button = new QPushButton("Close", &window);
    window.setCentralWidget(button);

    QObject::connect(button, &QPushButton::clicked, &window,
&QMainWindow::close);

    window.show();
    return app.exec();
}
```

Explanation:

This C++ code snippet is an example of a simple GUI (Graphical User Interface) application created using the Qt framework, a popular cross-platform application development framework. The program creates a window with a single button that, when clicked, closes the window. Here's a breakdown of its functionality:

Key Components

- **QApplication**: This class manages application-wide resources and is necessary for any Qt GUI application. It handles initialization and finalization, event handling, and more. An instance of **QApplication** is created at the beginning of **main**. It requires the command-line arguments **argc** and **argv** to handle platform-specific initialization.
- **QMainWindow**: Represents the main application window. This class provides a framework for building the application's main interface. In this code, a **QMainWindow** object named **window** is created.
- **QPushButton**: A widget that creates a clickable button. Here, it's created with the label "Close" and is set to be the central widget of **window**. The parent of the button is specified as **&window**, meaning the button will be contained within and automatically deleted with the main window, adhering to Qt's parent-child memory management.
- **setWindowTitle**: Sets the title of the main window to "Qt Application".
- **setCentralWidget**: This method of **QMainWindow** sets the primary widget of the window. In this case, the button becomes the central widget of **window**.
- **QObject::connect**: Establishes a connection between the button's **clicked** signal and the window's **close** slot. This means that when the button is clicked (**clicked** signal is emitted), the window's **close** method (**close** slot) is called, causing the window to close. Signals and slots are a fundamental part of Qt's event handling mechanism, allowing for easy and flexible communication between objects.
- **show**: Displays the main window and its contents. Until this method is called, the window will not be visible.
- **app.exec()**: Enters the main event loop and waits for user interaction. It returns an exit code when the application is closed. This method is responsible for processing events such as clicks and key presses, ensuring the application remains responsive.

Execution Flow

1. Initializes the **QApplication** object with command-line arguments.
2. Creates a main application window (**QMainWindow**).
3. Adds a "Close" button (**QPushButton**) as the central widget of the main window.
4. Connects the button's **clicked** signal to the window's **close** slot, linking the button click to closing the window.
5. Displays the window with **show()**.
6. Enters the application's event loop with **app.exec()**, waiting for user actions.

Result:

When run, this program displays a window titled "Qt Application" with a single button labeled "Close". Clicking the button will close the window, demonstrating basic interaction within a Qt application. This example provides a simple introduction to creating GUI applications with Qt, showcasing window creation, widget usage, and signal-slot connections for event handling.

Exercise 9: Game Development With SDL

- **Task**: Write a simple SDL program that opens a window and fills it with a solid color.
- **Answer**: Similar to Exercise 8, setting up an SDL project involves specific setup and library linking that goes beyond plain C++ code snippets. Please consult SDL documentation for initial setup.

```
#include <SDL.h>
#include <iostream>

int main(int argc, char* argv[]) {
    if (SDL_Init(SDL_INIT_VIDEO) < 0) {
        std::cerr << "SDL could not initialize! SDL_Error: " << SDL_GetError()
<< std::endl;
        return 1;
    }

    SDL_Window* window = SDL_CreateWindow("SDL Tutorial", SDL_WINDOWPOS_UNDE-
FINED, SDL_WINDOWPOS_UNDEFINED, 640, 480, SDL_WINDOW_SHOWN);
    if (!window) {
        std::cerr << "Window could not be created! SDL_Error: " << SDL_GetEr-
ror() << std::endl;
        return 1;
    }

    SDL_Renderer* renderer = SDL_CreateRenderer(window, -1, SDL_RENDERER_AC-
CELERATED);
    SDL_SetRenderDrawColor(renderer, 0xFF, 0x00, 0x00, 0xFF); // Fill with
solid red
    SDL_RenderClear(renderer);
    SDL_RenderPresent(renderer);

    SDL_Delay(2000); // Wait two seconds

    SDL_DestroyWindow(window);
    SDL_Quit();

    return 0;
}
```

Explanation:

This C++ code demonstrates the basics of creating a graphical window using SDL (Simple Direct-Media Layer), a popular cross-platform development library designed for handling graphics, events, audio, and more. The program initializes SDL, creates a window, fills the window with a solid color (red), and then closes after a short delay. Here's a breakdown of its functionality:

Key Components and Flow

- **SDL_Init**: Initializes the SDL library. The **SDL_INIT_VIDEO** flag is passed to specify that SDL's video subsystems should be initialized. If SDL fails to initialize, an error message is printed, and the program exits with a return value of **1**.
- **SDL_CreateWindow**: Creates a window with the specified title ("SDL Tutorial"), position (undefined, letting the window manager decide), size (640x480 pixels), and flags (**SDL_WINDOW_SHOWN** to ensure the window is shown). If window creation fails, an error message is printed, and the program exits.
- **SDL_CreateRenderer**: Creates a renderer for the window, which allows drawing graphics in the window. The **-1** parameter automatically chooses the graphics driver that supports the flags given, **SDL_RENDERER_ACCELERATED** requests a hardware-accelerated renderer which should be faster than a software renderer.
- **SDL_SetRenderDrawColor and SDL_RenderClear**: These functions set the drawing color for the renderer (solid red in this case, using RGBA values) and clear the window with the current drawing color, effectively filling the window with red.
- **SDL_RenderPresent**: Updates the window with any rendering performed since the last call, making the red fill visible on the screen.
- **SDL_Delay**: Pauses the program for a specified duration (2000 milliseconds, or 2 seconds), keeping the window open long enough to be seen.
- **Cleanup**: Before exiting, the program cleans up by destroying the created window and quitting SDL to release resources.

Execution Flow

1. **Initialize SDL**: The video subsystem is initialized to allow graphical operations. An error check ensures SDL started correctly.
2. **Create a Window**: A 640x480 window titled "SDL Tutorial" is created. The program checks if the window was successfully created.
3. **Create a Renderer**: A hardware-accelerated renderer for the window is created.
4. **Draw a Solid Color**: The renderer is set to draw in solid red, and the window is filled with this color.
5. **Display and Wait**: The window updates to show the red color, and the program waits for 2 seconds.
6. **Clean Up and Exit**: The window is destroyed, SDL is cleaned up, and the program exits.

Error Handling

The program includes basic error handling for SDL initialization and window creation. If either of these operations fails, SDL provides an error message (**SDL_GetError()**), which is printed to the standard error stream, and the program exits with an error code.

Conclusion

This code is a simple demonstration of using SDL to create a graphical window and perform basic rendering. It introduces fundamental concepts needed for more complex graphical applications and games using SDL, such as window management, rendering, and event handling (not covered in this snippet).

Exercise 10: Network Programming With Boost.Asio

- **Task**: Implement a Boost.Asio asynchronous TCP echo server that echoes back any received messages to the client.
- **Answer**: Due to the complexity and dependencies on the Boost.Asio library, please refer to the Boost.Asio documentation for a detailed example of setting up an asynchronous TCP echo server.

```
#include <boost/asio.hpp>
#include <iostream>

using boost::asio::ip::tcp;

class session: public std::enable_shared_from_this<session> {
public:
    session(tcp::socket socket): socket_(std::move(socket)) {}

    void start() { do_read(); }

private:
    tcp::socket socket_;
    enum { max_length = 1024 };
    char data_[max_length];

    void do_read() {
        auto self(shared_from_this());
        socket_.async_read_some(boost::asio::buffer(data_, max_length),
            [this, self](boost::system::error_code ec, std::size_t length) {
                if (!ec) do_write(length);
            });
    }

    void do_write(std::size_t length) {
        auto self(shared_from_this());
        boost::asio::async_write(socket_, boost::asio::buffer(data_, length),
            [this, self](boost::system::error_code ec, std::size_t /*length*/)
{
                if (!ec) do_read();
            });
```

```
    }
};

class server {
public:
    server(boost::asio::io_context& io_context, short port)
       : acceptor_(io_context, tcp::endpoint(tcp::v4(), port)) {
        do_accept();
    }

private:
    tcp::acceptor acceptor_;

    void do_accept() {
        acceptor_.async_accept([this](boost::system::error_code ec, tcp::socket
socket) {
            if (!ec) std::make_shared<session>(std::move(socket))->start();
            do_accept();
            });
    }
};

int main(int argc, char* argv[]) {
    try {
        if (argc != 2) {
            std::cerr << "Usage: async_tcp_echo_server <port>\n";
            return 1;
        }

        boost::asio::io_context io_context;
        server s(io_context, std::atoi(argv[1]));
        io_context.run();
    }
    catch (std::exception& e) {
        std::cerr << "Exception: " << e.what() << "\n";
    }

    return 0;
}
```

Explanation:

This C++ code demonstrates an asynchronous TCP echo server using Boost.Asio, a cross-platform C++ library for network and low-level I/O programming. The server listens for incoming TCP connections on a specified port, reads data from each connection, and then writes the data back to the sender, effectively "echoing" the received messages. The code is structured around the asynchronous programming model provided by Boost.Asio to handle multiple connections efficiently without blocking. Here's a breakdown of its components:

Key Components

- **Boost.Asio Headers**: The program includes the necessary Boost.Asio header for networking functionality.
- **session Class**:
- Represents a single connection from a client.
- Contains a **tcp::socket** for the connection and a buffer for the data.
- The **start()** method initiates the read operation.
- **do_read()** asynchronously reads data from the socket into **data_**. Upon successful read, it calls **do_write()** to write the data back to the client.
- **do_write()** asynchronously writes the data back to the socket. Upon successful write, it calls **do_read()** again to read the next piece of data, thus continuing the echo functionality.
- Both asynchronous operations maintain a shared pointer to the **session** object (**self**) to ensure the **session** remains alive for the duration of the asynchronous operations.
- **server Class**:
- Sets up an asynchronous accept operation to wait for new connections.
- Contains a **tcp::acceptor** configured to listen on a specified port.
- **do_accept()** initiates the accept operation. Upon accepting a new connection, it creates a new **session** for that connection and starts it.
- **Main Function**:
- Checks command-line arguments for the server port number.
- Creates an **io_context** object, which provides core I/O functionality.
- Creates a **server** object, passing it the **io_context** and the port number.
- Calls **io_context.run()**, which enters the processing loop to handle all asynchronous operations set up by the server and sessions.

How It Works

1. The program starts by checking for a port number provided as a command-line argument.
2. It initializes the Boost.Asio I/O context and creates a **server** object that begins listening for incoming connections on the specified port.
3. For each incoming connection, **do_accept()** in the **server** class asynchronously accepts the connection, creates a new **session** for it, and calls **start()** on the **session**.
4. Each **session** asynchronously reads data from its socket. Once data is received, it is echoed back to the sender using asynchronous write operations.
5. The echo cycle continues for each **session** with **do_read()** and **do_write()** calling each other upon successful completion of their respective asynchronous operations.
6. The server runs indefinitely, handling multiple asynchronous connections, until it's terminated.

Key Concepts Illustrated

- **Asynchronous I/O**: Boost.Asio allows for efficient asynchronous I/O operations using a proactor design pattern. This pattern decouples I/O operations from their completion handling, allowing a single thread to manage multiple concurrent operations without blocking.
- **TCP Server**: The example implements a fundamental TCP server pattern, accepting connections, reading data, and writing data back.
- **Echo Protocol**: A simple protocol where the server sends back whatever data it receives from the client.
- **Error Handling**: The code includes basic error handling for I/O operations and reports exceptions that might be thrown during the server's operation.

This example is an illustration of creating networked applications with Boost.Asio, emphasizing asynchronous operations for scalable I/O-bound tasks like network servers.

Case Study

Creating a detailed real-world application encompassing various advanced topics from Chapter 9 (presumably covering advanced C++ concepts such as networking with Boost.Asio, asynchronous programming, and more) would require extensive code and explanations. Here's a conceptual outline for a chat server application using Boost.Asio, showcasing asynchronous operations, TCP networking, and handling multiple clients – aspects that are often part of advanced C++ networking topics.

Application Overview: Asynchronous Chat Server

The proposed application is an asynchronous chat server that allows multiple clients to connect and exchange messages in real-time. This server listens for incoming TCP connections, accepts clients, and then reads and broadcasts messages from any client to all connected clients.

Key Concepts Demonstrated

- **Boost.Asio for Networking**: Utilizes Boost.Asio for asynchronous networking operations.
- **TCP Socket Programming**: Manages TCP connections for real-time communication.
- **Asynchronous Operations**: Employs asynchronous read and write operations to handle multiple clients without blocking.
- **Thread Safety**: Ensures that shared resources among asynchronous handlers are accessed safely.
- **Session Management**: Tracks connected clients and handles their lifecycle and message passing.

Application Components:

1. **Server**: Orchestrates the network operations, accepting connections and managing active client sessions.
2. **Session**: Represents a single client connection. Handles reading messages from the client, writing messages back, and notifying the server of activity.

3. **Client Manager**: Maintains a list of active sessions and provides functionality to broadcast messages to all connected clients.

Simplified Code Structure:

Note: Implementing the full application is beyond the scope of this response due to complexity. Instead, a high-level overview and snippets are provided.

```
// Requires Boost.Asio
#include <boost/asio.hpp>
#include <iostream>
#include <set>
#include <memory>
#include <mutex>

using boost::asio::ip::tcp;

class ChatMessage { /* Message handling logic */ };

class ChatSession: public std::enable_shared_from_this<ChatSession> {
    /* Handle individual client connections */
};

class ChatServer {
public:
    ChatServer(boost::asio::io_context& io_context, short port)
       : acceptor_(io_context, tcp::endpoint(tcp::v4(), port)) {
        do_accept();
    }

private:
    void do_accept() {
        // Asynchronously accept connections
    }

    // Other server logic
};

int main(int argc, char* argv[]) {
    try {
        if (argc != 2) {
            std::cerr << "Usage: chat_server <port>\n";
            return 1;
        }
```

```
        boost::asio::io_context io_context;

        ChatServer server(io_context, std::atoi(argv[1]));

        io_context.run();
    }
    catch (std::exception& e) {
        std::cerr << "Exception: " << e.what() << "\n";
    }

    return 0;
}
```

High-Level Functionality

- **Server Setup**: Initializes the server on a specified port and starts asynchronously accepting client connections.
- **Session Handling**: Each client connection is wrapped in a **ChatSession**, which reads incoming messages and broadcasts them to all other connected clients.
- **Message Broadcasting**: When a message is received from a client, the server distributes it to all active sessions.

Real-World Application Considerations

- **Security**: Implementing TLS/SSL to encrypt communication.
- **Scalability**: Managing a large number of concurrent connections efficiently.
- **Robustness**: Handling network errors and client disconnections gracefully.

This chat server example illustrates the application of advanced C++ topics in a networked context, providing a foundation for building complex, real-time, and asynchronous applications.

Explanation:

The provided C++ code snippet outlines the foundational structure for an asynchronous chat server using the Boost.Asio library. While the code is not complete, it demonstrates the initialization and basic setup necessary for handling TCP connections in a chat application. Let's break down the key components and their intended functionality:

Key Components

- **Boost.Asio**: A cross-platform C++ library used for network and low-level I/O programming. It supports asynchronous operations, which are crucial for writing efficient network applications that handle multiple connections simultaneously without blocking.
- **tcp**: A namespace alias for **boost::asio::ip::tcp**, representing the TCP protocol. TCP (Transmission Control Protocol) is a reliable, stream-oriented protocol used for establishing a connection-oriented communication link between hosts.

- **ChatMessage Class**: Intended to handle the logic for chat messages, such as formatting, serialization, and deserialization. This class is a placeholder in the provided code snippet and would need to be implemented with methods for managing chat message data.
- **ChatSession Class**: Represents a single connection with a client. It is derived from **std::enable_shared_from_this<ChatSession>** to allow the session to manage its own lifetime through **std::shared_ptr**. This setup is essential for asynchronous operations, ensuring that a **ChatSession** instance remains alive as long as there are operations pending that involve it. The actual implementation of handling client connections, reading from and writing to the socket, would go here.
- **ChatServer Class**:
- **Constructor**: Takes a **boost::asio::io_context** reference and a port number as parameters. The **io_context** is a central object in Boost.Asio applications, providing core synchronous and asynchronous I/O functionalities. The server initializes a **tcp::acceptor** to listen for incoming connections on the specified port.
- **do_accept Method**: Starts an asynchronous operation to accept incoming connections. When a new connection is accepted, it should ideally create a new **ChatSession** to handle the connection and then wait for another connection in a loop. This method is a key part of the server's functionality but is left unimplemented in the snippet.
- **main Function**:
- Checks if a port number is provided as a command-line argument. If not, it prints a usage message and exits.
- Initializes a **boost::asio::io_context** object and a **ChatServer** instance, then runs the **io_context**'s event loop by calling **io_context.run()**. This call blocks and processes all asynchronous operations initiated by the server, such as accepting connections and handling client data.

Flow and Functionality

The program defines the basic structure for an asynchronous chat server capable of handling multiple client connections. The server listens on a specified port for incoming connections, accepts them asynchronously, and processes each connection in its session. The **ChatMessage** and **ChatSession** classes are placeholders indicating where message handling and session management logic should be implemented.

Execution:

Upon execution, the server starts and listens for incoming connections on the provided port. For each connection, it should create a session to handle communication. The actual chat functionality, including message broadcasting to clients, would need additional implementation in the **ChatSession** and **ChatServer** classes.

This code serves as a starting point for building a more complete and functional asynchronous chat server using Boost.Asio.

SUMMARY

This comprehensive guide delves into advanced C++ programming, offering a deep exploration of its modern features, practical integration with various frameworks and libraries, and real-world applications. Aimed at enhancing software development practices, the book is structured into three main sections, each focusing on crucial aspects of advanced C++ programming and its application in today's technological landscape.

Introduction: The book begins with an overview of advanced C++ features, highlighting the significance of modern C++ practices in software development. This section sets the stage for the detailed exploration that follows, emphasizing the importance of keeping abreast with C++'s evolving capabilities to write efficient, maintainable, and high-quality software.

Section 1: Modern C++ Language Features: This section covers the core language features that define modern C++, including lambda expressions, move semantics, smart pointers, and more. Each topic is dissected to explain its syntax, uses, benefits, and best practices. Special attention is given to type deduction, writing compile-time functions with **constexpr**, implementing flexible functions with variadic templates, and the exploration of template metaprogramming techniques. These concepts are crucial for writing efficient code and leveraging C++'s full potential.

Section 2: Integration with Frameworks and Libraries: Moving beyond language features, this section introduces the integration of C++ with various frameworks and libraries, essential for GUI development, game development, network programming, numerical computations, and web development. It provides introductions to working with Qt, SDL, Boost.Asio, the Eigen library, and CPPRESTSDK, respectively. Each subsection not only guides the reader through the basics but also illustrates how C++ serves as a backbone for developing complex applications in diverse domains.

Section 3: Practical Applications and Case Studies: The final section bridges theory with practice, presenting comprehensive case studies and practical applications. It covers building cross-platform GUI applications, developing and optimizing a 2D game engine, creating high-performance web servers, implementing efficient matrix operations for engineering applications, and designing as well as deploying RESTful web services. These real-world examples showcase the application of advanced C++ features and the integration with frameworks to solve complex problems, highlighting the versatility and power of C++ in software development.

Overall, this guide is an invaluable resource for software developers seeking to deepen their understanding of advanced C++ and its application in contemporary software projects. It not only broadens the reader's programming knowledge but also provides practical skills and insights for developing high-quality C++ applications across various domains.

Quiz Questions

Question 1: What does the following lambda expression return?

```
[](int x) { return x * x; }(5);
```

A) 10
B) 25
C) 5
D) 15
E) None of the above

Question 2: Which part of a lambda expression is used to specify variables from the surrounding scope that it can access?

A) Parameter List
B) Capture Clause
C) Function Body
D) Return Type
E) Mutable Specification

Question 3: What do move semantics in C++ primarily optimize?

A) Program correctness
B) Compilation time
C) Memory usage
D) Source code readability
E) Compile-time type checking

Question 4: Which of the following is true about the move constructor?

A) It always copies the data from the source object.
B) It is called when an object is passed by value to a function.
C) It leaves the source object in a valid but unspecified state.
D) It can only be used with primitive data types.
E) It requires the source object to be const.

Question 5: What is the main purpose of **unique_ptr** in C++?

A) To share ownership of an object between multiple pointers
B) To manage dynamic arrays
C) To ensure only one owner for dynamic memory
D) To break circular references
E) To count the references to a dynamically allocated object

Question 6: How does **weak_ptr** help in the context of **shared_ptr**?

A) By allowing multiple owners of an object
B) By providing temporary ownership of an object
C) By reducing the memory footprint of **shared_ptr**
D) By breaking circular references among **shared_ptr** instances*
E) By automatically deallocating associated resources

Question 7: Which function should you use to safely create a **unique_ptr** that manages a new object?

A) **new**
B) **std::make_shared**
C) **std::make_unique**
D) **std::shared_ptr**
E) **std::allocate_shared**

Question 8: What is a primary advantage of using **weak_ptr**?

A) It can be used to manage arrays.
B) It allows multiple ownership of an object.
C) It prevents memory leaks by breaking circular references.
D) It automatically deallocates its associated object.
E) It increases the reference count of **shared_ptr**.

Question 9: What does **auto** do in C++?

A) Automatically initializes variables to zero.
B) Generates automatic storage duration.
C) Deduces the type of a variable at compile-time from its initializer.
D) Automatically deallocates memory.
E) Declares a variable as automatic type without needing an initializer.

Question 10: Which statement is true about **decltype**?

A) It deduces the type of a variable at runtime.
B) It requires an initializer to deduce the type.
C) It is used to define the return type of functions based on its arguments.
D) It deduces the type of an expression without evaluating it.
E) It can only deduce types for literals and not for complex expressions.

Question 11: What is the primary benefit of using **constexpr** for functions in C++?

A) They can be executed asynchronously.
B) They guarantee no exceptions will be thrown.
C) They can be evaluated at compile time, potentially improving performance.
D) They automatically generate inline assembly.
E) They provide automatic memory management.

Question 12: Which of the following is a requirement for a function to be **constexpr**?

A) The function must be virtual.
B) The function must return **void**.
C) The function must use dynamic memory allocation.
D) The function must have a return type and all parameter types as literal types.
E) The function must be a template function.

Question 13: What feature do variadic templates use to accept an arbitrary number of template arguments?

A) Template specialization
B) Template overloading
C) Ellipsis (...)
D) Template instantiation
E) Lambda expressions

Question 14: Which of the following is a use case for variadic templates?

A) To create functions that can only accept a fixed number of arguments of the same type
B) To define classes that require static member variables only
C) To implement functions or classes that can handle a variable number of arguments of different types
D) To avoid using templates in modern C++ programming
E) To replace all uses of function overloading

Question 15: What is the main advantage of template metaprogramming in C++?

A) It simplifies syntax for template declarations.
B) It allows running C++ code in interpreted mode.
C) It enables computations to be performed at compile-time, reducing runtime overhead.
D) It automatically generates documentation for the code.
E) It facilitates dynamic memory management.

Question 16: Which template metaprogramming technique allows for compile-time type checking and selection?

A) Overloading
B) Polymorphism
C) Type traits
D) Lambda expressions
E) Template specialization

Question 17: Which of the following is true about Qt?

A) It only supports GUI development for Windows.
B) It uses JavaScript as its primary programming language.
C) It provides tools for both GUI and non-GUI development.
D) It cannot be used for mobile application development.
E) It exclusively supports the Model-View-Controller (MVC) design pattern.

Question 18: How do signals and slots in Qt facilitate event-driven programming?

A) By allowing direct function calls between objects.
B) By enabling compile-time checking of event connections.
C) By using a callback mechanism that does not require object instances.
D) By providing a mechanism for objects to communicate with each other via events and responses.
E) By automatically generating code for event handling at runtime.

Question 19: What does SDL stand for?

A) Simple DirectMedia Layer
B) Standard Development Library
C) Secure Digital Licensing
D) Systematic Design Language
E) Simple Design Logic

Question 20: Which SDL function is used to initialize the SDL library?
- A) SDL_Start()
- B) SDL_Init()
- C) SDL_Begin()
- D) SDL_Setup()
- E) SDL_Launch()

Question 21: What is Boost.Asio primarily used for?
- A) Parsing XML and JSON documents
- B) Managing database connections
- C) Cross-platform network and low-level I/O programming
- D) Graphics rendering
- E) Multithreading and concurrency management

Question 22: Which of the following is true about asynchronous operations in Boost.Asio?
- A) They block the execution thread until the operation completes.
- B) They require manual management of threads for scalability.
- C) They allow the program to perform other tasks while the operation is in progress.
- D) They are less efficient than synchronous operations for network I/O.
- E) They can only be used with TCP protocols.

Question 23: What is Eigen primarily used for?
- A) Creating graphical user interfaces
- B) Network programming
- C) Numerical computations and linear algebra
- D) Parsing XML documents
- E) Writing operating systems

Question 24: Which of the following is true about Eigen?
- A) It can only perform operations on fixed-size matrices.
- B) It requires a third-party GUI library to display results.
- C) It offers high performance for matrix and vector operations through template metaprogramming.
- D) It is written in Python and requires a C++ wrapper for integration.
- E) It exclusively supports integer data types for matrix operations.

Question 25: What is the primary use of the CPPRESTSDK library?
- A) Creating desktop GUI applications
- B) Developing games
- C) Building and consuming RESTful web services
- D) Performing complex numerical computations
- E) Managing database connections

Question 26: How does CPPRESTSDK handle asynchronous operations?

A) Using the **async** and **await** keywords
B) Through the use of callbacks
C) Utilizing the PPL (Parallel Patterns Library) for futures and promises
D) By employing a custom threading model unique to CPPRESTSDK
E) It does not support asynchronous operations

Question 27: What is the primary benefit of using a cross-platform GUI framework?

A) It allows applications to bypass the operating system's security features.
B) It provides native integration with mobile devices only.
C) It enables developers to write code once and run it on multiple operating systems.
D) It significantly increases the application's performance.
E) It restricts the application to use only web-based technologies.

Question 28: In the context of cross-platform GUI application development, what is a "slot" in Qt?

A) A memory location reserved for application data.
B) A function or method invoked in response to a signal.
C) A placeholder within the layout for dynamic content.
D) A special type of data structure for storing UI elements.
E) The process of compiling the application for different platforms.

Question 29: What is the primary function of the rendering system in a 2D game engine?

A) To manage the game's soundtrack and sound effects.
B) To process user input from devices like keyboards and gamepads.
C) To handle the loading and management of game assets.
D) To manage the drawing of sprites and animations on the screen.
E) To simulate physical interactions and movements within the game.

Question 30: Which of the following is a common technique for optimizing a 2D game engine?

A) Increasing the number of game entities to enhance realism.
B) Using higher resolution textures for all game assets.
C) Minimizing CPU and GPU workload through efficient algorithms and data structures.
D) Storing all game assets in memory at the start of the game to reduce loading times.
E) Implementing complex AI algorithms for all game characters to improve gameplay.

Question 31: What is a key feature of C++ that allows for efficient low-level network handling in web server development?

A) Garbage collection
B) Dynamic typing
C) Direct system calls and socket management
D) Built-in HTML parser

Question 32: What C++ feature can significantly improve the performance of matrix operations through parallel execution?

A) Templates
B) Operator overloading
C) Dynamic memory allocation
D) Multi-threading and parallel algorithms
E) Exception handling

Question 33: Which of the following is crucial for optimizing matrix operations in C++?

A) Reducing the use of conditional statements within loops
B) Increasing the size of matrices to maximize hardware utilization
C) Choosing appropriate data structures and algorithms for the task
D) Using only integer types for matrix elements
E) Compiling the program with the oldest available C++ standard for compatibility

Question 34: Which HTTP method is typically used to retrieve data from a RESTful web service?

A) POST
B) GET
C) PUT
D) DELETE

Question 35: What is a common format for sending data to and from a RESTful web service?

A) CSV
B) YAML
C) XML
D) JSON

Advanced Questions

1. **Lambda Expressions**: Write a C++ program that uses lambda expressions to filter and print only the even numbers from a **std::vector<int>**.
2. **Move Semantics**: Implement a C++ class that demonstrates the use of move constructors and move assignment operators to efficiently transfer resources between objects.
3. **Smart Pointers**: Create a C++ program that manages a dynamic array of integers using **std::unique_ptr** and demonstrates automatic resource management.
4. **Smart Pointer Best Practices**: Modify the previous program to use **std::shared_ptr** and **std::weak_ptr** to implement a simple cache system that avoids memory leaks and dangling pointers.
5. **Type Deduction with Auto**: Write a C++ function that takes a container (like **std::vector** or **std::list**) as input and prints its elements using **auto** in a range-based for loop.
6. **Decltype**: Create a C++ template function that adds two numbers and uses **decltype** to automatically determine the return type based on its arguments.
7. **Constexpr Functions**: Implement a **constexpr** function in C++ that calculates the nth Fibonacci number and use it to initialize a compile-time constant.

8. **Variadic Templates**: Write a C++ function template that takes a variable number of arguments and prints them to the console.
9. **Template Metaprogramming**: Develop a C++ metafunction that computes the factorial of a number at compile time and use it in a static assertion.
10. **GUI Development with Qt**: Design a Qt application with a button and a text label. When the button is clicked, the label should display the current time.
11. **Game Development with SDL**: Create a simple 2D game using SDL where the player controls a square that moves across the screen with arrow keys.
12. **Network Programming with Boost.Asio**: Write a C++ program using Boost.Asio to implement a TCP server that echoes back any received messages to the client.
13. **Numerical Computations with Eigen**: Implement a C++ program that uses the Eigen library to solve a system of linear equations.
14. **Web Development with CPPRESTSDK**: Develop a RESTful API in C++ using CPPRESTSDK that supports CRUD operations on a resource, such as books, including endpoints to create, read, update, and delete a book.
15. **Cross-Platform GUI Application**: Extend the Qt application to be cross-platform, ensuring it compiles and runs identically on Windows, macOS, and Linux.
16. **Optimizing a 2D Game Engine**: Enhance the SDL game by implementing double buffering to optimize rendering performance.
17. **Creating a High-Performance Web Server**: Optimize the Boost.Asio web server for high performance by integrating a thread pool to handle requests concurrently.
18. **Implementing Efficient Matrix Operations**: Use the Eigen library to perform and benchmark the multiplication of two large matrices, comparing the performance with and without optimization techniques like expression templates.
19. **Designing and Deploying RESTful Web Services**: Enhance the CPPRESTSDK RESTful service to include JSON Web Token (JWT) authentication for secure access to the API endpoints.
20. **Advanced Template Metaprogramming**: Implement a C++ program that uses template metaprogramming techniques to generate a compile-time type-safe state machine framework.

About the Authors

Shams Al Ajrawi earned her Ph.D. in Electrical and Computer Engineering from the University of San Diego and San Diego State University (JDP), San Diego in March 2021, after receiving her M.S. from the New York Institute Technology University in 2009. She earned her bachelor's degree in 2005 from the University of Technology. She had full Fellowship (SDSU/UCSD/NSF) in the field of Electrical and Computer Engineering, in 2016 for five years. She has been an editor and reviewer at many IEEE Transaction journals and she has published many research papers in BCI field. Her research interest lies in Brain Computer Interface Application includes Wireless Network Communication, Artificial Intelligent, Advanced Signal Processing, Machine Learning, and Cybersecurity. Dr. Al Ajrawi holds many teaching positions over the last 15 years, from being lead and core faculty at Coleman university and an adjunct faculty at San Diego State university, University of California San Diego, University of San Diego, University of North Texas, CMU, MiraCosta college, Grossmont, and Miramar college.

Charity Jennings is Senior Associate Faculty at University of Phoenix and serves as Assistant Chief Academic Officer at Center Education Group for the Center for Allied Health Education and City College. Dr. Jennings is a strategic education leader with a record of achieving measurable results as a dean, director, and professor. Focused in the areas of program and course design, change management, academic operations, accreditation and product management.

Paul Menefee is a successful technology leader with 25 years experience and a passion for solving customer challenges. Proven ability to quickly understand and align products, technology and market research.

Wathiq Mansoor is an esteemed Professor at the University of Dubai, renowned for his extensive academic leadership experience in esteemed universities worldwide. He holds a Ph.D. in Computer Engineering from Aston University in the UK, where his research focused on the design and implementation of multiprocessor systems and communication protocols for computer vision applications. With a strong foundation in Computer Engineering, Dr. Mansoor's current research interests lie in the domains of Artificial Intelligence, intelligent systems, and security. He leverages his expertise in neural networks and deep learning models to develop innovative solutions for various applications. Dr. Mansoor's contributions to the field of Computer Science and Engineering are widely recognized, evident in his impressive publication record comprising over 200 journal and conference papers. In recent years, his work has particularly emphasized the advancements and applications of Artificial Intelligence. He consistently strives to push the boundaries of knowledge and promote cutting-edge research in this rapidly evolving field. Apart from his scholarly pursuits, Dr. Mansoor is an accomplished organizer of international and national conferences and workshops. His ability to bring together experts and researchers from diverse backgrounds demonstrates his commitment to fostering collaboration and knowledge sharing within the academic community. Furthermore, Dr. Mansoor actively engages in mentoring and supervising the next generation of computer engineers and innovators. He has successfully guided numerous Ph.D. and undergraduate projects, empowering students to contribute meaningfully to the field. Additionally, he has co-supervised several postgraduate students through research collaborations with international research groups, enabling them to benefit from global perspectives and expertise. Overall, Dr. Mansoor's remarkable contributions to the field of Computer Science and Engineering continue to inspire and shape the minds of students and professionals alike. His dedication to research, teaching, and academic leadership is instrumental in driving advancements in Artificial Intelligence and fostering innovation in the field.

Mansoor Ahmed Alaali became President of Ahlia University in 2015. He joined Ahlia University in 2009 after 20 years at the University of Bahrain. Prof. Mansoor held many academic and industrial senior positions over the last thirty years. Professor Mansoor's research interest is in applied computer science, data mining, algorithm, Artificial Intelligence and Ethics. Graduating from the University of Teesside (UK), he gained his Master of Science and PhD at the University of Aston in Birmingham (UK). A member of several academic and professional bodies. An editor and reviewer of international refereed journals, Professor Mansoor has written several books and numerous journal and conference articles; delivered keynote speeches; and is a committee member of local, regional and international conferences. Professor Mansoor was a member of Bahrain National Qualification Framework's Verification Committee; previous roles include external consultant for international off-campus programmes of the University of Greenwich (UK) and the University of Sunderland (UK); and IT strategy and training Adviser to Bahrain's Minister of Labour and Social Affairs.

Index

D

E

F

G

I

L

M

N

O

www.ingramcontent.com/pod-product-compliance
Lightning Source LLC
LaVergne TN
LVHW080113011026
849160LV00013B/1087
* 9 7 9 8 3 6 9 3 4 9 9 8 4 *